PSYCHOLOGICAL AND SOCIAL ASPECTS OF PSYCHIATRIC DISABILITY

EDITED BY

LEROY SPANIOL

CHERYL GAGNE

MARTIN KOEHLER

CENTER FOR PSYCHIATRIC REHABILITATION

SARGENT COLLEGE OF HEALTH AND REHABILITATION SCIENCES

BOSTON UNIVERSITY

Published by:

Center for Psychiatric Rehabilitation
Sargent College of Health and Rehabilitation Sciences
Boston University
940 Commonwealth Avenue West
Boston, MA 02215

Printed in the United States of America

Book design and photo illustration by Linda Getgen

Library of Congress Catalog Card Number: 96-85675
ISBN 1-878512-06-4

Published January 1997— Second printing July 2001

contents

CHAPTER 5   THE HELPING CULTURE

CHAPTER 6   SELF-HELP

PREFACE

The psychological and social approach to understanding physical disability has a long tradition (Marinelli & Dell Orto, 1991; Shontz, 1975; Wright, 1983). There has been a deliberate attempt in the field of physical rehabilitation to understand how a person is affected by the disability, as well as how the person with a disability affects and is impacted by family, friends, the helping system, and society in general. The focus of research and demonstration efforts in the area of physical disability has been both on the experience of the person and on the barriers in the environment that prevent functioning fully and autonomously in the community. While information and resources have been available to assist the person with his or her disability, the emphasis has been on increasing his or her capacity to function independently.

In the field of psychiatric disability the traditional focus has been on treating the illness, rather than the person who has the illness. Hospitalization, medication, and therapy have been used as the primary interventions to treat the illness and to reduce positive symptoms. Negative symptoms have been seen as part of the illness, or as resistance on the part of the person, rather than as attempts by the person to cope with the illness, medication, and the effects of his or her environment. Traditional treatment approaches have not acknowledged the wholeness and integrity of the person with the disability. They have not acknowledged important dimensions of the internal recovery process that follow the onset of mental illness, as with any significant trauma (Deegan, 1988). They have not acknowledged the impact of the helping system, and society in general, on the person who is struggling to recover. They have not acknowledged the impact on the

families of people with psychiatric disability, including parents, spouses, siblings, and children of parents with psychiatric disability. While there has been some effort to understand the person's experience of the illness, the impact of society on the person's ability to function, and the need for new skills and supports to function more effectively, this effort has not become widespread and has not been effectively integrated into the helping process. Research and service efforts that have been narrowly focused on what seemed to impact on the illness and on the symptoms, have begun to focus on the person's functioning in a variety of environments of choice.

The newly emerging information on psychological and social aspects of psychiatric disability represents an additional approach to understanding people with mental illness. The approach focuses on understanding the experience of the person, the impact of the environment on the person, how the person copes, how the person moves on with his or her life, and what the barriers and facilitators are to this process. We want to present ways to identify and to support the strong and fiercely tenacious spirit of people with psychiatric disability.

Language usage has changed dramatically over the last several years in the field of psychiatric rehabilitation (*Guidelines for Reporting and Writing About People With Disabilities,* 4th edition, 1993; *Information for Writers,* NAMI, 1995; also see Spaniol & Cattaneo in chapter 7 in this book). In most cases, we did not update the language originally used in the articles selected for this book. The articles reflect this gradual change toward language that is more respectful of, and consistent with, how people with psychiatric disability view themselves.

We would like to thank the many students, family members, consumers, and professionals with whom we piloted this book. They shared their experiences willingly and generously, knowing that others might benefit from what they have learned.

We would like to give special thanks to Kristen Cronk for her tireless efforts in scanning and preparing the manuscript and Linda Getgen for her many useful suggestions on the text and for her wonderful design and typesetting expertise.

LeRoy Spaniol, Ph.D.
Cheryl Gagne, M.S.
Martin Koehler, B.S.

References

Deegan, P. (1988). Recovery: The lived experience of rehabilitation. *Psychosocial Rehabilitation Journal, 11* (4), 11-19.

Marinelli, R. P. & Dell Orto, A. E. (Eds.) (1991). *The psychological and social impact of physical disability, 4th ed.* New York: Springer Publishing Company.

National Alliance for the Mentally Ill. (1995). *Information for writers.*

Research and Training Center on Independent Living. (1993) *Guidelines for reporting and writing about people with disabilities, 4th ed.* University of Kansas: Author.

Shontz, F. C. (1975). *The psychological aspects of physical illness and disability.* New York: Macmillan.

Wright, B. (1983). *Physical disability—A psychosocial approach, 2nd ed.* New York: Harper & Row.

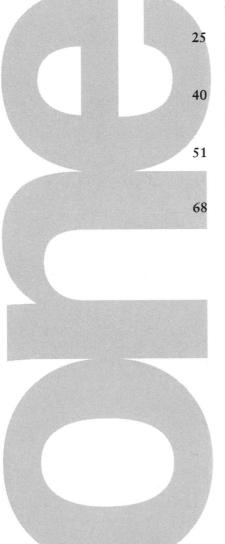

THE COURSE OF PSYCHIATRIC DISORDER, III: LONGITUDINAL PRINCIPLES

John S. Strauss, Hisham Hafez, Paul Lieberman, and Courtenay M. Harding

THIS ARTICLE ORIGINALLY APPEARED IN THE *American Journal of Psychiatry*, 1985, 142(3), 289-296, AND IS REPRINTED WITH PERMISSION.

The authors studied 28 patients hospitalized for functional psychiatric disorder in an attempt to explore systematically the course of psychiatric disorder. Data collected over the 2-year period following discharge suggested the existence of eight longitudinal principles for understanding the course of psychiatric disorder. These principles reflect identifiable phases and some of the factors involved in a patient's remaining in one phase or moving on to a new phase. The clinical and research implications of these principles are described.

Current views about the course of psychiatric disorder appear to be both incomplete and distorted. Two research practices have contributed to these shortcomings, which have limited the base of systematic inquiry underlying clinical practice. The first of these research strategies is the almost exclusive attention to outcome rather than course of disorder. The second is the tendency to look at course of disorder in a relative vacuum. This tendency leads to inadequate consideration of the disorder as taking place in a person evolving over time, a person who lives in an environmental context. In this report, we describe a study that attempted to reduce these shortcomings to provide a more complete perspective on the course of psychiatric order and the factors that influence it.

It is our contention that until such a broad perspective is developed, an understanding of the nature of psychiatric disorder and the ability to provide optimum treatment will be severely limited.

Conceptualizations of the course of psychopathology fall into three groups: the natural history model, the diathesis-stress model, and the clinical model. The natural history model was brought to psychiatric thinking by Kraepelin, who focused on outcome of disorder (more than on the intervening course) as a way of identifying specific psychiatric diseases. Although noting its different courses, he defined dementia praecox essentially as a disease in which several different syndromes could be considered as representing a single disease because they all had a narrow range of outcomes.

The natural history model has been extremely important in the field of medicine generally and has contributed much to psychiatry. Although it has some validity, the validity is limited by certain problems. One of the most significant of these is that systematic data have recently become available indicating that even patients with the disorder for which the natural history model was established, schizophrenia (dementia praecox), do not all have the same outcome (Strauss & Carpenter, 1974; Ciompi, 1980; Harding & Strauss, in press). Another problem for this model is that it does not have within it a structure for considering environmental impact. Recent research has shown that, even for schizophrenia, family environment (Vaughn & Leff, 1976) and perhaps life events (Day, 1981), social supports (Cohen & Sokolovsky, 1978), and psychosocial treatments (Maher & Gunderson, 1979) may have major effects on outcome.

A more recent model of the course of disorder, one more suitable for reflecting outcome heterogeneity and environmental impact, is the diathesis-stress model. This model, building on the natural history paradigm, suggests that although there is an underlying vulnerability for a disorder, its continued manifestation or recurrence is influenced by stress. This model provides a foundation for considering such factors as the impact of family environment and life events, but it too has certain shortcomings suggested by recent data. One major problem is the difficulty in defining diathesis and stress specifically. Events that could he predicted to be stressful, such as a death in the family, may for some people mobilize functioning and reduce symptoms rather than cause decompensation.

In addition to the problems with definition, the diathesis-stress model does not in itself provide a basis for thinking about the possibility that patients might play an active role in influencing the course of their disorder. And yet, even in psychotic disorders, it is highly likely that patients play a significant part in controlling their symptoms (Breier & Strauss, 1983; Lazarus, 1981). People also select their environments (which may be more or less stressful) and collaborate or "comply" with their treatment (or do not do so). The diathesis-stress model does not offer a basis for considering such patient contributions. Finally, the diathesis-stress model does not emphasize possible shifts in vulnerability over time. If the patient becomes less likely to relapse under a given "stress" as time progresses, one must assume that there are changes in the patient that help to account for this shift in pathologic response.

Building on the natural history and diathesis-stress models to provide a structure that can define vulnerability and stress more specifically and account for change and the active role of the patient, we have described the Interactive Developmental Model (Strauss & Carpenter, 1981). This model has two major principles: 1) The course of disorder is strongly affected by interactions between the individual and the environment. In these interactions, either

the individual or the environment can be the initiator. 2) The individual develops over time. By develop we mean that the person's strengths and vulnerabilities change over time, frequently in the direction of human development more generally. This development, we hypothesize, influences the course of psychiatric disorder (Strauss, Kokes, Carpenter et al., 1978).

However, the Interactive Developmental Model was generated originally as a general and speculative statement to meet the data that wcre available. It is necessary next to construct this model in more detail and from an empirical base. Such a step requires an exploratory study to identify relevant variables and suggest longitudinal processes. In previous reports, we have outlined key variables (Strauss, Loevsky, Glazer, et al., 1981) and discussed methodologic issues (Strauss & Hafez, 1981). In this report, we describe the longitudinal processes in the course of psychiatric disorder that have been suggested by our research. These processes are divided into two major types: 1) longitudinal patterns and 2) individual-environment interactions that contribute to these patterns.

Method

To explore systematically the course of psychiatric disorder, we carried out an intensive follow-along study of psychiatric patients. Twenty-eight patients hospitalized for functional psychiatric disorders were interviewed shortly after admission. Following discharge the subjects were interviewed at bimonthly intervals over the period of 1 year, and again at 2 years following discharge. The interviews focused on collecting data on symptoms and social functioning as they evolved across a variety of life "contexts" such as work, family, friendships, and treatment. Information was also collected on a range of environmental factors that might influence shifts or stabilities in these areas.

The interview schedules used in the study included open-ended and structured questions. After the interviews, ratings were made using several standard scales (Strauss & Carpenter, 1974; Endicott, Spitzer, Fleiss, et al., 1976; Overall & Gorham, 1962), and a narrative description of the previous 2 months' events and sequences was written.

Patients in the study were between the ages of 18 and 55 years, had a functional psychiatric disorder, and lacked any history of major problems with organic brain disorders or substance abuse. Because one focus of the study was the role of work following hospital discharge, another criterion for participation in the study was that the patient had worked at some time in the year before admission. Basic clinical and demographic characteristics of subjects in the sample are presented in Table 1.

TABLE 1.
CHARACTERISTICS OF 28 PSYCHIATRIC PATIENTS IN A STUDY OF COURSE OF DISORDER

Subject	Age (yrs)	Sex	Marital Status	Social Class[a]	Diagnosis[b]
1	31	F	Single	III	Schizoaffective disorder
2	26	M	Single	IV	Schizophrenia, paranoid type
3	24	M	Single	V	Schizophrenia, Paranoid type
4	28	F	Single	III	Bipolar disorder, mixed type
5	37	F	Single	V	Schizophrenia, Undifferentiated type
6	37	F	Divorced	II	Schizoaffective disorder
7	39	M	Divorced	II	Bipolar disorder, mixed type
8	26	F	Single	III	Bipolar disorder, manic type
9	43	F	Single	III	Schizoaffective disorder
10	34	F	Divorced	IV	Bipolar disorder
11	24	M	Separated	III	Schizoaffective disorder
12	37	M	Divorced	I	Major depression
13	26	F	Married	III	Major depression
14	39	F	Married	IV	Bipolar disorder, depressed type
15	26	F	Single	III	Major depression
16	23	F	Single	V	Major depression
17	20	M	Single	V	Bipolar disorder, manic type
18	38	M	Married	III	Atypical depression
19	28	F	Separated	V	Schizoaffective disorder
20	55	F	Married	III	Major depression
21	25	M	Single	IV	Major depression
22	22	F	Single	IV	Schizoaffective disorder
23	20	F	Single	IV	Schizoaffective disorder
24	28	M	Single	III	Bipolar disorder, manic type
25	29	M	Single	III	Schizophrenia, paranoid type
26	20	M	Single	V	Dysthymic disorder
27	24	F	Single	III	Schizophrenia, paranoid type
28	26	M	Single	III	Affective disorder, bipolar type

[a]Hollingshead-Redlich scale.
[b]According to *DSM-III*.

Results

We have been able to find no published account of a similar research project that followed subjects and their environmental situations repeatedly over time. Regular observation of the evolution of our subjects and their disorders in relation to their environment allowed us to document the course, for example, of a subject who, when rehospitalized, recovered rapidly from one episode of a recurrent psychosis following her original discharge. She functioned well for 3 months, then, following a success at work, had an exacerbation involving increased symptoms and diminished ability to work. The subject took more medication, got assistance from family and co-workers, and improved somewhat. She stabilized over the next several months.

Our review of sequences such as these (which are so commonplace in clinical experience), using systematically collected data and follow-up, suggested a set of eight longitudinal principles. These principles are grouped into two categories: longitudinal patterns and individual-environment interactions (see Table 2).

Longitudinal Patterns

Principle 1: Nonlinearity of Course

Concepts of course of disorder drawn from previous research have sometimes been strange indeed. For example, a traditional 1-year outcome study of patient 14 in our sample would suggest the course shown in Figure 1. However, our bimonthly assessment of this patient produced the curve shown in Figure 2. The two points in Figure 1 are not incorrect, but assuming a straight line between them is inadequate and misleading when the goal is to understand longitudinal processes. In our sub-

TABLE 2.
LONGITUDINAL PRINCIPLES IN THE COURSE OF DISORDER

A. Longitudinal patterns
1. Nonlinearity of course
2. Identifiable phases
   a. Moratoriums
   b. Change points
   c. Ceilings
3. "Mountain climbing"
4. Time decay of vulnerability
5. Phases of environmental response
   a. Convalescence
   b. Backlash

B. Individual-environment interactions
6. Identifiable sequences of individual-environment interaction
   a. Exaggerating feedback
   b. Corrective feedback
   c. Cumulative effect
7. The active role of the patient
8. The meaning of environmental events and personal behaviors

jects the course of disorder and recovery over the 2 years as measured by the Global Assessment Scale (Endicott, Spitzer, Fleiss, et al., 1976) and the Level of Function Scale (Strauss & Carpenter, 1974) never followed a straight line.

Principle 2: Identifiable Phases

This principle states that particular kinds of differentiated phases can be identified within the nonlinear courses of disorder. One common pattern for subjects in our study is shown in Figure 3.

Three commonly occurring phases can be discerned in such patterns. They are designated as moratoriums, change points, and ceilings.

Moratoriums. During certain periods, patients in our study experienced stability in symptoms and function. During such periods little measurable behavioral or symptom change was noted. We call these periods "moratoriums." Somewhat like the

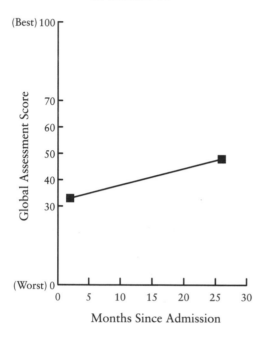

FIGURE 1.
TRADITIONAL ONE-YEAR OUTCOME STUDY
OF PATIENT 14

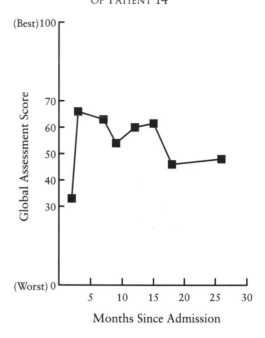

FIGURE 2.
BIMONTHLY ASSESSMENT OF OUTCOME
OF PATIENT 14

psychoanalytic concept of latency, the moratorium often appears to involve many important, although relatively hidden, changes. In such a case, patients often seemed to be reconstituting their identity, accumulating supports, or strengthening their skills in subtle ways. The following are three examples of moratoriums.

> After her discharge, patient 1 went to work as a sales clerk in a store run like a large family. The job itself was well below the status of those she had achieved at her prehospitalization peak, but it felt "comfortable." The low demand of the job tasks and the warmth and support she received from several co-workers and from her boss contributed to this comfort.

> Patient 22 stayed home with her parents and did very little socially or occupationally for 3 months following hospital discharge. After that period, she returned to work and increased her level of social and occupational function steadily over a 3-month period to a point well above the level she had lived at for several years before the onset of her psychiatric symptoms.

> Patient 10, who may have been in a prolonged moratorium period, was rehospitalized because of an exacerbation of her longstanding anxiety and auditory hallucinations following an increase in her job responsibilities. After admission, these symptoms dropped rapidly to their usual level. Following 1 week at this plateau, she returned to her job, which had been adjusted to be less stressful. She was discharged from the hospital a few days later and remained without further incident at her pre-exacerbation moratorium level of functioning.

FIGURE 3.
COMMON PATTERN OF THE COURSE OF PSYCHIATRIC DISORDER IN 28 PATIENTS

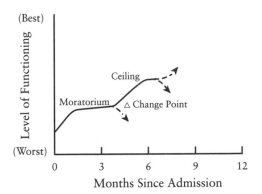

The existence of moratoriums following an episode of disorder appears to be universal, but their timing and duration vary widely. These variations may be related to the severity of illness and the number of previous episodes, among other things.

Change points. Change points involve considerable shifts in functioning or symptoms over a brief period.

> Patient 1, who had been working as a sales clerk in the family-like store, decided she needed to move on to a job with more future and better pay. She found such a job, and as she planned to begin it she also started to consider using the increased money she would receive to move from her parents' house to an apartment where she could have more personal freedom to date, cook, and function more autonomously.

Change points can be stimulated by the patient's own desires for moving on or by family or other pressures. These points appear to follow the principles of crisis theory, which postulate that at such a time patient can either improve markedly or decompensate. It is extremely difficult at this stage in our knowledge (since these points had not previously been identified and hence studied) to predict which direc-

tion the patient's course will take. Knowledge of the person's earlier patterns of response to stress, his or her other skills and needs, and the availability of social supports may help us anticipate the patient's future course however. Predicting the direction of change is especially difficult because symptoms frequently become worse at a change point, whether the person goes on to improvement or exacerbation. This phenomenon of temporal symptom exacerbation at such a point has also been noted by McCrory and associates (1980). An additional problem with change points emerges when the patient or clinician has to decide when symptom exacerbation is a prodromal sign of decompensation or simply a normal reaction to life's exigencies.

> Patient 12, who had been diagnosed as having a major depression, started to become depressed 2 months after hospital discharge and wondered if he was becoming ill again. He had been considering a major career change that involved a lower-status but more lucrative job. When seen at follow-up 2 months later, he reported the symptoms to have disappeared and the job change to be well under way.

Ceilings. The ceiling is defined as the highest level of functioning reached in a given period of time. It is not an impenetrable level, but it is often particularly difficult for the person to surpass the ceiling without experiencing major decompensation and symptom exacerbation.

> Patient 5 was a subject who would return rapidly to work following discharge from each of her several hospitalizations. She was very competent, but each time she was going to be promoted she would once again start to become psychotic.

Several subjects in the study experienced further progress beyond their ceiling after discharge, but also found such progress particularly stressful.

The irregular patterns in the course of disorder and the moratoriums, change points, and ceilings have several treatment implications. For example, patients, clinicians, and family members often become frustrated during moratoriums, seeming to expect that there should be a more or less straight line of progression and improvement. But excessive pressure for improvement during moratoriums might sometimes be deleterious, not allowing patients to gather their resources before approaching a change. In fact, patients may need all the moratorium time they can get because changes, when they do come, rarely come singly. If people get jobs, they have to deal with work settings, get used to a change in identity, shift roles with friends, perhaps take on new responsibilities in the family, and manage transportation.

Once the phases are noted, educational intervention by the clinician may be helpful, analogous to the interventions in family interactions described by Vaughn and Leff (1976) and Liberman (1982). Related adjustments to the quantity and quality of support, encouragement, and demand as well as possible shifts in medication and training using behavioral rehearsal may also be helpful.

Principle 3: "Mountain Climbing"

The course of disorder and its phases thus far have been described as a single process. In fact, as has been shown elsewhere (Strauss & Carpenter, 1977), there are several different processes occurring simultaneously and operating as open-linked systems. Symptoms, social relations functioning, and occupational functioning are three such systems that are relatively independent of each other while also having some intercorrelation. In reviewing the evolution of disorder and recovery in our subjects, it appeared that these systems often reflected a pattern that we termed "mountain climbing." When a subject was

well established in one context, such as social relations, perhaps following a period of moratorium he or she might attempt a change point in another context, such as work. This pattern of establishing a foothold in one area before attempting to make progress in another was relatively common.

Principle 4: Time Decay of Vulnerability

There appears to be a time decay phenomenon associated with vulnerability to various life events and situations during recovery from a symptomatic episode. The more recent the episode, the more vulnerable the person seems to be. This declining vulnerability may have an important biological analog. Post and Kopanda (1976) have written about the possibility of a "kindling" phenomenon through which repeated exposure to certain chemicals may increase physiological reactivity to them rather than produce habituation. A time decay phenomenon might reflect the reversal of this process, an "unkindling," or reduced reactivity.

Principle 5: Phases of Environmental Response

Just as there are several longitudinal phases in the patient's disorder and functioning, there appear to be predictable phases of environmental responses as well.

Convalescence. Many patients reported that they are implicitly allowed a convalescence of about 2-4 months following discharge from the hospital. During this time demands are generally limited, and patients are given assistance and permission to reenter the stream of life gradually.

Backlash. When the implicit convalescent period ends, however, there often is a backlash during which family, friends, and clinicians appear to demand even more than they had before the exacerbation or onset of the illness. These demands often come as a surprise to patients who think that they have been doing well. The backlash phenomenon often causes considerable distress for all involved. An understanding of the patient's moratorium, change point, and ceiling phases during the post-discharge period would help those persons in the patient's environment titrate their own reactions and expectations more appropriately.

It is possible that as such environmental phases are clarified further, they may be found to include the same kind of moratoriums and change points seen in the individual. In fact, correspondences of certain individual and environmental phases may be crucial influences on the patient's improvement.

Individual-Environmental Interactions

Principle 6: Identifiable Sequences of Individual Environment Interaction

At a level more microscopic than the broad patterns described earlier, the subjects' experiences can be seen to reflect identifiable sequences in which they and their environments interact. Several types of cause-effect   sequence appear to take place, including exaggerating and corrective feedback cycles and cumulative impacts.

Exaggerating feedback. In exaggerating feedback cycles ("positive feedback," in general systems terms), each event in the sequence exaggerates the situation further in a cyclic fashion. Feedback is used here to indicate the process by which a change in the person or the environment itself generates subsequent changes, which in turn influence the initial change.

> Patient 12 found that when he started to get depressed before a psychotic episode, he became preoccupied with astrology, paid less attention to work, performed more poorly, became more depressed, and became more preoccupied and progressively more disturbed.

Corrective feedback. In corrective feedback situations ("negative feedback," in the terms of general systems theory), a sequence of events occurs that returns a person to a previous, more modulated state.

> Patient 1, a young woman with schizoaffective disorder, noted that as she became more hyperactive on the job a co-worker would say things like, "Why don't you slow down? I'll help you with those customers. This intervention appeared to help the subject regain control of her activity level.

Cumulative effect. Cumulative impacts of more or less separate environment-individual interactions are common.

> Patient 11 moved, changed jobs, and separated from his family all within a few weeks. Then he was involved in an automobile accident (not through his fault) that left him without transportation for work or social contacts. This group of events was followed by a recurrence of symptoms.

Principle 7: The Active Role of the Patient

Many views of psychiatric disorder portray the patient as passive. Although such concepts of illness go back at least to Newton (Toulmin, 1982 unpublished paper), the principle described here suggests that the patient often has an active role in the process of decompensation and recovery.

Our subjects persistently described the role they took in affecting the course of their disorder both directly and through influencing their environment. This principle was noted, for example, in a patient's determination to function in spite of frightening symptoms, participation in a treatment regimen, attempts to undermine that regimen, or consumption of symptom causing street drugs. The importance of the patient's active role is suggested by studies of patients' giving up on efforts to get better (Schmale, 1964) and of their treatment participation (Van Putten & May, 1978). Besides giving up on improving and their participation in therapy, patients also have a major role in terms of their many ways of helping to control their symptoms, methods that appear to be most useful when symptoms are at low or moderate levels of intensity (Breier & Strauss, 1983).

Principle 8: The Meaning of Environmental Events and Personal Behaviors

The implications to the person of the environmental event or situation will influence the course of the disorder (Lazarus, 1981; Lieberman & Strauss, 1984). For instance, a job failure may free the person to pursue a new line of work more compatible with certain basic needs.

> Patient 6 was a very proud woman who quit her administrative job because she just couldn't take the pressures. Although job problems had previously been followed by a recurrence of her schizoaffective disorder, on this occasion her symptoms did not reappear. Rather, she found a job as a clerk in an office. In this job she pursued in comfort, and for the first time in her life, her interest in developing better relationships with co-workers.

Just as the meaning of the environmental situation affects the person's response, so the meaning of the person's behavior influences environmental responses.

> When patient 6 was later laid off from her new job because of the deteriorating economy, her boyfriend threatened to break up with her because she was no longer contributing to the household.

These then are the longitudinal principles of the interactive developmental model. It should be noted that not all eight principles were identifiable in all subjects, but each principle was found often enough to warrant routine attention for clinical

and research purposes. It also appears that there are interactions among the principles. For example, a moratorium may be most likely to end after time decay of vulnerability has reached a certain level.

An Illustrative Case

How do these various longitudinal principles operate together to influence the course of disorder for a particular patient?

> Patient 14, mentioned earlier, was a 39-year old married white woman with a 4-year history of bipolar disorder and three previous psychiatric hospitalizations. She was admitted to the hospital for the fourth time for a severe depressive episode when we first saw her as a research subject. In a schematic comparison of only her functioning level on admission and at 1-year follow-up, the line is straight, as shown in Figure 1. In fact, her course was far more complex, as shown in Figure 2.
>
> When admitted to the hospital, the patient was extremely depressed. She said she was "no good" and was distanced from the people in her environment. She fended off practically all attempts to make contact with her.
>
> In the course of treatment, both psychosocial and pharmacologic, she became less depressed, and her interactions with the environment increased. These changes made it possible for her to be discharged from the hospital. She returned to living with her family, which consisted of her husband and two children.
>
> Because her job had been a very helpful part of her life, she returned to work immediately. Her supervisor and co-workers were supportive and were pleased to have her back, and they told her so. She in turn began joking with them again, completing an exaggerating feedback sequence moving her further away from her depressed state. She was very effective at her computer programming job, shouldered more than her share of the work, and even suggested effective procedural

changes to help the group be more productive. If a moratorium occurred at all with this patient, it did so in the hospital and was of very brief duration. In fact, she returned very quickly to her prehospitalization ceiling of function.

During a plateau at this ceiling level (perhaps a second moratorium at a higher level), she did well for several months. In fact, she even pushed through her previous ceiling within the family context (mountain climbing). She lived in a very difficult family situation. Her children had minor but troublesome problems with the school authorities, and her husband had been diagnosed as having a major illness. With the support of her successes at work, the patient assumed a more active role in the family. She became more assertive than she had ever been and insisted that family members help with the housework. They responded well, and the situation improved. Thus, successes in the job and family contexts resulted in a positive cumulative impact on the patient.

At this time, however, the economy was on the decline and the regional office of the manufacturing company that employed the patient laid off many employees. She was lucky, however, or so it seemed. She did continue on the job, but in spite of the fact that her abilities were superior to those of several other workers, her hours were reduced and she was transferred to the evening shift.

The patient had a longstanding problem with not being very assertive. She had become more assertive at home, but she did not transfer her new advances at home to the work context. If she had taken a more active role in protesting the reduction of and change in hours, perhaps she would have avoided the shift in the job situation. Unfortunately, the job

The existence of moratoriums following an episode of disorder appears to be universal, but their timing and duration vary widely.

change had a major negative impact on her self-esteem and social contacts. There was only one co-worker, a rather dour and withdrawn woman, on the evening shift. There was no joking or praise for work well done. In addition, the cutback in hours reduced her salary and she felt less valuable for what she could contribute to the hard pressed family finances.

The patient became less assertive at home. While hoping for more praise and recognition from the family, she received more criticism instead. Before long, she was back in the hospital with a severe depression. The exaggerating feedback sequence (reduced work→reduced money→reduced self-esteem→reduced active role→reduced self-esteem) appeared to have contributed to the recurrence.

This patient's situation illustrates how the course of compensation and recovery in psychiatric disorder may be a complex evolving process. For her, a sequence involving positive changes in self-esteem, active role, and social contacts in the work setting led to increased ability to deal with another context, the family. But with the change of the economy, the role of her work in meeting, or at least not frustrating, certain needs was reduced. The snowball effect that apparently was set into motion had aroused more desperate coping mechanisms in the patient, perhaps the kind of conservation withdrawal described by Engel (unpublished 1972 paper). It is processes such as these that seem to influence the directions, timing, and structure of the moratoriums and change points, and the degree of vulnerability to decompensation.

Discussion

The need for a more adequate model to reflect the evolution of a psychiatric disorder is especially glaring now that increasing evidence has been generated showing that even people with the most severe and chronic mental illness may experience major changes, often with partial or full recovery. Furthermore, there is increasing evidence that these changes may be related to environmental factors such as family behavior and expectations, psychosocial treatment, social networks, and stressful life events. Thus, we know that a person with a psychiatric disorder may, over time, go from point A to a very different point B. and we know of some factors that may be involved in that change. But almost nothing is known about the processes by which the person gets to point B and the sequence of phenomena that may be involved.

Actually, the lack of information on the evolution, in contrast to the outcome, of psychiatric disorder is not so surprising: the problem of doing truly longitudinal research has been noted in developmental psychology, a field where there might have been an even more intensive focus in this direction (Elder, 1983 unpublished paper). Apparently the multiple cross-sectional model, with its assessment at no more than a few points in time and its ease of data collection and analysis, has been so seductive that the more complex understanding of the evolution of sequential processes has been all but ignored.

But the issues of sequence and patterns cannot be neglected indefinitely: they potentially hold answers for too many crucial questions. Are there critical periods in the recovery process when stressful life events may have an especially powerful impact? Is there a particular point in a chain of happenings during which a specific intervention, such as helping a patient return to work or starting intensive psychotherapy,

may be especially helpful or noxious? Are there particular sequences of events in the evolution of disorder that in themselves lead to recurrence of the disorder? Although there are many clinical impressions regarding these essential questions, there has been almost no systematic research to help validate or correct the clinical impressions and to develop them further.

One of the major features inhibiting research on the evolution of disorder and recovery is the complexity involved. What characteristics should be studied? When should data be collected? To begin resolving these questions, it was essential to carry out exploratory research focused on identifying patterns and delineating key variables. Through such research, it is possible to begin to establish a truly longitudinal framework for understanding the processes of psychopathology. It is important in such an inquiry, as in any scientific effort, to be faithful to the phenomena being studied, even though this may lead to shifts in research method (Strauss & Hafez, 1981; Bakan, 1973; Skinner, 1972).

The Interactive Developmental Model of the course of psychiatric disorder has grown out of such efforts. With its longitudinal principles, it attempts to describe variables and processes to provide a structure for integrating and furthering what is known about the course of psychiatric disorder.

References

Bakan, D. (1973). *On Method: Toward a reconstruction of psychological investigation.* San Francisco: Jossey-Bass.

Breier, A., & Strauss, J. S. (1983). Self-control in psychiatric disorders. *Archives of General Psychiatry, 40,* 1141-1145.

Ciompi, L. (1980). The natural history of schizophrenia in the long term. *British Journal of Psychiatry, 136,* 413-420.

Cohen, C., & Sokolovsky, J. (1978). Schizophrenia and social networks: Expatients in the inner city. *Schizophrenia Bulletin, 4,* 546-560.

Day, R. (1981). Life events and schizophrenia: The "triggering" hypothesis. *Acta Psychiatrica Scandinavica, 64,* 97-122.

Endicott, J., Spitzer, R. L., Fleiss, J. L., et al. (1976). The Global Assessment Scale: A procedure for measuring overall severity of psychiatric disturbance. *Archives of General Psychiatry, 33,* 766-771.

Harding, C. M., & Strauss, J. S. (in press). The course of schizophrenia: an evolving concept. In M. Alpert (Ed.), *Controversies in schizophrenia.* New York: Guilford Press.

Lazarus, R. S. (1981). The stress and coping paradigm. In C. Eisdorfer, D. Cohen, A. Kleinman et al. (Eds.), *Models for clinical psychopathology.* New York: Spectrum Publications.

Liberman, R. P. (1982). Social factors in schizophrenia. In L. Grinspoon (Ed.), *Psychiatry 1982: The American Psychiatric Association annual review.* Washington, DC: American Psychiatric Press.

Lieberman, P., & Strauss, J. S. (1984). Recurrence of mania: environments factors and medical treatment. *American Journal of Psychiatry, 141,* 77-80.

Maher, L., & Gunderson, J. (1979) Group, family, milieu, and community support systems treatment for schizophrenia. In I. Bellak (Ed.), *Disorders of the schizophrenic syndrome.* New York: Basic Books.

McCrory, D.J., Connelly, P. S., Hanson-Mayer, T. P., et al. (1980). The rehabilitation crisis: The impact of growth. *Journal of Applied Rehabilitation Counseling, 11,* 136-139.

Overall, J., & Gorham, D. (1962). The Brief Psychiatric Rating Scale. *Psychological Reports, 10,* 799-812.

Post, R. M., & Kopanda, R.T. (1976). Cocaine, kindling, and psychosis. *American Psychiatry 133,* 627-634.

Schmale, A. H. (1964). A genetic view of affects with special reference to the genesis of helplessness and hopelessness. *Psychoanalytic Study Child 19,* 287-310.

Skinner, B. F. (1972). A case history in scientific method. In *Cumulative Record,* (3rd ed). New York: Appleton-Century-Crofts.

Strauss, J. S., & Carpenter, W. T., Jr. (1974). Characteristic symptoms and outcome in schizophrenia. *Archives of General Psychiatry, 30,* 429-434.

Strauss, J. S. , & Carpenter, W. T., Jr. (1977) Prediction of outcome, III: Five year outcome and its predictors. *Archives of General Psychiatry, 34,* 14-20.

Strauss, J. S., & Carpenter, W. T., Jr. (1981) *Schizophrenia.* New York: Plenum.

Strauss, J. S., & Hafez, H. (1981). Clinical questions and "real" research. *American Journal of Psychiatry, 138,* 1592-1597.

Strauss, J. S., Kokes, R. F., Carpenter, W. T., Jr. et al. (1978). The course of schizophrenia as a developmental process. In I. C. Wynne, R. I. Cromwell, & S. Matthysse (Eds.), *Nature of schizophrenia: New findings and future strategies.* New York: John Wiley & Sons.

Strauss, J. S., Loevsky, L., Glazer, W., et al. (1981). Organizing the complexities of schizophrenia. *Journal of Nervous Mental Disorders, 169,* 120-126.

Van Putten, T. & May, P. R. A. (1978). Subjective response as a predictor of outcome in pharmacotherapy: The consumer has a point. *Archives of General Psychiatry, 35,* 477-480.

Vaughn, C. E., & Leff, J.,P. (1976). The influence of family and social factors on the course of psychiatric illness. *British Journal of Psychiatry 129,* 125-137.

A Long and Winding Road: The Process of Recovery From Severe Mental Illness

William Patrick Sullivan

WILLIAM PATRICK SULLIVAN, PH.D., IS AN ASSOCIATE PROFESSOR AT INDIANA UNIVERSITY.

THIS ARTICLE ORIGINALLY APPEARED IN *Innovations and Research*, 1994, 3(3), 19-27, AND IS REPRINTED WITH PERMISSION.

Longitudinal and cross-cultural studies confirm that recovery is a possible outcome for those facing severe mental illnesses. Indeed, recovery has been offered as the guiding mission for mental health services in the 1990s. If recovery is a process that can be influenced by the behavior of self or others it is important that this phenomenon is explored. This paper represents a preliminary step in the effort to decode the recovery process. Specifically, 46 former and current consumers of mental health services were asked to identify those activities, attitudes, and behaviors, initiated by self or others, that are essential to their success. These factors are explored drawing from informant accounts and tentative implications of the findings are offered.

In two recent articles, Anthony (1991, 1993) has offered recovery as the guiding mission for mental health services in the 1990s. This declaration is timely, for a host of longitudinal and cross-cultural studies continue to challenge the concept of chronicity—formerly a dominant conceptual anchor in our understanding of severe mental illnesses (Harding, Brooks, Takamaru, Strauss & Breier, 1987a, 1987b; Harding, Zubin & Strauss, 1987; Marsella, 1988; McGlashan, 1988; Sartorius, Jablensky, Ernberg, Leff, Korten & Gulbinat, 1987; Warner, 1983). The simple

recognition that there are a range of possible outcomes associated with severe mental illness provides the necessary foundation for the concept of recovery to secure legitimacy. Certainly, recovery may reflect the natural course of illness for select individuals due to biophysical reasons that cannot be discerned given the current state of knowledge and technology (Wynne, 1988). However, if recovery is an outcome that can be influenced by the actual behaviors of self or others, a fresh research agenda is suggested. For example, the acceptance of schizophrenia as a chronic condition may direct attention to those factors that cause or predict relapse. In contrast, a research paradigm guided by the vision of recovery strives to reveal those processes that undergird success. And, it is inappropriate to assume that the forces that promote recovery are merely the flip side of those factors which predict relapse.

At this juncture recovery is an illusive concept. Anthony (1993) notes that recovery is a deeply personal, unique process of changing one's attitudes, values, feelings, goals, skills, and/or roles. It is a way of living a satisfying, hopeful, and contributing life even with the limitations caused by illness. Recovery involves the development of new meaning and purpose in one's life as one grows beyond the catastrophic effects of mental illness. (p. 15)

If the concept of recovery can supply the needed vision to guide mental health professionals and programs into the next century, it is crucial to unveil key elements of this deeply personal experience. It is hoped this exercise can clarify those personal and professional activities which support this journey. This paper represents a preliminary step in the effort to decode the recovery process. Specifically, former and current consumers of mental health services were asked to identify those activities, attitudes, and behaviors, initiated by self or others, that are essential to their success. What follows is a discussion of the discrete factors identified by these experts. Additionally, these factors, as well as the personal narratives of respondents, provide the groundwork for a description of the recovery process from a developmental perspective. Throughout this paper offers tentative implications of the findings for consumer's, professional helpers, and mental health service delivery.

The Study

Fifty-four current and former consumers of mental health services participated in a semistructured interview that lasted approximately 1 hour. Data were collected between May, 1990, and January, 1992. Respondents were predominantly recruited from three community mental health centers in the Midwest, a chapter of the Alliance for the Mentally Ill, and a consumer-operated support group. Other interviews were conducted with individuals who learned of the project through personal sources or at various mental health workshops. Representatives of the participating organizations notified potential candidates about the study to solicit informants. All respondents were paid for sharing their expertise on the recovery process.

To be included in the study, respondents matched the criteria for severe and persistent mental illness originally offered by the Steering Committee on the Chronically Mentally Ill (1981) and captured in the basic dimensions of diagnosis, disability, and duration. Furthermore, these clients were viewed by self and/or others as successfully surmounting the illness on the basis of their participation in some form of vocational activity, residence in at least a semi-independent setting, and having avoided psychiatric hospitalization for at least 2 years. This definition of success (or recovery) is consistent with the common mission and goals of community-based

TABLE 1.
MEAN SAMPLE CHARACTERISTICS

(*N* = 46)

Gender

Female	22	(48%)
Male	24	(52%)

Diagnosis

Schizophrenia	74%
Bipolar	17%
Other	9%

Age

Total Sample	39	(S.D. = 9.5)
Female	42.7	(S.D. = 10.9)
Male	35.6	(S.D. = 6.5)

Age at First Hospitalization

Total Sample	24	(S.D. = 6.6)
Female	27.3	(S.D. = 7.3)
Male	21	(S.D. = 4.0)

Average Number of Previous Hospitalizations

Total Sample	5.6	(S.D. = 5.2)
Female	4.1	(S.D. = 2.7)
Male	7.0	(S.D. = 6.5)

Average Years Since Last Hospitalization

Total Sample	6.3	(S.D. = 5.5)
		(Median = 4.0)
Female	6.5	(S.D. = 5.5)

Average Years Between First and Last Admission

Total Sample	8.7	(S.D. = 5.6)
Female	8.5	(S.D. = 6.3)
Male	9.0	(S.D. = 5.0)

mental health services. It is certainly arguable that this criteria is skewed by focusing narrowly on actual activities and the outward manifestations of a process that has internal dimensions as well.

Of the original cohort of informants interviewed, 46 met all criteria for inclusion in the study. Table 1 provides a glimpse of demographic characteristics and historical data provided by informants. While the use of self-reports undoubtedly introduces some error into these statistics, it is now common for consumers to be informed of their diagnoses, and they have also proven to be reliable historians in the area of hospitalization episodes (Cutting, & Dunne 1989; Distefano, Pryer & Garrison, 1991). A review of the data indicates that the sample is closely divided by gender and predominantly white. In addition, the majority of respondents have been diagnosed with schizophrenia (74%), were hospitalized for the first time in early adulthood (mean, 24), and experienced an average of 5.6 hospitalizations (range 0-30) over a period of 8.7 years. It is noteworthy that as a group informants have not been hospitalized for a psychiatric reason for over 6 years.

All interviews were recorded and transcribed verbatim. All informants were queried about their initial involvement with the mental health system, their assessment of the quality of the care received to date, and what factors have contributed to their success in dealing with a mental illness. Responses to the latter question were analyzed using elements of Spradley's (1979) ethnographic research method. Accordingly, the factors for success identified by informants were grouped into a series of overarching domains. Given the kinds of questions posed to participants and the nature of their responses, the creation of these domains did not demand great conceptual abstraction. The use of qualitative methodology was consciously chosen in order to elicit data entirely from the respondents' perspective. This method allows for unforeseen data to emerge and also recognizes the consumer as the expert on the recovery process (Strauss, 1989). Hatfield and Lefley (1993) note that continued advancements in basic research and rehabilitation strategies rest, in part, on our ability to understand the subjective experience of those who face severe mental disorders.

Keys for Success: Consumer Perspectives

In the following section the key domains identified by at least 30% of respondents as important to their success are briefly described and illustrated by the use of their words. Table 2 lists these domains and the percentage of informants who specifically identified each area as important to their success. The number of discrete factors identified by respondents ranged from 1 to

TABLE 2.
FACTORS ASSOCIATED WITH SUCCESS

(N = 46)

Medication	72%
Community Support Service/ Case Management	67%
Self-Will, Self-Monitoring	63%
Vocational Activity (Including School)	46%
Spirituality	43%
Knowledge About the Illness/ Acceptance of the Illness	35%
Mutual Aid Groups—Supportive Friends	33%
Significant Others	30%

10, with an average of 4.7 per informant. The response pattern of informants was similar across diagnostic categories and gender.

Medication

The importance of medication in the treatment of severe mental illness has been amply documented. Indeed, the failure of consumers to comply with medication regimens is a common source of frustration for professionals and family members. In this study, 72% of consumers identified medication as critical to their success. For example, one respondent noted: "When I started taking the medication again it was like night and day for me. I felt different. I felt happy. I didn't feel like people were setting me up."

However, respondents also noted their frustration working with professionals in the effort to find the right medication and dosage levels. One informant noted that "it is important to get a doctor who will listen. So many of them...won't listen to what you are saying." Another former consumer described her experience with medication beginning in the 1970s:

> At first there was a higher dosage...and that made me sleepy and sluggish and things like that. But when they started reducing it then I thought—Well, I really do have a brain and it's going to function. That I was really going to come around and not be drugged out all my life.

These respondents remind us anew of the importance of active listening, education, and patience on the part of professionals as critical factors in medication compliance (Goldstein, 1992). The data also suggest that, with time, those who find a medication they are comfortable with, and who learn from previous unsuccessful attempts to succeed without psychotropic drugs, begin to recognize the centrality of compliance to the recovery process.

Self-Will/Self-Monitoring

Understanding severe mental illness as a neurobiological disorder can lead one to conclude that the afflicted individual has little power to control the illness process.

Most need, as do all of us, someone who will take their concerns seriously and who displays a willingness to treat their feelings and concerns with compassion.

Perhaps the most stunning finding from this study was the high percentage (63%) of respondents who described their ability to control or a least successfully monitor the illness. The potential for consumers to manage symptomatology has been postulated by Breier and Strauss (1983) and has been suggested in the personal account of Esso Leete (1989).

Many of the respondents describe their success as a matter of attitude or drive: "I made up my mind that I was going to be normal. I have a fighting spirit—a persistence." Echoing a similar sentiment one respondent noted: "As long as I don't give up is the secret I think. I've met people who kind of [gave up], they don't know which way to go or anything to do."

A key to success lies in the ability to recognize symptoms and to take action to counteract them. Some of the strategies used by respondents are likely to seem absurd to outsiders. Consider the divergent manner in which two informants describe their approach to dealing with hallucinations: "When I threaten them bad enough [the voices], usually they try to get worse with me, but if I just make it serious enough [his threats] they will leave me alone." This informant speaks of actually shouting at his voices when they disturb him. In contrast, a different informant takes a more passive but equally effective approach: "When I have been irritated by my voices I will just listen to some of my favorite music and just keep playing it, playing it, playing it, until it goes away."

Others learn to watch for particularly predictive signs of relapse. "I know what to look for," or specifically, "I start feeling like—perceptions, sensitivity to stuff to—it looks a little different. So then I know that I had better talk to somebody." These informants, vigilant to changes in feelings and behaviors, also learn to strategically use professional helpers, particularly psychiatrists who may make modifications in their medication. The myriad of ways that persons cope with hallucinations has been noted by Romme and Escher (1989). Obviously, it behooves professionals to learn of these idiosyncratic signs from consumers and family members and, subsequently, to go over a plan of action with those with whom they are working.

Community Support/ Mental Health Services

The emergence of this factor is undoubtedly influenced by the preponderance of respondents still associated with a community mental health center. Nonetheless, it is still meaningful that these consumers view services as an important vehicle to success. The interesting data here, however, are reasons why the consumers viewed these services as helpful. Consider these responses: "I feel safe up there"; "They make you feel welcome"; "It gave me a place to go when I was disappointed that I didn't finish college"; and "They never turned their back on me."

Similar themes emerge when the informants describe the importance of case managers and therapists: "She's a friend, not only a caseworker, but she's a friend. We sometimes go out to eat. She sees that my apartment is okay and she sees that I'm okay, physically or mentally"; "He just looks after me...he takes me seriously"; and "I'll never forget that vision when he stood there, and he always stands there with his hands in his pockets, and at that time with a pipe in his mouth. And he said, I'm not giving up on you...do you hear me? I'm not giving up."

Great efforts have been made to develop a range of effective services and programs to help consumers in community settings. Yet, these informants suggest that much of the power of helping still comes in the form of a relationship (see Mosher & Burti, 1992; Saleebey, 1991). However, the manner in which the professional helps is not by being dispassionate, detached, or objective. Rather, the professional helps when s/he joins with the consumer, engaging and working in partnership and treating the individual in a respectful and normalized manner.

Where specific services of community support programs were identified as helpful, it was in the provision of tangible aid and the ability to offer structure. In the words of one participant, the program was helpful by "setting me up in an apartment, helping me get my furniture, helping me pay off my medical bills, [and] getting medicine." Illustrating the power of structure, one current consumer notes that "they give you activities in such a way that it keeps you busy and you don't have that time to become sick."

Vocational Activity

From an historical perspective probably no single element has been more closely linked with rehabilitation and recovery from mental illness than work. Far from simply being a preoccupation among professionals, work is commonly identified by consumers as both a goal and a force in recovery (Arns & Linney, 1993). In this study, vocational activity was construed broadly to include attending school and homemaking activities. For this sample, work serves the same purposes as it does for others, from providing for basic needs to an essential ingredient to the sense of selfworth. Work also provides structure: "It helps your routine"; "It keeps me busy"; "I'm forced to concentrate; It gets me out of the house."

Work also represents goal-directed behavior and the sense that one is making a contribution. To be successful in this area is to have some sense that life can become manageable: "When I got that chance to be stable and grab a few classes and to be rewarded for finishing the classes, getting the grades—it didn't take very long before that's what I wanted to do more than go manic."

The words of one informant speak of the link between work and self-esteem:

Well I guess I sort of feel like you can accomplish something and get your work done and if you have troubles your mind doesn't dwell on them so much. So at least you're successful in one thing so your not such a terrible or dumb or lazy person.

Spirituality

The sheer number of respondents who indicated the power of spirituality as important to their success was not anticipated. Here, a broad definition of spirituality is employed which includes participation in organized religious activities. Upon reflection it would seem that the identification of this variable as important to the lives of informants mirrors the centrality of spirituality for many Americans. Spirituality provides solace during illness, is a mechanism used to reduce the burden of the illness, and is a source of social support (Sullivan, 1993).

The following quotes illustrate the themes identified above:

I'm a Christian and so I began praying and asking God to help me through those times;" "They're [the congregation] going to help me overcome this obstacle of shying from people;" "A lot of times at night I'll see different things, you know, and I'll just close my eyes and say a prayer, and pretty soon I will open my eyes and it will be gone.

There have been close relationships, at various points in history, between mental health professionals, pastoral counselors, and clergy. This tradition may have waned. The re-establishment of these relationships and the active effort to educate clergy and congregations could prove to be a fruitful enterprise (Shifrin, Cohen, & Kraft, 1990).

Mutual Aid Groups/Supportive Friends

Mutual aid or support groups, developed by professionals and/or consumers, have become an integral part of the recovery process and the mental health system. These groups differ in the degree of their formality but are formed to provide supportive and educational functions. What became apparent in this study is that there are clear instances where groups of current and former consumers, like most people, develop natural support systems among themselves. These natural networks, while not formally organized, appear to serve similar functions as designated support groups.

The emergence of this factor is clearly influenced by the sample. First, several members of a support group for bipolar disorders are included in the survey. Second, the development of a strong natural helping network was found among two groups of individuals participating in supportive housing programs.

The informal support networks that developed in these apartment programs are particularly significant. So often the concept community integration implies the need to ensure that persons facing severe mental illness are geographically and emotionally dispersed throughout the community. Yet, given the choice to select a housing option, most people prefer to live in proximity to those with whom they can easily relate to. Here, clients are able to develop symmetrical relationships (in terms of power) with peers that are, as Estroff (1981) notes, markedly different from the asymmetrical relationships often endured with professionals and those deemed normal. The following quote is illustrative of the culture that developed in these settings:

I have a group of friends now...we call each other and we do things together. We help each other. We talk on the phone. If we get scared or paranoid, then we talk on the phone and they're usually very nice to try and help me.

There are things that I'm not able to do for myself, or think that I can't do for myself. And when I'm doing for someone else that is putting out something that I should be doing for myself but can't—but I can do it for other people. And it's healing. It [is] healing to get your mind off yourself and be able to love and help someone. It's really good therapy.

The beneficial impact of formal consumer support programs, similar to the illustrations above, is manifested through the opportunity to give and receive support and the chance to assume leadership roles that are often denied in other settings (Rappaport, Reischl, & Zimmerman, 1992). These helpful aspects of participation in formal support groups were also identified in this study. Of particular importance is how these groups provide a level of comfort and understanding that is not experienced in other relationships. Consider the following observations:

"There's just some things that somebody without this disorder can't and won't ever be able to understand. But the support group, they understand...." "If I say something, they understand exactly what I'm talking about;" and "Being around other people who have it [bipolar disorder] and understand you is very important—we use fewer words when we talk. We know you understand." Finally, how these groups augment professional support is clear in this report: "This is my main system. And it literally kept me out of the hospital this spring. If I had not had the outside support I would have been in the hospital somewhere."

Significant Others

This domain encompasses the informants' personal relationships outside their family of origin. While the sustenance these relationships offer (support, tangible aid, and so forth) may be conceptually indistinct from other significant relationships, including family, the flavor of the narratives indicates that differences exist. Certainly, the role of the family as caregivers has received considerable attention in the past decade. Have attention to the basic needs of love and affection, and the opportunity for sexual expression been lacking in psychosocial rehabilitation? For example, the *Cumulative Index* for *Psychosocial Rehabilitation Journal,* covering a 15-year period, reveals only three articles devoted to sexuality, with none appearing since 1984. Simply stated, one informant noted: "It just matters, being loved."

In this study informants provided a variety of examples of how their partners had helped them, from offering support during difficult times to having a positive impact on their self-esteem; "He keeps me happy. I mean he is always joking around and he tells me that it's not always as bad as I think it is;" and "When I met [my wife] she introduced me to the idea that I was somebody that someone else could get enjoyment from and I made quantum leaps after that because my self-image was poor."

Learning how to forge and maintain deeply personal relationships is a vexing developmental task for most people. The difficulty that many current and former consumers face in this area is obviously amplified by illness and is a function of the period of life in which these illnesses commonly strike. Some consumers may lack basic knowledge and skills. Most need, as do all of us, someone who will take their concerns seriously and who displays a willingness to treat their feelings and concerns with compassion.

Knowledge/Acceptance of the Illness

This area, learning about the illness and accepting one's situation, quite possibly undergirds all of the domains listed previously. The reports of the respondents' suggest that understanding the illness prompts one to comply with medication, avoid overly stressful situations, monitor symptoms, strive to live a healthier lifestyle, and eliminate or reduce alcohol and drug use (these two domains were listed separately by 15% and 17% of respondents respectively). The interconnectedness of increased knowledge of the illnesses and subsequent changes in behavior is reflected in the following observations:

> I think the most important thing that I've done or could have happened to me is realizing and accepting the fact that I am mentally ill. That's the most important part. Because without that realization, I might not take my medication.

> Well one of the things that you have to do is realize that you can't accept or can't handle stress as well as you could before you got sick. And you might have to plan your day accordingly not to put too much stress on you, because stress is one of the triggers.

Sometimes it all comes down to a simple revelation: "In other words, what I'm doing in this whole process is realizing that I have a disability and anytime you have a disability you have to live according to it. That's all there is to it."

Estroff (1989, p. 193) has pondered the relative effect of accepting an illness label as synonymous with self (I am a schizophrenic) versus viewing oneself as a person with an illness: "Is good prognosis associated with separation from self, a preserving of a person who has but is not an illness? Or does the individual fare better by embracing and incorporating schizophrenia as within and of the self?"

No clear answers can be offered here. It would seem that knowledge and acceptance of the illness can be empowering for some but inhibiting to others. However, the way in which the self understands and relates to the illness, and the specific manner in which professionals, where involved, impart knowledge about the course and prognosis of the illness, may prove to be important factors in the recovery process.

Summing Up

This exploratory study has obvious limitations. Perhaps the most critical limitation of all is our incomplete knowledge of illnesses like schizophrenia. It is certainly possible that this sample reflects those individuals destined to have a relatively benign course and/or those who gain maximum benefit from medication. Nonetheless, the respondents described here vividly portrayed periods of confusion and despair and experienced considerable periods of confinement due to mental illness. Some did not use medication.

The results may also be skewed by the sample. Different results may emerge if individuals were solicited from alternative sources, for example, those who have steadfastly avoided contact with the mental health system. A more diverse sample, geographically and culturally, would have also strengthened the study.

It is important to affirm that these results should not be construed as offering a recipe for recovery. The study represents

The sheer number of respondents who indicated the power of spirituality as important to their success was not anticipated.

a preliminary attempt to distill data from the individual recovery story of respondents. While some domains may seem to be prerequisite to others, it is more likely that there is a synergistic and kaleidoscope-like aspect to the recovery process. For example, reflection on the nature of each discrete domain presents a paradox in that countervailing forces may be operating simultaneously. For example, there are several instances where respondents underscore the importance of accepting the limitations of the illness but also assert the power of their will in ameliorating the impact of the illness. They describe the importance of avoiding stress but also identify as key to their success activities that can produce high levels of anxiety, such as working and involvement in a significant personal relationship.

What these informants describe are efforts to actively adapt their lifestyle to deal with a challenging situation. In daily life they draw sustenance from a higher power, helping professionals, friends and lovers, and their own strength. They make choices that are consistent with their desires and goals while remaining cognizant of what is needed in the management of a serious illness. This ability to make such informed choices may be captured in a single word: maturity.

In fact, several respondents directly or indirectly noted their maturation as a critical element of their success:

> [I worked] so hard at the Breakthrough house to do good, you know, to learn how to accept myself and assume responsibility for things you know. Growing up and all that.

> I was lonely, I didn't understand, I would feel so—I don't know whether it would be nasty or what...I was so new to the situation. I was depressed. I didn't know where I was going. I had anxiety real bad. You said what changed me? Well, I stopped trying to run from it and [instead] get around on it and try to meet it head on.

Some recognize the changes they have made in their life:

> I think I'm a different person than I was back then . . . Because I've learned to take care of myself. I've learned to take my medicine.

Others can recall a seminal event that precipitated the change:

> I was off my meds and up all night. I was reactive, irritable, all that stuff—and that's when I made the decision, because [my wife] was right there and she called my mother and said...right in front of me, I can't really do anymore for him—and so my mother...who had done this so many times, sitting up all night, doing what we did to go through it. And that's when that voice kind of went inside me and I said I've got some responsibilities here, and I can't keep doing this stuff.

There have been a number of attempts to study the natural course of illnesses like schizophrenia. McGlashan (1988) reports that while schizophrenia can be viewed as a chronic illness, this does not mean that functioning progressively deteriorates over time. Instead it appears that functioning levels or plateaus approximately 5 to 10 years after the onset of the illness. Using hospitalization data as a proxy measure for the onset of illness, the profile of the respondents in this study seems consistent with this finding. Here, consumers averaged over five and one-half hospitalizations in roughly a 9-year period before life seems to have evened out. Strauss, Hafez, Lieberman, and Harding (1985) have offered the Interactive Development Model hypothesizing that there are variations (ceilings, moratoriums, change points) in the course of the illness for each individual and that an understanding of these phases may provide clues to treatment and recovery. Wynne (1988), taking a longitudinal perspective, notes that it is unclear if late-life improvements in schizophrenia are the result of the natural history of the illness, changes in the personality, or a reduction in environmental demands. While there are still more questions to address than available answers McGlashan (1988) states that "an important fact remains: a lot of people recover from schizophrenia" (p. 528).

While it is inappropriate to draw firm conclusions from this study, the reports of these informants posit a key role for the individual in the recovery process. Strauss (1989) has hypothesized that oftentimes consumers are not passive victims to a disease process but, instead, actors who engage in goal-directed behavior, whose feelings and interpretations about the illness impact the phases of the disorder, and who call upon regulatory mechanisms to adapt. Understanding the relationship between the person and the illness may provide important data about the recovery process. Yet, a wider net must be cast, for chronicity and recovery are probably best understood as interactional phenomena involving the cultural milieu, professional response, self, and the illness process. At any point in time one factor may exert greater negative or positive force in relationship to the others.

Revisiting the role of the environment and self may seem dangerous to some. Could the clock be turned back and the way paved for assessing blame to the person and family? We have come too far in the area of basic research and studies of the brain to dismiss the central role of neurobiology in severe mental illness. Still, the focus here is not on the cure or cause of illness but on the ability to manage, adapt, and recover. The data presented here were offered by those most knowledgeable about this process, those who have lived with these illnesses. John Strauss (1993), who has been a leader in studying the phenomenology of mental illness, has observed:

> I personally believe...that the psychological and experiential can have as much impact on the biological as the reverse,

and the arrows of cause in severe mental disorder involve a wide range of complex sequences of direction and interaction, most of which we do not yet understand. The starting points are far from clear. But no matter what theory or theories are eventually found to be correct, such discovery will depend on the dictum that, like the customer, "the patient is always right." (p.vi)

References

Anthony, W. (1991). Recovery from mental illness The new vision of service researchers. *Innovations and Research, 1*(1), 13-14.

Anthony, W. (1993). Recovery from mental illness The guiding vision of the mental health system in the 1990s. *Psychosocial Rehabilitation Journal, 16*(4), 11-23.

Arns, P. & Linney, J. (1993). Work, self, and life satisfaction for persons with severe and persistent mental disorders. *Psychosocial Rehabilitation Journal, 17*(2), 63-79.

Breier, A. & Strauss, 1. (1983, October). Self-control in psychotic disorders. *Archives of General Psychiatry, 40,* 1141-1145.

Cutting, J. & Dunne, F. (1989). Subjective experience of schizophrenia. *Schizophrenia Bulletin, 15*(2), 217-231.

Distefano, M. K., Pryer, M. & Garrison, J. (1991). Validity of psychiatric patients self-report of rehospitalization. *Hospital and Community Psychiatry, 42*(8), 849-850.

Estroff, S. (1981). *Making it crazy.* Berkeley University of California Press.

Estroff, S. (1989). Self, identity, and subjective experiences of schizophrenia In search of the subject. *Hospital and Community Psychiatry, 15*(2), 189-196.

Goldstein, M. (1992). Psychosocial strategies for maximizing the effects of psychotropic medications for schizophrenia and mood disorder. *Psychopharmacology Bulletin, 28*(3), 237-240.

Harding, C., Brooks, G., Takamaura, A., Strauss, J. & Brier, A. (1987a). The Vermont longitudinal study of persons with severe mental illness 1: Methodology, study sample, and overall status 32 years later. *American Journal of Psychiatry, 144*(6), 718-726.

Harding, C., Brooks, G., Takamaura, A., Strauss, J. & Brier, A. (1987b). The Vermont longitudinal study of persons with severe mental illness 11: Long-term outcome of subjects who retrospectively met *DSM-III* criteria for schizophrenia. *American Journal of Psychiatry, 144*(6), 727-735.

Harding, C., Zubin, J. & Strauss, J. (1987). Chronicity in schizophrenia: Fact, partial fact, or artifact? *Hospital and Community Psychiatry, 38*(5), 477-486.

Hatfield, A. & Lefley, H. (1993). *Surviving mental illness.* New York: The Guilford Press.

Leete, E. (1989). How I perceive and manage my illness. *Schizophrenia Bulletin, 15*(2), 197-200.

Marsella, A. (1988, Suppl, 344). Cross-cultural research on severe mental disorders: Issues and findings. *Acta Psychiatrica Scandinavica, 78,* 7-22.

McGlashan, T. (1988). A selective view of recent North American longterm followup studies of schizophrenia. *Schizophrenia Bulletin, 14*(4), 515-542.

Mosher, L. & Burti, L. (1992). Relationships in rehabilitation: When technology fails. *Psychosocial Rehabilitation Journal, 15*(4), 11-17.

Rappaport, J., Reischl, T., & Zimmerman, M. (1992). Mutual help mechanisms in the empowerment of former mental patients. In D. Saleebey (Ed.), *The strengths perspective in social work* (pp.8497). New York: Longman.

Romme, M. & Escher, A. (1989). Hearing voices. *Schizophrenia Bulletin, 15*(2), 209-216.

Saleebey, D. (1991). Technological fix: Altering the consciousness of the social work profession. *Journal of Sociology and Social Welfare, 18*(4), 51-67.

Sartorius, N., Jablensky, A., Ernberg, G., Leff, J., Korten, A. & Gulbinat, W. (1987). Course of schizophrenia in different countries: Some results of a WHO international comparative 5 year follow-up study. In H. Hafner, W. F. Gattaz, & W. Janzarik (Eds.), *Search for the causes of schizophrenia* (pp. 107-113). Berlin: Springer-Verlag.

Shifrin, J., Cohen, J. & Kraft, F. (1990). *Pathways to partnership: An awareness and resource guide on mental illness.* St. Louis, MO: Pathways to Promise.

Spradley, J. (1979). *The ethnographic interview.* New York: Holt, Rinehart, & Winston.

Steering Committee on the Chronically Mentally 111 (1980). *Toward a national plan for the chronically mentally ill.* Washington, DC: Department of Health and Human Services.

Strauss, J. (1989). Subjective experiences of schizophrenia: Toward a new dynamic psychiatry: 11. *Hospital and Community Psychiatry, 15*(2), 179-187.

Strauss, J. Foreword. (in) Hatfield, A. & Lefley, H. (1993). *Surviving mental illness.* New York: The Guilford Press.

Strauss, J., Hafez, H., Lieberman, P. & Harding, C. (1985). The course of psychiatric disorders, 111: Longitudinal principles. American *Journal of Psychiatry, 142*(3), 289-296.

Sullivan, W. P. (1993). "It helps me to be a whole person": The role of spirituality among the mentally challenged. *Psychosocial Rehabilitation Journal, 16*(3), 125-134.

Warner, R. (1983). Recovery from schizophrenia in the Third World. *Culture, Medicine, and Psychiatry, 16*(1), 85-88.

Wynne, L. (1988). The natural histories of schizophrenic process. *Schizophrenia Bulletin, 14*(4), 653-659.

Sense of Self in Recovery from Severe Mental Illness

Larry Davidson and John S. Strauss

LARRY DAVIDSON, PH.D. IS WITH THE DEPARTMENT
OF PSYCHIATRY, SCHOOL OF MEDICINE,
YALE UNIVERSITY, NEW HAVEN, CT

JOHN STRAUSS, M.D. IS WITH THE DEPARTMENT
OF PSYCHIATRY, SCHOOL OF MEDICINE,
YALE UNIVERSITY, NEW HAVEN, CT

THIS ARTICLE ORIGINALLY APPEARED IN THE
British Journal of Medical Psychology, 1992, 65, 131-145,
AND IS REPRINTED WITH PERMISSION.

This report, based on research interviews conducted with persons struggling to recover from prolonged psychiatric disorders, suggests that the rediscovery and reconstruction of an enduring sense of the self as an active and responsible agent provides an important aspect of improvement. This process of developing a functional sense of self in the midst of persisting psychotic symptoms and dysfunction is described, and its implications for understanding severe mental illness and processes of change are discussed. It is suggested that viewing the development of a dynamic sense of self as central to the improvement process provides a coherent thread which ties together diverse research findings concerning factors influencing course and outcome of illness. It is also suggested that for treatment and rehabilitation to elicit and foster a more functional sense of self, models of improvement will need to allow for, and encourage, a more active and collaborative role for the person with the disorder.

What I need to learn is the work of recovery (woman with mental illness speaking to interviewer).

Research interviews conducted with persons struggling to recover from prolonged psychiatric disorders suggest that the process of rediscovering and reconstructing an enduring sense of the self as an active and responsible agent provides an important, and perhaps crucial, source of improvement. This process of becoming aware of a more functional sense of self and building upon it in the midst of persisting psychotic symptoms and dysfunction is alluded to over and over again by persons suffering from these disorders. They note that an enhanced sense of self provides them with both a refuge from their illness and a foundation upon which they may then take up the work of recovery in a more active and determined fashion.

In the following report we will describe this process as it is revealed in the self-reports of research subjects participating in the Yale Longitudinal Study of Prolonged Psychiatric Disorder (Strauss, Hafez, Lieberman & Harding, 1980). Following this description, we will then consider the implications of this phenomenon for understanding severe mental illness and processes of improvement. We will suggest that the process of developing a functional sense of self provides a kind of Archimedean point upon which to rethink a variety of diverse research findings concerning factors influencing course and outcome of these disorders. In conclusion, we will address implications of this research for developing models of psychiatric treatment and rehabilitation.

The notion of the self has a long and distinguished career in understanding and treating schizophrenia and related disorders. It played a central role in the classical theories of schizophrenia offered by such pioneers in the field as Emil Kraepelin (1904), Eugene Bleuler (1950), Karl Jaspers (1963), and Adolf Meyer (1950), and was also given a prominent place in earlier psychoanalytic accounts (e.g. Freud, 1910; Fromm-Reichmann, 1950; Schilder, 1976; Sullivan, 1940). While a distortion in sense of self remains to this day an essential phenomenological characteristic of schizophrenia as described in the *DSM-IIIR* (American Psychiatric Association, 1987), it has received considerably less attention in recent years with the increasing support for "descriptive" and biological approaches to severe mental illness. Recent publications deriving from a variety of theoretical perspectives, however, have argued trenchantly for renewed attention to this earlier notion. From social psychology and medical and cross-cultural anthropology (e.g. Estroff, 1989; Fabrega, 1989a, 1989b) to cognitive psychology (e.g., Warner, Taylor, Powers & Hyman, 1989) and the self-psychology of Kohut (e.g., Pollack, 1989), investigators have suggested that sense of self continues to provide a key theoretical construct in the understanding and treatment of these disorders.

Additional support for the importance of the construct of the self in severe mental illness is provided by considerable data from investigations of other psychiatric and non-psychiatric conditions. These investigations suggest that sense of self also plays an important role in the management of and recovery from somatic illnesses, the effects of stressful life-events and depression. Many investigators have noted the way in which aspects of an enhanced sense of self, such as a sense of self-efficacy and an internal locus of control, can help to ameliorate various aspects of disorder and encourage efforts at coping and adaptation in the context of chronic illness or stressful life-events (e.g., Burish & Bradley, 1983; Dohrenwend & Dohrenwend, 1981; Forsyth, Delaney & Gresham, 1984; Lazarus & Folkman, 1984; Rodin, 1989; Strickland, 1978). In addition, Brown, Bifulco and Andrews (1990) have recently suggested a causal relationship between positive self-esteem and recovery from depression.

While the importance of such constructs as self-efficacy, locus of control, and self-esteem have now been demonstrated in understanding processes of coping and recovery with somatic conditions, the effect of life-events and depression, these aspects of sense of self have, with few exceptions (e.g., Warner et al., 1989), yet to be explored in the case of coping with severe mental illness (Davidson, 1995, 1996). Bringing such theoretical constructs to bear in investigations of coping with prolonged psychiatric disorder promises to provide a basis for a more comprehensive understanding of the nature and impact of the active role which people may play in managing, compensating for and recovering from their disorders (Strauss, Harding, Hafez & Lieberman, 1987).

Far from being only a theoretical notion restricted to the conceptual approaches of scientific investigators, however, sense of self appears to be a major component in the everyday experience of severe mental illness. It is a component that people with these disorders often describe, and which they often see as a core factor in processes of illness and change. Nowhere is this as clear as in persons who are struggling to improve. We thus propose to complement earlier, more theoretical, approaches by using the recurrent references to the self made by the subjects involved in our study to explore from an empirical base the ways in which sense of self may provide an essential aspect of improvement in severe mental illness. In order to describe the process of developing and employing a functional sense of self as it unfolds in the everyday experience of our subjects, we have chosen to quote from their self-reports and to retain as much as possible their own terminology. It may be possible, in future publications, to attempt an integration of these subjective findings with existing theoretical approaches to the self.

Method

Data in this report were obtained through a series of intensive, semi-structured, follow-along interviews conducted over a 2- to-3-year period with each of 66 subjects. The subjects had been hospitalized for severe mental disorders and were between the ages of 20 and 55. Persons with organic brain disorders or major problems with substance abuse were excluded. Basic demographic and diagnostic characteristics of these subjects are summarized in Table 1.

TABLE 1.
SUBJECT CHARACTERISTICS

(*N* = 66)

Age
M	29
Range	20-55

Gender
Male	34
Female	32

Marital Status
Single	47
Married	7
Separated	2
Divorced	10

Hollingshead-Redlich Scale of Social Class
M	3.7 (III)
Range	I-V

Diagnosis *(DSM-IIIR)*
Schizophrenia	25
Schizoaffective	17
Major affective disorder	24

Initial interviews had been obtained while the subjects were hospitalized in order to collect clinical, personal, and demographic data. Following discharge, subjects were then interviewed bimonthly for 1 year and at yearly intervals afterwards. Interviews focused on subjects' past and recent experiences with work and social relations functioning, symptoms, treatment, living situation, and coping efforts. All interviews were recorded on audiotape. After the interviews, extensive ratings were made using several standard scales (e.g., Endicott, Spitzer, Fleiss & Cohen, 1976; Overall & Gorham, 1962; Strauss & Carpenter, 1974a) and narrative summaries of each interview were dictated and transcribed. For this report, completed research protocols and selected interview tapes were reviewed to collect information relevant to the process of rediscovering and reconstructing a functional sense of self and its role in the improvement process.

Of the 66 subjects in this study, 32 (48.5%) showed an improvement in overall functioning of 20 or more points on the Global Assessment Scale between their initial interview and their last follow-up. Practically all of these subjects in one way or another described experiences involving the rediscovery and reconstruction of a dynamic sense of self at different points in the course of their illness. While for some subjects this was a process which was just beginning and which was described as tentative, for others it was a process well under way which already appeared to have produced beneficial results. One subject in particular (whose name and other identifying information have been changed) described the overall process in detail in a particularly informative fashion. Her report will be utilized to furnish concrete examples of each of the aspects of the process involved and will be supplemented by additional material provided by other subjects in the study.

Betty is a 27-year-old, single Caucasian woman with a 10-year history of severe mental illness. She has been diagnosed *(DSM-IIIR)* as having schizophrenia and has been hospitalized on six occasions for auditory hallucinations, ideas of reference, and delusions of control. Currently living in a supervised apartment and working part time, Betty spoke at length in interviews concerning the "work of recovery." Hospitalized for her first psychotic episode just prior to when she would have started college as a promising young artist, she has joked that as a result of her illness she has "majored" in psychiatry rather than art, and has compared her familiarity with the local mental health community and its agencies and professionals with the kind of connections she would have to have made with artists and gallery owners had she been able to pursue her initial career interest. Although still hopeful for further improvements in functioning, Betty has stated that she is too proud of the work she has had to do in improving to see herself simply as a failure in other, formerly important, areas of her life such as art. She appears to be someone who has been relatively successful in establishing a dynamic and efficacious sense of self in the midst of a devastating mental illness, and in employing this self as an important resource in her struggle to improve.

Review of the self-report data from Betty and other subjects in the study revealed four basic aspects of the recovery process which may be seen as involving the rediscovery, reconstruction, and utilization of a functional sense of self. These four aspects are: 1) discovering the possibility of possessing a more active sense of self; 2) taking stock of the strengths and weaknesses of this self and assessing possibilities for change; 3) putting into action some aspects of the self and integrating the results of these actions as reflecting one's actual capabilities; 4) using an enhanced sense of self to provide some degree of refuge from one's illness and the detrimental elements of one's social milieu (e.g., stigma) and to provide a resource with which to battle them. While these four aspects have been

separated for ease of presentation and comprehension, that does not suggest that a person may only be involved in any one issue at a time, or that people move in an orderly progression from the first aspect to the second, and then on to the third and fourth in a clearcut, linear fashion. These four aspects rather are related and overlapping, and are perhaps interactive in nature as well.

Discovering a More Active Self

The first aspect of this process appears to involve a person's discovery that there is at least the possibility that there is an active sense of self in the midst of dysfunction. For some people this experience may involve a rediscovery of aspects of the self which remain unaffected by the illness and which may thus be employed independently of it. For others, however, it may involve coming to discover previously unknown and untapped aspects of the self which have not yet been affected by the illness and which thereby offer areas for competence which have thus far been unexplored. For still others this experience may involve a gradual acceptance of the illness as an entity which is separate from the person, thus allowing for a new sense of the self to arise which is no longer identified with the effects of the illness. While for some subjects these experiences involved a gradual reawakening after an extended period of passivity and withdrawal, for others there was more of a timely returning to areas of functioning which were intact prior to an acute and relatively brief episode of dysfunction. The common thread throughout all of these variations is a dawning awareness of an additional aspect of the self not currently in operation which holds promise for a more active sense of self than that identified with one's illness.

There are several such instances of discovery in Betty's report of her struggles with her illness. The first discovery came at a particularly low point in the course of Betty's illness, when she had been overwhelmed by persisting psychotic symptoms for some time. Having been so paralyzed and crippled by her fears and delusions, she had been placed in locked seclusion and denied access to unit activities. She describes this situation as culminating in her increased sense, partly due to the interventions of her nurse, that she could *do more* than remain within the confines of the seclusion room. Betty describes:

> It may have been because [my nurse] really seemed to pay a lot of particular attention to me and I started waking up and I started knowing that there were possibilities for life outside that room and things really started opening up for me And she knew I had potential and talent and all this and that I could get better, and I knew it too. And I just woke up. I wasn't hallucinating as much, and I was active and eager, and I was also more social....She ended up being very helpful in that she let people know, "Well, Betty's ready to come out, Betty can attend unit meetings, Betty can take a half hour out twice a day."

What appears to be crucial in this instance is that Betty, with the help of her nurse, came to believe that there was a self who was capable of being more active and efficacious apart from, or in addition to, the passive, helpless and hopeless self who was confined to seclusion. Betty's "discovery" at this point involved her growing sense that there was at least the potential for a more functional self; that she need not forever remain engulfed in impotence and despair.

Practically all of these subjects in one way or another described experiences involving the rediscovery and reconstruction of a dynamic sense of self at different points in the course of their illness.

This dawning awareness of a sense of self beyond one's illness ranges from being solely intuitive, as in simply having a "felt-sense" of potential, to being completely thought out and conceptualized. Its content may range from a vague and undefined sense of being able to do better than one is currently doing, to a fairly well circumscribed direction that one is compelled to pursue. One research subject, for example, described getting a vague but persuasive feeling one day at a day treatment center that he simply could *do better* than all of the "chronic" patients he saw around him, while for another subject his dawning awareness of a sense of self involved the clear conviction that he should return to college. Regardless of the degree to which this awareness is processed cognitively, it appears to offer the person a sense of hope that s/he will improve and would seem to provide the first opening on to the road of recovery. Rather than providing an experience which happens only once at the beginning of the improvement process, however, this dawning of hope for a more dynamic sense of self appears to recur in the course of improvement to provide additional windows on to new paths at crucial points further down the road.

Betty attributed some credit for this achievement in her improvement to her nurse. Persons who improve appear often to give some credit for this awakening of hope to significant others in their lives whom they see as having "believed in them" or as having "had faith" at crucial points that they could do better. One patient said that what she appreciated most about her clinician was that no matter how "down and out" or despondent she felt about herself and her ability to manage, he maintained confidence in her. This suggests at least one way in which social supports and psychotherapeutic interventions can be helpful in fostering and facilitating improvement.

Taking Stock of the Self

The second aspect of this process involves a person's pausing to take stock of his/her perceived strengths and limitations prior either to engaging in new behaviors and taking on new projects or to returning to projects put on hold by the disruption created by the illness. Subjects repeatedly point to the importance of securing for themselves a grasp on perceived or sensed possibilities for change before manifesting behaviorally renewed motivation for, or interest in, taking new risks. Once a person begins to believe in or hope for a more active and efficacious sense of self, it appears imperative to conduct a kind of personal inventory to see what this self is and is not capable of before actually putting it to use. Whether this occurs at a very basic level, as in "Do I have what it takes to leave the seclusion room and attend a unit meeting?," or again at a more advanced level, as in "Do I have what it takes to move from a part-time to a full-time job?" this inventory appears to be taken with a specific goal in mind. It may be thought of as an attempt to determine what "fits" and whether or not one's present self "measures up" to a

Persons who improve appear often to give some credit for this awakening of hope to significant others in their lives whom they see as having "believed in them" or as having "had faith" at crucial points that they could do better.

desired level of competence before concrete steps are taken to achieve a goal. As in the first aspect described above, this determination may range from a cognitive appraisal based on prior experience to a largely affective sense of what is "right." In most cases it involves a combination of these, being based partly on what one thinks one has learned about oneself and partly on the sense that one has on a more intuitive level.

In describing her experiences of this aspect of recovery, Betty provides an example which blends both of these elements into a coherent whole. She offers the analogy of taking stock of one's kitchen prior to baking a cake. Not only must you be sure that you have acquired all of the essential ingredients for the cake, she points out, but you must also feel comfortable enough with your own level of experience or practical knowledge in putting the kitchen and its contents to use. You must, in other words, have a good "feeling" about the project you are undertaking; it must "fit." She describes:

> I have a good will, it just takes the right amount, the um, the kitchen has to be right, so to speak, before I do the endeavors. The feeling has to be right, everything has to be right before you can make a cake. If you don't feel like buying the flour for six months then you don't feel like it. Then you get your flour, and then you notice you don't have enough cinnamon, so you wait a while.

As Betty suggests in this analogy, the process of taking stock of one's self prior to embarking on new tasks can be a gradual and stepwise procedure of accumulating and consolidating the skills and strengths needed to achieve one's goal. If, in the process of taking inventory, a person begins to feel that s/he does not currently possess a required skill, s/he may either change the goal or pause in his/her pursuit of it in order to pick up the skill along the way. While this aspect of the process is described as taking place during a pause between the discovery of a more positive sense of self and the demonstration of activity, this is only meant to indicate its apparent mediating function and not to suggest a normative length of time. The process of taking stock of oneself and trying out one's strengths in order to feel on firmer ground prior to taking on new challenges may be extended over a considerable length of time before it is followed by any demonstrable results.

The inventories that people take of their selves need not always be accurate or realistic, however, nor may people always be aware of, or even stop to consider, all of the skills required for a given task. Betty, for example, may not consider ahead of time the social skills and level of comfort in social situations which will be required if she is to sit successfully through a drawing class at a local community college. In addition, this process of assessing one's strengths and limitations ordinarily occurs in a social context. People involved in this aspect of the process may find themselves in confusing or difficult positions if their own self-appraisals, or their own sense of what is right for them, markedly differ from the views of those around them. This can, of course, work in various directions. One patient, for example, considered himself more capable of working than either his family or the staff at the day hospital where he was being treated, resulting in his leaving treatment against their advice to take a job at a diner which turned out to be a highly successful experience for him. Another subject reported feeling relatively unsupported by his treaters and family in a direction which he felt compelled to pursue, while feeling more supported in directions which held no attraction for him. Opposite instances could of course occur as well.

In any case it is important to recognize the influence of others' appraisals—whether spoken or implicitly conveyed through actions and attitudes—on the person's own process of taking stock of the self. It appears that having a less secure sense of self may at times render a person more vulnerable to others' input. This provides an important point at which stigma, a highly critical family milieu, and/or pessimistic clinicians can have an undermining impact on a person's efforts at improvement.

Putting the Self Into Action

The third aspect of this process of developing a sense of self appears to involve a person's experiences of putting his/her newly (re-)discovered and inventoried self into action and reflecting on and incorporating the results of these actions. Once the kitchen is adequately stocked and prepared, it is possible to bake the cake. How well the cake is baked will then, in addition, be taken to reflect on one's ability as a cook. A positive outcome may enhance the sense of self by affirming its strengths, while a negative outcome may undermine a newly emergent and still tentative sense of self. As in the first two aspects discussed above, the actions, reflection and integration which are entailed in this aspect can take place with varying degrees of cognitive and/or affective involvement. They may also take place on a number of levels of complexity and at various times in the course of the illness and improvement process.

Betty describes one instance in her own struggle in which this process took place on what is perhaps the most basic level. On this level, exerting one's newly discovered self provides one with "evidence" (in Betty's terms) of the ability simply *to be* active and efficacious. Doing something as apparently trivial as turning on her radio, for instance, proves to Betty that she can in fact do things for herself. She describes:

> It is being active, and I take pride and I'm independent to a certain extent like in my jazz music, like *I'll* turn on my jazz radio, and *I'll* love it...it's *my* interest. I turn the radio on myself, no one had it going to nourish *them*selves, to entertain *them*selves, like parents would at a house. *I* turn it on, *I'm* responsible, *I* enjoy the music, *I* make notes and draw while I'm hearing it then I turn it off, then I have some evidence, I've got something done, I've been productive, I have the drawings to look at. Maybe they're damn fine drawings.... It was for me and by me. My own nurturing. So I'm proud of this effort, but I do need that active state of mind to be steady, to be constant.

Betty emphasizes that what was most important for her in this instance was that it was *she* who was acting on her own behalf; that she was effective in taking care of herself and therefore no longer needed to be solely the recipient of the actions of others. It appears to be only under this condition that Betty is able to gather confirming evidence that she possesses a self capable of responsible, self-directed, action.

Getting someone simply to "comply" with treatment may in fact end up having an effect opposite to the one intended, for example, if it leaves the patient continuing to feel controlled from the outside, only now by her/his doctor rather than by her/his hallucinations.

Were the goal to stem from another source (e.g. her therapist), or the action to be undertaken by someone else (e.g. her mother), then Betty could not be as sure of her self as a source of initiative and agency, nor could she be proud of her accomplishments and integrate them into her sense of self.

As Betty describes in this passage, for someone at this early stage of developing a sense of self the feeling that one can be active and function autonomously at all is not something that is steady or constant. For her and others in similar conditions, it will take more work in building upon these kinds of gradual steps before that sense is established firmly and integrated into the already existing, fragmented, passive, and dependent sense of self which accompanies the illness. The discovery that the self can be active at all, can take steps in the world to accomplish even extremely simple tasks, thus appears to provide a kind of developmental achievement particularly important for some persons struggling with severe mental illness. This kind of evidence is required before more difficult and complex tasks can even be considered.

Once the person has acquired such evidence, putting into action more complex desires and pursuing more difficult goals may also provide opportunities for further enhancement of the sense of self by integrating those new aspects of the self required by the tasks at hand. Such an enhanced sense may then lead to new, and more advanced, goals. One patient left a day treatment center to take a part-time job as a dishwasher at the diner where he frequently ate his meals alone. In finding that he was able to handle this job adequately, he affirmed those parts of himself which were required by the job: skills such as maintaining sufficient attention and concentration and tolerating the stress of having time pressures and a boss. In his self-report, this patient also described his pleasant surprise at being able, unexpectedly, to broaden his sense of self by integrating *in addition* several aspects of himself which he only discovered while carrying out this task. He found that in being able to wash dishes he was not only demonstrating better mental controls, but also demonstrating a level of social competence in making friends with his co-workers that astonished him. As a result, he started to eat some of his meals with his new friends and found his social life to be expanding beyond his prior expectations.

Betty emphasized that for her the activity must stem from her own sense of initiative for it to be effective in helping to establish and enhance her sense of self. The example she provided also demonstrated that this process may often be carried out through very small and apparently trivial steps. These aspects of her report suggest additional perspectives from which to consider the important contributions of significant others in a person's life. Getting someone simply to "comply" with treatment may in fact end up having an effect opposite to the one intended, for example, if it leaves the patient continuing to feel controlled from the outside, only now by her/his doctor rather than by her/his hallucinations. Similarly, being critical of or devaluing small but self-initiated steps taken by a patient because they do not approach more lofty expectations may undermine what progress s/he has been able to make and thereby diminish the likelihood of future achievements of a more advanced goal.

Appealing to the Self

In the last aspect of this process, a more functional sense of self may be utilized by a person in coping with the symptoms and effects of the illness and in compensating for areas of functioning adversely affected by it. As a somewhat enduring sense of self as agent arises which is experienced as separate from the illness, it appears to become available to a person to serve as a refuge from the illness and the other detrimental influences related to it such as stress and stigma. As suggested by the research on coping with physical illnesses and life events cited in the introduction to this paper, an established sense of agency may then also be employed by the person as a resource in coping with, and compensating for, the illness.

Betty provides an example of how securing a stable sense of self can create a buffer against some of the ravages of the illness and be employed in coping with its symptoms. She relates an incident which took place at the group home where she previously lived in which she was becoming overstimulated by the social interactions which were taking place in the kitchen. In this instance Betty found that she could make use of her newly enhanced sense of self in coping with the anxiety and suspiciousness which she had learned by this time were symptoms of her illness. She describes:

> So then I drink the coffee, it's not all that awful, I'm in a contest of will with the world, with nature, whatever, and I say to myself: "Well, damn it, you just calm down and drink your coffee." And I say to myself: "You'll just have to wait five minutes." So I wait. And then the roommate's still bugging me out and then I have the

control, the self-esteem, the confidence, and it's manageable. Then I just proudly walk to my room and take space. I mean, it's successful.

What comes across as crucial in this vignette is Betty's sense that she is capable of surviving and even contending with what she experiences as external or foreign pressures. Having the confidence that she will now have a voice in what happens to her, she successfully diverts her attention away from her symptoms to what she herself can control.

When one has a consistent sense of self apart from illness one can in this way appeal to the self as enduring in the midst of symptoms as a reminder that they are in fact only symptoms of an illness and thus need be neither so threatening nor interminable. In stressful situations one may appeal to a functional sense of self to recall what has been helpful in such situations in the past in lowering the level of anxiety or in eliminating the source of tension. And once there is a sense of self that can be seen as responsible for managing the illness, it then also becomes possible for the person to take a more active and determined part in his/her social and vocational rehabilitation, developing coping mechanisms (Brenner, Boker, Muller, Spichtig & Wurgler, 1987; Carr, 1988; Falloon & Talbot, 1981; Thurm & Hainer, 1987) and learning to exercise self-control over symptoms (Breier & Strauss, 1983).

The discovery that the self can be active at all, can take steps in the world to accomplish even extremely simple tasks, thus appears to provide a kind of developmental achievement particularly important for some persons struggling with severe mental illness.

As with the other aspects of this process already discussed, employing a sense of self in dealing with difficulties is an interactive endeavor, open to the influence of the illness itself, significant others in the person's life, and the world in general. Had Betty's sense of self still been too tentative or fragile to withstand the onslaught of the stress and symptoms described above, she would probably have lost her battle with her illness, at least for the time being, and emerged with a diminished sense of self, perhaps as a result more vulnerable in the future to destabilization and decompensation. Alternatively, even if Betty were to have such a tentative and fragile sense of self, were she fortunate enough to have a supportive rather than annoying roommate she still might be able to survive the destabilizing effects of her social milieu. For another subject in the study, it took obtaining drumming lessons from an experienced musician and teacher to turn his love of drumming from a stressor which invariably precipitated episodes of relapse into a productive avenue for the learning of coping skills. What is primarily involved in all of these variations is the function of a person's sense of self as an important tool in the monitoring, managing, and compensating for illness in a social context.

Betty reports that she now knows that her symptoms serve as warning signs that there are things that she needs to attend to in her immediate environment which might threaten her. Once she can discover or become aware of the source of her distress, she can then evaluate its merits and decide on an appropriate response. Each step of this process provides a point at which we might see Betty's sense of self as furnishing her with a resource with which to evaluate and respond to the events and relationships in her life which are either directly or indirectly related to her illness. It is at this point in the process that the existing research literature on the role of self-efficacy, locus of control, and self-esteem in coping efforts (Brown et al., 1990; Burish & Bradley, 1983; Dohrenwend & Dohrenwend, 1981; Forsyth et al., 1984; Lazarus & Folkman, 1984; Rodin, 1989; Strickland, 1978) becomes both relevant and applicable. Attempting to apply research findings in these areas to persons with severe mental illness who have yet to achieve an enduring sense of self may be premature and may overlook the fact that developing a more internal locus of control and sense of efficacy may be required in such cases before more advanced coping tasks become possible (Davidson, 1996).

Discussion

The process of rediscovering and reconstructing a functional sense of self in the midst of dysfunction described above may be particularly important in shedding light on two aspects of severe mental illness and the process of improvement. The first area is that of interpreting the research findings concerning the variety of factors influencing the course and outcome of the illness. The second area is that of developing models of clinical treatment and psychiatric rehabilitation.

Research has suggested several factors which influence the course and outcome of severe mental illness, ranging from premorbid social functioning (Strauss & Carpenter, 1977; Zigler & Phillips, 1960)

and duration of disorder (Strauss & Carpenter, 1974b, 1977) to the detrimental effect of expressed emotion in families (Brown, Birley & Wing, 1972; Brown, Monck, Carstairs & Wing, 1962; Vaughn & Leff, 1976), the beneficial effect of a supportive social network (Beels, 1981; Hammer, 1981; Hammer, Makiesky-Barrow & Gutwirth, 1978), and the role of stressful life-events (Birley & Brown, 1970; Brown & Birley, 1968; Rabkin, 1980) and the broader cultural context (Cooper & Sartorius, 1977; Warner, 1985; Waxler, 1979) in precipitating episodes of relapse. Without considering the process of developing a dynamic sense of self described above, these factors present a diverse array of unrelated concepts, each of which appears to act independently of the others. Viewing the development of a functional sense of self as central to the improvement process can provide a coherent thread which ties these divergent concepts together and situates them within a shared context as interrelated aspects of a unitary process. As such, it provides a kind of Archimedean point upon which to rethink factors influencing outcome in terms of their relevance for the process of improvement. The following are a few examples.

Expressed Emotion and Social Support Research

It was noted in the above discussion that the development of a sense of self takes place in a social context, with the significant others in a person's life contributing to this process in either a positive or negative fashion. The existing research literature on the effects of expressed emotion in families (Brown et al., 1972; Brown et al., 1962; Vaughn & Leff, 1976) and social support networks (Beels, 1981; Hammer, 1981; Hammer et al., 1978) on course and outcome of disorder may be considered as providing two examples of how the social milieu exerts an impact on a person's efforts at recovery through its influence on his/her developing sense of self. A highly critical and overinvolved family milieu can be seen as interfering with the development of an active sense of self by fostering negative appraisals and undermining a person's efforts at establishing his/her own sense of agency. On the other hand, a supportive social network can be seen as facilitating the development of a positive sense of self by providing one with a sense of self-worth through belonging and by nurturing self-initiated action.

Research on Open-linked Systems and "Mountain Climbing"

Studies have suggested that areas of functioning such as work, social relations, and symptom management can be best thought of as "open-linked systems," with each area existing relatively independently of the others (Strauss & Carpenter, 1977). In this sense, premorbid social functioning, for example, provides the best single predictor of recovery of functioning in that area, while premorbid work functioning serves as a better predictor of recovery of work functioning. Research has also shown, however, that interactive effects do occur, with gains made in social functioning, for example, having a kind of overflow effect on work or symptom management — a process we have called "mountain climbing" (Strauss at al., 1985). One way by which to understand both the relative autonomy of areas of functioning and their potential for interaction is to view the sense of self as the central and mediating factor. Different aspects of the self may be considered to be relatively independent of each other, with each being developed and employed in its respective area of functioning with its own degree of confidence and efficacy. However, by contributing to a heightened sense of efficacy, successes in one area, e.g. work, may engender efforts to be effective in other areas such as social relations or symptom management. In the example provided earlier, functioning well as a dishwasher gave the person enough confidence in himself to start taking risks in making friends with his co-workers.

Implications for Treatment

With respect to treatment and rehabilitation, acknowledging a central role for the development of the patient's sense of self encourages an integration of an active role for the patient in his/her own improvement. Models of illness and recovery which offer only a passive or reactive role for the patient (as reflected, for example, in the common phrase "treatment compliance") can be seen in this context as setting up further obstacles to the patient's rediscovery and reconstruction of his/her sense of self (Romme & Escher, 1989). Models which, on the other hand, incorporate the patient as an active collaborator in treatment and rehabilitation elicit and foster a more functional sense of self and may contribute positively to improvement (Davidson & Strauss, 1995). As mentioned in the above discussion, interventions which instill hope, foster positive and yet realistic appraisals of self, encourage building on existing strengths, and assist in the process of monitoring and managing symp-

A possible direction has been suggested by one patient who gently reminded one of the authors that "psychotic people can learn from mistakes too.

toms and compensating for areas of dys-function may help to stabilize and enhance a patient's sense of self. It is quite possible, on the other hand, that chronicity, passivi-ty, and dependence are somewhat fostered by strategies which move in the opposite direction, instilling hopelessness and help-lessness and fostering negative appraisals of self by emphasizing weaknesses and limita-tions (Davidson, in press; Estroff, 1989).

Clinicians, of course, would not willing-ly or knowingly act to instill hopelessness or negative self-appraisals in their patients. It may be, however, that in order to treat the patient as a full collaborator in the treatment and rehabilitative process fairly basic issues in the design and practice of clinical care will have to be reconsidered. An example of the kinds of issues raised by an appreciation of the sense of self as a central factor in improvement are the issues of control and responsibility. How can you treat patients as responsible and self-direct-ed agents and at the same time act to ensure their safety and well-being? How can you avoid demanding simple compli-ance from patients and at the same time help them to avoid relapse by managing their medications? Who does know best, at what times and concerning what areas? Such questions raise many unsettling and difficult issues which require additional thought and clarification. A possible direc-tion has been suggested by one patient who gently reminded one of the authors (LD) that "psychotic people can learn from mis-takes too." Maintaining too much control as a clinician would seem to deprive patients of this very human and very important opportunity for learning, while also possibly impacting negatively on their efforts to develop a functional sense of self.

Conclusion

Sense of self may provide an essential thread which ties together various aspects of functioning, both with respect to course and outcome of illness and to effective treatment interventions and rehabilitation strategies. If the woman quoted at the out-set of this report is right, it may in fact be possible to learn the "work of recovery." Betty suggested that she had learned much and made much progress in her own improvement by replacing art as her career with the work of separating herself from, and then learning about, managing and recovering from, her illness. A similar direction has been suggested by two people involved in the mental health consumer movement. An anonymous mental health consumer and provider who contributed to the *Schizophrenia Bulletin*'s "First Person Account" series (Anon, 1989) wrote that accepting that he had an illness which he could neither will nor wish away made it possible for him then to look to the sense of self which remained apart from this ill-ness so that he could "hope again and move forward in life." And Pat Deegan (1989), another mental health consumer and provider, has argued that the most important vocation for persons struggling with severe mental illness is the work of becoming one's true self in spite of one's ill-ness and other demoralizing factors such as stigma. Listening to these veterans of severe mental illness, and exploring in more depth and detail the processes involved in the work of developing a functional sense of self in the midst of disorder, may provide a key to understanding processes of improve-ment and to improving psychiatric treat-ment and rehabilitation.

Acknowledgements

This report was supported in part by NIMH Grant MH 00340 and by a grant from the National Association for Research on Schizophrenia and Depression (NARSAD). The authors wish to thank Hisham Hafez, MD, Courtenay Harding, PhD, Paul Lieberman, MD and Jaak Rakfeldt, PhD for their collaboration in the Yale Longitudinal Study, and two anonymous journal reviewers for their comments on an earlier draft of this paper.

References

American Psychiatric Association. (1987). *Diagnostic and statistical manual of mental disorders, 3rd ed, rev.* Washington, DC American Psychiatric Association

Anonymous. (1989). How I've managed chronic mental illness. *Schizophrenia Bulletin, 15,* 635-440.

Beels, C. C. (1981). Social support and schizophrenia. *Schizophrenia Bulletin, 7,* 58-72.

Birley, J. L. T. & Brown, G. W. (1970). Crisis and life changes preceding the onset or relapse of acute schizophrenia: Clinical aspects. *British Journal of Psychiatry, 116,* 327-333.

Bleuler, E. (1950). *Dementia praecox or the group of schizophrenias.* New York: International University Press.

Breier, A. & Strauss, J. S. (1983). Self-control in psychotic disorders. *Archives of General Psychiatry, 40,* 1141-1145.

Brenner, H. D., Boker, W., Muller, J., Spichtig, L. & Wurgler, S. (1987). On autoprotective efforts of schizophrenics, neurotics and controls. *Acta Psychiatrica Scandinavica, 75,* 405-414.

Brown, G.W., Bifulco, A. & Andrews, B. (1990). Self-esteem and depression. IV. Effect on course and recovery. *Social Psychiatry and Psychiatric Epidemiology, 25,* 244-249.

Brown, G.W. & Birley, J.L.T. (1968) Crisis and life changes and the onset of schizophrenia. *Journal of Health and Social Behavior, 9,* 203-214.

Brown, G.W., Birley, J.L.T. & Wing, J.K. (1972). Influence of family life on the course of schizophrenic disorders: A replication. *British Journal of Psychiatry, 121,* 241-258.

Brown, G.W., Monck, E.M., Carstairs, G.M. & Wing, J.K. (1962). Influence of family life on the course of schizophrenic illness. *British Journal of Preventive and Social Medicine, 16,* 55-68.

Burish, T.G. & Bradley, L.A. (1983). *Coping with chronic disease.* New York: Academic Press.

Carr, V. (1988) Patients' techniques for coping with schizophrenia. *British Journal of Medical Psychology, 61,* 339-352.

Cooper, J. & Sartorius, N. (1977). Cultural and temporal variations in schizophrenia. A speculation on the importance of industrialization. *British Journal of Psychiatry, 30,* 50-55.

Davidson, L. (1996). Recovery of the self as an aspect of coping with schizophrenia (Article submitted for publication).

Davidson, L. & Strauss, J.S. (1995). Beyond the biopsychosocial model. I. Models of disorder, health and recovery. *Psychiatry, 58,* 44-55.

Davidson, L. (in press). Phenomenological contributions to models of recovery from severe psychiatric illness. In D. Knowles, E. Murray & R. Rojcewicz (Eds), *Phenomenological psychology and clinical practice.* Stonybrook, NY: State University of New York Press.

Deegan, P. (1989). *A letter to my friend who is giving up.* A keynote address. Unpublished address delivered to the Connecticut Conference on Supported Employment, Cromwell, Connecticut.

Dohrenwend, B. S. & Dohrenwend, B. P. (1981). *Stressful life events and their contexts.* New York: Prodist.

Endicott, J., Spitzer, R.L, Fleiss, J.L. & Cohen, J. (1976). The global assessment scale: A procedure for measuring overall severity of psychiatric disturbance. *Archives of General Psychiatry, 33,* 766-771.

Estroff, S.E. (1989). Self, identity, and subjective experiences of schizophrenia: In search of the subject. *Schizophrenia Bulletin, 15,* 189-196.

Fabrega, H. (1989a). On the significance of an anthropological approach to schizophrenia. *Psychiatry, 52,* 45-65.

Fabrega, H .(1989b). The self and schizophrenia: A cultural perspective. *Schizophrenia Bulletin, 15,* 277-290.

Falloon, I.R.H. & Talbot, R.E. (1981). Persistent auditory hallucinations: Coping mechanisms and implications for management. *Psychological Medicine, 11,* 329-339.

Forsyth, G.L., Delaney, K.D. & Gresham, M.L. (1984). Vying for a winning position: Management style of the chronically ill. *Research In Nursing and Mental Health, 7,* 181-188.

Freud, S. (1910). *Psychoanalytic notes on an autobiographical account of a case of paranoia.* Vol xxii, pp 3-82. London: Hogarth Press, 1958.

Fromm-Reichmann, F. (1950). *Principles of intensive psychotherapy.* Chicago: University of Chicago Press.

Hammer, M. (1981). Social supports, social networks, and schizophrenia. *Schizophrenia Bulletin, 7,* 45-57.

Hammer, M., Makiesky-Barrow, S. & Gutwirth, L. (1978). Social networks and schizophrenia. *Schizophrenia Bulletin, 4,* 522-545.

Jaspers, K. (1963). *General psychopathology.* (Translated by J. Hoenig & M. Hamilton). Chicago: University of Chicago Press.

Kraepelin, E. (1904). *Clinical psychiatry, 6th ed.,* (Translated by A.R. Deffendorf). New York: Macmillan.

Lazarus, R. S. & Folkman, S. (1984). *Stress, appraisal, and coping.* New York: Springer.

Meyer, A. (1950). *The collected papers of Adolf Meyer.* Baltimore, MD: Johns Hopkins University Press.

Overall, J. & Gorham, D. (1962). The brief psychiatric rating scale. *Psychological Reports, 10,* 799-812.

Pollack, W.S. (1989). Schizophrenia and the self: Contributions of psychoanalytic self-psychology. *Schizophrenia Bulletin, 15,* 311-322.

Rabkin, J.G. (1980). Stressful life events and schizophrenia: A review of the research literature. *Psychological Bulletin, 87,* 408-425.

Rodin, J. (1989). Sense of control: Potentials for intervention. *The Annals of the American Academy of Political and Social Science, 503,* 29-42.

Romme, M. & Escher, A. (1989). Hearing voices. *Schizophrenia Bulletin, 15,* 209-216.

Schilder, P. (1976). *On psychosis.* New York: International Universities Press.

Strauss, J.S. & Carpenter, W.T. (1974a). Characteristic symptoms and outcome in schizophrenia. *Archives of General Psychiatry, 30,* 429-434.

Strauss, J.S. & Carpenter, W.T. (1974b). The prediction of outcome in schizophrenia.II. Relationships between predictor and outcome variables. *Archives of General Psychiatry, 31,* 37-42.

Strauss, J.S. & Carpenter, W.T. (1977). Prediction of outcome in schizophrenia. III. Five-year outcome and its predictors. *Archives of General Psychiatry, 34,* 159-163.

Strauss, J.S., Hafez, H., Lieberman, P. & Harding, C. (1985). The course of psychiatric disorder, III. Longitudinal principles. *American Journal of Psychiatry, 142,* 289-296.

Strauss, J.S., Harding, C.M., Hafez, H. & Lieberman, P. (1987) The role of the patient in recovery from psychosis. In J.S. Strauss, W. Boker & H. Brenner (Eds), *Psychosocial treatment of schizophrenia,* pp. 160-166. New York: Hans Huber.

Strickland, B.R. (1978). Internal-external expectancies and health-related behaviors. *Journal of Consulting and Clinical Psychology, 46,* 1192-1211.

Sullivan, H.S. (1940). *Conceptions of modern psychiatry.* New York: Norton.

Thurm, I. & Hafner, H. (1987). Perceived vulnerability, relapse risk and coping in schizophrenia. *European Archives of Psychiatry and Neurological Sciences, 237,* 46-53.

Vaughn, C.E. & Leff, J.P. (1976). The influence of family and social factors on the course of psychiatric illness: A comparison of schizophrenic and depressed neurotic patients. *British Journal of Psychiatry, 129,* 125-137.

Warner, R. (1985). *Recovery from schizophrenia: Psychiatry and political phenomenon.* New York: Routledge & Kegan Paul.

Warner, R., Taylor, D., Powers, M. & Hyman, J. (1989). Acceptance of the mental illness label by psychotic patients: Effects on functioning. *American Journal of Orthopsychiatry, 59,* 398-409.

Waxler, N.E. (1979). Is outcome for schizophrenia better in nonindustrial societies? The case of Sri Lanka. *Journal of Nervous and Mental Disease, 167,* 144-158.

Zigler, E. & Phillips, L. (1960). Social effectiveness and symptomatic behaviors. *Journal of Abnormal and Social Psychology, 2,* 231-238.

Self, Identity, and Subjective Experiences of Schizophrenia: In Search of the Subject

Sue E. Estroff

SUE E. ESTROFF, PH.D., IS ASSOCIATE PROFESSOR, DEPARTMENT OF SOCIAL MEDICINE, UNIVERSITY OF NORTH CAROLINA, CHAPEL HILL, NC.

THIS ARTICLE ORIGINALLY APPEARED IN THE *Schizophrenia Bulletin*, 1989, 15(2), 189-196, AND IS REPRINTED WITH PERMISSION.

Schizophrenia is an I am illness—one that may overtake and redefine the identity of the person. This essay explores concepts of personhood and subjectivity from social science that are useful in understanding the experiencing subject in schizophrenia. Relationships between the self and sickness have not been investigated adequately with reference to their influence on prognosis. Chronicity is conceived of as a loss of self and of positive social roles and identity. Methods for the study of self and identity in relation to schizophrenia include analysis of illness-identity representations made by persons with schizophrenia.

> Something has happened to me—I do not know what. All that was my former self has crumbled and fallen together and a creature has emerged of whom I know nothing. She is a stranger to me....She is not real—she is not I...she is I—and because I still have myself on my hands, even if I am a maniac, I must deal with me somehow. (Jefferson, 1974, pp. 11-25)

As Lara Jefferson's narrative illustrates, schizophrenia (and other severe, persistent psychiatric disorders) is more than an illness that one *has*; it is something a person *is* or may *become*. Unlike having other debilitating, enduring disorders such as cancer or heart disease, having schizophrenia also may entail "becoming a schizophrenic." Having schizophrenia includes not only the experience of profound cognitive and emotional upheaval; it also results in a transformation of self as known inwardly, and of person or identity as known outwardly by others. Schizophrenia, like epilepsy and hemophilia is an *I am* illness, one that is joined with social identity and perhaps with inner self, in language and terms of reference. A comprehensive account of schizophrenia would include the person, the subject, the self that both *has* and *is* this (or these) disorder(s). To study the subjective experience of schizophrenia, we must identify and know the subject. These tasks require substantial adjustments in the ways we think about and respond to persons who have schizophrenia.

This essay outlines a rationale and some means for taking the subject, the person, back to the center of inquiries into the nature and consequences of schizophrenia. This is not a new project. It is more of an "intellectual renewal project," meant to renovate and rejuvenate preexisting but neglected areas of inquiry. Concepts of the self and identity have been central concerns in the study of schizophrenia before. A disturbed sense of self and "extreme perplexity about one's own identity" remain as symptoms of schizophrenia in *DSM-III-R* (American Psychiatric Association, 1987, p. 189). What is different about our efforts is emphasis, careful attention to experience and phenomenology of self, interdisciplinary collaboration and trespass, and a particular enthusiasm for developing rigorous methods with which to investigate these difficult topics The articles in this issue of the *Schizophrenia Bulletin* present evidence in abundance that the pursuit of subjectivity, identity and person is not only possible, but illuminating and amenable to scholarly inquiry.

While the study of selves and subjectivity may have become peripheral to psychiatry as Strauss (1989) argues, sociomedical and social psychological scientists continue to devote considerable attention to these areas. It is my intention to synthesize, translate, and apply those formulations that I find of most relevance to the study of persons with schizophrenia. Both Fabrega (1989) and Lally (1989) discuss cultural and psychological perspectives on the self, identity, and mental illness, and this essay anticipates and complements those contributions. Then building on this foundation, a person-centered, self-conscious formulation of chronicity is proposed. Reference to relevant research and conceptualizations is selective rather than comprehensive; the formulations and puzzlements here are intended to be more evocative than conclusive, more interrogative than declarative.

A Conceptual Inventory of the Subject

To begin, there are several basic tenets of social psychology and symbolic interactionism that have long informed and framed understandings of identity formation and transformation. I cannot hope to convey here the complex debates and conceptualizations that characterize the study of self, person, and identity (Lee 1982; Lapsley & Power, 1988). Despite the verbal density and near unintelligibility of many of these conceptual propositions, there are general domains of agreement about selves and others, subjectivity, and the social construction of personhood and identity that are salient. These are probably oversimplified and abbreviated below.

Others provide the contrast that permits definition of self—the object (out there, not me) delineates the subject (in here, I, self). At the same time, we participate with others in what Crapanzano (1982, p. 192) calls a "conspiracy of 'understanding'"

about who we are and what categories we belong to, about the labels given and received. This is a fluid process, the pace and rhythm of which varies over time and by context or audience. There are periods of self/other agreement and confirmation, and contexts of convergence. Phases of renegotiation and change occur; signals from others that are discrepant with inner experience contribute to customary developmental processes as well as unexpected evolutions of self. In some contexts—for example, the family—we occupy permanent *roles*, even while our experienced selves change.

The levels or layers of person are divided typically into at least two facets. There is a private subject and a public person, a self known to self and the person known to and identified by others. Despite various schemes and labels promoted by contesting schools of thought, the principle is the same: inner and outer; secret and shared; individual and social; subjective and objective. While separable heuristically (and in some way separate actually), these layers must overlap to some extent. When they do not, the individual is likely to experience the "radical estrangement" or "hyperalienation" (Kovel, 1987, p. 334) of self so characteristic of schizophrenia. This lack of agreement or constructive interaction between self and others *about* self may also result in an incomprehensibility of person, identified by Rosenberg (1984) as the hallmark of psychosis.

Finally, there is the idea of reflexivity, the ability we have to consider ourselves as an object. Reflexive thought and speech include our observations of ourselves, our self-consciousness, our ability to refer to ourselves in the third person, and our ability to engage in a relationship with our selves. It is the capacity that allows us to write autobiographies and to engage in psychotherapy. With these principles in mind, we examine more closely some ideas of self, identity, and subjectivity applicable to schizophrenia.

What does a concept of subject, of self, of person entail? First there is the dimension of *time,* of personal history (Frankenberg, 1987). There is a configuration of self that exists over time: an enduring entity that precedes, transcends, outlasts, and is more than an illness or diagnosis. While clinical accounts often document the course of an illness, they seldom provide a narrative of the person through time, in time—both personal and social. The "psychiatric history" is only a portion of personal history, yet it must be located, situated in the *lifetime* of the person now experiencing schizophrenia.

The individual and his or her relatives have a different notion of personal time and history than the clinician. Part of the agony of relatives must stem from their richer, longer, and rather different sense of history of the person who has schizophrenia. Clinicians meet and know patients after a disorder is present, when there is a disordered person. Unlike the friend or relative, clinicians did not have a different life course in mind, nor did they see or know the prior, perhaps more successful efforts to lead a life, to be a different person than the one now encountered in a clinic or hospital ward. But, is that person so different, so altered, or so absent as we have thought? Is there a missing person associated with schizophrenia or is the person present but obscured from our recognition? Does schizophrenia alter that basic private biography, the developing but continuous logic of self, the privately known and lifelong embodi-

Schizophrenia, like epilepsy and hemophilia is an I am *illness, one that is joined with social identity and perhaps with inner self, in language and terms of reference.*

ment of one's uniqueness? Brody (1987, p. x) describes this "dual nature of sickness—the way it can make us different persons while we still remain the same person." At present we lack information about what is the same and what is different about and within persons who have schizophrenia.

Considering time and personhood leads to the related topic of before and after. Who and what existed *before* the illness, and who and what endure *during and after?* Some do not accept that there is an "after" with schizophrenia, only before. This question seems to be rather crucial and may be answered most accurately by one seldom asked—the individual with schizophrenia. It is an area in which discrepancy abounds between clinician and patient, between relatives and diagnosed individual. We may see rather different changes than does the individual. Often referred to as "insight or denial" (see Greenfeld et al., 1989), the patient's protest or rejection of redefinition via diagnosis (or confinement) could signal something altogether different from pathology. It could be a cry for recognition of persisting, healthy, trying-to-survive self and personhood. In research in progress, we are finding that most of the patient-participants acknowledge symptoms and disturbances of thought and emotion. What they resist and reject are notions that those signs mean they are incompetent, failed, or somehow revised individuals because of these problems. Many make what we call "normalizing statements" in order, we hypothesize, to stress and reassert their similarities with others and to retain claim to their persisting, unrecognized, not-disordered selves.

We know too little about conceptions and recollections of the self and time before voices were heard, and before thinking was derailed; before the "others" noticed and the interventions began. The articles by Cutting and Dunn (1989), Romme and Escher (1989), and Lally (1989) provide ample evidence that changes are felt and tracked, that losses and gains in function, relationships, and social situations are felt keenly. So often, when relatives tell their story, they begin with a description of their loved one *before,* when there were accomplishments and successes, a known, knowable, and welcomed presence. And then the narrative of loss begins—the tale of the new, strange, disturbed and disturbing, not-really-who-they-were-before-but-still-somehow-the-same person.

The stories of individuals who have schizophrenia vary on this topic. Jefferson describes clearly a loss and change of self. Others protest redefinition saying, "You are not your illness. Find another role besides mental patient" (*Lighthouse,* 1988, p. 2). An essay in the same consumer newsletter asks, "Is there recognition and identity after mental illness?" (p. 3). Is there identity after mental illness? That the question is asked at all illustrates the need for studies of the processes and experiences of change, loss, and persistence of self accompanying schizophrenia.

Sickness in our culture implicitly alters the self (see Herzlich and Pierret, 1987). We say, "I'm not feeling like-myself," when we are ill. Others say, "You don't sound like or seem like yourself," when we are infirm or injured. We say, "I'm feeling much more like myself," on recovery. Others say, "You sound and seem much more like yourself these days." We are *not ourselves* in some profoundly cultural and symbolic way when we are sick or injured. Yet, of course, we are. The implication is

that we reject the dysfunctional self of sickness *as not me,* as other than a familiar or claimed self. This is all well and good if illness or injury is temporary, and we can return to or reclaim ourselves. When sickness persists, when injury and resulting impairment linger, when others have in the meantime grieved the loss and perhaps buried the former self, what then? When sickness overtakes one's biography, what remains? French sociologists Herzlich and Pierret (1987, p. 178) explain:

> By enforcing inactivity, illness thus prevents individuals from "playing their role," marginalizes them, and can even provoke a feeling of loss of identity "Who am I?" the sick person wonders. These questions sometimes reveal a feeling of total annihilation of the personality....

There are two interrelated dilemmas here: First, when being "not myself" *is* my self, that is, illness persists. Second, when the most self-seeing, self-knowing, self-confirming others lose, alter, or put away the person's prior, not-sick self so that it is unverifiable to and with them. And thus appears the double discrepancy, the double dilemma described in part by Erikson (1957):

> The patient has to seek definition as acutely sick and helpless in order to achieve a measure of public validation for his illness—and simultaneously has to use all his remaining strengths to struggle against that illness—a dilemma is posed which he may resolve by simply giving up the struggle altogether and *submerging himself* in the sick definition permanently (p. 271. emphasis added).

This "struggle" *for* self and *with* self that may epitomize schizophrenia goes on on two fronts: privately and publicly, in terms of inner sense of self and in terms of social identity. The interaction of these two spheres may make a reclaimed and restored self, and an accepted, agreed-upon identity nearly impossible to achieve for the symptomatic or hospitalized individual. The individual may experience self as persisting but with some new features or incapacities (symptoms). She or he may claim to be essentially "the same." But if others acknowledge a revised person, shifting the terms of the conspiracy of understanding, an undermining conflict between self and others *about* self may arise. At present, we lack sufficient data and reflection on this aspect of the experience of schizophrenia to engage in more than informed speculation.

To continue with the inventory of self and person, we include also social place and space. We have roles, and we belong by virtue of kin ties, for example, to groups, usually at least a nuclear family. Sylvia Frumkin (Sheehan, 1982) is a daughter and a sister. Lara Jefferson was someone's child. These kinship and other roles exist in the social world, and we fill them when we happen along with our own particular version of daughterhood or being a sibling. Belonging in a normative way to a larger group or groups both conveys and constitutes a sense of self, provides an identity in relation to others and by virtue of others' acknowledgment of us. Each of us claims and is assigned membership in a variety of cultural categories and social roles. These contribute to what we experience, the meaning or significance of those events or emotions, with whom we validate or share those experiences, and among whom we come to know ourselves and become known to others.

Gender, age, and ethnicity are aspects of person, other categories to which we belong and from which we know who we are and what we are. Maleness and femaleness, youth and old age, blackness or whiteness, all contain and convey prescriptions and models for behavior and expected characteristics. They are part of the inventory of person. While kinship, gender, ethnic, and age categories transcend individual versions, our portrayal is expected to be unique. There may be others *like* us, but no one else *is* us. We are supposed to have exclusive claim on one such self for a lifetime.

Bolstering this expected uniqueness at the larger societal level, person-specific legal and administrative identities are created. We have Social Security numbers, drivers' license numbers, and hospital identification numbers. These constitute so-called administrative selves (Douglas, 1983) that accompany and mark us over a lifetime as the *same person,* at least in the political, legal, and bureaucratic arenas.

There is also a core of meaning and knowing in the person. By this I mean the ways in which we attach significance to events; the ways we learn and remember, hope or regret; the ways we know what is real, what we prefer or disdain. Each of us has (and in some way *is*) these belief and symbol systems; these enduring though evolving clusters of meaning, experience, and knowledge. These are, like other aspects of self and identity, derived over time, in and from culture, from the experiences we have alone and with others. Here, I am referring to the meaning-making, world-knowing, experience-having self that forms part of the core of each of us. For the person with schizophrenia, this part of the self is thought to be perhaps the most altered, most vulnerable, most hidden or obscured.

In this issue of the *Bulletin,* each of the articles seeks to retrieve this dimension of

We are not ourselves *in some profoundly cultural and symbolic way when we are sick or injured.*

the person by asking, What is the meaning of this illness for this person? How profoundly and extensively is the person changed by having this illness? How can we best inquire about those meanings and learn from and about them? The subject, the person who experiences schizophrenia, may be more enduring than we have thought. The article by Bouricius (1989) presents a poignant and effective challenge in this regard. At the very least, these should be empirical questions deserving rigorous answers.

Chronicity is a transformation of a prior, enduring, known, and valued self into a less known and knowable, relatively recent, devalued, and dysfunctional self.

To sum up, schizophrenia is a disease, like others, that afflicts a person who has a history, an identity, kin and social roles, gender, age, hopes, ambitions, and these inner and outer selves. But because schizophrenia affects profoundly both how we present *and* experience ourselves, often the person and the disease or diagnosis become joined in scientific and social thinking in the realms of intervention and identity. To this point, I have outlined the more prominent aspects of self and personhood relevant to the study of individuals with schizophrenia. Next, we examine some proposed methods and concepts for a self-conscious, person-centered understanding of prognosis and the construction of chronicity.

Perhaps different facets of self are more durable, if less visible or knowable, than others. If there are special vulnerabilities, special sensitivities of the self to destructive influences, clinical work needs to be informed and focused on self-protection and preservation. If there are special strengths and durabilities of self that can aid healing and functioning, these require acknowledgment and encouragement—not engulfment in a patient role, label, or medication regimen, however well-intentioned. For example, Mann (1986, pp. 235-236) describes the treatment of a young man with schizophrenia as focused on filling in the "gaping maw of nonentity," of healing the "lesion" of identity from which he suffered. This was accomplished by retrieving and recreating an identity with and for the patient, within the therapeutic relationship. Pollack (1989) argues similarly that the quintessence of psychotherapy with persons who have schizophrenia is the construction (or reconstruction) of a coherent self first between therapist and patient, and eventually within the patient.

Investigating Prognosis With Self-Conscious Concepts and Methods

Several questions arise here. Is it inevitable that a person who has schizophrenia becomes schizophrenic? Is the self necessarily engulfed by the disease, identity taken hostage by the diagnosis? How does the individual view himself or herself in relation to the illness? Is good prognosis associated with a separation from self, a preserving of person who *has* but *is not* an illness? Or does the individual fare better by embracing and incorporating schizophrenia as within and of the self? Since we have paid so very little attention to subjective experiences and to the experiencing self of schizophrenia, we do not yet have empirically derived answers to these questions. We are apparently much more skilled at identifying evidence of illness than we are at recognizing and assessing the presence of person and condition of self.

Strauss (1989) suggests that individuals have a relationship with their disorders that influences course end outcome. Benjamin (1989), taking the hallucinated voice as a representative of the illness, describes the various coherent relationships individuals develop with those voices. These are significant contributions to the study of self and schizophrenia to which I wish to add, conceptually and methodologically.

Conceptually, we can posit two propositions about the relationship of self to sickness that apply in the Western World: 1) Loss or absence of self results in or constitutes an illness, and 2) sickness results in a loss of and change in self. Clinicians such as Kohut (Kohut & Wolf, 1978; Wolf , 1982) and others (Levin, 1987) articulate the first position, suggesting that there is no formed or cohering self in schizophrenia. Social scientists such as Erikson (1957), Charmaz (1983), and Goffman (1963) tend, not coincidentally, to emphasize the second perspective, describing the transformation of self, and identity that results from serious mental illness, especially that which is prolonged.

In clinical formulations, both psychological and biological pathology are located within the person, and they destroy or prevent the development of a self. In more social perspectives, external factors—such as responses to the individual by others and the individual's experiences with symptoms and treatment—erode, diminish, and otherwise alter the self and social identity. Neither approach ignores the contributions of factors emphasized by the other, but neither has been able to demonstrate empirically the relative influence of these various forces. Goffman, for example, persuades via elegant argument, compelling vignette, and logical precision that total institutions alter the internal selves and external identities of inmates. Yet, controversy continues in the research arena because empirical tests of this assumption have produced such equivocal results (Doherty, 1975; Townsend, 1976; Weinstein, 1983).

These disputes will not be settled here. The point has been to highlight underlying assumptions about the relationship of illness to identity and of sickness to the self. In so doing, perhaps more direct inquiry can proceed to test these hidden but influential propositions.

The second conceptual proposal concerns how individuals locate or situate their illnesses and symptoms in relation to themselves. I find Kohut's object relations notion of a continuum between self→self-object→object helpful as a way of representing this dimension. It seems entirely possible that for some individuals, the illness is experienced as an object, and for others it is more of a self-object, while for others it is inseparable from self. We would then seek some means for determining where a particular person fits along this dimension, investigating how or if prognosis was related.

Is good prognosis associated with a separation from self, a preserving of person who has but is not an illness? Or does the individual fare better by embracing and incorporating schizophrenia as within and of the self?

Methodologically, there are several techniques for examining these dynamics. Several innovative means, such as Structural Analysis of Social Behavior (Benjamin, 1989), Lally's (1989) scale and phase and more conventional strategies such as Strauss' (1989) semistructured interview are promising. Careful analysis of first person accounts of schizophrenia (Sommer & Osmond, 1983) or illness narratives (Kleinman, 1988) that focus on the self-sickness dimension is long overdue. We lack rigorous inquiries into how individuals with schizophrenia represent themselves in these texts and in speech; whether they describe loss or persistence of self; how these remain apart from or join with their illnesses; and what others say and do that influences those processes.

In ongoing research, we are investigating what we call *illness-identity statements*. We ask patient participants a series of open-ended questions about their explanations for and understandings of their problems; if they have names for the problem; how they think it works; what their doctors call it; and whether they consider this a mental illness. In response, many patients make *I have* statements, such as "I have a bipolar disorder." Others make *I am* statements, such as "I'm crazy. I'm not crazy. They say I'm crazy. I don't know." We are also interested in *you have* or *you are* indications that come from others, especially clinicians, and the responses of patients to these. These questions are repeated and the discussions are continued five times over 2 years.

Not only are we interested in how these individuals represent themselves in speech, but we use these data to locate them along the self-sickness continuum suggested above. As we track their functioning and experiences over time, we seek to establish whether prognosis or course bears any systematic relationship to this dimension.

Results from this investigation are far too preliminary to report, but the point has been to make a methodological contribution to the pursuit of subjectivity and subjects, and of self-schizophrenia relations. In that regard, two lessons are already apparent. First, on the basis of the obviously pained and sometimes forceful reactions of participants to these questions, we are convinced that these are not only crucial, but very private matters. The latter interviews in the sequence yield progressively richer, more detailed information. As the interviewer becomes better known to the participant, there is less hesitance and discomfort surrounding these topics. Second, the participants' formulations change over time: as they experience successes and failures in daily life, as they take or do not take medications, as they experience differing levels of symptoms, and as they respond to others' responses to them. As several articles in this issue demonstrate, there is a coherent process of reflexive assessment that occurs as individuals attempt to make sense of their symptoms, their lives, and their selves.

Chronicity as Loss of Self and Defeat of Person

Where, one might justifiably ask at this juncture, does this leave and lead us? As promised, with more questions than answers. I have thus far suggested that our failure to identify and know the experiencing subject, their meanings, and the sense they make of schizophrenia represents a debilitating deficit in our understandings and responses via treatment. Ironically, the loss and disorder of person so characteristic of our conceptions of schizophrenia may be at least party our own invention, and one of many ways in which we desert the person who has schizophrenia. We may both compound and create the isolation of inner and social self by failing to investigate and acknowledge the persistence of person.

In my view, the social and personal processes of having schizophrenia are not and need not be equivalent to the disease or having the disease. *Becoming a schizophrenic* is essentially a social and interpersonal process, not an inevitable consequence of primary symptoms and neurochemical abnormality. At the same time, I am not suggesting that schizophrenia is any sort of personal or cultural fiction. The point is that there are simultaneous, equally influential neurophysical, social, and personal processes at work. Within this conceptual frame work, chronicity is a transformation of a prior, enduring, known, and valued self into a less known and knowable, relatively recent, devalued, and dysfunctional self. This process, I have argued, occurs among and in the eyes of others, and internally, within the person.

One of the ways that this occurs is through what we call progressive role constriction. As individuals cease to have a job, withdraw from school, and lose contact with friends and family, they also lose valued social roles, and the acceptable identities compiled and derived from those roles. The patient role is often one of the few that remain. These cumulative experiences and situations result in necessary reformulations by the person, and can result in their becoming part of a new category, that is, schizophrenic. This category, which is as profoundly cultural and transcendent as the others identified above, carries implicit verification that the person is not who or how we may have thought the person was before. Instead of becoming *part* of the inventory of person, the category of schizophrenic engulfs or pervades the person.

Many parents and siblings wonder in agony where their son or brother went, once schizophrenia occurs. There is this partial stranger who is also their child, their sib. Perhaps it is this sometimes paradoxical persistence of the person, along with the person's symptoms and incomprehensible behaviors, that leads to confusion

and wildly varying hope and despair about recovery. Our clinical and cultural conceptions of schizophrenia create the capacity to obscure and redefine individuals who have the disease, as surely as the primary symptoms alter their cognitions and perceptions. While it has been by no means established that preserving valued roles and retaining a positive personhood contribute to more positive outcome, it is difficult to imagine that the suffering and despair of individuals would not be lessened.

As Strauss (1989) has already noted, the idea that individuals have a relationship with their disorders, or representations of their disorders, poses some problems. This perspective presumes the existence of separate entities of self and sickness. Fabrega (1989) demonstrates that this conception is culture-bound and of perhaps limited relevance to schizophrenia. Indeed, our cultural and clinical conceptions of schizophrenia lead to conflicting and contradictory positions. On the one hands we suspect that the disease alters and even overtakes the self. On the other, we envision schizophrenia as a disease and biological entity, presumably separable from self, situated in the body.

The idea of fighting the disease, having distance from symptoms, making the separation between a sick or not sick self—all these require an intellectually unacceptable separation of symptoms from subject. Even if this is a scientifically or philosophically disquieting position, we mast ask whether it is, however, realistic phenomenologically, and whether it is valid experientially and subjectively. In anthropological terms, we proceed ethnographically and inductively to learn the concepts, meanings, and experiences of our expert informants. At that point, our tasks as researchers are to seek associations, causal links, patterns, and implications.

To conclude, I have argued here that we have failed to pose and pursue several essential questions about the subjective experience of schizophrenia. How do the pervasive cultural, clinical, and personal symbols, metaphors, and meanings of schizophrenia influence prognosis? How do individuals with schizophrenia understand and locate themselves in relationship to the symptoms, labels, and responses? What contributes to a person's ability to separate himself or herself from this sickness, and does this facilitate or even constitute recovery? In some sense, I am wondering if loss of self, personal and social, to schizophrenia *is chronicity*. Is survival of the self to oneself and in the eyes of others a necessary condition of positive outcome and favorable course? Because we often fail to know, cannot comprehend, or irreversibly alter our own notions of the person with schizophrenia, we may be unnecessarily, wastefully contributing to chronicity and the construction of schizophrenic patients. Continued careful pursuit of the subject will, we hope, answer some of these questions.

Acknowledgments

Preparation of and data for this article were supported in part by research grant MH-40314 from the National Institute of Mental Health. The author appreciates the contributions of John Strauss, the Triangle Mental Health Survey staff, and Lorna Benjamin for the thoughts conveyed here and in the longer term project of which it is part.

References

American Psychiatric Association. (1987). *DSM-III-R: Diagnostic and Statistical Manual of Mental Disorders. 3rd ed., revised*. Washington, DC: The Association.

Benjamin, L.S. (1989). Is chronicity a function of the relationship between the person and the auditory hallucination? *Schizophrenia Bulletin, 15*, 291-310.

Bouricius, J.K. (1989). Negative symptoms and emotions in schizophrenia. *Schizophrenia Bulletin, 15*, 201-208.

Brody, H. (1987). *Stories of sickness*. New Haven, CT: Yale University Press.

Charmaz, K. (1983). Loss of self: A fundamental form of suffering in the chronically ill. *Sociology of Health and Illness, 5*, 168-197.

Crapanzano, V. (1982). The self, the third, and desire. In B. Lee (Ed.), *Psychosocial theories of the self* (pp 179-206). New York: Plenum Press, 179-206.

Cutting, J. & Dunn, F. (1989). Subjective experience of schizophrenia. *Schizophrenia Bulletin, 15*, 217-231.

Douglas, M. (1983). How identity problems disappear. In A. Jacobson-Widding (Ed.), *Identity: Personal and sociocultural* (pp 35-46). Atlantic Highlands, NJ: Humanities Press.

Doherty, E.G. (1975). Labeling effects in psychiatric hospitalization: A study of diverging patterns of inpatient self-labeling processes. *Archives of General Psychiatry, 32*, 562-568.

Erikson, K.T. (1957). Patient role and social uncertainty: A dilemma of the mentally ill. *Psychiatry, 30*, 263-274.

Fabrega, H., Jr. (1989). The self and schizophrenia: A cultural perspective. *Schizophrenia Bulletin, 15*, 277-290.

Frankenberg, R. (1987). Life cycle, trajectory or pilgrimage? A social production approach to Marxism, metaphor and mortality. In A. Bryman, B. Bytheway, P. Allatt & T. Keil, (Eds.), *The life cycle* (pp 122-138). London: MacMillan.

Goffman, E. (1963). *Stigma: Notes on the management of spoiled identity*. Englewood Cliffs, NJ: Prentice-Hall.

Greenfeld, D., Strauss, J.S., Bowers, M.B. & Mandelkern, M. (1989). Insight and interpretation of illness in recovers from psychosis. *Schizophrenia Bulletin, 15*, 245-252.

Herzlich, C. & Pierret, J. (1987). *Illness and self in society*. Baltimore: The Johns Hopkins University Press.

Jefferson, L. (1974). *These are my sisters: A journal from the inside of insanity*. Garden City, NY: Anchor, Doubleday.

Kleinman, A. (1988). *The illness narratives: Suffering, healing and the human condition*. New York: Basic Books, 1938.

Kohut, H. & Wolf, E.S. (1978). The disorders of the self and their treatment: An outline. *International Journal of Psychoanalysis, 59*, 413-425.

Kovel, J. (1987). Schizophrenic being and technocratic society. In D.M. Levin (Ed.), *Pathologies of the modern self: Postmodern studies on narcissism, schizophrenia, and depression* (pp. 330-348). New York: New York University Press.

Lally, S.J. (1989). Does being in here mean there is something wrong with me? *Schizophrenia Bulletin, 15,* 253-265.

Lapsley, D.K. & Power, F.C. (Eds.). (1988). *Self, ego, and identity: Integrative approaches.* New York: SpringerVerlag.

Lee, B., (Ed.). (1982). *Psychosocial theories of the self.* New York: Plenum Press.

Levin, D.M., (Ed.). (1987). *Pathologies of the modern self: Postmodern studies on narcissism, schizophrenia and depression.* New York: New York University Press.

Lighthouse Newsletter. (1988). Report on national mental patients' conference, October/November, 2-3.

Mann, D.W. (1986). Six months in the treatment of two young chronic schizophrenics. *Psychiatry, 49,* 231-240.

Pollack, W.S. (1989). Schizophrenia and the self: Contributions of psychoanalytic self-psychology. *Schizophrenia Bulletin, 15,* 311-322.

Rosenberg, M. (1984). A symbolic interactionist view of psychosis. *Journal of Health and Social Behavior, 25,* 289-302.

Romme, A.J. & Escher, A.D.M.A.C. (1989). Hearing voices. *Schizophrenia Bulletin, 15,* 209-216.

Sheehan, S. (1982). *Is there no place on earth for me?* Boston: Houghton Mifflin Company.

Sommer, R. & Osmond, H. (1983). A bibliography of mental patients' autobiographies, 1960-1982. *American Journal of Psychiatry, 140,* 1051-1054.

Strauss, J.S. (1989). Subjective experiences of schizophrenia: Toward a new dynamic psychiatry, II. *Schizophrenia Bulletin, 15,* 179-187.

Townsend, J.M. (1976). Self-concept and the institutionalization of mental patients: An overview and critique. *Journal of Health and Social Behavior, 17,* 263-271.

Weinstein, R.M. (1983). Labeling theory and the attitudes of mental patients: A review. *Journal of Health and Social Behavior, 24,* 70-84.

Wolf, E.S. (1982). Comments on Heinz Kohut's conceptualization of a bipolar self. In B. Lee (Ed.), *Psychosocial theories of the self* (pp. 23-42). New York: Plenum Press.

CHRONICITY IN SCHIZOPHRENIA: REVISITED

Courtenay M. Harding, Joseph Zubin and John S. Strauss

COURTENAY M. HARDING, PHD, ASSISTANT PROFESSOR
OF PSYCHIATRY, DEPARTMENT OF PSYCHIATRY,
UNIVERSITY OF COLORADO SCHOOL
OF MEDICINE, DENVER, USA.

JOHN S. STRAUSS, MD, PROFESSOR OF PSYCHIATRY,
DEPARTMENT OF PSYCHIATRY, YALE UNIVERSITY
SCHOOL OF MEDICINE, NEW HAVEN.

JOSEPH ZUBIN, PHD, THE LATE DISTINGUISHED
RESEARCH PROFESSOR OF PSYCHIATRY, VETERANS
ADMINISTRATION MEDICAL CENTER, PITTSBURGH, PA.

THIS ARTICLE ORIGINALLY APPEARED IN THE
British Journal of Psychiatry, 1992, 161, 27-37
AND IS REPRINTED WITH PERMISSION.

Derived simply from the Greek work chronos, *meaning time, the label "chronic" denotes an illness of long duration or one of frequent recurrence. However, when chronic is paired with schizophrenia, as in "this person is a chronic schizophrenic," the connotation becomes an expectation of deterioration, defect, or deficit states (Cutting, 1983). These perceptions about schizophrenia have pervaded and guided clinical judgements (Feighner et al., 1972; American Psychiatric Association, 1980, 1987), treatment programming (Bachrach, 1979; Lamb, 1981; Strauss & Glazer, 1982), policy formulation (Greenblatt, 1978; Talbott, 1979), and decisions about priority for funding (Kraft, 1981). These perceptions have also stripped hopes of recovery from patients and their families (Chamberlin, 1979; Lovejoy, 1984). Further, the use of phrases such as "deinstitutionalization of chronic mental patients" glosses over the large heterogeneity of patient types, courses of illness and recovery, and the actual shifts in composition* *and migrations of groups of patients within society (Lamb, 1979; Leighton, 1982; Harding & Ashikaga, 1982).*

This report summarizes a century of research and clinical evidence (or lack thereof) about the concept of chronicity in schizophrenia. In addition, alternative ideas will be presented which provide different views of the disorder and of the recovering person. Such changes in the perceptions of the complex processes involved in schizophrenia carry strong implications for the patient, the clinician, the family, and the mental health system.

Why the Profession is Pessimistic About Schizophrenia

The Effect of Biased Clinical Observation

Before the turn of the century, clinicians adopted the then new scientific system for classification of disease entities which was based on the linear unfolding sequence of cause, onset, course, and outcome as an inflexible natural history of the disorder. In 1896, Kraepelin (1899) carefully described case after case of dementia praecox, combining a group of mental disorders into a single disease entity because of their relentless, downward, deteriorating course and thus uniformly poor outcome. After initially reporting 13% lasting recovery, Kraepelin later revised his estimate to only 2.6 to 4.1% (Shapiro & Shader, 1979). Dementia praecox was identified by characteristic symptoms and by a poor longitudinal course. In 1899, these factors differentiated dementia praecox from manic depression which, in contrast, was thought to be marked by a good longitudinal course and expectations of recovery. Prognosis confirmed diagnosis. If the person who had all the symptoms of dementia praecox improved, then Kraepelin routinely considered the patient to have been originally misdiagnosed—an interesting tautology.

Just after the turn of the century, Eugene Bleuler (1911, translated 1950) widened Kraepelin's concept of dementia praecox by shifting the overall focus from the course of the disorder to that of differentiating primary and secondary symptoms, as well as incorporating Freudian concepts of psychopathology. He postulated a group of psychoses called "the schizophrenias"—a pluralism often forgotten.

During his long study of such patients, Bleuler (as translated) appeared to have begun with some optimism about outcome and to have become more pessimistic over time. The course of the schizophrenias was described by Bleuler, early in his career, as varying considerably because an individual could be "both qualitatively and temporally rather irregular. Constant advances, halts, recurrences, or remissions are possible at any time" (Freyhan, 1958). Freyhan also stated that Eugene Bleuler's "emphasis on range, variability, and most crucial, reversibility of schizophrenic manifestations, form the cornerstone of his concept" (p. 770). In a follow-up study, Bleuler reported 60% as having achieved a state of only "mild deterioration" (i.e. capable of self-support), while 18% had moderate and 22% severe deterioration (Freyhan, 1958). However, these findings have been generally dismissed as not surprising because the heterogeneity was to be expected, given the inclusiveness of his diagnostic criteria and

Classical descriptions of course and outcome for schizophrenia, on which the bulwark or psychiatric thinking was built, were probably not representative of the complete range that is possible for this disorder.

the difficulty of applying them reliably. Later, Bleuler himself declared that there was never "full *restitutio ad integrum*" in his patients who were classified as having one of the schizophrenias (Bleuler, 1911; Shapiro & Shader, 1979). Rephrased, this statement appears to have become the adage, "once a schizophrenic, always a schizophrenic."

The pessimistic views of these seminal writers about the course and outcome of schizophrenia have been taught to generations of psychiatric trainees. As an example, the newest diagnostic guides in psychiatry, the *Diagnostic and Statistical Manual (DSM-III*; American Psychiatric Association, 1980), and its revision the *DSM-III-R* (American Psychiatric Association, 1987), states the following expectations about the course and outcome of schizophrenia: "The most common course is one of acute exacerbations with increasing residual impairments between episodes" and "A complete return to premorbid functioning is unusual—so rare, in fact, that some clinicians would question the diagnosis" (*DSM-III*, 1980, p. 185).

Until recently, few teachers or clinicians ever questioned whether the original descriptions and conclusions were based on a balanced and representative sample of all those with the disorder (M. Bleuler, 1978; Harding, 1984; McGlashan, 1988). Both Kraepelin and Bleuler may have had biased samples from which they described their hospital in-patients. Before the turn of the century, Kraepelin's patients came into hospital and for the most part stayed in custodial care (Scull, 1979; Jones, 1983).

The historians Alexander and Selesnick (1966) have described the situation as follows: "Kraepelin's stress on the morbid outcome of dementia praecox led to a fatalistic compliance with a predestined course. Once a label of dementia praecox had been affixed to a person, he became a case number awaiting the ultimate fate of deterioration. Custodial care, even though humane, did not change the nihilistic attitude of the staff caring for the unfortunate victim" (p. 164). The effects of such continuous hospital stay on the levels of functioning in patients has been vividly described in reports on institutionalization by Barton (1959), Goffman (1961), and Wing and Brown (1970), among others. Further bias might have been introduced by the strong possibility that Kraepelin included in his samples patients with tertiary syphilis and other organic disorders, for which tests were unavailable until 1911 and later (Davison & Bagley, 1969) .

Contrary to the German policy of custodial care, the Swiss developed strategies of early release and foster family placement as early as 1905 (M. Bleuler, 1978). Therefore, for E. Bleuler, it was a case of "out of sight, out of mind." His son, Manfred Bleuler (1978), attributes his father's pessimism regarding the outcome of schizophrenia to such a bias. His description of it is as follows:

> From 1886 to 1898, E. Bleuler dedicated himself completely to his community of schizophrenics as director of the remote psychiatric clinic of Rheinau, which was then in an isolated, rural sector of Switzerland. Two decades later, during and after the First World War, he went back to Rheinau to visit about once a year, usually when the weather was fine during the summer. His former schizophrenic patients always greeted him warmly and enthusiastically. Much as these greetings pleased him, he usually made the painful observation. "Most of them did seem to have deteriorated."

> Then depressed, he would ask, "Is there really nothing that can stop this disease?" If he spent all his life wrestling with the question whether there was an "organic process" at the basis of schizophrenia, it was mainly because of experiences like the above. But E. Bleuler did not know how many improved patients were out for their Sunday walks during his visits, and certainly not how many had been released and were living at home, recovered. Had he known, and if he had not continued to meet only the most severe cases among his old problem children, his assessment of the schizophrenias would have been strongly influenced. A number of generations of clinical psychiatrists had experiences similar to his. (M. Bleuler, 1978, p. 413)

The available evidence points to the fact that Kraepelin's sample was culled selectively from those patients who remained continuously institutionalized, while members of Bleuler's sample were often lost to follow-up, leaving only the ones who remained to be noticed. Both investigators also had samples which included those patients who would meet criteria for other organic diagnostic categories. Thus, the classical descriptions of course and outcome for schizophrenia, on which the bulwark or psychiatric thinking was built, were probably *not* representative of the complete range that is possible for this disorder.

Today, many clinicians also have a biased sampling, because of their predominantly short-term caseloads. Perhaps only a certain segment of the entire population of people who once were diagnosed as schizophrenic continue to need and receive care, but this is rarely noted. The group which the clinician continues to see and treat mistakenly appears to represent the entire picture of schizophrenia (Cohen & Cohen, 1984). Further, if a particular patient enters a caseload and functions only marginally for 5 to 10 years, with repeated episodes of illness, the tendency for the clinician is to think that this level will continue or worsen; with short-term caseloads, not enough additional time elapses to check that assumption. Such patients are often regarded as fairly unresponsive to early efforts at treatment, and when they continue to be marginal, are viewed as failures in whom the disorder has obtained the upper hand. If such a person drops out of the caseload, a busy clinician often assumes that he/she has simply transferred to another clinician's caseload or is living a marginal existence. Rarely is a forward movement towards better functioning and reintegration into the community assumed. There is no built-in systematic feedback to clinicians about successes: they receive only negative messages, signalled by the reappearance of those patients with new episodes.

However, there are clinicians, such as M. Bleuler (1955, 1963, 1968, 1969, 1972a, 1972b, 1974, 1978, 1983) at Burghölzli Hospital in Switzerland and G. Brooks (Brooks, 1959, 1960, 1961a, 1961b, 1966, 1981; Brooks & Deane, 1960, 1965; Brooks et al., 1963, 1970) at Vermont State Hospital who have stayed in one setting over decades. They have followed-up prospectively those patients in an intact cohort who were also discharged to the community. These clinicians, and others like them, report that a number of once-chronic patients significantly improve and recover across their life course.

The Effect of Contradictory Research Evidence

To compound these problems of biased sampling, short- and long-term follow-up studies presented over the years have been both contradictory and confusing (Rennie, 1939; Rupp & Fletcher, 1939; Holt & Holt, 1952; Astrup & Noreik, 1966; Brown et al., 1966; Achté, 1967). Some of these studies reported poor outcome, while others did not. Many reviews of the literature (Strömgren, 1961; Stephens, 1970;

Bachrach, 1976; Shapiro & Shader, 1979) have outlined reasons why such contradictions have existed:

a) different samples are selected because of different criteria for the diagnosis of schizophrenia

b) "schizophrenia" is often not defined

c) different length of follow-up periods

d) outcome is often defined only as "recovered" or "unrecovered"

e) there are varying sources of data in follow-up (e.g. case records vs. actual interview)

f) lack of "blindness" in data collection procedure (e.g. that the investigators knew previous history of the subjects)

g) use of clinical non-structured interviews

h) single cross-sectional assessments

i) too many missing or deceased subjects

(Reprinted from *Hospital & Community Psychiatry* [1987] 38, 478.)

It appears that the confusing empirical data and clinical descriptions from potentially biased samples, available since schizophrenia was described less than 100 years ago, have not provided much clarification or accurate information about the long-term course and outcome of the disorder.

Current Investigations and Concepts

The Five Recent Long-term Studies of Schizophrenia

Within the last decade, a number of systematic studies of the short- and long-term outcome in schizophrenia have examined the range of methodological issues mentioned above. All five have found heterogeneity in outcome functioning, rather than simply marginal or deteriorated states. These very long-term follow-up studies

TABLE 1.
FIVE LONG-TERM STUDIES

Study	Sample Size	Average Length in Years	% Subjects Recovered and/or Improved Significantly
M. Bleuler (1972a, 1972b) Burghölzli, Zurich	208	23	53%–68%
Huber et al. (1979) Bonn Studies	502	22	57%
Ciompi & Müller (1976) Lausanne Investigations	289	37	53%
Tsuang et al. (1979) Iowa 500	186	35	46%
Harding et al. (1987a, 1987b) Vermont	118	32	62–68%

reported since 1972 have produced astonishingly similar results, which appear to override their differences in design (Harding et al., 1987c). Each of them found at least half of each cohort had significantly improved or recovered, when assessed at 20-, 30-, and 40-year follow-up. Two were those mentioned above as the research cohorts of long-term directors of hospitals, M. Bleuler and G. Brooks. Table 1 summarizes these five studies.

Manfred Bleuler (1978) followed 208 patients who were either first admissions or readmissions for 23 years, as a representative cohort admitted to Burghölzli Hospital during 1942 to 1943. He found that 53% of the entire group significantly improved or recovered: when the first admissions were separated out, 68% were found to have recovered or improved.

In the United States, the most recent long-term study was the prospective/retrospective longitudinal study across an average of 32 years by Brooks at Vermont State Hospital. His sample contained 269 very chronic subjects (Chittick et al., 1961). This included an in-depth current assessment completed by Harding and associates (1987a, 1987b). At the time of their selec-

tion in the mid-1950s, Brooks' subjects averaged 16 years duration of illness, 10 years of total disablement, and 6 continuous years of hospital stay (Chittick et al., 1961). At follow-up, half to two thirds of all cohort sub-samples (whether alive or deceased and whether diagnosed for schizophrenia by *DSM-III* or *DSM-I*) had achieved significant improvement or recovery (Harding et al., 1987b).

The Vermont subjects were matched by age, gender, diagnosis, and length of chronicity to patients residing at Augusta, Maine State Hospital in the 1950s. Co-directed with Michael De Sisto, this effort represented the first attempt in the world literature to match subjects on key variables and follow them up with the same protocols. The essential difference between the two cohorts was the presence or absence of a rehabilitation program. The Maine replication averaged 37 years of followup. This study (National Institute of Mental Health #40032) has recently been completed and will be reported soon.

The results of The Burghölzli and Vermont longitudinal studies have been supported by the three other long-term studies, which were cross-sectional assessments or cohorts selected retrospectively from old case records. A Swiss study, by Ciompi and Müller in 1976, assessed 289 subjects at an average of 36.9 years after first admission; 53% of the study subjects were found to be significantly improved or recovered. The Bonn Study, conducted by Huber and associates (1975), examined 502 subjects at an average of 22.4 years after admission, and found 57% recovered or significantly improved (Huber et al., 1980). The later study concluded: "schizophrenia does not seem to be a disease of slow progressive deterioration. Even in the second and third decades of illness, there is still potential for full or partial recovery" (p. 595).

Finally, another study in the United States, "The Iowa 500" (Winokur et al., 1972; Tsuang et al., 1979), also produced similar results, but they were not obvious because only the subsamples who did not improve were reported. This investigation followed 186 subjects who had been admitted consecutively between 1934 and 1944 to the University Psychiatric Hospital in Iowa City. At an average of 35 years later, 46% recovery and improvement was found in their schizophrenic sample, who met the relatively narrow Feighner and associates (1972) criteria for schizophrenia.

Thus, recent, more methodologically-sound studies have found that one half to two thirds of over 1300 subjects studied for longer than 20 years achieved recovery or significant improvement. These results represent a major challenge to the current prevailing concept of outcome in schizo-

Severe psychiatric disorder has been found not to be a unitary, linear, unfolding process, but one that ebbs and flows at different rates across different areas of functioning.

phrenia as invariably resulting in marginal levels of functioning or a downward deteriorating course.

Persistent Findings of Heterogeneity Across Areas of Outcome Functioning

Among shorter-term studies, the work of Strauss & Carpenter (1972, 1974, 1977; Strauss et al., 1974) also revealed that outcome was not a unitary process, but consisted of a set of "open-linked" systems, such as occupational functioning and social competence, which operate semi-independently of each other and of symptoms and length of time in hospital. Further work by the same team also found wide heterogeneity of outcome functioning, even at the 5-year follow-up point (Hawk et al., 1975). This variation across outcome domains has been found by many others (e.g., Bland & Orn [1978] in their 14-year Alberta Hospital follow-up study; Gardos and associates [1982] in their Boston State Hospital study of 12 years follow-up [if one balances their findings with good outcome refusals]; and cross-culturally in the World Health Organization [1979] International Pilot Study of Schizophrenia, a 2- and 5-year follow-up).

In addition to these studies of hospital admissions, there has been a recent epidemiologically-based population study of all people diagnosed as having schizophrenia drawn from the county of Buckinghamshire, north of London. This catchment area of approximately 500,000 people used a single mental hospital (Watt et al., 1983). The sample (n = 121) consisted of both first-admission and readmission patients with schizophrenia. At the 5-year point, 99% were followed-up and 48% had achieved a good outcome. Of the first admissions 58% had a good outcome.

The Failure of Diagnostic Criteria to Predict Long-term Functioning

Major efforts to reduce the observed heterogeneity of outcome have revolved around the definition of who is *really* schizophrenic and who is not. Two types of strategies have been undertaken in attempts to clarify these issues. The first has been focused on narrowing the criteria to achieve a homogeneous group with "core," "nuclear," "process," or "true," schizophrenia; these include Feighner and associates (1972), Langfeldt (1937), Schneider (1959), the RDC by Spitzer and associates (1975), and *DSM-III* (American Psychiatric Association, 1980). The second strategy has been to change the diagnosis of schizophrenia to another category if subjects recovered or improved, as in Langfeldt's "schizophreniform psychosis" (1939), Jaspers' (1963) "reaction psychosis," or Leonhard's (1961) cycloid psychosis.

Both strategies have been tested by constructing samples on the basis of these systems of criteria, and conducting outcome studies. In every case where careful methods were used, the outcome was found to be heterogeneous, with half or more of the subjects displaying significant improvement. The diagnosis of schizophrenia has not been confirmed by association with outcome, beyond a limited degree. In fact, empirical data tend to validate Vaillant's contention that "prognosis and diagnosis are two different dimensions of psychosis" (see footnote 1 and also Vaillant, 1978).

Evidence points to the fact that beyond "outcome" even the evolution of the course of schizophrenia is not a foregone conclusion: there appears to be a wide spectrum of possible courses that patients follow. Huber and associates (1975) for example, identified 73 different courses and later reduced them to 12 composite forms, while Ciompi (1980a, 1980b) and Bleuler (1978) have established a minimum of 8. Research is just beginning to provide an understanding of the determinants of the evolution of the disorder and of improvement over time, since previously, not even the heterogeneity of outcome had been widely recognized.

Thus, even if there is a natural history for schizophrenia tending toward an expected outcome, the roles of patient personality and of the environment, both in and out of the hospital, in aiding or interfering with the expected outcome are too powerful to permit uniformity (Strauss et al., 1988). No matter what diagnostic system is employed, many patients get better. Misconceptions from the past which have hindered the ability to judge more accurately the full picture of the disorder have been dispelled. Such misconceptions, said E. Bleuler, "are the greatest obstacles to the progress of science" (Freyhan, 1958).

The Difficulties of Separating the Effects of the Environment From the Effects of Schizophrenia

As early as 1960, Brown noted that the number of patients residing in hospitals for over 2 years (the criterion for chronicity proposed by Kramer and associates [1955], in the classic Warren State Hospital study) had decreased from two thirds in the 1920s to one third in the 1930s. By the 1950s in the United Kingdom, only 12 to 13% of schizophrenic patients were in hospital for over 2 years. Wing (1962) concluded that institutionalization itself had contributed to the picture of disability for those who stayed. Patients were rarely reviewed for

---

1. In the paper entitled a *Ten-Year Follow-up of Remitting Schizophrenia* presented at the 129TH Annual Meeting of the American Psychiatric Association, Anaheim, CA, May 1975.

discharge after 2 years because their loss of social skills was perceived as persistent psychopathology, when in fact it may have been an independent feature, caused by long-term hospital stay itself.

In 1971, Ludwig studied an in-patient sample and itemized a "case of chronicity" which vividly described how institutionalized people become socialized into a "good patient" role. His list included: "to be dull, harmless, and inconspicuous; to evade responsibility, minimize stress, ignore others, to retain the right to behave unpredictably and have a certain 'diplomatic immunity.'" These acquired skills may have made life easier for both patients and staff as a compromise in an untenable situation, but were inimical to social integration into the community. The following description was collected from the current literature to describe the "pool of chronic patients" in caseloads today. The chronic mental patient is: unproductive; surviving in low standard housing; emotionally isolated; maintained on medication; generally dull and colorless or erratically flamboyant; unable to generalize learning; chronically ill; slightly disheveled; a victim or victimizer; frustrating; dependent; apathetic; unemployed or unable to work in competitive market; a tax drain; and has poor quality of companionship. It is remarkable how much of this description overlaps with Ludwig's code.

To understand these characteristics, Strauss and Glazer (1982) have described some of the processes in the chronic patient which can helpfully be differentiated. Rather than seeing chronicity as a single attribute, they noted four separate aspects: "a) chronicity of symptoms; b) chronicity of dysfunction in occupational and relationship spheres; c) chronicity of receiving treatment; and d) the "chronic attitude," a sense of hopelessness, of having given up, of having settled into being bizarre or disabled" (p. 208).

In attempting to understand this picture of chronicity, it has been difficult to separate out the *residual effects of the disorder* (such as negative symptoms) (Strauss et al., 1974; Andreasen, 1982); the effects due to *institutionalization* (Wing & Brown, 1970; Ciompi, 1980b); the socialization into the *patient role* (Goffman, 1961; Haley, 1969; Ludwig, 1971); the lack of *rehabilitation* (Anthony, 1977; Strauss, 1980); *reduced economic opportunities* (Brenner, 1973; Warner, 1985); reduced *social status* (Hollingshead & Redlich, 1958; Dunham, 1976); the *side-effects of medication* (Gardos & Cole, 1980; Mandell et al., 1982), and the role of lack of *staff expectations* (Chittick et al., 1961; Lamb & Goertzel, 1972), self-fulfilling prophecies (Rosenhan 1973; Houghton, 1980), and *loss of hope* (Lovejoy, 1984).

Given the many factors contributing to chronicity in "chronic mental patients" and the fact that the group under treatment at any time represents only a fraction of persons who have had episodes of schizophrenia (Cohen & Cohen, 1984), a doubt must arise as to whether chronicity is a necessary and inherent outcome of the disorder.

Some Suggested Concepts About Improvement and Recovery in Schizophrenia

In the search for new perspectives, several concepts about the course of schizophrenia and recovery from it have been developed by investigators who have spent most of their professional lives living and working with, as well as treating and learning from, people with this illness. These concepts include the possible ameliorative effects of ageing and the deleterious effects of psychosocial events, the probability that schizophrenia is primarily a prolonged illness rather than a chronic one, a focus on the person who has the disorder and ways of reaching that person, and consideration of the person's illness-environment interaction in disorder and recovery.

Drawing on his experience in conducting the longest follow-up to date (catamnestic period ranging up to 64 years after first admission), Ciompi (1980a) suggests that the natural ageing process is an ameliorative factor in the dissipation of the illness in later years. He speculates that biological factors dampen the effects of the illness, which allow the once-afflicted person to resume a more normal life-course. In addition, Ciompi perceives chronicity to be due primarily to psychosocial artifacts, introduced by such forces as institutionalization and under-stimulation, over-stimulation by family members, labelling, life events, expectations of significant others, and the "general psychosocial inertia" exhibited by patients to reduce "insecurity, fear, and tension" (1980b). Ciompi further cites the variability of long-term courses, the lack of specificity of negative symptoms for schizophrenia, the sparsity of genetic evidence, and the reversibility of residual states, to strengthen his case for psychosocial causes of chronicity. He concludes that "the development of a person who was once psychotic must be viewed more as an open life process than as a disease process" (1980b).

In assessing the impact of schizophrenia across a person's lifetime, Harding and Strauss (1984) have concluded that the disorder is primarily a prolonged illness rather than a chronic one. Harding cites many other "chronic" disorders—rheumatoid arthritis, ankylosing spondylitis, epilepsy, asthma, urinary-tract infections, peptic

Recent, more methodologically-sound studies have found that one half to two thirds of over 1300 subjects studied for longer than 20 years achieved recovery or significant improvement.

ulcers, alcoholism, and heroin addiction—which have heterogeneous outcomes that include significant improvement or recoveries; the list is by no means all inclusive.

A person can be quite disabled with certain forms of arthritis and yet play tennis again (Calabro, 1979; Cousins, 1979; Gilliland & Mannik, 1983). Many young people with serious seizure disorders for 10 years or more, requiring heavy dosages of anticonvulsants, recover and move on to normal lives without further medication or seizures (Vick, 1976; Swaiman & Wright, 1982). Many early-onset asthmatics go about their lives later, free of the disorder (Daniele, 1982; Simpson et al., 1984), as do some people with "chronic" forms of alimentary-tract ulcers (Bockus, 1974) or urinary-tract disorders (Kraft & Staney, 1977). In the field of psychiatry, Vaillant has tracked the recovery of alcoholics (1980) and heroin addicts (1969) who had long histories of severe disorder.

Speculations could be made about the roles of the body's seeming ability to right itself (Cannon, 1963; Harding & Strauss, 1984b), the persistence of the human psyche, the developmental evolution of coping strategies, and a changing environment which is more or less helpful in promoting the return to health. Alterations in any of these factors could account for the heterogeneity of outcome for people with the same disorder.

Zubin believed that schizophrenia has become increasingly benign during the last century, with a significant reduction in cases showing a catastrophic downhill course (Bleuler, 1963; Zubin et al., 1983). He viewed schizophrenia as primarily an episodic disorder. Zubin and Spring (1977) considered the patient to be a person with a persistent underlying vulnerability—an essentially well person with intermittent episodes of illness, rather than a sick person with intermittent episodes of good health. Chronicity, as well as the negative symptoms which mark it, was seen to be an artifact caused by: a) the iatrogenic and nosocomial effects of treatment, as well as b) the cold reception which the former schizophrenic patient receives when he returns to his often noxious ecological niche, resulting in a rapid return to chronicity, or c) a return to an inadequate premorbid personality. Separation of the behavior due to premorbid status from the focal disorder of schizophrenia needs recognition, and has become a task for ongoing research (Zubin, 1983).

Focusing on the person, as Zubin did, M. Bleuler (1978) states, "In the schizophrenic psychoses... the old intellectual competence, warmth and emotional depth are discernible behind every serious state of morbidity, time and time again" (p. 453). Based on his view of the person and the disorder, Bleuler has suggested that genetic components of any form of treatment should be "stimulat-

A system which offers opportunities for multiple levels of functioning in housing, occupational, and social skills, with allowance for people making use of these offerings on an as-needed basis may work better in the long run than a lock-step rigid process which expects either recovery in a short time or lifetime custodial care, with not much in between.

ing and appealing to the patient's healthy element, in particular to his need to make contact with others...[Favorable influences]...are in essence the same forces that develop a healthy personality from childhood on and keep it healthy. They include active participation in the community of his fellow men and the natural unfolding of the abilities with which the patient was endowed" (p. 298).

In a recent example illustrating the idea of trying to reach the person behind the disorder, the Extended Treatment Service Division of New York Hospital developed a program which looked beyond treatment of an illness to trying to find evidence that "the person is still there." Signs of "aliveness" were seen as glimmers of light, shining out through openings or cracks in the exterior psychosis; treatment consisted of encouraging more of the light to filter through. This viewpoint was directly opposed to a prevalent one, which pictures the person disappearing into a central core of illness and the crack is widened to shore the light in (K. Terkelsen's personal communication to C. Harding, 1983).

As another clinician who followed his patients over decades, George Brooks in Vermont also came to see the person behind the disorder. In reflecting upon the turnaround of many of his once very chronic patients, Brooks identified four primary ingredients of the Vermont rehabilitation program which appeared to reduce chronicity. "Drugs relieved the anguish and fevered mental activity. People were trusted and hence expected to be capable. Goals (jobs, homes, companions) were a new experience of hope for many. People were allowed, even encouraged, to show compassion (aide to patient, patient to patient, patient to aide)" (personal communication to C. Harding, 1984).

The present state of the art does not permit clinicians to predict *who* will not turn around towards health. Therefore, since many patients eventually do move in the direction of recovery, early closure of assessment needs to be avoided. Brooks (1981) has eloquently pleaded for the "right to rehabilitation" for each patient as an integral part of every treatment plan, in order to encourage the turnaround.

The Person-Illness-Environment Interaction

In studying a person's struggle back from a psychotic episode, Strauss and colleagues in the Yale Longitudinal Study have conducted intensive observations during the first year after an episode, with a follow-up after the second year (Breier & Strauss, 1983, 1984; Harding & Strauss, 1984a, 1984b; Strauss et al., 1985). Their findings suggest that multiple interactions occur between persons and their environments to shape the recovery process. Severe psychiatric disorder has been found not to be a unitary, linear, unfolding process, but one that ebbs and flows at different rates across different areas of functioning. Furthermore, patients appeared to be active participants in shaping their own recovery process (Harding & Strauss, 1984b; Strauss et al., 1987). As an example, Breier and Strauss (1983) have recorded ways in which people have learned to control their own incipient psychotic symptoms, such as delusions and hallucinations; they suggested a way to teach these skills to other patients.

These findings have led Strauss (Strauss & Hafez, 1981) to speculate that the form of the traditional diagnosis needs to be revised, in order to reflect this dynamic process in the individual-environment interaction. Multi-axial "patterns" of premorbid functioning could be incorporated into the diagnostic formulations, to help predict better both morbid processes and ongoing future patterns in the pursuit of recovery. Thus, diagnostic classification would move from a static snapshot to a longitudinal working hypotheses.

Conclusions

Current expectations, including those stated in *DSM-III*, have depicted the person with repeated episodes of schizophrenia as having a chronic, deteriorating course with residual symptoms and deficits in functioning such as work, social relations, and basic self-care. These expectations have been challenged above by providing evidence about the field's misconceptions, both historical and recent, upon which these assumptions were made.

In addition, we have presented both research data and many newer concepts which have evolved about the causes and course of chronicity in schizophrenia and about the person with the disorder. These data demonstrate the existence of a more flexible, dynamic process, in which the person is not a mere passive actor but a more active participant than has been appreciated. Recently, more systematic research has found significant improvement over time, with widely heterogeneous levels of functioning, even within the same person. This improvement over time means that the illness is more a prolonged one than a chronic one. Traditional diagnostic criteria continue to be relatively non-specific in predicting long-term outcome. However, a suggestion is made to revamp the diagnostic system into one of multiaxial patterns across time. Multiple contributions to the formation of and recovery from chronic states and behavior are seen as stemming primarily from biopsychosocial sources, as well as from the effects of underlying vulnerability, ageing, and developmental growth. The focus has been shifted back from the disorder to the person, who is seen as a vulnerable human being living a life with intermittent episodes of schizophrenia. These episodes may taper off across time, as the person gathers his/her energies to redevelop and improve levels of basic functioning such as self-care, work, and social relations.

Implications

The revival of rational hope for improvement and recovery re-empowers patients and their families, as well as changing the way clinicians perceive their tasks (Harding, 1988). The evidence summarized above demands the return of patients' control over their own lives, by permitting a collaboration in treatment decisions. The provision of opportunities for patients to learn or re-learn social and occupational skills, self-management of psychotic symptoms, and handling of medication, as well as ways to fine tune their environments to meet the needs of particular vulnerabilities, would encourage the turn-around to health and competence.

Further, with the return of patients to the community, many families have become the primary case managers. Any kind of support which can be provided to augment families' understanding of the nature of schizophrenia, to increase skills of dealing with returned relatives, and to procure respite services would enhance the education of families, coping abilities, and feelings of competence, must also be considered a priority (Anderson et al., 1980).

The restructuring of service delivery systems to accommodate slow, uphill returns to health may be more cost-effective in the final analysis. Over time, the person who represents a tax drain in day treatment facilities can become a taxpayer and an active citizen. A system which offers opportunities for multiple levels of functioning in housing, occupational, and social skills, with allowance for people making use of these offerings on an as-needed basis (going in and out, and up and down, through these multiple levels) may work better in the long run than a lock-step rigid process which expects either recovery in a short time or lifetime custodial care, with not much in between. It has been shown (e.g., Harding & Ashikaga, 1982) that eventually, many people can move out of the mental health system and utilize natural supports in the community. Flexible, longitudinal program strategies are essential to meet the needs of a person struggling with a fluctuating disorder across time.

Acknowledgements

This work has been partially supported by NIMH Grants #29575, #40607, and #34365, the Medical Research Service and the Health Services Research and Development Division of the Veterans Administration. Another version of the first part of this article was originally published in Hospital & Community Psychiatry, 1987, 3(5), 477-486.

The authors thank George W. Brooks, MD, Luc Ciompi, MD, and Kenneth G. Terkelsen, MD for their helpful comments as well as Nancy Ryan and Donna M. Gill for typing this manuscript.

References

Achté, K.A. (1967). On prognosis and rehabilitation in schizophrenia and paranoid psychoses. A comparative follow-up study of two series of patients first admitted to hospital in 1950 and 1960 respectively. *Acta Psychiatrica et Neurologica Scandinavica.* (suppl. 196), 1-217.

Alexander, F.G. & Selesnsick, S.T. (1966). *This history of psychiatry: An evaluation of psychiatry thought and practice from prehistoric times to the present.* New York: Harper & Row.

American Psychiatric Association (1980). *Diagnostic and statistical manual of mental disorders (3rd ed.) (DSM-III).* Washington, DC: APA.

American Psychiatric Association (1987). *Diagnostic and statistical manual of mental disorders (3rd ed., revised), (DSM-III-R).* Washington, DC: APA.

Anderson, C.M., Hogarty, G.E. & Reiss, D.J. (1980). Family treatment of adult schizophrenic patients: A psychoeducational approach. *Schizophrenia Bulletin, 6,* 490-505.

Andreasen, N.C. (1982). Negative symptoms in schizophrenia. Definition and reliability. *Archives of General Psychiatry, 39,* 789-794.

Anthony, W.A. (1977). Psychological rehabilitation: A concept in need of a method. *American Psychologist, 32,* 658-662.

Astrup, C. & Noreik, K. (1966). *Functional psychoses: Diagnostic and prognostic models.* Springfield: Charles C. Thomas.

Bachrach, L.L. (1976). A note on some recent studies of released mental hospital patients in the community. *American Journal of Psychiatry, 133,* 73-75.

Bachrach, L.L. (1979) Planning mental health services for chronic patients. *Hospital & Community Psychiatry, 30,* 387-393.

Barton, R. (1959). *Institutional neurosis.* Bristol: Wright.

Bland, R.C. & Orn, H. (1978). Fourteen-year outcome in early schizophrenia. *Acta Psychiatrica Scandinavica, 58,* 327-338.

Bleuler, E. (1911). *Dementia praecox or the group of schizophrenias.* Translated (1950) by J. Zinken. New York: International Universities Press.

Bleuler, M. (1955). Research and changes in concepts in the study of schizophrenia, 1941-1950. *Bulletin of the Isaac Ray Medical Library, 3,* 1-132.

Bleuler, M. (1963). Conception of schizophrenia within the last fifty years and today. *Proceedings of the Royal Society of Medicine, 56,* 945-952.

Bleuler, M. (1968). A 23-year longitudinal study of 208 schizophrenics and impressions in regard to the nature of schizophrenia. In D. Rosenthal & S.S. Kety (Eds.), *The transmission of schizophrenia.* Oxford: Pergamon Press.

Bleuler, M. (1969). The genesis and nature of schizophrenia. *Psychiatry Digest, 30,* 17-26.

Bleuler, M. (1972a). *Die schizophrenen Geistesstörungen im Lichte lanjähriger Kranken-und Familiengeschichten.* Stuttgart: Georg Thieme. Translated (1978) by S. M. Clemens as The schizophrenic disorders, long-term patient and family studies. New Haven: Yale University Press.

Bleuler, M. (1972b). Die schizophrenen Geistesstörungen im Lichte langjähriger Kranken-und Familiengeschichten. Stuttgart: Georg Thieme; as reviewed (1978) by G.C. Teschke. *Schizophrenia Bulletin, 4,* 48-55.

Bleuler, M. (1974). The long-term course of the schizophrenic psychoses. *Psychological Medicine, 4,* 244-254.

Bleuler, M. (1983.) Schizophrenic deterioration (a multi-author discussion section). *British Journal of Psychiatry, 143,* 78-79.

Bockus, H.L. (1974). Perspective prognosis in peptic ulcer. In H.L. Bockus (Ed.) *Gastroenterology* (3rd ed.), Philadelphia: Saunders.

Breier, A. & Strauss, J.S. (1983). Self-control in psychotic disorders. *Archives of General Psychiatry, 40,* 1141-1145.

Breier, A. & Strauss, J.S. (1984). Social relationships in the recovery from psychotic disorder. *American Journal of Psychiatry, 141,* 949-955.

Brenner, M.H. (1973). *Mental illness and the economy.* Cambridge: Harvard University Press.

Brooks, G.W. (1959). Opening a rehabilitation house. In M. Greenblatt & B. Simon (Eds.) *Rehabilitation of the mentally ill.* Washington DC: American Association for the Advancement of Science.

Brooks, G.W. (1960a). Rehabilitation of hospitalized chronic schizophrenic patients. In L. Appleby, J. Scher & J. Cumming (Eds.), *Chronic schizophrenia*. Chicago: The Free Press.

Brooks, G.W. (1961a). Rural community influences and supports in a rehabilitation program for state hospital patients. In M. Greenblatt, D. J. Levinson & G. L. Klerman (Eds.), *Mental patients in transition*. Springfield: Charles C. Thomas.

Brooks, G.W. (1961b). Motivation for work in psychiatric rehabilitation. *Diseases of the Nervous System, 22*, 129-132.

Brooks, G.W. (1981). Vocational rehabilitation. In J.A. Talbott (Ed.), *The chronic mentally ill: Treatment, programs, system*. New York: Human Sciences Press.

Brooks, G.W. & Deane, W.N. (1960). Attitudes of released chronic schizophrenic patients concerning illness and recovery as revealed by a structured post-hospital interview. *Journal of Clinical Psychology, 16*, 259-264.

Brooks, G.W., Deane, W.N., Lagor, R.C., et al (1963). Varieties of family participation in the rehabilitation of released chronic schizophrenic patients. *Journal of Nervous & Mental Disease, 136*, 432-444.

Brooks, G.W. & Deane, W.N. (1965). The chronic mental patient in the community. *Diseases of the Nervous System, 26*, 85-90.

Brooks, G.W., Deane, W.N., & Laqueuer, H.P. (1970). Fifteen years of work therapy. *Diseases of the Nervous System (GWAN Supp), 31*, 161-165.

Brown, G.W. (1960) Length of hospital stay and schizophrenia: a review of statistical studies. *Acta Psychiatrica et Neurologica, 35*, 414-430.

Brown, G.W., Bone, M., Dalison, B., et al . (1966). *Schizophrenia and social care*. London: Oxford University Press.

Calabro, J. J. (1979). Juvenile rheumatoid arthritis. In D.J. McCarthy (Ed.), *Arthritis and allied conditions: A textbook on rheumatology* (9th ed). Philadelphia: Lea & Febiger.

Cannon, W.B. (1963). *The wisdom of the body*. New York: WW Norton.

Chamberlin, J. (1979). *On our own—Patient controlled alternative to the mental health system*. New York: McGraw-Hill .

Chittick, R.A., Brooks, G.W., Irons, F.S. et al (1961). *The Vermont story*. Burlington: Queen City Printers.

Ciompi, L. (1980a). Catamnestic long-term study on the course of life and aging schizophrenics. *Schizophrenia Bulletin, 6,* 606-618.

Ciompi, L. (1980b). Is chronic schizophrenia an artifact? Arguments and counter-arguments. *Fortschritte der Neurologie—Psychiatrie, 48,* 237-248.

Ciompi, L. & Müller, C. (1976). *Lebensweg und Alter Schizophrener. Eine katamnestische Langzeitstudie bis ins Alter.* Berlin: Springer Verlag. Translated (1984) as *The life course and aging in schizophrenia: A catamnestic longitudinal study into advanced age* by E. Forsberg for the Vermont Longitudinal Research Project.

Cohen, P. & Cohen, G. (1984). The clinician's illusion. *Archives of General Psychiatry, 41,* 1178-1182.

Cousins, N. (1979). *Anatomy of an illness as perceived by the patient: Reflections on healing & regeneration.* New York: Norton.

Cutting, J. (1983). Schizophrenic deterioration (a multi-author discussion of the topic). *British Journal of Psychiatry, 132,* 77-84.

Daniele, R.P. (1982). Asthma. In J.B. Wyngaarden & L.H. Smith (Eds.), *The textbook of medicine*. Philadelphia: W. B. Saunders.

Davison, K. & Bagley, C. (1969). Schizophrenic-like psychoses associated with organic disorders of C.N.S.—a review of the literature. In Current problems in neuropsychiatry (ed. R.N. Herrington). *British Journal of Psychiatry, Special Publication No. 4,* Ashford: Headley Brothers.

Dunham, H.W. (1976). Society, culture, and mental disorder. *Archives of General Psychiatry, 33,* 147-156.

Feighner, J.P., Robbins, E., Guze, S.B., et al. (1972). Diagnostic criteria for use in psychiatric research. *Archives of General Psychiatry, 26,* 57-63

Freyhan, F.A. (1958). Eugen Bleuler's concept of the group of schizophrenias at mid-century. *American Journal of Psychiatry, 114,* 769-779.

Gardos, G. & Cole, J.O. (1980). Overview: public health issues of tardive dyskinesia. *American Journal of Psychiatry, 137,* 776-781.

Gardos, G., Cole, J.O.& Labrie, R.A. (1982). A twelve-year follow-up study of chronic schizophrenics. *Hospital & Community Psychiatry, 33,* 983-984.

Gilliland, B.C. & Mannik, M. (1983). Rheumatoid arthritis. In R. G. Petasdorf (Ed.), *Harrison's principles of internal medicine.* New York: McGraw-Hill.

Goffman, E. (1961). *Asylums: Essays on the social situation of mental patients and other inmates.* New York: Doubleday Anchor .

Greenblatt, M. (1978). *Psychopolitics.* New York: Grune & Stratton.

Haley, J. (1969). The art of being schizophrenic. *In The power tactics of Jesus Christ and other essays.* New York: Avon Books.

Harding, C.M. (1988). The outcome of schizophrenia. *The Harvard Medical School Mental Health Letter, 4,* 3-5.

Harding, C.M. & Brooks, G.W. (1980). Longitudinal assessment for a cohort of chronic schizophrenics discharged twenty years ago. *The Psychiatric Journal of the University of Ottawa, 5,* 274-278.

Harding, C.M. & Ashikaga, T. (1982). *Utilization of community mental health clinics, the state hospitals, and social support networks by the Vermont Story Cohort-Twenty Years After Deinstitutionalization.* Report prepared for Dr. R. Surles, Department of Mental Health, Vermont.

Harding, C.M. & Brooks, G.W. (1984). Life assessment of a cohort of chronic schizophrenics discharges twenty years ago. In S.A. Mednick, M. Harway & K.M. Finello (Eds.), *The handbook of longitudinal research, Vol. 2.* New York: Prager Press.

Harding, C.M. & Strauss, J.S. (1984a). Changing views about prognosis in schizophrenia. *Biological Psychiatry, 19,* 1597-1600.

Harding, C.M. & Strauss, J.S. (1984b). The course of schizophrenia: An evolving concept. In M. Alpert (Ed.), *Controversies in schizophrenia: Changes and constancies.* New York: Guilford Press.

Harding, C.M., Brooks, G.W., Ashikaga, T., et al. (1987a). The Vermont longitudinal study of persons with severe mental illness: 1. Methodology, study sample, and overall status 32 years later. *American Journal of Psychiatry, 6,* 718-26.

Harding, C.M., Brooks, G.W., Ashikaga, T., et al. (1987b). The Vermont longitudinal study: 11. Long-term outcome of subjects who retrospectively met *DSM-III* criteria from schizophrenia. *American Journal of Psychiatry, 144,* 727-735.

Harding, C.M., Zubin, J. & Strauss, J.S. (1987c). Chronicity in schizophrenia: fact, partial fact or artifact? *Hospital & Community Psychiatry, 38,* 477-486.

Harding, C.M., Brooks, G.W., Ashikaga,T., et al. (1987d). Aging and social functioning on once-chronic schizophrenic patients 22-62 years after first admission: The Vermont story. In N. Miller & G.D. Cohen (Eds.), *Schizophrenia and aging: Schizophrenia, Paranoia, and schizophreniform disorders in later life.* New York: Guilford Press.

Hawk, A.B., Carpenter, W.T. & Strauss, J.S. (1975). Diagnostic criteria and five-year outcome in schizophrenia: A report from the International Pilot Study of Schizophrenia. *Archives of General Psychiatry, 32,* 343-347.

Hollingshead, A.B. & Redlich, F.C. (1953). *Social class & mental illness.* New York: Wiley.

Holt, Jr., W.L. & Holt, W.M. (1952). Long-term prognosis in mental illness: a thirty year follow-up of 141 mental patients. *American Journal of Psychiatry, 108,* 735-739.

Houghton, J. (1980). One personal experience before and after mental illness. In J.G. Rabkin, L. Gelb & J.B. Lazare (Eds.), *Attitudes toward the mentally ill: Research perspectives.* DHSS, Washington DC: Government Printing Office (80-1031).

Huber, G., Gross, G. & Schüttler, R. (1975). A long-term follow-up study of schizophrenia: Psychiatric course of illness and prognosis. *Acta Psychiatrica Scandinavica, 52,* 49-57.

Huber, G., et al. (1980). Longitudinal studies of schizophrenic patients. *Schizophrenia Bulletin, 6,* 592-605.

Jaspers, K. (1963). *General psychopathology.* Translated from the German by J. Hoenig & M. W. Hampton. Chicago: University of Chicago Press.

Jones, W.L. (1983). *Ministering to minds diseased: A history of psychiatric treatment.* London: Heinemann Medical.

Kendell, R.E., Brockington, I.F. & Leff, J.P. (1979). Prognostic implications of six alternative definitions of schizophrenia. *Archives of General Psychiatry, 35,* 25-31.

Kraepelin, E. (1899). *Psychiatrie.* Leipzig: Barth.

Kraepelin, E. (1902). *Clinical psychiatry. A textbook for students and physicians* (6th ed.) (translated by A.R. Diefendorf). New York: Macmillan.

Kraft, J.K. & Stainey, T.A. (1977). The natural history of symptomatic recurrent bacteriuria in women. *Medicine, 56,* 5560.

Kraft, A.M. (1981). Discussion: systems for the chronically mentally ill. In J.A. Talbot (Ed.), *The chronically mentally ill. Treatment, programs, systems.* New York: Human Sciences Press.

Kramer, M., Goldstein, H., Israel, R.H., et al. (1955). A historical study of the disposition of first admissions to a State Hospital. Experiences of the Warren State Hospital during the period 1916-1950. *Public Health Monograph #32.* Washington DC: U.S. Department of Health, Education & Welfare.

Lamb, H.R. & Goertzel, V. (1972). High expectations of long-term ex-state hospital patients. *American Journal of Psychiatry, 129,* 471-475.

Lamb, H.R. (1979). Staff burnout in work with long-term patients. *Hospital & Community Psychiatry, 30,* 396-398.

Lamb, H.R. (1981). What did we really expect from deinstitutionalization? *Hospital & Community Psychiatry, 32,* 105-109.

Langfeldt, G. (1937). The prognosis in schizophrenia and the factors influencing the course of the disease. *Acta Psychiatrica et Neurologica Scandinavica, suppl. 13,* 1-228.

Langfeldt, G. (1939). *Schizophreniform states.* Copenhagen: E. Munksgaard.

Leighton, A. (1982). *Caring for mentally ill people.* New York: Cambridge University Press.

Leonhard, K. (1961). Cycloid psychoses: Endogenous psychoses which are neither schizophrenic nor manic depressive. *Journal of Mental Science, 107,* 633-648.

Lovejoy, M. (1984). Recovery from schizophrenia: A personal odyssey. *Hospital & Community Psychiatry, 35,* 809-812.

Ludwing, A.M. (1971). *Treating the treatment failures: The challenge or chronic schizophrenia.* New York: Grune & Stratton.

Mandell, M.R., Severe, J.B., Schooler, N.R., et al (1982). Development and prediction of post psychotic depression in neuroleptic-treated schizophrenics. *Archives of General Psychiatry, 39,* 197-203.

McGlashan, T. (1988). A selective review of recent North American long-term follow-up studies of schizophrenia. *Schizophrenia Bulletin, 14,* 515-542.

Rennie, T.A.C. (1939). Follow-up study of five hundred patients with schizophrenia admitted to the hospital from 1913-1923. *Archives of Neurology & Psychiatry, 42,* 877-891.

Rosenhan, D. (1973). On being sane in insane places. *Science, 179,* 250-258.

Rupp, C. & Fletcher, E.K. (1939). A five to ten year follow-up study of 641 schizophrenic cases. *American Journal of Psychiatry, 96,* 877-888.

Schneider, K. (1959). *Clinical psychopathology.* Translated (1959) from the German by M. W. Hamilton & E.W. Anderson. New York: Grune & Stratton.

Scull, A.T. (1979). *Museums of madness.* New York: St. Martin's Press.

Shapiro, R. & Shader, E. (1979). Chapter II Selective review of results of previous follow-up studies of schizophrenia and other psychoses. In World Health Organization (Ed.), *Schizophrenia: An international pilot study.* Chichester: Wiley.

Simpson, H., Russell, G. & Forfor, J.O. (1984). Respiratory disorders. In J.O. Forfor & F.C. Arneil (Eds.), *Textbook of paediatrics, Vol. I* (3rd edn). Edinburgh: Churchill-Livingstone.

Spitzer, R.L., Endicott, J. & Robins, E. (1975). *Research diagnostic criteria (RDC).* New York: Biometrics Research.

Stephens, J.H. (1970). Long-term course and prognosis in schizophrenia. *Seminars in Psychiatry, 2,* 464-485.

Strauss, J.S. (1980). Chronicity: Causes, prevention, and treatment. *Psychiatric Annals, 10,* 328-332.

Strauss, J.S. & Carpenter, W.T. (1972). The prediction of outcome in schizophrenia: 1. Characteristics of outcome. *Archives of General Psychiatry, 27,* 739-746.

Strauss, J.S., Carpenter, W.T. & Bartko, J.J. (1974). Speculations on the processes that underlie schizophrenic symptoms. *Schizophrenia Bulletin, 11,* 61-70.

Strauss, J.S. & Carpenter, W.T. (1974). The prediction of outcome in schizophrenia: 11. Relationships between predictor and outcome variables. *Archives of General Psychiatry, 31,* 37-42.

Strauss, J.S. & Carpenter, W.T. (1977). Prediction of outcome m schizophrenia: 111. Five-year outcome and its predictors. *Archives of General Psychiatry, 34,* 159-163.

Strauss, J.S. & Hafez, H. (1981). Clinical questions and "real" research. *American Journal of Psychiatry, 138,* 1592-1597.

Strauss, J.S., Lovesky, L., Glazer, W., et al (1981). Organizing the complexities of schizophrenia. *Journal of Nervous & Mental Disease, 169,* 120-126.

Strauss, J.S. & Glazer, W. (1982). Treatment of the so-called chronically psychiatrically ill. In J.H. Masserman (Ed.), *Current psychiatry therapies*. New York: Grune & Stratton.

Strauss, J.S., Hafez, H., Lieberman, P., et al . (1985). The course of psychiatric disorder: III. Longitudinal principles. *American Journal of Psychiatry, 142,* 289-296.

Strauss, J.S., Harding, C.M., Hafez, H., et al. (1987). The role of the patient in recovery from psychosis. In J. Strauss & H. Brenner (Eds.), *Psychosocial management of schizophrenia*. Toronto: Hans Huber.

Strömgren, E. (1961). Recent studies of prognosis and outcome in the mental disorders. In P. Hoch & J. Zubin (Eds.), *Comparative epidemiology of the mental disorders*. New York: Grune and Stratton.

Swaiman, K.F. & Wright, F.S. (1982). Seizure disorders. In F.S. Wright, F.E. Dreifus & G.J. Wolcott, et al. (Eds.), *The practice of pediatric Neurology (2nd ed.)*. St. Louis: Mosby.

Talbott, J.A. (Ed.) (1979). *The Chronic mental patient: Problems, solutions, and recommendations for a public policy*. Washington DC: APA.

Tsuang, M., Woolson, R. & Fleming, J. (1979). Long-term outcome of major psychoses: 1. Schizophrenia and affective disorders compared with psychiatrically symptom-free surgical conditions. *Archives of General Psychiatry, 36,* 1295-1301.

Vaillant, G.E. (1969). The natural history of urban narcotic drug addiction: some determinants. In H. Steinberg (Ed.), *Scientific basis of drug dependence*. London: J. & A. Churchill.

Vaillant, G.E. (1978). A ten-year follow-up of remitting schizophrenics. *Schizophrenia Bulletin, 4,* 78-85.

Vaillant, G.E. (1980). Adolf Meyer was right: Dynamic psychiatry needs the life chart. *Journal of the National Association of Private Psychiatric Hospitals, 11,* 4-14.

Warner R. (ed.) (1985). Recovery from schizophrenia. In *Psychiatry and the political economy*. London: Routledge & Kegan Paul.

Watt, D.C., Katz, K. & Shepherd, M. (1983). The natural history of schizophrenia: A five-year prospective follow-up of a representative sample of schizophrenics by means of a standardized clinical and social assessment. *Psychological Medicine, 13,* 663-670.

Wing, J.K. (1962). Institutionalism in mental hospitals. *British Journal of Social & Clinical Psychology 1,* 38-51.

Wing, J.K. & Brown, G.W. (1970). *Institutionalism and schizophrenia*. London: Cambridge University Press.

Winokur, G., Morrison, J., Clancy, J., et al. (1972). The Iowa 500: 11. A blind family history comparison of mania, depression and schizophrenia. *Archives of General Psychiatry, 27,* 462-464.

World Health Organization. (1979). *Schizophrenia: An international follow-up study*. New York: Wiley.

Zubin, J. & Spring, B. (1977). Vulnerability: A new view of schizophrenia. *Journal of Abnormal Psychology, 86,* 103-126.

Zubin, J., Magaziner, I. & Steinhauer, S.R. (1983). The metamorphosis of schizophrenia: From chronicity to vulnerability. *Psychological Medicine, 13,* 551-571.

Consumer-Practitioners and Psychiatrists Share Insights About Recovery and Coping

Andrea Blanch, Daniel Fisher, William Tucker, Dale Walsh, and Janet Chassman

ANDREA BLANCH, MAINE DEPARTMENT OF MENTAL HEALTH, MENTAL RETARDATION AND SUBSTANCE ABUSE SERVICES, AUGUSTA, ME.

DANIEL FISHER, EASTERN MIDDLESEX OUTPATIENT CENTER, WAKEFIELD, MA.

WILLIAM TUCKER, NEW YORK STATE OFFICE OF MENTAL HEALTH, ALBANY, NY.

DALE WALSH, CENTRAL NEW HAMPSHIRE COMMUNITY MENTAL HEALTH SERVICES, CONCORD, NH.

JANET CHASSMAN, NEW YORK STATE OFFICE OF MENTAL HEALTH, ALBANY, NY.

THIS ARTICLE ORIGINALLY APPEARED IN *Disability Studies Quarterly*, 1993, 13(2), 17-20 AND IS REPRINTED WITH PERMISSION.

In the field of medicine, discussion between doctors and patients about how they can best collaborate in dealing with a particular illness has not generally been the norm. However, medical sociologists have recently begun to argue that "the experience of illness" is central to an understanding of the sociology of health care (Zola, 1991), and that the manner in which individuals define their own symptoms and act to alleviate them is critical to an understanding of "illness behavior" (Mechanic, 1986). Similarly, the doctor-patient relationship is currently being re-examined. Candib (1987) suggests that although there are risks associated with self-disclosure, physicians who are willing to share their personal experiences as patients may increase both empathy and reciprocity in the doctor-patient encounter.

In mental health, dialogue between psychiatrists and persons diagnosed with a mental illness is, if anything, even less common. However, even here some steps have been taken. The growth of the consumer/ex-patient movement during the last 20 years has allowed people to articulate the vital importance of stating their needs in their own words, making choices, and taking responsibility for their own treatment. Professionals and policymakers have responded with efforts to redesign professional roles (e.g., Smith & Ford, 1986) and to create forums for discussion and exchange of perspectives. For example, a recent series of "Pioneer Dialogues" brought consumers/ex-patients and state mental health administrators together to discuss system reform (Loder & Glover, 1992).

Dialogue with mental health clinicians entails some unique difficulties. Many ex-patients are angry at treatment they have received or witnessed in the mental health system (Chamberlin, 1978). In addition, mental health professionals are sometimes criticized for embracing a theoretical framework which reinforces a "deficit" model of human problems (Gergen, 1990). However, a growing number of people with a psychiatric history are entering the mental health field, and some professionals have started to disclose their own psychiatric histories. As these "consumer-practitioners" openly discuss their own process of recovery, they express many of the ideas developed by the consumer/ex-patient movement in a context and a language that encourages professionals to listen.

The Dialogue Process

In New York State, an ongoing dialogue has been created between seven psychiatrists and nine "consumer-practitioners." The dialogue process is intended to accomplish three goals: 1) To create a forum for psychiatrists and ex-patients to exchange perspectives; 2) To begin developing a shared vision of recovery and; 3) To consider ways in which the treatment relationship could be more collaborative.

The dialogue was initially structured around five questions: 1) What does "recovery" mean in the context of a diagnosis of serious mental illness? 2) What are the most important factors facilitating a recovery process? 3) What are effective ways to recognize and manage recurrent symptoms? 4) What roles can the recipient and the practitioner play in developing and using client-specific coping strategies? 5) What personal experience led you to this understanding about recovery and coping? These questions focused the discussion of issues where both groups could be expected to offer insights.

Points of Controversy

Several points of controversy emerged during the dialogue process. First, there were different perceptions of the social distance between psychiatrists and the people they serve. Some individuals felt social distance is no greater than that in general medicine, while others referred to the two groups as representing "two different worlds." Psychiatrists were also surprised by the degree to which people recounted negative experiences within the mental health system, and raised questions about the representativeness of the participants.

Second, psychiatrists appeared to view medication and diagnosis as important tools, and compliance (and in some cases, even control) as positive factors in treatment. In contrast, most consumer-practitioners expressed the opinion that all use of coercion or control is countertherapeutic, and criticized the medical model and the current diagnostic system as disempowering and detrimental when used to the exclusion of other explanatory frameworks. They also strongly advocated choice in the taking of medication and stressed the importance of being informed by the psychiatrist about the negative and positive aspects of each drug. Third, the two groups expressed differences of opinion concerning aspects of timing in the treatment and recovery process. Psychiatrists are often under extreme time pressures, and may feel responsible for offering quick treatment in order to reduce pain or because delay in treatment of a psychotic episode may adversely affect outcome. An alternative view was presented by several consumer-practitioners, who expressed the need for psychiatrists to take time to know the individual in depth before intervening, and who suggested that eliminating pain (or symptoms) prematurely may cut off the recovery process.

Hope is perhaps the most fundamental factor in recovery. Moreover, psychiatry has a key role to play in fostering hope.

Despite these differences, the two groups had much in common. Many individuals expressed surprise at how similar their experiences had been, and at how willing both groups were to listen and respond thoughtfully to each other. Getting to know each other as individuals appeared to be important. As one individual noted: "Revealing our personal histories helped me to connect with the psychiatrists and other recipients on a more human level. That connection served to contain the turmoil I felt during later confrontations."

Recovery and Coping

This dialogue was initiated in response to the recognition that the concepts of recovery and coping have not been widely incorporated into clinical practice for persons diagnosed with serious mental illness. One psychiatrist noted after a conversation with a recipient: "He said that from time to time he still has symptoms, which amazed me. He doesn't look symptomatic, and he has a very important job....The fact that he does coping exercises, this was new to me. Fifty years in psychiatry and I had never heard this."

Clinical researchers have recently begun to investigate the process of recovery from serious mental illness. Breier and Strauss document the importance of social relationships (1984) and self-control over psychiatric symptoms (1983) in recovery. Other studies have demonstrated the effectiveness of personal coping strategies (Cohen & Berk, 1985; Wiedl & Schottner, 1991). The vision of recovery emerging from the dialogue process is consistent with much of this earlier work. However, the direct participation of recovering individuals alters both language and conceptual orientation in subtle but potentially important ways. The following observations and quotations occurred during the first 5-hour dialogue, and were subsequently reviewed and revised during the second dialogue.

> "*Recovery*" relates not only to the experience of symptoms, but also to the secondary assaults of stigma, discrimination, and abuse: One person noted that "Dealing with internalized stigma was almost as difficult and took as much away from my life as the symptoms did."

1) Recovery is an active, ongoing, and individual process. It occurs internally, is often very distinct from "treatment," and takes many different forms. As one individual stated, "I'm not recovered. I'm in an active process of recovery."

2) "Recovery" relates not only to the experience of symptoms, but also to the secondary assaults of stigma, discrimination, and abuse: One person noted that "Dealing with internalized stigma was almost as difficult and took as much away from my life as the symptoms did."

3) Hope is perhaps the most fundamental factor in recovery. Moreover, psychiatry has a key role to play in fostering hope. As one person put it, "It's important that when people are admitted they *immediately* learn there's hope. The psychiatrist—the gate keeper—is the best person to do this."

4) The establishment of a sense of control or free will is critical to recovery: "For many years I subscribed to the 'please fix me' model. Only when I became involved in recovery did I realize that no one is going to heal me, I'm going to be the person to do that." Conversely, the lack of sense of control can impede progress. One psychiatrist recounted a patient who had stated: "I've learned that I have a biological disease and until you find a cure, I'm not going anywhere."

Developing some sense of a "healthy" self appears to be critical for retaining a sense of control rather than being engulfed by one's symptoms. As one person said, "there are always islands of clarity. We need to train the mind to have a center, so that the person can control symptoms."

5) "Remembering your track record"—learning from observing your own mental and emotional behavior—is critical for coping. Although problems may recur repeatedly, giving the appearance of little progress, incremental learning may in fact be taking place.

6) Self-directed coping strategies are effective and can be learned. For example, training oneself to meditate may make it possible to let delusional thoughts go. Most individuals reported having developed coping skills on their own, although one noted that his psychiatrist had pointed out some of the things he was doing to cope.

7) Maintaining or developing connections to valued activities and people is critical to the recovery process: "Don't give up *anything* that you value." Psychiatrists noted that many people can continue normal activities such as work even when they are in the hospital.

8) Connecting with other people on a human level was also seen as important. Overcoming attitudinal and interpersonal barriers may be the most significant barriers in promoting recovery, since it requires professionals to examine their own inner process and coping strategies, sometimes a painful process.

9) Recovery is a process of "finding meaning in your experience." Each person's construction of meaning was different, but the capacity to find something instructive about the personal experience of mental illness appears critical to recovery.

Toward a Collaborative Doctor-Patient Relationship

Gillick (1992) argues that public confidence in the medical profession is eroding, and that physicians are increasingly disillusioned with their profession. She suggests that "the mutual mistrust and even suspicion that currently poisons so many patient-doctor relationships can only be allayed if there is a shared conception of the ground rules and if there are well-defined avenues of communication" (p. 83). The dialogue described in this paper demonstrates that mutual discussion on difficult issues can be productive, and lends support to the hypothesis that understanding the subjective experience of mental and emotional distress may be critical to formulating an effective response. In addition, the dialogue appears to have had a personal impact on many of the participants. For the consumer-practitioners, the dialogue was "very healing to be involved in," but also personally difficult and painful: "It threw me back into the belly of the experience... It took me years to get perspective, but now I need to revisit it." Psychiatrists were also personally affected by the experience. One noted: "I have started listening to patients differently. When they say, 'What can I do between now and next session if I become symptomatic?' I used to pass it off. Now I listen and respond with suggestions."

Conclusion

The dialogue process has allowed participants to understand what they have in common as well as how their experiences differ. This communality of experience reduced social distance, allowed members of both groups to see each other as individuals, and led to the articulation of a set of shared principles about recovery. In addition, the dialogue modeled a process of collaboration that could potentially form the basis for a different relationship between psychiatrists and the people they serve. Finally, although still in an early stage, the discussion also raises the possibility of a wider involvement of consumer-practitioners and other ex-patients in a variety of roles in the treatment of individuals diagnosed with serious mental illness.

References

Breier, A. & Strauss, J.S. (1983). Self-control in psychotic disorders. *Archives of General Psychiatry, 40,* 1141-1145.

Breier, A. & Strauss, J.S. (1984). The role of social relationships in the recovery from psychotic disorders. *American Journal of Psychiatry, 141* (8), 949-955.

Candib, L.M. (1987) What doctor; tell about themselves to patients: Implications for intimacy and reciprocity in the relationship. *Family Medicine, 19,* 23-30.

Chamberlin, J. (1978) *On our own: Patient-controlled alternative to the mental health system.* New York: Hawthorne Books.

Cohen, C.I. & Berk, LA. (1985) Personal coping styles of schizophrenic outpatients. *Hospital and Community Psychiatry 36 (*4), 407-410.

Gergen, K.J. (1990) Therapeutic professions and the diffusion of deficit. *The Journal of Mind and Behavior, 11 (*3 & 4), 353[107]-368[122].

Gillick, M.R. (1992) From confrontation to cooperation in the doctor-patient relationship. *Journal of General Internal Medicine, 7,* Jan.-Feb., 83-86.

Loder, A. & Glover, R. (1992) New frontiers: Pioneer dialogue between consumers/survivors and commissioners. *MHSIP Updates.* November.

Mechanic, D. (1986) Illness behavior: An overview. In Sean McHugh & T. Michael Vallis (Eds.), *Illness Behavior: A Multi-disciplinary Model.* New York: Plenum.

Smith, M.K & Ford, J. (1986) Client involvement: Practical advice for professionals. *Psychosocial Rehabilitation Journal, 2* (3), 25-34.

Wiedl, KH. & Schottner, B. (1991). Coping with symptoms related to schizophrenia. *Schizophrenia Bulletin, 17* (3), 525-538.

Zola I.K (1991). Bringing our bodies and ourselves back in: Reflections on a past, present and future "medical sociology." *Journal of Health and Social Behavior, 32* (1), 1-16

RECOVERY AS A JOURNEY OF THE HEART

Patricia Deegan

PATRICIA DEEGAN, PH.D., IS PROGRAM DIRECTOR, NORTHEAST INDEPENDENT LIVING PROGRAM, LAWRENCE, MASSACHUSETTS, AND CONSULTANT, NATIONAL EMPOWERMENT CENTER, LAWRENCE.

THIS ARTICLE APPEARED IN THE *Psychiatric Rehabilitation Journal*, 1996, 19(3), AND IS REPRINTED WITH PERMISSION.

THIS ARTICLE WAS ORIGINALLY PRESENTED AT THE ALLIANCE FOR THE MENTALLY ILL OF MASSACHUSETTS/DEPARTMENT OF MENTAL HEALTH OF MASSACHUSETTS CURRICULUM AND TRAINING COMMITTEE CONFERENCE AT THE MASSACHUSETTS STATE HOUSE ON MAY 10, 1995.

I would like to thank you for this opportunity to speak with you today. I am especially pleased to be speaking to so many faculty and field supervisors. Your task is very important. You are teaching students who will become tomorrow's mental health professionals. The message I would like to bring to you today is that it is not enough to merely teach them facts and figures and knowledge. We must also help students to seek wisdom.

There is a difference between knowledge and wisdom. The etymological root of the word *knowledge* comes from the Middle English, *to recognize*. And indeed students in the various mental health related disciplines are required to recognize and to master a specific field of knowledge. They are required to know how to conduct empirical inquiry, to formulate findings, to contribute to theoretical models, to learn clinical skills, etc. However students are not required to seek wisdom. Wisdom comes from the Greek *eidos* and *idein* which means *to see the form or essence of that which is*. Thus most students emerge from their studies full of knowledge or the

ability to recognize things, but they lack wisdom or the ability to see the form or essence of that which is.

For example, when we teach our students about the heart we teach them that the heart is a pump; a type of organic machine with valves and chambers. And indeed, in time they learn to recognize the anatomical heart in all its detail. After successfully passing their final anatomy exam we say, "This student knows about the heart." But in wisdom we would have to doubt this statement.

Wisdom would seek the form or essence of the heart. In wisdom we would see that the anatomical heart, which we have given our students to study, is no*body's* heart. It is a heart that could belong to any*body* and therefore it belongs to no-*body*. Wisdom would have us understand that there is another heart. There is a heart that we know about long before we are taught that the heart is a pump. I am speaking here of the heart that can break; the heart that grows weary; the hardened heart; the heartless one; the cold heart; the heart that aches; the heart that stands still; the heart that leaps with joy; and the one who has lost heart. Wisdom demands that we teach students of the human sciences about the essence of this heart. The human heart. Not the pump that beats in *any body* but the one that lives in *my body* and in *your body*.

In a similar fashion we pass on knowledge about mental illness. Students emerge from school with knowledge about neurotransmitters and schizophrenics and bipolars and borderlines and multiples and OCDs. They become experts in recognizing illness and disease. But this is where we so often fail them. We fail them because we have not taught them to seek wisdom to move beyond mere recognition in order to seek the essence of what is. We have failed to teach them to reverence the human being who exists prior to and in spite of the diagnosis we have placed upon them. Just as the generic, anatomical heart does not *exist*, neither does the "schizophrenic" or "the multiple" or the "bipolar" exist outside of a generic textbook. What exists, in the truly existential sense, is not an illness or disease. What exists is a human being and wisdom demands that we see and reverence this human being before all else. Wisdom demands that we whole heartedly enter into a relationship with human beings in order to understand them and their experience. Only then are we able to help in a way that is experienced as helpful.

Those of us who have been labeled with mental illness are first and foremost human beings. We are more than the sum of the electrochemical activity of our brain. Our hearts are not merely pumps. Our hearts are as real and as vulnerable as valuable as yours are. We are people. We are people who have experienced great distress and who face the challenge of recovery.

The concept of recovery is rooted in the simple yet profound realization that people who have been diagnosed with mental illness are human beings. Like a pebble tossed into the center of a still pool, this simple fact radiates in ever larger ripples until every corner of academic and applied mental health science and clinical practice are affected. Those of us who have been diagnosed are not objects to be acted upon. We are fully human subjects who can act and in acting, change our situation. We are human beings and we can speak for ourselves. We have a voice and can learn to use it. We have the right to be heard and listened to. We can become self determining. We can take a stand toward what is distressing to us and need not be passive victims of an illness. We can become experts in our own journey of recovery.

The goal of recovery is not to get mainstreamed. We don't want to be mainstreamed. We say let the mainstream become a *wide* stream that has room for all of us and leaves no one stranded on the fringes.

The goal of the recovery process is not to become normal. The goal is to embrace our human vocation of becoming more deeply, more fully human. The goal is not normalization. The goal is to become the unique, awesome, never to be repeated human being that we are called to be. The philosopher Martin Heidegger said that to be human means to be a question in search of an answer. Those of us who have been labeled with mental illness are not de facto excused from this most fundamental task of becoming human. In fact, because many of us have experienced our lives and dreams shattering in the wake of mental illness, one of the most essential challenges that faces us is to ask, "who can I become and why should I say 'yes' to life?"

To be human means to be a question in search of an answer. However, many of us who have been psychiatrically labeled have received powerful messages from professionals who in effect tell us that by virtue of our diagnosis the question of our being has already been answered and our futures are already sealed. For instance, I can remember such a time during my third hospitalization. I was 18 years old. I asked the psychiatrist I was working with, "What's wrong with me?" He said, "You have a disease called chronic schizophrenia. It is a disease that is like diabetes. If you take medications for the rest of your life and avoid stress, then maybe you can cope." And as he spoke these words I could feel the weight of them crushing my already fragile hopes and dreams and aspirations for my life. Even some 22 years later, those words still echo like a haunting memory that does not fade.

Today I understand why this experience was so damaging to me. In essence the psychiatrist was telling me that my life, by virtue of being labeled with schizophrenia, was already a closed book. He was saying that my future had already been written. The goals and dreams that I aspired to were mere fantasies according to his prognosis of doom. When the future has been closed off in this way, then the present loses its orientation and becomes nothing but a succession of unrelated moments. Today I know that this psychiatrist had little wisdom at that time. He merely had some knowledge and recognized me as "the schizophrenic" who had been handed down through the generations by Kraeplin and Bleuler. He did not see *me*. He saw an illness. We must urge our students to seek wisdom, to move beyond mere recognition of illness, and to wholeheartedly encounter the human being who comes for help. It is imperative that we teach students that relationship is the most powerful tool they have in working with people.

Beyond the goals of recovery, there is the question of the process of recovery. How does one enter into the journey of recovery? Today I would like to begin a conceptualization of recovery as a journey of the heart. We will begin in that place where many people find themselves; in that place of being hard of heart and not caring anymore.

Prior to becoming active participants in our own recovery process, many of us find ourselves in a time of great apathy and indifference. It is a time of having a hardened heart. Of not caring anymore. It is a time when we feel ourselves to be among the living dead: alone, abandoned, and

Giving up was not a problem, it was a solution. It was a solution because it protected me from wanting anything. If I didn't want anything, then it couldn't be taken away. If I didn't try, then I wouldn't have to undergo another failure. If I didn't care, then nothing could hurt me again. My heart became hardened.

adrift on a dead and silent sea without course or bearing. If I turn my gaze back I can see myself at seventeen years old, diagnosed with chronic schizophrenia, drugged on Haldol and sitting in a chair. As I conjure the image the first thing I can see are that girl's yellow, nicotine stained fingers. I can see her shuffled, stiff, drugged walk. Her eyes do not dance. The dancer has collapsed and her eyes are dark and they stare endlessly into nowhere.

People come and people go. People urge her to do things to help herself but her heart is hard and she cares about nothing except sleeping, sitting, and smoking cigarettes. Her day consists of this: At eight in the morning she forces herself out of bed. In a drugged haze she sits in a chair, the same chair every day. She begins smoking cigarettes. Cigarette after cigarette. Cigarettes mark the passing of time. Cigarettes are proof that time is passing and that fact, at least, is a relief. From 9 A.M. to noon she sits and smokes and stares. Then she has lunch. At 1 P.M. she goes back to bed to sleep until 3 P.M. At that time she returns to the chair and sits and smokes and stares. Then she has dinner. Then she returns to the chair at 6 P.M. Finally it is 8 o'clock in the evening, the long awaited hour, the time to go back to bed and to collapse into a drugged and dreamless sleep.

This scenario unfolds the next day and the next and then the next, until the months pass by in numbing succession, marked only by the next cigarette and the next...

During this time people would try to motivate me. I remember people trying to make me participate in food shopping on Wednesday or to help bake bread or to go on a boat ride. But nothing anyone did touched me or moved me or mattered to me. I had given up. Giving up was a solution for me. The fact that I was "unmotivated" was seen as a problem by the people who worked with me. But for me, giving up was not a problem, it was a solution. It was a solution because it protected me from wanting anything. If I didn't want anything, then it couldn't be taken away. If I didn't try, then I wouldn't have to undergo another failure. If I didn't care, then nothing could hurt me again. My heart became hardened. The spring came and went and I didn't care. Holidays came and went and I didn't care. My friends went off to college and started new lives and I didn't care. A friend whom I had once loved very much came over to visit me and I didn't care. I remember sitting and smoking and saying almost nothing. And as soon as the clock struck 8, I remember interrupting my friend in mid sentence and telling her to go home because I was going to bed. Without even saying goodbye I headed for my bed. My heart was hard. I didn't care about anything.

I trust that the picture I am painting here is familiar to many of us. We recognize this picture of apathy, withdrawal, isolation, and lack of motivation. But if we go beyond mere recognition in search of wisdom we must dig deeper. What is this apathy, indifference, hardness of heart that keeps so many people in a mode of survival and prevents them from actively entering into their own journey of recovery? Is it merely the negative symptoms of schizo-phrenia? I think not. I believe that becoming hard of heart and not caring anymore is a strategy that desperate people who are at the brink of losing hope, adopt in order to remain alive.

Hope is not just a nice sounding euphemism. Hope and biological life are inextricably intertwined. Martin Seligman's (1975) work in the field of learned helpless offers us great insight into the chiasmic intertwining of hope and biological life. He sights two examples. The first is a published report by Dr. H. M. Lefcourt (1973):

> This writer witnessed one such case of death due to a loss of will within a psychiatric hospital. A female patient who had remained in a mute state for nearly 10 years was shifted to a different floor of her building along with her floor mates, while her unit was being redecorated. The third floor of this psychiatric unit where the patient in question had been living was known among the patients as the chronic, hopeless floor. In contrast, the first floor was most commonly occupied by patients who held privileges, including the freedom to come and go on the hospital grounds and to the surrounding streets. In short, the first floor was an exit ward from which patients could anticipate discharge fairly rapidly. All patients who were temporarily moved from the third floor were given medical examinations prior to the move, and the patient in question was judged to be in excellent medical health though still mute and withdrawn. Shortly after moving to the first floor, this chronic psychiatric patient surprised the ward staff by becoming socially responsive such that within a two week period she ceased being mute and was actually becoming gregarious. As fate would have it, the redecoration of the third floor unit was soon completed and all previous residents were returned to it. Within a week after she had been returned to the hopeless unit, this patient...collapsed and died. The subsequent autopsy revealed no pathology of

note and it was whimsically suggested at the time that the patient had died of despair. (p.182–183)

The second example is that of an army medical officer named Major F. Harold Kushner. Major Kushner was shot down over North Vietnam and he was interned in a prisoner of war camp from 1968 to 1973. Here is how Dr. Seligman relates the story:

When Major Kushner arrived a First Camp in January 1968, Robert has already been captive for two years. He was a rugged and intelligent corporal from a crack marine unit, austere, stoic, and oblivious to pain and suffering. He was 24 years old...Like the rest of the men, he was down to a weight of ninety pounds and was forced to make long, shoeless treks daily with ninety pounds of manioc root on his back. He never griped...Despite malnutrition and terrible skin disease, he remained in very good physical and mental health. The cause of his relatively fine shape was clear to (Major) Kushner. Robert was convinced that he would soon be released. The Viet Cong had made it a practice to release, as examples, a few men who had co operated with them... Robert had done so, and the camp commander had indicated that he was next in line for release, to come in six months...

The [designated] month came and went, and [Robert] began to sense a change in the guards' attitude toward him. Finally it dawned on him that he had been deceived, that he wasn't going to be released. He stopped working and showed signs of severe depression: he refused food and lay on his bed in a fetal position, sucking his thumb. His fellow prisoners tried to bring him around. They hugged him, babied him and, when this didn't work, tried to bring him out of his stupor with their fists. He defecated and urinated in bed. After a few weeks, it was apparent to Kushner that Robert was moribund: although otherwise his gross physical

shape was still better than most of the others, he was dusky and cyanotic. In the early hours of a November morning he lay dying in Kushner's arms. For the first time in days his eyes focused and he spoke: "Doc, Post Office Box 161, Texarkana, Texas. Mom, Dad, I love you very much..." Within seconds, he was dead. (p. 168)

Seligman (1975, p. 168) goes on to comment:

Hope of release sustained Robert. When he gave up hope, when he believed that all his efforts had failed and would continue to fail, he died. Can a psychological state be lethal? I believe it can. When animals and men learn that their actions are futile and that there is no hope, they become more susceptible to death. Conversely, the belief in control over the environment can prolong life.

To paraphrase I would say that when those of us with psychiatric disabilities come to believe that all of our efforts are futile; when we experience that we have no control over our environment; when nothing we do seems to matter or to make the situation better; when we follow the treatment teams' instructions and achieve their treatment goals for us and still no placement opens up in the community for us; when we try one medication after another after another and none of them seem to be of any help; when we find that staff do not listen to us and that they make all of the major decisions for us; when staff decide where we will live, with whom we will live; under what rules we will live, how we will spend our money, if we will be allowed to spend our money, when we will have to leave the group home, and at what time we will be allowed back into it, etc. etc. etc., then a deep sense of hopelessness, of despair begins to settle over the human heart. And in an effort to avoid the biologically disastrous effects of profound hopelessness, people with psychiatric disabilities do what other people do. We grow hard of heart and attempt to stop caring. It is safer to become helpless then to become hopeless.

Of course, the great danger is that staff will fail to recognize the intensity of the existential struggle that the person who is hard of heart is struggling with. The danger is that the staff will simply say, "Oh, this person just has a lot of negative signs and symptoms and that's a poor prognosis and we mustn't expect much from this person." Or staff may become judgmental and dismiss us as simply being lazy and unmotivated. Or the staff may succumb to their own despair and simply write us off as being "low functioning."

It is imperative that the instructors and field trainers of the next generation of mental health professionals help today's students to avoid these pitfalls. It is imperative that students be helped to understand that being hard hearted and not caring are highly motivated, adaptive strategies used by desperate people who are at great risk of losing hope. We must help students understand and empathize with the deep existential struggle that is at the heart of this dark night of despair.

There are a number of things I tell students about how to work with people who appear to be hard of heart, apathetic, and unmotivated. First I help the student understand the behavior in terms of its existential significance. I want the student to grasp the magnitude of what it is they are asking a person to risk when they ask them to start to care about something again. I want

Our greatest challenge is to find a way to refuse to be dehumanized in the age of managed profit, and to be bold and brave and daring enough to remain human hearted while working in the human services.

them to understand that under the hardened heart lies the breaking heart. How much suffering, how much loss can a human heart hold before it breaks? It is not a crazy thing to try to protect such a vulnerable heart. Students must be helped to honor the strategy of giving up and to understand that perhaps that person shall never risk again. In any case, it is only the person whom we are trying to help who has the power to take the risk, to care about something—something as simple perhaps as caring enough to put a poster on their bedroom wall, or caring enough to wear some new clothes or to try a job placement. These may seem like small things but if we understand their full existential significance, such acts are small steps toward caring, toward admitting that I just might want to participate in the human community again.

Secondly, I ask students to suspend their perception of people as chronic mental patients and to try to see the individual as a hero. I ask them, could you have survived what this individual has survived? Perhaps this individual has done what you could not do. Perhaps they are not weak and fragile sick people. Perhaps those of us with psychiatric disabilities are incredibly strong and have fiercely tenacious spirits. Could you live on $530 a month and cope with a disability at the same time? If a student can momentarily drop out of his or her distanced professional posture and, in true humility, come to see a person with a psychiatric disability as a hero who has survived, then I say there is a good prognosis for that student. That student has a chance of being human hearted while working in the human services and this is no small accomplishment.

Finally, I try to help students understand that although they do not have the power to change or motivate the person with a psychiatric disability who is hard of heart, they do have the power to change the environment, including the human interactive environment, in which that person is surviving. When working with a person with a psychiatric disability who is hard of heart, who has given up and who is motivated not to care anymore, we must understand that this is a person who feels they have no power. They experience all the power to be in the hands of others. They experience what psychologists call an external locus of control. For such people it is imperative to create an environment in which there are choices to be made. I am speaking here, not of forced choice such as either you take your medications or you go back to the hospital (this is little more than coercion), but of real choices. I am speaking here of all types of choices, from small concerns such as what flavor ice cream you want, to what coffee shop you want to go to, to what kind of vocational goals you might want to pursue, etc.

The person with a hardened heart will reject, reject, and reject again these invitations to choose. However the staff must not fall into despair, feel like their efforts are futile, grow hard of heart, and stop caring themselves. If they do this, then they are doing exactly what the person with a psychiatric disability is doing. Staff must avoid this trap. They must do what the person cannot yet do. Staff must

I want the student to grasp the magnitude of what it is they are asking a person to risk when they ask them to start to care about something again.

role model hope and continue to offer options and choices even if they are rejected over and over again.

Additionally, environments must include opportunities for people to have accurate information. Information is power and information sharing is power sharing. People who feel powerless can increase their sense of self efficacy by having access to information. People who feel powerless also feel that what they say does not matter. Taking the time to listen to people and to help them find their own unique voice is important. Having a voice in developing rules, as well as having a say in the hiring and evaluation of staff, are important ways of exercising a voice that for too long has been silenced. Finally, it is important to have other people with psychiatric disabilities working as paid staff. Role models provide hope that maybe I, too, can break out of this hardened heart and begin to care again. People who are defending themselves against the possibly lethal effects of profound hopelessness must see that there is a way out and that actions they take can inch them ever closer to their desired goal. They need to see that the quality of life can get better for people who have been similarly diagnosed. They need to see that there are opportunities for improving their situation. That is why hiring people with psychiatric disabilities as mental health professionals and staff is so important. It is also why exposure to peer support, self help, and mutual support are so important.

Choice, options, information, role models, being heard, developing and exercising a voice, opportunities for bettering one's life: these are the features of a human inter-active environment that support the transition from not caring to caring, from surviving to becoming an active participant in one's own recovery process. Creating such environments are the skills that tomorrow's mental health professionals must master.

As for myself, I cannot remember a specific moment when I turned that corner from surviving to becoming an active participant in my own recovery process. My efforts to protect my breaking heart by becoming hard of heart and not caring about anything lasted for a long time. One thing I can recall is that the people around me did not give up on me. They kept inviting me to do things. I remember one day, for no particular reason, saying yes to helping with food shopping. All I would do was push the cart. But it was a beginning. And truly, it was through small steps like these that I slowly began to discover that I could take a stand toward what was distressing to me.

I know that anger, especially angry indignation, played a big role in that transition. When that psychiatrist told me the best I could hope for was to take my medications, avoid stress and cope, I became enraged. (However, I was smart enough to keep my angry indignation to myself because rule #1 is never get enraged in a psychiatrist's office if you're labeled with chronic schizophrenia!) I also remember that just after that visit I made up my mind to become a doctor. I was so outraged at the things that had been done to me against my will in the hospital as well as the things I saw happen to other people, that I decided that I wanted to get a powerful degree and have enough credentials to run a healing place myself. In effect, I had a survivor mission that I felt passionately about.

I was also careful not to share my new-found aspiration with anyone. Imagine what my psychiatrist would have said to me if I had announced at age 18, having

virtually flunked out of high school, with a combined GRE score of under 800, with a diagnosis of chronic schizophrenia, that I was planning on getting my Ph.D. in clinical psychology. "Delusions of grandeur!" But in essence that is precisely what I did. Starting with one course in English Composition at the local community college I slowly made my way. Dragging my textbooks into the mental hospital with me or trying to read with double vision due to Prolixin, I inched my way forward. I had a strong spirituality that really helped. I had a strong therapeutic alliance with a psychotherapist. I lived with really weird hippies who had tolerance for lots of weird behavior including my psychotic episodes. After some experimenting in my early teens, I somehow intuited that drugs and alcohol were bad news for me and I did not use them even though the people around me did. In retrospect, I know this was a wise decision. I read tons of books about healing and psychopathology and personality theory in an effort to understand myself and my situation. I was always trying new ways of coping with symptoms including my relentless auditory hallucinations. And perhaps most importantly of all, when I got out of bed in the morning, I always knew the reason why I had a purpose in life, I had been called, I had a vocation, and I kept saying yes to it. Even in the present I must make a daily affirmation of my vocation in order to keep going. The temptation to give up is still strong sometimes.

My journey of recovery is still ongoing. I still struggle with symptoms, grieve the losses that I have sustained, and have had to get involved in treatment for the sequela child abuse. I am also involved in self help and mutual support and I still use professional services including medications, psychotherapy, and hospitals. However, now I do not just take medication or go to the hospital. I have learned to *use medications* and to *use* the hospital. This is the active stance that is the hallmark of the recovery process.

There is more to the recovery process than simply recovering from mental illness. We must also recover from the effects of poverty and second class citizenship. We must learn to raise our consciousness and find our collective pride in order to overcome internalized stigma. Finally, many of us emerge from mental health treatment settings with traumatic stress disorders related to having sustained or witnessed physical, sexual, and/or emotional abuse at the hands of staff. As one long term veteran of mental health services wrote:

> The stuff I've been through was like a nightmare. Sometimes I go back into the nightmare. I cry every night about it. Remembering it is like being in the nightmare again...Sometimes I scream at night because I dream about the hospital I was raped in or some other hospital I've been in. (LaLime 1990)

Sometimes recovering from mental illness is the easy part. Recovering from these deep wounds to the human heart takes much longer.

Recovery does not mean cure. Rather recovery is an attitude, a stance, and a way of approaching the day's challenges. It is not a perfectly linear journey. There are times of rapid gains and disappointing relapses. There are times of just living, just staying quiet, resting and regrouping. Each

We must urge our students to seek wisdom, to move beyond mere recognition of illness, and to wholeheartedly encounter the human being who comes for help. It is imperative that we teach students that relationship is the most powerful tool they have in working with people.

person's journey of recovery is unique. Each person must find what works for them. This means that we must have the opportunity to try and to fail and to try again. In order to support the recovery process mental health professionals must not rob us of the opportunity to fail. Professionals must embrace the concept of the dignity of risk and the right to failure if they are to be supportive of us.

In closing, I would like to add that all around the world, people who have been psychiatrically labeled are organizing. We are organizing on the local, state, national, and international level. We are developing a collective voice and are fighting to overcome oppression, poverty, discrimination, and stigma. We are saying no to second class health care, poor or non existent housing, and to the indignities that so often come with psychiatric hospitalizations including the barbaric use of restraint and seclusion. We are sitting at the table in dialogue with service providers and policy makers to find alternatives to involuntary treatment. We are joining with other disability groups to form a broad coalition of 40 million Americans with disabilities to achieve equity in healthcare, support services, and entitlements.

We are also beginning to define our experiences in our own terms and to educate mental health professionals about our experience and what helps. We are fortunate to have the National Empowerment

Center in Lawrence, Massachusetts. The National Empowerment Center is a completely consumer run and controlled national technical assistance center supported through funding from the Center for Mental Health Services. We have developed many innovative trainings and resources. For instance, we have a new training available that is entitled *Hearing Voices That Are Distressing: A Simulated Training Experience and Self-help Strategies*. In this workshop designed for mental health practitioners and students, participants listen to an audiotape that was designed by people who hear voices to simulate the experience of hearing voices that are distressing. Participants listen to the tape while having to undergo a series of tasks including a mental status exam, a community outing, a day treatment activity group, and psychological testing. After the simulated training participants have the opportunity to learn many self-help strategies that help to control or eliminate distressing voices.

A new age is upon us. We must help the students of today to understand that people with psychiatric disabilities are human beings with human hearts. Our hearts are as real and as vulnerable and as valuable as yours are. Understanding that people with psychiatric disabilities are first and foremost people who are in process, growing and changing is the cornerstone of understanding the concept of recovery. We must not let our hearts grow hard and calloused toward people with psychiatric disabilities. Our role is not to judge who will and will not recover. Our job is to create environments in which opportunities for recovery and empowerment exist. Our job is to establish strong, supportive relationships with those we work with. And perhaps most of all, our greatest challenge is to find a way to refuse to be dehumanized in the age of managed profit, and to be bold and brave and daring enough to remain human hearted while working in the human services.

References

LaLime, W. (1990). Untitled speech used as part of Lowell MPOWER's anti-stigma workshop, Lowell Massachusetts.

Deegan, P. (1990). Spirit breaking: When the helping professions hurt. *The Humanistic Psychologist, 18*(3), 301-313.

Lefcourt, H. M. (1973). The function of the illusions of control and freedom. *American Psychologist, 28*, 417-425.

Seligman, M. E. P. (1975). *Helplessness: On depression, development and death*. San Francisco: Freeman.

Finding Myself and Loving It

Jeanine M. O'Neal

JEANINE M. O'NEAL IS A STUDENT AT THE UNIVERSITY OF PITTSBURGH, PITTSBURGH, PA. SHE WILL BE RECEIVING A B.A. DEGREE IN SPANISH IN APRIL 1984.

THIS ARTICLE ORIGINALLY APPEARED IN THE *Schizophrenia Bulletin*, 1984, 10(1), 109-110.

When my first episode of schizophrenia occurred, I was 21, a senior in college in Atlanta, Georgia. I was making good grades, assistant vice president of my chapter in my sorority, president of the Spanish club, and very popular. Everything in my life was just perfect. I had a boyfriend whom I liked a lot, a part-time job tutoring Spanish, and was about to run for the Ms. Senior pageant.

All of a sudden things weren't going so well. I began to lose control of my life and, most of all, myself. I couldn't concentrate on my schoolwork, I couldn't sleep, and when I did sleep, I had dreams about dying. I was afraid to go to class, imagined that people were talking about me, and on top of that I heard voices. I called my mother in Pittsburgh and asked for her advice. She told me to move off campus into an apartment with my sister.

After I moved in with my sister, things got worse. I was afraid to go outside and when I looked out of the window, it seemed that everyone outside was yelling "kill her, kill her." My sister forced me to go to school. I would go out of the house until I knew she had gone to work; then I would return home. Things continued to get worse. I imagined that I had a foul body odor and I sometimes took up to six showers a day. I recall going to the grocery store one day, and I imagined that the people in the store were saying "Get saved, Jesus is the answer." Things worsened—I

couldn't remember a thing. I had a notebook full of reminders telling me what to do on that particular day. I couldn't remember my schoolwork, and I would study from 6:00 P.M. until 4:00 A.M., but never had the courage to go to class on the following day. I tried to tell my sister about it, but she didn't understand. She suggested that I see a psychiatrist, but I was afraid to go out of the house to see him.

One day I decided that I couldn't take this trauma anymore, so I took an overdose of 35 Darvon pills. At the same moment, a voice inside me said, "What did you do that for? Now you won't go to heaven." At that instant I realized that I really didn't want to die, I wanted to live, and I was afraid. I got on the phone and called the psychiatrist whom my sister had recommended. I told him that I had taken an overdose of Darvon and that I was afraid. He told me to take a taxi to the hospital. When I arrived at the hospital, I began vomiting, but I didn't pass out. Somehow I just couldn't accept the fact that I was really going to see a psychiatrist. I thought that psychiatrists were only for crazy people, and I definitely didn't think I was crazy yet. As a result, I did not admit myself right away. As a matter of fact I left the hospital and ended up meeting my sister on the way home. She told me to turn right back around, because I was definitely going to be admitted. We then called my mother, and she said she would fly down on the following day.

I stayed in that particular hospital for 1 week. It wasn't too bad. First I was interviewed, then given medication (Trilafon). There I met a number of people whose problems ranged from depression to having illusions of grandeur. It was quite interesting. I had a nice doctor, but he didn't tell me that I had schizophrenia—only that I had an "identity crisis." I was then transferred to a hospital in Pittsburgh. I did not care for my doctor. He told me that I was imagining things and constantly changed my medication. For instance, if I had a stomach ache, he would say I imagined it. At this stage of my recovery I was no longer imagining things, but I was afraid. I feared large crowds of people and therefore avoided going shopping, dancing, or riding buses (anywhere large crowds existed). It took me from September until March to recover. By the way, this particular doctor diagnosed my case as an "anxiety-depression reaction." In the meantime my family was very supportive of me.

In April, I decided that I was well and didn't need medication anymore (not knowing that I had schizophrenia and that it was incurable), and I also stopped going to the doctor's office. I got a job, from which I was terminated after a week. I became hypertensive and nervous without realizing it. My friends and family said I was behaving strangely, but I took no notice. I went out dancing practically every night to make up for the time lost while being afraid. I felt as if I were on top of the world—as if I were free.

The summer passed quickly. I had decided to return to Atlanta in the fall and complete my senior year. After all, I only had 1 measly year toward my Bachelor of Arts degree in Spanish, and I wanted to complete my education at the college where my education began. My parents, however, suggested that I finish in Pittsburgh, in case anything else might occur. I didn't listen, and somehow thought they were plotting against me. Next, I found myself in Atlanta and sick once again. I was taken to another psychiatric hospital. This time things were twice as bad as the first. I no longer heard voices but the things I saw and dreamed about were far more traumatic. I recall at one point thinking I was Jesus Christ and that I was placed on this earth to bear everyone's sins.

My stay in that particular hospital was absolutely terrible. Each time I saw things I was placed in seclusion. They constantly used me as a guinea pig to discover which medicine would best suit my needs. However, I met many people (patients), some of whom became very close friends. I remained in the hospital 1 month and 2 days and was finally prescribed Loxitane, which I am presently taking.

After I was released, I returned to Pittsburgh and became an outpatient at Western Psychiatric Institute and Clinic. My doctor is very good and I respect her a lot. She's really a great person. It took me 6 months to recover. Again I was afraid of crowds of people, and I avoided them whenever I could.

Now I have been taking Loxitane for almost 2 years with considerable results. All of the symptoms seem to have vanished. I have my own apartment, I am back in college in Pittsburgh, president of my chapter of my sorority, and, above all, more confident and happier than I have ever been in my life. I reflect back on the pains of the past and consider them a learning experience. I foresee the future as a bright challenge. My doctor once asked me what do I think taking medicine means and I replied, "not being sick." Today I take my medicine daily, just as a person with high blood pressure or a diabetic does. It doesn't bother me. Today I am really free!

Maintaining Mental Health in a Turbulent World

Joan F. Houghton

JOAN F. HOUGHTON IS SOCIAL SCIENCE RESEARCH
ANALYST, MENTAL HEALTH EDUCATION BRANCH,
NATIONAL INSTITUTE OF MENTAL HEALTH,
ROCKVILLE, MD, AND A DOCTORAL STUDENT IN
COUNSELING EDUCATION.

IN MEMORY OF INA JEAN, A FRIEND, WHOSE LAUGHTER
CONTINUES TO RING IN OUR HEARTS AND WHOSE
HOPE WAS LOST IN THE STRUGGLE TO SURVIVE IN A
TURBULENT WORLD.

THIS ARTICLE ORIGINALLY APPEARED IN THE
Schizophrenia Bulletin, 1982, 8(3), 548-552.

My mother and I sat next to each other in the waiting room while my father investigated admission procedures. A young man was seated near us. Perspiration dripped across his brow and down his cheeks. In silence I took a tissue from my purse, moved close to him, and gently wiped the moisture from his face. I reassured him that everything would be fine.

Soon my father rejoined us. We went together to a small room where I met Kay, the psychiatric social worker assigned to my case, and a psychiatrist (whose name I don't recall). We talked a few minutes. I was presented with a piece of paper and instructed to sign my name. Obediently, I wrote "Saint Joan" on the paper, not realizing that I was voluntarily admitting myself to a state mental hospital.

This is a preview of a tragedy in my life which I find difficult to remember 5 years later. The difficulty is a function of the fact that my reality is your reality—that I, like you, struggle to cope and survive each day in a turbulent world. The difference between us is an experience which has changed every aspect of my life. It is the changes and not the experience that I want so much to share with you.

In order to replace mental illness with mental health, considerable learning and relearning had to occur. To survive and cope, I had to begin my life over again, to adopt a new, healthier style of living. By learning more about myself, my limits, and weaknesses and strengths, and by making changes in my way of life, I have been able to maintain my health and prevent a recurrence of mental illness. My first psychotic episode and the hospitalization experience set the conditions for these changes to happen cataclysmically.

At the time of my hospitalization I had both a sense of death and a rebirth about me. My first psychotic episode appeared as a private mental exorcism, ending with the honor of sainthood and the gifts of hope and faith. Fortunately, this sense of power became a source of tremendous strength during my recovery and sustains one even today.

Then, and in my memory, my hospitalization was an entombment; the medications were an embalmment. I walked among the living dead. It was not so much cruel as morbid and morose. It lasted 5 eternal weeks.

In the real world the sense of death remained for years, until I stopped ingesting medications. The transformation was extraordinary: My face was no longer swollen; extra pounds began to melt away; my hair grew thicker and more manageable; my movements were no longer mechanical and forced; my energy level increased. I had a tremendous sense of rebirth.

To maintain a sense of well-being, I have had to change my lifestyle and my priorities. My illness taught me (the hard way) the importance of meaningful work, good patterns of rest and sleep, exercise, diet, and self-discipline. Once freed from the regulating shackles of medications, I had to substitute their positive effects—a reasonable routine, a slower pace, and a calm atmosphere.

I began my new life by setting up a schedule for myself, by providing a structure for everyday living. I put the schedule for "the ideal day" and "the ideal week" in a small black notebook which I kept in my purse or briefcase. The notebook also stored a calendar and addresses and phone numbers, and a running list of tasks to be accomplished. It reminded me of what was important.

Although I no longer carry the notebook, parts of it remain recorded in my thoughts. Even now, I schedule in "down time" at the end of the day—about 30 minutes to an hour of quiet before bedtime to read, write in my diary, lounge in a tub of hot water. Because television, phone calls, rock music, exercises or other mentally or physically stimulating activities can disturb my sleep patterns, I avoid them whenever possible before bedtime.

Although my daily eating habits have not changed that drastically, I give careful attention to dieting. I never eliminate a food group—balanced meals are essential to good health, mental and physical. I minimize consumption of foods which have proved harmful to me—sugar, coffee, and other stimulants. For me, sugar intake is a critical indicator of my general health and well-being. When I crave sweets, especially sugar candies, I am typically very tired and working under stress. This is a sign to take a day off from work and rest. Coffee, cokes, and other caffeinated beverages are rarely consumed because they generate nervous energy. I reluctantly take medications, even aspirin, unless I am physically very ill or in great pain. Occasionally, if I have trouble sleeping, I drink a glass of wine. When I'm feeling "down," I give in to my one dietary weakness: potato chips. (Food frustrations can be very harmful, in my opinion.)

Exercise and physical activity not only strengthen the body but serve as an emotional safety valve. A tennis racket, a softball bat, or a golf club is an excellent means for displacing anger. Running is often effective in alleviating depression. Dancing and swimming can be equally beneficial for lethargy and withdrawn personalities.

*M*y illness taught me (the hard way) the importance of meaningful work, good patterns of rest and sleep, exercise, diet, and self-discipline.

From my perspective, mental illness is often negative energy turned inward; exercise provides a healthy release for this energy. Physical activity serves in a paradoxical way to build and exhaust the body. A well-balanced exercise program is as essential as a well-balanced meal—too much, too little, or the wrong types of exercise can be as detrimental as too much, too little, or the wrong types of food.

My own exercise program is varied because I like to participate in most sports. Because some activities, such as tennis, frustrate me, I avoid matches which are too competitive. Since my back and knees cry out in pain when I run, climb steep mountains, or exercise too long, I minimize these activities. A bike ride or hike in the woods can be very emotionally and mentally rejuvenating.

The second major area of my life in which I learned to change involved my mental processes and intellectual development.

Psychotic episodes have the effect of "playing" mental messages on 78+ and frequently switching stations. Disorganized thoughts are often best managed in organized environments. Impulsive obsessive-compulsive behaviors have been a critical indicator that my mental world is not well ordered. I have learned to manage this by a process I call "mental purging."

If I have had a particularly busy day, if someone has upset me, or if I have a great deal to accomplish in a short period of time, I reach for paper and pen. When I have a great deal to do, I list the tasks to be accomplished, establish priorities, and try to set up a reasonable time frame in which to get them done. When my emotions have been tested, I make an entry in my diary. When I have spent a lot of myself and my energy on the needs and problems of others, I write a letter focusing on all that's good in my life. I view writing as a healthy form of transference. It purges my mind of information that interferes with action and helps to organize my thoughts into patterns of action.

Another essential change in my life has been learning to set reasonable goals and to reach them. (I still struggle with what's "reasonable.")

When I left the hospital, I felt as though I could do nothing. Reaching a goal wasn't even an issue when getting out of bed was my greatest challenge. I had no desire to set a goal because I had no desire to live.

To relieve her own pain of watching me waste away, my mother taught me to crochet. The goal was a poncho cape. She coached me while I struggled with a skein of wool which seemed to have no end. My therapist became a cheerleader along the sidelines, encouraging me to finish the cape, to do a row a week, and to bring it to his office for periodic checkups. It took 3 years, but I finished it! I won the game against that part of me that was already defeated.

In addition to mental purging and reasonable goal-setting, I have endeavored to remain mentally stimulated. At first I had the sense that I had suffered a mental (heart) attack—a stroke of the brain. My body movements were slow and mechanical; my brain functions were retarded. In general, I was on slow speed.

Not only was I painfully aware of the differences in my mental and physical abilities, but I felt helpless to rehabilitate myself. When I returned to work and to graduate school, I had great difficulty attending to lengthy oral instructions and concentrating on written material. In spite of the challenge, I endured. In time, especially after I discontinued medications, I was more academically proficient than I had been before my illness. Being back in school forced me to think about something other than myself. As a psychology graduate student, my course work put my illness into perspective, and my illness provided a special leaning and direction for my education and training.

When I returned to work, school, and the stresses of "normal" living, the importance of defining my own limits and setting reasonable goals became apparent. I learned through two subsequent episodes that I could not permit others to push me, and more importantly, that I could not push myself without suffering serious consequences. I learned that any change—such as a business trip or vacation—which drastically altered my routine was stressful. Deadlines, other- or self-imposed, were harmful, especially if they were unrealistic.

I had to learn that my body rhythm had been reset at a slower speed and that I could no longer work and play at my previous rate without suffering a physical or mental "breakdown." I was indeed much like the patient recovering from a heart attack. If I were to avoid another "attack," I had to change my physical pace and my mental attitude about myself and my abilities.

Socially, I also experienced changes and with these changes I had to learn new social skills which would not only help me but others to cope with my illness and hospitalization.

Because I was a mental health professional, I assumed that my colleagues would be intensely interested in my experiences as a patient. I felt no reason to closet myself because of my illness—I had done nothing wrong. I had gotten sick, had a mental (heart) attack. My desire to detach and withdraw grew more from a sense of physical ugliness than from my episode and hospitalization. I wanted and I expected to be embraced for my suffering, not rejected because of it.

A condition, which I call "justifiable paranoia," developed from experiences of rejection (covert and overt), persecution, and discrimination. Others simply did not know how to relate to me as a recovering psychotic. Does one send a get-well or a thinking of you card? Does one visit? What does one say to a business associate who is shuffling around on Haldol? What tasks should a supervisor assign to an employee who is having feelings of uselessness? Can universities accredit students as psychologists who receive part of their education (without credit) in a mental hospital? If not for many advocates (whom I will discuss later), I might not have been able to endure the answers to these questions. I was forced, for my survival, to learn—for the first time in my life—to fight. No longer could I turn the other cheek. My friends have remained my friends. New acquaintances—people who accept me for my strengths, my weaknesses, tragedies, successes, and failures—are vitally important to me. They reassure me that "I'm OK."

Former patients live in emotional straightjackets simply by the nature of their illness.

Those who continue to struggle for a sense of mental health, who call or write asking for hope, inspire me.

I have been told that some call me names, say I'm "crazy" and unfit" to counsel young people. While these words hurt me deep, I have acquired such a strong sense of self that they no longer interfere with my progress. I know who and what I am. I am sufficiently content to forgive them. I am still learning how and when say "no," "I can't," and "I don't want to." I have learned to speak about my illness only when I'm asked about it. I rarely volunteer my "confession" of sins as a mental patient. Most important, I learned to laugh about my experiences, to say the word "crazy" and know that it doesn't apply to me. I have learned when to closet myself and when to open my closet door. Occasionally I even shake my skeleton and know that others are laughing with me and not at me.

In the emotional dimensions I have also had many lessons: I have learned to cry.

A few years after my illness I met someone who permitted me to talk about my hospitalization. As I described the experience, I cried. A gentle touch that said, "It doesn't matter; we can still be friends" was worth years of therapy. That moment was an emotional breakthrough for me. That person gave me a very precious gift—hope.

Many emotional lessons in anger have yet to be learned. I often "sit on it." It's there; I feel it; but I don't express it well. All too often it's displaced and misplaced. It's a problem I share with much of our society.

Former patients live in emotional straightjackets simply by the nature of their illness. To others, misplaced anger may be a sign of repressed violence. Tears, a state of sadness, may be misread as an impending state of depression. Laughter may be heard as mania. Emotional extremes create fear, especially in those who only know of our history rather than our personalities.

My spirit is stronger, more determined. It permits me to "tune in" to myself and the world around me.

Some of the most beneficial changes for maintaining my mental health have been environmental. Learning when to move has not been an easy lesson. It has always been costly financially but with a substantial benefit emotionally.

Six months after my hospitalization I decided to take a leave of absence from my job and live in Seattle, Washington, with friends. The time away was very therapeutic. I used it to write an overdue research paper for one of my graduate courses, to rest, relax, and assess my life. It helped me to see how the stresses of my everyday lifestyle had contributed to my illness.

The most crucial change for me occurred in the workplace about 2 years after my hospitalization. I moved from an office setting which was stifling and destructive to one which continues to be supportive and creative. In this new work environment I have found meaning to my life. I have been permitted to grow and develop with an abundance of nurturance, encouragement, and support.

Repeatedly, I have pointed out the importance of the workplace, particularly for the recovering patient. For most of us, the workplace is the primary source of ego strength. We spend our young life preparing to work and the majority of our awake, adult life at work. Some of us work by the Protestant ethic; others of us develop identities around job titles and organizational affiliations. We work to survive as well as to enjoy life. It is often a source of stress and a source of socializing. It provides our bread and butter, our meat and potatoes. Without a meaningful job, we lack meaning. We become parasites on society by chance rather than by choice. Worst of all, we have no self-worth.

I, like you, struggle to cope and survive each day in a turbulent world. The difference between us is an experience which has changed every aspect of my life.

I have been extremely fortunate in this regard. My education, training, and diversified work experiences occurred before my illness. I was hospitalized as a respected mental health professional and honor student in graduate school. There was a fair share of security attached to my job, and there were opportunities for career advancement before my illness.

My episodes and hospitalization undermined my own accomplishments. Not only was I experiencing a rebirth emotionally, physically, mentally, and socially, but I was as an infant in the arms of my employer.

My work and work environment had contributed significantly to my "breakdown," but I was ill equipped to move into a new job situation when I returned to work. At the same time that I needed to relocate organizationally, I was clinging to what was known and familiar to me.

In time, as I grew stronger and could recognize the destructive aspects of my work situation, I challenged the injustices. My struggle against management resulted in a most satisfactory job transfer to the Mental Health Study Center of the National

Institute of Mental Health. The first steps toward the reconstruction of my dormant ego and infantile identity were taken when the Chief of the Child and Youth Programs Section, Dr. Milton Shore, reviewed my job application and resume, invited me in for an interview, expressed an interest in having me work with him, and engaged the system to hire me. It was as though he had injected me with hope.

The new job situation only improved over time. Special arrangements were made and approved for me to complete my graduate work while conducting research and providing counscling to students in a high school. My on-site supervisors, whom I subsequently told of my experiences as a mental patient, applauded my excellent work and assured me of a continued place on the staff. If there was discrimination, it was in my favor. My consulting assignments broadened to all areas of the school; my counseling caseload was increased; I was asked to develop staff training programs on sensitivity and caring. They rewarded me for my own intense sensitivity to kids and my ability to help them find solutions (rather than to "wallow" in problems). I set my own limits and priorities. I was given opportunities to translate my own personal tragedies into something meaningful for others.

Many people have served as my advocates these past 5 years. I have mentioned only a few of them here.

My family and friends have continued to give love in abundance. They coached, encouraged, cried, and laughed with me. They have been my army against those who were denying me my place as a productive, worthwhile member of society.

My therapist, Jeremy P. Waletzky, M.D., has become a friend. He has permitted me to be his teacher.

Norman Rosenberg, my attorney at the Mental Health Law Project, validated my sanity. He was my armor in the battles against a university which was denying me readmission to graduate school and against a supervisor who threatened me with disability retirement.

My supervisors have restored a sense of meaning and purpose to my life. By giving me a place to give to others, I believe they have given many places to many people like me.

RECOVERY: THE LIVED EXPERIENCE OF REHABILITATION

Patricia E. Deegan

PATRICIA DEEGAN, PH.D. IS PROGRAM DIRECTOR, NORTHEAST INDEPENDENT LIVING PROGRAM, LAWRENCE, MASSACHUSETTS, AND CONSULTANT, NATIONAL EMPOWERMENT CENTER, LAWRENCE.

THIS ARTICLE ORIGINALLY APPEARED IN THE *Psychosocial Rehabilitation Journal*, 1988, 11(4), 11-19 AND IS REPRINTED WITH PERMISSION.

This paper distinguishes between recovery and rehabilitation. Persons with psychiatric disabilities do not "get rehabilitated" but rather they recover a new and valued sense of self and of purpose. Through the recovery process they become active and responsible participants in their own rehabilitation project. The experiences of recovery as lived by a man with a physical disability and a woman with a psychiatric disability are discussed. Recommendations for creating rehabilitation environments that facilitate the recovery process are also given.

The application of rehabilitation approaches and technologies to adults with psychiatric disabilities is a relatively new and exciting development in our field. The discovery and application of rehabilitation models allow us to think about this population in new and exciting ways. Of significance is the fact that, from the perspective of the rehabilitation approach, it is no longer necessary to isolate persons with psychiatric disabilities as being totally different from other groups of persons with disabilities. Today, artificial boundaries between groups of persons experiencing different types of disabilities can be bridged through the understanding that most people with disabilities share the same fundamental needs and aspirations: The need is to meet the challenge of the disability and to reestablish a new and valued sense of integrity and purpose within and beyond the limits of the disability; the aspiration is to live, work, and love in a community in which one makes a significant contribution.

It is important to understand that persons with a disability do not "get rehabilitated" in the sense that cars "get" tuned up or televisions "get repaired." They are not passive recipients of rehabilitation services. Rather, they experience themselves as *recovering* a new sense of self and of purpose within and beyond the limits of the disability. This distinction between rehabilitation and recovery is important. Rehabilitation refers to the services and technologies that are made available to persons with disabilities so that they might learn to adapt to their world. Recovery refers to the lived or real life experience of persons as they accept and overcome the challenge of the disability. We might say that rehabilitation refers to the "world pole" and that recovery refers to the "self pole" of the same phenomenon.

The recovery process is the foundation upon which rehabilitation services build. This is most evidenced in the simple observation that we can make the finest and most advanced rehabilitation services available to the individuals with psychiatric disabilities and still fail to help them. Something more than just "good services" is needed, e.g., the person must get out of bed, shake off the mind-numbing exhaustion of the neuroleptics, get dressed, overcome the fear of the crowded and unfriendly bus to arrive at the program, and face the fear of failure in the rehabilitation program. In essence, they must be active and courageous participants in their own rehabilitation project or that project will fail. It is through the process of recovery that persons with disabilities become active and courageous participants in their own rehabilitation project.

We see then that recovery is an important and fundamental phenomenon upon which rehabilitation efforts depend. It is therefore surprising that very little has been written in our professional and scientific journals regarding it. Perhaps the phenomenon is elusive precisely because it is so fundamental. Perhaps it is because the recovery process cannot be completely described with traditional scientific, psychiatric, or psychological language. Although the phenomenon will not fit neatly into natural scientific paradigms, those of us who have had a disability know that recovery is real because we have lived it. At a recent conference that brought together persons with diverse disabilities, I had the pleasure of talking with Brad, a man who has paraplegia. We shared our stories of recovery.

Our denial was an important stage in our recovery. It was a normal reaction to an overwhelming situation. It was our way of surviving...

The Experience of Recovery

At a young age we had both experienced a catastrophic shattering of our world, hopes, and dreams. Brad had broken his neck and was paralyzed and I was diagnosed as being schizophrenic. We recalled the impact of those first days following the onset of our disabilities. He was an athlete and dreamed of becoming a professional in the sports world. I was a high school athlete and had applied to college to become a gym teacher. Just days earlier we knew ourselves as young people with exciting futures, and then everything collapsed around us. As teenagers, we were told that we had an incurable malady and that we would be "sick" or "disabled" for the rest of our lives. We were told that if we continued with recommended treatments and therapies, we could learn to "adjust" and "cope" from day to day.

Needless to say, we didn't believe our doctors and social workers. In fact, we adamantly denied and raged against these bleak prophesies for our lives. We felt it was all just a mistake, a bad dream, a temporary setback in our lives. We just knew that in a week or two, things would get back to normal again. We felt our teenage world was still there, just waiting for us to return to it. Our denial was an important stage in our recovery. It was a normal reaction to an overwhelming situation. It was our way of surviving those first awful months.

The weeks passed us by but we did not get better. It became harder and harder to believe we would ever be the same again. What initially had seemed like a fleeting bad dream transformed into a deepening nightmare from which we could not awake. We felt like ships floating on a black sea with no course or bearings. We found ourselves drifting farther and farther away from the young, carefree people we had been. He lay horizontal and in traction while his friends were selected to play ball for prestigious colleges. I stood drugged and stiff in the hallways of a mental hospital while my classmates went off to their first year of college.

We experienced time as a betrayer. Time did not heal us. Our pasts deserted us and we could not return to who we had been. Our futures appeared to us to be barren, lifeless places in which no dream could be planted and grow into a reality. As for the present, it was a numbing succession of meaningless days and nights in a world in which we had no place, no use, and no reason to be. Boredom and wishfulness became our only refuge (Knowles, 1986).

Our denial gave way to despair and anguish. We both gave up. Giving up was a solution for us. It numbed the pain of our despair because we stopped asking "why and how will I go on?" (Harrison, 1984). Giving up meant that for 14 years he sat in the day rooms of institutions gazing at soap operas, watching others live their lives. For months I sat in a chair in my family's living room, smoking cigarettes and waiting until it was 8:00 p.m. so I could go back to bed. At this time even the simplest of tasks were overwhelming. I remember being asked to come into the kitchen to help knead some bread dough. I got up, went into the kitchen, and looked at the dough for what seemed an eternity. Then I walked back to my chair and wept. The task seemed overwhelming to me. Later I learned the reason for this: when one lives without hope, (when one has given up) the willingness to "do" is paralyzed as well.

All of us who have experienced catastrophic illness and disability know this experience of anguish and despair. It is living in darkness without hope, without a past or a future. It is self-pity. It is hatred of everything that is good and life giving. It is rage turned inward. It is a wound with no mouth, a wound that is so deep that no cry can emanate from it. Anguish is a death from which there appears to be no resurrection. It is inertia that paralyzes the will to do and to accomplish because there is no hope. It is being truly disabled, not by a disease or injury, but by despair. This part of the recovery process is a dark night in which even God was felt to have abandoned us. For some of us this dark night lasts moments, days, or months. For others it lasts for years. For others, the despair and anguish may never end.

Neither Brad nor I could remember a specific moment when the small and fragile flame of hope and courage illuminated the darkness of our despair. We do remember that even when we had given up, there were those who loved us and did not give up. They did not abandon us. They were powerless to change us and they could not make us better. They could not climb this mountain for us but they were willing to suffer with us. They did not overwhelm us with their optimistic plans for our futures but they remained hopeful despite the odds. Their love for us was like a constant invitation, calling us forth to be something more than all of this self-pity and despair. The miracle was that gradually Brad and I began to hear and respond to this loving invitation.

For 14 years Brad slouched in front of the television in the hell of his own despair and anguish. For months I sat and smoked cigarettes until it was time to collapse back into a drugged and dreamless sleep. But one day, something changed in us. A tiny, fragile spark of hope appeared and promised that there could be something more than all of this darkness. This is the third phase of recovery. This is the mystery. This is the grace. This is the birth of hope called forth by the possibility of being loved. All of the polemic and technology of psychiatry, psychology, social work, and science cannot account for this phenomenon of hope. But those of us who have recovered know that this grace is real. We lived it. It is our shared secret.

It is important to understand that for most of us recovery is not a sudden conversion experience. Hope does not come to us as a sudden bolt of lightning that jolts us into a whole new way of being. Hope is the turning point that must quickly be followed by the willingness to act. Brad and I began in little ways with small triumphs and simple acts of courage: He shaved, he attempted to read a book, and he talked with a counselor; I rode in the car, I shopped on Wednesdays, and I talked to a friend for a few minutes. He applied for benefits, he got a van and learned to drive; I took responsibility for my medications, took a part-time job, and had my own money. He went to college so he could work professionally with other people experiencing disabilities; I went to school to become a psychologist so I could work with people experiencing disabilities. One day at a time, with multiple setbacks, we rebuilt our lives. We rebuilt our lives on the three cornerstones of recovery—hope, willingness, and responsible action. We learned to say: "I am hopeful;" "I am willing to try;" and "I discover that I can do" (Knowles, 1986). This is the process of recovery that is the ground from which springs effective use of rehabilitation services.

Recovery does not refer to an end product or result. It does not mean that Brad and I were "cured." In fact, our recovery is marked by an ever-deepening acceptance of our limitations. But now, rather than being an occasion for despair, we find that our personal limitations are the ground from which spring our own unique possibilities. This is the paradox of recovery, i.e., that in accepting what we cannot do or be, we begin to discover who we can be and what we can do.

Recovery does not refer to an absence of pain or struggle. Rather, recovery is marked by the transition from anguish to suffering. In anguish Brad and I lived without hope. We experienced anguish as futile pain, pain that revolved in circles, pain that bore no possibility other than more pain, and pain that lead nowhere. However, when we became hopeful, our anguish was transformed into true suffering. True suffering is marked by an inner peace, i.e.,

We rebuilt our lives on the three cornerstones of recovery—hope, willingness, and responsible action.

although we still felt great pain, we also experienced a peace in knowing that this pain was leading us forward into a new future. A biologist who has spina bifida captures this spirit of true suffering in recovery when she writes: "Suffering is peaceful. You know the pain may kill you, but it won't destroy you. In a very risky way, you are safe" (Harrison, 1984).

For many of us who have disabilities, recovery is a process, a way of life, an attitude, and a way of approaching the day's challenges. It is not a perfectly linear process. At times our course is erratic and we falter, slide back, re-group and start again. Our experience of recovery is similar to that described by the poet Roethke (1948/1975) who himself experienced major mental illness:

CUTTINGS
...One nub of growth
Nudges a sand-crumb loose,
Pokes through a musty sheath
Its pale tendrilous horn.

CUTTINGS
(later)
This urge, wrestle, resurrection of dry sticks,
Cut stems struggling to put down feet,
What saint strained so much,
Rose on such lopped limbs to a new life?...(p.35)

Recovery is the urge, the wrestle, and the resurrection. Recovery is a matter of rising on lopped limbs to a new life. As professionals we would like nothing more than to somehow manufacture the spirit of recovery and give it to each of our program participants. But this is impossible. We cannot force recovery to happen in our rehabilitation programs. Essential aspects of the recovery process are a matter of grace and, therefore, cannot be willed. However, we can create environments in which the recovery process can be nurtured like a tender and precious seedling. Some of the principles for creating such environments in rehabilitation programs are given below.

Recovery in Rehabilitation Programs

As we have seen, recovery is not a linear process marked by successive accomplishments. The recovery process is more accurately described as a series of small beginnings and very small steps. To recover, persons with psychiatric disabilities must be willing to try and fail, and try again. Too often, rehabilitation programs are structured in such a way as to work against this process of recovery. These programs tend to have rigid guidelines for acceptance. They tend to have linear program designs in which a person must enter at point "A" and move through a series of consecutive steps to arrive at point "B." Failure at any point along the way will require that participants return to entry level. Finally, some of these programs define failure in absolute terms, e.g., a program participant dropped from a vocational placement for failing to attend work for X number of days is simultaneously dropped from the program and must completely re-apply to the program when ready to accept the program's rules and expectations. In all of these ways, the design and structure of

Rehabilitation programs can be environments that nurture recovery if they are structured to embrace, and indeed expect, the approach/avoid, try/fail dynamic that is the recovery process.

rehabilitation programming can work against the process of recovery.

Rehabilitation programs can be environments that nurture recovery if they are structured to embrace, and indeed expect, the approach/avoid, try/fail dynamic that is the recovery process. This means that rehabilitation programs must have very flexible entry criteria and easy accessibility. The design of rehabilitation programming must be nonlinear, i.e., with multiple points of entry and levels of entry into programming. The real challenge of rehabilitation programs is to create fail-proof program models. A program is fail-proof when participants are always able to come back, pick-up where they left off, and try again. In a fail-proof environment where one is welcomed, valued, and wanted, recovering persons can make the most effective use of rehabilitation services.

A second point regarding the establishment of rehabilitation environments conducive to the recovery process derives from the understanding that each person's journey of recovery is unique. Of course, there are certain fundamental constituents of the process of recovery that are similar in all persons with a disability, e.g., the experience of despair and the transition to hope, willingness, and responsible action. However, people with disabilities are, above all, individuals and will find their own special formula for what promotes their recovery and what does not. Therefore, it is important to offer persons in recovery a wide variety of rehabilitation program options from which to choose, e.g., supported work programs, social clubs, transitional employment programs, consumer-run drop-in centers and businesses, workshops, skill training programs, and college support programs.

Consumer-run self-help groups, self-help networks, and advocacy/lobbyist groups can also be important resources for persons in recovery and should be available as options. Of course, these important resources can only be established and maintained by persons recovering from psychiatric disability. Creating these resources, as well as linking with other persons with disabilities and sharing existing resources, is one of the greatest challenges that face those of us who are recovering.

Additionally, if we truly hope to offer a wide variety of rehabilitation programs to persons with psychiatric disabilities, then it is important to examine the values upon which so much of our programming is based. Too often we project traditional "American" values on people with disabilities, e.g., rugged individualism, competition, personal achievement, and self-sufficiency. Too often our program models have tacitly adopted these, and only these, values. We might ask ourselves: Are all of our local area's vocational rehabilitation programs built on a competitive model in which individual achievement is stressed more than cooperative group efforts? Are our residential rehabilitation programs all geared toward preparing people to live independently?

For some people with psychiatric disabilities, especially those who relapse frequently, these traditional values of competition, individual achievement, independence, and self-sufficiency are oppressive. Programs that are tacitly built on these values are invitations to failure for many persons in recovery. For these persons, "independent living" amounts to the loneliness of four walls in the corner of some rooming house. For these persons, "individual vocational achievement" amounts to failing

one vocational program after another until they come to believe they are worthless human beings with nothing to contribute. For these persons, an alternative type of rehabilitation program, and even lifestyle, should be available as an option. Instead of competitive vocational training based on individual achievement, a cooperative work setting stressing group achievement could be established. The value here is cooperation in the achievement of work goals and the sharing of responsibility for work production so that the group or work community can compensate for the individual during periods of relapse. Residential program options should include the possibility for communal living situations such as the L'Arche communities pioneered by Jean Vanier (Dunne, 1986; Vanier, 1979; Vanier & Wolfensberger, 1974). When these types of options are made available and exist alongside rehabilitation programs based on more traditional values, then we can feel confident that we are offering a truly comprehensive network of services from which persons in recovery can choose their own course of rehabilitation.

The third recommendation for creating programs that enhance recovery involves recognition of the gift that people with disabilities have to give to each other. This gift is their hope, strength, and experience as lived in the recovery process. In this sense, persons with disabilities can become role models for one another. During that dark night of anguish and despair when individuals live without hope, the presence of other persons in recovery can challenge that despair through example. It becomes very difficult to continue to convince oneself that there is no hope when one is surrounded by others with disabilities who are making strides in their recovery!

Hope is contagious and that is why it is so important to hire people with disabilities in rehabilitation programs. Because recovery is a phenomenon that is similar for all people with disabilities, it can be very effective to have persons with divergent disabilities act as role models for one another. Additionally, a person need not be "fully recovered" in order to serve as a role model. Very often a person with a disability who is only a few "steps" ahead of another person can be more effective than one whose achievements seem overly impressive and distanced.

Finally, and perhaps most fundamentally, staff attitudes are very important in shaping rehabilitation environments. There are a number of common staff attitudes that are particularly unhelpful to persons in recovery. For instance, too often staff attitudes reflect the implicit supposition that there is the "world of the abnormal" and the "world of the normal." The task facing the staff is to somehow get the people in the "abnormal world" to fit into the "normal world." This creates an us/them dichotomy wherein "they" (persons with disabilities) are expected to do all of the changing and growing. Such an attitude places staff in a very safe position in which they can maintain the illusion that they are not disabled, that they are not wounded in any way, and that they have no need to live the spirit of recovery in their own lives. Indeed, when the us/them attitude prevails, "staff" and "clients" are truly worlds apart. Such an environment is oppressive to those individuals with disabilities who are struggling with their own recovery.

If a rehabilitation program is to be a dynamic setting that promotes and nurtures the recovery process, then the rigid walls separating the "world of the disabled" and the "world of the normal" must be torn down. Staff members must be helped to recognize the ways in which they, too, are deeply wounded. Perhaps they have experienced anguish in their lives or perhaps they have known personal tragedy or struggle. To embrace and accept our own woundedness and vulnerability is the first step toward understanding the experience of persons with disabilities. In so doing we discover that we share a common humanity with them and that we are not "worlds apart."

A dynamic rehabilitation environment is one in which staff members are vitally involved in their own personal growth and/or recovery. Therefore, they empathize deeply with the woundedness and vulnerability that persons with disabilities experience. They understand that in some mysterious way to be human means that all of us must "rise on lopped limbs" to a new life.

References

Dunne, J. (1986). Sense of community in L'Arche and in the writings of Jean Vanier. *Daybreak Monograph 20.* Richmond Hill, Ontario: Daybreak Publications.

Harrison, V. (1984). A biologist's view of pain, suffering and marginal life. In F. Dougherty (Ed.), *The deprived, the disabled and the fullness of life.* Delaware: Michael Glazier.

Knowles, R. T. (1986). *Human development and human possibility: Erikson in the light of Heidegger.* Lanham: University Press of America.

Roethke, T. (1948/1975). The lost son and other poems. In *The collected poems of Theodore Roethke.* New York: Anchor Press/Doubleday.

Vanier, J., & Wolfensberger, W. (1974). Growing together: *Daybreak Monograph 2.* Richmond Hill, Ontario: Daybreak Publications.

How I Perceive and Manage My Illness

Esso Leete

ESSO LEETE IS THE FOUNDER OF THE DENVER SOCIAL SUPPORT GROUP, ONE OF THE OLDEST PEER-RUN GROUPS IN DENVER. AS A PRIMARY MENTAL HEALTH CONSUMER, SHE IS ON MANY LOCAL COMMITTEES AND BOARDS. SHE SERVED AS FIRST VICE-PRESIDENT OF THE CLIENT COUNCIL OF THE NATIONAL ALLIANCE FOR THE MENTALLY ILL. SHE HAS BEEN DESIGNATED A NATIONAL SWITZER SCHOLAR AND HAS RECEIVED AN AWARD FOR THE MOST OUTSTANDING CONSUMER ADVOCATE IN COLORADO FOR THE LAST 25 YEARS. SHE HAS BEEN EMPLOYED FOR 11 YEARS AS A MEDICAL RECORDS TRANSCRIBER AT THE COLORADO MENTAL HEALTH INSTITUTE AT FORT LOGAN..

THIS ARTICLE ORIGINALLY APPEARED IN THE *Schizophrenia Bulletin,* 1989, 15(2), 197-200.

The article describes some of the ongoing problems psychiatric patients encounter on a daily basis as perceived by an individual who has lived with schizophrenia for more than 25 years. Specific carefully planned coping strategies which are seen as critical to the recovery process are presented.

More than by any other one thing, my life has been changed by schizophrenia. For the past 20 years I have lived with it and in spite of it—struggling to come to terms with it without giving in to it. Although I have fought a daily battle, it is only now that I have some sense of confidence that I will survive my ordeal. Taking responsibility for my life and developing coping mechanisms has been crucial to my recovery. I would like to share some of these with the reader now.

To maintain my mental health, I found I had to change my priorities and take better care of myself. I modified my attitudes, becoming more accepting and nonjudg-

mental of others. In addition, I altered my behavior and response to symptoms. I have also had to plan for the use of my time. When one has a chaotic inner existence, the structure of a predictable daily schedule makes life easier. Now, obviously structured activity can be anything, but for me it is work—a paying job, the ultimate goal. It gives me something to look forward to every day and a skill to learn and to improve. It is my motivation for getting up each morning. In addition, my hours are passed therapeutically as well as productively. As I work, I become increasingly self-confident and my self-image is bolstered. I feel important and grownup, which replaces my usual sense of vulnerability, weakness, and incompetence. Being a member of the work force decreases stigma and contributes to acceptance by my community, which in turn makes my life easier.

Research continues to show that one of the differences between the brain of a "normal" person and one who has schizophrenia is a major difficulty filtering or screening out background noises. I am hyperalert, acutely aware of every sound or movement in my environment. I am often confused by repetitive noises or multiple stimuli and become nervous, impatient, and irritable. To deal with this, I make a deliberate effort to reduce distractions as much as possible.

I often have difficulty interacting with others socially and tend to withdraw. I have found I feel more comfortable, however, if I socialize with others who have similar interests or experiences to my own. To counteract my problem with poor eye contact, I force myself to look up from time to time, even if I have to look a little past the person with whom I am speaking. If I do become overwhelmed in a social situation, I may temporarily withdraw by going into another room (even the restroom) to be alone for a while.

I attempt to keep in touch with my feelings and to attend immediately to difficulties, including symptoms like paranoia. For example, instead of constantly worrying about the police surprising me, I always choose a seat where I can face the door, preferably with my back to a wall instead of to other people. In general, instead of working myself up emotionally over some threatening possibility, I will check out reality by asking the people I am with questions like who they are calling, where they are going, or whatever. It clears the air immediately, and usually I am satisfied with their answer and can go on about my business. In other words, I cope by recognizing and confronting my paranoid fears immediately and then moving on with my life, freeing my mind for other things. Also, I have learned to suppress paranoid responses, and I make an effort not to talk to myself or to my voices when others are nearby. It can be done through self-discipline and practice.

In addition, I suffer from feelings of isolation, alienation, and loneliness. This is difficult to deal with because on the one hand I need to be with people, but on the other hand I am frightened of it. I have come to realize my own diminished capacity for really close friendships, but also my need for many acquaintances. An ongoing and reliable support system has been extremely important. I have gained much practical information, insight, and support from my peer-run support group, a very comfortable means of coming to accept and deal with mental illness. Also, it has been invaluable to have someone I trust (often my husband) with whom I can "test

We struggle constantly with our raging fears and the brutality of our thoughts, and then we are subjected as well to the misunderstanding, distrust, and ongoing stigma we experience from the community.

reality." I let him know my perceptions and he gives me feedback. I am then able to consider the possibility that my perceptions may not be accurate, and I modify my response accordingly if I wish. In this way I can usually acknowledge more conventional ways of thinking, instead of automatically incorporating outside information into my delusional system.

A common complaint from persons with a mental illness is that of impaired concentration and memory. This can make holding a job or even completing a thought very difficult. To overcome the effects of a poor memory, I make lists and write down all information of importance. Through years of effort I have managed to develop an incredible amount of concentration, although I am only able to sustain this for relatively brief periods of time.

Sometimes I still find it difficult to keep my thoughts together. I therefore request that communication be simple, clear, and unambiguous. It helps me if the information is specific, as vague or diffuse responses only confuse me. When speaking to someone I may need more time to think and understand before responding, and I take this time. Likewise, I have learned when working on a task to be careful, perhaps taking more time than others, and to concentrate fiercely on what I am doing. And I must be persistent.

Many times when becoming acutely ill, I am frightened of everything, feeling small and vulnerable. When I am in distress, I do whatever makes me feel better. This may be pacing, curling up into a ball, or rocking back and forth. I have found that most of these behaviors can be accomplished without appearing too strange, believe it or not. For example, I can pace by taking a walk, I can curl up when I sleep, and I can rock in a rocking chair or hammock or even by going to an amusement park. I am often able to relax by physically exercising, reading, or watching a movie. In general, then, I think I am discovering how to appear less bizarre.

I find it crucial to schedule time between events rigidly. For example, I will not agree to give two talks on the same day. I find I must also give myself as much time as I can in which to make decisions; I have an enormous amount of ambivalence, and pressure to come to a decision quickly can immobilize me. (It is not a pretty picture.) Too much free time is also detrimental. Therefore, I find it useful to structure my leisure time and to limit it. Perhaps some day I will be able to handle it in greater increments, but for now I find it best to keep very busy, with minimal amounts of leisure time.

Perhaps the coping strategy I use the most is compulsive organizing. I think a controlled environment is probably so important to me because my brain is not always manageable. Making lists organizes my thoughts. It also increases self-esteem, because when I have accomplished something and crossed it off my list, it is a very concrete indication to me that I am capable of setting a goal, working toward it, and actually accomplishing it. These "small" successes build my confidence to go out and try other things. As a part of this process, I break down tasks into small steps, taking them one at a time. Perhaps organizing and

There is nothing more devastating, discrediting, and disabling to an individual recovering from mental illness than stigma.

giving speeches about my illness is another coping skill—and the audience response is a type of reality-testing.

In general, then, I believe I do have an irritable brain. I am supersensitive to any stimulus. My behavior is sometimes erratic, and I am easily frustrated and extremely impulsive. I regret that I still have times of uncontrollable angry outbursts. I cope with these and other symptoms by taking low doses of medication. Before I came to realize the role medications could play in my illness, I was caught in a vicious circle. When I was off the medication, I couldn't remember how much better I had felt on it, and when I was taking the medication, I felt so good that I was convinced I did not need it. Fortunately, through many years of trial and error, I have learned what medication works best for me and when to take it to minimize side effects based on my daily schedule. Increasing my medication periodically is one means I often use for stabilization during a particularly stressful period.

I want to emphasize that stress does play a major role in my illness. There are enormous pressures that come with any new experience or new environment, and any change, positive or negative, is extremely difficult. Whatever I can do to decrease or avoid high-stress situations or environments is helpful in controlling my symptoms. In general terms, all of my coping strategies largely consist of four steps: 1) recognizing when I am feeling stressed, which is harder than it may sound; 2) identifying the stressor; 3) remembering from past experience what action helped in the same situation or a similar one; and 4) taking that action as quickly as possible. After I have identified a potential source of stress, I prepare mentally for the situation by anticipating problems. Knowing what to expect in a new situation considerably lowers my anxiety about it. In addition, I try to recognize my own particular limitations and plan in advance, setting reasonable goals.

Please understand that these are the kinds of obstacles that confront individuals with a psychiatric disorder every day. Yet we are perceived as weak. On the contrary, I believe we are among the most courageous. We struggle constantly with our raging fears and the brutality of our thoughts, and then we are subjected as well to the misunderstanding, distrust, and ongoing stigma we experience from the community. Believe me, there is nothing more devastating, discrediting, and disabling to an individual recovering from mental illness than stigma.

Life is hard with a diagnosis of schizophrenia. I can talk, but I may not be heard. I can make suggestions, but they may not be taken seriously. I can report my thoughts, but they may be seen as delusions. I can recite experiences, but they may be interpreted as fantasies. To be a patient or even ex-client is to be discounted. Your label is a reality that never leaves you; it gradually shapes an identity that is hard to shed. We must transform public attitudes and current stereotypes. Until we eliminate stigma, we will have prejudice, which will inevitably be expressed as discrimination against persons with mental illness.

We rarely read about people who have successfully dealt with their emotional

I cope by recognizing and confronting my paranoid fears immediately and then moving on with my life, freeing my mind for other things.

problems and are making it, and they will not usually identify themselves to us because they are all too aware of the general attitude. The current image the public has of the mentally ill must be changed, not to mention that of the individual himself. We have grown up in the same society and have the same feelings about mental illness, but we must also live with the label.

Ultimately we must conquer stigma from within. As a first step—and a crucial one—it is imperative for us as clients to look within ourselves for our strengths. These strengths are the tools for rebuilding our self-image and thus our self-esteem. I found that I first had to convince myself of my worthiness, then worry about others. Each time I am successful at a task it serves to reinforce my own capabilities and boost my confidence. Just this way, persons with mental illness can and must change the views and expectations of others.

Obviously, education about mental illness is critical for all parties involved, especially for the patient. I have made an extensive study of my disorder and have found education invaluable in understanding my illness, coming to terms with it, and dealing with it. We must conscientiously and continually study our illnesses and learn for ourselves what we can do to cope with the individual disabilities we experience.

Many of us have learned to monitor symptoms to determine the status of our illness, using our coping mechanisms to prevent psychotic relapse or to seek treatment earlier, thereby reducing the number of acute episodes and hospitalizations. My own personal warning signs of decompensation include fatigue or decreased sleep; difficulty with concentration and memory; increased paranoia, delusions, and hallucinations; tenseness and irritability; agitation; and being more easily overwhelmed by my surroundings. Coping mechanisms may include withdrawing and being alone for a while; obtaining support from a friend; socializing or otherwise distracting myself from stressors; organizing my thoughts through lists; problem-solving around specific issues; or temporarily increasing my medication.

Yet too many times our efforts to cope go unnoticed or are seen as symptoms themselves. If others understood us better, perhaps they would be more tolerant. We did not choose to be ill, but we can choose to deal with it and learn to live with it. By learning to modulate stress, we will more effectively manage our illness, thus endowing ourselves with an ongoing sense of mastery and control. I find my vulnerability to stress, anxiety, and accompanying symptoms decreases the more I am in control of my own life. Unfortunately, our progress continues to be measured by professionals with concepts like "consent" and "cooperate" and "comply" instead of "choose," insinuating that we are incapable of taking an active role as partners in our own recovery.

I see my schizophrenia as a mental disorder with a genetic predisposition, predictably expressing itself in times of extreme stress, but often exacerbated by rather ordinary fluctuations in my environment. Mental illness is a handicap with biological, psychological, and social ramifications, making it a formidable obstacle to be overcome. I understand that life may be more difficult for me than for others and that I must preside over it more attentively for this reason. As with other chronic illnesses, it has demanded that I work harder than most. I know to expect good and bad times and to make the most of the good. I take

my life very seriously and do as much with it as I can when I am feeling well, because I know that I will have difficult times again and will likely lose some of my gains.

Although there is no magic answer to the tragedy of mental illness, I contend that we need not be at its mercy. Appropriate treatment can help us understand our disease and we can learn to function in spite of it. We can overcome our illness and the myths surrounding it. We can successfully compensate for our disabilities. We can overcome the stigma, prejudice, discrimination, and rejection we have experienced and reclaim our personal validity, our dignity as individuals, and our autonomy. To do this, we must change the image of who we are and who we can become, first for ourselves and then for the public. If we do acknowledge and seriously study our illnesses; if we build on our assets; if we work to minimize our vulnerabilities by developing coping skills; if we confront our illnesses with courage and struggle with our symptoms persistently—we will successfully manage our lives and bestow our talents on society, the society that has traditionally abandoned us.

The Schizophrenic Inside

Patricia J. Ruocchio

PATRICIA J. RUOCCHIO, B.A., IS A
WRITER WHO HAS PUBLISHED ARTICLES IN THE
*American Journal of Psychiatry, Hospital and Community
Psychiatry, The New York Times, and Schizophrenia Bulletin.*
MS. RUOCCHIO ALSO WRITES FOR TRADE PUBLICATIONS
AND HAS BEEN SELECTED TO APPEAR IN
Who's Who Among U.S. Writers, Editors, and Poets.

THIS ARTICLE ORIGINALLY APPEARED IN THE
Schizophrenia Bulletin, 1991. 17(2), 357-360.

There are many things that cannot be adequately said about schizophrenia, things to which language greatly pales. No one can know what fills the empty spaces of blocked thoughts, what hell lurks within the unyielding walls of a skull that traps the schizophrenic inside his own torturous mind. My greatest fear is this brain of mine, which torments me in times of psychosis, always threatens me, and seems to always be laughing at me, scorning my vulnerability. The worst thing imaginable is to be terrified of one's own mind, the very matter that controls all that we are and all that we do and feel.

Initially what led me to want to say what cannot be said about my illness was a desire to communicate the chaos that goes on beneath the veneer of what is called "thought blocking." For the outsider looking on, the patient is talking and simply stops, the idea he was trying to communicate simply terminated. But this is not so. The idea has not been obliterated, but conquered by forces in the brain that have the power to halt meaningful communication and block the schizophrenic's connection with the very person or persons he wishes so desperately to hold on to. He is tortured as his voice turns mute and he sees his lifelines being cut by his own inability to complete the fervent thoughts that now choke him. I am often caught in guttural struggles with my own voice as I try to get the words out. These aborted thoughts not lost, but taken over by a more powerful chaos, are among the things that cannot be said.

Sometimes what is even more telling, though less painful for me, are what the clinicians call "loose associations"—one blocked thought following quickly on the heels of another. At least if I am loose associating I am communicating something, even if it is the disorganization of my mind and its desire to keep me from focusing. This kind of talking is a shield that prevents me from talking about something that is greatly troubling to me, so desperately wanting to get out and make itself coherent to someone else, but for some reason lost in a hodgepodge of miscellaneous half sentences. Just as I struggle with my voice when thoughts are blocked and trapped, I battle to gain control over the unwieldy words that pour from my mouth, confusing me, frustrating me, and literally tying me down and making me prey once again to the whims of what my brain chooses to allow my lips to utter.

There is agony in not being able to communicate one's mind. The destined target is there, within physical touch, but a thousand miles away if he cannot be touched with words, cannot hear what is in my head. The abysmal aloneness I feel is only made worse by the physical closeness of someone with whom I am trying so desperately to connect. I want to infuse my mind into his, to show him what is happening in there, but I am blocked by the limitations of inadequate words, a brain that scrambles thoughts, and a bony structure that will not let me pass beyond its boundaries.

Most devastating is the anger or impatience I have felt from friends and less practiced mental health workers in response to my psychotic ramblings. I tend to repeat the same things from one episode to another, ask the same questions, and be confused by the same ideas. My concerns are the same, the conflicts blocked before are blocked again and therefore remain uncommunicated, unexpressed in the way I am trying so desperately to convey them. It is hard for people to tolerate my always asking the same questions, repeating the same phrases, being troubled by the same abstractions of the world which make no sense to me. If only they could know that when I repeat certain things each time, it is not these words I am trying to express. These repeated ramblings rather are code words for things that send me into psychosis because of their unbearable torture but then cannot be revealed within that realm either. Not only am I alone with my demons, but I also cannot depict them and can only repeat the same code words over and over, putting off those who can stand to hear them only so many times.

I picked up the words interpersonal terror years ago and have clung to them as perhaps the most apt description of what the schizophrenic experiences—a fear of reaching out and an even greater fear of allowing anyone to get close.

My own inadequacy to use language to express what lies buried so deeply inside me, even when I am lucid, makes words a curse that blocks the proverbial light within the tunnel, and I am alone with my darkness. There are things that happen to me that I have never found words for, some lost now, some which I still search desperately to explain, as if time is running out and what I see and feel will be lost to the depths of chaos forever. With each uncommunicated experience the darkness grows. For each light that is turned on when I can make someone understand, there is another that lies inside me, unable to make itself known, a thing that keeps me from ever showing the totality of my mind to anyone. Perhaps this is my protection, for in this way I remain an island unto myself.

This disconnection is not conscious, even if it be by choice. I cannot control what can or cannot be conveyed. I can only continue the struggle to make my inner being known to those I feel safe with, suffering through the blocks where no words come, fighting to get control of a wandering mind. When I am blocked by confusion, or a total scrambling of my thoughts, interjections of obtuse phrases, and coded associations I cannot explain, I can only go through it and accept it as what my brain does. The triggers are so infinite and arbitrary it is difficult to pin them down or anticipate them. There is a kind or sadness mixed with the frantic effort to escape from the waters closing over my head. For a while at least, my mind wins and I drown, if I am able, allowing myself to ride with it, become passive for the duration, saving my energy for the long and painful process of resuscitation and revival.

It is this temporary giving in to death that is so difficult when one feels such terror. But when it can happen, it is with a great sadness that one resigns oneself to the illness It feels like a defeat, but it is also an acceptance and a working with the psychosis to realize that this is where your mind needs to be at this time. For me, it always runs its course. I always come around again, but to stop the wild thrashings of the drowning victim takes trust, the ability to live with excruciating pain and terror, and the ability to call upon a self that has learned about its own nature. I do not think anyone can truly come to a feeling of peace about giving in when it is necessary, but to learn to do it reserves the strength needed for the next time.

Between the drownings and flowing with the tide, I still strive as much as I can to visualize the inner mind that has claimed me as its own. I attempt to reproduce its image with the most accurate words I know to give to my therapist. The reason I do this after so much time and so many visions lost to chaos and unreason is that if I am to survive this maelstrom called schizophrenia, I must continuously try to gain the comprehension I need to withstand each plunge into darkness and find a way to share as much as I can in a way that will make me feel the least alone. And so I continue to try to say what cannot be said about schizophrenia, for I believe that if I search long and hard enough, the words will someday come.

The Psychological Phenomenon

Although one cannot deny the role of biological function, or rather malfunction, in the origins of schizophrenia, the interplay between psyche and brain matter cannot be denied. In fact, it is often fascinating as one learns how the physiology of the illness can trigger emotional changes and vice

My own inadequacy to use language to express what lies buried so deeply inside me, even when I am lucid, makes words a curse that blocks the proverbial light within the tunnel, and I am alone with my darkness.

versa. Sometimes there is a chain reaction where one component will be set off and then the other becomes disturbed and on and on until you find yourself spiraling into a maze of insanity.

Sometimes in going forward in our understanding it is most helpful to go backward to earlier perceptions of the illness that developed before medications were available that effectively curbed the most debilitating symptoms. I say this because in looking back at literature from the 1960s and 1970s, I find that although much of my pathology has been aided by medication, I retain many of the basic psychological beliefs that the completely regressed schizophrenic experiences. For example, I was quite surprised to learn that my safety shield, the wall of glass that separates and protects me from the world when it gets too frightening, has always been noted in schizophrenics and is actually called by some the "wall of glass syndrome." Even more interesting is the belief I share with many schizophrenics that I am real and the rest of the world unreal. The two realities have become my secret, to be shared only with those I am closest to. The sharing of my secret realities feels painful and arduous as I try to explain what I experience to my therapists.

The urgent need to have another person understand exactly what I experience inside is another psychological state that goes beyond curtailment of overt symptoms. Although on the outside things seem to have calmed down greatly, on the inside there is a storm raging, a storm that frightens me when I feel that I am alone in it. The desperate need for complete and total understanding of the workings of one's brain leads to an intense desire to merge with another human being. So powerful is this desire that I often speak fervently of the wish to place my therapist inside my brain so that he can just know what is happening inside me. It is perhaps a sign of growing health that I will now occasionally speak of taking my brain out and laying it on the floor for him to see, thus giving him access to and understanding of all that I am while the two of us remain separate beings. Gradually, over the course of many years of hard work, my ego is becoming stronger.

There is agony in not being able to communicate one's mind.

However, this improvement usually manifests itself with treaters, and my fear of people, or as some have called it, "interpersonal terror," remains. I picked up the words *interpersonal terror* years ago and have clung to them as perhaps the most apt description of what the schizophrenic experiences—a fear of reaching out and an even greater fear of allowing anyone to get close. Bizarre, even violent, behavior on the part of schizophrenic individuals is a vehicle by which they can "frighten away" other people so that they do not have to experience this interpersonal terror. I tend to try to frighten people with my hostile stares or the glazed, crazy look that can come into my eyes when I myself am frightened and become disoriented. On a more conscious level, I will sometimes make the profuse scars on my arms very visible and watch for a reaction from anyone that sees them. I usually want people to be repulsed and awed by these signs or violence.

If I cannot actively make people around me disappear, I try to disappear myself, I tend to withdraw more than attack, sometimes feeling myself melt into an inanimate object, actually becoming a chair or a wall, and sometimes just withdrawing my consciousness back to the time when I was psychotic all the time, living in a world that existed only to me. I do not willfully become psychotic, but there are many times that I feel so vulnerable that I need to pull away from the rest of the world and let my mind take over. The wall and the glass dome that isolated my world and made me the only being in existence. The Creator and the Sufferer have been internalized. Although I now recognize that other people exist and forces do not swirl from within trees, the psychological basis for creating such a world still exists and the forces have changed over time into The People in my head who come out to torture me. Although medication has curtailed the activity of The People, there have been times when they have subliminally tempted me to stop my medications so that they could once again appear. Now in times of stress I feel them as demons, less powerful, but presences nonetheless that make me know that despite outwardly normal behavior, my psyche has not yet totally healed.

Schizophrenia: Some Issues

Jill Stainsby

JILL STAINSBY WAS FIRST DIAGNOSED AS HAVING
SCHIZOPHRENIA IN 1977. IN 1991 SHE EARNED A
MASTER'S DEGREE FROM SIMON FRASER UNIVERSITY,
BURNABY, BRITISH COLUMBIA, CANADA. SHE IS
CURRENTLY EMPLOYED AS A UNION COORDINATOR.

THIS ARTICLE ORIGINALLY APPEARED IN THE
Schizophrenia Bulletin, 1992, 18(3), 543-546.

Schizophrenia is real. Mental illness is a medical event. As David Ransom (1990) wrote:

> In the 1960s and 1970s many people like me who thought of themselves as "progressive" came to believe that mental illness did not exist. There was a strange comfort in the idea that a society of everyone except ourselves was "manufacturing" mental illness. But when we faced its devastating impact on the lives of people we knew, we had no idea what to do. Too often we chose to forget they existed rather than acknowledge they were mentally ill. We blamed "psychiatry" and ran away. [p. 5]

This avoidance of the issue of mental illness can, unfortunately, often be found among people who have not had much experience with mental distress. For many of us, however, being involved when someone among our family or friends has experienced mental trauma, occasionally to the point where they have needed medical treatment or hospitalization, has been very challenging. Several of us have tried to keep people out of the medical system when they were not coping because of mental or emotional dysfunctions. We have also tried to stay out of hospitals or off drugs ourselves when we were in such a state. Several of us have come home from our experience of medical intervention and denied we needed it or described the experience as unnecessary torture. I do not intend to negate anybody else's experience.

At the same time, I do not expect others to refuse me the right to my beliefs regarding mind-suffering. Saying that mental illness is a result of social pressures and is therefore somehow not real is like saying a broken leg does not need fixing because it's the scaffolding that you fell off that was unsafe. The fact is, the unsafe scaffolding created a situation in which your leg broke, and you need a cast. To assert anything else is to risk having the leg mend crookedly or not at all. Our society does tend to provide the precondition of stress that may be required before a person develops schizophrenia. Once that has happened, that person needs help in dealing with the illness.

People who are experiencing hallucinations, delusions, or thought disorders of any disorienting kind need care: and if their condition is deteriorating rather than improving, they need increasing levels of care. I think this is straightforward. If they can maintain themselves as they are, then they need only whatever help they ask for.

Schizophrenia is a chronic or episodic family of illnesses that responds to various treatments. Approximately one third of the people who are diagnosed as experiencing it recover and do not experience another episode of disjunction from reality, according to mental health workers; one third respond positively to drugs; and one third continue to have symptoms, whether drugged or not. It's that middle third of those of us who are diagnosed with schizophrenia who are served badly by political or personal arguments against intervention by the medical establishment. To be told "your fiends will help you get over this" is to deny that perhaps the leg I described above is really broken. This denial also puts a severe strain on those friends.

I do not disagree with the "antipsychiatry" movement completely. I agree that many therapies are at best useless and at worst dangerous and destructive. I believe that psychoanalysis and Freudian theory are both more damaging and dishonest than helpful for people who are questioning their own world view. What serves as therapy can be hurtful rather than positive. The image of psychiatry as a mechanism for social control, especially of women, has been altogether too accurate at times. I realize that there is good therapy, though it is rare, and certainly people should not take drugs in isolation, without care and monitoring.

Whether or not a person should be hospitalized depends on his or her ability to cope in the outside world. Only a small percentage of people living with mental stress deteriorate to the point of "genuine madness," and it is only those who suffer from genuine madness that I am concerned with here.

I do not believe that a schizophrenic episode will necessarily and naturally end in due time (though for some people it apparently does), and I do not believe that there are insights gained through experiencing that kind of dysfunction. That idea is perhaps a fantasy born of the experience, rather than a reflection of reality.

The medical model of schizophrenia (Dewitte & Ralph, 1989) is that nerve endings in the brain emit too much of the substance called dopamine and other neurotransmitters, so that the brain nerve cells "fire" too often, sending too many impulses. "Antipsychotic drugs appear to block the action of neurotransmitters, particularly dopamine, at receptor sites, thereby limiting impulse transmission" (p. 9). Antipsychotic drugs have an effect only on people who experience delusions, hallucinations, or thought disorders (i.e., random thoughts occurring in quick succession). They tend to make people feel "dopey," dry-mouthed, shaky, and stiff-jointed. There are further medications to stop the

side effects, which have no other apparent effects. The potential long-term effects include involuntary muscle tics.

While over-medication of women with minor tranquilizers is justifiably famous in feminist discourse, current medical opinions regarding the use of these drugs has swung the other way.

> Anti-anxiety agents and sedative-hypnotics: Drugs from this group, given in moderate to low doses help to alleviate anxiety and tension. In higher doses they will help to induce sleep. Usually these drugs are indicated for short-term treatment of anxiety and/or insomnia. Their long-term use is not recommended. [Dewitte and Ralph 1989, p. 2]

I would like to put the emphasis here on the statement that long-term use is not recommended and that it is a mental health workers' manual that says this. Medical opinions have changed, though I hate to be an apologist for the system in any sense. I believe it is public concerns, including feminist beliefs, that have caused this change in doctors' prescribing habits. I do contend, however, that there are a substantial number of individuals whose symptoms are relieved by drugs rather than therapy. I think people who show symptoms of dramatic brain disorientation should try them. They should also be given all the care and monitoring that they require. It is difficult to imagine recovering from severe hallucinations or thought disorders without a structured lifestyle and therapy, if required, to help sort out the confusion these individuals have been suffering. It is also crucial that their perceptions of their health and their wishes be central in any treatment program. While there is no cure for schizophrenia at present, antipsychotic drugs do their job well. I'm here to tell you that I have been prescribed one of these drugs for most of the past 13 years, and I'm doing just fine. It is difficult to make a statement that indicates I have schizophrenia because of the social stigma attached to the label. Besides that, I do not necessarily identify myself just as a "schizophrenic." No, I "have schizophrenia," an incurable but controllable disease, in much the same way as diabetes is controllable. I also have a dog, a horse, a partner, and just recently I earned a second university degree.

Since doctors have started prescribing these drugs, more than one ethical question has cropped up. One interesting question is, should a person with schizophrenia who has been violent when she or he is in an acute stage of the illness be permitted to be free and to work and to live a normal life? The question is not whether they should be punished as vengeance serves no purpose, but whether they can be trusted. I was never violent toward others while I was psychotic, but I can certainly tell you that my mind does not work the same way with medication as it does without it. Mainly, I don't experience irrational panic and fear or believe I'm hearing things I'm not. I can keep track of a thought as long as I want to. The world makes sense—or at least there are such things as logic and consistency. I am happy; I can be left alone safely, I can pursue and achieve long-term goals. I am not a threat. I believe that it is possible that other people who have been violent can be trusted once they have stabilized on medication. The tricky question, of course, is how to define "successfully medicated," when to believe the person has truly stabilized, and who gets to decide.

Another important ethical question is, should psychotic schizophrenics, violent or otherwise, be forced to take medication?

I do not necessarily identify myself just as a "schizophrenic." No, I "have schizophrenia," an incurable but controllable disease, in much the same way as diabetes is controllable.

The local resource for mental health care, which I attend, is the Greater Vancouver Mental Health Service, represented by Mental Health Teams throughout metropolitan Vancouver. They cannot require that individuals take drugs and can only hospitalize them if two psychiatrists agree that that is an appropriate course of action. The Mental Health Teams are a service dedicated to maintaining individuals' quality of life. As Linda Bouma, a Broadway Team nurse, reported:

We're a voluntary service, we can't force anybody to take anything or do anything that they don't want to do, and we will still monitor them if they go off their drugs. (We can't hospitalize anybody) unless they're certifiable.

"Certifiable" means that an individual is determined, by two psychiatrists, to be a danger to themselves or to others. This is a tenet of the provincial Mental Health Act, which is currently undergoing revision. It will be tightened up, according to Linda, "Which will make our jobs more difficult." Her understanding of the new regulations is that it will become more complicated to medicate or hospitalize someone against their will in the future, and that it will be very difficult for her, as a mental health worker, to watch people who could benefit from drugs deteriorate instead. Her analysis is that those who refuse all drugs even though they have repeated episodes of dysfunction are those with "little insight." Given the intensity of the psychotic experience, it is quite likely that some people have little energy for "insight," which may in fact work against them. It is a matter of a person perceiving the symptoms and diagnosing themselves accurately as having the illness, while suffering from hallucinations, fantasies, or frantic brain activity. This is a difficult task, but I would not want the medical system to force drugs or hospitalization on anyone who was not endangering themselves or others. At the same time, there can be a great deal of pain and distress associated with the mental trauma of schizophrenia, and anything that can be done to alleviate this suffering should be actively promoted by a person's caregivers. But decision-making power must be left in the hands of the individual. On June 28, 1991, the Ontario Court of Appeal ruled that even involuntary (i.e., incarcerated) incompetent psychiatric patients, who had previously, when mentally competent, asserted their desire not to be treated with antipsychotic drugs, must have that right respected. The issue was whether the patients' "best interests" overrode their "prior competent wishes," and the court ruled that they did not. The ruling further stated that:

> In my view, although the right to be free from nonconsensual psychiatric treatment is not an absolute one, the state has not demonstrated any compelling reason for entirely eliminating this right, without any hearing or review.... To completely strip these patients of the freedom to determine for themselves what shall be done with their bodies cannot be considered a minimal impairment of their Charter right.

In other words, the Ontario Court of Appeal found that the point at which a psychiatric patient can be forced to receive medical treatment, if they themselves have previously stated, while competent, that they do not wish to be so treated, has to do with whether they are a threat to themselves or others. Nobody can legally be given drugs they consistently refuse, except in emergency situations or when they are a danger. Whether an individual's refusal of drugs is a good or bad idea depends com-

pletely on their physical reaction to the drugs. My considered opinion is that the drugs are worth trying as they can have a profoundly calming and normalizing effect on the workings of a mind. As I say, I prove that assertion every week, as I take my medication and continue my life without mental distress.

Schizophrenia, or madness, is a topic that is guaranteed to bring complete silence to most groups of people. I would ask these people to consider whether they honestly believe that the illness does not exist and/or does not incapacitate people. Or are they afraid of the illness, of the pain and dysfunction that has happened to their friend or colleague? Are they afraid it will happen to them?

Schizophrenics need empathy, support (both in terms of emotions and finances as well as, often, structured living arrangements), acceptance, and as much autonomy as we are capable of managing. We are victims, not typically threats. Refusal to accept the illness, either on the part of the individual or on the part of her or his family and community, often causes unnecessary stress and suffering. The illness is grievous enough, without denial. It is not good enough to "let them be," to turn away from schizophrenics and justify this by saying, "I don't want to be the one who locks them up." We have a social responsibility to take care of each other. And a person suffering from schizophrenia certainly needs our care.

References

Dewitte, B. & Ralph, I. (1989). Psychotropic Agents: *A Handbook for Mental Health Workers*. 5th ed. New Westminster, BC: Bipublications.

Ransom, D. (1990). Learning to live with the fear of madness. *New Internationalist*, 209:5.

The History and Outcome of My Encounter With Schizophrenia

Ross B. Fortner with Christine Steel

ROSS B. FORTNER, J.D., IS AN OUTPATIENT AT THE
VETERANS ADMINISTRATION MEDICAL CENTER
OUTPATIENT CLINIC, PORTLAND , OR. MR. FORTNER HAS
SUCCESSFULLY COMPLETED WORK AS A TELEPHONE
RECRUITER FOR THE MARCH OF DIMES AND IS NOW A
TRAINEE WITH THE PRIVATE INDUSTRY COUNCIL OF
PORTLAND, OREGON, AT A WORK STATION IN THE
TELEPHONE RECRUITING OFFICE OF
THE AMERICAN RED CROSS.

THIS ARTICLE ORIGINALLY APPEARED IN THE
Schizophrenia Bulletin, 1988, 14(4), 701-706.

Schizophrenia is a mental disease which usually strikes in adolescence or early adulthood. The disease is a complex and sometimes terrifying one in which the patient may have paranoid delusions that people are plotting against him, hear voices controlling his thoughts, and act inappropriately in social situations. One out of every one hundred people develops schizophrenia. I was one of the unlucky ones.

Some say that schizophrenia is caused by a chemical imbalance in the brain or a difference in the brain's structure or metabolism. Often, symptoms are touched off by an emotionally stressful period in the patient's life. Like many physical diseases, schizophrenia can come and go. Over time, however, chronic schizophrenic patients often suffer progressive deterioration of their mental processes.

I experienced my first symptoms not long after I graduated from law school. For many years, my treatment was as confusing and bewildering as the mental states I was experiencing. My first treatments of early drugs and shock therapy failed miserably and, if anything, added to my paranoia. Then I was treated for an anxiety condition

rather than schizophrenia. Although this helped me keep my feelings of anxiety under control, it did not help the isolation, withdrawal, and paranoia I also experienced. When I came under treatment for schizophrenia again, my first doctor was insensitive and ill-informed, treating me with talk sessions only and no drug therapy. Today, with a combination of drug therapy, psychological counseling, and vocational counseling, I am able to lead a normal lifestyle and even share with you my experiences in coping with this bewildering disease.

When I left Whitman College in the spring of 1953, I had no idea what I would do next. I knew that I first had to complete my military service obligation. That summer, I worked as chief timekeeper for the Green Giant Canning Company in Waitsburg, Washington, and then in August, a few days after the end of the Korean War, I became a draftee in the U.S. Army.

At my preliminary duty station, Fort Lewis, Washington, I passed all mental and physical tests and turned down the opportunity to attend Officers Candidates School. After that decision, I was sent to Fort Bliss, Texas, for basic training and preliminary instruction in radar operations. Upon completion of radar school, I was transferred to Fort Jackson, South Carolina, where I was reclassified as a clerk typist and then assigned to Fort McClellan, Alabama.

When I was discharged from active duty in June of 1955, I decided to go to law school in the Pacific Northwest. I was admitted to the College of Law at Willamette University in Salem, Oregon. After a summer working in a box factory in Baker, Oregon, my hometown, I matriculated there in the fall of 1955.

I graduated with a 2.0 grade point average and, after taking the bar exam, which I failed by two points, I went to Work for the State Supreme Court as a temporary law clerk. After 1 month, I was made a permanent staff member to the State Attorney General. It was then that my life began to fall apart.

After my successful stint in the military and my hard work and graduation from law school, I was struck down by a serious mental disease—paranoid schizophrenia. The Attorney General, for whom I was working, sensed that I was becoming increasingly disturbed. One day, he drove me out to the state mental hospital in Salem. There, he and the hospital superintendent encouraged me to become a patient.

I had no idea what they were talking about. I tried to drive myself to follow my normal routine until I broke down. I became upset and tense, thinking that the world was a pretty awful place and that people were watching and talking about me. I felt that people were trying to get rid of me...they wanted to freeze me in the snow...that the radio programs and movies and television programs were talking about me. At night, I thought people were driving around my apartment building, honking horns, hooting and jeering, and ridiculing me. My speech and manner were preoccupied and vague. Scared, I went to my cousin's home in Portland to find refuge. My father came to Portland and convinced me to commit myself to the Oregon State Hospital for 60 days. That was the hardest decision I have ever made. Entering a state mental hospital is a terrifying proposition for even the most mentally unstable—to put yourself in such hands when you are already suffering terrible fear and paranoia is an unbelievable experience. The hospital records stated:

> The patient relates with difficulty and is quite suspicious. He sits tensely in the chair at the interview, and rather rambling

I experienced my first symptoms not long after I graduated from law school.

insists that he does not feel that the trouble is with him, but with the things that have been going on around him. He vaguely over-intellectualizes most of the material he discusses. Intellectually he seems well above average in intelligence, but is certainly not functioning at this level at the present time. His memory is unimpaired, although remembered events are frequently misinterpreted. His thought content is mostly preoccupation with ideas of persecution mixed with vague sexual preoccupation and feelings of guilt. He has no insight and his judgment is grossly impaired by his illness. There is considerable difficulty in abstract thoughts, and proverbs are vaguely and inaccurately, as well as often bizarrely, interpreted.

I was considered to be a danger to myself and placed on a closed ward. I underwent 13 electroshock treatments. The shock treatments were particularly difficult for me. I had to lie on a table in an old section of the hospital while the doctors touched electrodes to my temples. This would knock me out. I became so fearful of losing consciousness that they eventually had to wrestle me onto the table and force me into position for the treatments. After the electroshock therapy, I graduated to an open ward and then was released to my parents to return with them to Baker.

I started seeing a doctor at the university and a consultant at the Department of Vocational Rehabilitation. I was again diagnosed as a paranoid schizophrenic, and the new doctor sent to the state hospital for my records. When he received these, he applied to the Social Security Administration and secured disability income for me. He told me I should not try to work for a time. Up to that point, he was on the right track. But in what I now realize was a grave error, he took me off all medications and started me on his therapy of free association. I would go to sessions with him and just talk about everything I had on my mind. He would tell me I had a thought disorder and then sit and listen to what I said. That was the full extent of my treatment.

At the same time, I began seeing a counselor at the State Department of Vocational Rehabilitation. The counselor was in constant contact with my doctor, and together they tested me and laid the groundwork for me to retrain myself for employment. I was advised that I should not work in an employment agency because there was too much pressure in that field for someone with an emotional illness. Neither did they encourage me to pursue the field of law. Instead, I underwent training in bookkeeping at Goodwill Industries. The doctor and counselor both seemed to feel that this training would enable me to enter the business world in some occupation other than as an employment agency counselor.

Before I began the bookkeeping classes, I followed the counselor's advice and became a volunteer at the United Good Neighbors. There, I found the work confusing and beyond my ability. Unable to cope, my confidence in my doctor shaken, I was taken by my coworkers at United Good Neighbors to the mental health ward at Woodland Park Hospital. After a few days, I was taken to the VA hospital's psychiatric ward and became a patient there.

My treatment at the VA hospital in 1974 was inconclusive because I was only in a state of confusion, fear, and low self-

For many years my treatment was as confusing and bewildering as the mental states I was experiencing.

esteem, but was not paranoid. The doctors put me on a major tranquilizer, Haldol, and observed my adjustment to the drug. While I was on the psychiatric ward, the counselor continued to visit me and we laid plans for me to remain a client of the Department of Vocational Rehabilitation when I was released from the hospital.

The counselor suggested I go to the St. Vincent dePaul Rehabilitation Center for Work adjustment training in a sheltered workshop. Not being able to find anything else, I began to work in that organization in 1977. There, I was assigned various assembly jobs and paid on a piecework basis. After a time, I could not stomach this type of employment and was preparing to quit the program when someone at St. Vincent advised me to volunteer at one of the thrift stores. I followed this suggestion and began working on the floor of the main retail salvage store.

From my first day at the thrift store I was considered a good worker, and soon thereafter I was hired as a regular employee. I continued in this work, eventually being assigned as a clerk in the downtown store until I quit 2 years later.

St Vincent dePaul had served as a place to get some work experience and be employed for a long enough time to satisfy the trial period of work under the Social Security Administration's regulations. When I left there, I was no longer considered disabled and therefore was no longer eligible to receive disability income or help from the Department of Rehabilitation.

With a new feeling of confidence and independence, I began searching for a new job. I first interviewed with several law firms for a position as a law clerk or legal assistant, but I found that I did not have the experience needed to do that kind of work. I sent my resume to different businesses and answered advertisements in the newspaper. Since I had gained some knowledge of collections in law school and had done some collections work while employed by my parents in Baker, I applied at a collection agency and was hired in August of 1979.

I was assigned to collect small accounts and spent my days tracing and telephoning debtors to try to get them to pay their bills. I soon tired of the work. In addition to the lack of challenge in the work itself, I was unable to get along with a fellow collector in the office who kept interfering with my work. One day, in the winter of 1980, discouraged with my work and dissatisfied with my life, I became confused and frustrated and called on an old law school roommate for help. He invited me to his office to talk. When I arrived, he advised me that he had tried to reach the VA by telephone but could not, and was calling around the city to various psychiatrists to find help for me. That resulted in my being seen by a private doctor who, after interviewing me, declared an emergency and ordered me to go to the psychiatric ward of Providence Hospital. Another attorney friend from the same law firm drove me through the ice and snow to the hospital where I was admitted in the early evening hours. Because my medical insurance at the collection agency did not cover me, my tenure was short-lived. After 2 days, I was admitted to the psychiatric ward of the VA Hospital in nearby Vancouver, Washington, and my attorney friend engaged a taxi cab to drive me to Vancouver. I was immediately admitted and came under the supervision of several doctors there.

Again, like the last time I was admitted to the VA Hospital in Portland, I was suffering from confusion, frustration, and low self-esteem. But I was not paranoid. The doctors changed my medication to Loxitane, a tranquilizer used in the treatment of schizophrenia, and observed me for several days. They decided that I could go back to work and they discharged me.

I returned to Portland and the collection agency, still confused and frustrated. After trying to cope with the office again for a few days, I gave up and isolated myself in my apartment, with only a little cheese, soup, and milk to eat for 2 weeks. I grew quite paranoid and thought I was starving myself to death. This was the situation when my brother happened to come to Portland from eastern Washington. He found me mentally and physically sick and, after conferring with my cousin and mother, took me to a VA Hospital in Portland where I was again admitted to the psychiatric ward.

This time, unlike my two previous hospitalizations, my symptoms were schizophrenic. I imagined that people were out to cremate me. I thought the city of Portland was against me. The ward doctor experimented with the drug, Lithium, to see if it would help. This medication cleared up my fears and allowed me to think clearly again. However, its side effects caused my hands to tremble and other involuntary muscle movements in my body.

After I has stabilized on the new drug, the doctor next referred me to a social worker in the hospital. She took a history of my case and advised me to move from my apartment to a group home. With the help of the hospital staff, I found a group home and moved into the new quarters upon discharge from the hospital. Again, I became an outpatient of the VA Mental Health Clinic in downtown Portland. With the stress of cooking meals and maintaining an apartment removed, I devoted myself full time to finding another job in the community.

By chance one day, while I was at the outpatient clinic, I met a blind doctor who worked part time for the VA. His manner of handling my case was so insightful that I asked to become a permanent patient under him. The request was granted and proved to be the smartest decision I had made since coming to Portland in 1961. This doctor was an expert in treating schizophrenia. He was the first doctor to explain what schizophrenia meant. It was, he said, an illness that tends to make you isolate yourself, withdraw and have paranoid feelings. He said it was a group of mental disorders that basically disturb thought and action. Its symptoms include quick and violent temper, loneliness, and depression. The personality changes and thoughts of people plotting against you or people stealing your thoughts may prevail. A schizophrenic may become strongly religious, withdrawn and isolated from family and friends, and unable to work or take care of himself. He or she sometimes turns to drugs and alcohol.

He was the first doctor to explain what schizophrenia meant.

Once the doctor had explained the illness, he told me that my former doctor had been right to teach me relaxation skills and prescribe muscle relaxants because that had kept the anxiety and fears of my schizophrenia down. But he said the doctor who had used the technique of free association with me had been punitive and detrimental to my mental health. He said that I had a chemical imbalance in my brain and needed medication and counseling to enable me to make use of the parts of my brain not affected by the disease.

The doctor continued me on Navane and outlined to me the need to establish priorities, with socialization being first, communication being second, and confidence around people being third. To accomplish these goals, I would need to work; to have religious, cultural, and sports interests; to gain the support of relatives, friends, acquaintances, and mental health professionals; and to adopt hobbies such as music, movies, shows, and light reading. He told me that if I could accomplish these objectives, I would have good mental health again.

I applied to the VA under the Emergency Job Training Act and was told that I should continue to do volunteer work because of my need for experience and references. After a search which took me through the Volunteer Bureau and other sources, I located a volunteer job as an intake worker with the Volunteer Lawyer Project of the Multnomah County Bar Association. I worked there from the fall of 1984 until July of 1985.

While working for the Volunteer Lawyer Project, I was encouraged to enroll in legal assistant courses at Portland Community College. I took Legal Investigation Techniques and Law Office Management. I worked hard at those courses and the job. In June of 1985, I completed the course work with good grades and a short time later quit the intake worker's position at the project when the director who had hired me resigned.

When I quit the Volunteer Lawyers Project, I had intended to become a full-time student in Legal Assistant studies at the community college. Before classes were to begin in the fall, I planned a trip to visit a cousin in San Francisco, California. At this time, I was assigned a new doctor at the VA mental health clinic because my regular doctor for the past 5 years had resigned in order to work in private practice. The new doctor, a psychiatrist working full time for the VA mental health clinic, reviewed my medical charts and determined that I might be tried on a lower dose of Navane.

As I was looking forward to my trip and then my studies, I had a paranoid episode. I first began to be anxious and fearful while I was at a large shopping mall on the Saturday afternoon of Labor Day weekend. I thought people were talking about me so I returned quickly to my apartment. There, I felt guilty about the way I had quit the Volunteer Lawyers Project.

Unable to sleep, I spent the night reading and watching TV. I called the VA hospital and talked to a doctor. I was told that I needed socialization and was ordered to call the Metro Crisis Center. The person on duty there advised me to contact the Solo Center, which I could not do because it was not open. Again, I called the doctor who then advised me to sit tight and wait until my cousin returned from her weekend outing Monday night. I had another restless night on Sunday. Upon awakening Monday morning, I drank a glass of water. Soon, I had a tremendous pain in my stomach. I was sure that Bob Packwood and the Republican Party had broken into my apartment and put poison in my drinking glass. I called the poison center. They advised me to drink lots of water and wait for the pain in my abdomen to stop. When the pain persisted, they advised me to call the hospital. The doctor there told me the pain was caused by stress and that I should try to relax for the rest of the day. I followed these directions and read a book by Norman Vincent Peale. This relaxed me so much that I did not feel the need to call my cousin Monday night. All that remained of the schizophrenic episode was the guilt feeling over how I left the Volunteer Lawyers Project. The doctor told me I would feel better when I had apologized to the office manager.

By Tuesday morning the anxieties were no longer with me and I reported to the officer of the day at the mental health clinic. He reviewed the weekend's events with me and advised me to go ahead with the apology. Later that day, I called the Volunteer Lawyers Project and said I had left because I did not feel well received by the other workers in the office. I also said I was uncomfortable with the change in leadership the office was going through. That done, I set out to evaluate what I had gone through during the past 72 hours. I knew that my mind had been affected by this experience, but did not realize the full importance of this turn of events until after my trip to San Francisco, which my doctor had urged me to take despite the paranoid episode I had.

When I returned from 10 days of fun and relaxation in San Francisco, I began Legal Assistant classes at the community college. It was then that I discovered my memory had been impaired by the stress episode I had been through over Labor Day. Unable to concentrate or to retain the material being taught, I had to withdraw from classes. My doctor ordered a CT (Computed Tomography) scan to determine if my brain had been affected by the breakdown. Although the results of the test showed my brain was normal and that I had not suffered a stroke, the doctor ordered a staff clinical psychologist to give me a series of tests to determine my state of mind and the extent of memory loss I was suffering from.

First, I took a test called the MMPI (Minnesota Multiphasic Personality Inventory), which showed that I had some depression and anxiety, that I had a tendency to worry and a feeling of being unable to cope with life and that everything was impossible. Then, I took the inkblot test, which confirmed that I was a worrier and anxious in addition to being schizophrenic. The other tests showed my memory was not completely gone but was below average and not likely to improve. It was in the lower 10TH percentile of the population. Two other tests showed that although I could change conceptual sets and had a fairly good ability to switch from one task to another I performed below average. Finally, the tests showed my IQ to be above average. The psychologist said that although I would have a harder time working and would be eliminated from some jobs, he would refer me for vocational training as a clerk in a private concern where stress was low and I could work at my own pace. He thought the best kind of work would be part time, seasonal, or volunteer so I could build up my confidence for another full-time job.

My doctor, taking these findings into consideration, changed my Navane dosage back to its former level. In addition, he advised me to enter the day treatment program again. Through the day treatment program I took courses in veterans' benefits, assertiveness training, managing your mental illness, problem solving, leisure education, physical fitness, productive living, communications, stress management, building friendships, cooking, and music therapy.

In January of 1987 I once again became active as volunteer employment specialist with the Urban League of Portland. At the present time, I divide my time between the day treatment Program and the Urban League. The courses I am participating in now at the day treatment center are problem solving, communications, music therapy, and brown bag lunch. I also work weekly with a counselor there to set goals and discuss my moods or any problems I might have. I report to the office administrator at the Upon League, doing such tasks as filing, calling applicants and employers, writing up job orders, and operating office machines.

I feel that I have been on the leading edge of the medical breakthroughs in the treatment of schizophrenia. Although I experienced numerous setbacks and dead ends in mental treatment and in life itself, I have never been a quitter. Luckily I picked myself up and kept slugging away at life enough to find a place and a purpose for myself in society.

My Schizophrenia

Roberta L. Payne

ROBERTA L. PAYNE, PH.D., RECEIVED A B.A. IN CLASSICS
AND AN M.A. IN COMMUNICATION FROM STANFORD
UNIVERSITY; AN M.A. IN ITALIAN FROM THE UNIVERSITY
OF CALIFORNIA, LOS ANGELES; AND HER PH.D. IN
COMPARATIVE LITERATURE FROM THE UNIVERSITY OF
DENVER. SHE HAS TAUGHT AT THE UNIVERSITY OF NEW
ORLEANS, THE UNIVERSITY OF DENVER, IOWA STATE
UNIVERSITY, AND SOUTH DAKOTA SCHOOL OF MINES
AND TECHNOLOGY. DR. PAYNE'S WRITING EXPERIENCE
INCLUDES A BOOK PUBLISHED IN 1990,
The Influence of Dante on Medieval English Dream Visions,
AND A BOOK CURRENTLY IN PRESS ENTITLED,
The Elegy of Madonna Fiammetta.
SHE IS CURRENTLY A VOLUNTEER EDITOR AT THE
SCHIZOPHRENIA PROJECT AT THE UNIVERSITY OF
COLORADO HEALTH SCIENCES CENTER,
DENVER, COLORADO.

THIS ARTICLE ORIGINALLY APPEARED IN THE
Schizophrenia Bulletin, 1992, 18(4), 725-728.

I am an unusual schizophrenic in that I have a Ph.D. and have taught in several universities. I am also a typical schizophrenic of my generation (I am 46), in that both my mother and I have been blamed for my schizophrenia. Finally, my recovery from alcoholism and clinical depression has been essential for the recovery of my mental health in general, for I have what is called a "multiple diagnosis."

I first became ill when I was 22, and I spent 3 months in a mental hospital near Stanford, where I was a graduate student. I was told that I had depression. While I was in the hospital, I was in searing psychic pain. It did not help when the director of the hospital said, "Roberta, you may have a master's degree, but you are not master of yourself." But it was my mother who received the brunt of the blame. I was encouraged to blame every negative aspect of my childhood on her. For instance, if I got bad grades in high school, it was

because she had ruined my self-esteem; if I got straight A's, it was because she was pushy and domineering. I yelled accusations at her (in Colorado) over the phone when I was in that hospital; and then when she was too hurt to come to California to see me, my psychologist said she was rejecting me. My father was dealt with more summarily: I was told that I might have to pay him back what he spent on my education (5 years at Stanford) if I wanted to be free of him.

When I left that hospital, I was no better and no worse for the "talking cure." Unable to hold down a job, I moved in with my parents and lived with them (angrily) on and off for several years. I eventually hit a lull in my illness and decided to get my Ph.D. I spent 1 year at Harvard and received straight A's, but the cost to me was enormous. I felt as though I was being ostracized by the other students, but, looking back, I can easily see how I was so poorly adjusted that no one would want to become my friend. I suffered from anxiety and fear of the future, and my drinking progressed from social drinking to drinking myself to sleep at night. The very first thing I did when I woke up in the morning was to smoke a joint of marijuana and, smoking all day, I remained high until I went to bed. All that time, I was suffering from symptoms that eventually turned into schizophrenia.

One day I simply could not stand my anxiety any longer, so I went to Harvard's student health office and asked to see a therapist. I was desperately afraid. Only one therapist could see me, and he could see me for only 5 minutes. He was on crutches because of a tennis injury and was in a very, very bad mood. He told me I would have to make up my own mind about whether I wanted to continue working on my degree. And that was that! It took me many years to see that I may have been coloring that episode with paranoia.

After all these years, I simply cannot tell you what happened that day, except that I needed help and may not have presented that clearly.

I left Harvard after a year and went to teach at the University of New Orleans for several years. These were years primarily of alcoholism and depression (the alcohol temporarily killing the depression) for me. I stopped using marijuana because it made me paranoid; in fact, I would have to say that it made me the most paranoid I have ever been, even more so than I was with LSD. I spent 3 years in New Orleans, years of alcoholism, with all its symptoms.

The anxiety came back again. This time I got a respite from it by returning to Denver, my home city. The only job I seemed to be able to get there was typesetting. I worked the night shift in a warehouse, and during my coffee breaks I used to go out to my car and quickly drink a whole bottle of wine. I had to do that because I needed steady hands for typing. During those years I had extraordinarily vivid visual hallucinations. For instance, once while I was driving I visualized the road full of dogs and cats that had been run over but not killed, and I had to work my way through them in my car. One psychiatrist later told me that was a symptom of advanced alcoholism, but another said he thought it was schizophrenia because I had been drinking heavily just before I drove that time, which was true of my other hallucinatory episodes as well. Another symptom I had in those years that could have been from either schizophrenia or alcoholism was TV broadcasting. For instance, my television and the people at the TV station "forced" me to watch the movie *Days*

I felt as though I had been pushed deep within myself, and I had little or no reaction to events or emotions around me.

of Wine and Roses. At such times it felt as though I was not the only person in my living room.

I thought that going back to get my Ph.D. would take me out of all of that, so I enrolled at the University of Denver. Alcohol no longer helped me get through the day. I taught after I had been drinking, and I was unable to write papers. Finally, one night police stopped (but did not arrest) me for drunken driving. This gave me the impetus I needed to call for help. I joined Alcoholics Anonymous (AA) and have remained sober ever since: I had my 10th "birthday" last August. Although I am an agnostic, I am able to receive the help I need from AA, which has a spiritual basis.

A couple of pleasant, active years passed for me. Eventually, though, I fell into a very bad depression, the kind that hurts just to remember years later. I thought of getting help. Perhaps the student health center at Denver University was better than the one at Harvard. I realized that I could not continue in that condition, so I called them.

A psychologist named Dan saw me. He was a kind and gentle young man. In his office there was a huge, carved wooden chair I could nestle in; from this chair I spoke about my life. Dan was a tremendously good listener, and his questions challenged me. I learned that dysfunctional traits could exist in people who were deeply lovable, and that it was not appropriate to blame or call myself or others bad. Dan sent me to the university psychiatrist, Ellen, who placed me on an antidepressant that has worked wonderfully. I am on a minimum dose and have not been depressed again.

At the beginning of my last year at Denver University, "feelings" began to descend on me as they did at Stanford years before. I felt distinctly different from my usual self. I would sit for hours on end staring at nothing, and I became fascinated with drawing weird, disconnected monsters. I carefully hid my drawings, because I was certain I was being watched. Eventually I became aware of a magical force outside myself that was compelling me in certain directions. The force gained power as time went on, and soon it made me take long walks at 2 or 3 o'clock in the morning down dark alleys in my high-crime neighborhood. I had no power to disobey the force. During my walks I felt as though I was in a different, magical, four-dimensional universe. I understood that the force wanted me to take these walks so that I might be killed.

I do not clearly understand the relationship between the force and the Alien Beings (alas, such a name!) but my universe soon became populated with them. The Alien Beings were from outer space, and of all the people in the world, only I was aware of them. The Alien Beings soon took over my body and removed me from it. They took me to a faraway place of beaches and sunlight and placed an Alien in my body to act like me. At this point I had the distinct impression that I did not really exist, because I could not make contact with my kidnapped self. I also saw that the Aliens were starting to take over other people as well, removing them from their bodies and putting Aliens in their place. Of course, the other people were unaware of what was happening; I was the only person in the world who had the power to know it. At this point I determined that the Aliens were involved in a huge conspiracy against the world.

The thought of going back to Dan appealed to me. But I held back because the Alien Beings were gaining strength and had given me a complex set of rules. The rules were very specific and governed every aspect of my behavior. One of the rules was that I could not tell anyone else about the Aliens or the rules, or else the Aliens would kill me. Another of the rules was that I had to become utterly, completely mad. So now I was living in a world of great fear.

I had a number of other symptoms as well. I felt as though I had been pushed deep within myself, and I had little or no reaction to events or emotions around me. Almost daily the world became unreal to me. Everything outside of me seemed to fade into the distance; everything was miles away from me. I came to feel that I had the power to influence the behavior of animals; that I could, for instance, make dogs bark simply by hooking up rays of thought from my mind to theirs. Conversely, I felt that certain people had the capacity to read my mind. I became very frightened of those people and tried my best to avoid them. Whenever I saw a group of two or three people, I was sure they were talking about me. Paranoia is a very painful emotion. But when I saw crowds of people (as in a shopping mall), I felt an acute longing to wander among them, singing hymns and nursery rhymes.

> *I learned that dysfunctional traits could exist in people who were deeply lovable, and that it was not appropriate to blame or call myself or others bad.*

It wasn't until several months later that I had the power to break out of my secret world. One day I was sitting at an AA meeting when I completely lost contact with reality. It felt as though an enormous whirlwind seized me, and the pain was excruciating. (Being in a whirlwind is not a very good metaphor for that experience, but I have trouble finding words to describe it.) When it was over, I got in my car and drove home. It was difficult to drive because I was only partially aware of reality. I went to bed and listened to the singing of a bird outside my window. I was convinced that as long as I was able to be aware of the bird singing I would not lose my mind. I realized that I could not continue like this, so I called Dan.

First he sent me to Ellen, who placed me on thiothixene. My symptoms gradually subsided over about 2 weeks, and in the meantime I told Dan about the Aliens and the rules. It was terrifying, because I was convinced I would be killed. Each session I told him a little more, until finally I had let him in on my secret world.

I got my Ph.D. about 1 year later, with the help of many people at the student health center. Some just listened to me while I cried; and then there was Dan, who, through weeks and months of work, taught me, among many other things, to love my parents, especially my mother, again.

All of a sudden, the "real world" was in front of me. I went to teach in a university in South Dakota, but the result was disastrous. Many of my symptoms returned, and there was no one like Dan there. I came to realize that the quality of psychologists and psychiatrists does vary greatly. I barely finished the year. At the beginning of the next academic year, I had delusions and paranoia again, and all of my minor symptoms. I was put in the mental health ward of the small local hospital, where I remained for 5 weeks, grateful that I no longer had to stand in front of the students, who terrified me. There were creatures from 400 million (or is it billion?) light years away who told me through their brainwaves what an evil thing I was and how they were going to persecute me. This time there was something new: I could not think properly, and other people were aware of this. I could not think my way through a sentence. I got lost. More to the point, I was slipping and sliding around when I thought.

I formally withdrew from my job and returned to Denver. This time my convalescence has taken several years. I have not worked for 3 1/2 years, and, to be frank, I am afraid at this time to think of going back. I do, however, lead a very rich life, in which both of my parents, as well as many friends, are included. I have furnished, and take care of, my own condominium. Best of all, I have published my dissertation *The Influence of Dante on Medieval English Dream Visions* and have a translation from medieval Italian, *The Elegy of Madonna Fiammetta,* at the publishers; I am currently working on a second translation.

I am now taking clozapine and am very pleased with its effects, especially on my paranoia. I find, however, that the changes it brings—such as an increased ability to question, to follow maps, to hold intricate conversations, and to be interested in things outside of myself—are usually very subtle.

This is not the life I thought I would live, but it is a comfortable one, filled with kind people and the opportunity to write.

How I've Managed Chronic Mental Illness

Richard Weingarten

RICHARD WEINGARTEN IS CURRENTLY DIRECTOR OF PEER SUPPORT AT THE CONNECTICUT MENTAL HEALTH CENTER IN NEW HAVEN, CONNECTICUT.

THIS ARTICLE ORIGINALLY APPEARED IN THE *Schizophrenia Bulletin,* 1989, 15(4), 635-640.

A California doctor once compared my mental illness to diabetes. "You have a chronic illness," he said. "You will have to take medication for it, probably all the rest of your life. But it will keep your illness manageable and under control." It took me several years and three more hospitalizations before I heeded that doctor's advice. But when I did, I discovered that medication alone was not the only factor that made me feel well, nor was it therapy either. I had to create a life that gave me the structure, support, and meaning I needed to resume normal living.

I would like to emphasize that only after I accepted the illness as a chronic one could I really do something about improving my life. I had to learn that I could not "wish" away the illness; I could not "will" it not to be so. That is a process that took time and many internal struggles. When the struggle was finished and I heard the doctor's advice of years ago, then I could hope again and move forward in life. That is what I would like to share.

What I am about to say may sound like a well person's story, and perhaps it is because I am feeling mostly well these days, and have regained hope. For the last 6 months I've held a part-time job that I enjoy and am successful at. The social network that I constructed over the past year or two gives me much satisfaction and support. Relations with my family are tranquil. It feels as if I'm on a roll while at the same time I'm apprehensive that my luck may run out. I know where I have come from and do not want to return.

On the other hand, I still have bad days when I lack enthusiasm for my work and daily activities. These, I've noticed, are fewer and further between than before I began working. Getting a good night's sleep frequently seems like a crap shoot and I'm ever on the alert for paranoia, sensory overload, depression, and the other symptoms I have learned to associate with my illness.

Feeling well is a rather recent experience. For the past 13 years or so I was a truly sick person. I was hospitalized five times during psychotic episodes. I felt deep depression, extreme paranoia, destructive inner voices, delusions, sensory overload, hopelessness and despair, auditory and visual hallucinations, etc. These things plagued me at the times when I was acutely ill as well as between hospitalizations.

I believe my problems stemmed largely from a difficult adaptation at puberty and were then set in motion in a very repressed adolescence. My academic and athlete performance fell off noticeably at about age 13. The biggest blow then was the devastating estrangement I felt from my father. Not knowing how to give me the love and affection that I needed, my parents sent me to a boarding school. There, and at the monastic all-men's college I later went to, I built a thick wall around myself. At graduation, I didn't know what I wanted to do or could do, and I feel that I could have had real trouble at that point. Luckily, I went into the Peace Corps and landed in Latin America. The easygoing Latin American lifestyle and culture agreed with me, and I was able to be the adolescent I never allowed myself to be or was permitted to be at home. I met an unusual Latin American girl and developed trusting relationships with a few of the other volunteers. In Latin America, the wall came down, I regained contact with a feeling of well-being I had known as a child and led a pretty normal life.

When I returned to the United States, I was unable to build on the gains I made in Latin America. I dropped out of a graduate program in Latin American studies (still not knowing what I wanted to do), broke off my engagement to my Latin American fiancee, and moved to an East Coast city where some college friends were living and working. In the city I became very depressed and could not motivate myself in any positive direction. The depression forced me to go into therapy.

In therapy I worked on the developmental issues I missed in prep school and college. My negative self-image was a central issue. My therapist, with whom I developed a good working relationship, postulated that if I reconstructed a positive self-image for myself, I could withstand the symptoms of my illness and lead a "normal" productive life. But my depression continued to be a major concern, and I discovered other problems too—most significantly, sensory overload and paranoia. I had at least two psychotic episodes in the city but was not hospitalized there. During these episodes I formed delusions that completely absorbed my thinking and took over my life. For example, I believed that there was an undeclared citywide civil war going on and that I played an important but undefined part in it. I also believed that I had telepathic powers and spent hours lying on my bed "communicating" with my therapist and his wife, whom I had never met. I usually emerged from these episodes after a few days. I wasn't taking medication then. But the delusionary symptoms were

I discovered that medication alone was not the only factor that made me feel well, nor was it therapy either. I had to create a life that gave me the structure, support, and meaning I needed to resume normal living.

never very far away and neither was the paranoia that accompanied them.

I improved enough in the East Coast city to think about completing my education. I moved to a West Coast city where I planned to get a master's degree in education and teach at the elementary school level.

Out of therapy and without medication, the roof fell in on me 6 months after I arrived on the West Coast. This time I got caught up in a delusion where I thought a right-wing takeover of the country was bringing about another holocaust. Everything: billboards, radio, television, people, random sounds, and my own thoughts and actions fed into this delusion. I left the job I had and drove to San Francisco to seek out an old high school flame (for protection, I think). Depressed, suicidal, and without sleep, I spent a few terrifying days driving around the bay area talking to myself. I finally committed myself to a local hospital. I was put on medication, Haldol, I think, and released after a few days.

I stayed 5 more years in California and suffered three similar psychotic episodes for which I was hospitalized and misdiagnosed a paranoid schizophrenic. The episodes followed periods of increased stress, or perceived stress, when I went off my medication. After my second hospitalization, I reentered therapy. I later began taking lithium and other psychotropic medications. The medication kept me out of the hospital but I functioned at a low level. It was a huge struggle to be with people and get through the day. I labored 2 1/2 years to finish a master's thesis that should have taken 6 months to do. In despair and defeat (I was too stressed out to teach) and still not knowing what I could or wanted to do, I returned to Cleveland, Ohio, near where I grew up.

My hospitalization (in Cleveland) occurred immediately after I took myself off lithium. My former East Coast therapist told me in a phone conversation that he didn't think I needed it. This hospitalization was preceded by several days of depression and sleeplessness. A harshly critical voice, always a problem, got the upper hand, and I slipped into another terrifying depression. I was able to be taken off the lithium in the hospital, and put on Prolixin. However, the uncomfortable, long (5-week) hospitalization frightened (I had never been in the hospital for more than 2 weeks) and demoralized me. This last hospitalization occurred in spring of 1986. Since then, it's been a slow climb "back." It's this climb back I'd like to describe now. When I was discharged, I had no job, no friends to speak of, and very few family supports. I was alone in my apartment, isolated from the world, and very depressed over the emptiness that was my life.

My first break was seeing a "consumer" activist on a morning talk show. I called this consumer, and he told me about the various consumer activities in the Cleveland area. I began going to meetings of the various groups. One suburban group was interested in opening a consumer-operated clubhouse or drop-in center. This idea interested me, and for the next year or so I worked with this group helping them to organize their social activities. Within a year, this group, with financial help from a parents' support group, opened its own clubhouse on a 3-day-a-week basis. The same consumer activist directed me to a private mental health agency where there were some part-time job openings. The jobs had been filled by the time I got there, but the director of

the agency told me about a consumer self-help group that was working on a discharge handbook for mental patients being discharged from area hospitals. I joined this self-help group, began going to their weekly meetings, and gradually took a leadership role. This self-help project turned out to be a really good thing. It brought me into contact with the social service professionals who worked at the agency. It also brought me into contact with other consumers, many of whom I felt were much sicker than I. Seeing their needs and engaging them in good give-and-take exchanges was an experience that I grew to like a great deal. All of these contacts gave me the feeling that I was back in society (not stuck in my apartment) and doing something constructive. The publication of the discharge handbook I edited was the culmination of a year's work. That it was well received by patients, family members, and professionals was very gratifying.

At the same time the handbook was nearing completion, I luckily heard about a new mental health outreach team that was being formed at a private social service agency. I applied for the consumer's position on the team and was hired for the half-time job. This 3-day-a-week position gave me structure and a useful role to play, and also helped me get back on my feet. While trying to help others get connected to services and resources, I have certainly helped myself. The job has given me much confidence, has increased my self-esteem, and has enabled me to embark on new relationships, most of which are outside the mental health community.

Although this job has furthered the process that I call a "return to normalcy" (it feels as if I have been through a war), I have put several other things in place that have provided me with the support system that I needed. I would like to tell you about these as well as other relevant issues.

Psychiatrists. I have been fortunate in two ways. First, I've been able to go to psychiatrists since I became severely ill. Second, I've had some very good doctors. At various times my doctors have been therapists, mentors, friends, and allies. I really needed their loyalty and support when I had to confront the destructive forces within my immediate family. My father, for example, often berated me for having done "nothing" since returning from Latin America. Living alone and often out of work, I was isolated from normal social contact. I relied on my doctors to serve as good friends as well as a link to society. The weekly meetings became a high point for me. One therapist in particular showed me the important place that loss had in my life. I could go on and on about the good I derived from therapy.

On the negative side, I wish some of my doctors would have shown more faith in me. One doctor told me the only job I could do was that of a dishwasher. Very few were capable of what Erikson has termed "judicious indignation" and therefore didn't seem as real to me as therapists who were. Some were quite formal and distant. I felt like a "patient," not a person. Therapists need to understand that "patients" need the human touch or compassion just as much as they need the technical expertise of the professional. And I wish it wasn't left up to me to blow the whistle on relationships that weren't going anywhere or that weren't helpful to me.

Medication. Medication has been a serious and complicated issue for me. I resisted taking it for years, believing I wasn't really sick and could do without it or could medicate myself when I needed it. Unfortunately, this didn't work out and I wound up in the hospital three or four times. Since one of my goals is to stay out of the hospital, I now take medication on a regular basis.

It took me a long time to trust doctors who wanted to prescribe medication for me. I wish the doctors had anticipated my fears and questions about the medication and had given me as much information as they had. My present doctor has me on a maintenance dosage of Prolixin. I am grateful that medication is available for my condition.

I now counsel other consumers to take medication. However, I advise them that they must work closely with their doctors when taking it. Even considering the side effects, which are very real, taking medication is better than being in the hospital, I tell them. It is the lesser of many evils.

Social support. I grew up with a real sense of neighborhood. Later, when I was living on the West Coast, I felt the absence of neighborhood. I moved back to Cleveland. I tried to re-create the sense of living and belonging to a real neighborhood. It worked. I became known at the drug store, bank, gas station, supermarket, library, barber shop, etc. It was a good feeling to leave my apartment and greet friendly Midwestern faces every day. I've recently read that this kind of "network therapy" has been successfully employed with chronically mentally ill people in other parts of the country. We should not underestimate those friendly "hellos," "good mornings," and small talk. They provide a sense of being, belonging, and acceptance in our lives.

Writing. After my service in the Peace Corps, I got a job as a foreign news correspondent with an American wire service bureau. Writing has been an enjoyable part of my life and identity ever since. Since I've been ill, I've kept a journal off and on. I usually write in it at nights when I am reviewing (trying to make sense out of) my days. I'm shakier at nights, and this activity has a stabilizing effect on me.

After much time and practice, I've been able to concentrate on positive thoughts and let the negative ones go. I believe this has resulted in new habits of thinking. I also focus on relationships, on changes in myself and my life, on development issues, and on whatever else catches my interest.

Sometimes I just try to work on the craft of writing. I've found that poetry allows me to cast my experience, past and present, in a new light and to explore new thoughts and feelings.

Identity. I learned from my Peace Corps experience that I needed a vocational identity that would make me credible and respected by the local citizenry. So when I became ill and was unemployed, I knew I needed another vocational identity to satisfy the curiosity of the people living around me. I told people I was a freelance writer. I enjoyed having this identity, having worked as a journalist, and it fit well with my long-term aspirations to become a writer. It also explained why I was not working conventional hours. At job interviews, it helped explain away the gaps in my employment record.

My friends who knew of my goal to become a professional writer reinforced this identity by talking about writing with me or by commenting on something I'd written. They often introduced me to their friends as a "journalist." My girlfriend was very supportive. After I told her an anecdote or story from my days as a Peace Corps volunteer, she would exclaim, "You're a writer, Richard!"

People stood by me. My first therapist, Aaron Lazare, M.D., stayed in contact with me by letters and phone calls through good times and bad for many years after I stopped seeing him. Later, as I grew healthier, I would send Dr. Lazare articles that I had written and he would answer my letters with helpful comments on the articles. Also, as I grew healthier, John Strauss, Hank Tanaka, Karen Unger, and Mieko Smith, all

Therapists need to understand that "patients" need the human touch or compassion just as much as they need the technical expertise of the professional.

mental health professionals, took an interest in my work and encouraged me. These people were a positive and uplifting presence in my life for several years. They accompanied my growth and recovery when few people were interested in me. They validated my progress and pointed a way to the future.

Stigma. I am a normal-looking and normal-acting person and have had little trouble with stigma personally. But on a few occasions I have been stigmatized and know the shame, humiliation, rejection, and confusion that occur when people find out that you have a mental illness. One girlfriend refused to see me after I got out of the hospital. She said she saw no potential in me and that I had no future. I was deeply ashamed, but also half believed her. Now I'm selective in whom I tell about my illness. It's got to be pertinent to the conversation or I have to feel that I can trust the person I am talking to.

In my work as an outreach worker, I can identify myself as an ex-mental patient or consumer and try to help my clients deal with stigma. I've counseled people on how to write job resumes, conduct themselves at job interviews, and otherwise present themselves so they can avoid being stigmatized. I'm also aware of how professionals stigmatize people and how consumers stigmatize each other, and I try to counter it when I see it.

I wrote an article on stigma for the discharge handbook, and am now putting together a videotape on the subject. I think supportive, stigma-free environments like consumer operated drop-in centers have great value. Consumers don't have to pretend to be someone they aren't at these kinds of places; rather, they are accepted for who they are. Stigma is a serious problem for most consumers and keeps them from taking their rightful place in the society. A lot more needs to be done to eliminate it.

Social situations. I feel enormous pressures when I encounter new experiences, environments, and people, so it is easy for me to become overstimulated at these times. I've learned to overcome these situations by 1) avoiding them when possible, and 2) going back to them until I mastered them (i.e., have not felt overstimulated but "natural"). When I became more in touch with feelings of anger and rage, and my aggression in general, and was able to be more in the present, sensory overload became much less of a problem for me.

Paranoia. It was hard for me to see and admit the extent to which my paranoid outlook took over my life, but it did and led to many hospitalizations. The paranoia has lessened thanks to more positive feelings about myself. The more I can trust myself, the more I can trust others. Creating a secure, stable, friendly environment around me reduced the paranoia. Sorting out real fears from imagined ones in therapy also helped.

Ideals. It was my strong desire and conviction to work for social justice that caused me to become an activist in the Civil Rights Movement of the 1960s. This desire and conviction was also responsible for my becoming a Peace Corps volunteer in Latin America. After my Peace Corps experience, the ideal of service informed my decisions first to work as a journalist and then to teach and work with disadvantaged youths. I later reconnected with both of these ideals when I became involved with the Mental Health Consumer Movement and began to speak out, write, and work on behalf of mental health consumers, who I saw as an oppressed and voiceless minority.

Getting involved in jobs and activities that were consistent with my longstanding ideals helped me find and keep a focus when my day-to-day life was in turmoil due to the illness. Also, serving a cause that was greater than myself helped me get through those nights when the outcome and consequences of my activism were uncertain or problematic.

Spiritual. Although I was raised in the Jewish faith, I have been away from organized religion since college. After my last hospitalization, I began attending services at the Unitarian Church. The liberal religious services gave structure to my Sunday mornings. I enjoyed singing the hymns and taking part in the fellowship hour that followed the service. I often met other consumers who went to services. The services usually raised my spirits. Later I took an active role in a Central American family sponsored by the church. This drew on my Spanish-speaking ability and gave me more to do at a time when I needed the activity. Now that I'm feeling stronger and am seeing a woman on the weekends, I do not feel the same need to go to services. But I still serve on the refugee committee and recently took part in an American study group sponsored by another Unitarian Church.

Food. I gained 15 pounds during my last hospitalization. Taking off the weight when I didn't have a job and had to stay home a lot was very difficult. Eating was one of the central pleasures of my life, and no matter how hard I tried, I couldn't cut down. Then I began working and wasn't so dependent on my cravings. I reduced my portions and eliminated between-meal snacks. I lost the 15 pounds and felt much better about myself.

Sleep. Sleep remains a mystery to me. I don't know when I'll have a good night's sleep, although I usually know when I won't sleep well. It's as if the psychological ups and downs of my previous day, and my previous life, affect my sleep. This much I've learned: I need a minimum of 6 hours of sleep to be able to function well the next day, and a good night's sleep is worth its weight in gold.

Recreation. Fortunately, I've always been interested in sports, as a participant and as a fan. Physical fitness has always been a high priority, and I've usually belonged to a YMCA or health club wherever I've lived. When I moved back to Cleveland, I joined a community health center at an adjusted-fee membership, I've enjoyed the center's facilities and go there to exercise three or four times a week. I've made friends with the people I meet there. When I wasn't doing well, going to jog or swim was an important part of my day. Completing the workout I set out for myself bolstered my self-esteem.

Courage. I've had the courage to face up to my problems. Inwardly, I've come to terms with many thoughts, feelings, and sensations that I didn't want or even know that I had. Outwardly, I've usually gone to my appointments and prescheduled activities even when I wasn't feeling "right." I've had the courage to do what I wanted to do—pursue my recovery and my writing when many people didn't understand or approve of what I was doing (why I wasn't working a regular job). A few therapists admired the way I had gone through so many ordeals brought on by the illness. A few of them encouraged me to deal with my problems by telling me stories of how they met adversity or how other patients had. I was also pleased to hear their acknowledgment that therapy was often hard work, which it was.

Change. Based on my illness, my involvement with consumer groups, my work with the chronically ill young adults, and what I know about people in general, I have few illusions about change. Change doesn't come fast, it doesn't come easily, and most people resist it. But change does occur and it should be acknowledged when it does. For example, one therapist told me I looked much better than I did when I started seeing him a year earlier. I once remarked to the same therapist that I heard a distinct sadness in his voice. Much later, he commented that he heard a sadness in my voice when I recalled the times I played golf as a child.

Given the great ambivalence, uncertainty, and hopelessness brought on and magnified by the illness, I know how slow and irregular improvement can be. But change, no matter how small, fans the flames of hope—a rare and precious commodity for the chronically ill person. For example, for me, being able to feel distance and calm in a telephone conversation with my father was a clear sign of progress.

Mourning. I've had to mourn for the dreams I've had that I wasn't able to realize and for the expectations my family had for me that I couldn't fulfill. I've seen college friends pass me by in their careers and in the growth of their families. I've seen my own gains wiped out by bad days and weeks and recurrent hospitalizations. Interestingly, the passing of old dreams has been followed by new ones.

I feel that I am managing my illness successfully. Two things in dealing with my illness stand out. It helped me at first to feel that I could become my own therapist, and then to know that I did learn to help myself. Also, I saw the community around me as a valuable resource, and I was creative in finding ways to interact with it. I think others can do the same thing for themselves.

As far as aftercare services are concerned, I was lucky that with the exception of Social Security Disability Insurance, I did not have to depend on the public mental health system. Had I had a suitable job sooner, and appropriate social activities, I think I would have gotten to this point much earlier.

For the first time since childhood I am optimistic about my future. I see myself as having a future, working in the field of journalism or the area of community mental health. In my work with the chronically mentally ill, I see quite a few clients whose illnesses and situations are not so different from my own. I hope my story has meaning for them.

Behind the Mask: A Functional Schizophrenic Copes

Anonymous

THIS ARTICLE ORIGINALLY APPEARED IN THE *Schizophrenia Bulletin*, 1990, 16(3), 547-549.

A little knowledge, people say, is a dangerous thing. My problems first started when I decided to go back to college at the age of 27. My education and exposure to different lifestyles led to discontent with my life and especially my marriage. After taking a psychology course, I recognized signs of stress in myself and went for help to a school psychologist. He advised me to take some weeks away from home and consider a divorce. However, at the end of that time, I was convinced that I could not support myself alone and resigned myself to what seemed a problematic marriage; I came home in despair. It was on this ride home that I first heard messages over the car radio that I was sure were meant for me. I thought my old boyfriend was sending the messages.

That summer I had a very negative perception of my husband. In reflecting back on it, I realize that this did not have much basis in reality. There were quite a number of times that he tried positively to mend the relationship, but I didn't recognize it then. I attributed it to my state of mind. I began to relate incidents that were totally unrelated. A friend of mine talked about my neighbor suing a large company. A week later, the neighbor's daughter, who taught a summer class at college, defended the neighbor's right to sue. I thought it more than coincidence. I felt these two were part of a group of people who were probing my reactions in the process of gathering information about me. I felt that the world was beginning to revolve around me.

In the fall, I threw myself into schoolwork to drown out the unhappiness. I was taking 16 credits, working full time in my business which was a day-care center, and taking care of my children in the absence of their father. He was working out of town and came home on weekends. This load was to cause a major breakdown, though no one noticed my illness, including myself, for 9 months.

During that school term, certain remarks made by my professors led me to the conclusion that they were all working to rescue me from what they thought was an abusive marriage. And I, contrarily, was convinced that I wanted to stay married. I realized that I loved my husband and needed his love in return.

This perception of what I thought was going on caused me to feel a great deal of fear and insecurity. I felt particularly influenced by a foreign language instructor. Because of my loneliness due to my negative feelings toward my husband and his absence, I had transferred my emotional feelings to this man and was prey to a full-blown infatuation which intensified into a very real moral battle within myself.

I was convinced that this professor and I had a private means of communication and, because of this, interpreted most of what he said in class as personally relating to me. Sometimes the things I heard in class were bizarre and had no relation to the class purpose. One time the professor asked the room at large, "So your husband used to be a minister?" I had not divulged that information to him, but because I had recently told my babysitter that, I felt the incident was more than coincidence. I felt that there was a large network of people finding out about me, watching me on the street for some unknown reason. This feeling of lack of privacy soon grew into thinking my house was bugged, a fear I would have off and on for the next 8 years. The bizarre and illogical statements I heard people make were later dismissed as auditory hallucinations. They seemed very real to me, however.

On one occasion, I saw a personal experience of mine written on the blackboard in French and English. I had dropped a history class because I had gone to a party instead of to a required class and so missed an important test I could not make up. All this was written on the board. I did not recognize it as a hallucination at that time. These things caused me considerable anguish, but I continued to act as normal as I could for fear that any bizarre behavior would cause me to lose my job. I did not talk about these things, so the only noticeable signs of my illness were that I became silent and withdrawn, not my usual ebullient and smiling self. I did not think I was sick, but that these things were being done to me. I was still able to function, though I remember getting lunch ready very slowly as if working in molasses, each move an effort. However, my ability to study and write were not impaired because I got A's and B's for that semester.

By Christmas I heard an actor call me a liar over the TV, and I felt sure the media also knew about me. I was displaying considerable insecurity and fear, which caused my husband to quit his job and come home to look after me. However, my job became even more important to me then, and I continued to work though I quit college for a time. I continued to have recurring cycles of delusion and normality. I felt the language teacher was still conveying messages to me through the radio and would spend hours tuned to it. I found messages from my husband in the way things were arranged on the dresser or on the bookshelf. When I went to the store, I bought things that symbolically meant something else to me; each fruit, flavor, or color had a meaning that tied in with my delusion. For example, I would not buy Trix cereal, because it was associated with prostitution in my mind, but I bought a lot of Cheerios to make my day happier. The world of

delusion soon became a world of imagined depravities that were a torment to my moralistic mind. I felt I was the only sane person in the world gone crazy.

Finally, my sleeplessness and delusions led to an inability to function at all. That spring I was supposed to go on a trip. I drove aimlessly around town, afraid to leave, calling my husband frantically and speaking of the fears that bound me. I was hospitalized for 7 days after a checkup by my doctor, and I was referred to a psychiatrist.

Though the Navane he prescribed did help me function again, and I regained my trust in people and my smile, the delusions were always in the background. My husband and children wrapped me in arms of love and acceptance, taking on household duties so I would not be stressed. I continued to hold down my job, after a short rest, but still lived in two worlds. The psychiatrist never asked me about my delusional world, so I never talked about it. Actually, the psychiatrist did not tell me the extent of my illness, only saying that I had a chemical imbalance for which I needed pills. While this gave me the confidence to resume my job and normal living, it also allowed me to believe my delusional world was real. When I finally did some research on my own about the chemical dopamine, he told me I was schizophreniform. After my second acute episode 2 years later, he told me this illness was for life. At this time I joined a very nurturing civic theater drama group. This increased my confidence and memory skills preparatory to going back to college. In the last 3 years, I have returned to college part time while working, and have been successful.

The world of delusion and symbols is as real to me as the normal world. When coincidences happen or people speak in a strange way, I am very likely to take what they say as applying to my delusional world even though I do not usually act on those delusions. Most of the time I see my delusional world superimposed on the real world. At times, the network of people who watch me seem to be benevolent. At other times, I feel controlled and manipulated by my delusion and become so afraid and tormented that I have considered suicide or running away from home to escape. I still have trouble with making up symbols that I compulsively act on to appease my inner needs. For example, when I need to be close to my grandfather, I buy blackberries.

Several years ago, I had visual images of gross, sexual, or obscene images floated in front of my eyes when I least expected them. This mortified me, especially as I thought others could see these images of mine. The experiences really unnerved me until my therapist gave me Theodore Rubin's *Compassion and Self-Hate* (1975) to read. I learned to like myself and accept myself in spite of the ugly tricks my mind plays. Now I do not claim these images—I laugh at them and they go away. They haven't bothered me much since then.

This winter, I was acutely sick for the third time with 7 sleepless nights. I continued to work even though I was convinced that my work was part of an extrasensory perception (ESP) project designed to make me a teacher of ESP. All the remarks the children and other teachers made were integrated into and reinforced by my delusion. However, I continued to behave in a very conservative and rational manner, purposely avoiding behavior that might brand me as different. The abundance of sensory input during this time made the delusions run wild and added to the cumulative effect of the delusions. I wonder now if I wouldn't have been better off to have taken time off from work and waited until the added medication took effect. Perhaps, I could have avoided the sensory input which seemed to have intensified the construction of delusions.

Now, 3 months later, I am free from the delusions for the first time in many years. I find I am able to fight the delusional thinking better by discussing it with people. It also helps me to hear other patients in my Emotions Anonymous (E.A.) group talk about their delusions, because then I realize that I am sick and not the victim of some plot. My illness has caused me to grow in my inner self to discover who I really am with the help of my therapist. There are many unsung heroes and heroines behind the scenes in this saga of mine. I have not been in this battle alone. My family and relatives have offered financial and emotional support throughout my illness. I have a widespread circle of nurturing friends in church, E.A., the civic theater, work, and college. The acceptance I have found gives me courage and fulfills my life in a way no fantasy can. When my delusions threaten to turn to paranoia, I remember my friends and dare to trust, to reach out, and to be vulnerable.

Reference

Rubin, T.I. (1975). *Compassion and self-hate: An alternative to despair.* New York: David McKay Co., Inc.

Schizophrenia: A Pharmacy Student's View

Anonymous

THIS ARTICLE ORIGINALLY APPEARED IN THE
Schizophrenia Bulletin, 1983, 9(1), 152-155N.

On my first day of externship at a hospital I was waiting for the pharmacy to open since I was early by an hour. I was sitting in a lobby wearing a white lab coat and required name tag and catching a cat-nap. A young male patient approached me.

> Excuse me, miss. Do you know that every morning when I get out of bed I feel there is danger everywhere?

Because I had a white coat, he assumed I had an answer to this problem, or at least that I was not in his situation and could offer some assistance. I was taken off guard by this psychiatric patient but said, "You sound very frightened." He said, "Yes. Are you sad or just resting?" I felt he was seeing right through me. "No," I replied, "I'm not sad; I'm just very tired." "Oh," he said, "then I'll leave you alone," and he walked away. My white coat and name tag offered me no immunity from schizophrenia. Pharmacy students are vulnerable just as everyone else is, in spite of the fact that we are taught about all diseases as if we were an immune group. Inside, while I spoke to this patient I wanted to say:

> Yes, I too sense danger everywhere, each morning and all day. It's hard for me to get out of bed, to go out of the house, to talk to people, it's hard just to get dressed and get outside and function. I'm afraid of people, of change. I'm sensitive to sunlight and noise. I never watch the news or read a newspaper because it frightens me.

Talking to this patient had made the conflict within me very obvious. This young man and I are related in a way I cannot share with him, with my fellow students, or with faculty. Yes, I am a pharmacy student. But, yes, I have been diagnosed as schizophrenic and have been hospitalized on three occasions when I could not function. Yes, I am on neuroleptics and must see a psychologist at least once a week, and sometimes more often, in order to function. I wanted to tell him, "Yes, I know how it feels, and isn't it terrible?" Realization of this fact makes my role as a pharmacy student seem artificial—almost as if I must pretend and cover up to get by and pass as "normal"—and then there is always that danger that under stress or pressure my schizophrenia will get out of control and I will be found out. In lectures on antipsychotic drugs I want to tell faculty and fellow students what it feels like to take these medicines and have to depend on them to function "outside" and what it is like to be titrated as an individual to the proper medication and dosage and the problems involved. I want to talk about schizophrenia and let them know it is not so far removed from them and correct some of the common misconceptions held about people who have schizophrenia.

Let me explain some of the major problems and pressures that schizophrenia has presented to me in getting through pharmacy school.

During my first semester of pharmacy school I was on 2 mg of Haldol and 2 mg of Cogentin h.s. as prescribed for me after hospitalization the summer before entry to school. My condition improved psychologically and I seemed to be in remission until I entered school. I found I could neither read the board nor my notes; everything was blurred no matter where I sat. I called the psychiatrist who had prescribed the drugs and remembered his suggesting that I should take 2 more mg of Cogentin. I complied and the next few days I not only had blurry vision, but I could not even see the lines on my notebook paper nor my writing—it was all one blur. In fact, the paper looked colorless. After 2 to 3 days of this, I called the physician back and told him I just could not take this medicine any more, because I could not read or see with it. I could not even tell if I was taking notes on the lines. This side effect, he said, was as he expected; his recommendation now was to drop down to only 2 mg of Cogentin and switch from Haldol to Stelazine 6 mg every day.

This was a compromise solution because, although I could now read and write, my schizophrenia was not so well controlled. I wanted to drop out of school 3 weeks into the semester; I was afraid to go outside and felt as though I did not belong in pharmacy school or would not be able to overcome the stresses to be faced there. Fellow students were remarking to me that I seemed to be more impatient, hyperactive, and depressed. I also had problems with what a friend of mine called "the Stelazine stroll"—akathisia. I continued to go out of the city once a week to see my psychologist who helped me with aspects of the pressures I could not face alone or only with the drugs.

In an effort to be self-destructive, and perhaps as part of the uncontrolled disease process, I stopped my psychotherapy and medication for 3 months. I was a pharmacy student with probably one of the worst compliance problems possible. I should have known better, but the intellectual knowledge I had gained was applicable to everyone except myself. I was not even at this point entirely aware of why I was so noncompliant except that I was self-destructive. The schizophrenia worsened and I became depressed in addition, due to my inability to cope. After pushing myself to the point of a psychotic break, I finally called my psychologist 3 months later and leveled with him about not being on medication. He worked with me about starting it up again. It was now the second semester of my first year in pharmacy school, a semester in which the schizophrenia remained in control with therapy and medication.

Summer school started and I was doing relatively well until there was a personal crisis to which I responded by going off medication. After all, all these other people around me were making it without meds, why couldn't I? So I went on and deteriorated during the summer and into fall until the choice became 4 to 8 weeks of hospitalization (and dropping out of pharmacy school as a consequence) or taking the medicine. I chose the latter, saying to my psychologist that I didn't like either choice.

I was then in my first semester of my second year. I had just restarted Stelazine at 8 mg h.s., an increased dose, and began having what I thought were seizures. In my classes I experienced an aura and then a wave hit me. I felt overstimulated and could hear a lecture but not process the information and take notes. My hand tremor was so bad during these episodes that I could not write. My psychologist suggested a consultation with the psychiatrist who had supervised my previous hospitalizations and prescribed the medications.

It is not clear whether the psychiatrist misunderstood my reason for calling or whether I misunderstood his advice about Cogentin. However, I later learned that Cogentin makes blurred vision worse, not better.

Although the psychiatrist was hesitant to give me the label for what was happening, I insisted, and he said it was "transient psychotic episodes." The problem with this development was that it began after I had already been taking an increased amount of the medication. Where could we go from here? The psychiatrist recommended titration, increasing the dose of Stelazine. However, it didn't work. He then suggested taking Stelazine along with another antipsychotic drug with more milligram potency (Navane 5 mg h.s.), but I was still having acute psychotic episodes in my classes. I had taken to sitting in the back of the classroom, although I could not see the board, because I needed to be able to leave the room when this occurred, at the suggestion of the psychiatrist that I not sit there and suffer through it. I had explained away my change in seating to the other students by saying I felt I was going to have a seizure or by joking and saying I had decided I didn't care to see what teachers were writing on the board any more.

When I got up in the morning, I could predict that the episodes would occur and where—I had a prodrome. There were many frantic long distance calls to my psychologist after these episodes. I had to tell someone who could help me with what was happening to me. I, at this point, felt scared enough that never again would I have a compliance problem. I didn't want to lose all I had worked for in pharmacy school. I noticed the episodes were worse when emotionally volatile material was discussed in classes, such as antipsychotic agents, characteristics of schizophrenia, depression—all problems I had to cope with daily and that remained unresolved for me.

Because of my response, the psychiatrist suggested 5 mg of Navane in the morning and 5 mg of Navane h.s. with 2 mg of Cogentin h.s. From October to December, I suffered the psychotic episodes and the problems of getting properly titrated on the medicine until psychotic episodes no longer occurred. Only the so-called "aura" remained.

As a consequence of the psychotic episodes and occasionally having to leave the classroom, I missed a lot of notes in my classes. All this work had to be made up. This increased the pressure I was under, which in turn worsened the schizophrenic symptoms and almost forced me into a hospitalization. I did not want to drop out of school or receive too many incomplete grades, which would have been the result of 4 to 8 weeks of hospitalization to get properly titrated on the medication and to

decrease disease symptoms. However, most of my instructors had rigid rules about missing exams and taking make-up exams. To reduce the pressure, I told the professor with whom I was doing independent study that for medical reasons I would not be able to finish the paper due in that course. I decided to tell him why and he allowed me the incomplete grade without requiring a medical letter on file, saving me the possible consequences of having this information on written record. And, most importantly, he did not treat me differently as a result of knowing. This reduced my stress and gave me time to make up work and take my final examinations. It also allowed me to work on my independent study paper during vacation and to do a good job on it while I was finally beginning to get a positive response to the medication.

I enjoyed winter break and finished my independent study project without incident, but as second semester approached I began to fear the room we had classes in, all the people and stimulation, and to fear recurrence of these episodes. What scared me most was the fact that this disease could prevent me from doing something I really wanted to do and needed to do to be psychologically healthy—that is, complete pharmacy school—and the knowledge that schizophrenia does this to many people's lives. I could not accept the fact that intellectually I could be capable of something that I may not at times be capable of emotionally.

When classes started, I still felt overstimulated and again had prodromes of psychotic episodes. I could not process information when people were talking; everything just seemed like noise. I was now on 5 mg of Navane b.i.d. and 2 mg of Cogentin h.s. I got up enough courage to sit in front of the class again, but I was very fearful. My psychologist explained that I had begun to associate that classroom with these episodes and that extreme anxiety was causing dissociation reactions in me: I felt I was outside my body; I was watching everything. I wanted an antianxiety agent to get rid of these feelings and that constant impending feeling that a psychotic episode would begin. The psychiatrist prescribed 5 mg of Valium in the morning and at bedtime when necessary. I took it only in the morning when I could not restructure my environment and situation to reduce the anxiety. For the first several weeks I was falling asleep in my first class and had double vision because I could not keep my eyes open. Finally, I became tolerant to the sedative effect.

So this is the answer right now for me: neuroleptics, an anti-anxiety agent, an anti-Parkinson agent, and intense long-term psychotherapy with my psychologist. And I still look around at my fellow students and say to myself, "they do it without medicine, or doctors, or going to a psychiatric ward," but I needed all these things to cope with the pressure and stress of pharmacy school and life.

What I have been trying to express here is the actual reality of what being "individually titrated to an antipsychotic medication" and having schizophrenia means to someone personally going through it as opposed to how objectively and easily it is expressed in pharmacy classes. My instructors have stated that "antipsychotics alleviate symptoms but do not cure psychoses," but this matter-of-fact statement has a very personal meaning for me. It involves internal conflicts and many complicated adjustments—getting to a psychologist outside the city, or if the necessity of hospitalization occurs, getting hospitalized outside the city so fellow students and the pharmacy school will not have access to that information about me. It means never being able to see well because of the side effects of the medication. It also means enormous medical bills and debts.

I recall a teacher, a Pharm.D., telling the class that schizophrenics tend to have low IQs. He was wrong; the research does not support this. They probably do tend, because of the disease, to be more environmentally deprived and have interruptions in their schooling.

I have heard fellow students talking about violent crimes saying, "Oh, you know that person was schizophrenic." No one is teaching these health professionals what the word means, what it does to people, and that schizophrenics are generally less violent than the rest of the general population.

Finally, I heard a teacher in one class talk about long-term chronic illness such as schizophrenia in a way that suggested the teacher knew something about the disease and had looked beyond the myths. Through this class, I began to understand a little better my own noncompliance with the psychotropic drugs; how unacceptable my illness was not only to me, but would have been to others if they had known my diagnosis. I didn't take the medicine at times because I didn't want the disease, its problems, and its stigma. I wanted to be normal. And even now in 1980, in a professional pharmacy school, it would probably shock many people to know a schizophrenic was in their class, would be a pharmacist, and could do a good job. And knowledge of it could cause loss of many friends and acquaintances. So even now I must write this article anonymously. But I want people to know I have schizophrenia, that I need medicine and psychotherapy, and at some times I have required hospitalization. But, I also want them to know that I have been on the dean's list, and have friends, and expect to receive my pharmacy degree from a major university.

When you think about schizophrenia next time, try to remember me; there are more people like me out there trying to overcome a poorly understood disease and doing the best they can with what medicine and psychotherapy have to offer them. And some of them are making it.

PAST THE STRUGGLES OF MENTAL ILLNESS, TOWARD THE DEVELOPMENT OF QUALITY LIVES

Donna Orrin

DONNA ORRIN, M.S.W., PRESIDENT OF CREATIVE CONNECTIONS, PRESENTS WORKSHOPS FOR CONSUMERS, FAMILIES, AND PROFESSIONALS. ADDRESS CORRESPONDENCE TO HER AT CREATIVE CONNECTIONS, P.O. BOX 7044, ANN ARBOR, MI 48107

THE THERAPIST REFERRED TO IN THE ARTICLE, BOB EGRI, M.A., C.S.W., IS CO-DIRECTOR OF COUNSELING RESOURCES OF ANN ARBOR, 2645 PETERS ROAD, DEXTER, MICHIGAN 48130.

THIS ARTICLE ORIGINALLY APPEARED IN *Innovations and Research*, 1994, 3(3), 41-45 AND IS REPRINTED WITH PERMISSION.

Often mental health professionals, with a strong sense of personal and professional missions to provide optimum services, hear of the failure of the system to meet the needs of those they serve. It is important to take a look at, and celebrate, the difference professionals can and do make in the lives of those who so courageously work hard to survive and overcome the struggles of mental illness.

Although I have struggled with chronic mental illness for the past 26 years, I have also been fortunate enough at times, to have incredible support from family, friends, and mental health professionals. As a result, I have been able to accomplish a great deal, despite my illness. Of course, sometimes, when reaching out to friends or family members, there have been times that doors have slammed in my face, phones have slammed down after expressions of anger, and people have avoided me and abandoned me as "hopeless" or "undesirable." It has, at times, been an excruciatingly painful, difficult, and impossible journey. Yet, other times, I have achieved great successes and have felt happy with my life.

In fact, at times, chosen goals have even been easy, effortless, and enjoyable, thanks to the years of therapy with my therapist, Bob Egri, that have so greatly benefited me, and the therapeutic work I have done. While my life has been so full of ups and downs, I now have, what I consider to be, a true "quality of life." Fortunately, Bob has given his best (and then some) to provide me with the respect, acceptance, compassion, understanding, and inspiration to not only overcome tremendous obstacles, but also to eventually lead me to a place where I can and do now create the life of my choice.

My illness has taken many forms in the last 26 years. The difficulties, the successes despite the illness, the work with my therapist in overcoming crises, and the eventual development of a quality of life has taught me that, with support, great progress is possible.

Basic attitudes in mental health professionals, such as respect, acceptance, humor, a sense of hope, and teamwork between therapist and client enable an individual to cope with mental illness.

Assisting individuals in identifying their personal needs and wants and assertively discussing them in their relationships and varied aspects of life bring opportunities for an improved life. This often begins in therapy, at the prompting of the therapist so the client feels safe in discussing any upsetting feelings about therapy or the therapist.

Strategies, such as contracts, letters to self, recognition of symptoms, appreciation of successes, goal setting, and taking credit for working on the recovery process, are helpful tools to lead someone through severe crises. In the event of suicidal ideation, understanding and non-judgmental support is essential.

Experiences I have faced in the last 26 years enable me to state with conviction that the above-mentioned characteristics and strategies can make an incredible difference. My illness began when I first left home for college. I became seriously depressed, attempted suicide, and dropped out of school. Actually, during the first 18 years of my life, I experienced constant, negative, self-critical thoughts, although I never shared this with anyone. After dropping out of college, I experienced the manic highs of my illness and began to experience psychotic symptoms. I remained in denial and refused hospitalization despite the strong efforts of friends and family to convince me I needed help. Eventually, I did agree to hospitalization and began a 24-year cycle of manic-depression with psychotic symptoms.

While I have been hospitalized about 30 times in the last 26 years, and have lived in four different group homes (with the length of stay varying from 2 weeks to 4 months), I have also earned my bachelor's degree in communication. I have worked 10 years (on and off, due to my illness), as a media specialist. I have also received my M.S.W. from the University of Michigan and worked 2 years as a social worker on a psychiatric in-patient unit. During this same time period of the 24 years, I have also spent 8 months laying on my mother's couch, thinking of all the mistakes I made in my life. (And it took me months to think of all my mistakes!) I didn't even watch TV or listen to the radio. (That was too painful, for it brought up sad memories, or reminded me of what my life lacked). My mother encouraged me to take a short walk with her once a day. If she hadn't insisted

Basic attitudes in mental health professionals, such as respect, acceptance, humor, a sense of hope, and teamwork between therapist and client enable an individual to cope with mental illness.

and offered to go with me, I wouldn't have left the couch. It was a struggle for her, believe me. I spoke with only one friend, 1 hour each week. She had no idea about my condition or life-style as we basically had intellectual talks. Prior to the last 2 years, I was unemployed and did not engage in any volunteer activities for 4 years, due to my disability. I had become devastated and experienced symptoms of chronic mental illness after the unexpected and sudden death of my twin brother.

I was in and out of hospitals. I had suicidal ideation, and attempted suicide twice. Thanks to the help of my therapist, I was able to get control over the suicidal ideation. The suicidal thoughts lingered, and were very strong, but strategies I will discuss later, helped me to stop myself from following through with the suicidal urges.

During these years, there were long, dragged out months, where I only spoke with my mother on the phone, 5 minutes a day. She begged me to say one—just one— positive thing during these short talks, but I was unable to do so. She threatened to stop talking to me if I could not say one positive thing, as this dragged her down so. Her high blood pressure increased. However, she did still talk to me, despite my inability to find anything positive to say. During this time, I also went to therapy for 1 hour per week.

Mostly, I would wander aimlessly, lost in a deep morass. Eventually, I began a program at a partial hospital. That was very helpful, but the real difference began after I had ECT almost 4 years ago. It isn't for everyone, but it worked for me. My depression lifted, ruminating, negative thoughts ceased, suicidal thoughts disappeared, I lost the hostility I had toward my family, I became more active, and therapy once again, became extraordinarily helpful for me. In fact, it benefited me more than it ever had. I want to emphasize what works for one individual does not work for another, but ECT was the pivotal point in my life. However, if I had not continued with my therapy after the ECT treatments, I would not be doing as well as I am now.

My life has gone from a miserable, mere existence to a full life. I now have excellent friendships and good relationships with most of my family. (Not everybody, but we can't expect too many miracles, can we?) I also have meaningful, enjoyable work, a balanced life including solitude, entertainment, recreation, spiritual development, personal growth, stability, and a good dose of self-esteem.

I now have my own business, and publish articles and present workshops related to mental illness on local, state, and national levels. I address professionals, family members, and consumers, dealing with a vast variety of issues. During the past 3 years, I have served as a Community Mental Health Board Member for Washenaw County in Michigan and recently was appointed by the governor to the Michigan Rehabilitation Advisory Council. I co-produced an award winning documentary based on a discussion/writing workshop I developed, and produced a workshop manual, audiocassete, a photo-poetry book, and a poetry book about the benefits of treatment.

This progress did not come easy, by any means. Often, it was a matter of reminding myself that three steps forward and

Relapse is a part of recovery. It is not a failure.

two steps back, is still progress. Other times, it has been necessary to try to conceive of the fact that three steps forward and five steps back, is still progress. Such moments have provided the opportunity to work through important issues in therapy, where I could then become more self-aware and eventually, more in control of my life. Relapse is a part of recovery. It is not a failure.

Mental health professionals have helped me to make the transition from struggling with a chronic mental illness to coping with it and living a good life.

Basic attitudes and characteristics can make a huge difference in a client's life, especially for someone who does not necessarily get the kind of acceptance, respect, and sense of equality that is so important in anyone's life. Appreciation, encouragement, and sensitivity go a long way toward enabling an individual to have the courage to do the kind of self-evaluation that is so essential for coping with difficult times.

Another important trait, I've found, is humor. Humor can improve any situation. Laughter eases the pain, is enjoyable, and gives an opportunity to work on concerns with less stress. For example, when I first started therapy, I was very troubled by intense, traumatic experiences. I felt a burden and pain that I was convinced would last forever. My therapist said, "Someday, you're going to laugh at this." I then began to laugh at the absurdity of such a suggestion. Bob quickly said, "See, you're laughing already." His constant wit has sustained me through many hard times.

There have been times that the vast majority of people in my life have given me up as "hopeless." During these dry spells, when I floundered, my therapist continued to try to give me a sense of hope. He has never given up on me, even when I was strongly immersed in a sense of hopelessness. As the situation worsened and remained seemingly hopeless to me and others, Bob kept his firm belief in my ability to overcome symptoms and move toward an enriching life. To be persistent, through such longstanding severe crises, must be extremely difficult for the therapist. Nonetheless, eventually, it can have its great rewards for therapist and client alike.

In contrast, a lack of hope has the danger of almost paralyzing a person, or preventing them from going after their dreams. Once, as I was being discharged from a hospital, my social worker told me, "Face the facts. You'll only be a store clerk a few months out of each year. As you get older, you'll have more and more hospitalizations. You're just not being realistic, Donna, if you expect anything more than that."

It was after that, that I earned my M.S.W. and worked as a social worker both in a state hospital and the psychiatric ward of a private hospital. Luckily, I had enough trust in my therapist, and felt enough respect from him, that I shared with him, one day, my dream of going back to school. I had not spoken of that goal with anyone, although it was a goal I had long thought about. Bob was encouraging, and we worked toward overcoming stresses or obstacles in obtaining my goal.

One of the most helpful results of my therapy has been my growing ability to identify and discuss my needs and wants, as well as concerns I may feel about my relationships. This ability began with the encouragement of my therapist to discuss any concerns or upsetting feelings I had about therapy or about him, as my therapist. He also encouraged me to vent the anger I had bottled up. As a result, I felt safe enough to voice my upsetting feelings. We have worked through many difficulties in this realm. Since Bob made it safe for me to voice and work through my concerns, I have learned I can express my needs and

wants with others in a way that is respectful to others as well as to myself. This process has enabled me to improve all my relationships: friendships, family relationships, and interactions with coworkers are easier and more fulfilling. There is, at times, an ease with identifying and discussing important elements within the relationships.

There are some needs and wants that could be easily overlooked. The "little things," which may not be so little, have also provided me with great pleasure. As I work through the recovery process, with my therapist, I begin to appreciate sitting by ponds with ducks and seagulls, watching sunsets, taking walks through woods, listening to music and appreciating art. Identifying these sort of needs are also important.

Another significant need to identify is that of a well-balanced amount of solitude. Certainly, as a mental health consumer, there have been countless times, that I have wished for more socialization and activity in my life. Nonetheless, I am aware I need some quiet times for myself as well. Such moments have brought a sense of peacefulness in my life. These are times I get to know myself better and to relax. I listen to myself at these times. Socrates, the greatest thinker of all times, said, "Know thyself." You don't get to know yourself by dashing from one activity to the next. The best way I have found to know myself, is during those moments to myself when I can look inside. Many ideas come to me at these times, as well. Still, it is not always necessary for me to think about things. There is a poster that states, "Sometimes, I sits and thinks, and sometimes, I just sits!"

The recognition of individual needs, for me, has also included the awareness of the importance for me to listen to my body. To use an old phrase, "Go with the flow." But I am not referring to the flow of society. I am referring to my own internal flow. I have discovered that I know when I want to be with a friend, when I want to browse through a store, when I want to write or go for a walk, when I want to work on a project or a therapy exercise. I also knew when I was ready to return to work after working on my recovery. By listening to myself, and following the promptings that come from myself, I find I am happier. I accomplish more in the long run, because I work on my projects when I am emotionally prepared to. I am able to live in the manner I most enjoy.

I try to be kind to myself, rather than hard on myself, as I so often have been. This includes treating myself well. I give myself little "treats" that I enjoy.

There are also a vast variety of strategies that can help a client through difficulties and lead to personal growth. One strategy that has been helpful for me is utilizing contracts. Bob and I discuss the situation, then I write a contract for the appropriate situation. For example, writing a contract was one of the tools that kept me from acting on the urges to kill myself. I gave a copy to my therapist and kept a copy for myself, in a constantly visible place. The contract read, "I agree to call Bob if I am about to use nearby materials to kill myself. At the time, I may not be compelled to follow through with this commitment. I may feel I want to take advantage of a possible opportunity to end what may appear to be an endlessly painful and hopeless life. Depression leads to such irrational thoughts. In fact, I have always risen from depression to once again embrace life. Regardless of how valid or invalid this argument may sound to me at the time, this agreement alone commits me to contacting Bob if I am about to kill myself. It is my understanding that we are embarking on a deeper, more effective form of therapy designed to deal with core issues, and that this new treatment would not be initiated without this serious and sincere commitment."

On the more light-hearted side, I have found that acknowledging and appreciating successes along the way can be a real boost. There is a cartoon where two people are standing beside a ladder. There is a sign above the ladder that states this ladder is the "ladder of success." One person says to the other, "Frankly, I was hoping for an elevator."

There are no elevators. That makes it more important to appreciate each gradient step along the way. The therapist and client can then further appreciate the progress they make as a team, and the significance of the process along the way.

Rather than judge an individual who attempts suicide, supporting that person in a positive manner may well provide the life preserver so desperately needed at that time.

My therapist has also helped me to recognize my symptoms. Not just the usual symptoms, but also the unique, individual symptoms. For example, I start to think squirrels are evil when I begin to become psychotic. Whenever I notice any symptoms, I call my therapist and psychiatrist immediately, so I can "nip my illness in the bud." While I have experienced psychotic, manic, and depressive symptoms in the last 2 years, I have handled the situations swiftly. After a few days of increased medication, I have been able to return to my maintenance dosage. I used to decompensate quickly and my symptoms would escalate rapidly and I would land in the hospital even though I had eventually learned to recognize my symptoms before anyone else did. I now act quickly enough to prevent that escalation. As I said earlier, I have not been hospitalized during the last 3½ years. I quickly get to a safe environment that is not overly stimulative and take care of basic needs for sleep, proper nutrition, exercise, as well as any psychological needs. With a multidisciplinary approach, I have gotten control over symptoms when they appear.

I also let friends, family members, and some co-workers know what my symptoms are. They know they can gently take me aside and speak to me about any concerns they may have. They also have the number of my therapist, in the event I may escalate too quickly to identify the symptoms and reach a point of denial. However, as I said, after all these years of experience, I am now able to easily identify symptoms, and take the appropriate actions quickly.

Another useful strategy I have long employed has been to set short-term and long-term goals. If I am not doing well, I may just dream for awhile and let myself turn them into goals when the time is right. Sometimes, if I am suicidal, I only try to find one thing to look forward to. Sometimes, it is as simple as looking forward to a cold glass of water in the morning. Other times, I may need to look further ahead, because nothing immediate appears at all pleasurable. For instance, I once envisioned the flowers that would appear on the trees in one month. It was the only thing I had to look forward to for the next 4 weeks, and it helped me get through those difficult, extremely painful days. However, if I am living a full life, I select goals for seven different areas of my life: mental, emotional, spiritual, physical, social, financial, and professional.

It has also been important to give myself credit for the recovery process. Working through recovery is a great accomplishment; far greater than earning any degree you can hang on the wall or any project you can hope to complete. People deserve credit for their courage, persistence, and stamina. Other accomplishments can occur later. As Bob has often told me, "Once you have mastered yourself, you can master anything. First, you must master yourself." Therapy has given me the opportunity to work through issues as well as crises, and address internal and external obstacles in my recovery process. I have gained far more than I expected to by facing difficult personal concerns in therapy. My self-awareness and control over my thoughts, feelings, actions, and life have increased dramatically.

Another useful strategy has been writing letters to myself. When I am feeling well, I think about what I would like to say to myself if I feel depressed, hopeless, or in need of hospitalization, but feeling like I don't want to admit myself.

I have also written a letter to myself in case I ever again feel suicidal. It reads, in part, "More than once, I have felt completely hopeless, only to rise again like the Phoenix. It is far too easy to believe the negative thoughts. But history does not support them. I have risen each and every time I have fallen, to once again reach a time where I felt glad to be alive."

What can I give myself to make it through struggles that strip me of all of my self-esteem? To know that these thoughts may come again and just to push them aside. "Oh, it's you again. It's no new news that you're back, but I'm not going to delve into you, ruminating about you, over and over."

The negative thoughts can be so overwhelming, so strong and powerful, so all-encompassing. It is difficult to ignore them until you can deal with them and get totally rid of them.

But I can choose not to believe them. ('Oh, there's that thought again. Let it go. We'll get rid of it. I've thought that before, and it proved not to be true. It's like when I have psychotic symptoms. I hear voices, but now I know they are a symptom and not real, although they appear real and I used to think they were real.')

The negatives have never proven to be true in the long run; although they seem so apparent and real at the time.

Consider the negativity only as symptoms of an illness. A temporary crisis that I can and will and have in the past, overcome. Even if the temporary crisis last months or years (as it sometimes has), it is still only temporary..."

When I am suicidal, my poverty of thought and therefore, lack of conversation, convinces me I have nothing to offer. I feel like "I am nothing," a burden to all, unworthy of living and totally worthless. Each moment is filled with terror and pain. I feel as if there is no escape.

Once, I needed to get my stomach pumped in order to continue living. I had taken enough pills to kill myself. As my stomach was being pumped, I prayed that I would live. I wondered at this time, why I had attempted suicide if I really wanted to live. Actually, I hated life, but feared the unknown of death more. Criticism or anger from others at this time, or afterwards, about the attempt, was not helpful. It only made matters worse. It proved to me that I really was a burden to others and gave me more reason to attempt suicide. It strengthened the already strong, negative thoughts I had about myself (which were the symptoms of my illness, not a personal sign of weakness). As important people in my life yelled at me and criticized me, my illness worsened. Support, sensitivity, and understanding is essential to my well-being; indeed, to my life, at such times. As William Styron has said, "Condemning a person who attempts suicide is like condemning a wild animal for gnawing off its foot to escape a trap."

Rather than judge an individual who attempts suicide, supporting that person in a positive manner may well provide the life preserver so desperately needed at that time.

In fact, accepting, supportive, positive people are important to the entire recovery process. There is already enough negativity provided by the illness itself.

It is my hope that people will recognize that the impossible is possible, and that they will believe in the abilities of persons who may be experiencing what often appears to be insurmountable odds. With help, the debilitating effects of a most serious illness can be cast aside and individuals recovering from mental illness can not only dream like anyone else, they can actually achieve their dreams. Mental health professionals play a significant part in the development of quality lives. Their understanding, sensitivity, respect, and support is essential. In fact, it can be the cornerstone building block for helping others not only survive great crises, but also for helping people move beyond the terror, pain, and struggle of mental illness to arrive at a place where they can create the lives of their choice. Strategies such as recognizing symptoms, appreciating successes, using contracts, letters, goal setting, and helping individuals give themselves credit for the arduous task of working through the recovery process, can go a long way toward enabling great progress. During periods of suicidal ideation, non-judgmental support is especially essential and the mental health professionals can help by encouraging family members to do their best under a most distressing, frustrating, helpless time.

Mental health professionals, who work so hard, and put in so many long hours, under a most demanding schedule, deserve great credit for the mission they have selected. Their decisions to help others in their struggle to transform pain into joy, is worthy of far more commendation than anyone could ever offer.

Twelve Aspects of Coping for Persons with Serious and Persistent Mental Illness

Frederick J. Frese

FREDERICK J. FRESE, III, PH.D., CURRENTLY SERVES AS SECOND VICE PRESIDENT OF THE NATIONAL ALLIANCE FOR THE MENTALLY ILL AND IS PAST PRESIDENT OF THE NATIONAL MENTAL HEALTH CONSUMER' ASSOCIATION.

THIS ARTICLE ORIGINALLY APPEARED IN *Innovations and Research*, 1993, 2(3), 39-46 AND IS REPRINTED WITH PERMISSION.

As with the acquisition of most skills, learning to cope with a disability is a function of experience and guidance from others. The author, diagnosed with schizophrenia at age 25, is now a psychologist who works with persons hospitalized with mental illness. He has frequently delivered presentations about coping with schizophrenia during the past 3 years. His ideas are based on his personal experience of living with the disorder, his experience with his patients, and that which "rings true" to his thoughts on twelve aspects of learning to live with this serious mental disorder.

When people lie, sparks are set off in the brain, thus melting brain chemicals which may be the conscience and pride. "I was 2 years old when I got my doctorate, an M.D. from Harvard. I got a Ph.D. in comparative literature and a law degree at the same time, as well as a phi beta kappa in care-giving from Sunny Acres."

The above is a paraphrased sample of speech from one of my actively psychotic schizophrenic friends. She is really a very nice person and has a lot of good ideas, but obviously something is not quite right with the way she is thinking.

I, too, am a person with schizophrenia. I am not currently psychotic but I have been in the state of psychosis frequently enough to have become somewhat familiar with the trips there and back.

After years of keeping my experiences with schizophrenia a secret, a few years ago I decided to become open about my condition. Initially I revealed my background during talks I was giving locally. Later, at the invitation of various groups of professionals, consumer/survivors and family members, I began giving talks around the country. At first I gave a talk calling for partnership between consumer/survivors, professionals, and family members. The speech was fairly well received. But at the annual convention of the South Dakota Alliance for the Mentally Ill, I was asked to give two different speeches to the same audience. I decided to give the second speech on coping skills. In doing so I learned consumers and family members would far more like to hear about how to go about living with schizophrenia than about more theoretical or political aspects of caring for the mentally ill.

My first speech in South Dakota was given almost 3 years ago. Since then I have given the same basic talk several dozen times in about half the states. The speech has evolved considerably since it was first delivered, as audience members contributed comments that I felt were particularly valuable.

My talk addresses twelve aspects of coping with schizophrenia. I have organized it a little differently for this article, but I still keep the basic twelve aspects as the organizational framework for the presentation. What follows is the essence of the basic speech, adapted for publication.

1.) Denial, Acceptance, and One's Belief Structure

I cannot tell you how difficult it is for a person to accept the fact that he or she is schizophrenic. Since the time when we were very young we have all been conditioned to accept that if something is crazy or insane, its worth to us is automatically dismissed. We live in a world that is held together by rational connections. That which is logical or reasonable is acceptable. That which is not reasonable is not acceptable.

The nature of this disorder is that it effects the chemistry that controls your cognitive processes. It affects your belief system. It fools you into believing that what you are thinking or what you believe is true and correct, when others can usually tell that your thinking processes are not functioning well.

I had been hospitalized five times before I was willing to consider the possibility that there might be something wrong with me. We are all conditioned from birth not to accept that which is crazy or insane. That which is insane is beyond the pale of that which those in our human family will accept. We accept that which is logical, that which is rational and reasonable. That which is crazy is dismissed. Therefore it is very difficult for us to accept that what we are thinking is in fact crazy. Psychosis is a "catch 22." If you understand that you are insane then you are thinking properly and are therefore not insane. You can only be psychotic if in fact you believe that you are not. Therefore almost everyone with this disorder initially denies that they have it. Some deny it all their lives. Most of the 300 patients I have in the hospital where I work will tell you that they are not mentally ill. Denial of the disorder comes as part of the territory for most of us who have it. Some of those who have the disorder not only deny that they have it but also deny that it exists.

It is exceedingly difficult for you to admit to yourself that your mind does not function properly. It fools you. With this disorder you develop an epistemological structure that is not consonant with that of the vast majority of those in the larger, majority population.

But if one does not acknowledge that they have the disorder, how can it be helped? Why would anyone want to be cured of a disorder that they do not believe they have ?

I find that a good approach for persons in such denial is to point out that, even though they may not have the disorder, it is true that they have been treated by others as though they do have mental illness. They will usually agree with this thesis, especially if they have been hospitalized. Often these folks will accept being referred to with a term like, "survivor." Once they have accepted the fact that others may view them as mentally ill, they then have some motivation to learn more about the disorder.

It is generally best not to try to make a "frontal assault" against denial. Try to establish a trusting relationship and gradually chip away or "defreeze" the rigid cognitive defensive structure that constitutes the denial.

2.) Knowledge of the Disorder

In this, the "Decade of the Brain," evidence continues to mount that viewed from an objective, or, scientific perspective, schizophrenia is a brain-based disorder. It can be best conceptualized as an imbalance in the biochemistry of the brain's neurotransmitting systems (Gershon & Rieder, 1992; Wong et al., 1986). Studies are published with great frequency now, further establishing the neurophysiological correlates and consequences of serious mental illness. As articulated by one prominent psychiatrist, "Patients have to be taught to accept the fact that they are ill, that this is not a mystical experience but a disease—an illness that needs treatment." (Cancro, 1992).

From the viewpoint of the person with the disorder, however, the phenomenon can be very much like a mystical experience. The young psychiatrist, Carol North (1987), describes herself as being in a parallel reality or at a cosmic juncture. I (Frese, 1993a) have referred to one of my breakdowns as "cruising the cosmos." David Zelt (1981) describes himself as being "constantly in touch with the infinite and the eternal."

The nature of the disorder is that it affects the brain's thought and belief systems, it affects a person's confidence in what is truthful. There-fore, to the person who is experiencing the disorder it very much can be a mystical journey where poetic relationships and metaphorical associations dictate truth. To the person who is experiencing the disorder, these subjective experiences are very real indeed.

Therefore, while one should try to understand as much as possible about how the disorder is accompanied by biochemical irregularities, one should also understand that for the person who has the schizophrenia, it indeed can be a mystical or even a religious experience.

Often these mystical experiences can be most seductive. One has the feeling that he is having special insights and even special powers. One is no longer restricted by the rigid control of rationality. One begins engaging in what experts have called paleo-logic (Arieti & Brody, 1974) or parataxic thinking (Sullivan, 1953). Many consumer/survivors prefer the term, "poetic" logic.

Because our disability is one of a biochemical imbalance, it is reasonable that our "crutch" is chemical. For us, our crutch is the neuroleptic medications that we take.

3.) Medication, Chemicals

Persons with serious mental illness are disabled, just like people who are blind, deaf or crippled. Like others who are disabled we can be helped by artificial support. Where the blind may have a cane or a seeing eye dog, the deaf may be helped with a hearing aid, and the crippled may be helped with a wheelchair or a crutch, we, too, can be helped by artificial means. Because our disability is one of a biochemical imbalance, it is reasonable that our "crutch" is chemical. For us, our crutch is the neuroleptic medications that we take. In order to keep our brain's neuro-chemical processes properly balanced, we need the assistance of helpful chemicals, prescribed medications. Certainly without having such medications available, I would not be able to function as I do today. True, there are side effects of these drugs: akathisia, akinesia, dyskinesia, dystonia, et cetera, and these can be quite problematic, even disabling. But the medications are becoming better. Around the country I have met dozens of persons who have been helped by clozapine, which has only been widely available in this country for a relatively short time. The drugs Risperidone, Roxiam, and Olanzapine, which may be widely available during the next few years hold out further hope for those of us who are disabled with mental illness. Those of us who are dependent on these drugs should attempt to learn all we can about them and their side effects, both short term and long term. These medications hold such hope for us. But just as some chemicals function to assist us, others are harmful to us. Such "street drugs" as PCP and amphetamines are much more likely to cause a recovered schizophrenic to relapse into psychosis than they are to have a similar effect on a "normal" individual. Likewise, marijuana and alcohol also increase the likelihood that persons with these vulnerabilities are going to experience mental breakdowns. Those of us with these vulnerabilities to breakdowns in our biochemical systems need to learn as much as possible about the effects of drugs so that we can utilize and avoid them in a judicious manner.

4.) "Paleologic" or Delusional Thinking

When a healthy individual functions in a normal manner, encountering moderate degrees of stress and pressure, his or her physiological systems operate in a healthy manner. But when stress increases and is sustained, physiological systems begin to wear and weaken. Eventually they malfunction. They break.

Different individuals react in different ways. Some people react more with blood pressure increases, others more readily react with sweaty palms. Still others react with increased gastro-motility, their stomachs "churn." Psychophysiologists refer to this as "response specificity," and point out that people tend to develop symptoms in the physiological systems in which they are most reactive (Sternbach, 1966). Blood pressure reactors develop hypertension, skin reactors develop hives, stomach reactors develop ulcers.

From this perspective it is not unreasonable to view some of us as neurotransmitter reactors. When we are functioning in a normal manner, we are rational, but we tend to overreact to stress with our emotions and our cognitions. Ordinarily we

reason as others do. Our mechanisms for processing information in a logical, rational manner are intact. We are said to use linear logic and Aristotelian reasoning. When our systems encounter pressures, our physiological/mental processes react as a defense. Our mental processes react in such a manner as to defend against the stressors. We may become more vigilant, more suspicious. Our thinking may speed up, our minds may begin to race. We may start developing new, more original ways of thinking about things. Our coping mechanisms begin to strain. At some point our minds begin to break. At first they just crack a little. They craze. Then we begin to "go crazy." We lose our ability to remain rational. Instead our minds revert to an evolutionarily earlier way of functioning.

Beneath our centers for rational processing in the brain resides the paleocortex, the limbic cortex, the reptilian brain. Here are the centers of emotions, of anger, of fear, of humor and of love. Ordinarily from this paleocortex, emotional activity affects us as when we are moved to tears by a story or to laughter by a joke. But we rapidly recover control and are guided by rationality. We remain confident that that which is reasonable or logical is true. We can believe that which strikes us as rational.

But when our rational processes break, our cognitions become dominated by the activities of the paleocortex. Our mental processes begin to become dominated by paleologic (Arieti & Brody, 1974) activity. We begin to lose our confidence in rational processing and begin to see truth in nonlinear relationships.

5.) Social Deficits

Miller and Flack (1990) presented an interesting paper recently. In observing schizophrenics in social interaction and comparing us with normals, they found that we tend not to look at the person to whom we are talking. From our perspective there is good reason for this, of course. We are more easily distracted and if we look at others while we are talking we will see their facial reactions, making it more difficult to focus on what we are saying. This naturally can be most disconcerting to the person with whom we are conversing. Normals expect signs of interaction when they are speaking with others. Since we often fail to respond in the expected manner, we throw them off.

Miller and Flack also point out that compared to normals we schizophrenics are much less likely than normals to nod in agreement or move our hands in rhythm with our partner's speech. Often when we do nod appropriately it will be later in the course of talking than is usually expected. The reason for such delaying is that we spend a longer time processing information than normals. Such delays of course tend to throw off the rhythms of a conversation. Normals find this disconcerting. They often do not realize that our failure to send and receive the expected cues during conversation is part of our disability.

Normals send other signals in conversational encounters. They use short statements at the beginning and end "How are you?" or "See you Wednesday" and longer statements in the middle. They also lower the pitch of their voice to indicate they are finished. Schizophrenics tend not to do this. We seem to have a defect in our cue signalling mechanisms. As a result we often have difficulty in knowing when we should be ending a conversation or how to do it. Miller and Flack feel we are defective in our capacity to engage in shared (conversational) activities. I would agree but I feel if we know the nature of these defects and

I cannot tell you how difficult it is for a person to accept the fact that he or she is schizophrenic.

those with whom we come in frequent contact know about these deficits, we can better work together to overcome them.

Others (Lysaker, Bell, Milstein, Goulet, & Bryson, 1993) have reported that schizophrenics' deficits in social communication skills interfere with their functioning in vocational settings. They point out that schizophrenics may perceive a joke as a threat, or otherwise misinterpret communications by coworkers and employers. Often persons with schizophrenia can perform the work as well as normals, but due to their deficits in social and communication skills they have more difficulty in the work setting, often to the point of even losing the employment.

Clearly, those of us with schizophrenia need to know more about our deficits and those who frequently interact with us need to know about our deficits in social interaction. Together we can work to better compensate for them.

6.) Replaying/Rehearsing

Often when you visit a psychiatric hospital you will see patients who seem to be talking to people who are not there. In their one-sided conversations they will often become quite animated. Because they are talking to people who are not there, it is usually assumed that they must be hearing voices and talking back to them. Although this may sometimes be the case, often something quite different is at play.

Those of us with schizophrenia are very sensitive to having our feelings hurt. Insults, hostile criticism, and other forms of psychological assault wound us deeply, and we bear scars from these attacks to a much greater degree than do our normal friends.

Because we have this hypersensitivity, naturally enough we try to protect ourselves and prepare ourselves from possible future attacks. By way of this, one of the things we do is replay in our minds situations where we have been hurt, trying to develop strategies of response so that if we find ourselves in similar situations again we will not be so damaged again. What we are doing in our minds is saying to ourselves, "What I should have said was..." or "I should have told that guy that I am just as good as he is." We rehearse or replay situations over and over in our minds, and we often find ourselves speaking in an audible fashion when we are doing this. We have a definite compulsion to engage in this sort of behavior.

Many years ago my wife became so bothered by my tendency to do this, that we worked out an agreement that I would try to engage in this behavior only when I was in the shower in the morning and while I was mowing the lawn. The lawn mower motor tended to drown out the sound of my mumbling.

Persons with schizophrenia need to know that we have this tendency to talk to ourselves and that this behavior tends to upset normals. I recommend that whenever we have a need to do this that we do the same thing that we do when we have other physiologically based needs to function in a manner not welcome in polite social circumstances. We should excuse ourselves, withdraw to a restroom, or other area where we can be in private and rehearse/replay until we get the urge to do so out of our system.

Despite this advice, I frequently find myself in social situations where I am talking to myself, usually in a soft tone. It is at times like these that I am most gratified that others know that I am disabled with schizophrenia. Because of this I think others expect me to be a little different. So when they see me talking to myself they do not seem to be quite so perplexed.

7.) Expressed Emotion

The Expressed Emotion (EE) concept was developed by George Brown and his associates in the Institute of Psychiatry in London in the 1950s (Brown, Carstairs, & Topping, 1958). Brown's studies focused on the relation between family variables and the likelihood of relapse on the part of persons with schizophrenia who had recently been released from the hospital. Those investigators found that patients who went to live with family members who were highly emotionally involved were much more likely to relapse than those patients who went to families who were less "hostile," or who exhibited less "expressed emotion." Furthermore, the relationship between emotional involvement and relapse was not related to the severity of symptoms at the time of discharge.

High EE was defined as involving three factors. These are from the Camberwell Family Interview (Brown & Rutter, 1966):

1.) Statements of resentment, disapproval, or dislike, and any comments expressed with critical intonation that is, a critical tone, pitch, rhythm, or intensity in their voice.

2.) Hostile remarks indicating personal criticism.

3.) Emotional overinvolvement, constant worrying about minor matters, overprotective attitudes, intrusive behavior.

Additionally, warmth, expressed in terms of positive comments and voice tone, appear to be added protection for persons discharged to low-EE environments and dissatisfaction, even when not expressed in a critical or hostile manner, appeared to increase relapse risk in high-EE households.

It is my experience that those of us with schizophrenia are indeed very sensitive to hostile criticism and other forms of expressed emotion. But it is not only in the family context. Whenever persons with schizophrenia encounter criticism, insults, or other forms of psychological oppression, we tend to be damaged in a manner that increases the likelihood of our relapsing into psychosis. This vulnerability tends to be part of the disorder. Those who have this disorder need to know that they are vulnerable in this manner. Other persons who come into frequent contact with the mentally ill also need to know that we are particularly sensitive in this regard.

As with those in the AA organization, those of us with schizophrenia need to avoid the persons, places, and things where we are likely to encounter expressed emotion. But of course, we will not always be able to avoid such circumstances. For those times when we are going to encounter hostile criticism, etc., I recommend that we be prepared to protect ourselves by developing a mechanism for communicating to others something about the nature of our disability. Some years ago I developed a card which I carry in my wallet. When I find myself being faced with unfair criticism I will present the person doing the criticizing with my card, which has these words written on it:

> Excuse me. I need to tell you that I am a person suffering from a mental disorder. When I am berated, belittled, insulted, or otherwise treated in an oppressive manner I tend to become emotionally ill. Could I ask that you restate your concern in a manner that does not tend to disable me? Thank you for your consideration.

While I don't use this card frequently, I do find it gives me assurance to have it with me.

8.) Stress and Excitement

Not long ago three former patients at our hospital were the focus of a local TV news program on mental illness. All three performed very well for the program but unfortunately within 3 weeks each of them had relapsed and were back in the hospital. My own breakdowns frequently occur while I am attending conferences or shortly thereafter. I often find that visits to a shopping mall where there is much stimulation causes me too much stress.

Persons with schizophrenia should realize that they can become overstimulated by exciting circumstances as well as by stressful circumstances. We need to develop techniques to limit the effects that overstimulation may have on our systems. I find that when I begin to become overstimulated it is often helpful to politely excuse myself and withdraw from the situation. If I am at a conference I can withdraw to my room or if I am at a mall I can withdraw to a less stimulating environment.

I find that if I know ahead of time that I am going to be in a stressful or exciting situation for an extended period of time it is helpful to increase the dosage of my medication prior to involving myself in such events.

At meetings where there are often sharp exchanges between the participants, I find that it is helpful to withdraw from the circle of participants and sit at a distance from the verbal exchanges. It is less taxing to be out of the line of verbal fire that often occurs during meetings where important issues are being discussed.

9.) Music and Hobbies/ Woodshedding

Because the nature of our disorder is such that our ability to sustain our rational processes is damaged, it is often helpful if we engage in activities that do not tax our logical abilities. Music, art, and poetic type endeavors are often easier for us to handle. For this reason I encourage persons disabled with schizophrenia to engage in these forms of expressions as a way of communicating.

As Tim Woodman (1987) relates in describing his disorder: "What really helped was art therapy. I got a lot of satisfaction out of painting, and it seemed to me to go some way toward answering my unspoken desire for personal harmony" (p. 330).

In my own case I find that dancing for extended periods of time can be very therapeutic. There is something about being able to express yourself in a nonrational manner that helps release pressures that have built up from stresses that have been encountered. Often these musical or artistic expressions come forth in a manner that is not readily appreciated by others. Nevertheless, the fact that we are expressing ourselves can be most therapeutic. A term that has been adopted for such activity is "woodshedding." (J. S. Strauss, personal communication, December 17, 1990.) This term is taken from jazz, where a musician will go out away from others to a woodshed and experiment with various sounds until the sounds begin to form patterns that can be appreciated by others. For those of us with schizophrenia, engaging in woodshedding activities, whether they be in art, music, or poetry, can be a viable method for building a bridge back to the world of normality.

Not long ago a patient of mine who engages frequently in writing poetry wrote a poem that I feel carried a particularly insightful message to mental health workers. She wrote:

> Be my teacher
> Not a preacher,
> And as I learn,
> Give me a turn.

The nature of the disorder is that it affects the brain's thought and belief systems, it affects a person's confidence in what is truthful.

10.) Stigma/ Discrimination

Traditionally those of us who were struck with mental illness were ejected from society and placed in isolated asylums. The words "crazy," "insane," and "nuts" have come to mean those things that can be immediately dismissed as unimportant by the members of the normal population. Until about 30 years ago those of us who were determined to be insane were removed and not expected to return to society. When we did start returning we were not generally welcomed. As I pointed out in a recent article (Frese, 1993b), the movies have a tradition of portraying the mentally ill as monsters. The news media also primarily addresses mental illness when one of us has killed or has committed some other form of bizarre crime.

While normals can speak openly and even casually about cancer or heart disease, the topic of schizophrenia elicits primarily emotional reactions like fear or derisive humor. Normals are not comfortable with the thought of a seriously mentally ill person living in their neighborhood, being in school with them, or being in their workplace. We still frighten them. They do not know what to expect from us.

Recently the National Mental Health Consumer's Association adopted a six-part national agenda. One of that organization's six designated issues is discrimination, for which the following is stated, "Discrimination, abuse, ostracism, stigmatization and other forms of social prejudice must be identified and vigorously opposed at every opportunity." Likewise there has been established a National Stigma Clearinghouse (275 Seventh Ave., 16th Floor, New York, NY 10001) which monitors and challenges media stereotypes of the mentally ill.

For those of us who have returned and have found that we are not as welcome as we would like to be, we have a challenge. We must work together to change the image we have with those in what I sometimes refer to as the "chronically normal community." As more and more of us are becoming open about the nature of our disability, we have an obligation to share with others as much as we can about mental illness so that there is less fear and greater understanding and acceptance. To help counter the negative images, it is of course helpful to have positive images of the mentally ill to put forth. Mike Jaffe (1993) and his family have done us all an outstanding service by producing and widely distributing posters highlighting "people with mental illness (who) enrich our lives." They point out that such persons as Robert Schumann, the composer, Vaslov Nijinski, the dancer, Eugene O'Neill, the playwright and many other accomplished individuals, suffered from serious mental illness.

Of course I cannot leave the topic of discrimination without mentioning the Americans with Disabilities Act (ADA). This recent legislation is seen as a significant step forward for us in the area of employment opportunities, building on legislation that has been evolving during the past two decades.

Numerous consumer/survivor activists have stated that the stigma that accompanies serious mental illness in many ways is worse than the illness itself.

11.) Revealing/Covering

Since deciding to become open, and even public, about my condition, I have received quite a bit of media coverage. One consequence of this is that recovered mentally ill persons, including many professionals, who have not been open about their condition, contact me and ask if it is wise to share such information with others, particularly their employers. Some time ago I developed a strategy for approaching others such as employers.

The consumer/employee takes an article about myself or another recovered person and shows it to the boss. If the boss's reaction is positive, saying something like, "That person must be very brave and is probably making a real contribution," then you know it may be safe to share with him or her about your own background.

If, on the other hand, the boss's reaction is more along the lines of, "I'm sure glad we don't have a 'nut case' like that working here," then you might want to be a little more cautious. Interestingly enough, those who have tried this strategy in mental health settings have received both types of reaction. Those who receive a positive reaction generally follow up and reveal that they, too, are recovered persons. Usually this is a therapeutic relief for them. It is very difficult to carry a "shameful" secret with you. When we consumers meet at conventions and elsewhere I often hear statements like, "I am so tired of hiding," from those who are not open to others about their condition.

However, as a practical matter, many persons probably should not be too open about their past. The ADA affords some protection and even advantage to officially stating that you have a disability but there is still much discrimination.

If you decide not to reveal to others, how do you cover for the time you were in the hospital? If you are unemployed how do you answer when asked what you do for a living? Many consumers find these very difficult questions to handle.

I advise that you respond by saying you are a writer, an artist, a (mental health) consultant, or perhaps that you "free lance," depending on how you have been spending your time. None of these responses are lies, per se, but they leave considerable latitude for interpretation and they do not require that you have a specific employer or work location.

Whether you decide to reveal or not is a serious personal decision. If you are older, established in a career, particularly in the mental health field, it is probably safer to become open about your condition. Obviously, the closer you are to retirement age the better. But if you are younger, just starting out, you might want to be very careful about becoming too open about being a person with serious mental illness. One important thing to remember is that once you tell others about yourself, you cannot untell them. Once you become open, there will be insults, subtle and otherwise. If you decide to reveal, be prepared to do a lot of educating of our "chronically normal" friends.

12.) Networking/Consumer Groups/ Self-help

Whenever I was released after being hospitalized, I always knew that there were others who were like me, those who had received psychiatric inpatient treatment and were now in the community. But I had no way of knowing who these people were. Everything was clouded in secrecy. There was no practical way for one to meet others who had similar experiences. As a result, being a recovering mentally ill person was a very lonely experience. As I did, too many discharged persons spend too much time alone in a room watching television or just looking at walls.

Fortunately this situation is changing. Fourteen years ago the National Alliance for the Mentally Ill (NAMI) was founded and regular meetings of family members now occur in virtually all of the states and larger cities in the country and in many smaller ones. Many of these groups encourage involvement of recovering persons themselves as well as family members. Indeed, NAMI has a national network of recovered persons called the Consumer Council. Recently members of this network have been gaining more influence within NAMI and as of this writing they occupy three positions on the NAMI Board of Directors.

In addition to the consumers active with the NAMI organization there are two independent national consumer organizations which are active in networking and advocating for recovered persons. The National Association of Psychiatric Survivors (NAPS) is active in advocating for the rights of consumers, but takes a position in opposition to any form of forced treatment, a stance that some recovered persons are not comfortable with.[1]

The third nationally active organization for recovered persons which has been regularly recognized in discussions of public policy involving the mentally ill is the National Mental Health Consumers' Association (NMHCA).[2] This organization is also independent and it has traditionally taken no formal position concerning the forced treatment issue.

All three organizations have been active in articulating news of persons who have received treatment for serious mental illness. Depending on one's degree of comfort with the family movement and feelings about the forced treatment issue, the activities of one or more of these groups could be of interest to recovered persons wanting to become more active in advocating for bettering conditions for persons with mental illness.

---

[1] The NAPS organization went out of existence in 1995.

[2] NMHCA is theoretically functioning but does not have a working address.

In addition to these national groups, most cities and states have consumer organizations with which one can affiliate. It has been my experience that recovering persons benefit greatly from associating with others with similar disabilities.

In some areas consumers have taken the initiative to establish facilities for recovering persons that are operated by themselves. They may or may not work in concert with traditional mental health providers, but control of these operations remains in the hands of recovered persons themselves. These are usually referred to as self-help efforts and are generally found to be cost effective and much appreciated by the consumers who are involved with them. Indeed, recently when the board members of the NMHCA organization were asked to identify their highest priority in restructuring the delivery of mental health care in this country, they unanimously identified self-help as their major issue. With this kind of enthusiastic support, it is likely that self-help consumer-run drop-in centers, social clubs, and crisis facilities will become more widely available.

References

Arieti S., & Brody, E. (1974). *American handbook of psychiatry, (Vol. 3)* (2nd ed.). New York: Harper and Row.

Brown, G. W., Carstairs, G. M. & Topping, G. G. (1958). Post-hospital adjustment of chronic mental patients. *Lancet, 2,* 685-689.

Brown, G. W. & Rutter, M. (1966). The measurement of family activities and relationships: A methodological study. *Human Relations, 19,* 241-263.

Cancro, R. (1992). Researchers see a time of hope for schizophrenia breakthrough. *OMH News. 3,* 3-6.

Frese, F. J. (1993a). Cruising the cosmos, part three: Psychosis and hospitalization. A consumer's personal recollection. In A. B. Hatfield & H. P. Lefley (Eds.), *Surviving mental illness.* New York: Guilford Press.

Frese, F. J. (1993b). The movies and the mentally ill. *The Journal of the California Alliance for the Mentally Ill, 4,* 8-10.

Gershon, E. S. & Rieder, R. O. (1992, September). Major disorders of mind and brain. *Scientific American, 267,* 126-133.

Jaffe, M. (1993). Posters posters. *The Journal of the California Alliance for the Mentally Ill, 4,* 61-62.

Lysaker, P. L., Bell, M. D., Milstein, R. M., Goulet, J. G. & Bryson, G. J. (1993). Work capacity in schizophrenia. *Hospital and Community Psychiatry, 48,* 278-280.

Miller, D. R. & Flack, W. F. (1990). *A sociopsychological approach to understanding schizophrenia.* Paper presented at the annual convention of the American Psychological Association, Boston, MA.

North, C. S. (1987). *Welcome silence: My triumph over schizophrenia.* New York: Simon and Schuster.

Sternbach, R. A. (1966). *Principles of Psychophysiology.* New York: Academic Press.

Sullivan, H. S. (1953). *The interpersonal theory of psychiatry.* New York: Norton.

Woodman, T. (1987). First person account: A pessimist's progress. *Schizophrenia Bulletin, 13,* 329-331.

Wong, D. F., Wagner, H. N., Tune, L. E., Dannals, R. F., Pearlson, G. D., Links, J. M., Tamminga, C. A., Brouselle, E. P., Ravert, H. T., Wilson, A. A., Toung, J. K. T., Malat, J., Williams, J. A., O'Tuana, L. A., Snyder, S. H., Kuhar, M. J. & Gjedde, A. (1986). Positron emission tomography reveals elevated D-2 dopamine receptors in drug-naive schizophrenics. *Science, 234,* 1558-1563.

Zelt, D. (1981). First person account: The messiah quest. *Schizophrenia Bulletin, 7,* 527-531.

Spirituality and Serious Mental Illness: A Two-Part Study

Karen N. Lindgren and Robert D. Coursey

KAREN N. LINDGREN,PH.D., RECEIVED HER DOCTORATE
FROM THE UNIVERSITY OF MARYLAND AND IS
CURRENTLY EMPLOYED AT NORTHWEST CENTER,
A COMMUNITY MENTAL HEALTH ORGANIZATION
IN PHILADELPHIA.

ROBERT D. COURSEY, PH.D., IS AN ASSOCIATE PROFESSOR
OF PSYCHOLOGY, UNIVERSITY OF MARYLAND AT
COLLEGE PARK(COLLEGE PARK, MD 20742). HE IS THE
CHAIR OF THE MARYLAND TRAINING CONSORTIUM ON
SERIOUS MENTAL ILLNESS.

THIS ARTICLE ORIGINALLY APPEARED IN THE
Psychosocial Rehabilitation Journal, 1995, 18(3), 93-111
AND IS REPRINTED WITH PERMISSION.

There is increasing evidence that spiritual beliefs can have a positive role in clients' lives. Using 30 members who were interested in spirituality from three psychosocial rehabilitation centers, a four-session course-development study was run with six groups. The highly structured psychoeducational program was designed to help clients utilize their spiritual beliefs to foster a healthy self-esteem.

Significant pre-post changes were reported on the spiritual support scale, but not on measures of depression, hopelessness, self-esteem, nor purpose in life. This finding was not significant when the program participants were compared with wait-list control members, but the analysis had very low power (n of 13 vs. 15). Suggestions about improving the program are made. The results of an interview given prior to the program are reported. The survey presents data on the participants' religious service attendance, on their prayer and religious thoughts, on the discussion of spirituality in therapy, the effect of their spirituality on their illness and on their lives, and unusual spiritual experiences.

Recently, researchers have proposed that spiritual support, like social support, can have a stress-buffering effect. Spiritual support is defined as "the perceived, personally supportive components of an individual's relationship with God" (Maton, 1989, p. 310). Maton suggests spirituality provides support via two pathways: cognitive mediation and emotional support. Cognitive mediation refers to the interpretation and meaning that spiritual beliefs give to events; emotional support refers to the feeling of being cared for and valued. Maton (1989) found that spiritual support was positively related to personal and emotional adjustment in a high life-stress college freshman group.

Research also suggests that spiritual beliefs can help individuals adjust to such stressful events as physical illness. Research with terminally ill individuals suggests that they are better able to cope with their illness if they hold spiritual beliefs (Epperly, 1983; Gibbs & Achterberg-Lawlis, 1978).

Tebbi and his colleagues (1987) found that spiritual beliefs provided a purpose in life and gave meaning to illness for cancer patients. Spiritual beliefs can also help people cope with other high-stress life events. For instance, Wright and his colleagues (1985) found that relatives of Alzheimer's patients who rated high on a measure of "spiritual support" reported lower caregiver burden. Maton (1989) found that religiosity was positively related to self-esteem and inversely related to depression in a high-stress group of recently bereaved parents.

In this study, it was hypothesized that another high-stress group, people with serious mental illnesses, may benefit from a sense of spiritual support. Unfortunately, little research has been done to investigate the different aspects of spirituality in serious mental illness. The majority of studies have focused on the relationship between psychopathology and religious beliefs and practices (e.g., Kalf & Hamilton, 1961; Koenig, George, Meador, Blazer, & Ford, 1994; Lowe, 1954; Gallemore, Wilson, & Rhoads, 1961; Meador, Koenig, Hughes, Blazer, Turnbull, & George, 1994). A noteworthy exception to this is the recent study by Sullivan (1993). Forty-eight percent of the individuals in his sample reported spirituality as central to coping with their serious mental illness. He suggests that spirituality positively impacts individuals through three pathways (two of which are similar to Maton's [1989] cognitive mediation and emotional support). Sullivan found that spirituality provided a framework for understanding life events (similar to Maton's cognitive mediation), and a source of social support (similar to emotional support). However, in Sullivan's model, social support encompasses the support of others, the support of a higher power, and the sense of belonging to a community. Sullivan also found that individuals utilized spirituality as a coping mechanism, affecting how individuals evaluated the meaning of events and how individuals chose to cope with them.

The purpose of this study was to investigate how spirituality has affected the thoughts, illness, and lives of individuals with serious mental illness, and to understand if a discussion of spirituality could have a therapeutic benefit in terms of self-esteem, depression, hopelessness, purpose in life, and spiritual support. This was done in two ways. First, individuals were interviewed about their spiritual beliefs and how they felt these beliefs affected their lives and their illness. Second, a four-session spirituality group was designed. Individuals with serious mental illnesses participated in the group and were given pre- and post-group measures to complete. The results of each will be presented.

Method

Subject Recruitment

Participants were recruited from persons who regularly attend three psychosocial rehabilitation centers in Maryland. The announcement described a four-session group focusing on spiritual beliefs. The letter also explained that data would be collected on the group in order to test the program's effectiveness. Lastly, all denominations and members of all faiths were encouraged to join. It is important to note that only individuals who were interested in spirituality are represented in this study.

Procedures

Persons who chose to participate first met with the first author (Karen Lindgren). During this time, the program was described, the reasons for collecting data explained, and the consent form was reviewed. The consent form specified that diagnosis and current medications would be provided to the researcher by the rehabilitation center staff. After this, participants completed the questionnaire packet and were interviewed for demographic and religious background variables. (About half of the participants were interviewed first and about half filled out the questionnaires first.) The questionnaire packet was completed in the presence of a research assistant or staff member not familiar with the experiment.

The packet consisted of the Rosenberg Self-Esteem Scale, the Beck Depression Inventory (Beck, et al., 1961), Beck Hopelessness Scale (Beck et al., 1974), Crumbaugh's Purpose in Life Scale (Crumbaugh, 1968), and Spiritual Support Scale (Maton, 1989). The Rosenberg Scale is considered the best measure of the self-acceptance aspect of self-esteem and reliability and validity are reported in Robinson and Shaver (1973). The Beck Depression Inventory assesses 21 symptoms of depression, and has excellent validity and reliability (Beck, Steer & Garbin, 1988). The Beck Hopelessness Scale measures the extent to which individuals feel they will be unable to overcome difficult life situations, and also has strong reliability and validity (Beck et al., 1974; Mendoca, Holden, Mazmanian, & Dolan, 1983). Crumbaugh's Purpose in Life Test (1968) measures the degree to which individuals experience a sense of meaning and purpose in life, and has good psychometric properties including norms for psychiatric populations. Finally, the Spiritual Support Scale measures the degree to which an individual perceives a supportive, loving relationship with God (Maton, 1989). In addition, the Short Christian Orthodoxy Scale (Hunsberger, 1989) was administered to participants who reported Christian beliefs.

A research assistant or staff member reviewed the packet with the participant and remained with him or her until the questionnaires were completed. The interview included demographic information, history of illness, and religious information. Part of the information collected, i.e., spiritual beliefs, was used to make the group more relevant. That is, the basic structure and themes of each session were not altered, but examples and illustrations were tailored to fit the religious beliefs of each particular group. This was done to enhance participation among group members and to make the experience as meaningful as possible.

Individuals were then randomly assigned to the first or second groups. One group (the wait-list control group) was put on a wait-list and then participated in the program at a later date. This group was contacted either by phone or at the center 1 week before their first session in order to ensure participation.

The experimental group participated in 4¹/₂-hour sessions. Three experimental groups of five or six people each were run, and three wait-list control groups also received the same 4-week intervention. Participants were required to attend at least three of the four sessions in order for their data to be used in the analysis. After the first session, names and telephone numbers were collected. Persons who missed a session were either called or contacted at the center, and a time arranged to participate in a makeup session. This ensured that each individual was familiar with all of the material.

At the end of each session, participants filled out a brief questionnaire (15 items). The questionnaire was used to understand which components of the group were the most helpful to participants. It was designed to tap four areas of group process (universality, cohesion, self-learning, spirituality) plus the class material. Statements reflecting these five areas were written by the researchers, and then tested for face validity. Three of the five areas (universality, cohesion, self-learning) were chosen because they are important components of group process (Yalom, 1986). The fourth component, spirituality, was added as representative of the material discussed within each session. The class material questions were based on information from each class. This questionnaire is described in greater detail in the results section of this paper.

At the end of the fourth session, the questionnaire packet was readministered to both the experimental and wait-list groups. The experimental group also completed a questionnaire asking for feedback on the group sessions. This information was used to further improve the quality of future groups, but did not alter the program in any way for those who were waitlisted. After filling out a second packet of questionnaires, the wait-list group then participated in the intervention. At the end of the fourth session, they were given a third set of measures to complete. At this time, the experimental group received a 4-week follow-up measure.

Program Description

The four-session group focused on how spiritual themes could promote a sense of self-worth and support when one has a mental illness. The subject material for each class was outlined in a detailed manual. The goal for the first session was for individuals to become aware of how they judge their own self-worth. Members explored the differences between spiritual values and societal values as well as how spirituality affects their self-esteem. The second session focused on the spiritual meanings individuals had given to their illness. Participants discussed how these interpretations could positively or negatively affect their sense of self-worth. This session was also used to educate clients about the biological aspects of mental illness, and members discussed how this information could be integrated into their own spiritual framework. The third class had two purposes. First, individuals practiced forgiving themselves for their failures and celebrating their successes. Second, members explored what qualities they had to offer others. The final class dealt with the impact of their spiritual experiences on their feelings and symptoms. Members also discussed the social support aspect of spirituality and local resources were exchanged. For a complete description of the program, please contact the authors.

Use of Language

In current use, a distinction is sometimes made between "religion" which connotes a set of beliefs, practices, and rites associated with a particular church or denomination, and "spirituality" which connotes a set of more personal and less institutionalized beliefs and practices. However, at other times the words "religious" and "spiritual" are used interchangeably by members of specific denominations as well as by those without any affiliation. To achieve clarity, at the beginning of the interview, the interviewer discussed with the participants the meaning of the word "religious" (beliefs and practices associated with a specific church) and "spiritual" (a more non-church set of beliefs and practices). The participant was then asked what word he/she liked to use—religion, spirituality, faith, etc. The interviewer then used the participants' preferred word throughout the interview. However, in the class discussions, all participants spontaneously used the word "religion" and not "spirituality," and the leaders therefore followed that usage. In this paper, we have chosen to use the word "spirituality" throughout because we believe it better includes both meanings. We use "religion" only when we are referring to beliefs and practices specific to traditional religious institutions.

Results

Number of Participants and Demographic Variables

At each of the three rehabilitation centers, an experimental and wait-list control group was formed. After the wait-list control period, this group then received the spirituality intervention. Altogether, 49 individuals initially volunteered to take the spirituality class. Of these, 19 were unable to attend due to scheduling difficulties, decided not to attend, or did not attend at least three classes. Thirty participants were individually interviewed about their own and their family's spiritual/ religious beliefs. Two of these individuals' class evaluations were not usable. Thus, the interview results are based on 30 participants, and the class results on 28. The mean age was 41.2 (*sd* = 11.1), and there were 21 women and 9 men. Diagnoses included schizophrenia (67%), bipolar disorder (10%), unipolar depression (7%), schizoaffective disorder (3.3%), personality disorder (3.3%) and others (10 %) Demographic variables for each sample are presented in Table 1.

TABLE 1.
BREAKDOWN OF AGE, CHRONICITY, AND DIAGNOSIS BY CONTROL AND EXPERIMENTAL GROUP

VARIABLE	CONTROL	EXPERIMENTAL
Age[a]	40.69 (9.89)	41.60 (12.16)
Chronicity[a]	12.91 (11.95)	13.08 (8.54)
Diagnosis[b]		
Schizophrenia	8	11
Bipolar Illness	1	2
Unipolar Disorder	0	1
Schizoaffective Disorder	1	0
Personality Disorder	1	0
Other	2	1

[a] Means (Standard deviations)
[b] Actual *n* from each group

Psychoeducational Results

Preliminary tests for confounding variables and measurement effects were performed. There were no pre-intervention differences for location, sex, and no differences between experimental and control group. The pre-post measurement in the control sessions did not reveal any testing effects. Therefore, the data from the intervention component from both experimental and control groups were collapsed into one pre-post test. Groups were blocked on whether they had received the intervention first or second at each location.

Intervention effect. The main analyses examined the hypothesis that individuals who received the intervention would show positive change on measures of depression, hopelessness, spiritual support, self-esteem, and purpose in life. This was examined in two ways: a) pre- and post-intervention scores were compared using the entire sample, and b) those who participated in the intervention first were compared to the wait-list control group.

First, the data from the intervention component from both groups were collapsed into one pre-post intervention repeated measures MANOVA. Groups

were blocked on whether they received the intervention first or second at each location (that is, the experimental and wait-list group). The means and standard deviations for these groups are reported in Table 2 and the results of this analysis are reported in Table 3. The results of the multivariate tests indicated a significant pre-post difference: $F (5, 15) = 3.25$, $p < .04$ (see Table 2 for means). Examination of the univariate tests suggests this significant F was largely due to a significant change in the Spiritual Support Scale. The multivariate tests revealed no effects among the two groups (first and second at each center), nor any group by time interaction effects overall.

The univariate tests also revealed a significant group effect for self-esteem. That is, the group which received the intervention first (regardless of center location) had healthier scores on the self-esteem measure at both pretest and posttest than the groups that received the intervention second (see Tables 2 and 3).

TABLE 2.
PRE AND POST MEANS (STANDARD DEVIATIONS) FOR THE INTERVENTION PERIOD BY GROUP

	EXPERIMENTAL		WAIT-LIST	
	Pre	Post	Pre	Post
Purpose	54.0	50.4	46.9	46.9
in Life	(9.9)	(9.0)	(10.0)	(12.6)
Hopelessness	3.8	3.3	5.9	8.1
	(3.3)	(3.0)	(5.9)	(6.2)
Beck Depression	11.2	8.8	17.3	15.8
Inventory	(12 4)	(8.2)	(11.2)	(8.9)
Self-esteem	21.1	19.9	24.4	23.8
	(3.4)	(3.4)	(3.3)	(5.3)
Spiritual	10.8	11.8	9.0	10.6
Support	(3.6)	(35)	(3.4)	(3.6)

The next analysis conducted was to compare individuals who first participated in the intervention to individuals who were

TABLE 3.
MULTIVARIATE ANALYSIS OF VARIANCE TEST OF DIFFERENCES BETWEEN
PRE-INTERVENTION AND POST-INTERVENTION SCORES

MULTIVARIATE RESULTS

Effect	Hypothesis *(df)*	Error *(df)*	*F*	*p* Value
Group	5	15	.98	.46
Pre-Post Intervention	5	15	3.25	.035
Group X Pre-post	5	15	1.35	.295

UNIVARIATE RESULTS

Measure	Hypothesis *(MS)*	Error *(MS)*	*F*	*p* Value
Effect: pre-post intervention				
Spiritual Support	14.88	3.18	4.68	.04
Purpose in Life	52.60	39.34	1.34	.26
Hopelessness	2.88	5.55	.52	.48
Beck Depression	42.00	43.4	.97	.34
Self-esteem	9.52	3.36	2.83	.11
Effect: group				
Spiritual Support	22.14	21.87	1.01	.33
Purpose in Life	280.04	169.54	1.65	.21
Hopelessness	116.06	34.47	3.37	.08
Beck Depression	8.47	172.00	2.43	.14
Self-esteem	125.71	25.76	4.88	.04
Effect: group x pre-post intervention				
Spiritual Support	1.22	3.17	.38	.54
Purpose in Life	32.37	39.34	.82	.38
Hopelessness	19.25	5.54	3. 47	.08
Beck Depression	1.62	43.39	.04	.85
Self-esteem	.69	3.36	.21	.66

Note: *df* for all of the univariate tests = (1,19).

in the wait-list condition. This was to test if individuals in the spirituality groups had different scores from individuals participating in regular rehabilitation center activities. A repeated measures multivariate analysis of variance (MANOVA) was performed and the group by pre-post intervention was examined across all of the measures. There was no significant difference in the interaction effect.

Group process. Since there were significant results on the first main analysis, indicating a change in scores during the intervention period, the next stage of the analysis focused on discovering what aspects of the groups contributed to this outcome. All participants were given a group process measure in order to understand which components of the intervention were helpful. The measure was composed of five scales: cohesion, self-learning, universality, spirituality, and class-learning. Each scale was made up of three items, each of which had a range of 0 to 3. These three items were summed to get a scale score; thus, each scale had a possible score ranging from 0 to 9. Scales were correlated with change scores on the measures.

Change scores were used rather than post-test scores in order to control for the wide variability of scores at pretest. No correlations were significant; however, two correlations approached significance. These correlations were universality with change in the Beck Depression Inventory ($r = .42$, $p = .07$), and universality with change in the Spiritual Support Scale ($r = .41$, $p = .06$). The remainder of the correlations between the process measure and change on the tests were very low, ranging from $r = .02$ ($p = .47$) to $r = .30$ ($p = .13$). This may be due to the restricted range in the process scale scores: a close examination revealed very little variability on all of the scales except for universality.

Correlations Between Change Scores and Background Variables

Change scores on the measures were correlated with a number of different variables gathered in the interview (including age, sex, chronicity, education, whether an individual worked, score on the Short Christian Orthodoxy scale, amount of prayer, amount of time thinking about God, spiritual experiences, attending services, family's religious information, the effect of religion and spirituality on one's illness, on one's life, and how comfortable an individual was in talking about their spirituality). Bonferroni corrections were not applied to these correlations because of the exploratory nature of this section. Therefore caution must be exercised in interpreting them.

There were no significant correlations with the demographic variables nor with the Short Christian Orthodoxy Scale. However, change scores were correlated with some interview questions. Individuals who grew less depressed on the Beck Depression Inventory over the intervention thought about God more often ($r = .42$, $p < .05$). They also had families who attended services less frequently ($r = .41$,

$p < .05$). Individuals whose scores increased in hopefulness on the Beck Hopelessness Scale were those who felt religion had a positive effect when they were ill ($r = .41$, $p < .05$). Individuals who reported a spiritual experience had a greater positive increase on both the Rosenberg Self-Esteem Scale ($r = .39$, $p < .05$) and on the Spiritual Support Scale ($r = .38$, $p < .05$). Individuals who increased in spiritual support were also more likely to have families who attended services frequently ($r = .48$, $p < .01$). However, they were also less likely to think about God ($r = .64$, $p < .01$) and less likely to feel religion/spirituality had an overall positive effect on their life ($r = .41$, $p < .05$). It should be noted that no participant reported a negative effect of spirituality on their life, so this last correlation represents different degrees of positive effects.

Interview Results

The interviews took place before entrance into the class. Both the main researcher and three other assistants helped conduct the interviews. The interviews served four purposes: 1) a screening tool for individuals with active hallucinations or delusions; 2) a source of information about an individual's spiritual beliefs before the class, so that class examples could be made salient to different beliefs; 3) a way to understand how spiritual beliefs might impact serious mental illness in either a positive or negative way; and 4) a source of religious and demographic background variables which might contribute to success or failure in the class. The results of these interviews yielded many common themes which can give professionals an idea of the nature and types of beliefs clients hold, and how these beliefs may effect their illness. All of the interview results are presented in Table 4. Again, these are percentages of individuals who are interested in talking about their spirituality.

TABLE 4.
INTERVIEW RESULTS

Interview Questions	Specific Responses	Yes	No
1. Currently attend services?		57%	43%
If yes: How often do you attend?			
More than once a week	24%		
Once a week	41%		
Several times/month	6%		
Several times/year	29%		
If no: would you like to attend?		77%	23%
2. Ever discuss spirituality/religion with a clergy person?		38%	62%
3. Ever discuss spirituality/religion with a therapist?		33%	67%
4. Are you (would you be) comfortable discussing spirituality/religion with a therapist?			
Not comfortable at all	24%		
Uncomfortable	14%		
Somewhat comfortable	17%		
Comfortable	7%		
Very comfortable	38%		
5. Would you like to discuss spiritual/religious concerns in therapy?			
Never	34%		
No	3%		
Sometimes	24%		
Yes	3%		
Very much	28%		
6. Would you like more opportunities to discuss spirituality/religion with others? *(30% of "yes" responses made stipulations regarding when and with whom they would discuss it)*		67%	33%
7. Impact of spirituality/religion when ill?			
Harmed a great deal	7%		
Harmed somewhat	7%		
No effect	13%		
Helped somewhat	27%		
Helped a great deal	47%		
8. Impact of spirituality/religion on life?			
Harmed a great deal	0%		
Harmed somewhat	0%		
No effect	20%		
Helped somewhat	20%		
Helped a great deal	60%		
9. How often do you pray?			
Daily	57%		
Weekly	18%		
Monthly	3%		
Never	21%		
10. How often do you think about God or spiritual/religious matters?			
Daily	76%		
Weekly	7%		
Monthly	3%		
Never	14%		
11. Have you ever had a mystical or spiritual experience?		47%	53%

Service attendance. Fifty-seven percent of clients attend religious services currently. (See Table 4 for all percentages.) Of these 17 individuals, 65% (11/17) attended at least once per week. Worship (71%), social reasons (18%), or enjoyment of the music (12%) were listed as the main reasons for attending services. For instance, three individuals saw services as an opportunity to meet new people or socialize with people they already knew, e.g., friends or family. A few others reported the services had a general calming effect on their symptoms.

Of the 13 who did not attend any type of services, 77% (10/17) expressed a strong interest in attending; 9 of these cited practical reasons (either money, transportation, or some combination of the two) as the primary reason they did not attend services. The remaining 4 individuals either felt no desire to attend services, did not find a church they agreed with, or felt some embarrassment about attending.

Prayer and spiritual thought. Individuals were also asked how often they prayed and/or thought about spiritual matters. About half (57%) reported prayer as a part of their daily routine (43% prayed daily, and 14% prayed more than once a day). A larger percentage (76%) thought about spiritual matters on a daily basis. Fourteen percent never thought about spirituality. One of these individuals reported consciously choosing to avoid religious thoughts as it escalated her symptoms.

Sixty-seven percent of respondents said they would like more opportunities to discuss spirituality in a treatment setting, although 30% of these stipulated that it should be with individuals who shared their views.

Just as spirituality can provide a sense of emotional support, it can also be associated with negative emotions.

Spirituality in therapy. Thirty-three percent of the clients reported that they currently discussed spiritual concerns with their therapist, but they represented only half of those who wanted to discuss it. Thirteen percent (4/30) of all the participants reported wanting to discuss spirituality with their therapist "very much" and an additional 21% (6/30) wanted to occasionally, but neither group had done so.

When asked how comfortable they would feel discussing spiritual issues with their therapist on a scale of 1 (I would not feel comfortable at all) to 5 (I would feel very comfortable), the average rating was 2.21 (sd = 1.66) (I would not feel comfortable). However, 45% said they would feel comfortable doing so, and another 17% said they would feel "somewhat" comfortable. Thirty-seven percent (11/30) said they would not like to discuss spiritual concerns in therapy.

There were a few different reasons individuals would not feel comfortable discussing spiritual concerns in therapy. Three individuals felt their therapist could not understand their beliefs. Two cited their therapists' different religious background as the reason. Six additional individuals stated general uncomfortableness in therapy around the topic.

Effect of spirituality on illness. Participants were also asked if they felt their spirituality has had a positive or negative effect on their illness. On a scale of 1 (it has harmed a great deal) to 5 (it has helped a great deal), the mean rating was 4 (sd =.93) (spirituality has helped). Five (17%) individuals felt their spirituality harmed them while they were ill. Of these, three individuals cited involvement in a religious group as what was detrimental to them. The other two individuals felt their spiritual thoughts had a direct negative impact on their mental health i.e., it caused their symptoms to escalate.

The remaining 83% (25/30) felt spiritual beliefs had a positive impact on their illness. Twenty-four percent (6/25) felt their beliefs provided a direct intervention in their illness (e.g., provided a healing). Another 28% (7/25) reported that spirituality provided indirect interventions (e.g., through hope in a better future). The remaining 48% of these individuals (12/25) who felt that their spirituality had a positive effect on their illness suggested their beliefs provided them with comfort: in half of these cases, this feeling stemmed from a realization that they were not alone.

Effect of spirituality on life. Similar results were found when individuals were asked how their spiritual beliefs helped them in life: on a scale of 1 (it has harmed a great deal) to 5 (it has helped a great deal) the mean rating was 4.4 (*sd* = .72). Twenty percent (6/30) felt their spirituality helped them "get through" troubled times. Five additional people felt it provided a means to self-improvement and confidence; another 20% found it to be an important source of love. The final 43% of the sample suggested their religion had helped mainly through its social aspect. On the other hand, 13% of the respondents indicated guilty feelings stemming from their spirituality

Spiritual experiences. Forty-seven percent of individuals (14/30) reported having some type of mystical experience, ranging from an undefinable feeling to intense visions or dreams, and from experiencing help with common problems to experiencing life-changing events. These experiences were broken down as follows: 21% (3/14) reported "special," undefinable feelings; 14% reported they felt spiritual experiences helped them with a very specific problem; 29% reported intense visions which were life-changing experiences; 14% reported spiritual dreams. The remaining 21% (3/14) of the experiences had unusual components to them, and therefore were considered either delusional or hallucinatory by mental health professionals. One anomalous comment was made by an individual who felt her medications interfered with her ability to have spiritual experiences.

Discussion

Class Material

In general, feedback from the consumers and group leaders suggested that the material seemed appropriate for the population. The leaders' experience of the groups indicated that the clients' understood the material. In 15 post-class interviews, participants reported enjoying and understanding the material. When asked to recall material, about 65% (*n* = 8) recalled specific material, and another 15% (*n* = 4) recalled general ideas from the class. Three individuals (10%) did not remember any information from the class.

Intervention Effects

Two analyses examined the effect of the intervention. The first compared all individuals' scores prior to the intervention to their scores following the intervention. This produced a significant multivariate F, and examination of the univariate tests indicated a significant change in the Spiritual Support Scale from pretest to posttest.

The second analysis compared individuals who first participated in the intervention to individuals who were in the wait-list condition, and thus had not yet received the intervention. In contrast to the first analysis, this analysis produced no significant results. One possible explanation for the discrepancy is that the second analysis had very low power: the 13 individuals who participated in the intervention first were compared to 15 individuals who were wait-listed.

Relationship Between Background Variables and Change Scores

While these correlations provide some interesting hypotheses, caution must be exercised in interpretation because there was no correction for the large number of correlations run. Individuals who grew less depressed over the intervention thought about God more often; those who grew more hopeful on the Beck Hopelessness Scale were more likely to feel spirituality positively impacted their illness. Perhaps a discussion of spirituality validates it as a source of support, producing a positive impact.

Two of the correlations with change in the spiritual support scale were not in the expected direction. Changes in spiritual support were greater for individuals who initially felt less positive about the effect of spirituality on their life and who had thought about God less. One possible reason for this is a ceiling effect; that is, individuals who felt spirituality was a very positive influence on their life and who thought about God a great deal scored very high on the spiritual support scale both at pretest and posttest, producing very little change. On the other hand, those individuals who thought about God less and felt less positive about the impact of religion on their life (no individual felt the impact was negative) may have developed a greater sense of spiritual support, by having an opportunity to think about and discuss their beliefs, thereby producing a new positive experience and change. An examination of the data lends some support to this hypothesis. The Spiritual Support Scale ranged from 0–15, with 15 indicating the greatest sense of spiritual support. Of the six individuals who did not change on the scale, three scored a 15 and one additional person scored a 12. In addition, no individual who scored a 12 or higher at pretest changed more than 2 points on the scale at posttest. In this study, a high sense of spiritual support seemed to stay constant.

Interview Results: Implications and Integration

The interviews provided helpful information regarding the nature and importance of consumers' beliefs, the role it plays in their lives, and therapeutic issues which can stem from spirituality. It is important to reiterate that this information comes from individuals who expressed an interest in spirituality. Therefore, the percentages represented here may overestimate the interest in spiritual beliefs among individuals with a serious mental illness. However, an examination of the percentages indicates that for those who do express an interest, spirituality is an important part of their lives, often of their daily routines. As a salient aspect of some individuals' lives, it is an important variable for therapists to consider.

Only half of the individuals who wished to discuss spiritual concerns in therapy had done so. This raises two issues to be discussed below: a) is there therapeutic value in discussing spiritual concerns; and b) if so, how can therapists make a spiritual discussion comfortable?

Spiritual support and serious mental illness. First, is spirituality a topic appropriate for therapeutic discussion? The results of this project suggest that a discussion of spiritual concerns can be of therapeutic value. The main effect of the class seemed to be increasing an individuals' sense of spiritual support. A sense of spiritual support has been shown to be related to ability to cope with health-related issues (Maton, 1989), as well as coping styles in general (Pargament, 1986) and may be an important complement to social support (Maton, 1989). Persons with a serious mental illness often have little social support (e.g.

Hammer, 1981); thus spiritual support may be a useful resource.

Using Maton's (1989) model, spiritual support involves two concepts: emotional support and cognitive mediation. Therapists can use this model to explore the impact of spirituality on serious mental illness. The emotional support that spirituality provides may be very important. Of the 83% who believed that spirituality helped them in their illness, about half of these individuals indicated that it helped most through the comfort it provided, feelings of being cared for, and feelings that they were not alone. The support may come from the social networks associated with religious beliefs as well. Forty-three percent of individuals felt religion had helped their life mainly through its social aspect. This is similar to Sullivan's (1993) study, in which participants reported they found support in the social networks associated with religious organizations, in feeling connected to a larger community, and in being able to depend on a divine other. However, just as spirituality can provide a sense of emotional support, it can also be associated with negative emotions. In this survey, a few individuals indicated guilty feelings regarding the times they believed they had neglected their beliefs.

A second therapeutic avenue is cognitive mediation, that is, the understanding that spirituality can provide about mental illness. As part of the class, participants rated how strongly they believed various spiritual/religious beliefs. The most frequently-rated statements included: "Suffering is a punishment for something I did wrong," " If I tried harder to be good, I could get well," and "There must be some reason God has chosen me to suffer." These belief systems can provide meaning to an illness. However, these understandings can also have a positive or negative impact on the client's well-being. Therapists can help clients sort out the psychological impact of their beliefs and assist them in deciding whether alternative perspectives and practices might be more healing for them.

Spirituality and therapy. If clients can benefit from a discussion of their beliefs, how can therapists make therapy a comfortable place to do so? It is important to note that not all clients wanted to discuss their spirituality in therapy. Even in this group, composed of individuals interested in spirituality, 37% did not wish to discuss it in therapy. Thus, any discussion of spiritual issues needs to proceed cautiously and with mutual consent from the client.

If therapists are to discuss spiritual issues with clients, they should possess an understanding of the client's beliefs. Therapists need education not only about religious tenets but about the ethical issues involved in discussing spirituality in therapy (cf. Sheridan & Bullis,1991; Titone, 1991). In addition, clients may be hesitant in sharing spiritual concerns with therapists that do not share their beliefs. In this study, 37% of the interviewees felt they would not be comfortable discussing spiritual matters in therapy. Seventeen percent of the sample cited their therapists'

> *Respect for the clients' belief is crucial in developing trust for a spiritual discussion. This is particularly important when a client reports a belief which seems to have a delusional component to it.*

different religious background or fear of a lack of understanding as the reason for their discomfort. Along the same lines, Weisbrod, Sherman and Hodinko (1988) found that Jewish clients were more willing to share their psychological concerns with therapists who shared or understood their beliefs.

A therapist's reaction to spiritual beliefs can affect the therapeutic relationship. Two individuals reported that they sought new therapists after one had ignored their spiritual concerns. Similarly, a few individuals who experienced intense spiritual visions were hesitant to discuss them with their therapist for fear they would be devalued. Even in a respectful atmosphere, some clients reported that they would not feel comfortable. In these cases, it is important to have referrals available to various churches/synagogues and pastoral counselors for clients who wish to discuss their beliefs with a clergy person or counselor. An example of connecting religious and mental health professionals is the work being done by the Religious Outreach Network of the National Alliance for the Mentally Ill (NAMI).

Spiritual experiences vs. hallucinations. Respect for the clients' belief is crucial in developing trust for a spiritual discussion. This is particularly important when a client reports a belief which seems to have a delusional component to it. Initially, it may not be as important to evaluate the "delusionality" of the belief as it is to evaluate the importance of the belief to the client, and

Any discussion of spiritual issues needs to proceed cautiously and with mutual consent from the client. If therapists are to discuss spiritual issues with clients, they should possess an understanding of the client's beliefs.

the effect the belief has on the client's life. Clients who have experiences to which they give a spiritual meaning can feel special and may value their experiences. The experience can also boost self-esteem. To have a therapist infer that the belief was a product of the client's distortion or drugs or mental illness, can be a devastating blow. In this survey, clients who had experienced a devaluing of their experience felt anger at their therapists, and in some cases, closed further spiritual discussions in therapy. In addition, individuals who had a spiritual experience were more likely to change in a positive direction on both depression and spiritual support. Perhaps being able to discuss and having peers value their experience produced the positive change.

A therapist can be important in helping clients sort out the meaning of their experiences. As a part of the program, participants were taught ways to distinguish experiences which were helpful to them from ones which were harmful. One method was to find a "soul mate," a friend, counselor, or clergy person who could discuss and sort out the experience with them. Not one participant reported they currently had such a person in their life. In these cases, it is important for the therapist to discuss the experience with the client or to connect him or her with someone else.

Finally, the study revealed that clients can appreciate that although spirituality can have helpful components, they should not confuse this with symptoms of mental illness. In many cases, they had already distinguished the two for themselves. Many of those who registered for the class openly volunteered the limits they put on spirituality; for instance, one individual requested not to participate in guided imagery exercises. Another volunteered that she could not participate in organized religion, a third felt any discussion of spirituality caused her thoughts to race. Only one individual appeared actively confused and became angry about religion during the interview. She elected not to participate in the class. Thus, any fear on the therapist's part that a spiritual discussion will open a Pandora's box may be unrealistic. For those who have spiritual beliefs, they have, most likely, thought a great deal about them, and understand how their beliefs affect them.

Limitations and Future Directions

There are some limitations to this research. The sample was composed solely of individuals who were interested in discussing spirituality; thus, one cannot be sure how these results relate to other clients. While Sullivan (1993) did not ask clients about their spirituality, about half of the sample volunteered that they used it as a coping mechanism. Further research would need to examine more explicitly the spiritual beliefs of clients who do not express an interest in discussing spirituality in a group setting.

A second concern was the lack of participants of the Jewish faith. Three Jewish individuals were interviewed, however, none of them elected to take the class. As a side note, all three reported they would feel uncomfortable discussing their beliefs with their therapists, and all three reported they would not like such a discussion with others. Although this is a small number from which to generalize, it suggests that the program may not meet the needs of these clients. Research focused on what types of programs would be helpful to non-Christian clients would fill this gap.

Similarly, further research would need to examine how clients' specific beliefs interacted with the class. For instance, the leaders structured the present class to be untraditional, and it may be important to focus on individuals who hold more orthodox beliefs to understand how less traditional material impacts them.

Finally, there are limitations associated with the intervention methodology. First, the design did not incorporate a way of testing for leader effects. One way to do this would be to train two leaders, who then co-lead the classes with staff from the rehabilitation centers. The staff could be blind to the experimental hypotheses, thus limiting experimenter bias. Second, the methodology should include a way of separating out the effects of group process from the impact of the educational material. Ideally, group process could be evaluated by both the leaders and class participants and these ratings compared. Measures developed for use with individuals with a chronic mental illness would need to be piloted to ensure participants understand the measure, while providing a wider range of scores. But unless some way of measuring group process is developed, it will be impossible to evaluate fully the educational package alone.

References

Beck, A.T., Steer, R.S. & Garbin, M. (1988). The Beck Depression Inventory: Twenty-five years of evaluation. *Clinical Psychology Review, 8,* 77-100.

Beck, A.T., Ward, C.H., Mendelson, M., Mock, J. & Erbaugh, J. (1961). An inventory for measuring depression. *Archives of General Psychiatry, 4,* 561-572.

Beck, A.T., Weissman, A., Lester, D. & Trexler, L. (1974). The measurement of pessimism: The Hopelessness Scale. *Journal of Consulting and Clinical Psychology, 42,* 861-865.

Crumbaugh, J.C. (1968). Cross-validation of purpose-in-life test based on Frankl's concepts. *Journal of Individual Psychology, 24,* 74-81.

Epperly, J. (1983). The cell and the celestial: spiritual needs of cancer patients. *Journal of the Medical Association of Georgia, 72,* 374-376.

Gallemore, J, Wilson, W. & Rhoads, J. (1969). The religious life of patients with affective disorders. *Diseases of the Nervous System, 30,* 483 487.

Gibbs, H.W. & Achterberg-Lawlis, J. (1978). Spiritual values and death anxiety: Implications for counseling with terminal cancer patients. *Journal of Counseling Psychology, 25,* 563-569.

Hammer, M. (1981). Social support, social networks, arid schizophrenia. *Schizophrenia Bulletin, 7,* 45-57.

Hunsberger, B. (1989). A short version of the Christian Orthodoxy Scale. *Journal for the Scientific Study of Religion, 28,* 360-365.

Kalf, F.C. & Hamilton, J.G. (1961). Schizophrenia- a hundred years ago today. *Journal of Mental Science, 107,* 819-827.

Koenig, H.G., George, L.K., Meador, K.G., Blazer, D.G. & Ford, S. M. (1994). Religious practices and alcoholism in a Southern adult population. *Hospital and community Psychiatry, 45,* 225-231.

Lowe, W.L. (1954). group beliefs and sociocultural factors in religious delusions. *The Journal of Social Psychology, 40,* 267-274.

Maton, K. (1989). The Stress-buffering role of spiritual support Cross sectional and prospective investigations. *Journal for the Scientific Study of Religion, 28,* 310-323.

Meador, K.C, Koenig, G.H., Hughes, D.G., Blazer, D.G., Turnbull, J, & George, L.K. (1994). Religious affiliation and depression. *Hospital and Community Psychiatry, 43,* 1204- 1208.

Mendoca, J.D., Holden, R.R., Mazmanian, D. & Dolan J., l. (1983). The influence of response style on the Beck Hopelessness Scale. *Canadian Journal of Behavioral Science, 15,* 237-247.

Michelle, J.A. (1988). Spiritual and emotional determinants of health. *Journal of Religion and Health, 27,* 62-70.

Pargament, K.I. & Hahn, J. (1986). God and the just World: Causal and coping attributions to God in health situations. *Journal for the Scientific Study of Religion, 25,* 193-207.

Robinson, J.P. & Shaver, P.R. (1980). *Measures of social psychological attitudes.* Ann Arbor, Michigan: Institute for Social Research.

Sheridan, M. & Bullis, R. (1991). Practitioners' views of religion and spirituality: A qualitative study. *Spirituality and Social Work Journal, 2,* 2-10.

Sullivan, W.P. (1993). "It helps me to be a whole person": The role of spirituality among the mentally challenged. *Psychosocial Rehabilitation Journal, 16,* 125 134.

Tebbi, C., Mallon, J., Richard M. & Bigler, L. (1987). Religiosity and locus of control in adolescent cancer patients. *Psychological Reports,* 683-696.

Titone A. (1991). Spirituality arid psychotherapy in social work practice. *Spirituality and Social Work Communicator 2,* 7-9.

Weisbrod, A., Sherman, M.F. & Hodinko B. (1988). Impact of precounseling information: Therapist counseling style and similarity of religious values on religious Jewish clients. *Journal of Psychology and Judaism 12,* 60-78.

Wright, S D, Pratt, C.C. & Schmall, V.L.. (1985). Spiritual support for caregivers of dementia patients. *Journal of Religion and Health, 24,* 31-38.

Yalom, I.D. (1986). *Theory and practice of group psychotherapy.* New York: Basic Books.

Women: The Ignored Majority

Carol T. Mowbray, Daphna Oyserman, Catherine Lutz, & Rogeair Purnell

CAROL T. MOWBRAY, PH.D., THE UNIVERSITY OF MICHIGAN, SCHOOL OF SOCIAL WORK.

DAPHNA OYSERMAN, PH.D., MERRILL-PALMER INSTITUTE, WAYNE STATE UNIVERSITY.

CATHERINE LUTZ, DEPARTMENT OF PSYCHOLOGY. WAYNE STATE UNIVERSITY.

ROGEAIR PURNELL, THE UNIVERSITY OF MICHIGAN, SCHOOL OF SOCIAL WORK.

Introduction

The major thrust of psychiatric rehabilitation is to provide skill development and supports enabling individuals to function in their roles of choice. The model thus contains an underlying assumption that meaningful life roles are "chosen" roles. It therefore may tend to overlook the impact on persons' lives of the roles that they are given. These given or ascribed roles include those based on gender, ethnicity, and socioeconomic class. Self-definitions, behaviors, beliefs, attitudes, and values are all likely to be structured within such social roles, which can also serve as important social identities (Oyserman & Markus, 1993). In spite of increased awareness of gender as an issue, in current Western culture, gendered roles are those for which there are, perhaps, the least latitude. Yet, as we shall show, the field of psychiatric rehabilitation has paid little attention to the subject of gender differences. We reviewed the 1992–93 volumes of the *Psychosocial Rehabilitation Journal* and found that only 15 out of a total of 21 studies, which reported information on individuals who were recipients of psychiatric rehabilitation services, presented the gender composition of the study sample at all. Furthermore, of these articles, less than half ($N = 6$) tested for gender differences (40%). Thus, only 28% of the articles could inform their readers about whether men and women differed on the study results. It seems likely that when differences between women and men are not even examined, the result is likely to be a service model that is theoretically androgenous, but in actuality male-biased. Again, the psychiatric rehabilitation literature on service approaches bears this out. The primary domain considered in services is vocational. There has been some consideration of the generic topic of rehabilitation in housing choices. However, those domains where women are considered to occupy primary roles, e.g., the family, parenting, and interpersonal relationships (Miller & Stiver, 1993), have received scant attention (Oyserman, Mowbray & Zemencuk, 1996).

This lack of concern for possible gender differences in psychiatric rehabilitation overall and especially to those issues of primary concern to women, is not unique to this field, but may be seen to reflect the perspective of the entire psychiatric/mental health establishment. For decades, feminists scholars and advocates have decried sex bias in the treatment system. Early research by Broverman et al. (1970) established the negative perceptions of women held by clinicians and the double bind in which women were placed, in that the expected characteristics of a "healthy" adult varied markedly from those for an adult female. Similarly, Chesler (1972) contended that because gendered roles were so proscriptive of mental health, women were in double jeopardy; those who overconformed to female sex roles were likely to be viewed as mentally ill as well as those who violated "appropriate" gendered role expectations. Additionally, clinical and practice research has found gender biases in diagnosis (Loring & Powell, 1988) and in treatment, which serve to demean women (as dependent, passive, seductive, hysterical, etc.), foster traditional and limited sex roles, and respond to women patients as sex objects (Hankin, 1990).

An awareness of how such biases might affect services to women with long-term psychiatric disabilities is of more recent origin. Test and Berlin (1981) were apparently the first to point out that the "chronically mentally ill are regarded as almost genderless…" (p. 136). Although the research literature was limited, their review was able to identify the existence of significant gender differences in numerous domains of life functioning: instrumental roles, social and sexual roles, marital and family roles, and physical health. Several authors have elaborated on the problems raised in Test and Berlin's pivotal article (e.g., Bachrach, 1984; Bachrach, 1985, Bachrach & Nadelson, 1988). However, systematic attention to gender differences is still clearly lacking. For example, a 20-year metaevaluation of published treatment effectiveness studies involving aftercare services (Feis, cited in Mowbray & Benedek, 1988) found that 22% of studies did not indicate the gender composition of their sample and another 15% contained all male subjects. Over all the studies which did report gender ratios, there was a predominance of male participants (54.8%). A more recent review of 1992 issues of the *American Journal of Psychiatry* found that while a large proportion (84%) reported on the gender composition of their samples, less than half (46/99) tested for gender differences. Considering the significance of the topic of gender differences and the state of our practice ignoring women's special needs, more writing, discussion, and training are clearly mandated concerning psychiatric rehabilitation for women.

In this article, we will review the most recent literature concerning women with long-term, severe mental illness. The review has been organized to cover the same major topics earlier identified by Test and Berlin (1981) regarding role functioning. We will begin with a summary of gender differences in the target population on demographics and clinical characteristics. We end our review with a discussion of ways to improve both the treatment and knowledge bases.

Gender Differences in Demographics and Clinical Characteristics

Gender Differences in Diagnoses

It comes as no surprise to most rehabilitation and mental health providers that women far outnumber men in diagnoses of major affective disorders, especially depression. In fact, the lifetime prevalence for major depressive episodes in women is 1.67 times that of men—affecting a staggering 21.3% of the female population (Kessler et al., 1994)! What is much less commonly known, however, is that women actually outnumber men in all major *DSM-III* psychiatric diagnoses except one—antisocial personality disorder. This epidemiological finding was first established in the 1980 Epidemiological Catchment Area (ECA) studies from 5 sites (Robins, Locke & Regier, 1991) and more recently replicated in the National Comorbidity Study, using a national probability sample (Kessler et al., 1994). These gender differences upset conventional notions that men have higher rates of anxiety disorders and non-affective psychoses, such as schizophrenia and schizoaffective disorder, and that schizophrenia is primarily a disorder of young males. Comorbidity is another area in which conventional wisdom held that men outnumbered women. In fact, the National Comorbidity Study revealed that women, compared to men, have a higher prevalence of comorbidity of three or more disorders (Kessler et al., 1994). Women with either alcoholism or cocaine use diagnoses appear more likely to exhibit a concurrent depressive disorder than do males (Gomberg, 1993; Denier, Thevos, Latham & Randall; 1991, respectively).

Despite the overrepresentation of women in most categories of mental illness diagnoses, it is men who are overrepresented in more intensive treatment programs: women are more likely to receive outpatient treatment (Wilcox & Yates, 1993) and men inpatient care (Hankin, 1990). In a recent statewide study, females as compared with males with severe mental illness were served predominantly in the less intensive services of crisis/emergency and outpatient care; while males outnumbered females in use of case management and residential services (Mowbray & Benedek, 1988).

Gender Differences in Demographics

There are also major gender differences in the demographics of persons with severe mental illness. Several research studies have corroborated the fact that women in treatment with a mental illness diagnosis are significantly older than men (Test, Knoedler, Allness & Burke, 1985) and also that women have a later age of onset (Goldstein, Tsuang & Faraone, 1989). The latter gender difference may be particularly marked in schizophrenia (Greenwald, 1992). That is, the age of onset for schizophrenia is 27 for females versus 21 for males (Gottesman, 1991). Similar though less dramatic differences are found for unipolar depression (25 for females vs. 23 for males) and for bipolar disorder (20 for females vs. 18 for males) (Burke, Burke, Regier & Rae, 1990).

Research also consistently indicates gender differentials in marital status among persons with mental illness: National weighted estimates show that while a *minority* of men with serious mental illness marry (31% to 46% married), a *majority* of women do (55% to 75% married;

National Institute of Mental Health, 1986). In fact, in overall population studies, marriage has consistently been interpreted as serving a protective function in men, while in women its function is more questionable. Married men usually have the lowest rates of mental illness, especially depression; while single (never married) women are often *less* depressed than their married counterparts (Gove, 1979; Hankin, 1990).

Differences in the racial composition of male versus female populations diagnosed with mental illness have been explored, but so far no significant differences have been supported. However, the ECA data for one site indicated a four-way interaction of age, ethnicity, sex, and diagnosis; that is, higher prevalence rates for older Mexican-American women and younger non-Hispanic women, especially on alcoholism, drug abuse, phobias, and depression (Burnam et al., 1987).

Possible Reasons for Gender Differences

Explanations for gender differences in diagnosis have been posited, but none clearly established. For major affective disorders, a social roles explanation appears to be the best heuristic at present (Hankin, 1990). According to this explanation, women's socialization emphasizes relationships with others and de-emphasizes the importance of independence and personal autonomy. Women's social roles place multiple demands on them, but offer little status and few opportunities for personal gratification, and encourage minimization of their own needs. Combined, these factors make women more vulnerable to depression as they seek to meet role obligations and view problems in goal attainment as due to personal shortcomings.

Explanations for gender differences in schizophrenia are more diverse. A hormonal basis has been raised as a parsimonious way to account for the age differential. That is, female hormones may serve as protective factors for women disposed genetically or constitutionally to schizophrenia. Postmenopause, this protection disappears, thus explaining the two or three to one ratio of female to male schizophrenics in midlife and older age groups (Greenwald, 1992; Seeman, 1982). Hormonal differences have also been used to explain the supposedly better treatment outcomes observed for women schizophrenics; i.e., female hormones enhance the effectiveness of antipsychotic medication—an enhancement that ends postmenopause, when the sex differential in treatment outcomes is also thought to end.

Other nonhormonal explanations for these gender differentials have also been advanced: For one, that women's later age of onset produces better premorbid functioning and hence better outcomes. Secondly, women and men have been found to exhibit different types of schizophrenia. That is, men exhibit more negative symptomatology (such as withdrawal, amotivation, etc.), while women show more florid and affective symptoms, more acting out, and more overt hostility (Shtasel et al., 1992; Goldstein & Link, 1988). Women compared to men also appear to have more negative early life experiences, suggesting that schizophrenia for women may be more environmentally influenced (Greenwald, 1992). These differences in symptomatology and past history may reflect an actual difference in the underlying psychiatric illness (e.g., left hemisphere dysfunction and the deficit syndrome; Goldstein, Tsuang & Faraone, 1989); or they may reflect socialization and cultural proscriptions which affect how the illness is manifested.

It should be noted, however, that many of these studies about supposedly better outcomes for females versus males who are diagnosed with schizophrenia are flawed. That is, many of the studies use small samples which may not be representative; for example, including only first admission patients (so older women with greater disturbance are not studied) or recruiting solely from private psychiatric hospitals (in which middle to upper income women with insurance are overrepresented). Also, the measures of treatment outcomes or premorbid competence may not be valid; for example, common outcomes such as compliance with the treatment plan, attendance at day programs (Mowbray & Benedek, 1988), and adjustment ratings which include marital status as a major indicator (Angermeyer, Goldstein & Kuehn, 1989) may stack the deck in favor of women who follow their gender roles, are submissive to authority, and marry.

Thus, although usually ignored in treatment considerations, gender appears to play a major role in the etiology and manifestation of mental illness. At this point, more scientifically sound research is definitely needed to explain the gender differences which have been observed. However, the evidence does seem clear enough to mandate attention to gender differences on the basis of findings from clinical studies. We now turn our attention to research which has explored gender differences in role functioning.

Gender Differences in Instrumental Role Performance

Few studies have been conducted which focus explicitly on gender differences in functioning in or support needed for instrumental roles; such as employment, educational activities, home maintenance, etc. Some large-scale descriptive studies of populations with serious mental illness were located which happened to test for some of these gender differences. For the most part, no significant differences appear between men and women on education and employment, for North American groups studied (Herman et al., 1988; Shtasel et al., 1992; Test et al., 1985). This contrasts to dramatic vocational disadvantages for women reported by Test and Berlin in 1981. The lack of current differences may reflect methodological problems (e.g., not controlling for women's older ages and thus greater opportunities for vocational experiences). Or, it may reflect more subtle influences now operating. Even if real, a lack of gender differences in employment status may not necessarily be to women's advantage, given the competing family obligations faced by most working women, including those with severe mental illness. For example, Holstein and Harding (1992), in a small sample follow-up of individuals discharged from an inpatient psychiatric facility, found that 13 out of 14 women were working and of those, 6 reported having homemaking responsibilities for others. For the men, 7 of 10 were working and none of the 7 had responsibilities caring for others. The investigators suggest that women's multiple work roles may significantly increase their stress and consequent symptomatology.

Whether or not past or present labor force and educational status for persons with severe mental illness are affected by gender may thus be questionable. However, there are clear differences in services to males and females in rehabilitation agencies. Nationally, across all types of disabilities, women represent less than one third of the caseloads of vocational rehabilitation programs, with reported earnings at closure only 56% of those achieved by men (Menz et al., 1989). Cook and Roussel (1987) found that women in a psychiatric rehabilitation program were given fewer job placements before "graduating" and that they were retained in the agency longer before getting their first paid jobs. Once in these independent job placements, women received significantly lower salaries (Cook & Roussel, 1987). Examination of data from Fairweather Lodge programs (a psychosocial residential and employment program) indicates fewer female than males being served (37% vs. 63%) (Fergus, 1987). This may not be surprising, given the typical jobs available to Lodge members (e.g., janitorial, landscaping, construction, etc.). Perkins and Rowland (1991) report that for a psychiatric rehabilitation center in London, a minority of day program patients are women (41%). These women are underrepresented at the higher intensity service levels and show significantly less movement out of the program than men. Thus, despite an apparent lack of gender differences in education and work histories, or even an alleged "better premorbid functioning" for women versus men, women seem to be under-represented in vocationally-oriented programs. This may reflect cultural expectations that vocational performance is more important to men or higher staff expectancies for men's vocational activity (Bachrach, 1985). Such attitudes, implicitly tied to the social construction of gender, violate the rehabilitation principle of individualized treatment. It should also be pointed out that for many women, the full-time homemaker role does not offer the safety and comfort assumed, but rather presents many stressors which may increase symptomatology and decrease adaptive functioning.

The instrumental role of living independently has also been studied, albeit in a limited manner. Contrary to expectations, women appear to more often live in independent settings—alone, in houses or apartments (Mowbray & Chamberlain, 1986; Test, Burke, & Wallisch, 1990). For example, Cook and Jonikas (1993) found 41% of females but 29% of males living in normal housing 6 months after closing services from a psychiatric rehabilitation agency. While these differences may be reflective of women's experience and socialization in household maintenance and domestic chores, they may also reflect differences in age and maturity. Cook and

Jonikas also reported that when length of program participation was controlled for, gender differences in living arrangements disappeared. Gender differences in living arrangements may also reflect males' greater involvement in the criminal justice system (higher arrest records and days spent in penal settings) and in using substances (Mowbray et al., 1996; Test et al., 1990). Both of these factors would promote more assignment of males to dependent/ supervised living situations.

Social, Sexual, Marital, and Family Roles

Social and Sexual Roles

There is a relatively large body of literature linking females' socialization into gendered roles with depression: that is, while women are socialized to be nurturing of others, supportive of their needs and attentive to their desires; this other-directedness can come at the expense of their own sense of worth and efficacy (e.g., Oyserman & Markus, 1993). In fact, when women do focus on dissatisfactions with their family and social relationships, their treatment rarely addresses these issues (Zemenchuk, Rogosch, & Mowbray, 1995). Socialization practices through which women become centered on social connections and men on autonomy are not routinely explored, leaving women with a sense that their needs are not being met and that they are somehow to blame Thus, while the mental health of the family is oftentimes considered to be the responsibility of the mother, no one has responsibility for seeing that her needs are being met (Bernardez, 1984).

Cogan (1993) has reported that while women are more likely to utilize community mental health services, they are less likely to view them as helpful than men. In fact, these women are quite likely to rate these services as being of no help at all. Perhaps, as Cogan suggests, this is because these services were not designed with the real life needs and circumstances of women in mind. In fact, relatively little is known about the everyday life circumstances of women with a severe mental illness. Social and sexual roles, friendships, and intimate relationships are likely to be central supports and could also be stressors for anyone. However, information is rarely reported about the interpersonal connectedness of women with psychiatric disabilities. What supports do they receive from friends, neighbors, and acquaintances; who can they turn to when they need help?

A recent study by Test and associates (1990) suggests that the daily life circumstances of men and women with a severe mental illness differ in important ways. Women were more likely than men to be hospitalized for nonpsychiatric reasons. Women were also more likely to be: married or divorced, involved in heterosexual relationships, parents, and, when parents, actively involved in parenting. Men were more likely to be jailed and to commit suicide. Males and females did not differ in the number of friends they were in contact with, but females were more likely to report kissing, dating, and sexual activity. From this and

In overall population studies, marriage has consistently been interpreted as serving a protective function in men, while in women its function is more questionable.

other reports, it appears that women with a severe mental illness are likely to be sexually active. Thus, Test et al. (1990) report that in their sample of young adults, three quarters of women but only 40% of males were sexually active. In a survey of members of a large psychosocial rehabilitation agency (Cook et al., 1994), 39% reported that they were sexually active; on average, members reported having more than four sexual partners in the past 5 years. Less than half of the members reported more than occasional use of condoms. There were no differences between reports of men and women in this sample. Katz, Watts, and Santmann (1994), surveying a sample of persons with serious mental illness, also found no gender differences in high risk sexual behaviors. Sexual activity has also been documented for women in hospital settings (Mowbray, Oyserman & Zemencuk, 1995).

Verhuist and Schneidman (1981) report that, unfortunately, over time, stable sexual relationships may be replaced with casual sexual encounters. A recent study, focusing on the social and sexual roles of women with severe mental illness, found that the vast majority self-reported a need for help in dealing with difficult relationships—both in getting their emotional needs met and in dealing with emotional and sexual abuse (Cogan, 1993). Women with severe mental illness may be more at risk of experiencing unwanted sexual advances, harassment, and exploitation as will be discussed later

It does not appear that women with a severe mental illness can assume that the community mental health and psychosocial rehabilitation services they are offered or receive will focus on their needs as spouses, mothers, or family members.

in this chapter. However, sexuality also involves desired intimacy and attainment of adult roles.

Marital and Family Roles

Marital and family roles are major social roles since marriage and parenting are normative signs of adult status and reflect important developmental tasks (Belle, 1982; Cohler & Musick, 1983; Gizynski, 1985). In addition, it is often argued that women are particularly likely to view social connectedness and relationships with others as important and self-defining (Oyserman & Markus, 1993). Given their normative, social, and developmental centrality, these marital and family roles are particularly likely to be central to women's sense of who they are and what is possible for them. Success in this domain will therefore likely provide the self with a sense of worth and competence, while setbacks may be particularly stress inducing and straining, providing the basis for a variety of negative self images (Markus & Cross, 1990; Stott, et al., 1983).

Unfortunately, women with a mental illness appear likely to experience a variety of social stressors in their intimate and family relationships. These stresses may increase vulnerability; thus, for example, married women of low socioeconomic status with young children and no paid employment outside the home are at increased risk of developing a psychiatric disorder (Romans-

Clarkson, Walton, Herbison & Mullen, 1989). Mental illness in turn may increase stress in social relations. A recent review by Downey and Coyne (1990) suggests that marital conflict is likely to be high up to 4 years after a depressive episode and that divorce is common among depressed women. In addition, women with a mental illness are more likely to marry a spouse with a psychiatric disorder—a situation that increases risk of exacerbation of their own symptoms and severity of marital and family disturbance (Downe & Coyne, 1990).

As in other domains related to women and mental illness, information is scarce as to the marital and family roles women with a mental illness carry out and the successes and problems they may encounter in these roles. However, it appears that women with a severe mental illness have a greater number of children than average and are more often divorced or not married than the norm, thus increasing their chances of raising children as single parents (Mowbray, Oyserman, & Zemencuk, 1995). In their review of the literature, Hammen, Burge, and Adrian (1991) suggest that adverse socioeconomic conditions and lack of resources are part of the life circumstances of women with a severe mental illness. The stress of parenting under conditions of poverty, social isolation, and marital discord increases risks for disorders in children (e.g., Hammen et al., 1987). In fact a large literature exists suggesting that children of women with mental illness are at risk for a variety of behavioral and emotional problems (e.g., Downey & Coyne, 1990; Persson-Blennow, Binet & McNeil, 1988; Phillipps & O'Hara, 1991; Richters, 1992; Tronick & Gianino, 1986). In addition, these children make up a sizeable minority of children removed from home and placed in foster care or other out-of-home placements (Blanche, Nicholson & Purcell, 1944; Oyserman, Benbishty & Ben-Rabi, 1992). Of course,

these findings do not explicate the dynamic process through which illness and the perceived effectiveness of child rearing may be interrelated.

Parenting

A number of recent studies have examined aspects of mother-child relationships as these related to child outcomes and to mental illness status. These studies have documented risk in the quality of early dyadic relationships between mother and infant and the security of the infant's attachment to the mother (see Oyserman, Mowbray & Zemencuk, 1994, for a more complete review). In particular, mothers with affective disorders appear to be less able to synchronize their emotional and communicative efforts with the child's. However, while mothers with an affective disorder were found to be less responsive and less able to sustain social interactions with their children than comparison mothers, they were no less affectionate and tended to express this in physical play and touching. While some studies have suggested that mothers with affective disorders may be more rejecting and critical than comparison mothers, Conrad and Hammen (1989) suggest that depressed mothers are more accurate in their assessment of their children and more negative in their responses to their children's difficulties and shortcomings, perhaps because they find them to be more overwhelming. In general, mother's depressive episodes appear to have a negative effect on their children such that a temporal association between mother and child episodes of major depression has been documented (e.g., Hammen et al., 1991).

Many studies have compared depressed with nondepressed mothers but relatively few compare nonmentally ill mothers to both mothers with schizophrenia and mothers with an affective disorder. When such comparisons are made, a schizophrenia diagnosis appears to be related to higher probability of emotional unavailability and passive lack of responsibility in interactions with children (e.g., Goodman & Brumley, 1990). Women with schizophrenia were also found to be less likely to provide a stimulating and enriched child-rearing environment for their young children than comparison or depressed mothers.

Available supports and resources and the difficulties and stressors women experience are clearly likely to influence their ability to carry out the parenting role and also their perceived capacity to carry out other roles. Unfortunately, it does not appear that women with a severe mental illness can assume that the community mental health and psychosocial rehabilitation services they are offered or receive will focus on their needs as spouses, mothers, or family members. Parenting appears to be a particularly unsupported role for women with severe mental illness. First, the little empirical evidence that exists suggests that women are not even routinely asked if they are parents, let alone what help they may need to fulfill their parenting role (e.g., Cogan, 1993; DeChillo, Matorin & Hallahan, 1987; Zemencuk, Rogosch & Mowbray, 1995; Wallace, 1992). Our review of the literature (Oyserman, Mowbray & Zemencuk, 1994) suggests that few services exist to support mothers with severe mental illness and their children. Second, women may be hesitant to request services since they run the risk of having their children become wards of the child welfare system, entering foster care or other out of home placement (Cogan, 1993; Perkins, 1992; Wallace, 1992). The extent to which mothers with SMI lose custody of their children is unclear, although a few reports suggest that it may be high, especially for older children (Bazar, 1990; Coverdale & Aruffo, 1989; Miller, 1990 Spielvogel & Wile, 1986; Test et al., 1990). Analyses of state appeals court decisions of termination of parental rights hearings for

seriously mentally ill mothers suggest that these women may experience discrimination (*Mental and Physical Disability Law Reporter,* 1985; 1986a,b).

Until recently, there has been little published work focusing on women's perspectives on their family, parenting, and intimate/spousal roles. Our pilot work in the Detroit area (Mowbray, Oyserman & Ross, 1995) suggests that mothers with severe mental illness view parenting as central to who they are and that they have concerns about their functioning as parents. Unfortunately, these mothers are also attempting to cope in difficult economic and social circumstances, trying to provide for themselves and their children without much support. Recent work in Vermont (Cogan, 1993; Wallace, 1992) also focuses more directly on the concerns and issues of mothers with a severe mental illness, presenting difficulties experienced by those who need help in their parenting role. The centrality of family, intimate relationships, and motherhood issues to the lives of the women in these studies is clear. Women were articulate about the services they needed and the responses of the mental health system to these needs. A listing of their needs and the service options open to them is illuminating. In-home services, though desired, are not readily available. Foster care and other out-of-home services do not strengthen the mother's ability to parent once her children are returned home. Mothers felt they need help in concrete domains such as financial assistance, obtaining appropriate and nutritional food for their children and with child-rearing issues. Women who lost custody of their children felt they needed services to support them, to make visitation possible, and to help them deal with the loss of their children on an on-going basis.

In summary, the literature clearly indicates that women who are severely mentally ill are not their condition: they are mothers, wives, girlfriends, and even less discussed, also daughters, sisters, and members of family networks. Clearly more work must be done to provide us with a better and more complete picture of these women and the social roles they play and aspire to attain. This information will better allow us to plan for and carry out rehabilitative efforts. In so doing, we need to also examine the role of sociocultural context in framing the supports and stresses experienced by women with a severe mental illness. For example, it has been argued that African American women are more likely to give and receive help within extended family networks than are whites (Hogan, Eggebeen & Clogg, 1993). Yet the ability of family networks to provide support to subgroups of women with mental illness has not been investigated. Similarly, we do not know the extent to which cultural beliefs about the meaning of mental illness or acceptance of formal support systems may change women's perceived supports and stresses, or enable or disenable the uses of mental health of psychosocial rehabilitation services (Sue & Sue, 1987). Thus, many important topics related to social roles remain unexplored, hindering our ability to provide effective gender-relevant services.

The studies all support the conclusion that women with psychiatric disabilities have more health problems than their male counterparts.

Physical Health and Medication Use

Health Issues for Women With Serious Mental Illness

The inattention to women's problems by the health care delivery system has been documented, as has the inadequate treatment women in the general population receive from health providers (Dan, 1994). Since the comorbidity of physical and mental health problems is high, it might be expected that women with severe mental illness should experience health problems and differences in health care provision. Although this area of gender differences is not well-researched, enough information is available to indicate that such a conclusion is warranted.

Only a handful of research studies could be located which investigated indicators relevant to the physical health of women with severe mental illness. While few in number, the existence of these studies contrasts positively with coverage reviewed by Test and Berlin—who cited only one article in 1981. The studies all support the conclusion that women with psychiatric disabilities have more health problems than their male counterparts. Thus, Test and associates (1990), in their long-term study of Assertive Community Treatment clients, found that women spent significantly more time in general medical inpatient settings (for nonpsychiatric reasons). Similarly, in a hospitalized sample, Mowbray and Chamberlain (1986) reported that women received significantly more nonpsychiatric medical treatment, particularly related to cardiology, diabetes, dermatology, and X-rays. (Men received more treatment for broken bones and minor wounds.) In a hospitalized dually diagnosed sample, gender differences were found in medical problems and their rated severity (Mowbray et al., 1996). To some extent, increased medical problems may reflect the older ages of female versus male groups studied. In fact, the health difference reported by Mowbray and Chamberlain (1986) was no longer significant when age was controlled. However, age may not be a singular explanation since, in Mowbray et al. (1996), the female patients were younger than the males. The general literature on women's health problems suggests that oftentimes a woman's problems go unnoticed or unattended until a late treatment stage (Dan, 1994). Particularly with a psychiatric patient, health problems may be erroneously viewed as part of her delusional system (Mowbray & Benedek; 1988). Advocates concerning women's health needs have interpreted gender differences to reflect morbidity concerns for women and mortality concerns for men. This distinction seems to be maintained for persons with psychiatric disabilities wherein women have more health problems and complaints, but men have a higher suicide rate (Seeman, 1982; Test et al., 1990). Unfortunately, the medical establishment is less focused on morbidity issues, especially those requiring long-term care (Dan, 1994).

Women and Psychotropic Medications

Other studies (summarized by Bachrach, 1985) have described women with schizophrenia as having frequent complaints of weight gain, skin problems, constipation, pseudopregnancy, and menstrual irregularities. Many of these difficulties can be related to use of psychotropic medications, particularly neuroleptic drugs. Tardive dyskinesia, which is purportedly directly related to such drug use, is more frequent and more severe in females than in males. Cook and Jonikas (1993) suggest that medication side effects are often not considered by psychosocial rehabilitation programs, especially for women members. In focus groups, female members of a psychiatric rehabilitation program reported that their doctors never asked about problems of a sexual nature, e.g., vaginal dryness. In contrast, doctors appeared comfortable querying male members about ejaculation and other sexual performance issues. Thus, physical health issues, including those relat-

ed to medication use, appear to be significant but largely ignored for women.

Besides their effects on sexuality and menstrual problems for women, use of psychotropic medications poses unique problems for women who are pregnant, postpartum, or planning to have children. In general, the vast majority of research on drug use has been conducted on males. However, since nearly all drugs cross the placenta (and are present in lactation), doctors oftentimes feel that female psychiatric patients should discontinue psychotropic medications during pregnancy (and in the postpartum if they are nursing mothers) (Allen, 1994; Mowbray et al., 1995). In actuality, lithium carbonate is the only psychotropic whose teratogenicity on fetal development is well established (Schou, 1990). However, a chance of birth defects has been reported for antidepressants and minor tranquilizers in some studies, but contradictory findings are common. (See Allen, 1994; and Mowbray et al., 1995; for more information.) In general, this area has not been well-researched, similar to other topics concerning medications for women. Understandably, physicians often disagree as to the alternative risks to the fetus from maintaining psychotropic drug use versus untreated, severe maternal psychiatric symptoms, which could lead the woman to harm herself or her child directly or through neglect (Allen, 1994; Cohen, 1989). Obviously, psychiatric patients may have many concerns about these issues. However, it appears that most physicians assume it is their role to *make* medication decisions for their patients (Krener, Simmons, Hansen & Treat, 1989). In fact, Allen (1994) describes one study which found that few programs even required written informed consent from females receiving lithium during their childbearing years. Thus, women are denied involvement in a major topic concerning not only their own life course but that of their offspring. Such practices are, of course, contrary to psychiatric rehabilitation principles and should be addressed by psychiatric rehabilitation programs. However, it appears that few are doing so for their female members. Women who are pregnant or contemplating conception should be given information that is complete and understandable concerning the risks of use and non-use of psychotropics as well as treatment alternatives, and be given help in making their own decisions.

A major problematic factor concerning physical health is the fact that women, compared to men, are prescribed psychotropic medications more frequently and in greater quantities (Allen, 1994; Mowbray & Chamberlain, 1986; Seeman, 1982). The literature has been quite consistent in such findings both for women with psychological/emotional problems and for those with more severe disorders, and across many classes of psychotropic medications from minor tranquilizers to antipsychotics. These gender differences may reflect the general societal trend to take women's complaints of any sort less seriously, write them off as of psychosomatic origin, and inappropriately use medications to silence them (Dan, 1994).

Substance Abuse

Comorbid Substance Abuse and Mental Illness—Prevalence and Characteristics by Gender

Alcohol and illicit drug use and misuse is far more common in men than in women (National Institute of Drug Abuse, 1990). In a national study, Kessler and associates (1994) found that 35.4% of male respondents reported a lifetime history of substance dependence or abuse versus 17.9% of female respondents. Although the co-occurrence of alcohol and drug dependence and mental illness was not reported,

women have been found to be more likely to have a comorbidity of three or more disorders (Kessler et al., 1994). Consistent with gender differences in overall psychiatric epidemiology, among the most common comorbid mental disorders for those with a lifetime history of alcohol dependence or abuse are affective and anxiety disorders (although antisocial personality disorder is also prevalent; Regier et al., 1990). Among individuals seeking substance abuse treatment for a cocaine disorder, Ziedonis, Rayford, Bryant, and Rounsaville (1994) found that women had higher rates of current phobia and childhood attention deficit disorder. Another epidemiological study of a similar population (Halikas et al., 1994) reported that women exhibited significantly higher lifetime rates of all psychiatric diagnoses except antisocial personality disorder (ASPD). Finally, an examination of gender differences in psychiatric diagnoses at three substance abuse treatment programs found women, compared to men, were more likely to have a psychiatric problem other than a personality disorder (e.g., agoraphobia, dysthymia, anorexia, suicide attempts, and bulimia; Wilcox & Yates, 1993). Thus, several research studies concur that women are more likely to have a psychiatric disorder concurrent with substance abuse (although there is less agreement on the specifics of the psychiatric diagnosis). Explanations for these gender differences are usually consistent with social psychological theories on sex roles, in that "...female deviance tends to be inwardly directed whereas male deviance is more outwardly directed and antisocial...[suggesting] that substance abuse exerts a greater psychological impact on females but a greater impact on the social functioning of males" (Robbins, 1989, p. 126). In addition, childhood sexual abuse has also been correlated with adult females' addictive behaviors and could be hypothesized as a common cause for co-occurring psychological problems (Briere & Runtz, 1987; Briere, 1988). That is, substance abuse can be viewed as self-medication against depression or as chemically induced dissociation (Hamilton, 1990).

Few studies have examined differences other than diagnoses between males and females with a psychiatric disability and substance use disorder. Mowbray et al. (1996) found that among psychiatric inpatients with substance abuse problems, women were more likely to be younger, report a family history of drug use, be unemployed, have medical problems, and utilize self-help services than their male counterparts. Women were also more likely to have children and to have their children living with them. On the other hand, men had more legal problems, a greater number of residences in the past three years, higher alcohol severity ratings, and more employment problems within the last 30 days than female respondents. These gender differences among those with a dual diagnosis appear to be consistent with the social role theory of gender differences, explicated by Robbins (1989). However, another study of comorbidity at three substance abuse treatment programs found that most gender differences were age related. For example, alcohol was the drug of choice for older men and women, poly-substance use was more common among younger subjects, and ASPD traits were more often found among males under 40. Women also reported more depressive symptomatology, were more likely to abuse benzodiazepines (minor tranquilizers), and to have their drug of choice be something other than alcohol (Wilcox & Yates, 1993).

Treatment Issues

Although the number of women misusing alcohol or drugs is not greater than the number of men, chemically dependent women face many obstacles when seeking treatment. These obstacles are likely to be exacerbated when we consider that these women are also more likely to have a serious psychiatric problem. Mondanaro (1989) notes that for women, chemical dependency involves a unique set of issues. First, women may experience a greater number of psychological problems, such as lower levels of self-esteem, and more anxiety and depression. In addition, they may face more stigma associated with their chemical dependency than do men. Historically, legal drugs such as alcohol and tobacco were reserved for men. Although times have changed somewhat, women who use substances still suffer the residual effects of these attitudes. For African American women, the stigma may also be reinforced by racial stereotypes, suggesting that they are more likely to use street drugs than other women. In addition, the media has done little to address damaging and unsubstantiated stereotypes about African Americans using and selling drugs more than any other group of Americans.

Compounding the above problems, many women who abuse substances have lower educational levels and, therefore, decent employment may be hard to find (Mondanaro, 1989). In fact, combined with the traditionally lower wage scale for women, a poor job history may make earning a viable wage even more difficult. Due to lack of money, many women cannot afford substance abuse services or ancillary expenses which would facilitate their treatment, such as transportation and childcare. Third, issues of sexuality and intimacy are likely to be more significant for women. Sexual abuse, incest, rape and violence have been reported by many chemically

---

[1] A common definition of abuse used in the literature is: The involvement of dependent, developmentally immature children and adolescents in sexual activities they do not truly comprehend to which thy are unable to give informed consent, or that violate the social taboos of family roles.

dependent women (Mondanaro, 1989). Their addiction may represent their attempts to cope with past abuse (Root, 1989). In an analysis of the life histories of female substance abusers, Woodhouse (1990) found that violence and abuse were common themes. Fifth, due to feelings of powerlessness, some women may not be motivated or may feel unable to change (Mondanaro, 1989), as if they had done too many bad things to ever remedy them. Traditional 12-step programs, like Alcoholics Anonymous, may be less helpful to women because of their focus on giving up control—which many of these women have too little of anyway.

Mondanaro (1989) has also noted that women may not seek direct help for their substance abuse since they often view it as a secondary problem. Instead of chemical dependency treatment, they may seek help for problems of a physical or psychiatric nature. Men, on the other hand, are more likely to see substance abuse as a primary problem and to thus seek help directly for drug or alcohol use. Mondanaro's seventh point is sobering. Women may actually experience more physical problems due to their drug use than men who use drugs. Such problems include cirrhosis of the liver, digestive disorders, and circulatory disorders. Eighth, for pregnant substance abusing women, very few services exist. The scarcity of programs for these women is unfortunate due to the fact that many women are especially motivated to stop using drugs when they find out they are pregnant, but just cannot get

The incidence of childhood sexual assault among female psychiatric patients has reportedly ranged from 20–51% in inpatient settings and 22–54% in outpatient settings—as compared to 6–15% for the general population.

the help they need. As a result, their babies may be exposed to the deleterious effects of drugs for longer periods of time, simply because their mothers were unable to receive needed substance abuse counseling in an inpatient or residential setting. In this light, current legislative efforts to take punitive action against drug-addicted women found to be pregnant is unfortunate in that it may keep more women away from treatment rather than seeking what little treatment is currently available.

On a more positive note, according to a recent treatment review article, out of 80 studies, women and men appeared to have similar treatment outcomes (Toneatto, Sobell, & Sobell, 1992). Although, similar to the psychiatric literature, few (only 28%) studies actually examined gender differences.

Limitations

As in other literature cited, research and evaluation of the chemical dependency problems of women with serious mental illness has some significant limitations. Although more research is being conducted to explore dual diagnosis among women, studies vary greatly in the demographic characteristics of subjects, the substance use studied, comorbid mental disorders examined, the use of inpatient versus outpatient samples, examination of onset differences between mental illness and substance use comorbid disorders, and whether individuals studied were seeking mental health or substance abuse treatment. Without comprehensive studies exploring all aspects of the etiology of comorbid alcohol, licit and illicit drug use, and various types of mental illness among representative study populations, the development of effective treatment programs for dually diagnosed women will continue to be difficult. Again, the message to service providers is to improve their assessment techniques to better identify women with this concomitant problem. This may only be a partial solution, however, since substance abuse treatment resources for women are likely to be difficult to find or to access. Thus, psychiatric rehabilitation services may have to engage in more of their own program development activities.

Sexual Victimization

Another pressing, and yet often unaddressed issue affecting women with a serious mental illness is that of sexual abuse,[1] including childhood incest as well as current adult abuse. Research investigating the incidence rates of childhood abuse among mentally ill women suggests a higher occurrence than among the general female, adult population (Finkelhor, 1979; Russell, 1983; Siegel et al., 1987). Studies have also documented the relationship between childhood sexual assault histories and severity of symptomatology (Beck et al., 1987; Bifulco, Brown & Adler, 1991; Brownes & Finkelhor, 1987; Craine, Henson, Colliver & MacLean, 1988). Unfortunately, histories of current or past sexual abuse among severely mentally ill women are seldom explored by mental health professionals (Jacobson & Richardson, 1987) . This contributes to a poor knowledge base on this topic, as well as to ignoring important issues in treatment and rehabilitation programming.

Histories of Childhood Sexual Assault
The incidence of childhood sexual

assault among female psychiatric patients has reportedly ranged from 20–51% in inpatient settings and 22–54% in outpatient settings—as compared to 6–15% for the general population (Bifulco et al., 1991). Estimates vary for a number of reasons. First, definitions of sexual abuse vary, e.g., the amount of contact necessary to constitute abuse, the age of the victim, the use of force or coercion, and the relationship with the perpetrator (Bifulco, et al., 1991). Secondly, methods of obtaining the information also vary (Finkelhor, 1986). Common methods include interviews, surveys, and chart reviews. Although surveys and chart reviews pose the advantage of being less invasive and preserving confidentiality, an interview is more likely to yield complete information, depending on what questions are asked (Jacobson & Richardson, 1987). Questions phrased with innocuous wording such as, "sometimes when children are still young, someone does something sexual with them. Did anything like that happen to you?" are more likely to yield affirmative responses than those containing words such as "incest" or "abuse." Similarly, questions regarding specific abuse instances are more likely to yield information than more general questions (Finkelhor, 1986).

In the general population, a history of sexual assault has been linked to such problems as excessive aggression, sexual dysfunction, histories of adult victimization, hyperactivity, substance abuse, dissociative states, and chronic feelings of depression and helplessness (Beck & van der Kolk, 1987; Hamilton, 1990). The results of one study of 286 working class mothers in England revealed a strong relationship between childhood sexual abuse and clinically relevant levels of depression (Bifulco et al., 1991). Furthermore, over half of the participants who reported childhood sexual abuse experiences also reported other negative childhood experiences including lack of parental care, parental violence, and institutional stays prior to the age of 17. Although histories of child abuse were associated with depression in women who had not experienced other negative early experiences, it was fairly rare and constituted only 5% of the cases of depression in the sample as a whole. This suggests an important link between sexual abuse and parental neglect among severely mentally ill women.

Studies examining psychiatric populations have found even more severe symptoms among sexually abused patients than among other adult, female patients (e.g., Beck & van der Kolk, 1987; Craine et al., 1988). In one study of 26 female patients in a state hospital, those with sexual assault histories ($N = 12$) were more likely to experience sexual delusions, affective symptoms, substance abuse, suspected organicity, and major mental problems; and they spent more time in seclusion than other patients (Beck & van der Kolk, 1987). Similarly, in a study by Craine et al. (1988), 51% of an inpatient sample reported sexual abuse as children or adolescents. Of these women, 66% met criteria for posttraumatic stress disorder. In addition, every woman who was positive for all of the following six symptoms had been sexually abused: compulsive sexual behavior, chemical dependency, sadomasochistic sexual fantasy, sexual identity issues, chronic fatigue, and loss of interest in sex.

Although research on childhood sexual assault suggests high rates among women with severe mental illness, as well as more severe symptoms when compared with their non-abused counterparts, mental health professionals often remain unaware of assault histories among their female clients. Ann Jennings (1994) recounts the story of her daughter, who was not identified as a victim of early childhood sexual trauma until nearly 12 years of "treatment" in psychiatric hospitals, mainly with psychotropic drugs. Furthermore, even after the trauma was revealed, the reaction of mental health professionals was to ignore the information. In a study by Craine et al. (1988), 56% of abuse patients had never been identified as such during the course of their hospital treatment. Many of these patients remarked that they had never told any of the staff in the hospital because they had never been asked. This lack of awareness is likely to produce ineffective or inappropriate treatment for these women. In traditional therapy situations, unidentified abuse histories may lead to transference and countertransference issues with male therapists which are detrimental to the therapeutic process. Indeed, there is some concern that most adult women who are survivors of abuse be given female therapists because of their tendency to distrust men, perform for men, and/or give power away to them (Hamilton, 1990). In rehabilitation programs, lack of awareness of a prior abuse history may mean that programs do not develop effective strategies to enable women to fully function in roles of choice, e.g., because staff do not understand the barriers which the woman's past experiences are presenting. Gelinas (1983) contends that many adult survivors of incest are wrongly diagnosed as psychotic or borderline personality disorders (due to the dissociative states they display, their impulsivity and/or perceptual disturbances). Thus, failure to discover past abuse histories can be a very serious problem. Ten years and 15 mental hospitals after her disclosure, Ann Jennings' daughter committed suicide. Possible reasons for mental health and rehabilitation providers' failure to inquire about or deal with sexual assault histories include discomfort with the topic, the belief that such information is irrelevant, disbelief of women's reports, and the difficulty in obtaining reliable information.

Jacobson and Richardson (1987) argue

that in order to avoid inappropriate treatment for severely mentally ill women, routine inquiry into sexual assault histories is essential. She recommends that therapists develop standard times and ways of asking about different types of abuse. She emphasizes the importance of investigating the circumstances surrounding the abuse as well as the perceived effects of the abuse. Based on research findings, mental health workers should also inquire about specific levels of assault, since relatively less severe forms of abuse may have different effects on the client than do more severe forms (although this cannot always be assumed). Obviously, obtaining reliable abuse histories is dependent on the establishment of a trusting and safe relationship between the client and the mental health professional.

Although routine inquiry into the presence of early childhood sexual assault histories is an important first step in responsible treatment planning for women with severe mental illness, more basic questions in this area remain unanswered. The relationship between childhood abuse and adult psychiatric status is well documented. However, little is known regarding the nature of this relationship. Researchers in this area have relied primarily upon retrospective correlational studies. Inherent in such methods are memory biases. Furthermore, such studies are subject to multiple interpretations. For example, as mentioned above, some researchers have suggested that the important variable in psychiatric symptoms is not sexual abuse per se, but rather a generally unstable or neglectful environment in which parents fail to keep the child safe from harm (Bifulco et al., 1991; Muenzenmaier, Meyer, Struening & Ferber 1993). The high co-occurrence of neglect and child abuse is consistent with this interpretation.

Another ambiguity is whether varying levels of abuse may translate into varying levels of psychiatric symptoms. In other words, it is unclear at this point whether all forms of sexual abuse are equal in their deleterious effects. Finally, the existence of psychosocial risk factors which mediate the relationship between childhood sexual abuse and later onset of mental illness are yet unknown. Such risk factors might include family history of mental illness, socioeconomic status, or coping style.

Clearly, more in-depth research is needed in order to design effective prevention programs, and to coordinate services tailored to the special needs of victims of childhood or adolescent sexual assault. Unfortunately, few reports of intervention models for women with serious mental illness could be found in the literature. The most accepted model for adult survivors of incest is one patterned after treatment for posttraumatic stress disorder, in which the trauma memory and associated affects are slowly brought to the fore during outpatient therapy sessions. However, for clients who are likely to decompensate during this process (which could be the case for many women with existing psychiatric disability), this approach is not recommended (Gil, 1988). Herder and Redner (1991) describe an intervention designed for women with serious mental illness who have sexual assault histories, which incorporates case management, as well as a specific group therapy. They contend that this approach has shown initial favorable results. Group therapy is thought to be advantageous in that it enables these women to reestablish trusting relationships with others. The primary focus of their model is on psychosocial education and cognitive reframing of the abuse incident. Victims of childhood sexual assault are taught to view their symptoms as early attempts to cope with the abuse incident. This reframing of what are often viewed as dysfunctional reactions to the abuse is intended to increase feelings of self esteem and control over women's lives. Therapy then shifts to exploring alternative, more productive coping skills for the present. Although outcomes of this form of group therapy are based on subjective, anecdotal reports, they suggest that addressing the abuse incidence directly results in positive therapeutic change.

Adult Sexual Victimization

While we have thus far focused primarily on childhood sexual abuse, sexual and physical assault of women with severe mental illness in adulthood is also a topic of serious concern. Research indicates that more than a quarter of all women in North America have been beaten by a male partner—or 3 to 4 million American women annually. Battered women constitute 22-35% of women seeking care in emergency departments (Dan, 1994). In psychiatric settings, the prevalence of battering appears to be much higher (e.g., 50% of female psychiatric outpatients and 64% of psychiatric inpatients; cited in Dan, 1994). In fact, it has been alleged that for some women, a psychiatric condition may be directly produced by repeated current experiences of physical or sexual abuse. That is, women's health advocates have long contended that women's responses to coping with their battering situation are often misinterpreted and mislabeled with psychiatric diagnoses and treated with tranquilizers rather than addressing the abuse, per se. Women who are battering victims have been labeled as masochistic personality types and blamed for their abuse—contributing, of course, to an even greater feeling of lack of control and consequent depression on their part (Schechter, 1987). Once a woman is given a psychiatric label, she is less likely to be believed concerning specific abuse allegations, and she risks losing custody of her children (Dan, 1994).

As is the case with child assault, possible reasons for this scarcity of information concerning adult victimization are failure to inquire about these events, or failure on the part of mental health workers to believe reports from severely mentally ill women. Unfortunately, these failures can lead to physical as well as psychological harm. Research suggests that severely mentally ill women are at greater risk for adult sexual assault (Dan, 1994). Presumably this reflects an interaction between a greater tendency to exploit disenfranchised groups and a lack of security in the houses and neighborhoods where these women live. Interventions, therefore, might include the provision of safer low income housing or education for mentally ill women on strategies for protecting themselves against sexual victimization.

Past and present sexual assault is a serious problem facing severely mentally ill women. Intervention strategies need to target a wide area including appropriate assessment of survivors of childhood sexual assault and early intervention for child and adolescent sexual assault victims. Mental health providers and advocates also need to ensure the provision of safe, low income housing, sex education, and assault prevention training in order to reduce the occurrence of adult sexual assault. Finally, more in-depth research is needed to determine which intervention strategies are best suited to the special needs of severely mentally ill women who have suffered past or present abuse.

Conclusions

Research and practice in psychiatric rehabilitation have paid insufficient attention to the specific needs of women with psychiatric disabilities. However, gendered roles have a significant impact on individuals' social identities and their self-conceptions in our society—thus, they cannot be ignored. An expanding (but still less than adequate) clinical and empirical knowledge base documents that there are significant issues which must be addressed to achieve rehabilitation goals for female clients. The issue areas which require attention concern women's instrumental roles (vocational, household maintenance), social roles (friendships, sexuality, intimate relationships, marriage, family planning, parenting, and childcare), physical health problems, side effects of medications, substance use, childhood sexual abuse histories, and vulnerability to adult sexual victimization.

This literature review is but a beginning to helping psychiatric rehabilitation and mental health professionals improve services to female clients. Further steps will be needed, as follows:

1. Service providers need to expand their knowledge concerning issues of particular importance to women with severe mental illness. These involve:

a. Gender differences in age, diagnoses, and functioning and their possible etiologies.

b. Vocational and educational needs and the barriers of bias and discrimination which women may differentially encounter.

c. Women's relational needs and the potentially important roles in recovery played by social networks, friendships, personal relationships, etc.

d. Sexuality, including sexual safety, sexual education, family planning, etc.

e. Pregnancy and the postpartum period—the need for economic and social resources, as well as decision-making concerning medication risks, alternative treatments, etc.

f. Needs associated with parenting, such as economic and emotional support, training in household management and parenting skills, knowledge of child development, advocacy concerning custody, assistance with child-care arrangements, etc.

g. The physical health problems women experience, including unwanted side effects of psychotropic medications,

especially on menstruation and sexual functioning.

h. Substance use disorders in women and how they relate to psychological and emotional problems.

i. The aftereffects often experienced by adult survivors of childhood sexual abuse, as well as likely indicators of having experienced this trauma.

j. The dynamics of adult sexual victimization, including correlates of sexual assault and domestic violence experiences.

2. Service providers need to expand upon their initial and periodic assessment methods to ensure that issues significant to female clients are adequately considered, such as childhood and/or adult sexual and physical assault histories, substance use disorders, battering and other domestic violence victimization, and parenting needs. Since these are sensitive topics, staff should be given training and adequate supervision when they begin to do these assessments.

3. Service providers need to review their practices concerning referral, screening, and/or entry to programs and services to ensure that they do not discriminate by gender; e.g., are equal numbers of women and men referred to vocational rehabilitation? enrolled in training programs? provided access to independent living opportunities with enough support? Are the same prescribing policies followed for men and women? Are men and women equally able to gain access to appropriate substance abuse treatment?

4. Needs assessments should be periodically conducted to ensure that the needs of special subgroups of women are being met within regular programming. If not, new program components should be initiated, e.g., integrated treatment for women with dual diagnosis, educational programs to promote sexual safety, group treatment for victims of childhood sexual assault, parenting education, etc. Support services may also need to be added to meet women's special needs, e.g., respite care or babysitting access for children of female clients who are mothers, transportation to service locations, etc.

5. Research is needed on all the above topics. To address bias, researchers should utilize larger samples of clients, representative of those utilizing psychiatric rehabilitation and mental health services, including minority populations, lesbian women, and all age groups.

Our review indicates that women are an ignored population in psychiatric rehabilitation and mental health services. This situation has gone on for too long: many of the unmet needs identified in this review were also cited by Test and Berlin more than 10 years ago. It is clear that research and service provision should prioritize female clients to improve this situation before another review is completed 10 years from now! Since many of the changes needed involve awareness and assessment issues, this is also a significant area for educators and trainers in psychiatric rehabilitation.

References

Allen, S.C. (1994). *Risk versus gain: The use of psychotropic medication in women of child-bearing age.* Presentation at Young Adult Institute Conference, New York, April.

Angermeyer, M.C., Goldstein, J.M., & Kuehn, L. (1989). Gender differences in schizophrenia: Rehospitalization and community survival. *Psychological Medicine, 19,* 365-382.

Bachrach, L.L. (1985). Chronically mentally ill women: Emergence and legitimation of program issues. *Hospital and Community Psychiatry, 36,* 1063-1069.

Bachrach, L.L. (1984). Deinstitutionalization and women: Assessing the consequences of public policy. *American Psychologist, 39*(10), 1171-1177.

Bachrach, L.L. & Nadelson, C. C. (eds.) (1988). *Treating chronically mentally ill women.* Washington, D.C.: American Psychiatric Association Press.

Bazar, J. (December 1990). Mentally ill moms aided in keeping their children. *APA Monitor, 32.*

Beck, J.C & van der Kolk, B. (1987). Reports of childhood incest and current behavior of chronically hospitalized psychotic women. *American Journal of Psychiatry, 144*(11), 1474-1476.

Belle, D.E. (1982). The impact of poverty on social networks and supports. *Marriage and Family Review, 5*(4), 89-103.

Bernardez, T. (1984). Prevalent disorders of women: Attempts toward a different understanding and treatment. In Mowbray, C.T., Lanir, S., & Hulce, M. (Eds.). *Women and mental health: New directions for change* (pp. 17-28). New York: Haworth.

Bifulco, A., Brown, G.W., & Adler, Z. (1991). Early sexual abuse and clinical depression in adult life. *British Journal of Psychiatry, 159,* 115-122.

Blanche, A., Nicholson, J., & Purcell, J. (1994). Parents with severe mental illness and their children: The need for human services integration. *Journal of Mental Health Administration, 21*(4), 388-396.

Briere, J. (1988). The long-term clinical correlates of childhood sexual victimization. *Annals of the New York Academy of Sciences, 528,* 327-334.

Briere, J. & Runtz, M. (1987). Past sexual abuse trauma: Data and implications for clinical practice. *Journal of Interpersonal Violence, 2*(4), 367-379.

Broverman, I., Vogal, S., Broverman, D., Clarkson, F., & Rosenkrantz, P. (1970). Sex role stereotypes and clinical judgements of mental health. *Journal of Counseling and Clinical Psychology, 34,* 1-7.

Brownes, A. & Finkelhor, D. (1987). Impact of child sexual abuse: A review of the literature. *Psychological Bulletin, 99,* 66-77.

Burke, K.C., Burke, J.D., Regier, D.A., & Rae, D.S. (1990). Age at onset of selected mental disorders in five community populations. *Archives of General Psychiatry, 47,* 511-518.

Burnam, M.A. et al., (1987). Six-month prevalence of specific psychiatric disorders among Mexican Americans and non-hispanic whites in Los Angeles. *Archives of General*

Psychiatry, 44, 687-694.

Chesler, P. (1972). *Women and madness.* Garden City, N.Y.: Doubleday.

Cogan, J. (1993). *Assessing the community support services needs that women with psychiatric disabilities may have regarding relationships.* Burlington, VT: Center for Community Change Though Housing and Support.

Cohen, L.S. (1989). Psychotropic drug use in pregnancy. *Hospital and Community Psychiatry, 40,* 566-567.

Cohler, B.J., & Musick, J.S. (1983). Psychopathology of parenthood: Implications for mental health of children. *Infant Mental Health Journal, 4*(3), 140-163.

Conrad, M. & Hammen, C. (1989). Role of maternal depression in perceptions of child maladjustment. *Journal of Consulting and Clinical Psychology, 57,* 663-667.Cook, J.A. et al. (1994). HIV-risk assessment for psychiatric rehabilitation clientele: Implications for community-based services. *Psychosocial Rehabilitation Journal, 17*(4), 105-115.

Cook, J.A. & Jonikas, J. (1993). *Women's issues in psychosocial rehabilitation: Empowering staff and members.* Institute presented at the International Association of Psychosocial Rehabilitation Services Conference, Oakland, California.

Cook, J.A. & Roussel, A.E. (1987). *Who works and what works: Effects of race, class, age and gender on employment among the psychiatrically disabled.* Presented at the Annual Meetings of the American Sociological Association, Chicago, Illinois.

Coverdale, J.H. & Aruffo, J.A. (1989). Family planning needs of female chronic psychiatric outpatients. *American Journal of Orthopsychiatry, 146*(11), 1489-1491.

Craine, L.S., Henson, C.E., Colliver, J.A. & MacLean, D.G. (1988). Prevalence of a history of sexual abuse among female psychiatric patients in a state hospital system. *Hospital and Community Psychiatry, 39*(3), 300-304.

Dan, Alice. (Ed.). (1994). *Reframing women's health: Multidisciplinary research and practice.* Thousand Oaks, CA: Sage Publications.

DeChillo, N., Matorin, S., & Hallahan, C. (1987). Children of psychiatric patients: Rarely seen or heard. *Health and Social Work, Fall,* 296-302.

Denier, C.A., Thevos, A.K., Latham, P.K. & Randall, C.L. (1991). Psychosocial and psychopathology differences in hospitalized male and female cocaine abusers: A retrospective chart review. *Addictive Behaviors, 16,* 489-496.

Downey, G. & Coyne, J.C. (1990). Children of depressed parents: An integrative review. *Psychological Bulletin, 108*(1), 50-76.

Fergus, E. (1987). *A profile of Lodge program characteristics by region.* Ways of Working Conference, East Lansing, Michigan, March 26-27.

Finkelhor, D. (1979). *Sexually victimized children.* New York, Free Press.

Finkelhor, D. (1986). *A sourcebook on child sexual abuse.* California: Sage Press.

Gelinas, D. (1983). The persisting negative effects of incest. *Psychiatry, 46,* 312-332.

Gil, E. (1988). *Treatment of adult survivors of childhood abuse.* Walnut Creek, CA: Launch Press.

Gizynski, M.N. (1985). The effects of maternal depression on children. *Clinical Social Work Journal, 13*(2), 103-116.

Goldstein, J.M. & Link, B.G. (1988). Gender and the expression of schizophrenia. *Journal of Psychiatric Research, 22,* 141-155.

Goldstein, J.M., Tsuang, M.T., & Faraone, S.V. (1989). Gender and schizophrenia: Implications for understanding the heterogeneity of the illness. *Psychiatry Research, 28,* 243-253.

Gomberg, E. (1993). Women and alcohol: Use and abuse. *Journal of Nervous and Mental Diseases, 181*(4), 211-219.

Goodman, S. H. & Brumley, H. E. (1990). Schizophrenic and depressed mothers: Rational deficits in parenting. *Developmental Psychology, 26,* 31-39.

Gottesman, I. I. (1991). *Schizophrenia genesis: The origins of madness.* New York: W. H. Freeman and Company.

Gove, W.R. (1979). Sex differences in the epidemiology of mental disorder: Evidence and explanations. In E. S. Gomberg & V. Franks, (Eds.). *Gender and disordered behavior.* N.Y.: Bruner/Mazel.

Greenwald, D. (1992). Psychotic disorders with emphasis on schizophrenia. In Brown, L.S. & Ballou, M. (Eds.), *Personality and psychopathology: Feminist reappraisals* (pp. 144-176). N.Y. Guilford.

Halikas, J.A., Crosby, R.D., Pearson, V.L.,

Nugent, S.M., & Carlson, G.A. (1994). Psychiatric comorbidity in treatment-seeking cocaine abusers. *The American Journal of Addictions, 3*(1), 25- 35.

Hammen, C., Burge, D., & Adrian, C. (1991). Timing of mother and child depression in a longitudinal study of children at risk. *Journal of Consulting and Clinical Psychology, 59,* 341-345.

Hamilton, N. (1990). *A guide to the assessment and treatment of female adult survivors of childhood sexual abuse/incest.* Lansing, MI: Michigan Dept. of Mental Health.

Hankin, J. (1990). Gender and mental illness. *Research in Community and Mental Health, 6,* 183-201.

Herder, D.D. & Redner, L. (1991). The treatment of childhood sexual trauma in chronically mentally ill adults. *Health and Social Work, 16*(1), 50-57.

Herman, S.E., Amdur, R., Hazel, K., Cohen, S., Blondin, P., & Mowbray, C.T. (1988). *Clients with serious mental illness: Characteristics and typology.* Lansing, MI: Michigan Department of Mental Health.

Hogan, D., Eggebeen, D.J., & Clogg, C.C. (1993). The structure of intergenerational exchanges in American families. *American Journal of Sociology, 98*(6), 1428-1458.

Holstein, A.R. & Harding, C.M. (1992). Omissions in assessment of work roles: Implications for evaluating social functioning and mental illness. *American Journal of Orthopsychiatry, 62,* 469-474.

Jacobson, A. (1989). Physical and sexual assault histories among psychiatric outpatients. *American Journal of Psychiatry, 146*(6), 755-758.

Jacobson, A. (1990). The relevance of childhood sexual abuse to adult psychiatric inpatient care. *Hospital and Community Psychiatry, 41*(2), 154-158.

Jacobson, A. & Richardson, B. (1987). Assault experiences of 100 psychiatric inpatients: Evidence of the need of routine inquiry. *American Journal of Psychiatry, 144*(11), 908-913.

Jennings, A. (1994). Retraumatizing the victim. *Newsletter of the Resource Center of the Northeast, 6*(3), 11-15.

Katz, R.C., Watts, C. & Santman, J. (1994). AIDS knowledge and high risk behaviors in the chronic mentally ill. *Community Mental Health Journal, 30*(4), 395-402.

Kessler, R.C., McGonagle, K.A., Zhao, S., Nelson, C.B. et al. (1994). Lifetime and 12-month prevalence of *DSM-III-R* psychiatric disorders in the United States. *Archives of General Psychiatry, 51,* 8-19.

Krener, P., Simmons, M.K., Hansen, R.L., and Treat, J.N. (1989). Psycho-social stress and puerperal depression. *International Journal of Psychiatry in Medicine, 19,* 65-84.

Loring, M. & Powell, B. (1988). Gender, race, and *DSM-III*: A study of the objectivity of psychiatric diagnostic behavior. *Journal of Health and Social Behavior, 29,* 1-22.

Markus, H., & Cross, M. (1990). The willful self. Special issue: Centennial celebration of the principles of psychology. *Personality and Social Psychology Bulletin, 16*(4), 726-742.

Mental and Physical Disability Law Reporter. (May-June 1985). Termination of parental rights, Volume 9(3), 187-189.

Mental and Physical Disability Law Reporter. (March-April 1986a). Termination of parental rights—Mental Illness, Volume 10(2), 104-106.

Mental and Physical Disability Law Reporter. (May-June 1986b). Termination of parental rights—Mental Illness, Volume 10(3), 182-183.

Menz, F.E., Hansen, G., Smith, H., Brown, C., Ford, M., McCrowey, G. (1989). Gender equity in access, services and benefits from vocational rehabilitation. *Journal of Rehabilitation, 55,* 31- 40.

Miller, J.B. & Stiver, I. (1993). A relational approach to understanding women's lives and problems. *Psychiatric Annals, 23,* 424-431.

Miller, L.J. (1990). Psychotic denial of pregnancy: Phenomenology and clinical management. *Hospital and Community Psychiatry, 41*(11), 1233-1237.

Mondanaro, J. (1989). *Chemically dependent women: Assessment and treatment.* Lexington, Mass: Lexington Books.

Mowbray, C.T. and Benedek, E.P. (1988). *Women's mental health research agenda: Services and treatment of mental disorders in women.* (Women's Mental Health Occasional Paper Series) National Institute of Mental Health. Rockville, MD.

Mowbray, C.T. & Chamberlain, P.C. (1986). Sex differences among the long-term mentally disabled, *Psychology of Women Quarterly, 10*(10), 383-391.

Mowbray, C.T., Oyserman, D., & Ross, S. (1995). Parenting and the significance of children for mothers with a serious mental illness. *Journal of Mental Health Administration, 22*(2), 189-200.

Mowbray, C.T., Oyserman, D., & Zemencuk, J. (1995). The experience of motherhood for women with serious mental illness: Research on pregnancy, childbirth and the postpartum. *American Journal of Orthopsychiatry, 65*(1), 21-38.

Mowbray, C.T., Ribisl, K.M., Solomon, M., Luke, D.A., & Kewson, T.P. (1996). *Exploring the characteristics of dual diagnosis: An examination of individual, social and community domains.* Ann Arbor, Michigan: University of Michigan, School of Social Work.

Muenzenmaier, K., Meyer, I., Struening, E., & Ferber, J. (1993). Childhood abuse and neglect among women outpatients with chronic mental illness. *Hospital and Community Psychiatry, 44*(7), 666-670.

National Institute of Drug Abuse (NIDA). (1990). *National household survey on drug abuse: Population Estimates 1990.* Rockville, MD: U.S. Department of Health and Human Services.

National Institute of Mental Health. (1986). *Client/patient sample survey of inpatient, outpatient, and partial care programs.* Rockville, MD.

Oyserman, D., Benbishty, R., & Ben Rabi, D. (1991). Characteristics of children and their families at entry into foster care. *Psychiatry and Human Development, 22,* 199-211.

Oyserman, D., & Markus, H. (1993). The sociocultural self. In J. Suls (Ed.), *Psychological perspectives on the self, Volume 4.* Hillsdale, NJ: Erlbaum.

Oyserman, D., Mowbray, C.T., and Zemencuk, J.K. (1994). *Mothers with a severe mental illness: Contextual issues.* Detroit, MI: Wayne State University.

Perkins, R. (1992). Catherine is having a baby. *Feminism and Psychology, 2,* 110-112.

Perkins, R.E. & Rowland, L.A. (1991). Sex differences in service usage in long-term psychiatric care: Are women adequately served? *British Journal of Psychiatry, 158*(suppl. 10), 75-79.

Persson-Blennow, I., Binett, B., & McNeil, T. F. (1988). Offspring of woman with nonorganic psychosis: Mother-infant interaction and fear of strangers during the first year of life. *Acta Psychiatrica Scandinavica, 78*(3), 379-383.

Phillips, C. H. C., & O'Hara, M. W. (1991). Prospective study of postpartum depression: 4 1/2 year follow-up of women and children. *Journal of Abnormal Psychology, 100,* 151-155.

Redner, L.L. & Herder, D.D. (1992). Case management's role in effecting appropriate treatment for persons with histories of childhood sexual trauma. *Psychosocial Rehabilitation Journal, 15*(3), 37-45.

Regier, D.A., Farmer, M.E., Rae, D.S., Locke, B.Z., Keith, S.J., Judd, L.L., & Goodwin, F.K. (1990). Comorbidity of mental disorders with alcohol and other drug abuse: Results from the Epidemiologic Catchment Area (ECA) Study. *Journal of the American Medical Association, 264*(19), 2511-2518.

Richters, J. (1992). Depressed mothers as informants about their children: A critical review of the evidence for distortion. *Psychological Bulletin, 112,* 586-499

Robbins, C. (1989). Sex differences in psychosocial consequences of alcohol and drug abuse. *Journal of Health and Social Behavior, 39,* 117-130.

Robins, L.N., Locke, B.Z., & Regier, D.A. (1991). An overview of psychiatric disorders in America. In L.N. Robins & D.A. Regier (Eds.), *Psychiatric disorders in America: The Epidemiological Catchment Area Study* (pp. 328-366). N.Y.: Free Press.

Romans-Clarkson, S.E., Walton, V.A., Herbison, G.P., & Mullen, P.E. (1988). Motherhood and psychiatric morbidity in New Zealand. *Psychological Medicine, 18,* 983-990.

Root, M.P.P. (1989). Treatment failure: The case of sexual victimization in women's addictive behavior. *American Journal of Orthopsychiatry, 59,* 542-549.

Russell, D.E.H. (1983). The incidence and prevalence of intra-familial and extra-familial sexual abuse of female children. *Child Abuse and Neglect, 7,* 133-146.

Schechter, S. (1987). *Guidelines for mental health practitioners in domestic violence cases.* Washington, D.C.: National Coalition Against Domestic Violence.

Schou, M. (1990). Lithium treatment during pregnancy, delivery, and lactation: An update. *Journal of Clinical Psychiatry, 51,* 410-413.

Seeman, M.V. (1982). Gender differences in schizophrenia. *Canadian Journal of Psychiatry, 27,* 107-112.

Shtasel, D.L., Gur, R.E., Gallacher, F., Heimberg, C. & Gur, R.C. (1992). Gender differences in the clinical expression of schizophrenia. *Schizophrenia Review, 71,* 225-231.

Siegel, J.M., Sorensen, S.B., Golding, J.M. et al. (1987). The prevalence of childhood sexual assault: The Los Angeles epidemiologic catchment area project. *American Journal of Epidemiology, 126,* 1141-1153.

Spielvogel, A. & Wile, J. (1986). Treatment of the psychotic pregnant patient. *Psychosomatics, 27*(7), 487-492.

Stott, F. M., Musick, J. S., Clark, R., & Cohler, B. J. (1983). Developmental patterns in the infants and young children of mentally ill mothers. *Infant Mental Health Journal, 4*(3), 217- 234.

Sue, D. & Sue, S. (1987). Cultural factors in the clinical assessment of Asian Americans. *Journal of Consulting and Clinical Psychology, 55*(4), 479-487.

Test, M.S. & Berlin, S.B. (1981). Issues of special concern to chronically mentally ill women. *Professional Psychology, 12*(1), 136-145.

Test, M.A., Burke, S.S. & Wallisch, L.S. (1990). Gender differences of young adults with schizophrenic disorders in community care. *Schizophrenia Bulletin, 16,* 1990.

Test, M.A., Knoedler, W.H., Allness, D.J., & Burke, S.S. (1985). Characteristics of young adults with schizophrenic disorders treated in the community. *Hospital and Community Psychiatry, 36,* 853-858.

Toneatto, A., Sobell, L.C., & Sobell, M.B. (1992). Gender issues in the treatment of abusers of alcohol, nicotine, and other drugs. *Journal of Substance Abuse, 4,* 209-218.

Tronick, E. Z., & Gianino, A. F. (1986). The transmission of maternal disturbance to the infant. *New Directions for child Development, 34,* 5-11.

Wallace, Anne. (1992, Spring). *Mothers with mental illness: Unheard voices, unmet needs.* Burlington, VT: Trinity College, unpublished manuscript.

Wilcox, J.A. & Yates, W.R. (1993). Gender and psychiatric comorbidity in substance-abusing individuals. *The American Journal of Addictions, 2*(3), 202-206.

Wilsnack, S.C. & Wilsnack, R.W. (1990). Women and substance abuse: Research directions for the 1990s. *Journal of the Society of Psychologists in Addictive Behaviors, 4*(1), 46-49.

Woodhouse, L.D. (1990). An exploratory study of the use of life history methods to determine treatment needs for female substance abusers. *Response, 13*(3), 12-15.

Zemencuk, J., Rogosch, F. & Mowbray, C.T. (1995). The seriously mentally ill woman in the role of parent: Characteristics, parenting sensitivity, and needs. *Psychosocial Rehabilitation Journal, 18*(3), 77-92.

Ziedonis, D.M., Rayford, B.S., Bryant, K.J., & Rounsaville, B.J. (1993). Psychiatric comorbidity in White and African-American cocaine addicts seeking substance abuse treatment. *Hospital and Community Psychiatry, 45*(1), 43-49.

Coping With Hearing Voices: An Emancipatory Approach

M.A.J. Romme, A. Honig, O. Noorthoorn and A.D.M.A.C. Escher

M.A. J. ROMME, MD, PH.D., IS PROFESSOR OF SOCIAL PSYCHIATRY, UNIVERSITY OF LIMBURG.

A. HONIG, MD, PH.D., MRC PSYCH, CONSULTANT IN SOCIAL PSYCHIATRY, COMMUNITY MENTAL HEALTH CENTER, MAASTRICHT, LECTURER, DEPARTMENT OF SOCIAL PSYCHIATRY, UNIVERSITY OF LIMBURG.

E.O. NOORTHOORN, MD, RESEARCH FELLOW, DEPARTMENT OF SOCIAL PSYCHIATRY, UNIVERSITY OF LIMBURG.

A.D.M.A.C. ESCHER, MA, SCIENCE JOURNALIST, COMMUNITY MENTAL HEALTH CENTER, MAASTRICHT, THE NETHERLANDS.

THIS ARTICLE ORIGINALLY APPEARED IN THE *British Journal of Psychiatry*, 1992, 161, 99-103 AND IS REPRINTED WITH PERMISSION.

A questionnaire comprising 30 open-ended questions was sent to 450 people with chronic hallucinations of hearing voices who had responded to a request on television. Of the 254 replies 186 could be used for analysis. It was doubtful whether 13 of these respondents were experiencing true hallucinations. Of the remaining 173 subjects 115 reported an inability to cope with the voices. Ninety-seven respondents were in psychiatric care and copers were significantly less often in psychiatric care (24%) than non-copers (49%). Four coping strategies were apparent: distraction, ignoring the voices, selective listening to them, and setting limits on their influence.

Verbal auditory experiences or perceptions in clear consciousness without corresponding external stimuli are common symptoms of mental illness. Although schizophrenia is generally amenable to pharmacotherapy and social therapies, many chronic schizophrenic patients continue to hear voices (Falloon & Talbot, 1981). These persistent voices may be of a threatening or obscene nature, representing some outside evil power over which the patients feel they have no control. At other times the same voices may be regarded as good and pleasant companions. Some patients are so preoccupied with and reactive to the voices that social reintegration is hampered.

Hearing voices is considered to be a common sign of psychosis by all leading psychiatric textbooks. We are used to interpreting hallucinations within a psychodynamic, biological, or psychopharmacological frame of reference (Kaplan & Sadock, 1985). Hence, hearing voices is supposed to be accompanied by other psychiatric signs or symptoms. It is perceived as a sign of mental illness by the psychiatric profession and is accepted as such by both patients and lay people. However, it is questionable whether hearing voices is an unequivocal sign of mental illness. Many people know that hearing voices is considered to be pathological, and so are not likely to discuss their hallucinations openly, as they do not want to be perceived as a psychiatric patient.

In general, the aim of psychiatric treatment is to bring the patient back into our reality with antipsychotic medication, social therapies, and sometimes psychodynamic therapy. Acceptance of patients' reality is avoided as this might confuse them even further and increase their internal chaos. Thus, discussion of the subjective experiences of hearing voices is not encouraged even though these auditory experiences sometimes represent a large part of' the patient's daily life.

This paper explores the phenomenon of hearing voices and the way in which hallucinators discuss and cope with their voices.

Method

After an evening television talkshow in which a schizophrenic patient talked about her voices, viewers who heard voices were asked to telephone the Correlation Foundation (a non-profit organization with a staff of trained therapists which acts as an intermediary after "emotional" television programs. Seven hundred individuals responded, 450 of whom heard voices. The Foundation reported this to be an extremely high response rate (Langelaan, 1987).

A questionnaire was designed consisting of 30 open-ended questions. The questions were partly based around the accounts and themes mentioned by those who contacted the Correlation Foundation. The questionnaire was posted to the 450 persons who heard voices and 254 replies (56%) were received, of which only 186 (41%) could be used for a complete analysis. The other 68 were mostly extended letters about experiences which could not unequivocally be categorized. The questions were open ended as we were interested in people's own descriptions of their experiences and the effect of the voices on their lives.

The following are examples of the type of questions asked:

How many voices do you hear? Are the voices friendly, aggressive, advising, or otherwise? How do you interpret the voices? Who is stronger, the voices or yourself? Do the voices intrude in your daily contact with others? Do others know of your voices? Did you receive help in coping with the voices (e.g. psychiatrist, psychologist, clairvoyant, mesmerist)?

Results

Of the 186 respondents only 13 (7%) reported that they did not experience disruption of social contacts by the voices nor any other formal psychiatric symptoms.

TABLE 1.
RESPONDENTS WITH ADDITIONAL PSYCHIATRIC SYMPTOMS
OR WHO WERE DISTRESSED BY HALLUCINATIONS

	No. (%) of Subjects (n = 164)	No. (%) of Men (n = 49)	No. (%) of Women (n = 115)
Age: Years			
15–30	29 (18%)	8 (16%)	21 (18%)
30–40	56 (34%)	19 (39%)	37 (32%)
40–65	73 (45%)	19 (38%)	54 (47%)
65+	6 (4%)	3 (6%)	3 (3%)
Marital Status			
unmarried	41 (25%)	9 (18%)	32 (28%)
married	60 (37%)	20 (41%)	40 (35%)
divorced	26 (16%)	6 (12%)	20 (17%)
other	4 (2%)	1 (2%)	3 (3%)
data missing	33 (20%)	13 (27%)	20 (17%)
Employment			
paid	64 (39%)	22 {45%)	42 (37%)
not paid	33 (20%)	9 (19%)	24 (21%)
household	31 (19%)	1 (2%)	30 (26%)
vocational training	18 (11%)	14 (29%)	4 (3%)
no occupation	8 (5%)	0 (0%)	8 (7%)
data missing	10 (6%)	3 (5%)	7 (6%)

These 13 respondents said of their voices: "They stimulate me. They are friends. It is my guide and tutor." In this group 7 felt themselves to be paranormally gifted and described themselves as "clairaudient." These subjects were excluded from further evaluation as one might question whether these experiences were true hallucinations. We defined a hallucination as a disorder of perception which people describe as being located in the external world (ego-dystonic) and which has the same qualities as normal perceptions, that is, is vivid and solid in the absence of any actual sensory stimulus. The data reported in Table 2 refer to the remaining 173 respondents who fulfilled this definition of a hallucination.

Nine patients did not indicate their sex.

TABLE 2.
CHARACTERISTICS OF HALLUCINATIONS IN COPERS AND NONCOPERS

	No. (%) of Subjects (n = 173)	No. (%) of Copers (n = 58)	No. (%) of Noncopers (n = 115)
Duration: Years			
< 1	10 (6%)	2 (3%)	8 (7%)
1-5	40 (23%)	12 (22%)	28 (26%)
> 5	113 (65%)	40 (75%)	73 (66%)
data missing	10 (6%)		
Age of Onset: Years			
< 14	31 (18%)	11 (20%)	20 (18%)
15-30	58 (34%)	18 (33%)	40 (35%)
30-40	45 (26%)	12 (22%)	33 (30%)
>40	28 (16%)	12 (23%)	16 (14%)
data missing	11 (6%)		
**Who is Stronger ** **			
self	79 (46%)	39 (72%)	40 (38%)
voices	49 (28%)	5 (10%)	44 (42%)
other	29 (17%)	9 (16%)	20 (19%)
data missing	16 (9%)		
**Nature of Voices ** **			
positive	26 (15%)	16 (30%)	10 (10%)
contradictory	31 (18%)	14 (26%)	17 (16%)
negative	98 (57%)	23 (43%)	75 (73%)
data missing	18 (10%)		
Voices Commenting on Action			
yes	102 (59%)	32 (68%)	70 (70%)
no	49 (28%)	19 (32%)	30 (30%)
data missing	22 (13%)		
Voices Taking Over Thinking			
yes	88 (51%)	29 (54%)	59 (67%)
no	52 (30%)	24 (45%)	28 (32%)
data missing	33 (19%)		
Imperative Hallucinations**			
yes	44 (25%)	10 (20%)	26 (24%)
no	79 (46%)	38 (74%)	41 (38%)
sometimes	36 (21%)	3 (6%)	41 (38%)
data missing	14 (8%)		

** $p < 0.001$, for distribution between copers and non-copers.

More than two thirds of the respondents were women. The majority were 30 years or over and the respondents were predominantly married. Only a small proportion did not have an occupation (5%) (Table 1). The age and sex of respondents were similar to those of all the people who contacted the Correlation Foundation in 1987 although twice as many respondents were divorced and the proportion of respondents who were married was slightly less than half that of others who contacted the Foundation in 1987.

The data were analyzed with reference to ability to cope with voices. We divided the sample into a coping and a noncoping group according to their own statements in answer to the question "Are you able to cope with the voices or not?" Of the 173 respondents 115 (66%) reported an inability to cope with the voices. Table 2 shows some characteristics of the voices experienced by both groups. Most respondents had been hearing voices for 5 years or more with the onset peaking between 15 and 30 years of age. Demographic data did not differ significantly between copers and noncopers. The noncopers felt significantly less in control of their voices and experienced the voices more negatively. Imperative hallucinations were significantly more common among the noncopers.

The coping strategies described by the respondents were categorized into four groups. Of these, distraction was the only strategy used significantly more often by the noncopers, while selective listening and setting limits was only used by a few noncopers (Table 3) compared with copers.

Responses to the questions "Do others know about your voices? Do you talk about your voices with others? What is the reaction of others when you talk about your voices with them?" did not differ significantly between copers and noncopers.

Respondents in psychiatric care (patients) compared with others (nonpatients) perceived significantly less sup-

TABLE 3.
COPING STRATEGIES OF COPERS AND NONCOPERS

	No. (%) of Subjects	No. (%) Copers	No. (%) Noncopers
Distraction *			
yes	42 (24%)	10 (26%)	32 (43%)
no	72 (42%)	29 (74%)	43 (57%)
data missing	59 (34%)		
**Ignoring ** **			
yes	54 (31%)	31 (56%)	23 (25%)
no	57 (33%)	21 (37%)	36 (39%)
sometimes	37 (21%)	4 (7%)	33 (36%)
data missing	25 (14%)		
**Selective Listening ** **			
yes	30 (17%)	19 (46%)	11 (14%)
no	87 (50%)	22 (53%)	65 (85%)
data missing	56 (33%)		
**Setting Limits ** **			
yes	45 (26%)	19 (48%)	26 (30%)
no	79 (46%)	20 (51%)	59 (70%)
data missing	49 (28%)		

*$p < 0.05$, **$p < 0.01$, for distribution between copers and non-copers .

TABLE 4.
PERCEIVED SUPPORT AND DISCUSSION ON VOICES
BETWEEN PATIENTS IN PSYCHIATRIC CARE AND NONPATIENTS

	No. (%) of Nonpatients (*n* = 67)		No. (%) of Patients (*n* = 97)	
Sex				
male	16	(24%)	33	(34%)
female	51	(76%)	64	(66%)
Mean (*S.D.*) Age: Years *	37	(10.6)	43	(12.6)
Age of Onset: Years				
< 15	12	(18%)	19	(20%)
15-30	30	(45%)	28	(29%)
30-40	17	(25%)	28	(29%)
40-65	8	(12%)	20	(21%)
> 65	0	(0%)	1	(1%)
Employment				
paid	28	(42%)	41	(43%)
not paid	17	(25%)	18	(19%)
household	9	(13%)	22	(23%)
vocational training	3	(5%)	5	(5%)
no occupation	10	(15%)	9	(10%)
Marital Status *				
single	11	(19%)	30	(38%)
married	35	(60%)	31	(39%)
divorced	11	(19%)	15	(19%)
widowed	1	(2%)	3	(4%)
Duration: Years				
< 1	4	(6%)	6	(6%)
1-5	18	(27%)	22	(23 %)
> 5	45	(67%)	68	(71%)
Perceived Support **				
no	1	(2%)	47	(49%)
yes	69	(98%)	49	(51%)
Do Others Know About My Voices *				
no	2	(2%)	15	(14%)
yes	69	(98%)	86	(86%)
Discussion With Others About Voices				
no	35	(50%)	46	(48%)
yes	34	(50%)	50	(52%)
What Reaction Do People Have?				
positive interest	11	(19%)	24	(29%)
negative interest	23	(40%)	29	(35%)
no interest	1	(1%)	4	(5%)
other	23	(40%)	26	(32%)

Numbers do not add up to column totals as not all respondents gave the relevant information.
*$p < 0.05$, **$p < 0.01$, patients v. nonpatients.

port from others. They also reported significantly more often that others did not know about their voices.

The patients were older and were more frequently unmarried than the nonpatients (Table 4). Copers were significantly less often in psychiatric care (24%) than non-copers (49%) ($p < 0.001$).

Successful Coping Strategies

Twenty copers who gave a clear description of their problems and coping strategies were selected for further interview. Ten of these copers had never received any psychiatric care. Of these, two cases could be interpreted as pathological bereavement reactions as the onset of their voices coincided with the death of a child. Three copers had heard voices from childhood onwards. In the other five cases the onset of hearing voices started at different ages and in various circumstances. In none of these ten individuals could a definite psychiatric diagnosis be made. Four of the other ten individuals who were known to have a psychiatric history had been diagnosed with schizophrenia and four others with a dissociative disorder. In the other two cases we could not trace a formal psychiatric diagnosis.

The stages leading up to the acceptance of the voices, which precede the actual development of coping strategies, have been described by Romme & Escher (1989) and are not discussed here. Four main groups of coping strategies—distraction, ignoring, selective listening, and setting limits—were apparent.

Distraction

Two main forms were described: a) distraction by physical means (taking a shower, jogging, breathing exercises, watching a pleasant video) and b) distraction by more abstract means (drawing a cloak around yourself in your mind, meditation, yoga).

Ignoring

A 42-year-old housewife had been hearing one voice for 5 years. She had been diagnosed as suffering from schizophrenia and had been admitted four times following suicide attempts ordered by her voice. Eventually she discussed the voice with her husband. He compared the voice with that of a nagging neighbor and asked her if she would harm herself if this neighbor ordered her to do so. Since then, whenever the voice gives these orders, she ignores them. For instance, when she is peeling potatoes and is ordered to stab herself with the knife, she stabs a potato instead. Her control over the voice has increased dramatically and she has not been readmitted since.

Selective Listening

A 53-year-old divorcee had over the last 10 years been in contact with various psychotherapists and lay people in connection with her voices. She described voices which periodically predicted disaster which she could not prevent. At one stage she tried to eradicate the voice by "getting hold of it" lifting it in the air, and throwing it as far as possible, while saying "Go back to your own friends, there is no place for you here." This ritual proved useful and enabled her to select the positive from the negative voices, and control them.

Setting Limits

A 28-year-old woman had been in hospital several times and still saw her psychiatrist on an outpatient basis. She said: "I made a deal with the voices. After eight o'clock it is their time. I don't answer telephone calls and I don't meet other people from eight o'clock onwards. During the day they hardly bother me now and I am able to function much better in daily life."

Discussion

This sample of auditory hallucinators is unique, as we were able to contact people who were not patients who coped well with often potentially disabling hallucinations. Our results are not of an epidemiological nature, as the population was self-selected, not random, and the attrition rate was too high. However, this does not impair the clinical importance of the description of the variations in coping styles. The questionnaire was not studied for reliability or validity, and as yet no objective criteria have been applied to determine how many of the respondents actually were mentally ill according to formal standards such as the Present State Examination (Wing et al., 1974). Some of the demographic data reflect the general response trend of the Correlation Foundation rather than a specific trait of this research sample. All of these aspects of the method should be taken into account in the discussion of the data.

Because of the way we recruited our respondents, they included those who reported experiences which could hardly be described as auditory hallucinations, as well as chronic psychiatric patients, and those whose hearing of voices did not lead to psychiatric treatment. The first group was excluded from further analysis. The second group was divided into copers and noncopers. The copers experienced the voices more often as a positive phenomenon. They were able to keep the voices under control by communicating with them in a selective manner. This group sought less psychiatric help than the noncopers. These data give some indication that hearing voices does not always lead to a psychosocial handicap or to seeking psychiatric help. The voices commenting on action and taking over thinking were equally represented in the two groups, but imperative hallucinations were more common among noncopers.

Coping styles were more diverse in the copers. Distraction was used significantly more often by the noncopers. A similar proportion in each group discussed hearing voices with others, which does not support our hypothesis that the professional attitude to hearing voices limits wider discussion of them, although the perceived support from such a discussion was significantly less in the patient group.

In October 1987 we organized a meeting for the people who responded to the television program (Romme & Escher, 1989). As a result of this congress some participants founded a self-help association which they called "RESONANCE". So far the association has organized an emergency telephone service, workshops for people who hear voices, and regular lectures and discussion sessions for psychiatric nurses. The network has started to expand, with MIND in the UK setting up a national working group on hearing voices. Contacts within the association and the publicity following the congress have encouraged people who hear voices to accept them.

Exchanging information on hearing voices and enabling sufferers to organize themselves can help them to cope with chronic auditory hallucinations and experiences, which are not always sufficiently alleviated by traditional psychiatric treatment. Help of a more practical nature to master the voices, as in the examples above, should be encouraged. That hearing voices does not seem to be limited to psychiatric patients might prove helpful in the acceptance of hearing voices and the development of coping mechanisms.

One problem that needs further research is the differentiation between true and pseudo-hallucinations. When we defined true hallucinations as hearing voices coming from outside the mind and through the ears, none out of 20 were experiencing true hallucinations. This was also the case for the schizophrenic patients. When we defined true hallucinations as hallucinations that are clearly experienced as coming from somebody else, 18 (8 who had had psychiatric care and 10 who had not had psychiatric care) were experiencing voices as ego-dystonic. Most schizophrenic patients hear voices inside their head, but are not able to have a dialogue with them and do not feel they can cope with them.

In our experience hallucinators describe hearing voices initially as perceived through their ears. However, as time passes, this develops into a perception of these voices as inside their head or body.

Many chronic hallucinators who are not able to cope with their voices or show signs of mental illness end up in psychiatric care. Helping the patient to accept the voices and actively developing effective coping strategies with the patient may well prove an effective adjunct to psychiatric rehabilitation, as has been reported earlier (Falloon & Talbot, 1981; Strauss, 1989). We cannot assume that all hallucinations and hallucinators are the same. There are many more possible coping strategies than the four described by our respondents (McInnis & Marks, 1990). "Coping with hearing voices" should be included in psycho-education programs for relatives of people with schizophrenia. Another approach would be to help the hallucinators to share their experiences, as demonstrated in Holland by the television program and the subsequent congress.

This report justifies further and more formal psychiatric research, to gather epidemiological data on hearing voices in the general population, and to develop more diverse coping strategies. Communication between the families of patients who chronically hear voices and psychiatric staff should also be stimulated.

References

Falloon, I.R H. & Talbot, R.E. (1981). Persistent auditory hallucinations: Coping mechanics and implications for management. *Psychological Medicine, 11*, 329-339.

Kaplan, H.I. & Sadock, B.J.V. (Eds.) (1985). *Comprehensive textbook of psychiatry* (4th ed.). Baltimore: Williams and Wilkins.

Langelaan, M. (1987). Correlation Foundation hears more than 700 voices. *Maandblad Ceestelijke Volksgezondheid, 718*, 822-828 .

McInnis, M. & Marks, I. (1990). Audiotape therapy for persistent auditory hallucinations. *British Journal of Psychiatry, 157*, 913-914.

Romme, M.A.J. & Escher, A.D.M.A.C. (1989). Hearing voices. *Schizophrenia Bulletin, 15*, 209-216.

Strauss, J.S. (1989). Subjective experiences of schizophrenia: towards a new dynamic psychiatry II. *Schizophrenia Bulletin, 15*, 179-187.

Wing, J.K., Cooper, J.E. & Sartorius, N. (1974). *The measurement and classification of psychiatric symptoms*. Cambridge: Cambridge University Press.

Involuntary Commitment: A Consumer Perspective

Barbara Garrett and Tom Posey

Barbara Garrett is a vocational rehabilitation counselor at the Las Vegas Medical Center, Las Vegas, New Mexico.

Thomas M. Posey is a past president of NAMI.

This article originally appeared in *Innovations and Research*, 1993, 2(1), 39-41 and is reprinted with permission.

To Joe America, "commitment" means locking up mental cases because they are dangerous or shouldn't be seen in "polite society." Commitment to the families of those who have mental illnesses is a way of protecting their loved ones. Commitment to us is fear of keepers taking total control of our lives, treating us as criminals, and possibly placing us in danger at a time when we can least protect ourselves—for we are mental health consumers.

What commitment means and what it should mean will, to a great extent, depend on who you are and your personal experiences. And most with first hand experience, be they family or consumer, hold opinions and feelings about commitment passionately.

Perhaps some calm exploration of these opinions and feelings can wet the worst hot edges of passion and carry us further down the road as we seek legislative solutions to a complex medical problem. The few drops of thought we have to offer are from the consumer perspective and from the perspective of consumers who might, if conditions should change, have to commit a love one.

As consumers, we are caught between a rock and a hard place. Intellectually we know that commitment is necessary at times, but emotionally we understand the terror of putting people under lock and key who have committed no crime.

We know the legal commitment hearing, for example, may be close to a "kangaroo court." Even though we are entitled by law to an attorney, we may not see, much less talk to, the one that is appointed to represent us. Even though by law we are entitled to have a "friend of the respondent" who should be someone that we can trust, there may be no such person present—or the person that is filing the commitment proceeding may be acting in that role. Even though by law we are supposed to be in the courtroom and hear what is said against us and have the right to challenge that testimony, in many cases we will sit, shackled and alone, in an anteroom waiting to be told our fate.

We know what it is like to be transported to and from the court hearing and/or hospital in chains or straight jacket because we are ill. If we are female we know that the odds are considerable that we will be sexually molested by staff or fellow patients during the time that we are under commitment—and that if we report such incidents, we will be ignored. Regardless of our gender, we know that the odds are that we will be mentally or physically abused, in a majority of cases by staff, and, again, any reporting will be ignored.

We know that in a good number of the states we will be housed in ancient buildings that won't even meet today's health and safety codes. And we know that the chances are very good that we will be force medicated for staff convenience, see a psychiatrist for 10 minutes or less once every 3 or 4 weeks, and any of our other medical illnesses will be allowed to go untreated. We know that many in the treatment team that we come in contact with may not speak our native language or even be licensed to practice in the state except in the mental hospital.

We know that we may be put in "time out" rooms, in four-point restrains, for hours on end, regardless of what the law says and often times for the simplest of infractions. We know that we will run the risk of being housed in the same building and maybe even in the same room with criminally committed murders and rapists.

We know that there is a good chance that the treatment that we are given, if we are given any, will not work and we will be released, still sick, to the streets. And we know that, even if we are released to community treatment, we may have no place to stay, no food to eat, no funds for medications and other essentials, and months before we are seen by the community providers.

All of this we know, but we also know that there may be that time that commitment for us is necessary. What a hell of a choice society has given us.

The reader should not be complacent in thinking that the things listed above took place years ago and not today. Be aware that every one of the items listed above can be substantiated, by court records, as having happened in 1992.

It is possible to craft commitment laws that address what we know intellectually, but what consumers fear is the inability of laws to ad-dress the reasonable emotional fears they face when committed. So let us explore all sides of the question. What is the solution?

In our hearts we know it is right, if we are to be a humane society, to protect those among us who suffer from the ravages of a disease that renders them, at times, of danger to themselves or others. Our angry feelings about commitment are tempered by

Commitment to us is fear of keepers taking total control of our lives, treating us as criminals, and possibly placing us in danger at a time when we can least protect ourselves— for we are mental health consumers.

the knowledge that commitment, at times, is the only appropriate course. To save the life of the person with a mental illness or that of innocent bystanders is only right and humane. Common sense and reason dictates nothing else. Laws can be written, as they have, to confine someone of danger to self or others until such danger passes. What we cannot legislate is emotional protection of those we are seeking to save, but we can and must insist that society demands that such protection is in place and enforced.

Commitment is a very serious action, for we are restricting the liberty of someone who has committed no crime. It is claimed that no constitutional rights are removed, but any of us who have gone through the process know that, although rights may not be removed, they are drastically restricted. If the situation is sufficient to take such a drastic action, then it must be done in the most humane fashion possible; treating it as the equivalent of a criminal proceeding is not humane. Election or appointment does not make someone an expert on mental illness and the treatment of same. Leaving someone's fate in the hands of such a person, the judge, is to stack the deck against us from the very beginning.

We propose that commitment and the need for same must extend beyond the strict limits of the law. Humane consideration must also play a great part. People are "dying with their rights on," and there is no need for this. But the answer is not to change the law for fear of removing some of the protection that might be there but to realize that walking in 2 feet of snow with no shoes on is, in fact, "of danger to oneself." Also required, we believe, is that any medical testimony be given by a medical professional with extensive experience with the mentally ill. No longer should someone with a degree in counseling or social work be allowed to testify as to a biological condition.

A person's liberty may be taken away from them and that should never be done except on the advice of the most qualified to give that advice. *Cost should never be the controlling factor in the commitment process.* Again, remove the responsibility for judgement from one who has little knowledge of the illness and only knowledge of the law.

Commitment can be a very terrifying experience, for we are placing someone who has committed no crime under the total control of a third party. Again, if the situation is sufficient to take such a drastic action, then it must be done in the most humane fashion possible. Chain and straight jackets should never be permitted as a matter of course. The proceeding should never take place in a cold and austere courtroom. And, leaving the decision as to who will become our keepers in the hands of only a judge is not sufficient protection.

Commitment must never be viewed as the permanent or long-term solution. It must be considered a very drastic intervention that is taken only to protect and treat a person with the understanding that he or she will be returned to the community as soon as possible. Therefore, the person or persons making any decision must be versed in constitutional rights, humane and safe environments, and mental illness treat-

Commitment must never be viewed as the permanent or long-term solution.

ment modalities. No one person can meet all of those criteria.

Some states have established commitment panels composed of persons with expertise in all of the areas mentioned above—and, from the consumers' point of view, these panels should always contain a consumer. These panels not only determines if a person meets the requirements for commitment but determines where the commitment shall take place. A panel may decide that community commitment is better than institutionalization. They may even set limits on the type of treatment that can be given or that must at least be tried. The treatment providers are removed from the role of "keepers" and become accountable to the commitment panel. While not perfect, the commitment panel is much better than a single judge and should become the requirement for all states to adopt.

Major changes must also occur at the institutional level. If treatment is a treatment process rather than a punitive process, the best, not the cheapest, personnel must be doing the treating. As long as society sees commitment as necessary, then society must understand and be willing to pay for the process. For anything less there can be no excuse. In most states, criminals have better living conditions than do those in a mental hospital. The difference is that criminals have a federal agency that is concerned with their treatment, while the mentally ill must rely on whomever is willing to do it.

This then leads to the role of the family. We know of few family members who are satisfied with the commitment process, but many want only to make it easier to commit rather than looking hard at what they are wanting to commit to. This not only causes much unneeded friction and animosity between family and consumers, but also allows members of society to avoid the responsibility that is rightfully theirs.

There is not one state that does not need to review its commitment laws, and each should be putting a procedure in place to do this. But in no case should that procedure involve only one or two of the interests concerned with commitment. The procedure must include professionals, legal and social advocates, lawmakers, families, and consumers. Agreement must start to replace mistrust if the commitment process is ever going to be effective and humane.

Since commitment is such an extreme measure, extreme measures must be taken to insure that many of the abuses, both of process and of those committed, are eliminated. A change in the process will account for some of this, but an additional step is also necessary to monitor those places to which a person can be committed. And, whoever does this monitoring must have the power to put a stop to any abuse that occurs. Many states have monitoring boards, but these boards have no power and can only report to the institution administration, who does nothing. In some states the monitors report to the governor, who never reads the reports. Every state has a Protection and Advocacy Agency, but they have, for the most part, failed as their vision is limited by the blinder of law at the expense of human compassion.

The members of monitoring boards must have extensive knowledge of institutionalization and mental illness. Thus, a majority of the board members should be family and consumers. A monitoring board must have the power to request, of the proper official, that a person be removed from his or her job in cases of abuse or violation of consumers rights.

Unions must agree, in contract, that members who commit consumer abuse will not receive union protection. Monitoring boards must have unlimited and unannounced access to all parts of the facility and all records, etc. Their only function must be the protection of those committed and unable to protect themselves.

Until institutions become safe, commitment is not doing the job that it was intended to do and will continue to be feared. And a sorrier truth, which those who are seeking to "tighten up" our commitment laws are failing to acknowledge, is that commitment, as we know it today, means sentencing consumers to conditions that are unsafe. The fears of consumers facing commitment are legitimate. Unless we are willing to own up to that fact and do something about it, consumer opposition to commitment laws will continue. If we are to call ourselves a humane society, we must address these concerns.

AIDS Knowledge, Attitudes, and Risk Behavior Among People With Serious Mental Illness

Jim A. Cates, Gary R. Bond and Linda L. Graham

JIM A. CATES, PH.D., IS IN PRIVATE PRACTICE WITH PHOENIX ASSOCIATES, INC., IN FORT WAYNE, INDIANA.

GARY R. BOND, PH.D., IS DIRECTOR OF THE DOCTORAL PROGRAM IN CLINICAL REHABILITATION PSYCHOLOGY AT INDIANA UNIVERSITY–PURDUE UNIVERSITY INDIANAPOLIS.

LINDA L. GRAHAM, R.N., M.S.N., IS AN ASSOCIATE PROFESSOR IN THE NURSING DEPARTMENT AT INDIANA UNIVERSITY–PURDUE UNIVERSITY AT FORT WAYNE.

THIS ARTICLE ORIGINALLY APPEARED IN THE *Psychosocial Rehabilitation Journal*, 1994, 17(4), 19-29 AND IS REPRINTED WITH PERMISSION.

This study compares HIV/AIDS knowledge, attitudes, sexual behaviors, and behavioral intentions of persons with serious mental illness (SMI), with those of a community sample. Findings indicate that a subgroup of persons with SMI are sexually active and engage in HIV-risk behaviors. Despite higher levels of cognitive impairment among persons with SMI, no differences were found in level of knowledge about HIV/AIDS; both groups are relatively well informed about transmission routes, populations at risk, and medical facts. However, persons with SMI are more concerned about the possibility of HIV infection and perceive themselves as comparatively helpless in the face of the threat.

AIDS has not been perceived as a threat to persons with serious mental illness (SMI) because of the prevailing stereotype that they are asexual or not interested in sex. In rare instances when persons with SMI are sexually active, the contact is assumed to be heterosexual (Harvey &

Trivelli, 1990). These assertions are now being rebutted. Recent research has documented that interpersonal sexual behavior is frequent among persons with SMI living in the community (Lukoff, Gioia-Hasick, Sullivan, Golden, & Nuechterlein, 1986; Test, Burke, & Wallisch, 1990) as well as in inpatient settings (Wasow, 1980). Persons with SMI also report frequent homosexual behaviors (Rozensky & Berman, 1984).

Not only are persons with SMI more sexually active than once believed, they appear to be engaging in sexual behaviors that put them at high risk for HIV infection. In a recent study of 205 patients in an acute care inpatient unit, approximately 20% of the sample had engaged in HIV-risk behaviors, including homosexual contact and heterosexual contact with persons considered to be at high risk, such as intravenous drug users (IDUs) and/or prostitutes (Sacks, Silberstein, Weiler, & Perry, 1990). Among persons at risk but of unknown HIV status, the majority (56%) were unconcerned by the potential for infection. Another study examined 113 patients, ages 18 to 55, admitted to an acute care psychiatric facility, and found that 42% had engaged in HIV-risk behaviors during the five years prior to their admission and 19% were at high risk for infection.

A study of 40 persons with SMI receiving outpatient services found that their knowledge of basic sexual anatomy and functioning was incomplete and that they had a high prevalence of HIV-risk behaviors, other than IV drug use (Goisman, Kent, Montgomery, & Cheevers, 1991). In a study of 83 persons receiving partial hospitalization services, knowledge of HIV/AIDS was weakly correlated with frequency of HIV-risk behaviors; and, again, a significant number of persons with SMI engaged in at least one HIV-risk behavior (Steiner, Lussier, & Rosenblatt, 1992).

During a 1-year period among the 476 inpatients admitted to a state psychiatric hospital in New York City the HIV-infection rate was 14% among persons for whom HIV status was previously unknown (Volavka, Conirt, O'Donnell, Douyon, Evangelista, & Czobar, 1992). In another study, also conducted in New York City, 7% of 350 patients admitted and tested in a 7-month period were HIV infected (Sacks, Dermatis, Looser-Ott, & Perry, 1992).

Despite the growing recognition that persons with SMI may be a high-risk population for HIV, very little empirical research has targeted their knowledge of and attitudes toward HIV/AIDS. Brief questionnaires have been developed as an adjunct to epidemiologically-oriented research (e.g., Baer, Dwyer, & Lewitter-Koehler, 1988; Sacks, et al., 1992), but there appears to be no published study comparing the knowledge of persons with SMI with that of the general population. This study was designed to begin to address that issue.

The hypotheses guiding the research are straightforward. Based on previous research, this study first hypothesized a lower frequency of sexual behavior for sexually active persons with SMI when compared to a normative sample. More persons with SMI were also hypothesized to describe themselves more often as asexual, compared with a normative sample.

Among sexually active individuals, persons with SMI were hypothesized to engage more frequently in HIV-risk behaviors, compared with a normative sample, due to their less accurate knowledge and greater cognitive impairment of persons with SMI. Accordingly, persons with SMI who are sexually active are hypothesized to report less intent to abstain from sexual behavior or to decrease their risk when engaging in sexual behavior.

The second phase of the study was designed to determine attitudes toward HIV/AIDS. It uses Protection-Motivation Theory (PMT) as a conceptual framework to understand attitudes about HIV/AIDS (Rogers, 1975; 1983). According to the PMT model, recognition of a health risk initiates a dual cognitive appraisal (Self & Rogers, 1990). First, a person must perceive the threat as sufficiently severe to warrant action in order to initiate protection (Severity of Threat). Second, the individual must perceive a sufficient personal threat to motivate protective behaviors (Probability of Occurrence) (Prentice-Dunn & Rogers, 1986). Then, the person initiates a dual coping appraisal. Are the recommended means of protecting oneself (from HIV infection) effective (Response Efficacy)? And even if such protective responses work, does the person feel capable of performing them (Self-Efficacy)?

Persons with SMI were hypothesized to exhibit greater fear of HIV infection and less certainty as to efficacy, when compared with a normative sample. Attitudes were measured using the four components of PMT.

Sample

Persons with SMI in this study met the following inclusion criteria: 1) a primary psychiatric diagnosis of schizophrenia, mood disorder, or personality disorder, with the diagnosis being given at least 6 months prior to participation in the study; 2) a demonstrated psychiatric disability (e.g., an impairment in social or vocational functioning) as evidenced by participation in a community support program; 3) at least 1 psychiatric hospitalization; 4) 18 years of age or older; 5) neither married nor in a monogamous relationship for at least 6 months prior to participation in the study; 6) no dual diagnosis of SMI and retardation or developmental delay; and 7) symptomatology sufficiently severe to warrant admission to a community support program (CSP) provided through the local community mental health center.

The sample of persons without SMI (the normative sample) met the following inclusion criteria: 1) 18 years of age or older; 2) neither married nor in a monogamous relationship for a period of at least 6 months prior to participation in the study; 3) no present or past diagnosis of SMI; and 4) no past psychiatric hospitalization.

Quota sampling was used to ensure 25 males and 25 females in each group. Each was a sample of convenience, and all participants were compensated for their time. The CSP sample was recruited from a midwestern community mental health center serving a small city and the surrounding area. Participation was solicited at two sites, a day treatment program and a drop-in center.

Normative group participants were recruited from three separate sites, chosen to ensure a spectrum of levels of educational attainment roughly spanning the range found in the CSP sample. The sampling sites were: a community school's GED preparation program, introductory academic classes at a technical college, and introductory psychology classes at a local university. Demographic characteristics of the sample are presented in Table 1.

As can be seen, the CSP sample was significantly older than the normative sample and was significantly less likely to report a previous relationship, either marriage or co-habitation (χ^2[1, $N = 100$] = 5.09, $p <$ .05.). The proportion of minorities did not differ in the two samples nor did level of education. Diagnoses for the sample of persons with SMI were based on community mental health center records. Primary diagnoses included 27 with some type of schizophrenia; 1 with a psychotic disorder, not otherwise specified; 8 with schizoaffective

TABLE 1.
DEMOGRAPHIC CHARACTERISTICS OF SAMPLE

| | CSP ($n = 50$) | | Normative ($n = 50$) | | |
	M	*(SD)*	*M*	*(SD)*	*t*
Age	33.46	(7.84)	25.04	(8.68)	$t = 2.24$**
Gender					
Male	25		25		
Female	25		25		
Education (# Yrs.)	12.16	(20.7)	11.80	(2.28)	$t = 1.16$
	n		*n*		
Race					
White	41		35		
African American	8		10		
Hispanic	1		4		
Other	0		1		
Marital Status					
Single	25		36		
Divorced	10		8		
Separated	8		3		
Co-habitated	7		3		

*$p < .05$, **$p < .01$

disorder; and 6 with bipolar disorder, not otherwise specified. The remaining individuals were diagnosed with mood or personality disorders.

Measures

Participants were administered a semistructured interview, using attitude items obtained from previously published instruments and/or sources (Baer, Dwyer, & Lewitter-Koehler, 1988; Bouton, Gallaher, Garlinghouse, Leal, Rosenstein, & Young, 1987; Carmen & Brady, 1990; Cates & Markley, 1992; DiClemente, Zorn, & Temoshok, 1987; Herek & Glunt, 1991; Liberman, 1988; Rozensky & Berman, 1984). Internal consistency for the a priori scales was weak (mean r = .57); factor analysis was successfully used to increase the cohesion of scale items (mean r = .68) and appeared to retain independent factors (mean correlation = .14). Attitude items and behavioral intention were rated on a 5-point Likert scale, from 1 = *Strongly Agree* to 5 = *Strongly Disagree*.

Included in the definition of high-risk behavior is sexual behavior with a partner at-risk (e.g., persons with a blood clotting disorder [hemophilia], males who have sex with males, IDUs, or persons with multiple sex partners). Inconsistent use of a condom by oneself or a partner is also a risk factor (Sacks, Dermatis, Looser-Ott, & Perry, 1990). Degree of risk was calculated as a simple sum of the at-risk items positively endorsed. The potential score range was from 0 to 21.

Knowledge items were generated based on current educational interventions. Knowledge is defined as accurate awareness of the known facts regarding HIV in three areas: modes of transmission, high-risk behaviors, and medical evidence about the course of HIV/AIDS. Knowledge items were scored as 2 for an accurate answer, 1 if the respondent was uncertain, and 0 if the answer was inaccurate. The potential score range was 0 to 44.

Degree of cognitive impairment was screened using the Comprehension subtest of the Wechsler Adult Intelligence Scale-Revised (Wechsler, 1981), a frequent measure of such impairment among persons with SMI. The scale was considered particularly relevant to the current research since it measures application of past experience to everyday situations (Zimmerman & Woo-Sam, 1973).

Behavioral intention was assessed using a four-item scale constructed for this study. The first item measured intent to remain abstinent; the remaining three items measured intent to reduce risk if sexual behavior were pursued. Agreement with the first item did not preclude agreement with the remaining items.

Sexual history was assessed using 20 items that tapped sexual activity, sex of sexual partners, frequency and consistency of condom use, and the frequency with which participants risked exposure to HIV via sexual transmission routes. Sexual at-risk behaviors were dichotomous (yes, engaged in such behavior, or no), with the exception of condom use, which was a Likert scale item *(always, often, sometimes, never)*. Potential

*P*ersons with SMI were also hypothesized to engage more frequently in HIV-risk behavior; but no significant differences in condom use were found between the sexually-active CSP and normative samples.

range of scores was 0 to 22. The item on condom use was analyzed as a separate measure. (It is the only item in the sexual history scale that measures a behavior that reduces risk.) Data on the contributory risk factors of drug and alcohol use were also collected. The frequency with which prescribed medications interfered with sexual activity was also assessed.

Results

Persons in the CSP sample showed greater cognitive impairment than participants in the normative sample, using the Comprehension subtest. However, no differences were found between samples in knowledge about HIV and AIDS.

A multivariate analysis of variance (MANOVA) was used to determine differences in attitudes between the two samples. Using Wilks' criterion, the samples were significantly different at the multivariate level, $F(1, 95) = 5.08$, $p < .01$. The samples were significantly different at the univariate level in attitudes toward Probability of Occurrence, $F(1, 98) = 5.98$, $p < .05$, with the CSP sample perceiving greater probability of infection than the normative sample. The CSP sample also reported significantly less efficacy on the Self-Efficacy scale than the normative sample, $F(1,98) = 11.66$, $p < .01$ (see Table 2).

A MANOVA was also used to determine differences in behavioral intentions between the two samples. Using Wilks' criterion, no significant differences were found at the multivariate level, $F(1, 97) = 1.93$, $p > .10$. No significant difference was found at the univariate level for intent to practice reduced-risk behaviors, $F(1, 98) = .43$, $p > .10$, but a difference approaching significance was found in intent to remain abstinent, $F(1, 98) = 3.49$, $p < .10$, with the

TABLE 2.
COMPARISON OF CSP AND NORMATIVE SAMPLES ON
KNOWLEDGE, ATTITUDES, INTENTIONS, AND SEXUAL HISTORY

	CSP (*n* = 50)		Normative (*n* = 50)		
	M	*(SD)*	*M*	*(SD)*	*F*
Knowledge	31.98	(2.10)	33.66	(1.85)	.09
Attitudes[a]					
Threat	2.11	(0.40)	2.15	(0.41)	1.44
Probability	3.14	(0.59)	3.00	(0.56)	5.94*
Response	3.45	(0.59)	3.50	(0.60)	.88
Self-Efficacy	3.95	(0.58)	3.76	(0.60)	11.66**
Intent[b]					
Abstinence	3.22	(1.25)	3.66	(1.10)	3.49
Reduce Risk	2.32	(0.58)	2.50	(0.65)	.43
Sexual History					
At-Risk Behavior	12.82	(5.71)	11.54	(6.02)	1.32
Condom Use	2.50	(1.47)	2.08	(0.43)	1.06

*$p < .05$ **$p < .01$

[a] Potential range of values is 1 to 5; larger values represent greater Severity of Threat and Probability of Occurrence, and less confidence in Response and Self-Efficacy.

[b] Scores for all participants in each sample (lower scores associated with lower at-risk behavior; more consistent condom use; greater intent to remain abstinent; and greater intent to practice reduced risk sexual behaviors).

CSP sample more likely to express this intent than persons in the normative sample. The samples were not significantly different on the sexual history scale, $f(98) = 1.32$, $p > .10$. Contrary to expectations, equal numbers in each sample ($n = 5$) reported themselves asexual over the past 10 years, $\chi^2(1, N = 100) = .010$, $p > .10$. Of the CSP sample, 29 described themselves as not currently sexually active, compared with 20 in the normative sample. This finding approached significance, $\chi^2(1, N = 100) = 3.24$, $p < .10$. Among the CSP sample, 11 reported only one sexual partner in the past ten years, compared with 10 in the normative sample, a nonsignificant finding, $\chi^2(1, N = 100) = .18$, $p > .10$.

No significant differences were found in condom use between the two samples, $t(98) = 1.41$, $p > .10$.

Significant differences were found between the samples in reported interference in sexual functioning due to medication, $t(98) = 3.28$, $p < .05$. The difference was in the hypothesized direction (14% for the CSP sample, and 2% for the normative sample).

Persons in the CSP sample were less likely than persons in the normative sample to report using alcohol or recreational drugs prior to engaging in sexual activity, a finding approaching significance, $t(98) = -1.65$, $p < .10$ (8% of CSP sample, 12% of normative sample). Significant differences were found in weekly alcohol use, $t(98) = -3.12$, $p < .01$, and monthly, $t(98) = 4.18$, $p < .01$; persons in the CSP sample were less likely to report alcohol use. Significant differences were also found in reported weekly drug use, $t(98) = -2.29$, $p < .05$, and monthly, $t(98) = -2.00$, $p < .05$. The CSP sample was less likely to report use of drugs during either time period.

Discussion

Contrary to the first hypothesis, no significant differences in sexual behavior or history of abstinence were found. Within each sample, three subgroups were identified: asexual, single sexual partner over the past 10 years, and multiple partners. It was also hypothesized that the CSP sample would have a larger asexual subgroup than the normative sample, but this was not supported. Ten percent of the CSP sample and 12% of the normative sample reported current abstinence from sex and over the past 10 years. This finding suggests that there may be an equally small proportion of individuals within the two populations who are currently safe from HIV infection because of lack of exposure. Among those who continue to be abstinent, knowledge and attitudes toward AIDS may influence decisions to avoid sexual contact.

Percentages in the second subgroup (one partner in the past 10 years) were similar for the CSP sample (22%) and the normative sample (20%). The third subgroup—those with multiple partners (68% of the CSP sample and, by coincidence, 68% of the normative sample)—appears at greatest risk for HIV infection, and need of intervention to reduce their high HIV-risk behavior.

The data in this study suggest that risk is comparable among persons with SMI in a CSP and a normative sample. However, the results are based on a small, convenience sample which limits the generalizability. The CSP sample may not be reflective of the larger population of persons with SMI. Because of their voluntary attendance in a day treatment and/or drop-in center, they may be more treatment compliant and attuned to health concerns. Within the normative sample there were two selection biases suggesting possible confounds: age and alcohol/drug use.

Persons with SMI were also hypothesized to engage more frequently in HIV-risk behavior; but no significant differences in condom use were found between the sexually active CSP and normative samples. Both the CSP sample and the normative sample reported inconsistent use of condoms. Only 18% of persons in the CSP sample, and 17% in the normative sample reported consistent condom use during sex ("always"). An additional 13% of sexually active persons in the CSP sample, and 28% of the sexually active normative sample reported condom use "often." The remaining participants (69% of persons in the CSP sample, and 55% of the normative sample) reported sporadic or no condom use.

The hypothesis of less accurate knowledge was not supported; persons in the CSP sample displayed a level of knowledge commensurate with the normative sample. Persons in the CSP sample did exhibit a higher degree of cognitive impairment than the comparison sample, but the impact of this impairment was not increased engagement in HIV-risk behaviors.

Only 36% of the CSP sample and 18% of the normative sample reported the intent to remain abstinent. For persons in the CSP sample, only 36% reported the intent to attempt to reduce the risk of infection, which compared to 64% of the normative sample. (Persons expressing a strong intent to remain abstinent still responded to intent if they engaged in sexual behavior.)

No differences were demonstrated in the attitudes of the CSP and normative samples in perceived Severity of Threat or Response

Persons in the CSP sample showed greater cognitive impairment than participants in the normative sample... however, no differences were found between samples in knowledge about HIV and AIDS.

Efficacy. Persons in the CSP sample did exhibit greater concern regarding the Probability of Occurrence of HIV infection, consistent with previous research (Sacks, et al., 1990), but also perceived themselves as lacking Self-Efficacy in responding to the risk, when compared to the normative sample.

Items comprising the four attitude scales were examined for their content in an effort to determine possible causes of significant differences on two of the four scales. Items measuring Response Efficacy were drawn from knowledge likely to be gained from educational sources as well as the mass media. Items on Severity of Threat assessed the impact for the society as a whole and again opinions were based on opinions and attitudes frequently expressed in the mass media. In contrast, Probability of Occurrence addressed the potential for personal impact by HIV infection, and Self-Efficacy items appeared to measure personal responsibility to protect oneself. In other words, it is speculated that the strongest differences between the groups resulted from questions taken out of the hypothetical and made personally relevant. Logically, a person with multiple sexual partners, at high risk for HIV infection, can maintain attitudes that are closely aligned with those of a person who is celibate when the issue is the severity of the HIV pandemic or the efficacy of various techniques and instruments to lessen the risk. However, those two persons might differ markedly in their perception of personal risk (Probability of Occurrence) and ability to respond in an efficacious manner (Self-Efficacy).

These findings partially support the hypothesis of greater fear and less efficacy for persons with SMI, when compared with a normative sample, as well as provide support for Protection-Motivation Theory. The finding that persons in the CSP sample perceive greater Probability of Occurrence, and yet perceive themselves as less self-efficacious strongly suggests a sense of helplessness.

The 10-year retrospective report on sexual history did not attempt to assess changes in perceptions of risk over time. Instead, behavioral intentions were used as the primary indicator of the probability of ongoing at-risk behavior. The hypothesis that persons with SMI would express less intent to engage in reduced-risk behavior as a result of greater cognitive impairment and distortions in judgment, was not supported. Indeed, neither sample expressed a strong intent to reduce risk. This is consistent with previous findings in community samples and may reflect ambivalence, confusion, or denial, created by the threat of a fatal sexually transmitted disease.

Even though persons with SMI may be less sexually active than the general population, many of them are sexually active. They appear less likely than the general population to be in a monogamous relationship, engage more often in HIV-risk behaviors, use condoms inconsistently, and are ambivalent regarding both abstinence and reducing the risk of infection with a sexual partner. This study suggests that those with SMI in a CSP perceive greater risk of infection and see themselves as more helpless to reduce risk than members of the general population. The findings regarding less self-efficacious attitudes toward HIV/AIDS among persons with SMI suggest that interventions for this population may need to be tailored in a different manner than those provided for the general population, a view expressed by mental health consumers themselves (Baer, Dwyer, & Lewitter-Koehler, 1988). Fortuitously, the effort needed parallels an existing movement within the community of persons with SMI and the helping professions serving this community which places emphasis on consumer empowerment. Empowerment, taking control of one's own life, is an antidote to the helplessness expressed by the mental health consumers in this study. Persons with SMI need to recognize their risk and be empowered to reduce their risk.

References

Baer, J. W., Dwyer, P. C., & Lewitter-Koehler, S. (1988). Knowledge about AIDS among psychiatric inpatients. *Hospital and Community Psychiatry, 39*, 986-988.

Bouton, R. A., Gallaher, P. E., Garlinghouse, P. A., Leal, T., Rosenstein, L. D., & Young, R. K. (1987). Scales for measuring fear of AIDS and homophobia. *Journal of Personality Assessment, 51*, 606-614.

Carmen, E., & Brady, S. M. (1990). AIDS risk and prevention for the chronic mentally ill. *Hospital and Community Psychiatry, 41*, 652-657.

Cates, J., & Markley, J. (1992). Demographic and personality variables associated with male prostitution by choice. *Adolescence, 27*, 695-706.

DiClemente, R. J., Zorn, J., & Temoshok, L. (1987). The association of gender, ethnicity, and length of residence in the Bay area to adolescents' knowledge and attitudes about Acquired Immune Deficiency Syndrome. *Journal of Applied Social Psychology, 17*, 216-230.

Goisman, R. M., Kent, A. B., Montgomery, E. C., & Cheevers, M. M. (1991). AIDS education for patients with chronic mental illness. *Community Mental Health Journal, 27*, 189-197.

Harvey, D. C., & Trivelli, L. U. (1990). *HIV education for persons with mental disabilities* (Report No. 1). Washington, DC: National Association of Protection and Advocacy Systems.

Herek, G. M., & Glunt, E. K. (1991). AIDS-related attitudes in the United States: A preliminary conceptualization. *The Journal of Sex Research, 28,* 99-121.

Liberman, R. P. (1988). Coping with chronic mental disorders: A framework for hope. In R. P. Liberman (Ed.), *Psychiatric rehabilitation of chronic mental patients.* Washington, DC: American Psychiatric Press (pp. 1-28).

Lukoff, D., Gioia-Hasick, D., Sullivan, G., Golden, J. S., & Nuechterlein, K. H. (1986). Sex education and rehabilitation with schizophrenic male outpatients. *Schizophrenia Bulletin, 12,* 669-677.

Prentice-Dunn, S., & Rogers, R. W. (1986). Protection motivation theory and preventive health: Beyond the health belief model. *Health Education Research, 1,* 153-161.

Rogers, R. W. (1975). A protection motivation theory of fear appeals and attitude change. *Journal of Psychology, 91,* 93-114.

Rogers, R. W. (1983). Cognitive and physiological processes in fear appeals and attitude change: A revised theory of protection motivation. In J. T. Cacioppo & R. E. Petty (Eds.), *Social psychophysiology.* New York: Guilford Press.

Rozensky, R. H., & Berman, C. (1984). Sexual knowledge, attitudes, and experiences of chronic psychiatric patients. *Psychosocial Rehabilitation Journal, 8,* 21-27.

Sacks, M., Dermatis, H., Looser-Ott, S., & Perry, S. (1992). Seroprevalence of HIV and risk factors for AIDS in psychiatric inpatients. *Hospital and Community Psychiatry, 43,* 736-737.

Sacks, M.H., Silberstein, C., Weiler, P., & Perry, S. (1990). HIV-related risk factors in acute psychiatric inpatients. *Hospital and Community Psychiatry, 41,* 449-451.

Self, C. A., & Rogers, R. W. (1990). Coping with threats to health: Effects of persuasive appeals on depressed, normal, and antisocial personalities. *Journal of Behavioral Medicine, 13,* 343-357.

Steiner, J., Lussier, R., & Rosenblatt, W. (1992). Knowledge about and risk factors for AIDS in a day hospital population. *Hospital and Community Psychiatry, 43,* 734-735.

Test, M. A., Burke, S. S., & Wallisch, L. S. (1990). Gender differences of young adults with schizophrenic disorders in community care. *Schizophrenia Bulletin, 16,* 331-344.

Volavka, J., Convit, A., O'Donnell, J., Douyon, R., Evangelista, C., & Czobor, P. (1992). Assessment of risk behaviors for HIV infection among psychiatric inpatients. *Hospital and Community Psychiatry, 43,* 482-485.

Wasow, M. (1980). Sexuality and the institutionalized mentally ill. *Sexuality and Disability, 3,* 3-15.

Wechsler, D. (1981). *Manual for the Wechsler Adult Intelligence Scale-Revised.* New York: Psychological Corporation.

Zimmerman, I. L., & Woo-Sam, J. M. (1973). *Clinical Interpretation of the Wechsler Adult Intelligence Scale.* Grune and Stratton: New York.

WOMEN WITH SERIOUS MENTAL ILLNESS IN THE ROLE OF PARENT: CHARACTERISTICS, PARENTING SENSITIVITY, AND NEEDS

Judith K. Zemenchuk, Fred A. Rogosch and Carol T. Mowbray

JUDITH K. ZEMENCUK, M.A., IS AN ADVANCED GRADUATE STUDENT IN THE DEPARTMENT OF SOCIOLOGY, WAYNE STATE UNIVERSITY.

FRED A. ROGOSCH, PH.D., IS A STAFF PSYCHOLOGIST AT THE MT. HOPE FAMILY CENTER, UNIVERSITY OF ROCHESTER.

CAROL T. MOWBRAY, PH.D., IS AN ASSOCIATE PROFESSOR IN THE SCHOOL OF SOCIAL WORK, UNIVERSITY OF MICHIGAN.

THIS ARTICLE ORIGINALLY APPEARED IN THE *Psychosocial Rehabilitation Journal*, 1995, 18(3), 77-92 AND IS REPRINTED WITH PERMISSION.

While considerable numbers of women with serious mental illness give birth, many are at risk of losing custody of their children. We lack specific information, however, about who these women are, how they function in the parenting role, and their parenting needs and, thus, how to provide the appropriate support to strengthen their parenting skills. Forty-eight women with serious mental illness ranging in age from 17 to 50 years, each of whom had at least one child under age 13, were interviewed while hospitalized in state psychiatric facilities. Results show that the majority of women experienced risk factors which would be expected to compromise their parenting ability, i.e., they were of low socioeconomic status, poorly educated, not married, with few social supports and multiple hospitalizations, and had given birth at an early age. Current hospital treatment did not appear responsive to parenting needs. The parenting sensitivity of the majority of women, however, suggested adaptive ideas about parenting that could be supported and strengthened. The findings are used to suggest appropriate interventions that consider the parenting role of women with serious mental illness, enhance their parenting skills, possibly reduce the number who lose custody of their children, and build on motherhood as a chosen and normative role with rehabilitation potential.

Studies of mothers with serious mental illness, have typically focused on the impact a mother's illness has on her children. Considerable empirical evidence documents the fact that children of mothers with mental illness are at risk for psychological problems (Philipps & O'Hara, 1991; Sameroff & Seifer, 1983; Stein, Gath, Bucher, Bond, Day & Cooper, 1991) due to the parent being affectively unavailable to provide support or social interchange as well as frequent parent-child separations (Sameroff & Sniffer, 1983). While it is known that chronic stressors such as these can partly account for the initiation and/or maintenance of child disorders (Ghodsian, Zajicek, & Wolkind, 1984; Hammen, Gordon, Burge, Adrian, Jaenicke, & Hiroto, 1987; Hammen, Adrien, Gordon, Burge, Jaenicke, & Hiroto, 1987), little information is currently available concerning the impact of parenting upon the woman with serious mental illness herself. Parenting may cause additional stress and exacerbation of a pre-existing illness, and therefore seriously interfere with the woman's functioning, as an individual and as a parent.

Research addressing parenting issues of women with serious mental illness may assist in the amelioration of difficulties experienced both by the children of mothers with serious mental illness and the mothers themselves. It is thus essential to explore not only the impact on children of having a mother with a serious mental illness, but also the impact of parenting on the woman with a serious mental illness herself.

There is substantial agreement that women with serious mental illness are sexually active (Coverdale & Aruffo, 1989); have normal fertility rates (Saugstad, 1989); and have a greater number of children than average (Rudolph, Larson, Sweeny, Hough, & Arorian, 1990). The extent to which these mothers retain care responsibilities for the children they have is not clear; a number of studies indicate that many of these women experience custody loss of their children (Coverdale & Aruffo, 1989; Miller, 1990; Spielvogel & Wile, 1986). However, it has been suggested that a large percentage of these mothers could be successful in parenting if adequate support programs were available (Bazar, 1990), promoting an environment that is healthier for both the child and her/his mother and decreasing the number and length of parent-child separations. Furthermore, having contact with her children may be a positive motivator to improve a mother's own functioning (Oyserman, Mowbray, & Zemencuk, 1993), thus enhancing parenting quality.

As Test and Berlin (1981) noted, the special needs of women with serious mental illness who are mothers have not been recognized, and consequently, the provision of services to assist these women in their parenting role has been largely neglected. However, if appropriate services are to be provided, it is crucial to identify the characteristics of women with serious mental illness who are mothers, and contextual variables which may place them at risk for parenting problems, as well as their parenting style which may indicate how they cope with the difficulties inherent in the parenting role.

The present investigation was undertaken to better understand the manner in which women with serious mental illness who are mothers function in the parent role and to explore their parenting style. We present findings on these issues from interviews of a group of hospitalized mothers, and also report on demographic characteristics, family of origin variables, and psychiatric histories which may be risk factors for parenting problems.

Method

Participants

The participants were 48 women hospitalized in state psychiatric facilities. Hospital staff had identified all women at each of four facilities who were parents and who had at least one child under age 13 with whom they had been living prior to hospitalization. This age was selected in order to best match diverse cutoff points between childhood and adolescence presented by the various parenting instruments used in this study. Otherwise eligible patients were excluded if their current mental status was too unstable to allow them to be interviewed. Sixty-seven percent of potential participants agreed to be interviewed. The mothers who refused to participate did not differ significantly in regard to age, race, marital status, education, diagnosis, total number of hospitalizations, number of hospitalizations in the past three years, or age at first hospitalization.

Measures

Both standardized instruments and questionnaires designed for this study were utilized. Demographic characteristics of the participants were assessed by the Current Life Situation Questionnaire. The Early Life Questionnaire was utilized to ascertain with whom the participant lived during childhood, whether separations from either of her parents had occurred, and other childhood perceptions of relationships. Both of these instruments were developed by the second author. Perceptions of parents' behavior toward the participant as a child were assessed by the Children's Reports of Parental Behaviors Inventory (CRPBI) using positive involvement, negative control, and lax discipline subscales (Raskin, Booth, Reatig, Schulterbrandt & Odle, 1971). Internal reliability coefficients (Cronbach's alpha) were .90, .88, and .67 for those subscales, respectively. Level of social support was ascertained by the Social Support Questionnaire (SSQ) (Bogat, Chin, Sabbath & Schwartz, 1983). Based on Rosenberg's six-scale Guttman scoring of the Self Esteem Scale, internal reliability for this sample was .62. Aspects of the parenting role were examined through use of the Child Behavior Checklist (CBCL) (Achenbach & Edelbrock, 1983; Achenbach, 1986) which assesses the child's social competence in activities, school, and social behavior and child behavior problems in the two broad behavioral domains of internalizing behavior (e.g., depression, social withdrawal, schizoid tendencies, somatic complaints, immaturity) and externalizing behavior (e.g., hyperactivity, sex problems, delinquency, aggression, cruelty).

The Sensitivity to Children Questionnaire (STC) (Stollak, Scholom, Kallman & Saturansky, 1973), thought to be less subject to selection of socially appropriate responses, and thus a more adequate reflection of the mother's parenting style, presented the participant with five problematic parent-child situations to which she was asked to respond.

Procedures

Interviews were conducted (during 1985–1986) by advanced clinical psychology graduate students trained in the administration of the measures described above. Each interviewer discussed the content of the interviews with each eligible participant before proceeding and those who chose to participate signed an informed consent form.

Results

Description of the Sample

As presented in Table 1, the demographic characteristics of the participants generally indicated that the sample was of low socioeconomic status, unemployed, poorly educated, predominantly of minority race, and not married. The age of the participants ranged from 17 to 50 years with a mean of 31.4 years (SD=8.6). Sixty-five percent of the participants were black and the remainder were white. Twenty-one percent of the participants were currently married; the majority were not married (never married, 52%; separated or divorced, 27%). The mean number of children of the participants (range=1–6); 46% had one child.

Seventy-one percent of the sample were at or below 20 on Hollingshead's four-factor scale of socioeconomic status. Prior to admission, 88% had been unemployed. The participants varied in educational level, with 60% having graduated from high school.

Psychiatric History

Sixty-five percent of the participants were diagnosed with a schizophrenic disorder, 13% with a schizoaffective disorder, and 21% with an affective disorder. Collectively, the participants had a chronic history of hospitalization; the average number of psychiatric hospitalizations was 6.8 (SD=5.8). They had an average of 3.0 hospitalizations (SD=1.7) in the 3 years prior to the current admission. Ninety-one percent of the participants had previously been admitted to a psychiatric facility; most were admitted on court orders for 60- or 90-day hospitalizations. At the time of the interviews, the median length of the current stay was 61.5 days.

TABLE 1.
CLINICAL AND DEMOGRAPHIC CHARACTERISTICS OF SAMPLE

(N=48)

Age

Mean	31.4 Years
Standard deviation	8.57
Range	17–50 Years

Race

Black	65%
White	35%

Marital Status

Currently married	21%
Never married	52%
Separated/divorced	27%

Number of Children

Mean	2.1
Standard deviation	1.32
Range	1–6

Education

9th grade or less	13%
10th–11th grade	27%
High school graduate	31%
Some college	23%
College graduate	+ 6%

Diagnosis

Schizophrenia	65%
Schizoaffective	13%
Affective	21%

Hospitalizations *(number over lifetime)*

Mean	6.8
Standard deviation	5.8
Range	1–24

Experience in Family of Origin

Less than half of the participants (48%) had lived with both of their parents while growing up. Black participants were less likely than white participants to have lived with both parents ($\chi^2[1]$=4.11, p<.05; 35% vs. 71%). Forty-eight percent of the participants had experienced at least one divorce or separation of their parents and 31% had experienced at least one remarriage of the custodial parent. Thirty percent of the participants had experienced at least one separation from their mothers before age 13. Reasons for separation included placement of the participant in foster care, being sent to live with relatives, hospitalization of the participant's mother, etc. Six of the participants (12.5%) experienced loss of their mothers either by death or abandonment. Separation from the participants' fathers was even more prevalent; 58% of the participants had experienced at least one separation from their fathers before age 13.

Although 88% of the participants reported that there was someone to whom they felt close while growing up, only 31% of the participants' mothers were mentioned and only 17% of the participants' fathers. Siblings and other relatives were frequently identified as individuals with whom a close bond existed.

Parenting Variables

The mothers' average age at first pregnancy was 20.4 years (range: 11–36). Thirty-six percent had become pregnant and 29% had given birth to their first child before age 18. A multiple regression was conducted with age at first birth as the dependent variable and diagnosis (affective disorder vs. schizophrenic disorder), education, and age at first hospitalization as predictor variables. Schizophrenic diagnosis, less education, and earlier age of first psychiatric hospitalization related to giving birth at a younger age, and together accounted for 49% of the variance.

Many of the participants (69%) had given birth to a child without being married. Sixty-one percent of the participants' children were reported to be unplanned and 52% of the participants reported that none of their children had resulted from planned pregnancies. Psychiatric hospitalization occurred during a pregnancy for 34% of the participants. Forty-three percent had been hospitalized during the first year after birth for at least one of their children. Almost half (48%) had been hospitalized before their first child was born indicating that psychiatric difficulty often preceded the onset of parenthood status.

Current Parenting Context

Few of the participants were parenting their children with the support of a spouse, since only 21% were currently married. Among black participants, 94% were single parents as compared to 53% of the white participants. Seventy-one percent of the black participants as compared to 17.6% of the white participants had never married. These racial differences in marital status were statistically significant ($\chi^2(3)=16.5$, $p<.001$). Among the participants who had ever married, 77.8% of the black mothers and 42.9% of the white mothers were currently separated or divorced.

Marital status was related to who cared for the participants' children during the current hospitalization ($\chi^2(4)=25.5$, $p<.001$). Relatives, often the participant's mother, were relied on most frequently (66.7%) for child care. This was true particularly for single mothers (96%), and to a lesser extent for mothers who were no longer married (46.2%). Fathers of the children provided childcare most frequently for married mothers (70%). Foster care was seldom used in the overall sample (8.3%), but was used more frequently by no longer married participants (23%).

The majority of mothers were attempting to raise their children in impoverished circumstances. Forty-six percent of the participants reported that their financial resources were not adequate to provide for the needs of their families. Sixty-seven percent of the mothers were receiving some form of public assistance. Although 85% of the mothers had been employed in the past only 13% were employed immediately prior to the current hospitalization. Those unemployed had been so, on average, for 5.8 years, and 58% of these participants had been employed for less than a year at their last job.

Fifty-four percent of the participants lived in their own residences (rental or homeowner); the remainder lived with relatives or friends. Thirty-five percent of the participants lived with their own mothers.

Social Support

The social support networks reported by the mothers varied widely in size ($M=11.5$; range = 2–38) and were dominated by relatives (66.3%). On average, the participants reported 7.6 kin and 3.9 nonkin supporters. Sixty-two percent of the participants reported only 3 or fewer nonkin supporters.

The participant's mother was included as a supporter by 64% of the participants, whereas the participant's father was listed as a supporter by 30% of the sample. The participant's children were frequently included as providing support; all but 23% of the mothers listed their children as supporters.

Thirty-two percent of the participants included a professional as a supporter. Neighbors were included as supporters by 47% of the participants; 81% included individuals with whom they lived as providing support. On average, 20% of the supportive individuals in the participants' networks were persons with whom they lived.

Having more individuals who provide support in one area was generally related to having more supportive individuals in other areas. Forty-one percent of the supporters provided only one type of support, whereas 59% provided multiple forms. The percentages of supporters providing each type of support were: emotional support, 50%; companionship, 46%; child assistance, 34%; tangible aid, 34%, and information and advice, 28%. Most of the participants (70%) reported at least one individual who made their lives difficult; 51% of these stressful network members also were sources of positive support. Most of the network members (67%) were seen at least weekly, with 40% seen daily. Finally, the participants reported satisfaction with the majority of their supporters (78%).

Perception of Child Behavior Problems

The T-scores of the total child behavior problem scale of the CBCL indicated that mothers perceived a range of behavior difficulties in their children ($M=54.8$, $SD=11.9$, range = 33–74). The majority of mothers did not report adjustment difficulties in their children beyond that found in the general population; only four of the mothers (8%) indicated a degree of disturbance in their child within the clinical range (in comparison to scores reported by Achenbach & Edelbrock, 1983). A multiple regression was conducted to explore factors that would relate to the participant perceiving difficulty in her child. The participant's perception of negative control from her own mother as measured by the Children's Reports of Parental Behaviors Inventory (Raskin et al., 1971) and the number of social supporters reported providing child care assistance were positively related to higher levels of perceived difficulty in the child, whereas a composite measure of adequacy or satisfaction with aspects of the living situation derived from the Current Life Situation Questionnaire was negatively related to perceived child difficulty. Together, these factors accounted for 40% of the variance.

Although a range of differences was found for both perceived child difficulty and adequacy of the living environment, the majority of mothers did not acknowledge difficulty in these areas.

Measures of Parenting Style

Themes of the five situations from the Sensitivity to Children Questionnaire (Stollack et al., 1973) included conflicting mother and child needs, separation, resolving conflicts, moral dilemmas, child misbehavior, attention to child affect, and managing child-induced maternal stress. The conceptual framework for scoring openended responses was derived from Maccoby and Martin's (1983) two dimensional scheme for classification of parent-

ing styles. The first dimension represents features of being accepting, responsive, and child-centered versus rejecting, unresponsive, and parent-centered. The second dimension consists of parenting that is demanding and structuring versus undemanding and low in control attempts. The crossing of these two dimensions yields four quadrants characterizing different types of parenting styles, i.e., authoritative, authoritarian, indulgent, and neglecting.

This conceptual organization was used to score the participants' STC responses. Initially, responses to each of the vignettes were aggregated across participants. For each of the vignettes, two independent raters categorized each solution into one of the four parenting styles which most closely characterized the style of the response. An additional fifth category was required for those responses which were characterized by psychotic process and were unanalyzable based on the four categories alone. Interrater agreement for the coding of the responses as assessed by Cohen's (1968) weighted kappa[1] was .87. Following the coding of solutions, the responses were reaggregated by participant, and the number of responses in each of the parenting style categories was determined (see Table 2). Authoritative parenting (that is both demanding-structuring and also accepting-responsive) has been related to better child outcomes (Darling & Steinberg, 1993). However, Darling and Steinberg's review also points out that the effect of parenting style is socioculturally dependent. What is considered as authoritarian or indulgent may be a good fit for particular contexts and the constraints and affordances contained within them. Thus, in the present study, we were primarily concerned about responses coded as neglectful or psychotic.

The first hypothetical situation, in which a participant's daughter runs into the house and sobs that, "Some kids made fun of me. They said I was a baby and that I couldn't play with them" produced responses such

TABLE 2.
PARENTAL STYLE RESPONSES FROM SENSITIVITY TO CHILDREN QUESTIONNAIRE
(N=48)

	Vignette 1	Vignette 2	Vignette 3	Vignette 4	Vignette 5
Authoritative Solution	38.3%	40.4%	31.9%	21.3%	27.7%
Indulgent Solution	23.4%	4.3%	23.4%	23.4%	4.3%
Authoritarian Solution	10.6%	29.8%	14.9%	25.5%	51.1%
Neglecting Solution	19.1%	19.1%	25.5%	25.5%	12.8%
Psychotic/Intrusive Solution	8.5%	6.4%	4.3%	4.3%	4.3%

as: "I'd say, I don't understand why people do stuff like that. Why they said that. Maybe they won't be like that next time. You don't like to be called a baby. That makes you feel bad" (authoritative); "Say, 'You're Mama's big girl'" (indulgent); and "I'd go in the house and sit around and do nothing" (neglecting).

When the participant was asked to respond to the second situation in which she finds her daughter pushing her 2-year-old sister and making the younger child cry, responses included "'Sarah, why are you crying? May I help you please?' I'd approach Sarah because she was the one who was crying" (indulgent); "I'd let her woop Sarah" (neglecting); and "Get up and get some milk. Get up and change these clothes. Get up and get hygiene. Then I tell you, go to church, not by yourself. Bring your children, too" (psychotic/intrusive).

In the third scenario, the mother was preparing to go out for the evening, having hired a babysitter her son had previously enjoyed being with, when the participant's son exclaims "Please don't go. Please stay home tonight." To this, participants responded with "You must really want me to stay. But now I've made plans, and I've got to go. Maybe later we can do some-thing" (authoritative); "I'd stay home. I couldn't go out" (indulgent); "I'm going, and you're not going to stop me because I need some different scenery. I can't be mother, doctor, nurse, etc. all at the same time" (authoritarian).

When participants were asked to respond to a situation in which after having done laundry all day, their son comes to them with a big smile on his face to show them a finger painting he made and his hands, face, and shirt are covered with finger paint (vignette #4), responses included "The picture you drew is beautiful" (indulgent); "I'd tell him, 'There's no way you can be doing that. You have to be supervised by someone. Otherwise, you might destroy things around the house'" (authoritarian); and "Just let him go to bed with it on. I worked today and will get it off tomorrow" (neglecting).

The fifth scenario described a situation in which the participant finds her son putting her wallet down with a $10 bill in his hand. It is clear from his actions (looking shocked at her arrival, putting his hand with the money behind his back) that she has caught him stealing. Examples of responses included: "If you want money, just ask for it. You shouldn't be going in

---

[1]Weighted kappa was used as a measure of agreement because other analyses of the present data set utilized a composite measure of the adaptiveness of parenting orientation wherein different styles of parenting were weighted (i.e., authoritative was scored 1; authoritarian and indulgent, 0; and neglecting and psychotic, -1). See Rogosch, Mowbray & Bogat, 1992.

other people's wallets cause that's called stealing. Give me the money back. If you want money just ask for it'" (authoritative). Other responses were "Smack him in the mouth" (neglecting) and "Ask, 'What are you doing with that $10 bill? What are you doing in my purse? Stealing is a sin. I don't believe in thieves. I don't want a thief in my house"' (authoritarian).

An authoritative solution was the predominant response in three out of the five vignettes (from 31.9% to 40.4% of responses), while an authoritarian theme was most prevalent in one vignette and authoritarian and neglectful themes were most prevalent in the remaining vignette. Neglecting solutions encompassed between about one eighth and one quarter of responses across stories. Psychotic/ intrusive responses were seldom seen (from 4.3% to 8.5%).

Discussion

The limitations of the present study must, of course, be acknowledged. A relatively small number of women were interviewed, all from inpatient settings. Demographic features of the sample can be compared to those obtained on a large, statewide Michigan sample of people with serious mental illness (Herman et al., 1988). The statewide sample was older than our women (average age = 43) and somewhat better educated (68% were high school graduates). In the statewide sample, a lower overall percentage had previous hospitalizations (81%). However, their total length of stay (17 months) appeared to exceed that of our mothers, perhaps congruent with their older average age. Our sample included a high percentage of African American women, reflective of the urban sites utilized, but not of the population of women with serious mental illness in the state (which was only 25% black). Thus, our findings may be limited to women in urban settings and the associated

differences in patient characteristics and economic opportunities. However, our assessment of the validity of the findings is increased due to the congruence of some of our results with those from other studies.

Similar to other studies of women who were seriously mentally ill, the mothers in this study presented with multiple risk factors for parenting difficulties. The majority of their children were reported to be unplanned; other reports found 52% and 53% of inpatient women with serious mental illness who were pregnant or post-partum reporting unplanned pregnancies (Forcier, 1990; Buist, Dennerstein & Burrows, 1990). Only a minority of our participants were currently married; nearly 70% had given birth while unmarried and, consequently, were parenting without the support of a spouse. Other investigators have reported only between 12% and 38% of mothers with serious mental illness being married (Forcier, 1990; Krener, Simmons, Hansen & Treat, 1989; Miller, Resnick, Williams, & Bloom, 1990; Rudolph et al., 1990). The majority of our sample was living under economic hardship and only half reported that the area in which they were raising their children was a safe place to live. Other studies also find pregnant women with serious mental illness to be of lower socioeconomic status (Krener et al., 1989, Miller et al., 1990; Rudolph et al., 1990). Finally, our study found, like DeChillo, Matorin & Hallahan (1987), that a minority of treatment plans for these women even mentioned the patient's children.

Our study identified additional risk factors which women with serious mental illness present. First, that a large number of participants first became pregnant at an early age. Giving birth at a relatively young age, before a woman is prepared for the ensuing responsibilities, is difficult for the mentally healthy woman; for the seriously mentally ill woman, such circumstances may exacerbate her already precarious mental health status. We also found that less than half of our participants had lived with both of their parents while growing up and almost one third experienced separation from their mothers before adolescence— suggesting problems in availability of adequate parental role models. Finally, while the number of mothers' network members varied widely, on average, the number of supporters reported was dominated by relatives and smaller than that reported by well mothers (Bogat, personal communication; Hammer, Gutwirth & Phillips, 1982). Also, most of the networks contained negative as well as positive supporters—suggesting that social support was problematic. Less than two thirds mentioned their own mothers as supporters. This may produce particular difficulties for single mothers who reported using relatives almost exclusively for childcare when hospitalized. The literature on pregnant women with serious mental illness also suggests that many have conflicts with their mothers regarding finances, housekeeping and childrearing (Casiano & Hawkins, 1987).

Subjected to the multiple risk factors just described, it is remarkable that the women in our sample were continuing with mothering responsibilities at all. Yet we found that the majority of mothers reported that their child's adjustment did not differ significantly from that of normative samples. Furthermore, a considerable number of the mothers in our study furnished adequate responses on a composite measure of parenting style, with authoritative responses, generally considered the most adaptive, predominating in the majority of stories.

While most mothers in the sample appeared to be functioning adequately at the time of the study, this does not imply that such was always the case, nor that adequate functioning will continue into the future. That is, the results suggest that many of the women studied were not prepared for motherhood, either because of

their age, their mental illness, or lack of parental role models. Furthermore, their current situations were not likely to ameliorate the effects of problematic past histories, with an overwhelming majority not married and continuing to parent alone, under economic distress, and facing the probability of periodic hospitalizations producing separations and adversely impacting interactions with their children. Although not addressed in data from this study, others (Chester, 1991) have described how allegations of mental illness adversely and differentially affect women compared to men in child custody battles. Mothers who are single and enter a psychiatric hospital are faced with the possibility that their children will be placed in foster care. Once removed, even when the woman has recovered postdischarge, regaining custody may be a difficult if not impossible proposition. Some states have laws that allow a child to be removed from a parent for no reason other than that the parent has a mental illness (*Mental and Physical Disability Law Reports,* 1985, 1986a, b).

Service Implications

The multiple problems identified in past histories and in current life situations indicate that women who are seriously mentally ill need considerable support and assistance to deal with stressors that may put them and their child(ren) at risk. However, as found in the current study and several others, mental health treatment plans seldom even correctly identify what the woman's parenting situation is, much less address her needs in carrying out the mothering role. At the very least, service providers should provide counseling concerning the status of children and the mother's fears and anxieties about her children's well-being. Since extended family members are often utilized in childcare and as social supports, their involvement in such counseling should be a high priority. Additionally, many mothers need economic supports to ensure adequate living arrangements for themselves and their children and informational supports to help develop parenting skills. The development of specialized programs that bring together mothers and children for observation, assessment, training and other interventions may be ideal (see Oyserman, Mowbray & Zemencuk, 1994, for a discussion). However, even with restricted resource levels, staff in current inpatient or community programs could better incorporate parenting issues.

Since having multiple pregnancies, especially when unwanted, can also create stress and psychiatric problems for women (Brown & Harris, 1978), the study results also have implications for service providers concerning avoiding early, unwanted pregnancies. In this study, having a diagnosis of schizophrenia, less education, and earlier age of first psychiatric hospitalization related to becoming pregnant at a younger age. While not examined here, other studies have found that women with serious mental illness are seldom given adequate information on family planning or birth control (Rudolph et al., 1990). Our results suggest the need to include these topics in mental health service programs and provide help to identify the group of women for which these efforts could best be targeted.

Beyond the need for service providers to minimize the stressors which mothers with mental illness face, our results also suggest that motherhood itself may have important positive therapeutic implications for women with serious mental illness. Motherhood is important to the adult role for women (Belle, 1982). It is certainly as central to their sense of self-worth as the vocational role is to men. Thus, from a rehabilitation perspective, mothering needs and choices must be considered as part of clients' decisions about life goals.

Anecdotally, women with a serious mental illness have reported that having children can focus their lives and provide a reason to avoid drugs, alcohol, the streets or other dysfunctional behaviors (Mowbray, Oyserman & Ross, 1994; Schwab, Clark & Drake, 1991). From this study, we found that more than two thirds of all participants listed their children in their support networks. We felt that the majority of the women in our sample were carrying out parental responsibilities within acceptable ranges, at the time of data collection. Thus, parenthood can represent an opportunity to increase women's self-esteem, feelings of competence, and usefulness to others. In a prior publication concerning this research study (Rogosch, et al., 1992), the composite measure of parental style was reported to relate positively to the number of network members providing emotional support and negatively to having a recent history of psychiatric hospitalization. This suggests that to build on the therapeutic potential of this role, mental health programs need to: assure that help is available from others, including case managers or professionals; assist women to expand their positive social supports (especially increasing nonkin supports); and keep mothers out of the hospital, shorten their hospitalizations, and ensure early return of their children, so that the frequency of mother-child separations and negative impacts on the sense of parenting competency are minimized.

Conclusions

While many of the women we studied generally evidenced sensitivity in their parenting attitudes, we did find that certain variables related to increased difficulties. It appears likely that other aspects of the women's personal histories and/or social circumstances may contribute to parenting problems at a later time. Awareness of mental health service providers concerning the service needs related to parenthood and/or child caring for women with serious mental illness who are mothers appears critical, given this group's experience of multiple risk factors. Motherhood can represent a tremendous opportunity for women to develop competencies in a major life role. We urge academic researchers, administrators and others to consider the mothering role and clients' feelings about it in designing new research studies and service programs.

In 1981, Test and Berlin reviewed our knowledge base concerning issues relevant to "women with mental illness." They wrote at that time:

> A range of services should be made available to assist [mothers with mental illness]...Included should be opportunities to learn specific child-management skills, have access to resources that share child-rearing responsibilities...and obtain assistance... [with] personal needs. (p. 140)

Much has changed in awareness of client needs and service appropriateness over the past decade. While it may be a sad commentary that this vulnerable subgroup of women with children has been little affected, it is also clear that we *can* do more!

References

Achenbach, T. M. (1986). *The child behavior checklist for ages 2–3*. Vermont: University of Vermont.

Achenbach, T. M., & Edelbrock, C. S. (1983). *Manual for the child behavior checklist and revised child behavior profile*. USA: Queen City Printers.

Bazar, J. (1990). Mentally ill moms aided in keeping their children. *The APA Monitor*, December:32.

Belle, D. (ed.). (1982). *Lives in stress: Women and depression*. Beverly Hits, Sage.

Bogat, G. A., Chin, R., Sabbath, W., & Schwartz, C. (1983). *Social support questionnaire*. Unpublished instrument, Michigan State University, Psychology Department.

Brown, G.W. & Harris, T. (1978). *The social origins of depression: A study of psychiatric disorder in women*. London: Tavistock Publications.

Buist, A. E., Dennerstein, L., & Burrows, G. D. (1990). Review of a mother-baby unit in a psychiatric hospital. *Australian and New Zealand Journal of Psychiatry, 24*, 103-108.

Burr, W. A., Falek, A., Straw & Brown, S. B. (1979). Fertility in psychiatric outpatients. *Hospital & Community Psychiatry, 30*, 527-531.

Casiano, M. E., & Hawkins, D. R. (1987). Major mental illness and childbearing. *Psychiatric Clinics of North America, 10*, 35-51.

Chester, P. (1991). Mothers on trial: The custodial vulnerability of women. *Feminism & Psychology, 1*, 409-425.

Cohen, J. (1968). Weighted kappa: Nominal scale agreement with provision for scaled disagreement or partial credit. *Psychological Bulletin, 70*, 213-220.

Coverdale, J. H., & Aruffo, J. A. (1989). Family planning needs of female chronic psychiatric outpatients. *American Journal of Psychiatry, 1*, 1489-1491.

Darling, N. & Steinberg, L. (1993). Parenting style as context: An integrative model. *Psychological Bulletin, 113*, 487-496.

DeChillo, N., Matorin, S., & Hallahan, C. (1987). Children of psychiatric patients: Rarely seen or heard. *Health and Social Work*, Fall, 296-302.

Forcier, K. I. (1990). Management and care of pregnant psychiatric Patients. *Journal of Psychosocial Nursing, 28*, 11-16.

Ghodsian, M., Zajicek, E., & Wolkind, S. (1984). A longitudinal study of maternal depression and child behaviour problems. *Journal of Child Psychology and Psychiatry, 25*, 91-109.

Hammen, C., Gordon, D., Burge, D., Adrian, C., Jaenicke, C., & Hiroto, D. (1987). Maternal affective disorders, illness: Risk for. children's psychopathology. *American Journal of Psychiatry, 144*, 736-41.

Hammen, C., Adrian, C., Gordon, D., Burge, D., Jaenicke, C., & Hiroto, D. (1987). Children of depressed mothers: Maternal strain and symptom predictors of dysfunction. *Journal of Abnormal Psychology, 96*, 190-198.

Hammer, M., Gutwirth, L., & Phillips S.L. (1982). Parenthood and social networks: A preliminary view. *Social Science and Medicine, 16,* 2091-2100.

Herman, S.E., Amdur, R., Hazel, K, Cohen, S., Blondin, P., & Mowbray, C.T. (1988). *Clients with serious mental illness: Characteristics and typology.* Lansing, MI: Michigan Department of Mental Health.

Krener, P., Simmons, M. K., Hansen, R. L., & Treat, J. N. (1989). Effect of pregnancy on psychosis: Life circumstances and psychiatric symptoms. *International Journal of Psychiatry in Medicine, 19,* 65-84.

Maccoby, E. E, & Martin, J. A. (1983). Socialization in the context of the family: Parent-child interaction. In P. H. Mussen (Ed.), *Handbook of child psychology* (vol. 4), E. M. Hetherington (Vol. Ed.), Socialization, personality, and social development (pp. 1-101). New York: Wiley.

Mental and Physical Disability Law Reports, (1985). 9, 187-189.

Mental and Physical Disability Law Reports, (1986a). 10, 104-106.

Mental and Physical Disability Law Reports, (1986b). 10, 182-183.

Miller, L. J. (1990). Psychotic denial of pregnancy: Phenomenology and clinical management. *Hospital and Community Psychiatry, 41,* 1233-1237.

Miller, W. H., Resnick, M. P., Williams, M. H., & Bloom, J. D. (1990). The pregnant psychiatric inpatient: A missed opportunity. *General Hospital Psychiatry, 12,* 373-378.

Mowbray, C.T., Oyserman, D., & Ross, S. (1995). Parenting and the significance of children for women with a serious mental illness. *Journal of Mental Health Administration, 22*(2), 189-200.

Oyserman, D., Mowbray, C. T., & Zemencuk, J. K. (1994). *Mothers with a severe mental illness: Contextual issues.* Detroit, MI: Wayne State University.

Oyserman, D., Mowbray, C. T., & Zemencuk, J.K. (1994). Resources and supports for mothers with a severe mental illness. *Health and Social Work, 19*(2), 132-143.

Philipps, L. H. C., & O'Hara, M. W. (1991). Prospective study of postpartum depression: 4-1/2 year follow-up of women and children. *Journal of Abnormal Psychology, 100,* 151-155.

Raskin, A., Boothe, H. H., Reatig, N. A., Schulterbrandt, J. G., & Odle, D. (1971). Factor analyses of normal and depressed patients' memories of parental behavior. *Psychological Reports, 29,* 871-879.

Rogosch, F. A. (1987). Causal modeling of parenting attitudes in mothers with severe psychopathology. *Dissertation Abstracts International, 49, 919.*

Rogosch, F. A., Mowbray, C. T., & Bogat, A. (1992). Determinants of parenting attitudes n mothers with severe psychopathology. *Development and Psychopathology, 4,* 469-487.

Rudolph, B., Larson, G. L., Sweeny, S., Hough, E. E., & Arorian, K. (1990). Hospitalized pregnant psychotic women: Characteristics and treatment issues. *Hospital and Community Psychiatry, 41,* 159-163.

Sameroff, A. J., & Seifer, R. (1983). Familial risk and child competence. *Child Development, 54,* 1254-1268.

Saugstad, L.F. (1989). Social class, marriage, and fertility in schizophrenia. *Schizophrenia Bulletin, 15,* 9-43.

Schwab, B., Clark, N. E., & Drake, R. E. (1991). An ethnographic note on charts of parents. *Psychosocial Rehabilitation Journal, 15,* 95-99.

Spielvogel, A., & Wile, J. (1986). Treatment of the psychotic pregnant patient. *Psychosomatics, 27,* 487-492.

Stein, A., Gath, D. H., Bucher, J., Bond, A., Day, A., & Cooper, P. J. (1991). The relationship between post-natal depression and mother-child interaction. *British Journal of Psychiatry, 158,* 46-52.

Stollak, G. E., Scholom, A., Kallman, J., & Saturansky, C. (1973). Insensitivity to children: Responses of undergraduates to children in problem situations. *Journal of Abnormal Child Psychology, 2,* 169-180.

Test, M. A., & Berlin, S. B. (1981). Issues of special concern to chronically mentally ill women. *Professional Psychology, 12,* 136-145.

Dealing With Depression and Manic Depression for People With Mood Disorders and Those Who Love and Support Them

Mary Ellen Copeland

MARY ELLEN COPELAND, M.S., M.A., IS THE AUTHOR OF *The Depression Workbook: A Guide to Living with Depression and Manic Depression* AND *Living Without Depression and Manic Depression: A Guide to Maintaining Mood Stability.* THESE BOOKS ARE BASED ON HER ONGOING STUDIES OF THE SELF-HELP TECHNIQUES AND STRATEGIES USED BY PEOPLE WHO EXPERIENCE SYMPTOMS OF DEPRESSION AND MANIC DEPRESSION. SHE BEGAN THESE STUDIES FIVE YEARS AGO IN RESPONSE TO HER OWN FRUSTRATION WITH THE LACK OF RESOURCES TO GUIDE HER IN HER EFFORTS TO STABILIZE HER MOODS AND REGAIN CONTROL OVER HER LIFE. SHE CURRENTLY CONTINUES HER STUDIES AND TRAVELS EXTENSIVELY, LECTURING AND PRESENTING WORKSHOPS ON THIS TOPIC.

THIS ARTICLE ORIGINALLY APPEARED IN *Innovations and Research,* 1994, 3(4), 51-58 AND IS REPRINTED WITH PERMISSION.

History. In 1976 I was diagnosed with manic depression, the same illness that hospitalized my mother for 8 years when I was growing up. I had had episodes of deep depression interspersed with hypomania since childhood, but this was the first time I had reached out for help, and the first time anyone labeled my ups and downs. For the next 10 years I took lithium and continued to live a hectic, chaotic life.

Then in 1986 something happened that changed the course of my life. I had my first toxic reaction to lithium. Each time the doctors tried to reintroduce the lithium the symptoms of toxicity returned. Thus began 4 nightmarish years of upheaval with ongoing episodes of severe depression and mania, trials of various medication combinations, repeated hospitalizations, the loss of my career and the loss of many long time supporters.

My determination to get my life back never faltered. Through the foggy haze that my life had become, I searched for a light at the end of the tunnel. In desperation I asked my doctor for information on how people with manic depression cope on a day-to-day basis. He said he would get that information for me. I looked forward to my next visit with great anticipation. Finally some answers seemed close at hand. Imagine my disappointment when he told me no such information existed.

An idea began to form in my mind. Somehow I would gather this information for my own use, compile it, and share it with others. I envisioned an anecdotal survey that I would send out to volunteers who have been diagnosed with affective disorders. I would compile the information into a manual that I hoped I might get published. I took this idea to my vocational rehabilitation counselor. I expected her to tell me all the reasons this would be impossible. Instead she thought it was a great idea and introduced me to Social Security Plans to Achieve Self-Sufficiency to cover the costs of the project. Together we drew up a plan that would pay for printing of the study, postage, a computer to compile the data and funds for development of a manual. The plan was accepted and I was off and running. Well, not exactly running at this point. I was still having moodswings that limited my ability to concentrate and the amount of time I could work. My enthusiasm for the project helped to counteract these problems.

I located 120 volunteers by putting notices in newsletters of various mental health organizations. I developed three intensive studies that covered all the questions I had been trying to answer for years and allowed participants the opportunity to share any additional information they thought might be helpful to others. When the responses started coming in, I was amazed. People had so much to share.

They wrote in the margins, on the front and back covers, and added additional pages. Some even audiotaped their information.

The task of compiling this data was overwhelming, especially to someone with a foggy brain and unpredictable moods. But as I began to learn how others increased their wellness and stability, I incorporated many of their successful strategies and wellness techniques into my life. As I did this, I noticed I was feeling better and better. I could work more effectively and efficiently for longer periods of time. I even had energy left over for social and leisure time activities that I had been neglecting.

The most important message I got from this study, for myself and others like me, is that there is lots of hope. Those of us with mood instability get well, stay well for long periods of time, and end up doing what we want to with our lives. This message of hope came across loud and clear. We need our supporters, both family members and health care professionals, to reinforce this message of hope at every opportunity.

me," etc., etc., etc., "I would be fine." These people's lives were controlled by the moodswings.

The other group shared long intensive stories of the positive things they were doing to maintain and enhance their stability. They were starting and attending support groups, advocating for themselves and others, educating themselves and others about their illness, had developed a team of supportive health care professionals who helped them develop and maintain effective treatment scenarios, and they were searching for and finding answers to recurrent health problems. They knew that they could not count on any one person to solve their problems for them—they must rely first on themselves with help from others. These people who were taking responsibility for their own wellness were achieving the highest levels of wellness, stability, happiness, and control over their own lives.

Health care professionals, family members, and friends can help us to take responsibility for our own wellness by being supportive and encouraging our efforts.

> *The most important message I got from this study, for myself and others like me, is that there is lots of hope. Those of us with mood instability get well, stay well for long periods of time, and end up doing what we want to with our lives.*

Responsibility

As the data began coming in, I found that I could have divided the responses into two piles. One pile was from people who shared their "if only...," i.e. "if only my mother hadn't died," "if only my brother hadn't been mean to me when I was growing up," "if only they would find the right pill," "if only the doctor would listen to

Self-Advocacy

Those of us who have mood instability feel as though we have lost control over our own lives, rights, and responsibilities, and have lost the ability and right to effectively advocate for ourselves. Regaining our sense of control by successfully advocating for ourselves gives us back hope and self-esteem necessary to stability and wellness. The following steps are a guide to this process:

1. Believe in yourself. We may need to work on raising self-esteem to really believe in ourselves and become our own best advocates.

2. Know your rights. We are all entitled to equality under the law. Some of us who have episodes of depression and manic depression erroneously believe that we do not have the same rights as others. If we are uncertain about what our rights are, we can find out from our state protection and advocacy office.

3. Decide what you want. Clarifying for ourselves exactly what we need, helps us set goals and be clear with others.

4. Get the facts. When we advocate for ourselves we need to know what we are talking about. We need to be sure our information is accurate. Writing it down and keeping it where we can easily find it helps.

5. Plan the strategy. We need to figure out what we think will work and the steps necessary to achieve these goals. We strategize. We think of several ways to address the problem. We ask supporters for suggestions. We get feedback on our ideas. Then we choose the strategy that feels right.

6. Gather support. Ww work together with friends. We help each other and are mutually supportive. Nothing helps self-advocacy more than supportive friends. We join groups with common concerns. If necessary, we call our protection and advocacy organization for additional support.

7. Target your efforts. Who is the person, persons, or organization we need to deal with to get action on this matter? We talk directly with the person who can best assist us.

8. Express yourself clearly. Good communication skills are vital for effective self-advocacy. We learn effective communication so we can get our message across. We are brief. We stick to the point. We don't allow ourselves to be diverted or to ramble on with unimportant details. We state our concern and how we want things changed.

9. Assert yourself calmly. We stay cool. We don't lose our temper and lash out at the other person, their character, or the organization. We speak out, and listen. We respect the rights of others, but don't let them put us down or walk all over us.

10. Be firm and persistent. We don't give up! We keep after what we want. We always follow through on what we say. We dedicate ourselves to getting whatever it is we need for ourselves.

Education

Study participants said that it was absolutely essential to learn everything they could about their particular diagnosis and any proposed treatment scenarios. Education is part of taking responsibility for our wellness and facilitates appropriate decision making about all aspects of mood instability including treatment, lifestyle, education, career, relationships, living space, parenting, and leisure activities. It also helps us to ask the right questions and know where to look for answers. This educational process must be ongoing to keep us up to date on the latest findings.

Study participants educated themselves through extensive research of related resources, attending related workshops and seminars, participating in mental health organizations and support groups and subscribing to related newsletters. The resource list at the back of *The Depression Workbook* and after each chapter in *Living Without Depression and Manic Depression* is a compilation of books, audiotapes and videotapes which study participants have found useful. Many of them can be found in libraries.

Another excellent source of information is newsletters which are put out by mental health organizations. Addresses for many of the organizations that put out these letters are also found in my books. Send the organization a postcard asking for a complimentary copy of their newsletter. If you think it would be useful, subscribe.

It is important to share our findings with our health care professionals, family members, and friends. They can assist us in this educational process by providing us with information as they become aware of it.

Medical Care

We have learned that in some cases mood instability is caused by chronic or acute disease processes. Hypothyroidism, which can be discovered through a complete battery of thyroid tests, is one of the common biological causes of depression. Other endocrine or adrenal gland dysfunctions, chronic or acute disease processes, food allergies, or seasonal affective disorder may be part of the picture. Excessive exposure to electromagnetic radiation from electric blankets, water bed heaters, and video screens may also be part of the picture.

To insure appropriate treatment we have a complete physical examination. When we go for this physical, we take with us lists of all the medications and health care preparations we are using, symptoms and recent changes in our health and life, and a history of illnesses that have affected other members of our family. This facilitates the process of uncovering and treating the mood instability.

When mood instability is severe, we may be unable to make arrangements for such a medical evaluation. Supporters may have to take a directive approach, making arrangements for necessary appointments, arranging or providing transportation, and reminding us of dates and times. We may even want a supporter to go to the appointment with us to help us remember information and to advocate for us when we are unable to do this for ourselves.

We look to our physician to refer us to other health care professions such as a psychiatrist, endocrinologist, nutritionist, psychologist, etc. according to our specific needs; and to work closely with these health care providers to develop the most appropriate treatment scenario.

We want members of our health care team to:

- be willing and anxious to know and understand us very well;

- have experience and expertise in treating mood instability;

- be willing to consider and try alternative therapies such as light, exercise, and peer counseling;

- use drugs only as absolutely necessary; and,

- support, counsel, advise, advocate, understand, and care.

Many study participants said that initial denial of symptoms made initiation of treatment difficult. They preferred working with health care professionals who addressed alleviating current symptoms rather than those who stressed diagnosis and long-term projections.

Counseling

Seventy-three percent of the people in my studies use counseling as part of their overall treatment strategy. Before the discovery of today's medical treatments, counseling or psychotherapy was the only treatment for people with depression or manic depression. Today we have many more treatment choices, and counseling is often recommended as one of several strategies used concurrently with other treatments to address and relieve symptoms.

Most of us look at counseling as a confiding relationship we establish with a person specially trained in the field of counseling. It gives us a chance to share our experiences and predicaments. It often reduces symptoms and helps us feel better by assisting us in developing a deeper understanding of ourselves and teaching us new approaches to life situations. Counseling can include listening, encouragement, support, understanding, monitoring, feedback, advice, information, and education. Those of us who have had mood instability often benefit from this kind of professional support.

Hospitalization

Although none of the study participants wanted to be hospitalized, they felt it was sometimes helpful and necessary in the following circumstances:

- for safety and protection;

- if family members and friends are unable to provide care;

- for drug treatment which needs to be monitored initially;

- if time-out in a safe structured environment would be helpful; or,

- if symptoms include psychosis or severe agitation.

Many of us have expressed the need for safe, comfortable places in the community where we can go voluntarily to get support and services when our symptoms are severe.

Medications

Many of the volunteers in the study use medication as part of their overall wellness program. We know that appropriate medications must be determined on an individual basis. Medication effectiveness and side effects vary from person to person. By working closely with our physician, we can determine the medication which best suits our need.

Some people in the study reported that they resisted using psychiatric medications because they:

1. fear the long- or short-term side effects;

2. feel medications diminish quality of life;

3. feel that the medications interfere with normal functioning i.e., sexual function, memory, intellectual capacity, coordination, vision, digestion, etc.;

4. feel like a failure for having to use medications;

5. have ethical reasons for refusing medications; or,

6. experience intolerable side effects.

However, we realize the medications may be necessary for the short or long term to allow us to get control of our life and to enhance the rehabilitation process. Careful monitoring and management of medications along with education can alleviate fears and assure the best treatment response.

We manage our medication treatment carefully by:

1. being under the care of a physician or team of health care professionals who have extensive knowledge and experience in the use of psychotropic medications;

2. learning all we can about every medication we take; (We have a thorough discussion with our physician and other health care providers about all aspects of the suggested medication or treatment strategy. We keep all information about each suggested medication or treatment in a mental health file. If we cannot do this for ourselves, we ask our supporters to do this for us.)

3. having the regular blood tests required for the medication we are taking;

4. Not changing the amount of medication we are taking or stop taking the medication without consulting our

physician; (Systems for medication changes and discontinuation vary with each medication and must be monitored carefully to avoid potentially serious reactions.)

5. being completely honest with our physician about taking the medication i.e., forgetting to take the medication several times, not renewing the prescription on time, etc; (The physician needs this information to accurately assess medication dosage and effects.)

6. including our pharmacist as an active member of our health care team. (We deal with a pharmacy that has a good reputation, where the pharmacist knows us, and where computerized record-keeping systems are used. We purchase all medications at the same pharmacy.)

Systems to insure consistency in taking medications have been developed by those of us who take medications. Many of us find that taking medications becomes so routine that we can't remember whether we have taken our dose. Some of us use an empty egg carton with each egg container marked with the day of the week. The first day of each week, we fill the containers with the medications we need to take for each day of that week. A quick glance into the container will let us know whether or not we have taken that day's medications. Others set out their medications for the day in a series of cups, one for morning doses, one for noon doses, etc. Pharmacists have a variety of small containers that will fit in pocket or purse that can be used in the same way. A watch with a timer signal or a small inexpensive timer can be a helpful reminder for medications that have to be taken at a certain time of day.

Medication Side Effects
Those of us who use medications have discovered that a lifestyle that includes a high fiber, low fat diet, plenty of liquids (check with your doctor to find out how much liquid you need with the medication you are taking), daily exercise, adequate rest, and the regular use of stress reduction techniques reduces the incidence and severity of medication side effects in many cases. When life begins to get "out of control," the side effects tend to worsen.

Many medication side effects are most severe when first introducing the medication. After a week or two, the side effects may diminish or disappear. The physician can alert us if this is the case. We keep our physician advised of all symptoms that appear after we start taking medication. We don't assume that the symptom is a normal medication side effect and fail to report it. A serious condition that needs attention could be needlessly overlooked.

Family members and friends need to know about medications we are taking. They can help us monitor medication effectiveness and they can bring to our attention side effects that we may not be noticing such as tremor or lethargy.

Treatment Preference Plan
We take advantage of the "window of opportunity" between episodes to develop a Treatment Preference Plan. While such plans are not legally binding in all states, they do assist supporters and caregivers who must make decisions for us when our moods are so unstable we can't make them for ourselves. Treatment Preference Plans include:

1. symptoms which indicate we are not able to make decisions for ourselves;

2. the names and phone numbers of at least three people (including health care professionals and family members) whom we want to make decisions in our behalf;

3. a listing of preferred, acceptable, and unacceptable medications; treatments; and treatment facilities, including reasons for such.

This Treatment Preference Plan is kept in a mental health file along with information about diagnosis, medications and self-help strategies. Each supporter should have a copy of this plan.

Charting Moods

It is easier to treat mood instability when it is first beginning than when the episode has cycled into an out-of-control mania or a deep suicidal depression. Developing and keeping an Early Warning Signs chart facilitates this process.

Develop an awareness of symptoms that indicate the beginning of an episode of depression or mania. Family members, supporters, and health care professionals can help us identify these early warning signs. For instance, many people report that fatigue, isolating behaviors, and difficulty getting up in the morning are early warning signs of depression. Insomnia, racing thoughts, and talking fast may be signs of mania. Record the signs on a simple daily chart. Make copies of the chart for on-going use. Each evening before retiring, review the chart to see if any of the warning signs have come up. If they have, or if they recur for several days, take action to alleviate the symptoms.

Family members and supporters can help with this monitoring process. However, it is important that they not be overzealous in reporting symptoms that are just a normal part of everyday living. Those of us with mood instability find this very offensive.

Techniques to Alleviate Symptoms of Depression

Many of us have found that the following techniques often help to relieve early warning signs of depression:

1. Contact health care professionals.

2. Talk to a supporter.

3. Exercise—go for a walk, work in the garden, etc.,

4. Get outside and get light through the eyes.

5. Arrange a special counseling session.

6. Do something enjoyable or fun.

7. Do something nice for someone else.

8. Do extra relaxation exercises.

9. Get up and get going.

10. Assess lifestyle and make changes needed to reduce stress.

Techniques to Alleviate Symptoms of Mania

Many of us have found that the following techniques often help to relieve early warning signs of mania (many of the strategies are the same as those used to relieve depression):

1. Contact health care professionals.

2. Talk to a supporter.

3. Get some mild exercise.

4. Activities such as writing, painting, or crafts help.

5. Increase the number of times a day we do deep breathing relaxation techniques.

6. Avoid stimulating places (such as bars and shopping malls) and people.

7. Avoid making any major decisions.

8. If we have early warning signs of mania and we are not sleeping, we get help immediately. Lack of sleep worsens mania very quickly.

Diet

We have found that we feel best when we have a diet focused on foods that are high in complex carbohydrates. The optimum would be six servings a day of grains such as cereals, breads and pastas and five servings a day of vegetables (one serving of fruit may be substituted for a serving of vegetables). This can be supplemented with high protein foods such as dairy products and meats (especially fish and poultry). Restricting or avoiding sugar and caffeine helps to stabilize moods.

We keep on hand healthy foods that are easy to prepare such as frozen dinners and canned soups for those days when we don't feel like cooking. This helps us avoid eating junk foods or having a diet that is restricted to one or several foods (not necessarily healthy) that are easy to fix.

Light

Many of us find that as winter approaches, as the days get shorter and there are more cloudy days, we feel more and more depressed. Many of us have successfully eliminated this problem by increasing our exposure to light. We spend as much time as possible outdoors. When we work inside we work in a well lit space (preferably near windows) and many of us use supplemental light sources such as light boxes. Light therapy is a well recognized treatment for seasonal depression. *Winter Blues* by Dr. Norman Rosenthal has a listing of health care professionals who specialize in light therapy as well as a listing of light box manufacturers.

Exercise

Exercise is the least expensive and most available anti-depressant. A daily walk or some other kind of exercise we enjoy makes us feel better. We begin slowly if we have not been exercising regularly and increase the intensity and length of exercise sessions gradually. A 20-minute to one hour walk four or five times a week is sufficient. If we have any health problems, we contact the doctor for suggestions and limitations before beginning an exercise program.

Doing Things We Enjoy

When our moods are getting out of control, many of us forget to do the things we enjoy that make us feel better. It helps to make a list of things we enjoy doing for easy reference when we are having a hard time. The list might include playing the piano, listening to classical music, refinishing furniture, working in the garden, watching funny videos, reading a good novel, quilting—whatever it is that we "lose ourselves in." We make time to include one or more of these activities in our schedule regularly, daily if our moods are unstable.

Cognitive Therapy

Negative and distorted thoughts create a vicious cycle. They worsen mood instability, thereby creating more negative thoughts. Symptoms of depression such as low self-esteem and confidence, hopelessness, fear, guilt, and embarrassment may be relieved through an intensive program of cognitive therapy (changing negative thoughts to positive ones).

While many of us have successfully done this work on our own, those of us who had the opportunity to work with a counselor trained in cognitive therapy techniques found the ideas and support to be helpful. Resources such as *Thoughts and Feelings* by Patrick Fanning, Matthew McKay, and Martha Davis and David Burn's *Feeling Good* and *The Feeling Good Handbook* provide excellent ideas and structure for this work.

The first step in this process is identifying learned, negative thoughts. These thoughts are often in shorthand, ("I am a jerk," or "I am a loser"), idiosyncratic, and persistent. Carrying a notebook and jotting down such thoughts as they occur over several days, particularly in moments of stress, is a workable strategy. Then choose one or two of these thoughts to work on, saving the list of others to work on later.

Begin by analyzing the thoughts. The following questions help this analysis: "What do these words really mean?" "Are they true?" "Would I say them to someone else?" "What is the benefit of saying this to myself?" "What does it cost me to say this to myself?" It helps to check the validity of the statement with a friend. This analysis often does a great job of disarming the negative thought.

Next, develop a positive rebuttal to the thought. Examples of negative thoughts and positive rebuttals include:

Negative thought...Positive rebuttal.

I have never accomplished any thing...I have accomplished a great deal.

I am not a likable person...I am well liked by many people.

I am an idiot...I am a smart person.

I will never be well...I will be well.

Every time the thought comes up, replace it with the positive rebuttal. Say it over and over upon awakening, before going to sleep, while doing the dishes, when waiting in traffic, while waiting for an appointment, i.e., anytime you have a minute of extra time. Say it aloud whenever possible. Write it down ten or fifteen times each day. Make signs that say the positive rebuttal to hang around your house and read it every time you see it. Reinforce the positive thought in this way for 4 to 6 weeks. By that time it should be firmly established in your mind and the old negative thought should be passé. If it starts to recur, do more reinforcement techniques until you have rid yourself of the negative thought for good.

When you feel ready, begin work on one or two more negative thoughts. This work is often long term but it is well worth it.

Some of us who have episodes of depression and manic depression erroneously believe that we do not have the same rights as others.

Cognitive therapy is one aspect of an overall wellness program and should never be considered a substitute for a complete program of medical and psychological care.

Relaxation and Stress Reduction

Many of us have forgotten how to relax. Daily use of simple relaxation techniques that involve deep breathing and relaxing various parts of the body, and may include guided imagery, help many of us to decrease symptoms and develop an overall sense of well-being. These exercises may be learned by taking a course at a hospital or mental health center, or by using one of the many available self-help books such as *The Relaxation and Stress Reduction Workbook* by Elizabeth Eshelman, Matthew McKay, and Patrick Fanning.

These exercises must be learned when we are feeling well. They need to be practiced daily. Structured periods of intense relaxation (10–30 minutes) need to be built into the daily schedule. Then they can be used as a resource to effectively alleviate symptoms during times of instability.

Mood instability may be caused, triggered or worsened by chronic or acute stress, life issues, or traumatic events such as: child abuse, sexual abuse, spouse abuse, marital problems, overwork, lifestyle changes, rejection, violence, war, natural or man made disasters, accidents, personal loss and tragedy, not meeting career goals, the stigma of mental illness, and substance abuse (self or family member).

These issues need to be worked through in a good, long-term counseling program that focuses on reconnection, empowerment, and validation. The counseling process may be enhanced by attending a support group, peer counseling and using self-help books such as *I Can't Get Over It: A Handbook for Trauma Survivors* by Aphrodite Matsakis.

Developing and Keeping a Strong Support System

While most of us have an informal support system, those of us with depression or manic depression have found that we need a more structured support system to provide assistance when we are having a difficult time and to enrich our lives. Low self-esteem, the stigma of mental illness, poor social skills from years of mood instability, the unpredictability of the moods, and the draining nature of mood instability cause friends and family members to back away, leaving us isolated, lonely, and vulnerable.

We have found that we can rebuild our support systems and keep them strong by being mutually supportive, by keeping our moods as stable as possible, by taking good care of ourselves, through regular attendance at support groups, attending church and other community events, and by having many friends so we don't wear our supporters out.

When we identify a potential supporter, we discuss support with them, telling them exactly what we would like from them, that we would be supportive of them, and that we have other supporters so they would not be expected to always be available.

It helps to make a list of at least five people who we can call on when we need support. Five people are essential to prevent wearing any one person out and because people are not always available or capable of being supportive. These lists, including phone numbers, should be posted in convenient places because when we need support, we often cannot think of who our supporters are.

Those of us who experience recurring episodes of mood instability need and want love, understanding, acceptance, caring, support, activities, information, feedback, monitoring (reality checks), and protection from our supporters.

Family support is very important to all of us. We have found that we can enhance our relationships with family members by being supportive of them whenever we can, by promoting open discussion of family issues and problems, by planning activities and get-togethers with family members, sharing the good times as well as the bad, and by holding family meetings to discuss the kind of support we would like and to see how they feel about giving us this kind of support.

Peer Counseling

Many of us have found peer counseling, a structured form of mutual attention and support, to be a valuable technique that gives us an opportunity to express ourselves any way we choose, while supported by a trusted ally. For some of us, peer counseling is the key component of our wellness program. We have found that peer counseling, when used consistently, is a free, safe, and effective self-help tool that encourages expression of feelings and emotions. It puts us in control of our own healing process.

All of us encounter a wide variety of situations that can be disturbing and, if not addressed, worsen mood instability. If responses to past experiences, hurts, trauma, and misinformation are not examined to determine their validity, and if the resulting emotions are not expressed, we may experience ongoing episodes of depression, mania, mood instability, sadness, anxiety, fear, embarrassment, guilt, shame, low self-esteem, and lack of self-confidence.

Peer counseling gives us a forum where we can carefully and safely examine issues and express emotions. It is based on the premise that we are all fine, know what to do to heal ourselves, and can do what we need to do to heal ourselves. We all know, at some level, the solutions to our problems and the reality of our beliefs. Peer counseling helps us find those solutions and trust our beliefs.

In a peer counseling session, two people agree to spend a previously agreed upon amount of time together, dividing the time equally, paying attention to each other's issues, needs, and distresses. Sessions usually last one hour but can be shorter or longer. Half of the time is spent addressing each person's issues while the other person pays attention.

Peer counselors have an ongoing agreement to complete confidentiality. Judging, criticizing, and giving advice are not allowed.

Planning

Some of us have found that making daily plans helps when we are having a hard time maintaining our stability. We can do this on our own, but it helps to do this with the assistance of our counselor or other supporter. It helps us feel better if we get some chores done each day and do some things we enjoy. It also helps us to do all those things we need to do for ourselves to help us feel better.

Following is an example of a daily plan for someone who works who is having early warning signs of depression:

7–8:15AM Get up, shower, dress, 15 minutes of stretching exercises, eat breakfast (bagel with cream cheese, herb tea).

8:15–8:30 Contact supporters for lunch and evening activities.

8:45–9 Drive to work (listen to favorite classical music).

9–10:15 Work—focus on tasks that are easy and do not involve major decision making.

10:15–10:30 Snack (apple) and relaxation exercise.

10:30–12 Work.

12–1 Salad and bread in cafeteria, half-hour walk outside with member or supporter.

1–2:30 Work.

2:30–2:45 Snack (cheese crackers and fruit juice) and relaxation exercise.

2:45–5 Work.

5:10–6 Appointment with counselor.

6–8 Dinner at Chinese restaurant with member of support team.

8–8:30 Drive home listening to favorite classical music.

8:30–10 Watch light video with family member.

10 Take a warm bath and go to bed.

Suicide Warning Signs

Depression and manic depression are serious illnesses: 15% of us end our lives by suicide. Those of us who have attempted to take our own lives and were not successful are glad we lived. We want and need our supporters to help us stay alive.

Our supporters need to know:

• If we are talking about suicide or admit to suicidal thoughts the chances of a suicide attempt are high.

• A suicide attempt may follow the loss of an important person, people, position, or possessions.

• Social isolation, street drugs, and alcohol increase the risk of a suicide attempt.

• The beginning of recovery is a very risky time—though we may have high energy, our thought patterns may still be very negative and we may not be able to take action.

• We may be at risk if we have been depressed and are now getting everything in our life "in order," like updating our will and giving away possessions.

• Agitation is very painful and dangerous—help is needed immediately.

Family members and friends may have to take emergency action, even when we ask them not to. It may be necessary to save our life.

We have found that there are many things we can do to avoid suicide attempts. They include:

1. Insisting on treatment of depression early;

2. Putting systems in place, including a suicide support team, when we are well to prevent suicide when we are depressed (This system should insure that we are never alone when we are suicidal, even if we insist we want to be alone);

3. Disposing of all leftover medications;

4. Setting up a system with our pharmacist so we won't have excess medications on hand;

5. Not allowing any firearms to be kept in our home;

6. Keeping pictures of favorite people displayed to serve as reminders of why we want to live;

7. Keeping all appointments with all health care professionals; and,

8. Always having something planned to look forward to.

Conclusion

If you are determined to get your moods under control, and most of us are, there may be several paths you need to follow. You can follow these paths one at a time,

or you may choose to pursue several at once. This article gives you a brief introduction to some possibilities. You can't do it all at once. This is a process that takes time and patience. I am still working on keeping my moods stable and know that I will always have to do this. But I have my life back. And it is better than ever.

References

Burns, D. (1980). *Feeling good.* New York: W. Morrow.

Burns, D. (1989). *The feeling good handbook.* New York: W. Morrow.

Copeland, Mary Ellen. (1992). *The depression workbook: A guide to living with depression and manic depression.* Oakland, CA: New Harbinger Publications.

Copeland, Mary Ellen.(1994). *Living without depression and manic depression: A guide to maintaining mood stability.* Oakland, CA: New Harbinger Publications.

Davis, M., Eschelman, Elizabeth and McKay, M.(1988). *The relaxation and stress reduction workbook.* Oakland, CA: New Harbinger Publications.

Gorman, Jack M. (1991.) *The essential guide to psychiatric medications.* New York: St. Martin's Press, Inc.

Matsakis, Aphrodite (1992). *I can't get over it: A handbook for trauma survivors.* Oakland, CA: New Harbinger Publications.

McKay, M., Davis, M. and Fanning, P.(1981). *Thoughts and feelings: The art of cognitive stress intervention.* Oakland, CA: New Harbinger Publications.

Rosenthal, Norman (1993). *Winter blues.* New York: Guilford Press.

A Continuum of Care for People Who Are Elderly and Mentally Ill

Michael A. Bernstein and Susan Jenkins

MICHAEL A. BERNSTEIN, A.C.S.W., HAS BEEN CHAIRMAN OF THE FLORIDA STATEWIDE BLUE RIBBON TASK FORCE ON THE MENTAL HEALTH NEEDS OF THE ELDERLY, FLORIDA CHAPTER REPRESENTATIVE TO THE INTERNATIONAL BOARD OF DIRECTORS OF THE INTERNATIONAL ASSOCIATION OF PSYCHOSOCIAL REHABILITATION SERVICES (IAPSRS), PRESIDENT ELECT AND FOUNDING TRUSTEE FOR THE FLORIDA CHAPTER OF IAPSRS, BOARD MEMBER-AT-LARGE OF THE FLORIDA COUNCIL FOR COMMUNITY HEALTH, AND LIAISON TO THE FLORIDA COMMITTEE ON AGING.

SUSAN JENKINS, M.ED., HAS BEEN THE DIRECTOR OF PLANNING AND EVALUATION FOR GULF COAST JEWISH FAMILY SERVICE, INC. FOR OVER EIGHT YEARS. SHE IS A BOARD MEMBER OF THE FLORIDA CHAPTER OF IAPSRS AND A LICENSED MENTAL HEALTH COUNSELOR FOR THE STATE OF FLORIDA.

THIS ARTICLE ORIGINALLY APPEARED IN *Innovations and Research*, 1991, 1(1), 10-12 AND IS REPRINTED WITH PERMISSION.

A comprehensive continuum of care has been designed to meet the multi-faceted needs of people who are elderly and seriously mentally ill in the Tampa Bay area of Florida. The authors discuss a number of specialized programs implemented in response to the needs of this population in community based settings.

Gulf Coast Jewish Family Service, Inc. (GCJFS), a nonsectarian social service agency located in the Tampa Bay area (Hillsborough, Pinellas, and Pasco counties) of Florida, has provided specialized services to people who are elderly and seriously mentally ill for the past 11 years. Programming implemented through GCJFS has been geared to address the high suicide rate of people who are elderly as well as offering alternatives to unnecessary long-term state mental hospitalization.

Florida is leading the nation with regard to a dramatic aging phenomenon. The 10 oldest areas (in terms of median age) are all within the state of Florida. Nationally, it is estimated that the population over 65 will grow 102% during the period from 1980 to 2020. During that same period of time, the population over 65 within the state of Florida will grow by 186%.

It is estimated that as many as 7 million seniors are in need of mental health services; however, very few of these individuals are receiving the treatment they so desperately need and deserve.

Frequently, the elderly with mental health needs are not provided services until their problems are so severe that they require institutionalization. Unfortunately, one of the most obvious indicators of the need for increased community mental health services to this population is that of the high suicide rate among the elderly. While estimates differ on the percentage of suicides committed by older people, some researchers feel that as many as 30 to 40% of all suicides are committed by the elderly (Osgood, 1987).

Again, while the increasing rate of suicide among the elderly in the nation is alarming, the Tampa Bay area of Florida has the highest suicide rate for geriatrics in the country (U.S. Census Bureau, 1990). The unique demographic characteristics and high suicide rate in the Tampa Bay area of Florida combined with the need to develop appropriate community alternatives to institutionalization have resulted in the implementation of a continuum of care for the elderly who have a mental illness.

Background

In 1980, GCJFS implemented its Geriatric Residential Treatment System (GRTS) program in order to begin assisting seniors in state mental health hospitals to return to the community. This program offers a variety of services including case management, day treatment/rehabilitation and residential care in community settings. To date, the program has assisted 754 people who are elderly and seriously and persistently mentally ill. Of these, 402 have come directly out of state mental institutions and another 352 have been diverted from going into state hospitals. Over 91% of the 754 assisted have never had to return to state mental hospitals after 11 years of operation, while over half have gone on to even more independent living in the community.

As a result of the success of the program, other community-based programs were soon developed and implemented throughout the State of Florida. Community settings that are usually perceived as secure for people who are elderly, such as nursing homes, often can meet the medical and physical needs of clients, but are not equipped to handle the psychiatric problems encountered in residents. According to a White House Conference on Aging Report, 60% of nursing home elderly have mental health needs with an additional 40% of the total "mentally healthy" nursing home residents being at risk (White House Conference on Aging Report, 1981).

In 1986, GCJFS implemented the Mental Health Overlay to Nursing Homes program in response to:

1) the number of people who are elderly and who are often discharge-ready for long periods of time in traditional state mental hospitals, and who have a primary medical diagnosis, but were in need of mental health support, and

2) the significant lack of mental health support for people who are elderly currently residing in the standing population.

The program provides for a team consisting of a psychiatrist, a psychiatric RN, and social workers to provide mental health support to individuals in area nursing homes as well as training to nursing home staff. The program has proven to be extremely successful and has served 1,110 individuals since its inception. The program has also enabled 125 people who are elderly to leave state mental hospitals and to be placed in community settings near loved ones, family, and friends. One hundred eighteen remain successfully placed in community nursing homes.

The services provided through the Mental Health Overlay program include assessment, counseling, treatment planning, consultation and education, psychiatric services, discharge planning, and followup. After providing Mental Health Overlay services to nursing homes in the Tampa Bay area for over 5 years, GCJFS recently received additional funding in order to expand those services in the Tampa Bay area of Florida. These dollars will enable over 200 clients in 20 additional nursing homes to receive these needed services.

GCJFS realized that many people who are elderly and have serious and persistent

Unfortunately, one of the most obvious indicators of the need for increased community mental health services to this population is that of the high suicide rate among the elderly.

mental illness were living in retirement homes, foster homes, and private homes, and not receiving any type of mental health services. According to a report of the National Institute of Mental Health (NIMH), nursing homes are now the largest single setting for the care of people with mental illness in this country (Harper, 1981).

In addition to the needs of people who are elderly, those responsible for the day-to-day care of these individuals (nursing staff, ACLF staff, and many times, spouses) had no training or experience in mental health to prepare them for their role. Those in the role of caregiver to a person who is elderly and mentally ill found themselves in uncharted territory. Not only were they trying to cope with the needs of a person with mental illness, but they had no training or support for themselves. The stress inherent in caring for a person who is elderly and mentally ill in the home, without adequate support systems, frequently results in an unbearable burden on the caregiver.

Realizing the need for services to people who are elderly and their caregivers, in 1987, GCJFS received funding through NIMH's Community Support Division to develop and implement a Geriatric Mental Health Support Team.

This program not only provides day treatment and rehabilitation to people who are elderly and have a psychiatric diagnosis but also offers support and training to their caregivers. In the brief period of time since this program was begun, the project has provided training to 42 area retirement homes, day treatment and rehabilitation to over 375 clients, and training and support to more than 450 caregivers.

As a result of the initial success of the program, when the NIMH funding period ended, the State of Florida actually doubled funding for the program so that these services could continue.

As a leader in providing mental health services in the State of Florida, and based on our experience in working with people who are elderly and mentally ill and those who care for them, GCJFS recognized that additional housing alternatives in community settings were needed.

In some cases, people who are elderly and have psychiatric disabilities simply had no place to go after being discharged from a state or local mental health facility. Still others had successfully completed the various levels of care of the GRTS program and needed a long-term living arrangement.

GCJFS explored what was being done by other regions of the State of Florida and in other areas of the country in an attempt to find a solution to this housing problem. As a result of that research and based upon the agency's reputation for outstanding services to people who are elderly and mentally ill, GCJFS was recently funded to provide Therapeutic Foster Home and Alternative Family Program (AFP) services, thereby expanding the permanent housing options for people who are elderly and mentally ill in the Tampa Bay area to include permanent foster home care.

This concept provides "decent, humane, affordable housing accompanied by the

> *An Alternative Family home is a private residence where the homeowner invites a maximum of three individuals to live in the home in exchange for a fee.*

provision of trained, licensed, and monitored supervision based on psychosocial principles." The Alternative Family Program (AFP) concept fosters client independence and client choice and empowerment in a permanent housing setting. It is an economical alternative to other forms of residential treatment and has demonstrated effectiveness compared to traditional treatment models.

An Alternative Family home is a private residence where the homeowner invites a maximum of three individuals to live in the home in exchange for a fee. The homeowner becomes a sponsor and is responsible for the care, support, and well-being of the client or clients. The sponsor assumes an active role in the client's treatment process and as part of this process is required to cooperatively develop at least two treatment goals which can be addressed in the Alternative Family environment. Sponsors are also responsible for providing transportation to and from day treatment/rehabilitation or other community supports.

Respite care is an integral part of the AFP. The respite care provides a "backup" in the event of illness or vacation of the sponsor.

Prior to accepting AFP clients, sponsors must be licensed and certified. The licensure and certification process is thorough and designed to adequately ensure the suitability and appropriateness of the sponsors. Sponsors must successfully complete certification requirements through GCJFS and must meet licensure requirements set forth by the State of Florida, including: applica-

According to a report of the National Institute of Mental Health, nursing homes are now the largest single setting for the care of people with mental illness in this country.

tion to provide foster care; addendum application; agreement of partnership; applicant's statement of income and expenses; adult foster care responsibilities, qualifications and requirements; civil rights compliance; description of services to be provided; household rules; release of information; and physician's report. In addition, all requirements for licensure include: three character reference letters; proof of first aid certification; criminal records background check; sanitation inspection; fire safety inspection; and a home study.

A home study is completed which includes a description of the potential foster home family dynamics, financial aspects, medical information, family activities, physical aspects of the home, and other areas of importance and concern.

The licensed sponsor must also satisfy the conditions of the contract which include the following: proof of homeowner's insurance, proof of automobile insurance, proof of Florida driver's license and vehicle registration, proof of freedom from communicable disease, current CPR certification, 8 hours of pre-service training, and an agreement to participate in the client treatment planning process.

Once a client is referred to the AFP and the eligibility evaluation and assessment are completed, the Alternative Family Coordinator selects several potential sponsors who meet the holistic needs of the individual client. A visit is arranged by the coordinator that allows both the client and the potential sponsor to get to know each other, as well as to allow the client to see the home and neighborhood in which she or he would be living. After the visit, if both parties are agreeable, the process continues. A 14-day trial period begins as soon as arrangements can be made. During this trial period, frequent home visits are made by the AFP staff in order to monitor the situation and offer consultation and assistance. Before the trial period ends, individual interviews with the sponsor and the client are held to determine the success of the match. A final meeting is then held with all concerned to discuss the outcome.

Once the match is completed, the person who is elderly moves into the sponsor's home and is encouraged to take part in the foster family's social activities and daily responsibilities of the home, thus becoming "just another member of the family."

Summary

Given the unique characteristics of the Tampa Bay area of Florida with regard to the elderly and mentally ill, GCJFS has had an opportunity to develop specialized community-based care in response to the needs of this population. This area of Florida mirrors what other parts of the country will face in years to come.

It has been heartwarming to watch the development of new and exciting programs geared at providing the best quality of life possible for people who are elderly and mentally ill. The driving force behind this growth and success has always been the commitment to provide the best possible services to this most underserved population.

In a recent meeting with Dr. E. Fuller Torrey, he described people who are elderly and seriously mentally ill as one of the most neglected and underserved populations in the United States. In partnership with consumers, family members, advocacy organizations, and professionals, we can see more attention being focused both nationally and internationally on a group that is most entitled to our concern.

References

Harper, M. S. (1981). Care of the mentally ill in nursing homes. *Addendum to National Plan for the Chronically Mentally Ill.* Washington, D.C.: National Institute of Mental Health.

Osgood, N. (1987). Medical College of Virginia.

U.S. Census Bureau (1990).

White House Conference on Aging Report (1981).

CHAPTER 4   THE FAMILY

Family Burden and Family Stigma in Major Mental Illness

Harriet P. Lefley

HARRIET P. LEFLEY, PH.D., IS A PROFESSOR OF PSYCHIATRY AND BEHAVIORAL SCIENCES, UNIVERSITY OF MIAMI SCHOOL OF MEDICINE.

THIS ARTICLE ORIGINALLY APPEARED IN THE *American Psychologist*, 1989, 44(3), 556-560 AND IS REPRINTED WITH PERMISSION.

Mental illnesses are unique in their etiological attributions. They are categories of disorder treated by medical means but viewed as induced by the behavior of others. Despite increasing evidence of diathesis, on the one hand, and on the other, a wide range of nonfamilial environmental stressors that may trigger decompensation (Day et al., 1987), families continue to be viewed as primary toxic agents, particularly in schizophrenia. The hard data emerging from the replications of the expressed emotion (EE) research (Vaughn, Snyder, Jones, Freeman, & Falloon, 1984) and the documented success of correlative psychoeducational interventions (Hogarty et al., 1986) have shifted the emphasis from etiology to potential precipitants of relapse. The EE investigators have cautioned that their research neither implies causality nor explains the decompensation of patients who have little or no contact with families, so that extrafamilial environmental events must be explored (Vaughn et al., 1984). Indeed, many families are perturbed by the implication that, as primary targets of EE research and behavioral training, they may be viewed as the major caregivers of deinstitutionalized patients (Hatfield, 1987). This is an undesired social role with the potential for creating an at-risk population among aging parents, young children, and other relatives whose mental health may be affected by living with the stresses and sorrows occasioned by the psychotic disorder of a family member (Lefley, 1987b).

The question of predictive deviance in families of persons with schizophrenia continues to be an issue (Goldstein, 1985) although the research data invariably demonstrate that investigator-defined patterns of deviance are in no way modal or normative in this population. In the EE research, moreover, the calm, benign affects of low EE rather than the critical overinvolvement of high EE are the prevailing worldwide norms among families of schizophrenic individuals (Jenkins, Karno, de la Selva & Santana, 1986; Leff& Vaughn, 1985), a finding that tends to contradict stereotypes of schizophrenogenesis. Over the years, numerous authors have cautioned that deviance in families, when observed, might be reactive to the experience of living with an individual who has a psychotic disorder. The reactive viewpoint, however, has focused largely on sympathetic or isomorphic responses to the cognitive deficits and aberrant communicative styles of the schizophrenic family member, rather than on the catastrophic impact of mental illness on the family system. Although there are claims of "epistemological confusion" among those who infer directionality from systems-oriented approaches (Dell, 1980), the organizational/systems model, when contrasted with the biologically based stress/ vulnerability paradigm (Rohrbaugh, 1983), nevertheless assigns a functional value to the patient's symptoms and views them as precipitated and maintained for familial homeostasis. In contrast, a conceptualization of families of the mentally ill in terms of a model of stress, coping, and adaptation (Hatfield & Lefley, 1987) views familial behaviors as coping strategies. These represent modes of adjustment, both positive and negative, to the chronic strain of long-term psychosis and its attendant patterns of crises and remissions.

Life Stress and Family Burden

The literature on stressful life events devotes far less attention to continuous or chronic stressors than to discrete events (Kessler, Price, & Wortman, 1985). Yet, in surveying the most widely used scales, Angermeyer (1985) pointed out, "You will find every major event conceivable in an individual's life but you will miss the fact that a close relative has become mentally ill—one of the most devastating and catastrophic events that they can experience" (p. 473). Research on the strains of living with psychiatrically impaired persons is relatively sparse despite its pronounced social importance in an age of deinstitutionalization (Noh & Turner, 1987). Over the years, a small literature has developed on family burden, typically encompassing two descriptive categories. "Objective burden" deals with the actual, objective problems. and "subjective burden" with the psychological distress engendered by the illness. There is some evidence of commonalities of objective burden in families in which a member has a chronic developmental, mental, or physical disability. Frequently, families experience financial hardships due to medical bills and the patients' economic dependency, disruptions of household functioning, curtailment of social activities, and altered relationships with friends and relatives because of the excessive demands of caregiving. Typical also is an attentional focus on the patient together with time commitments that often lead to neglect of others in the family

Regardless of diagnostic category, there are cycles of exacerbation and remission of symptoms with concomitant patterns of hope and disappointment in family members.

(Black, Cohn, Smull, & Crites, 1985; Lefley, 1987a; McCubbin et al., 1982). In many cases, the illness necessitates role and occupational changes for the major caregiver. Thurer (1983) has defined deinstitutionalization as a feminist issue because care of the chronically disabled has historically been assigned to women. In today's world, this may mean a woman's career options will be limited with no commensurate rewards for playing a self-sacrificing role that no longer brings approbation from society. There are, however, components of objective and subjective burden that are specific to mental illness. Regardless of diagnostic category, there are cycles of exacerbation and remission of symptoms with concomitant patterns of hope and disappointment in family members. Objectively, this means failure of the patient to carry out age-appropriate role functions on any consistent basis. Families invest time and energy in help seeking and negotiating the intricacies of the mental health system, and their interactions with service providers are often frustrating, confusing, and humiliating (Hatfield, 1982; Holden & Lewine, 1982; Unger & Anthony, 1984). Families experience stressors in the form of periodic crises involving interactions with emergency services or the police, involuntary commitment procedures that pit families in an adversarial posture against their loved ones, and difficulties in finding appropriate alternatives to hospitalization, especially for persons with bizarre or abusive behavior. The negative impact of the patient's behavior on other family members, particularly children and adolescents is an ongoing concern and may result in a need for ancillary interventions and a new generation of psychotherapists' bills.

Behavior management issues are ongoing tensions between patients and families. Relatives frequently must contend with the patient's abusive or assaultive behaviors, mood swings and unpredictability, socially offensive incidents in public places, conflicts with neighbors, patterns of losing or squandering money, poor personal hygiene, property damage and fire hazards, sleep reversal patterns that keep the household awake, and rejection of medications despite known patterns of relapse. The patient's positive symptoms of paranoid ideation and unprovoked aggression may alternate with negative symptoms of amotivation or anhedonia, attentional deficits, and prolonged silences. In either case, family members are deprived of the rewards and reciprocities of human interaction that most people expect from those they love.

Surveys of family experiences show the effects of stress on the psychological and sometimes the physical health of caregivers, inability of caregivers to make or fulfill personal plans, and their worries about what will happen to the patient "when I am gone," particularly among elderly parents of chronic patients (Lefley, 1987a). Relatives also report the agony of decisions about involuntary commitment of persons whose behavior or self-neglect may be life-threatening and guilt about leaving a loved one in hospitals or community placements of inferior quality—unhappy choices that the patient may resent and hold against them.

Perhaps the most devastating stressor for families, however, is learning how to cope with the patient's own anguish over an impoverished life. Even regressed patients are often aware of their impaired functioning and poor future prospects in relation to others in their age group. Families often mourn the loss of the premorbid personality, perhaps once bright with promise, but

patients' own grieving for lost developmental stages of learning, failed aspirations, and restricted lives can be uniquely stressful for those who love them and can feel their pain.

Stigmatization of Families

Although there has been much discussion of stigmatization of the mentally ill, stigma also generalizes to their families. Social barriers are frequently erected against the relatives and households of negatively valued persons. The behaviors of persons with psychotic disorders may further isolate the family, diminish its reputation, and jeopardize relationships with friends and neighbors.

In the case of mental illness, moreover, there is also an iatrogenic component that may reinforce the self-stigmatization of families. Both the professional community and the society that reflects its values have given them a message of their own culpability in generating or precipitating the devastating illness of a loved one. Although many parents have overcome the Kafkaesque nightmare of trying to determine how, when, why, and under what conditions their behaviors could have led to such horrendous consequences and have decided they did not necessarily cause their offspring's illness (Hatfield, 1981), there is residual and often unjustified guilt. Family members frequently berate themselves for angry responses to provocation, demands that may have been too stressful, expectations that may have been too high, and failure to distinguish between volitional and avolitional behavior in someone retrospectively perceived as ill (Lefley, 1987b).

Stress From Mental Health Professionals

Parents of deinstitutionalized mentally ill adults, many of whom have been ill for 20 or more years, have endured the life strains of their adult children's illness during an epoch of theories of family pathogenesis and correlative treatment models. They have been informed by the media that there are "crazymaking families" and have been given messages by mental health practitioners that, in Goldstein's (1981) words, informed them that "the patient's illness was their fault and they should go away, shrouded in guilt, and leave the professional to undo the damage" (p. 2). Embedded in the emerging self-reports of families' experiences (Dearth, Labenski, Mott, & Pellegrini, 1986; Group for the Advancement of Psychiatry, 1986; Walsh, 1985; Wechsler, 1983) and inferable from some of the critiques of family research (Hirsch & Leff, 1975; Howells & Guirguis, 1985) are four possible sources of iatrogenic damage. These include the psychologically disturbing impact of avoidant or recriminative responses to familial overtures for information and support, particularly when the family is in a condition of great distress; double-binding messages; modes of intervention whose sequelae may alienate the patient's support system; and a self-fulfilling prophecy that may stimulate particular types of behavior in family-provider interactions.

Surveys of families indicate general dissatisfaction with the service delivery system in the treatment of persons with major mental illnesses (Hatfield, 1982; Holden & Lewine, 1982; Unger & Anthony, 1984). There is a pronounced failure of the system to provide substantive help or information to persons with a major role in caregiving or continuity of support. Families report frustrations in attempting to elicit answers to legitimate questions and in dealing with reluctant, ambiguous, and sometimes hos-

Perhaps the most devastating stressor for families, however, is learning how to cope with the patient's own anguish over an impoverished life.

tile communications from mental health professionals. In contrast to the earlier exclusion of family members, the contemporary practice is to catapult them into family therapy, often without clear information and explicit informed consent (McElroy, 1987). Many families perceive systems-oriented (as opposed to supportive and psychoeducational) family therapies as a superimposed and often irrelevant treatment model that ignores their expressed needs for developing appropriate expectations and managing difficult behaviors.

The iatrogenic double bind refers to the cognitive dissonance evoked by contradictory messages from mental health professionals. There is a confusion of options in dealing with multiple therapists of differing persuasions and treatment approaches (see Wechsler, Schwartztol, & Wechsler, 1988), and there are conflicting directives on the appropriate behavior of family caregivers. Thurer (1983) described the mental health risks of the overburdened caregiver, typically the mother of a deinstitutionalized adult patient. She is suffering from the pain of her child's illness, the stigmatization of having "caused" it, and the burden of overseeing a treatment plan that may be unrealistic in terms of time, energy, money, and demands from the rest of the family. At the same time, she is trying to balance conflicting advice from professionals.

> When things do not go smoothly, she is blamed. Should she discourage her child from unnecessary risks, she may be deemed overprotective. Should she encourage independence and seek residential placement, she may be deemed neglectful or rejecting. Should she demur

from following any professional advice, she may be called a "saboteur." (Thurer, 1983, p. 1163)

McFarlane and Beels (1983) have suggested that dual messages are often conveyed to families by basically disapproving clinicians.

If one accepts that double-bind interactions can create distorted, even irrational, communication, then many 'therapeutic' situations can be seen as pathogenic: For instance, covert blame of the family by professionals is often combined with overt attempts to help them, while the contradiction is denied. (p. 316)

When the clinician also conveys the message to a fragile patient that his or her symptoms are useful to others and fulfill some function in the family system and a longsuffering family member is confronted with hostility rather than gratitude for forbearance, this may pave the way for premature separation and loss of the patient's support system (Lefley, 1987b).

One also wonders whether the perceived negative attributions of clinicians evoke defensive strategies in family members that reinforce the clinicians' preconceptions of deviance. Does the family member's history of experiences with providers, which may span many years, generate expectancies of evasiveness, dissembling, deflection of questions, or attitudinal rejection? Do these expectancies in turn produce anticipatory aggressive or demanding behavior in order to receive answers or services? Or, alternatively, does the expected rejection reinforce

In the case of mental illness...both the professional community and the society that reflects its values have given [families] a message of their own culpability in generating or precipitating the devastating illness of a loved one.

a tendency to a) become overly submissive or b) withdraw from confrontation and accelerate the process of disengagement or even abandonment of the patient? Further, is there a "reciprocal Rosenthal effect" as a function of the family's awareness of etiological theory? Many families are exposed to popular media articles on childrearing and assumptions of parental culpability when children are emotionally disabled. Do these theories generate varieties of intrapunitive behavior that include fulfilling perceived negative expectancies of clinicians or researchers? Iatrogenic damage of some types of family theories has been discussed in the literature (Terkelsen, 1983), but these empirical questions of self-stigmatization in familial response have yet to be addressed.

Clinicians With Mentally Ill Relatives

There is some evidence that the basic determinants of family burden, including stigma, generalize across populations regardless of level of sophistication or ease of access to the treatment system. In a study of 84 experienced mental health professionals with chronically mentally ill family members, Lefley (1987c) found that clinicians did not differ from lay family members in their assessments of the psychological burden of patients' behaviors. Moreover, mental health professionals showed significant concordance with nonprofessional family members (Hatfield, 1979) in assigning priority to education on symptoms and medications, behavior management techniques, and involvement with a support group as the most important services that can be offered to families. Despite the fact that the respondents were predominantly involved in the practice of psychotherapy, they considered affiliation with a self-help group and residential separation from the patient more effective coping strategies than individual or family therapy. Most of these clinicians who had lived with the patient for many years and had observed the developmental and later course of illness questioned family pathogenesis. Siblings disputed this even more than parents (Lefley, 1985), suggesting that defensiveness about a putative role in etiology was not a major determinant of response. Some respondents expressed anger in their comments about the impact of the etiological theories of their early training and about the insensitivity of some colleagues to family pain. Yet, they were uncomfortable in discussing mental illness in the family with colleagues. Instructed to disregard personal reticence styles, only 26% of the sample indicated they would have no compunctions about talking openly about the situation, whereas another 26% expressed strong reluctance. More than 90% of the respondents reported that they frequently overheard colleagues make negative or disparaging remarks about family members. Yet, almost one third reported that although they generally disagreed they kept silent. Ambivalent about an appropriate role for a family member-clinician, the majority felt unable or unwilling to contribute information or expertise to successful treatment of the case. Overall, the group seemed uneasy about talking about their personal experiences or edifying colleagues. Although 72% had undergone personal psychotherapy to process the impact of their relative's illness, in some cases there was an apparent reluctance to disclose fully their feelings of anger and

cognitive dissonance to the therapist. Thus, for mental health professionals with seriously mentally ill relatives, family burden may be exacerbated by role conflict because of perceived stigma from colleagues or disturbing contradictions between experience and training.

Changing Perspectives

A number of converging historical events have generated a *zeitgeist* for more favorable attitudes, cognitions, and alliances between families and clinicians. New biogenetic research findings, a widening recognition of the dimensions of family burden, and the pragmatic needs of deinstitutionalization have led to a reconceptualization of family role in the mental health field. Depopulation of hospitals produces a need to reinvolve families as caregivers or support systems for long-term patients. Changes in levels of service funding require a grass-roots constituency for legislative advocacy at the state and federal levels. The remarkable growth and influence of the National Alliance for the Mentally Ill (NAMI) has been a propitious and timely development in this historical process. For the family members who comprise its base, the new organization has provided a vehicle for mutual support, information sharing, public education and advocacy, resource development, and investment in preventive research for future generations. For persons who have endured inordinate pain and distress, these are highly adaptive behaviors that must surely be confusing to professionals who are still reading an older literature on families of schizophrenics.

These developments have also paved the road for new and productive alliances between clinicians and families at both case-centered and societal levels. There are now mandates from regulatory agencies for family involvement in treatment and discharge planning. Increasingly, family members are being solicited to sit on advisory and governance boards, evaluate services, and participate in the mental health planning process. For the first time, both primary and secondary consumers are exercising some control over the services that affect their own lives. Family members are also sharing their experiences and expertise in clinical training and continuing education. In university programs throughout the nation, NAMI members have invited roles as lecturers, workshop conductors, discussants in grand rounds, and presenters at professional conferences. Clinical training grants from the National Institute of Mental Health have regularly required family and consumer input in developing curriculum materials on the seriously mentally ill patient.

This new collaborative model of clinician-family relationships has done much to destigmatize a formerly negatively valued group. It has also reoriented the thinking of many mental health professionals. Views of family pathogenesis are in many cases changing to admiration for coping strengths under conditions of great adversity.

The new respect from service providers and the growing self-confidence of families in their own capabilities as educators, advocates, and survivors may do much to alleviate the stresses of family burden.

References

Angermeyer, N. C. (1985). "Normal deviance"—Changing norms under abnormal circumstances. In P. Pichot, P. Berner, R. Wolf, & K. Thau (Eds.), *Psychiatry, the state of the art. Vol. 7.* Epidemiology and community psychiatry (pp. 473-479). New York: Plenum.

Black, M. M., Cohn, J. F., Smull, M. W., & Crites, L. S. (1985). Individual and family factors associated with risk of institutionalization of mentally retarded adults. *American Journal of Mental Deficiency, 90*(3), 271 - 276.

Day, R., Nielsen, A., Korten, A., Ernberg, G., Dube, K. C., Gebhart, J., Jablensky, A., Leon, C., Marsella, A., Olatawura, M., Sartorius, N., Stromgren, E., Takahashi, R., & Wynne, L. C. (1987). Stressful life events preceding the acute onset of schizophrenia: A cross-national study from the World Health Organization. *Culture, Medicine & Psychiatry, 11,* 123-205.

Dearth, N., Labenski, B. J., Mott, M. E., & Pellegrini, L. M. (1986). *Families helping families: Living with schizophrenia.* New York: Norton.

Dell, P. F. (1980). Researching the family theories of schizophrenia: An exercise in epistemological confusion. *Family Process, 19,* 321-335.

Goldstein, M. J. (1981). Editor's notes. In M J. Goldstein (Ed.), *New developments in interventions with families of schizophrenics.* San Francisco: Jossey-Bass.

Goldstein, M. Z. (1985). Family factors that contribute to the onset of schizophrenia and related disorders: The results of a 15-year prospective longitudinal study. *Acta Psychiatrica Scandinavica (Suppl.) 319,* 7-18.

Group for the Advancement of Psychiatry. (1986). *A family affair—Helping families cope with mental illness: A guide for the professions* (Report No. 119). New York: Brunner/Mazel.

Hatfield, A. B. (1979). Help-seeking behavior in families of schizophrenics. *Journal of Community Psychology, 7*(5), 563-569.

Hatfield, A. B. (1981). Coping effectiveness in families of the mentally ill: An exploratory study. *Journal of Psychiatric Treatment & Evaluation, 3,* 11-19.

Hatfield, A. B. (1982). What families want of family therapists. In W. R. McFarlane (Ed.), *Family therapy of schizophrenia* (pp. 41-65). New York: Guilford.

Hatfield, A. B. (1987). The expressed emotion theory: Why families object. *Hospital & Community Psychiatry, 38,* 341.

Hatfield, A. B., & Lefley, H. P. (1987). *Families of the mentally ill: Coping and adaptation.* New York: Guilford.

Hirsch, S. R., & Leff, J. P. (1975). *Abnormalities in parents of schizophrenics.* London: Oxford University Press.

Hogarty, G. E., Anderson, C. M., Reiss, D. J., Kornblith, S. J., Greenwald, D. P., Javna, C. D., Madonia, M. J., & Environmental/Personal Indicators in the Course of Schizophrenia Research Group. (1986). Family psychoeducation, social skills trainings and maintenance chemotherapy in the aftercare treatment of schizophrenia: I. One year effect of a controlled study on relapse and expressed emotion. *Archives of General Psychiatry, 43,* 633-642.

Holden, D. F., & Lewine, R. R. J. (1982). How families evaluate mental health professionals, resources, and effects of illness. *Schizophrenia Bulletin, 8,* 626-633.

Howells, J. G., & Guirguis, W. R. (1985). The *Family and schizophrenia.* Madison, CT: International Universities Press.

Jenkins, J. H., Karno, M., de la Selva, S., & Santana, F. (1986). Expressed emotion in cross-cultural context: Familial responses to schizophrenia among Mexican Americans. In M. J. Goldstein (Ed.), *Treatment of schizophrenia: Family assessment and intervention* (pp. 35-49). Berlin: Springer-Verlag.

Kessler, R. C., Price, R. H., & Wortman, C. B. (1985). Social factors in psychopathology: Stress, social support, and coping processes. *Annual Review of Psychology, 36,* 531-572.

Leff, J. P., & Vaughn, C. (1985). *Expressed emotion in families: Its significance for mental illness.* New York: Guilford.

Lefley, H. P. (1985). Etiological and prevention views of clinicians with mentally ill relatives. *American Journal of Orthopsychiatry, 55,* 363-370

Lefley, H. P. (1987a). Aging parents as caregivers of mentally ill adult children: An emerging social problem. *Hospital & Community Psychiatry, 38,* 1063- 1070.

Lefley, H. R (1987b). The family's response to mental illness in a relative In A. Hatfield (Ed.), Families of the mentally ill: Meeting the challenges *(New Directions in Mental Health Services No. 34,* pp. 3-21). San Francisco: Jossey-Bass.

Lefley, H. P. (1987c). Impact of mental illness in families of mental health professionals. *Journal of Nervous & Mental Disease, 175,* 613-619.

McCubbin, H. I., Nevin, R. S., Cauble, A. E., Larsen, A., Comeau J. K., & Patterson, J. M. (1982). Family coping with chronic illness. The case of cerebral palsy. In H. I. McCubbin, A. E. Cauble, & J. M. Patterson (Eds.), *Family stress, coping, and social support* (pp. 169-188). Springfield, IL: Charles C Thomas.

McElroy, E. M. (1987). The beat of a different drummer. In A. B. Hatfield & H. P. Lefley (Eds.), *Families of the mentally ill: Coping and adaptation* (pp. 225-243). New York: Guilford.

McFarlane, W. R., & Beels, C. C. (1983). Family research in schizophrenia. A review and integration for clinicians. In W. R. McFarlane (Ed.), *Family therapy in schizophrenia* (pp. 311-323). New York: Guilford

Noh, S., & Turner, R. J. (1987). Living with psychiatric patients: Implications for the mental health of family members. *Social Science & Medicine, 25,* 263-271.

Rohrbaugh, M. (1983, July-August). Family therapy and schizophrenia research: Swimming against the mainstream. *Family Therapy Networker,* pp. 29-31, 62.

Terkelsen, K. G. (1983). Schizophrenia and the family: II. Adverse effects of family therapy. *Family Process, 22,* 191-200.

Thurer, S. L. (1983). Deinstitutionalization and women: Where the buck stops. *Hospital & Community Psychiatry, 34*(12), 1162-1163.

Unger, K. V., & Anthony, W. A. (1984). Are families satisfied with services to young adult chronic patients? A recent survey and a proposed alternative. *(New Directions for Mental Health Services No. 21,* pp 91-97). San Francisco: Jossey-Bass.

Vaughn, C. R., Snyder, K. S., Jones, S., Freeman, W., & Falloon, I. R. H. (1984). Family factors in schizophrenic relapse. *Archives of General Psychiatry, 41,* 1169-1177.

Walsh, M. (1985). *Schizophrenia: Straight talk for families and friends.* New York: Morrow.

Wechsler, J. A. (1983). In a darkness. New York: Irvington.

Wechsler, J. A., Schwartztol, H. W., & Wechsler, N. F. (1988). *In a darkness: A story of young suicide* (2nd ed.). Miami, FL: Pickering Press.

Troubled Journey:
Siblings and Children of People With Mental Illness

DIANE T. MARSH, REX M. DICKENS, RANDI D. KOESKE,
NICK S. YACKOVICH, JANET M. WILSON, JAMI S.
LEICHLITER, AND VICTORIA McQUILLIS

DIANE T. MARSH, PH.D., IS PROFESSOR OF PSYCHOLOGY
AT THE UNIVERSITY OF PITTSBURGH AT GREENSBURG.

REX M. DICKENS IS A MEMBER OF THE BOARD OF
DIRECTORS OF THE SAC NETWORK.

RANDY D. KOESKE IS ASSOCIATE PROFESSOR AT UPG.

THE REMAINING CONTRIBUTORS WERE STUDENTS AT
UPG DURING THE PERIOD OF THE STUDY.

THE EXPERIENTIAL MATERIAL IS TAKEN
FROM THE FORTHCOMING BOOK BY
DR. MARSH AND MR. DICKENS,
*Troubled Journey: Coming to Terms With the Mental Illness
of a Sibling or Parent* (Tarcher/Putnam).

ADDRESS CORRESPONDENCE TO DIANE T. MARSH, PH.D.,
DEPARTMENT OF PSYCHOLOGY, UNIVERSITY OF
PITTSBURGH AT GREENSBURG, GREENSBURG, PA 15601.
APPRECIATION IS EXPRESSED TO MEMBERS OF THE
SIBLINGS AND ADULT CHILDREN (SAC)
NETWORK OF THE NATIONAL ALLIANCE FOR THE
MENTALLY ILL (NAMI).

THIS ARTICLE ORIGINALLY APPEARED IN
Innovations and Research, 1993, 2(2), 13-23
AND IS REPRINTED WITH PERMISSION.

*Two surveys were undertaken to explore
the impact of serious mental illness on
adult siblings and children of people with
mental illness. These family members
reported a pervasive impact on their personal and interpersonal lives, both as
young family members and as adults. The
following topics are discussed: a) the
impact of the mental illness on childhood
and adolescence; b) the legacy for adulthood; c) expressed concerns; d) the process
of coping and adaptation; e) needs of siblings and children; f) mental health problems among siblings and children; and g)
recommendations for siblings and children
and for professionals. Implications for professionals and for NAMI members are also
considered.*

The past decade has witnessed dramatic change in the relationship between
professionals and families of people with
serious mental illness. A number of factors
have influenced this transformation,
including deinstitutionalization, which has
resulted in a service delivery system that is
as much family-based as community-based;
new evidence regarding the biological substrate of serious mental illness; increasing
recognition that families have legitimate
needs and rights of their own that should
be addressed by the mental health system;
compelling documentation of the devastating impact of serious mental illness on families; greater recognition of their positive
contributions and expertise; expanded
knowledge of effective family-oriented
intervention strategies; developments on
the level of national policy and systems
planning that mandate the involvement of
consumers and families; and the consumer-
advocacy movement, which has moved
families into more assertive, informed, and
involved roles.

The ascendant mode of family-professional relationships is now that of collaborative partnerships designed to build on the
strengths and expertise of all parties; to
respect the needs, desires, concerns, and
priorities of families; to enable families to
play an active role in decisions that affect
them; and to establish mutual goals for
treatment and rehabilitation. Until relatively recently, these constructive developments
have had the greatest impact on parents of
people with mental illness, who have
become effective advocates for their children and, increasingly, full members of
multidisciplinary treatment teams. At present, there is an effort to further explore
the familial territory at the level of family
subsystems. Although individual family
members cannot be fully understood without reference to the family system, it is

equally true that their lives as individuals have an integrity and legitimacy that cannot be reduced to their status as family members, and that their experiences and needs are likely to differ significantly as a result of their roles and relationships within the family (Marsh, 1992a).

The current research was undertaken to explore the roles of siblings and children of people with mental illness. Because of their developmental status, young family members share a special vulnerability to the familial experience of mental illness. The disability of a family member can be viewed as an "energy sink" (Bubolz & Whiren, 1984) that consumes energy needed for normal development and that deflects these family members from their expected trajectory. Thus, the impact of mental illness depends on its timing in the life spans of the individual and the family and on the attributes of the illness itself (see Rolland, 1988). It would be expected, for example, that the mental illness of a close relative might undermine the acquisition of basic trust during infancy, the development of peer relationships and academic skills during childhood, and the establishment of a secure sense of identity during adolescence. A child who is confronted from birth with the mental illness of a primary caregiver may be vulnerable to all of these risks.

There are some valuable descriptions of the experiences of siblings and children in books written by and for family members (e.g., Dearth, Labenski, Mott, & Pelligrini, 1986; Garson, 1986; Vine, 1982; Walsh, 1985; Wasow, 1982; Wechsler, Schwartztol, & Wechsler, 1988), and by professionals (e.g., Bernheim & Lehman, 1985; Marsh, 1992a). There is also an expanding literature concerned specifically with siblings and children (e.g., Atkins, 1992; Brown, 1989; Carlisle, 1984; DeChillo, Matorin, & Hallahan, 1987; Dinner, 1989; Garmezy & Rutter, 1983; Guttman, 1989; Johnson,

1988). Of special value are the accounts of siblings and children themselves (e.g., Crosby, 1989; Moorman, 1992; Swados, 1991; Weisburd, 1992), and those that are empirically based (e.g., Horwitz, Tessler, Fisher, & Gamache, 1992; Goodman, 1987; Landeen et al., 1992; Riebschleger, 1991; Silverman, 1989). There have also been efforts to explore resilience among young family members who are coping with the mental illness of a relative (e.g., Anthony & Cohler, 1987; Beardslee & Podorefsky, 1988).

While this expanding literature offers many insights into the experiences and needs of young family members, there is a clear need for additional research designed to delineate their experiences more precisely, to explore the legacy of those experiences for their adult lives, and to elucidate their process of coping and adaptation. In turn, this knowledge can serve as the foundation for more effective and responsive services for siblings and children, both as young family members and as adults.

Method

Two surveys were conducted through the Siblings and Adult Children Network (SAC) of the National Alliance for the Mentally Ill (NAMI). The first survey included 60 subjects, consisting of siblings ($n = 28$), children ($n = 19$), and those who were both siblings and children ($n = 13$). Mean age of respondents was 37.6 years, with a range of 21 to 67 years. A majority were female ($n = 47$) and white ($n = 55$). All of their relatives were diagnosed as having a serious mental illness (most often schizophrenia), and almost one fourth (24.2 %) reported that more than one family member had mental illness, including extended family members. Reflecting the composition of the group, age of respondents at time of diagnosis ranged from birth to age 37 (mean age = 14.3). They had experienced the mental illness of a relative for an average of 23.1 years (range = 2 to 50 years).

The first survey consisted of both structured and open-ended questions. In addition to demographic data, structured questions were used to assess the relative importance of coping resources, ranging from 1 ("not helpful") to 5 ("extremely helpful"), and of needs, ranging from 1 ("not important") to 5 ("extremely important"). Open-ended questions probed the following: a) the impact of their relative's mental illness on their own childhood and adolescence; b) the impact on their adult lives; c) how they had been changed by the illness; d) what had been most difficult and most helpful; e) whether they had gone through stages as they adapted to the illness; f) whether they had experienced mental health problems themselves; and g) whether there had been any positive consequences of the illness. Respondents were also asked for suggestions for other family members and for professionals.

The second survey included 75 subjects; a majority were again female (77.6 %) and white (91.3%). Mean age was 40.6 years, with a range of 21 to 77 years. Consistent with the characteristics of NAMI members as a whole (Flynn, 1992), their educational level was very high (86.2% had completed college or graduate school). In this survey, we asked adult siblings and children to rate their frequency of concern with 24 issues that had emerged in the first survey (see

TABLE 1.
EXPRESSED CONCERNS OF SIBLINGS AND CHILDREN

(*n* = 75)

Expressed Concern	Mean Rating	Rating of 3 or higher	Rating of 4 or 5
1. Caregiving Concerns	3.83	94.4%	62.0%
2. Family Disruption	3.70	82.9%	64.3%
3. Trouble Balancing Needs	3.39	81.4%	51.4%
4. Own Needs Not Met	3.25	79.2%	48.6%
5. Grew Up Too Fast	3.25	66.7%	51.4%
6. Guilt	3.16	74.4%	45.8%
7. Helplessness & Hopelessness	3.12	75.3%	35.6%
8. Need to be Perfect	3.07	63.4%	46.5%
9. Poor Self-Esteem	3.04	75.0%	34.7%
10. Chronic Sorrow	3.03	63.9%	38.9%
11. Emotional Anesthesia	3.01	69.6%	43.5%
12. Trust Problems	3.01	68.6%	40.0%
13. Intimacy Problems	3.00	69.1%	42.3%
14. Unfulfilled Potential	2.93	64.3%	35.7%
15. Grief	2.87	63.4%	28.2%
16. Felt Abandoned	2.83	60.8%	39.1%
17. Socially Isolated	2.79	54.3%	30.0%
18. Identity Problems	2.78	59.2%	31.0%
19. Depression	2.73	65.7%	18.6%
20. Fear of Violence	2.72	57.0%	22.3%
21. Affected Choices	2.63	50.7%	29.6%
22. Fear of Suicide	2.62	52.1%	22.5%
23. Separation Problems	2.60	51.4%	34.3%
24. Fear of Mental Illness	2.47	44.5%	20.9%

Note. Rating scale: 1=never, 2=rarely, 3=sometimes, 4=often, 5=always.

Table 1), ranging from 1 ("never") to 5 ("always"). Respondents were also asked whether they had sought personal psychotherapy and, if so, whether it had been helpful, ranging from 1 ("not helpful) to 5 ("extremely helpful"). For both surveys, there was some missing data due to incomplete surveys and to the inapplicability of some questions concerning childhood among respondents whose exposure to mental illness commenced later in life.

Results

The surveys provided a rich array of data regarding the experiences, coping resources, and needs of siblings and children. Results will be discussed in connection with the following topics: a) the impact of the mental illness on childhood and adolescence; b) the legacy for adulthood; c) expressed concerns; d) the process of coping and adaptation; e) needs of siblings and children; f) mental health problems among siblings and children; and g) recommendations for other siblings and children and for professionals.

Impact on Childhood and Adolescence
Respondents who were dealing with the mental illness of a relative during their own childhood or adolescence reported a wide range of adverse consequences for themselves and their families. Some of the most important include the following: a) disruption of normal development (e.g., absence of a model of normal development, difficulty determining which experiences were "normal" and which were not); b) a subjective burden (e.g., intense feelings of grief and loss, empathic pain over the suffering of other family members); c) an objective burden (e.g., need to deal with symptomatic behavior and illness-related crises, stigmatization); d) altered roles and relationships (e.g., risk of "parentification" among children who assume responsibility for a parent

with mental illness, "replacement child syndrome" among siblings who strive for perfectionism to spare their parents more anguish); e) identity issues (e.g., fear of developing mental illness themselves, impaired sense of self); f) personal risks (e.g., mental health problems themselves, especially depression and anxiety); g) familial consequences (e.g., disruption and stress, retreat behind a facade of normalcy); h) relationships outside the family (e.g., impaired peer relationships, social isolation and discomfort); and i) school (e.g., poor school performance, superachievement at the expense of personal life).

> It's like a large cloud moved over all our heads and everyone was paralyzed for years.
>
> I became a perfect child to spare my parents more grief.
>
> The mental illness shaped my life—it revolved around her problems.
>
> I am a superachiever with a great big hole inside.

Legacy for Adulthood
Many negative sequelae were also reported for adulthood, including continuation of some of the difficulties experienced in childhood and adolescence, as well as the emergence of new concerns in later life. Some of the latter included the following: a) the personal legacy (e.g., impaired self-esteem and self-concept, arrested emotional development, "emotional anesthesia"); b) the interpersonal legacy (e.g., fear of rejection, excessive concern with pleasing others); c) problems related to intimacy, commitment, and sexuality (e.g., avoidance of intimacy, inability to trust others); d) marriage and childrearing (e.g., concern about genetic risks for own children, difficulty balancing responsibilities to families of origin and procreation); e) caregiving responsibilities (e.g., intermittent or continuous caregiving, sense of lifetime responsibility);

TABLE 2.
COPING RESOURCES OF SIBLINGS AND CHILDREN
DURING CHILDHOOD, ADOLESCENCE, AND ADULTHOOD

(*n* = 60)

	Coping resource	To age 10	Age 11-20	Over age 20
1.	Personal qualities	2.67	3.31	3.88
2.	Family	2.46	2.36	2.83
3.	Friends	1.77	2.56	3.17
4.	Professionals	1.04	1.53	3.08
5.	Other NAMI members	1.25	1.73	3.60
6.	A support group	1.00	1.52	3.47
7.	Clergy	1.17	1.25	1.67
8.	Other	2.25	3.50	4.38

Note. Rating scale: 1 = not helpful, 2 = somewhat helpful, 3 = helpful, 4 = very helpful, 5 = extremely helpful.

f) balancing family responsibilities and personal needs (e.g., sacrifice of personal life to meet family needs, loss of family relationships in the quest for self-preservation); and g) impact on career (e.g., sense of unfulfilled potential, effect on career choice).

> I shut down emotionally some time in my youth and this carried into adulthood.

> I feel like a perpetual outsider.

> I still feel like that little girl who had to take care of everything herself.

> Living with fear—fear that I would lose control and become ill, fear that my children would have it, fear of the unexpected.

Expressed Concerns

The open-ended questions allowed siblings and children to define their own reality and to portray their experiences in their own words. Their responses provide compelling testimony regarding the impact of mental illness on the lives of these family members. Complementing the experiential material, the second survey provided empirical data regarding the relative importance of specific concerns, as presented in Table 1.,

All of the items represent important concerns among adult siblings and children. In fact, the empirical results do not begin to convey the anguish behind the numbers. For example, one survey (returned too late to be included in the data analysis) included nine items with ratings of "5+" (e.g., feelings of guilt: "5+++"). The following were the ten most salient themes (in rank order): caregiving concerns, family disruption, trouble balancing needs, own needs not met, grew up too fast, guilt, helplessness and hopelessness, need to be perfect, poor self-esteem, and chronic sorrow. Over 50% of respondents reported concern with all but one of the 24 issues, at least sometimes. The exception was fear of mental illness (44.5%), an unsurprising finding in light of the age and educational level of the sample. At this point in their lives, respondents were likely to be aware of the late adolescent and early adulthood onset of serious mental illness; whatever their earlier concerns, they are past the period of greatest risk.

In describing their experiences with mental illness, these family members underscored the consequences of the illness for their own lives.

> I have spent the last 25 years trying to find confidence, love, acceptance. I am extremely sensitive and weep easily. I

avoid intimacy but crave it desperately. I want more friends but fear to trust.

I learned to be fearful of everything in my environment and to devalue myself. Inability to attach, to express emotions to others and to myself, and to trust.

I blame myself for anything that goes wrong, have trouble enjoying even the simplest things in life.

For years I thought no one would really want me because I came from a 'defective' family. I still have a tendency to hold back in relationships for fear that I will be abandoned or something unexpected will happen.

Many of the concerns were shared by these family members, with relatively consistent ratings across role and age at time of onset. For example, caregiving concerns was cited by almost all respondents. For some items, however, there were differences among siblings (n = 48), children (n = 15), and those who were both siblings and children (n = 10). Based on analyses of variance, there were significant differences on 12 of the 24 items (and on average impact); all of these reflected higher ratings among children (including those who were also siblings). Thus, as a group, children appear to be more vulnerable to the consequences of a close relative's mental illness than those who are just siblings.

In addition, there were differences in ratings as a function of age at the onset of their relative's illness. There were significant differences on 12 of the 24 items (and on average impact); 11 items received highest ratings by respondents who were age 10 or younger at the time of onset (the remaining item received higher ratings by the two younger groups). Thus, the younger the family member at the time of onset, the greater the susceptibility to the adverse effects of mental illness. Reflecting the importance of role and age at onset, family members who were both children and under age 11 at the time of onset had higher

ratings for the following expressed concerns: own needs not met, grew up too fast, need to be perfect, poor self-esteem, trust problems, intimacy problems, felt abandoned, identity problems, and depression.

Where do you go when you need to revamp your whole life. I have basically a wasted life.

I feel I missed out on being a kid. Now I miss what I didn't get, including friendships, sports, and learning to take better care of me.

I had a hard time moving away, felt guilty all the time. My mom still wants me to move home.

Before I went to a counselor, I did not realize I had suffered at all—I was numbed out, frozen.

Coping and Adaptation

Respondents were asked to rate the relative value of a range of coping resources during the three developmental phases (to age 10, from age 11 to 20, over age 20). Results are presented in Table 2.

During each of the phases, respondents reported that their personal qualities were their most important resource. It is noteworthy, however, that no resource was rated as helpful during the first 10 years (all ratings fell in the "not helpful" and "somewhat helpful ranges." In fact, aside from their personal qualities as adolescents, it is not until adulthood that siblings and children rate other coping resources as at least helpful. The absence of resources among the youngest family members is underscored by the differences in mean ratings for all resources (including "other") to age 10 (mean rating = 1.70: "not helpful"), from age 11 to 20 (mean rating = 2.22: "somewhat helpful"), and over age 20 (mean rating = 3.26: "helpful").

Several respondents cited additional resources that had been helpful, such as creative activity (e.g., painting, writing, theater); regular exercise; volunteer work;

and geographic separation from their relative. When they were asked whether they had gone through a series of stages as they adapted to the mental illness of a relative, 91.2% of respondents answered affirmatively, frequently offering descriptions of the stages they had experienced during their own process of adaptation. They also shared personal coping strategies.

Learn about yourself and the impact of mental illness on your life.

Don't keep the illness a secret—share with others you can trust.

Separate the relative from the illness and yourself from your relative.

Be compassionate, caring, and concerned, but take care of yourself.

Because of the potential for a resilient response to stressful events, siblings and children were asked whether there were any positive consequences as a result of the mental illness. A large majority answered positively (86.7%). They cited the following benefits: a) personal growth and development (e.g., increased tolerance, empathy, compassion, understanding); b) better self-concept (e.g., greater strength, discipline, personal stability); c) enhanced skills (e.g., effective coping skills); d) significant contributions (e.g., assistance to other family members); e) effective advocacy (e.g., reformation of the mental health system); f) improved family and social life (e.g., special closeness among family members); g) healthier perspective and priorities (e.g., knowledge of what is important); and h) greater appreciation of life and mental health (e.g., more cognizant of blessings).

It made me compassionate and understanding in my career.

It helped us to realize our abilities and talents, how precious life is.

Like the old aluminum foil ad, I am 'oven-tempered for flexible strength.'

It helped us to get our priorities straight—no phoniness or concern for status.

It is important to note, however, that these positive consequences never occurred in isolation; virtually all surveys attested to negative consequences.

Needs of Siblings and Children
Respondents were also asked to rate the relative importance of seven needs during the three developmental phases. Mean ratings for each of the needs are presented in Table 3.

TABLE 3.
NEEDS OF SIBLINGS AND CHILDREN DURING CHILDHOOD, ADOLESCENCE, AND ADULTHOOD

($n = 60$)

	Need to Age 10	Age 11-20	Over Age 20
1. Information about mental illness, etc.	2.70	4.22	4.59
2. Skills for coping with the illness, etc.	3.39	4.33	4.48
3. Support for yourself	3.61	4.28	4.13
4. Services for your relative	3.71	4.31	4.76
5. Meaningful involvement in your relative's treatment	2.22	3.20	3.77
6. Working through your own reactions to the illness	3.64	4.33	4.33
7. Contact with other family members	3.50	3.72	3.87
8. Other	4.50	5.00	5.00

Note. Rating scale: 1 = not important, 2 = somewhat important, 3 = important, 4 = very important, 5 = extremely important.

The number of subjects providing ratings varied for the three phases, since some respondents (particularly siblings) were not dealing with the mental illness of a family member until adolescence or adulthood. While there were some differences in rankings of needs during the three developmental phases, all of the needs received relatively high ratings. Throughout childhood, adolescence, and adulthood, their most compelling needs were for satisfactory services for their relative, for working through their own reactions to the illness, for skills to cope with the illness, and for personal support (mean ratings for these needs fell in the "very important" range).

The need for information about mental illness and related issues received similarly high ratings during adolescence and adulthood. In contrast, there was less consensus regarding their need for meaningful involvement in treatment, which received the lowest overall rating (mean = 3.06: "important"). Some respondents rated that need as "extremely important;" others wanted no involvement (one wrote: "Give us a break."). Some additional needs were also cited, including personal psychotherapy, validation of personal needs and plans, constructive relationships outside the family, and open communication within the family. The comments of respondents reflected all of these needs.

> Learn as much as you can.

> Join a support group.

> Learn to express your needs assertively.

> Resolve your own issues and be sensitive to their impact on adult relationships.

Personal Mental Health Problems

Many adult siblings and children reported personal mental health problems, primarily depression and anxiety. More than three-fourths (77.3%) had received personal psychotherapy. This high level undoubtedly reflects the anguish and demoralization experienced by family members of people who have serious mental illness. These family members reported a high level of satisfaction with therapy. A majority (62.7%) reported that therapy had been very or extremely helpful (mean rating = 3.6; only one respondent rated it as not helpful). Consistent with our findings regarding expressed concerns, the percentage of family members who sought psychotherapy varied with role (sibling = 77.1%, child = 80.0%, both roles = 90.0%), and with age at onset of relative's illness (to age 10 = 90.0%, 11-20 = 76.9%, over 20 = 77.3%)

Thus, although the overall level of personal therapy is very high for all adult siblings and children, family members who are both siblings and children or who are under age 10 at the onset of illness are more likely to seek personal psychotherapy.

> It was hell living at home. My sister and I were abandoned emotionally for many years. I was so depressed and lonely. I even thought of suicide. My needs were never important I was in counseling for many years.

> I've been in and out of therapy for depression. I've been looking for love in inappropriate people and ways, have a lot of trouble socially.

> As a child I tried desperately not to have a problem because our family had so many. So I became perfectionistic, hid my fears and concerns and needs from everyone. I've probably always had a certain degree of depression as a result of my mother's illness. When my father died, I suffered a major depression and went into therapy.

> I've been in counseling for four years now. I've realized how her illness has hurt me—low self-esteem, relationship problems, etc. Only through therapy have I started to turn things around.

Suggestions for Siblings and Children

Respondents were asked to make suggestions for other siblings and children.

They offered a range of constructive suggestions. These included the following: a) learn as much as possible (e.g., about mental illness, coping skills, community resources); b) join an existing support group for siblings and adult children (e.g., for sharing, for advocacy); c) begin a support group if none is available; d) expand activities and relationships outside of the family; e) do not let the mental illness of a relative take over your life; f) locate a good therapist; g) rid yourself of stigma; and h) become active in education and advocacy efforts.

> Learn whatever you can about the illness, talk to others. Don't be ashamed, care for the ill relative without giving up your needs, and become active in teaching the world about mental illness.

> I was helped by discovering NAMI. I've gained more information about mental illness through NAMI than I was ever given as a child or adolescent.

> Learn to set limits, to say no, to live apart, and not to feel guilty about it.

> I say positive affirmations every day—that I am worthy of the good things in life, of being loved.

Suggestions for Professionals

Suggestions for professionals included the following: a) become knowledgeable about the experiences and needs of all family members; b) visit an existing family support group and a SAC support group if available; c) form collaborative partnerships with family members; d) include adult siblings and children as members of the treatment team if they are interested and available; e) avoid blaming and pathologizing family members; f) address the needs of all family members as early as possible; g) be available to answer their questions and respond to their concerns; h) make referrals to existing support and advocacy groups; i) assist families in achieving a balance that meets the needs of all family members; j) offer services for family members in clinical settings; k) serve as a resource and consultant to existing family support and advocacy groups.

> Be kind and considerate—have time for them. Encourage them to open up and be accepting of their feelings. Don't stigmatize or label. Don't look at them and treat them like they're ill also. Listen to them. Involve them. Treat them with dignity.

> The entire family system needs to be addressed. All family members are affected by a loved one's mental illness.

> Allow us to grieve. Take us seriously but help us to take ourselves less seriously. Don't treat us like we're crazy. Help us to love ourselves.

> Be aware of our pain. I am angry at the doctors who blamed my parents, which hurt them as much as losing a daughter to mental illness.

Discussion

Initially, it is important to note the limitations of the current sample, which is primarily middle class, middle aged, and white (reflecting the membership of NAMI). Thus, it is essential to replicate the present findings with other socioeconomic, ethnic, and age groups. For example, research should be undertaken with young children and adolescents who can offer a current perspective on their experiences rather than the retrospective accounts provided by adults, and with adult siblings and children who are not members of NAMI.

In spite of these limitations, results of the present investigation offer compelling evidence for the pervasive impact of mental illness on the lives of siblings and children, both as young family members and as adults. Indeed, from the moment that mental illness erupts in their families, their lives are transformed by this catastrophic event and their journeys deflected from the normal developmental course. Our results provide insight into the nature of this transformation, which affects all aspects of their personal intrafamilial, and extrafamilial lives.

> I carry pain about my sister every day. I constantly battle low self-esteem and shame. Our family has lost a great deal to this illness.

Adult siblings and children recounted many detrimental effects of the mental illness for their own lives as young family members. These included disruption of normal development; the experience of a powerful subjective and objective burden; distorted roles and relationships; impaired self-esteem and personal identity; personal mental health problems, especially depression and anxiety; familial disruption and stress; social isolation and discomfort; unsatisfactory peer relationships and academic performance; and a sense of having grown up too quickly.

> I lost a sense of knowing what I wanted, and how to set my own agenda, control my own life, choose relationships.

These family members also reported a profound impact on their adult lives, which are affected by the continuing problems of their childhood and adolescence and by new concerns that emerge in adulthood. As adults, siblings and children reported a powerful personal legacy, including impaired self-esteem and self-concept, arrested emotional development, and a

I developed some exceptional coping skills: problem solving, soothing, getting along with difficult people, intellectual searching. I even learned to look inside myself and grow spiritually. And my siblings and I have a level of tolerance that is useful in our fast-changing society.

sense of unfulfilled potential. They also described a pervasive interpersonal legacy that affects all adult relationships and that undermines their capacity for intimacy, trust, and commitment. This interpersonal legacy may deter them from marriage, since over one third (37.3%) had remained single, a higher proportion than the 10% that the Census Bureau estimated in 1992 would never marry. When they do marry, siblings and children report difficulty balancing the demands of their families of origin and procreation, and often fear that their own children will develop mental illness.

> I was afraid to have children because I had a fear that they would be mentally ill like my dad.

Many of these concerns are shared by family members who are siblings, children, and both siblings and children, such as anxiety about caregiving for their ill relative. There are also differences among the three groups, who reported unique experiences and problems as well as shared concerns. For instance, siblings sometimes expressed resentment that the ill brother or sister had received so much attention. Based on our overall results, the most important variable appears to be age at onset of the relative's illness. There are inherent risks for young children who are exposed to a primary caregiver whose reality contact is impaired and whose energy is depleted by the mental illness. There are also risks for siblings who are confronted

TABLE 4.
EFFECTIVE COPING STRATEGIES

Accept the mental illness and its consequences.

Seek information about mental illness, services, and resources.

Develop realistic expectations for all family members.

Learn about the experiences of other siblings and children.

Reframe to focus on personal and familial strengths.

Develop communication, conflict resolution, and problem solving skills.

Develop stress management skills.

Learn to express your needs assertively.

Develop strategies and skills for coping with your relative.

Resolve your emotional burden.

Employ mature defenses.

Seek personal counseling when appropriate.

Assume a constructive role in the family.

Join an existing support group for siblings and adult children.

Start a support group if none is available.

Share feelings and coping strategies with other siblings and children.

Expand activities and relationships outside the family.

Strive to maintain a normal lifestyle.

Learn to set limits.

Do not let the mental illness of a relative take over your life.

Establish collaborative relationships with professionals.

Educate professionals about family experiences and needs.

Become active in advocacy efforts.

From Marsh and Dickens (in press).

---

during their early years with the ravaging aftereffects of the mental illness of a brother or sister.

Thus, it is not surprising that many adult siblings and children who were confronted with mental illness during their first decade of life reported problems related to trust, identity, parentification, separation, intimacy, and affective blunting. These results are consistent with epigenetic stage-based conceptions of development, which assume that disruption during a particular developmental phase may undermine the resolution of the issues associated with that phase. The earlier exposure of children to this catastrophic event may result in a greater residue of "unfinished business" from childhood and a commensurate reduction in the energy available for adulthood.

> I lost my identity in relationships. Have only just begun to identify what I want, who I really am.

The study also illuminated the process of coping and adaptation. Siblings and children reported that potential coping resources differed in usefulness during childhood, adolescence, and adulthood. Significantly, respondents did not find any resources helpful during childhood; during adolescence, they rated just their personal qualities as helpful. Only as adults are they able to make use of a number of coping resources, including their personal qualities, other NAMI members, a support group, friends, and professionals. Clearly, in spite of their greater vulnerability, young family members have fewer resources than adult siblings and children to assist them in coping with this cataclysmic event. In addition, from the perspective of professional practice, it is important to note that many respondents reported mental health problems themselves, primarily depression and anxiety. Many of these family members affirmed the value of personal psychotherapy, particularly individual therapy.

> My mother needed help and refused. So I was completely powerless and sank into depression. Because of her illness, I went into therapy. That helped me develop more healthily. That's the only good result I can see coming out of this tragedy.

Based on our surveys and on the general literature concerned with coping and adaptation, Table 4 summarizes a range of effective coping strategies.

Almost all respondents indicated that they had moved through a series of stages as they adapted to the mental illness of a relative. Their process of adaptation generally conforms to a three-stage structure similar to the one delineated by Rando (1984) in connection with bereavement: a) avoidance, which is characterized by feelings of shock, denial, and disbelief; b) confrontation, which is characterized by intense feelings of grief and loss and by a range of negative emotions, including anger, guilt, and despair; and c) resolution, which is characterized by understanding and acceptance of the mental illness and by

reinvestment of energy in one's own life. As is the case with the biological death of a relative, however, there is no single pattern of adaptation nor is there a universal and time-limited series of sequential stages (see Wortman & Silver, 1989). Furthermore, there is much evidence for the presence of "chronic sorrow" on a continuing basis (see Marsh, 1992a, for a discussion of these issues).

> It's like someone close died—but there's no closure. It's never over.

The study provided impressive evidence for resilience among siblings and children of people with mental illness. They reported many positive sequelae, including beneficial changes in self-concept and self-efficacy, in compassion and tolerance toward others, in contributions to society, in family relationships and social life, and in attitudes and priorities. Consistent with the literature concerned with familial stress (see Figley, 1989), it appears that a catastrophic stressor, such as mental illness, generally results in disintegration of existing modes of functioning, which in turn offers the opportunity for renewal and reintegration.

> I developed some exceptional coping skills: problem solving, soothing, getting along with difficult people, intellectual searching. I even learned to look inside myself and grow spiritually. And my siblings and I have a level of tolerance that is useful in our fast-changing society.

As is the case in the present study, however, positive responses to stress often exist concurrently with a wide range of negative reactions and feelings. Indeed, virtually every survey offered cogent evidence for the anguish that accompanies the mental illness of a relative.

> Any increased sensitivity to others or any other 'side effects' would be traded in a eyeblink for a healthy relative.

Results of our surveys underscore the importance of a number of central needs among siblings and children, including their needs for information, for skills, for support, for services for their relative, for resolving their own reactions to the illness, for contact with other family members (especially other adult siblings and children), and for maintaining the integrity of their own lives. Some siblings and children expressed a need for meaningful involvement in the treatment of their relative; others preferred not to be involved. These needs remain important throughout childhood, adolescence, and adulthood, although there were some differences in relative importance of the needs. From a life span perspective, the stability of these needs provides a cornerstone for effective professional practice, since services can be designed to address the needs of siblings and children throughout their lives.

For years I thought no one would really want me because I came from a 'defective' family. I still have a tendency to hold back in relationships for fear that I will be abandoned or something unexpected will happen.

Implications for Professional Training and Practice

These results have a number of important implications for professional training and practice with siblings and children as young family members and as adults. The initial step involves cognitive restructuring, as professional practice is reformulated to focus on all members of the family and as service delivery systems are redesigned to meet their continuing needs. It is noteworthy that 80% of respondents indicated that professionals were not helpful until they reached adulthood. If the needs of these family members had been met as they were growing up, the adverse legacy for their adult lives might have been diminished.

In addition, graduate programs for mental health professionals should be modified to prepare clinicians to work effectively with all family members. For example, existing curricula should be expanded to incorporate the relevant literature concerned with family burden and needs, with the unique perspectives of siblings and children, and with new modes and models of professional practice with families. In addition, internships should offer professionals in training an opportunity to develop the skills and strategies necessary for collaboration with family members, including siblings and children, and for meeting their needs.

Finally, a range of services should be available to meet the needs of all family members from the moment of diagnosis. Services for siblings and children should include five general components: a) a didactic component that provides information about mental illness and community resources; b) a skills component that offers training in communication, conflict resolution, problem solving, assertiveness, behavioral management, and stress management; c) an emotional component that provides opportunities for grieving, for sharing, and for mobilizing resources; d) a family process component that focuses on the impact of mental illness on the family system, family subsystems, and individual family members; and e) a social component that offers support, reinforcement for normal developmental experiences and goals, constructive role models, and opportunities for advocacy.

TABLE 5.
EDUCATIONAL PROGRAM FOR ADOLESCENT AND ADULT SIBLINGS AND CHILDREN

Week 1. Nature and Purpose of Program
Introductions; overview of educational program; description of agency program; written survey of needs and requests of family members.

Week 2. Mental Illness I
Diagnosis; etiology; prognosis; symptoms.

Week 3. Mental Illness II
Treatment; medication; diathesis-stress model.

Week 4. The Family Experience
Family burden; family needs; life span issues; family roles and relationships; special concerns of siblings and children.

Week 5. Developmental Perspectives
Normal child and adolescent development; peer relationships; separation.

Week 6. Stress, Coping, and Adaptation
The general process; resources and strategies; increasing coping effectiveness.

Week 7. Enhancing Personal and Family Effectiveness I
Behavior management; conflict resolution; communication; problem solving.

Week 8. Enhancing Personal and Family Effectiveness II
Stress management; assertiveness; achieving a personal and family balance.

Week 9. Family-Professional Relationships

Week 10. Services, Providers, and Resources
Comprehensive system of community-based care; support groups.

From Marsh and Dickens (in press)

There are two general forms of intervention: nonclinical and clinical. Nonclinical services are designed primarily to provide education and support. Examples include educational programs, support groups, and multimodal programs. See Table 5 for an example of an educational program for adolescent and adult siblings and children.

Clinical services are designed to provide treatment for problems that are reactive to the mental illness of a relative or for more serious mental health problems that may have been precipitated or exacerbated by current stress. Clinical formats include individual, marital, family, and group therapy.

Researchers have consistently found that family members (primarily parents) perceive nonclinical services as the more valuable form of intervention (e.g., Hatfield, 1981; Lefley, 1987). These results have not yet been replicated with siblings and children, however, and SAC members who responded to our surveys cited the benefits of both nonclinical and clinical intervention. Thus, it is important to inform siblings and children of all available services and to assist them in making an informed choice regarding their use of specific services. Given the diversity among family members, it is likely that some will prefer nonclinical services, that others will choose a course of psychotherapy, and that still others will benefit from both forms of intervention.

Our overall results support the value of a multimodal approach to intervention designed to meet all the needs of siblings and children, and of a group format that provides contact with other family members. Groups can meet essential needs for information, skills, and support, and can be designed for school age, preadolescent, adolescent, and adult members. Such groups also offer opportunities to improve self-esteem and self-confidence, to develop a greater sense of mastery and control, to enhance social interaction, to reinforce normal patterns of growth and development, to provide assistance with peer relationships, and to encourage constructive long-term goals. While few resources are currently available for professionals who wish to work with siblings and children of people with mental illness (e.g., Dickens, 1989), there are some resources concerned with professional practice with siblings who are dealing with other forms of disability (e.g., Marsh, 1992b; Powell & Gallagher, 1993).

Implications for NAMI

Results of this study also have important implications for NAMI, which was often cited by adult siblings and children as their most valuable resource. Most important, it is essential to reach out to young siblings and children as early as possible: to acknowledge their anguish, to address their needs, and to empower them in coping with this catastrophic event. Services should be responsive to their unique needs and concerns, to their developmental level, and to their changing needs throughout the life span.

Specific suggestions include increased support for siblings and children within NAMI and educational programs designed to sensitize families and professionals to the needs of young family members. Adult siblings and children are particular suited for offering a corrective emotional experience for young siblings and children, for facilitating support groups, and for developing and implementing new initiatives for this population. For example, adult siblings and children might serve as mentors for young family members in a program similar to Big Brothers and Big Sisters.

References

Anthony, E. J. & Cohler, B. J. (Eds.). (1987). *The invulnerable child.* New York: Guilford.

Atkins, F. D. (1992). An uncertain future: Children of mentally ill parents. *Journal of Psychosocial Nursing, 30,* 13-16.

Beardslee, W. R. & Podorefsky, D. (1988). Resilient adolescents whose parents have serious affective and other psychiatric disorders: Importance of self-understanding and relationships. *American Journal of Psychiatry, 145,* 63-69.

Bernheim, K.F. & Lehman, A.F. (1985). *Working with families of the mentally ill.* New York: Norton.

Brown, E.M. (1989). *My parent's keeper: Adult children of the emotionally disturbed.* Oakland, CA: New Harbinger.

Bubolz, M.M. & Whiren, A.P. (1984). The family of the handicapped: An ecological model for policy and practice. *Family Relations, 33,* 5-12.

Carlisle, W. (1984). *Siblings of the mentally ill.* Saratoga, CA: R & E Publishers.

Crosby, D. (1989). First person account: Growing up with a schizophrenic mother. *Schizophrenia Bulletin, 15,* 507-509.

Dearth, N., Labenski, B.J., Mott, M.E. & Pelligrini, L.M. (1986). *Families helping families: Living with schizophrenia.* New York: Norton.

DeChillo, N., Matorin, S. & Hallahan, C. (1987). Children of psychiatric patients: Rarely seen or heard. *Health and Social Work, 12,* 296-302 .

Dickens, R. (Ed.). (1989). *Siblings and Adult Children Network group facilitator's guide.* National Alliance for the Mentally Ill, Arlington, VA.

Dinner, S.H. (1989). *Nothing to be ashamed of: Growing up with mental illness in your family.* New York: Lothrup.

Figley, C.R. (1989). *Helping traumatized families.* San Francisco: Jossey-Bass.

Flynn, L.M. (1992). NAMI member survey offers advocacy tool. *NAMI Advocate, 3*(2), p. 12.

Garmezy, N., & Rutter, M. (Eds.). (1983). *Stress, coping, and development in children.* New York: McGraw-Hill.

Garson, S. (1986). *Out of our minds.* Buffalo, NY: Prometheus.

Goodman, S.H. (1987). Emory University Project on Children of Disturbed Parents. *Schizophrenia Bulletin, 13,* 411-423.

Guttman, H.A. (1989). Children in families with emotionally disturbed parents. In L. Combrinck-Graham (Ed.), *Children in family contexts: Perspectives on treatment* (pp. 252-276). New York: Guilford.

Hatfield, A.B. (1981). Coping effectiveness in families of the mentally ill: An exploratory study. *Journal of Psychiatric Treatment and Evaluation, 3,* 11-19.

Horwitz, A.V., Tessler, R.C., Fisher, G.A. & Gamache, G.M. (1992). The role of adult siblings in providing social support to the severely mentally ill. *Journal of Marriage and the Family, 54,* 233-241.

Johnson, J.T. (1988). *Hidden victims.* New York: Doubleday.

Landeen, J., Whelton, C., Dermer, S., Cardamone, J., Munroe-Blum, H. & Thornton, J. (1992). Needs of well siblings of persons with schizophrenia. *Hospital and Community Psychiatry, 43,* 266-269.

Lefley, H.B. (1987). Impact of mental illness in families of mental health professionals. *Journal of Nervous and Mental Disease, 175,* 613-619.

Marsh, D.T. (1992a). *Families and mental illness: New directions in professional practice.* New York: Praeger.

Marsh, D.T. (1992b). *Families and mental retardation: New directions in professional practice.* New York: Praeger.

Marsh, D.T. & Dickens, R.M. (in press). *Troubled journey: Coming to terms with the mental illness of a sibling or parent.* New York: Tarcher/Putnam.

Moorman, M. (1992). *My sister's keeper: Learning to cope with a sibling's mental illness.* New York: Norton.

Powell, T.H. & Gallagher, P.A. (1993). *Brothers a sisters: A special part of exceptional families (2nd ed.).* Baltimore: Brookes.

Rando, T.A. (1984). *Grief, dying, and death: Clinical interventions for caregivers.* Champaign, IL: Research Press.

Riebschleger, J.L. (1991). Families of chronically mentally ill people: Siblings speak to social workers. *Health and Social Work, 16,* 94-103.

Rolland, J.S. (1988). Chronic illness and the family life cycle. In B. Carter & M. McGoldrick (Eds.), *The changing family life cycle* (2nd ed., pp. 433-456). New York: Gardner.

Silverman, M.M. (1989). Children of psychiatrically ill parents: A prevention perspective. *Hospital and Community Psychiatry, 40,* 1257-1265.

Swados, E. (1991). *The four of us: The story of a family.* New York: Farrar, Straus, & Giroux.

Vine, P. (1982). *Families in pain.* New York: Pantheon.

Walsh, M. (1985). *Schizophrenia: Straight talk for family and friends.* New York: Warner.

Wasow, M. (1982). *Coping with schizophrenia: A survival manual for parents, relatives, and friends.* Palo Alto, CA: Science and Behavioral Books.

Wechsler, J.A., Schwartztol, H.W. & Wechsler, N.F (1988). *In a darkness* (2nd ed.). Miami: Pickering.

Weisburd, D.E. (Ed.). (1992). *The Journal of the California Alliance for the Mentally Ill, 3*(1).

Wortman, C.B. & Silver, R.C. (1989). The myths of coping with loss. *Journal of Consulting and Clinical Psychology, 57,* 349-357.

SUCCESSFULLY LIVING WITH MANIA: HELPFUL HINTS TO FAMILIES AND PROFESSIONALS

Mary D. Moller and Laura Geer Knudsvig

MARY D. MOLLER, M.S.N., A.R.N.P., C.S., IS AN ADVANCED
REGISTERED NURSE PRACTITIONER AND IS CERTIFIED
BY THE AMERICAN NURSES ASSOCIATION AS A
CLINICAL SPECIALIST IN ADULT PSYCHIATRIC
MENTAL HEALTH NURSING.

LAURA GEER KNUDSVIG, B.A., A HEADSTART TEACHER, IS
ALSO A WIFE, MOTHER, AND STEPMOTHER LIVING
SUCCESSFULLY WITH MANIA. A COMBINATION OF
PRIVATE PSYCHOTHERAPY AND SUCCESSFUL MEDICAL
INTERVENTION HAS PROMOTED SUCCESSFUL SYMPTOM
MANAGEMENT. LAURA AND HER HUSBAND ESTABLISHED
THE FIRST SUPPORT GROUP FOR INDIVIDUALS WITH
MOOD DISORDERS IN SPOKANE, WASHINGTON. MARY
AND LAURA WERE FEATURED WITH ANNA PEARCE (PATTY
DUKE) ON "GOOD MORNING AMERICA,"
FEBRUARY 24, 1993.

THIS ARTICLE WAS ORIGINALLY PUBLISHED IN
Innovations and Research, 1993, 2(2), 61-68
AND IS REPRINTED WITH PERMISSION.

Mania has been documented as having three distinct stages: hypomania, mania, and delirium. Many consumers have been misdiagnosed as having schizophrenia when they are in the second stage. Accurate reporting and history taking are essential in facilitating accurate diagnosis and appropriate medical intervention. Misdiagnosis leading to mismedication can be devastating for the consumer's effort to manage symptoms. Nine unique emotional, behavioral, and cognitive themes, each representing symptoms, have been factored from these stages. Typically these symptoms involve emotionally charged labels such as manipulation, denial, and superficiality that encompass behaviors disruptive to interpersonal relationships. These symptoms are usually not completely alleviated by medications and require ongoing assessment and management. This article, in collaboration with a consumer successfully managing mania, describes interpersonal interventions that families and professionals can use to assist in managing these difficult symptoms.

Understanding the manic phase of bipolar disorder is critical to facilitating successful management of the symptoms by both consumer and family. Their strength and love is severely strained as they struggle to manage this severe and persistent neurobiological disorder. Marriages frequently end in divorce. Families are torn apart when children distance themselves from ill parents because they are confused by feelings of empathy during depression, and anger, frustration and helplessness during mania. Symptoms of mania often remain undiagnosed and untreated, or misdiagnosed and mistreated as schizophrenia, personality disorder, or substance abuse.

A fundamental difficulty in obtaining accurate treatment is that mania is a set of symptoms as well as a discrete *DSM-IV* diagnostic category. As a set of symptoms it represents alterations in mood, affect, and behavior that effect cognition and socialization. Symptoms of mania can occur in the exacerbation of schizophrenia, as a result of substance use/abuse, and in a variety of anxiety and personality disorders. As a diagnostic entity, mania represents aspects of a disorder within the broad category of mood disorders.

The differentiation of mania as either a symptom or a discrete diagnostic category is essential to assure not only appropriate medical care but also successful management of the illness by both consumer and family. Accurate reporting and history taking are essential in facilitating an accurate diagnosis. Enlisting the help of the family can be the key to diagnostic accuracy. Misdiagnosis can lead to mismedication. Successful management of any illness cannot begin until an accurate diagnosis is made and symptom-appropriate medications are prescribed. Mismedication contributes to the undermining of credibility of both medication and psychiatry in the eyes of the consumer as well as the family. In addition to accurate diagnosis, successful treatment occurs when the illness symptoms, symptoms of medication side effects, and basic personality characteristics of the consumer are differentiated.

Stages of Mania

Although it is well documented that mania is a medical illness (Andreasen & Black, 1991; Goodwin & Jamison, 1990), symptoms are not monitored by typical medical tests such as blood pressure or laboratory tests. Symptoms appear as either subtle or dramatic changes in mood and affect. Mania is described as having three stages: hypomania, mania, and delirium.

TABLE 1.
STAGES OF MANIA

Stage One: Mild Elation/Hypomania

Affect (mood): Carefree, lively, happy, worry-free, witty, joking, euphoric, uncaring, unrealistic, confident, uninhibited, mood swings easily to anger and irritation—particularly when others respond with criticism or lack of enthusiasm.

Cognition (thinking): Racing, overconfidence in one's sexual abilities or wealth, ideas shift quickly from one subject to another, poor concentration, difficulty following through on projects, little or no insight into behavior.

Behavior (action): Busy, increase in all activity, excessive talking, joking, singing or teasing, changes in menstrual cycle, inappropriate behavior for age or place, purposeless activity (writing unnecessary letters), spending sprees, meddling, development of superficial relationships, increased smoking, frequent telephone use, increased alcohol consumption.

Stage Two: Acute Elation or Mania

Affect (mood): Elevated, exaltation, expansiveness, mood rapidly turns to anger if others exert control leading to cursing, screaming, hostility, anger, striking out with fury, suddenly bursting into tears and talking about failure when previously talking about success.

Cognition (thinking): Exploding thoughts, flight of ideas, thoughts explode in the brain, pressured speech, frequent rhyming and punning, disorganized, illogical associations (however, the associations will relate to the person's ideas and interests), grandiose and persecutory delusions, hallucinations.

Behavior (action): Uncontrollable. Inappropriate dress, women often wear too much makeup, elaborate jewelry, bright colors and clothes that don't match or fit the season, hair is often decorated with beads and flowers, poor personal hygiene, activity is very urgent, lots of meddling, constantly busy, rearranging furniture, remaking beds, endless vacuuming, frequently changing clothes, no appetite, little sleep even though there are obvious signs of exhaustion, inhibitions decrease, may use profanity and be sexually indiscreet, easily distracted by environmental noise or temperature changes, frequently misidentifies others.

Stage Three: Severe Elation or Delirium

Affect (mood): Panic, disoriented, incoherent, extremely agitated, desperate, panic-stricken.

Cognition (thinking): Psychotic. Delusions, hallucinations, totally illogical, incoherent.

Behavior (action): Frenzy, unable to stop moving, bizarre psycho-motor activity, may be dangerous to self or others, exhaustion and death possible from cardiac arrest and/or dehydration, clients must be protected from themselves.

(Carlson & Goodwin, 1973). Each stage has discrete, documentable characteristics that vary individually (Lipkin, Dyrud, & Meyer, 1970). Table 1 describes key characteristics noted to occur for most people during the stages and course of the manic portion of bipolar disorder.

Table 2 lists a variety of emotional and behavioral themes that emerge as symptoms during these stages (Haber, Hoskins, Leach & Sideleau, 1987). Typically these symptoms involve emotionally charged labels such as manipulation, denial, and superficiality and include behaviors disruptive to interpersonal relationships. These symptoms are usually not completely alleviated by medications and require ongoing assessment and management. Effective management requires all involved to collaboratively distinguish differences between symptoms indicative of hypomania and mania from basic personality characteristics. The purpose of this article is to describe symptom management techniques appropriate for these symptoms.

Interventions for Emotional and Behavioral Themes
(Moller, 1990)

Due to heightened sensitivity occurring in mania, the consumer is vulnerable to criticism and needs to feel accepted as a human being. When acute symptoms are stabilized, the family must be wary of labeling normal mood fluctuations as symptoms of mania. This can best be prevented with consumer input. Consumers frequently remark that, even with symptom stability, most statements they make are still viewed within parameters of illness instead of wellness. The family can benefit by evaluating their tendency to regard honest attempts by the consumer to reconstruct family relationships as manipulation. This is only accomplished by acknowledging the consumer as an equal member of the family

and engaging in discussion to identify changes in affect, mood, cognition, and behavior occurring with treatment. As a result, effective interventions for the emotional and behavioral symptoms will be designed, and improvement in family functioning can occur.

TABLE 2.
EMOTIONAL AND BEHAVIORAL THEMES
COMMONLY EXPERIENCED IN MANIA

1. Competitiveness
2. Strong dependency drives
3. Denial
4. Value system based on social conventionality
5. Hostility and aggression
6. Manipulation
7. Superficial relationships
8. Anxiety
9. Loss

---

1) Competitiveness

A common symptom of mania is grandiosity, particularly regarding success. A person experiencing grandiosity has problems accepting that others may have greater success with a given task. When this occurs the consumer may compete to the point of destroying a relationship or withdraw from it completely. This theme frequently emerges as a personality characteristic as well as a symptom and it is essential for the family unit to define the differences. It may be impossible for the family to make a point at the time the problem arises, but a helpful communication response is, "We just see things differently. Maybe we can resolve this another time." As one consumer stated:

> I am the best at playing my game and yours, too. Due to the intensity of my thinking I may have many points to say in my defense or understanding, but I tire and begin to argue out of frustration rather than logic. We need to agree on taking a break and come together later.

Communication points for families and professionals.

• Identify differences between symptoms and personality characteristics.

• Build on the consumer's strengths.

• Treat all family members as equals — be careful of patronization.

• Be honest and direct with your concerns.

• Negotiate differences in opinions at a mutually agreed upon time—preferably when illness symptoms are not exacerbating.

2) Dependency Issues

Most adults have difficulty acknowledging an inability to meet needs independently. Families also have difficulty admitting an inability to care for all the needs of each member. The exaggerated opinion of one's abilities occurring in mania makes it even more difficult for a consumer to rely on another. It is also difficult for families to acknowledge a need to rely on a system that traditionally has ignored the needs of families. This is illustrated by a consumer:

> When you think like a roadrunner it is very hard to believe a tortoise is going to get much done. I learned at a young age that other people, even some older than I, did not think through things as completely or as efficiently as I did. I may see and believe an alternative, better way to accomplish a goal and feel a dedication to it. I often believe my mind shows better ways to manage medications, run a household, or achieve business objectives. I owe it to myself and to the psychiatric care system to test my new methods and prove them right. My mind can grasp the feasibility of improvement and the moral reasoning for it. Believe it or not, I want to believe it is okay to not have to do everything — to be normal and ordinary.

The mental health system is an altogether new arena to be understood by both consumers and families. If information is given, it is seldom clear. Specific information requested includes services available from the system and/or the community, availability of financial help, information wanted by the psychiatrist, when the psychiatrist wants to be contacted, and what can be expected from treatment.

Communication points for families and professionals.

• Acknowledge the presence and effects of the illness—this helps assuage denial.

• Pursue education regarding the symptoms and similarities to "normal" behavior.

• Identify the "ok-ness" of needing help.

• Facilitate independence in managing the illness by identifying what is available and how to get it.

• Acquaint consumer with the workings of the medical and psychiatric systems and acknowledge weaknesses of the system.

• Utilize the pharmacist as a medication information resource.

• Discover ways to simplify life.

3) Denial

The acceptance of the medicalization of mania by our society has been slow. Consumers have often lived with secrecy because of social stigma. When symptoms are in remission, the consumer is literally his or her old self and denial is common. It is not easy to admit having an illness that usually requires lifelong management, particularly when the illness causes a person to say and do embarrassing things. When confronted with symptoms of denial, one may be exposed and vulnerable, and feelings of being scoffed at and questioned are intensified. What is intended in jest may evoke hostility in the consumer. Recognition of denial as a symptom can facilitate discussion of how to identify denial when it becomes an obstacle to effective treatment.

Communication points for families and professionals.

• Point out behaviors indicating mania between episodes; doing so at that time will be more effective than during the episode. Be tactful and polite. If the behavior is humorous, let the consumer initiate laughter.

• Express concern, not blame or fault. Refrain from pointing fingers at one another. Remember, no one is to blame, but everyone has a responsibility for the successful management of the illness. All members of the family and treatment team must arrive at a consensus on how the illness will be managed. If the consumer is captain or at least co-captain of the team there will be more compliance and willingness to disclose symptoms because of experiencing some measure of control of the treatment.

• Recording conversations may assist in identifying which behaviors or statements actually occurred. Any recording of conversations taped or written, must have the permission of all involved. Conversing on paper and/or journaling may be helpful. Journaling is particularly useful if there is a therapist involved who can assist in interpreting and explaining the comments.

4) Value System Based on Social Convention

Clients have described a chameleon-like ability to become similar to those around them. This becomes very challenging for families as they perpetually try to predict the likes, dislikes, interests, and values of their ill family member. It is easier for consumers with mania to change their belief system than to maintain one that is not congruent with their surroundings. Persons with mania are very sensitive to the feelings of others and may believe that others can project feelings onto them. As a result, the consumer may become distanced; adopt the affect of friends, family members, or a professional; and adopt mannerisms, intonations, and even styles of moving that compel others to believe that the consumer is agreeing with them. This trait occasionally convinces a family member or friend to adopt the likes/dislikes of the consumer!

Consumers are quick to grasp concepts of other cultures and religions, but they need practices to be congruent with beliefs. Individuals with mania have difficulty with inconsistencies such as divorced marriage counselors and Catholic women using birth control. They are quick to identify and point out hypocrisy. Consumers may continue to make changes in friends and caregivers as they search for illusive perfection. When paranoia is present, this pattern is intensified.

Communication points for families and professionals.

• Accept frequent changes as consumers experiment with how others react and search for those with whom they experience comfort. As the illness stabilizes many changes in values and personality expression may occur.

• Identify and discuss patterns and trends in changing value system. Current behavior may not actually indicate internal values.

• Clarify value system currently in operation.

• Confront incongruencies in belief system gently, openly, and honestly after determining the necessity for confrontation.

5) Hostility and Aggression

Hostility and aggression occur in any relationship due to frustration and inability to get needs met in a satisfying way.

Hostility has been described as a guise for a desire to be normal that is complicated by a drive for perfection. This ambivalence leads to frustration because at times perfection seems possible and the quest for normal is abandoned as it seems somehow substandard.

Mania is a life filled with chaos. Consumers need to finish their multiple projects. They need space, encouragement, and possibly even help which they may refuse if offered. What may appear as hostile and aggressive responses to others may actually be an attempt to simplify things and eliminate complex stimuli to promote peace of mind. Consumers also try to eliminate unnecessary tasks and projects, particularly those they believe to be trivial such as changing clothes, washing unnecessary clothes, and picking up clutter. It is important to remember that individuals with mania perceive the world very differently from the way others do. Consequently, they may not understand that the family's perception is different. The consumer may need and ask for quiet. When the family turns the television off in the family room, the consumer doesn't understand why they turn on a radio in another room. Consumers interpret this as inconsideration. This symptom also occurs with room temperature, light, amount of activity, blandness of food, intensity of smells, and need for conversation. Consumers frequently connect feelings with places and objects they find unpleasant and react accordingly. They may mistake the family's acceptance of the place or object as insensitivity, callousness, or even perversion.

Consumers may be unable to control the aggression and feel remorseful, as at times it is the only thing they can figure out to do. This is usually due to learned experiences and accelerated thinking that typically blocks logical reasoning and should not be confused with stubbornness. Thoughts may be racing at a pace consumers are unable to override. They know damage can be done to the family when they do not intend damage. Consumers repeatedly say,

> Please do not let me harm you or someone else. I do not know what I am really capable of and I do not want to find out. Don't let it slide as another one of my 'moments.' I don't want to be this way. Short of suicide, aggression may be my most desperate plea for help.

Communication points for families and professionals.

• Remember, consumers do not desire to be cruel or to harm others despite appearances. They may be reacting to perceived cruelness from other family members.

• Distinguish between the person and their behavior.

• Realize that motives may not be reflected in actions. Discovering the motive may be the key to finding a more satisfactory way of meeting the person's needs.

• Allow personal accusations to diffuse, let go of them and try not to react. Evaluate the need for space, time, quiet, medication. A helpful response is "What would help us settle down now so we can resolve this later?"

• Always focus on facts, not hearsay from others. A third party mediator can be helpful.

• Identify activities such as withdrawing from family activities as symptom management techniques instead of disruptive behaviors.

6) Manipulation
Manipulation, by definition, is to serve one's own purpose by artful or unfair means or to play upon another to one's own advantage. Examples include choosing

offensive words, initiating crisis, irresponsible medication management, and emotional outbursts. It frequently represents a paradoxical attempt to elicit caring and control from others because the consumer senses a loss of control.

For individuals experiencing mania, words are "their thing." They do not miss anything when another person talks. They take in every syllable and intonation. If the family is not careful, the consumer will have them saying things they never said! Sarcasm is wasted on individuals with mania. They can see through the malice in sarcasm they perceive others to have and will get a message of anger long before they will consider changing the behavior the family is addressing or insinuating.

The consumer is apt to sense, reveal, or exploit areas of covert sensitivity and weakness in others and can skillfully shift the focus of a conversation from themselves to others (Janowsky, El Yousef, & Davis, 1974). This often spotlights family problems and causes discomfort. Consumers who seem mean and sharp are often emotionally fragile and do not want to be traumatized. An individual with mania can intimidate and harass a family member to effect defense of the self. Both consumer and family member may win, but the consumer will never lose. Since bipolar disorder is often genetic, many consumers were raised by a parent experiencing mania and learned to practice laconic and manipulative communication from their earliest days.

Consumers have intuitively learned that they can maintain some control over their moods if they can control the environment. They realize that others' moods affect them directly so they attempt to control all behaviors. To some degree they are conscious of this manipulation, which makes diplomatic discussion difficult.

Compliments and flattery, especially when directed toward medical caregivers,

should not be confused with manipulation, even though the family reports the use of similar techniques. Consumers generally do not expect special favors from staff members, even though they may try. They actually see caregivers as safe persons to compliment and believe them to be too wise to fall for the manipulative techniques that worked with family members. Prior to meeting caregivers, consumers have experienced a living hell—unable to control their lives, words, feelings, and actions. Many fears expressed by families are actually projections of the terror experienced by consumers. To all caregivers reading this article:

> You are the one who administered the medications that gave me back my life, the one who realized I was sick, not bad. You are the one who listened, observed, and validated my worth as a person. You talked to me about getting well and the new person I was becoming. You delivered me from a form of death. I can't see you as anything other than a saint. Even though I was still afraid of myself, you treated me as a person.

Gifts and flattery that may appear to you as manipulation are my deepest expressions of gratitude. For years I waged a war against this illness before I received successful treatment. To finally be properly diagnosed and treated is like being given a new life. As the recipient of such gratitude you are being honored, thanked, and praised for this lifesaving act just as a doctor might be thanked by any other patient experiencing a chronic illness or undergoing lifesaving surgery. A person with mania is as human as a person with cancer. There is a fine line between flattery and the most immense gratitude.

Communication points for families and professionals.

• Collaboratively identify situations that trigger manipulative behavior—prevention is the key. Most humans are desirous of getting needs met at the time of the need, particularly when desperately trying to save face, even to the point of humiliation.

• Mutually establish clear expectations on behavior—be aware of the embarrassing problems of the illness, help consumers understand they are not thought less of because of this symptom.

• Follow mutually established rules regarding limit setting—say exactly what you mean. Statements involving the words "you," "can't," "shouldn't," "won't ever," and "don't understand" are barriers to effective communication.

• Utilize negotiations and compromise—give and take is essential. Talk with each other about things that are bothersome and be accepting if it is personal. Look for examples in your own life that may elicit similar feelings.

• Recognize flattery as potentially representing gratitude.

• Discuss how the behavior was manipulative and deduce alternative ways of meeting needs.

7) Reaction to Loss

In addition to the loss of normal biological functions, all chronic illnesses involve psychological, sociological, and spiritual losses. Biological adaptations to mania involve the five senses and include a decreased tolerance for noise, irritation from light, hypersensitivity to smells and tastes, and misinterpretation of touch. Medications may take away familiar mood swings and leave consumers feeling they have no personality. Additionally, consumers who respond positively to lithium feel reluctant to report symptoms of mania or depression because they are now in treatment and should no longer experience symptoms.

Psychological losses include no longer experiencing the luxury of having good and bad days or a normal anger response, as most behavioral responses are evaluated and interpreted in terms of having taken the proper dose of lithium. Mood-stabilizing drugs may induce a consistent feeling of sameness, which may be experienced as a loss of creativity. The consumer has to reestablish personal identity and self-confidence within the framework of a non-manic personality.

Socially, consumers experience stigma, embarrassment, and grief when apologizing for behaviors that occurred during an episode. There may be a need for temporary reframing of job, educational, or career expectations until stability is reached and previous proficiency is regained.

Within the nuclear family there may be rejection by parents and siblings and a loss of trust. Studies identify a genetic role that effects decisions regarding childbearing. Childrearing is affected by severity of illness symptoms and the need for hospitalization.

Spiritual losses include feeling a loss of independence, the loss of a creative high versus depression, loss of privacy, loss of hope. There is an increased need for spiritual assurance and being considered a "normal" member of society. Frequently consumers are under the false impression they have lost citizenship, the right to vote, and the right to drive as well as membership in a church and their relationship with God.

Nearly all consumers grieve the loss of the high, but do not miss the depths of the depressions. Most learn that consistency and stability of mood results in increased productivity due to an ability to channel energies into constructive endeavors. A new lifestyle literally emerges from the devastation.

TABLE 3.
Effects of Anxiety on the Bio-Psycho-Social-Spiritual Self

Biological

Arthritic joint pain	Muscular aches	High blood pressure
Menstrual difficulties	Nervous tics	Dizziness
Thyroid problems	Stuttering	Palpitations
Hypoglycemia	Wrinkled forehead	Increased sweating
Skin rashes	Tension headaches	Cold, clammy hands
Hyperglycemia	Grinding teeth	Rapid heart beat
Finger or foot tapping	Sudden bursts of energy	Jaw pain
Migraine headaches	Wild hand gestures	Chest pain
Many colds	Back pain	Frequent bouts with flu
Allergies	Low grade infection	Hives
Altered gait	Increased appetite	Decreased appetite
Nausea	Stomach pain or cramping	Ulcers
Constipation	Diarrhea	Frigidity or impotence
Dry mouth or throat	Difficulty swallowing	

Psychological

Feeling that things are getting out of control	Feeling desperate
Anxiety or panic	Feeling trapped
Frustration	Feeling blue or depressed
Anger and irritation	Lack of concentration
Feeling resentful	Low levels of enthusiasm
Feeling guilty	Suspicious attitude
Rigidity	Phobias
Poor memory	Mental confusion
Difficulty falling asleep	Indecisiveness
Difficulty staying asleep	Racing thoughts
Conviction that everything turns out for the worst	Feeling exhausted/fatigued
Decreased cooperativeness	Unable to make decision

Sociological

Distancing from family/friends
Search for transfer or relocation
Reduced physical contact with others
Increased, often random, activities

Spiritual

Heightened sense of responsibility	Having feelings of futility
Performing duties strictly by the book	Distrusting everyone and everything
Having a vague feeling that something is wrong	Inefficiency in work
Working harder and harder to accomplish less	Reduction in overall performance
Negative attitude	Feeling omnipotent
Justifying previously wrong acts	

Communication points for families and professionals.

• Offer yourself and use active listening in discussing consequences of this illness.

• Identify with each other's emotional pain.

• Identify the most severe losses and some ways of handling these losses. Are the emotional reactions congruent with feelings?

• Discuss activities that may offset grief.

• Talk with others who have experienced and worked through similar symptoms.

• Point out positive changes as periods of emotional stability increase.

8) Superficial Relationships

Mania generally causes trouble in all relationships. There is often difficulty maintaining close friendships due to the rapid mood changes and demands for attention caused by the illness. Deep friendships may form quickly, but they may hold greater significance for the ill person than the healthy one. Difficulties with sexual identity may also occur.

Based on the mood of social and family groups, the consumer can be remarkably amusing and entertaining or glum and morose. Their chameleon-like ability allows consumers to adapt their own personality to that of the group. While friends may find this humorous, they also find it disorienting and baffling. They may hesitate to pursue the consumer for an intimate relationship. Mania distorts the consumers' view of relationships and they may break them as quickly as they were created. The consumer may perceive having been tricked or lied to when in fact the other person perceives the consumer as having done the trickery. The consumer may then distance him or herself from previously close friends.

The illness can devour all aspects of daily living. A plan needs to be in place for emergencies such as rapid cycling, hospitalization, and the untoward effects of medications. It is especially helpful to have a contact person in social situations who has some understanding of the illness and the ability to recognize and deal with actual and potential crises. Consumers have expressed the need for one or two confidants who are able to take children in an emergency, confront them about changes in behavior, and talk openly with family members about their perceptions regarding the consumer's immediate needs.

Communication points for families and professionals.

• Identify one or two close friends who will provide open, honest feedback and who are prepared for the intense highs and lows caused by this illness.

• Identify one or two close friends who will stand by the consumer during relapse, hospitalizations, and ongoing treatment.

• Identify individuals who can take over childcare activities, confront the consumer regarding illness symptoms, and talk with family members about concerns.

• Educate friends and family members about the illness and the intensity of emotions.

• Provide reality checks and confront symptoms in a way that promotes trust.

9) Anxiety

The intensity of the bio-psycho-social-spiritual symptoms that accompany mania typically create high levels of anxiety as the consumer struggles to balance symptoms. Anxiety can be a psychological death sentence to the consumer and family who have learned that unmanageable anxiety commonly signals relapse. Anxiety in and of itself becomes paradoxical as the absence of anxiety may signal a developing depression and high anxiety can trigger a manic episode that actually may be craved.

Table 3 lists the bio-psycho-social-spiritual symptoms of anxiety that families and consumers need to be taught. By understanding that anxiety is experienced by all people, and by recognizing the signs of anxiety that trigger relapse, the consumer and family can learn to manage its many symptoms. When anxiety is managed, a new stability of mood is reached. The resulting peace and satisfaction aids family members in understanding the effects of anxiety on the illness and motivates them to make adjustments in daily activities. The serenity experienced by successful anxiety management results in greater life satisfaction.

Communication points for families and professionals.

• Identify levels of anxiety experienced, share observations, and solicit feedback.

• Identify and share personal experiences with anxiety.

• Identify sources of anxiety in order to modify both stimulus and response.

• Assist in the identification and maintenance of a calm atmosphere. Encourage and/or model anxiety relieving techniques.

• Notify physician and utilize prescribed medications.

Conclusion

This article has examined some of the many intense emotional issues involved in the management of mania. Consumers want the roller coaster ride to stop as much as the family does. They deserve the oppor-

tunity to assist in illness management and to be valued as an equal member of the treatment team. When it is realized that control of mood swings is a reality, consumers report feeling as though they had received a personality transplant! Feelings of loss, discomfort with change, and painful adjustments begin to fade. They need to be encouraged to do their best to make treatment as successful as possible and to be patient with others. Once symptom management becomes a way of life, the daily efforts of living with this illness become tolerable and a life of harmony is possible.

References

Andreasen, N. C. & Black, D. W. (1991). *Introductory textbook of psychiatry.* Washington DC: American Psychiatric Press.

Carlson, B. & Goodwin, F. K. (1973). The stages of mania. *Archives of General Psychiatry, 28,* 221-228.

Goodwin, F. K. & Jamison, K. R. (1990). *Manic-depressive illness.* New York: Oxford Press.

Haber, J., Hoskins, P., Leach, A. & Sideleau, B. (1987). *Comprehensive psychiatric nursing, 2nd ed.* St. Louis: McGraw-Hill.

Janowsky, D. S., El Yousef, M. K. & Davis, S. M. (1974). Interpersonal maneuvers of manic patients. *American Journal of Psychiatry, 131,* 250-255.

Lipkin, K., Dyrud, J. & Meyer, G. (1970). The many faces of mania. *Archives of General Psychiatry, 22,* 262-267.

Moller, M. D. (1990). *Understanding and communicating with a person experiencing mania.* Videotape and Study Guide. Nine Mile Falls, WA: Nurseminars, Inc.

The Family Recovery Process

LeRoy Spaniol and Anthony M. Zipple

LEROY SPANIOL, PH.D., IS SENIOR DIRECTOR OF THE CENTER FOR PSYCHIATRIC REHABILITATION AT BOSTON UNIVERSITY AND EXECUTIVE PUBLISHER OF THE *Psychiatric Rehabilitation Journal*.

ANTHONY M. ZIPPLE, SC.D., IS VICE PRESIDENT FOR MENTAL HEALTH SERVICES FOR THE VINFEN CORPORATION, A PRIVATE NONPROFIT AGENCY OPERATING IN MASSACHUSETTS AND A BOARD MEMBER OF THE INTERNATIONAL ASSOCIATION OF PSYCHOSOCIAL REHABILITATION SERVICES.

THIS ARTICLE ORIGINALLY APPEARED IN *The Journal of the California Alliance for the Mentally Ill*, 1994, 5(2), 57-59, AND IS REPRINTED WITH PERMISSION.

The onset of mental illness is frequently a traumatic experience for all the members of a family. While the mental illness in their family member may be lifelong, we have found that each individual member of the family can experience his or her own recovery from the trauma, just as the family member who has the mental illness can experience recovery. Thus, we are beginning to see recovery as a process of readjusting our attitudes, feelings, perceptions, and beliefs about ourselves, others, and life in general.

Recovery is a process of self-discovery, self-renewal, and transformation. All people experience recovery at various times in their lives. The more threatening the particular event, the more it shakes the foundation of who we are and how we experience our lives. These powerful events break personal connections we took for granted and shatter the expectations, dreams, and fantasies for which we had hoped. Clearly these are processes which involve profound adjustments in our lives and more intensive periods of recovery. Recovery is painful and difficult for all family members. Yet the outcome of recovery can be the emergence of a new sense of self which is more vital and connected to who we really are, to others, and to a greater sense of meaning and purpose in life.

While there is a growing literature on *consumer* recovery in the field of psychiatric rehabilitation, there is not a great deal of information about the recovery process in families. Understanding the recovery process can provide a welcome long-term perspective to family members. It can bring some relief when they are caught up in the many difficult daily events of caring for a family member with a mental illness. When we are caught up in a particular stressful event, it is hard to recognize it as a process because it seems as if the pain will never end.

Professionals also need to understand how family members react to the trauma of mental illness in a family member. This knowledge can help professionals understand the family's experience and respond to it in a more helpful way, giving family members a sense of hope about their lives and the life of their family member with a disability.

There are several general characteristics of the recovery of family members that should be noted.

1) Recovery is a growth process—a transforming process. While it may not feel transformative at the time, and can be very painful, it is still a powerful growth process.

2) The particular impact of the illness differs in family members. A mother's experience is different from a father's experience. A parent's experience differs from a sibling's experience. A younger sibling's experience is not the same as a sibling who is older than the family member with the illness.

3) Each person in the family recovers at his or her own rate. This means that

family members may be in different phases of recovery at any given time.

4) Families need to be aware of each other's phase of recovery. Each phase of the recovery process has its own reactions and its own developmental tasks. As family members acquire the knowledge, skills, and support to complete these tasks they grow personally.

5) Recovery is not linear, so family members will recycle themselves through the phases as they gradually complete tasks that will facilitate moving ahead.

6) Emotional reactions of family members during the recovery process, even intense ones, are natural reactions and do not imply that there is something wrong with the family members.

The recovery process of family members can be described as a series of stages. It is important to note that stages are only guidelines. While they help us to understand the process of recovery, they do not define the process for each individual. Each stage contains many tasks. People may cycle through the stages and then return to complete incomplete tasks. This is why family members may feel they are losing ground in their recovery process at times. They experience themselves returning to issues they feel they have resolved because important emotional, intellectual or physical tasks have not been completed. The following stages describe the experiences of family members.

At some point it becomes clear that family members need to continue on with their individual lives and begin to think of supporting their ill loved one over the long run. This is when coping begins to take the place of grieving.

Discovery/Denial

As family members begin to become aware of what is happening they may try to explain it away. Family members may believe that their loved one's disorder is not really so serious. They may have negative or exaggerated images of people with mental illness from the media and their family member may not conform to those images. They may develop alternative and more "acceptable" explanations for their family member's behavior such as alcohol, drugs, laziness, or bad friends.

An all too frequent lack of clarity and communication with professionals about what is happening makes the illness hard to accept. As the relationship with the family member begins to change, family tensions and frustrations increase. Family members often attempt to find answers through any possible source, such as friends, other families, clergy, and professionals. Denial can be persistent and can linger throughout other aspects of the recovery process. Each member of the family must deal with his/her own recovery. Members of the family can support one another but they cannot recover for one another.

Disbelief is sometimes a more accurate word than denial to describe the experiences of some families. Disbelief is primarily a conscious process and it implies some acceptance, but "It is hard to believe it is happening to us." Belief begins to set in gradually as the reality of the disability makes it difficult to avoid. Family members need to be supported during their disbelief and they need to be gradually helped to see the disability for what it is.

Recognition/Acceptance

Families do gradually become aware that their family member has a major mental illness. Initially this awareness increases their faith and hope in professionals because professionals are expected to know the answers. However, as awareness of the seriousness of the illness increases, so may feelings of guilt, embarrassment, and self-blame. Family members are part of the general culture which has supported these feelings. If family members encounter professionals who maintain that families are responsible for the illness, then family members will have a double burden, because their worst fears seem to be confirmed by an "expert."

As family members begin to accept that there is a serious long-term illness, they experience a deep sense of loss. Perhaps the most striking loss is the destruction of their image of the life that they had envisioned with and for their ill family member. This feeling of loss is also experienced by the family member who has the illness. All family members share and must come to terms with this deep sense of loss. Acceptance of the loss is often made more difficult by the cyclical nature of the illness. Improvement of the family member raises hope that he or she will return to normal previous functioning. This on-again, off-again experience becomes an emotional roller coaster ride for the entire family.

If family members encounter professionals who maintain that families are responsible for the illness, then family members will have a double burden, because their worst fears seem to be confirmed by an "expert."

As the persistence of the illness becomes obvious to the family, the grieving process can begin more fully as they let go of old hopes and expectations and begin to create new ones. It should be noted that this awareness also creates a crisis in meaning. Questions about oneself, one's relationships to others, to one's work, and to larger meanings or purpose in life become important. As these meanings change, family members change. As family members begin to develop new answers to these basic questions, which incorporate the reality of their loved one's disability, they often change in profound ways.

Coping

Coping implies struggling with a problem without adequate knowledge, skills or support. This is how family members begin to cope. At some point it becomes clear that family members need to continue on with their individual lives and begin to think of supporting their ill loved one over the long run. This is when coping begins to take the place of grieving. Family members cope with the disruption in normal family life, recurrent crises, the persistence of the illness, the loss of faith in some professionals and the mental health system, and the aspirations of their family member with the mental illness. Professionals may feel family members are "intrusive" at this stage because family members may become more angry and assertive. They may question professional competency and demand additional services.

Their anger at professionals and outrage at the mental health system derive from their frustrations when seeking adequate care. Sometimes their anger derives from poorly trained professionals or inadequate resources. However, it is important to be aware that the anger family members feel is augmented by the hopelessness they often feel. They cope with pessimism and despair.

As families persist in their coping, they experience more success. Belief in the expertise of other family members grows. Family members value the support of other families who are struggling with a family member with a mental illness and gradually learn to accept the limits of what they can do about the illness. They begin to focus increasingly on the management of symptoms and improving the functioning of their family member. They become more interested in improved inpatient care, community services, housing, and rehabilitation. They gradually identify professionals on whom they can rely, and work more closely with them. Family members come to see valued professionals as necessary, but not sufficient to their efforts to cope.

Personal and Political Advocacy

Gradually, family members come to a new awareness of themselves in the recovery process. This awareness can include a greater level of personal advocacy and increased assertiveness and confidence. Family members say they feel differently about themselves. Even though the illness of their family member continues, *they* have changed. They blame themselves less. They let go of what they can't change or don't want to change and become more

Family members come to see valued professionals as necessary, but not sufficient to their efforts to cope.

focused on efforts to bring about the changes they see as necessary. They work out new roles and relationships with professionals which are more collaborative and based on equality. Their interest in the training of professionals may increase. They become more persistent over the long run.

For many, political advocacy becomes more important. United action to change the system becomes more valued. Family members experience their power, often for the first time in their lives. They experience their ability to influence the systems that are supposed to support their family member. And, it is at this point, that they have integrated and/or deepened new meanings and values about themselves, others, their work, and the larger concerns in life.

Leaving Home: Separation Issues in Psychiatric Illness

Agnes B. Hatfield

AGNES B. HATFIELD, PH.D., IS PROFESSOR EMERITUS OF HUMAN DEVELOPMENT, COLLEGE OF EDUCATION, UNIVERSITY OF MARYLAND; FAMILY EDUCATION SPECIALIST FOR THE NATIONAL ALLIANCE FOR THE MENTALLY ILL; AND DIRECTOR OF THE FAMILY EDUCATION PROGRAM FOR THE STATE OF MARYLAND.

THIS ARTICLE ORIGINALLY APPEARED IN THE *Psychosocial Rehabilitation Journal*, 1992, 15(4), 37-47 AND IS REPRINTED WITH PERMISSION.

People with severe psychiatric illnesses often have considerable difficulty separating from their parents. This can be a source of conflict between parents and residential care providers who place high value on independence. This study provides parent perspectives on the barriers to separation and suggests practical guidelines for relating to parents during the stressful transition process.

Interest in the role that families play in the support and care of their mentally ill relatives, once very limited, has increased significantly to the point where essentially all facilities and agencies serving this population now seek ways to include families. The nature of this relationship varies with the kind of service being provided—with roles and relationships differing when the service is in the hospital, for example, rather than in a rehabilitation center, and differing when the person lives in a community residence rather than in the family home. Each program needs to work out relationships most appropriate for it.

In our experience, roles and relationships can be especially difficult when the man or woman with mental illness leaves the parental home to live in a community residence. Some providers have argued that families no longer have a role since the person is now leaving home and preparing to live independently. Family advocacy groups and some providers, however, have argued that there are still a number of important roles for families, and unless these roles are understood and agreed upon, conflict is possible (Hatfield, 1990). The roles of families are seen as follows:

1. Providing support. The family is the most basic sociological unit in our culture. People have their earliest and most continuous associations within their families. It is to the family that one usually turns for comfort and support; most families feel obligated to help other members whether or not their help is reciprocated. People with mental illnesses are especially dependent on their families, for they have difficulty maintaining support networks on their own. However committed they may be, staff members cannot substitute for the natural family. They tend to come and go in the life of the client and they have primary responsibilities for their own families. The quality of life for most clients depends to a large extent upon the degree of support families can give.

2. Providing information. Information passed from agency to agency in mental health is often sparse and incomplete. In many cases families have the most complete and continuous knowledge about care and treatment over the years. This can be enormously helpful to a person's new care providers.

3. Monitoring services. Even though agencies usually have mechanisms for quality control, families have the right and responsibility to observe the progress of their particular relative and to report their concerns to those in charge. This is not too different from families feeling obligated to monitor the care of ill relatives in nursing homes.

4. To advocate for services. Service providers are dependent upon such family advocacy groups as the National Alliance for the Mentally Ill (NAMI) to advocate for money for residential care services. Their willingness to do this depends upon good family-provider relationships and satisfaction with services being provided.

Because these roles and relationships seem so crucial to the well-being of men and women who have mental illness, we were concerned to find frequent negative feeling toward families. For example, in the Maryland Family Education Program we found some staff members who felt there was no role for families once their relative moved into a community residence. They expected rapid disengagement from parents and swift transition to the new home. When this did not happen there was much frustration and significant concern about "symbiotic relationships" and "enmeshment" with parents.

Staff members placed high value on independence and felt that the client, too, was struggling hard for independence from parents. We frequently heard families criticized for being "overprotective," "pathologically dependent on their offspring," or "dysfunctional." While this was by no means the attitude of all staff members, it occurred enough to threaten the likelihood that families would stay involved in the support of their relative.

A little reflection suggested that it should not surprise that dependence/independence issues arise in parent and staff relationships, for there are a number of factors that aggravate the issue. To begin with, our society generally has considerable ambivalence and confusion about independence and its relative importance in a scale of values. The issues are compounded when people have severe psychiatric disabilities and must necessarily depend on others a great deal of the time for care and treatment. In addition, parents and staff members come from different life experiences with mental illness; it has different meanings for them. Finally, staff members and parents both have roles to play in support and care, but these roles have never been clarified, so conflict between them is likely.

Independence in American Culture

Since independence and self-reliance are considered universal values by many, these values are taken for granted and are rarely discussed. However, cross-cultural studies show that cultural values and economic arrangements determine prevailing attitudes, and independence may be valued differently in other societies Shaffer, 1979). Few societies place such a strong emphasis on independence as American society. This is often explained by our long period of frontier existence during which self-reliance was vital for survival. Dependence posed a problem when all hands were needed.

We are no longer a frontier society and our strong emphasis on independence may not have the same relevance. Probably all Americans suffer significant degrees of insecurity and anxiety lest they someday be old, ill, or handicapped and have to depend on the largesse of others. This may be the negative side of an overemphasis on independence. Ours is a rapidly evolving society composed of an increasing variety of national and ethnic groups with differing views about dependence, independence, and self-reliance. Inevitably, traditional views will be challenged.

Human development specialists find that the process by which young adults gain independence in our society is often fraught with conflict. It is generally less gradual, more abrupt, and more stressful than in many other cultures. It begins earlier and is completed later, with our children experiencing an unusually long period of dependence. Conflicting messages are given to parents and offspring by schools, churches, and other socializers regarding the nature and timing of various independent behaviors. It is not surprising if parents become confused and inconsistent (Conger, 1977). Growing up in our society brings with it strong feelings about dependence and independence. The emotional intensity for some people is so great that rational discussion about the subject is scarcely possible.

There may be something inherent in the process of parenting that makes parent and child separation threatening (Darling & Darling, 1982). Parental energies are bound up in child rearing over a long period of time, often a couple of decades or more. The burden of responsibility falls almost exclusively on the parents, for our society provides few social supports, and extended families are infrequently involved. This responsibility weighs heavily on parents, making it difficult for them to let go or allow room for risk-taking.

Brown (1978) believes that parents can never be entirely free of the peculiar kinds of stress that separation engenders. Genuine commitment to another person brings with it an inevitable vulnerability to the loss of that person. Each developmental milestone of the child brings anxiety. This anxiety is heightened during adolescence and young adulthood when the process of individuation and separation moves forward rapidly.

Dependence Behavior in Mental Illness

If anxiety accompanies separation from offspring generally, considerable anxiety must surely accompany separation from a relative who has a psychiatric disability. Krauss and Slavinsky (1982) say that it is hard to think of another disorder in which dependency plays such a large and consistent role. It is infrequently written about but often encountered, they note, and it is difficult for families and clinicians to tolerate it. Roots for this dependence lie in the severity of the illness, resistance to change, and lack of personal and social resources.

The parent dilemma is cogently stated by Lefley (1987) in the following paragraph:

> The schizophrenic and dysfunctional bipolar adult is frequently still locked in the dependency-independence conflict of adolescence. He or she wants individuation, but is unable to function at a more mature level. Anger directed at the mother reflects the conflict of one who wants to move away from the life buoy, but is afraid of drowning. Yet if the parent removes the buoy, the child may indeed drown or else founder so miserably that his or her progress is impeded...Thus parents are locked in a balancing dilemma that persists far beyond the cutoff time of late adolescence or young adulthood. (p. 120)

Krauss and Slavinsky (1982) find that most providers are unprepared to deal with the level of dependence many clients exhibit and they feel considerable negativism about it. They are quite willing to "help people who help themselves" but they have considerable trouble accepting people who lack the capacity or will. They are frustrated by what they perceive as passive, clinging, and demanding attitudes and resistance to change.

Contrary views about dependence have been expressed by some professionals. For example, Dincin (1981) says that dependency in itself is not bad, especially if it prevents regression. He encourages dependency upon entering his agency, and feels that staff members can move that dependency toward growth at a later time. Anthony, Cohen, and Cohen (1984) believe that an increase in client dependency can eventually lead to independent functioning. Dependencies on people, places, or things, they point out, are normal.

Parent Perceptions of Barriers to Independence

This study relates, in part, to a survey of 308 attenders at a NAMI convention in

1986 regarding families' views as to where their relative who has mental illness should be living. Only 3% felt that the family home was the appropriate place for them (Hatfield, 1990). The tendency of providers to see families as overprotective seems at variance with these families' statements, and tends to be a source of tension and conflict.

In order to begin addressing the issue, a brief questionnaire was sent to 100 randomly selected members of the Alliance for the Mentally Ill of Maryland. The purpose of the study was to determine parents' perceptions of the barriers that prevent the separation of people with mental illnesses from their families. Forty-five questionnaires were returned, of which only 34 were from parents. While the final number of usable responses is very small, we believe that the responses do begin to address this heretofore unaddressed issue.

Demographic data for these respondents were similar to data from other studies that used members of NAMI as subjects (Spaniol, Jung, Zipple, & Fitzgerald, 1987; Hatfield, 1978, 1983, 1989). The average age of respondents was 64, with 79% being mothers. The average age of their relatives who have mental illness was 33, with 63% being male. A high number (85%) had a diagnosis of schizophrenia, with the rest having affective, obsessive compulsive, and personality disorders.

Parents (62%) were the primary caregivers of their relatives either in their homes (38%) or in other arrangements which they supervised. Only 26% of the relatives were living in supervised housing. Twelve percent were in the hospital. These data were comparable to that gathered in a larger study of Maryland families 3 years ago (Hatfield, 1989).

The purpose of the questionnaire was to ascertain parents' perceptions of barriers to movement from parental homes to supervised residences for people with mental ill-

nesses. Parents were asked to respond to three main questions:

1. To what extent are availability and adequacy of housing barriers to community placement?

2. To what extent are selected client characteristics barriers to community placement?

3. To what extent are selected parental characteristics barriers to community placement?

Each of the three questions had from seven to nine items for parents to rate using a scale of "never," "sometimes," and "often."

TABLE 1.
AVAILABILITY AND QUALITY OF HOUSING AS BARRIERS
($N = 22$)

	Never	Sometimes	Often
Housing unavailable		32%	68%
Housing quality poor		58%	42%
Housing is costly		59%	41%
Housing is unsafe	13%	73%	14%
Staff members not competent	12%	53%	35%
Staff members do not communicate with families	13%	54%	33%
Expectations not appropriate	7%	60%	33%

Availability and quality of housing as barriers. The potential for clients to separate from their parents depends to a large extent on the availability of housing. It is clear from Table 1 that most parents feel that housing tends not to be very available.

According to Table 1, the quality of housing, its cost, its safety, and staff competencies are sometimes considered unsatisfactory. One parent added that "staff try valiantly under trying circumstances."

The lack of certainty about the availability and adequacy of housing when needed can be a tremendous barrier for parents and clients who are trying to work through a process of gradual separation, and it can be equally frustrating to therapists trying to help them. It is difficult to develop the readiness and raise appropriate expectations in the face of so much uncertainty.

Client characteristics as barriers. Some providers feel that the availability of housing is not the only factor that delays transition to community living. How parents view their relative's willingness to leave home and his or her capacity to succeed elsewhere are factors. This becomes quite clear in the following table.

Parents most often identify their relative's being "fearful of leaving home" or being "too comfortable at home" as barriers to separation. Perceiving these kinds of dependencies plus the individual's "refusal to live with other people who have mental illness," undoubtedly places great stress on parents as they contemplate the need to separate from their offspring. While most parents strongly empathize with their relative's dilemma, they may be unwilling to add to his or her pain by insisting upon separation. They may be unable to counter their relative's pleas to be allowed to remain home. One 72-year-old father wrote in the margin of his questionnaire:

> Our T was terribly scarred by his mental illness, and has lost his self-confidence. Also, T has become very dependent on his parents—we are his "security blanket." Finally, we are uncertain of T's ability to maintain an independent living style, and as we age we are concerned as to who will help him cope with the world.

Parents note other barriers to their relative's transition to community residences. According to Table 2, parents feel that

being low functioning, being at risk for relapse, and having tendencies for volatile behavior are barriers to being placed in a residential setting. Strangely, problems of substance abuse were not identified as likely barriers.

TABLE 2.
CLIENT CHARACTERISTICS AS BARRIERS

	Never	Sometimes	Often
Fearful of leaving home	12%	17%	71%
Too comfortable at home	12%	25%	63%
Functioning is too low	10%	76%	14%
Functioning is too high	44%	44%	12%
Tends to be volatile	21%	53%	26%
At risk for relapse	6%	50%	44%
Substance abuse problems	44%	28%	28%
Non-compliance with medication	26%	48%	26%
Refuses to live with other mentally ill people	18%	27%	55%

Parents have the perception that community residential services tend not to take or retain difficult clients. If the perception is correct, much work needs to be done to develop the kinds of services that can accommodate those with significant problems. These are the most needy clients, those most in need of skilled care, and those least easily accommodated in a parental home. If the perception of the parents is wrong, there is need for better communication between parents and mental health workers.

Parents' concerns as barriers. Providers often see parents as the primary factor in delaying or preventing the independence of their offspring. Table 3 shows how parents view these parental factors.

TABLE 3.
PARENTS' CONCERNS AS BARRIERS

	Never	Sometimes	Often
Need the help of the client	61%	33%	6%
Need the help of client's income	50%	30%	20%
Lonely without the client	39%	56%	5%
Worry about the patient	9%	13%	78%
Feel they are better caregivers	28%	39%	33%
Get satisfaction in caregiving	20%	70%	10%
Disagreement about the client	44%	44%	12%
Conflicting advice from professionals	28%	33%	39%

Seventy-eight percent of respondents felt that parents' tendencies to worry about their relative could be a barrier to separation. This was by far the highest rating on any item in the questionnaire. Judging from studies of family burden published in the last few years (Hatfield 1983, 1990; Lefley, 1987), most families live with high levels of anxiety a good deal of the time. Risks involved in separation clearly aggravate the tension.

We need to know more precisely the nature of these parents' anxieties. What kinds of risks do they feel are involved in their relative's living elsewhere? Some ideas may be inferred from Table 1. There seems to be concern about safety, cost, and staff competence. Parents do not feel fully confi-dent that staff members will communicate with them or have the right expectations for their relatives.

Data on Table 2 suggest that families might worry about their relative's level of functioning and his or her ability to succeed in a residential program. They may agonize over their relative's likelihood of suffering another failure; one parent noted that "the patient took a severe downturn in the last group living attempt."

Data on Table 3 suggest that there may be additional reasons for delay in separation. Respondents suggested that some parents might be lonely without their relative and that some get satisfaction from caregiving. Parents responded more often in the negative, however, to the possibility that the need for their relatives' help or their financial support could be barriers to their letting go.

Factors Triggering Separation

Parents in the survey were asked to select from a list of six possible factors the three most likely to result in a decision to have their relative live elsewhere. The rank order of parents was as follows:

• Appropriate housing becoming available.

• *Excessive conflict with the person in the home.

• *Professional advice that the person should live elsewhere.

• Aging of parents and/or declining health.

• Relative's desire for freedom to live independently from parents.

• Parents' desire for freedom to live their own lives.

(* = Tied for second place.)

Of course, housing becoming available is a key factor in beginning the separation process. Other factors that trigger the process are: excessive conflict when the relative is home, and professional advice that separation is desirable. Parents see declining health as sometimes an impetus for separation, and they see as least significant either the parents' or relative's desire for independence or freedom from each other.

We need to diffuse the emotional baggage that surrounds the issue of independence so that everyone involved— parents, client, and provider—can explore the issues comfortably.

Implications of the Study

This can best be considered a pilot study because of the small number of subjects. It dealt only with parents' perceptions, even though clients' and providers' perceptions are surely just as influential. What was learned here suggests that further study is warranted and should include parents, other family caregivers, clients, and providers.

The perception of housing shortages is undeniably real. It is difficult to prepare someone for living away from home when there is no certainty that housing will be available. In addition, our study suggests that even when housing is available, there may be barriers to smooth separation unless changes are made:

1. We need to become more objective and more rational about independence/dependence issues and avoid using labels that arouse emotions but obscure the dynamics of what is going on in the family. We need to diffuse the emotional baggage that surrounds the issue of independence so that everyone involved— parents, client, and provider—can explore the issues comfortably.

2. The word "independence" may have little usefulness in the discussion because it has so many meanings. The goal, we believe, is to help the client become as self-reliant as possible and, where needed, to depend on the system rather than on the parents. The literature is still vague about the way self-reliance comes about. In mental health practice, crude approaches are sometimes used in which the buoy is removed precipitously and the individual is left to sink or swim. Failure may be frequent, and failure is rarely an effective teacher. Such approaches do not enhance the confidence of either client or parent. We need a better understanding of the way self-reliance develops, and we need to work toward it in a concerted way. Attribution theory is applicable here, where our goal is to help individuals shift away from feeling controlled by exterior forces and toward a recognition that they can control many forces in their lives (Strauss, 1989). This involves a subtle but powerful shift in thinking that may have ramifications for the person. Parents and providers could help make this shift if they were consistent in the messages they were giving.

3. While the separation of offspring from parents must eventually be accomplished, the timing and the process by which it takes place could be quite different in different families. This could be planned with clients and their parents in a way that is comfortable for all involved.

4. It is inevitable that some parents will

be highly anxious when their relative first leaves home. They need all the reassurance we can give about their concerns. They need considerable support from professionals or from family support groups as they go through this transition process.

References

Anthony, W., Cohen, M., & Cohen, B. (1984). Psychiatric rehabilitation. In J. Talbott (Ed.), *The chronic mental patient: Five years later* (pp. 137-158). New York: Grune & Stratton.

Brown, S. L. (1978). Functioning, tasks, and stresses of parenting: Implications for guidance. In L. E. Arnold (Ed.), *Helping parents help their children* (pp. 22-34). New York: Brunner/Mazel.

Conger, J. J. (1977). *Adolescence and youth: Psychological development in a changing world.* New York: Harper & Row.

Darling, R. & Darling, J. (1982). *Children who are different.* St. Louis: Mosby.

Dincin, J. (1981). A community agency model. In J. Talbott (Ed.), *The chronic mentally ill* (pp. 212-226). New York: Human Sciences Press.

Hatfield, A. (1978). Psychological costs of schizophrenia to the family. *Social Work, 23,* 355-359.

Hatfield, A. (1983). What families want of family therapy. In W. R. McFarlane (Ed.), *Family therapy in schizophrenia* (pp. 41-65). New York: Guilford Press.

Hatfield, A. (1989). Serving the unserved in community programs. *Psychosocial Rehabilitation Journal, 13,* 71-82.

Hatfield, A. (1990). *Family education in mental illness.* New York: Guilford Press.

Krauss, J. B. & Slavinsky, A. (1982). *The chronically ill psychiatric patient and the community.* Boston: Blackwell.

Lefley, H. (1987). Behavioral manifestations of mental illness. In A. Hatfield & H. Lefley (Eds.), *Families Of the mentally ill: Coping and adaptation.* New York: Guilford Press.

Shaffer, D. R. (1979). *Social and personality development.* Florence, Kentucky: Brooks/Cole.

Spaniol, L., Jung, H., Zipple, A., & Fitzgerald, S. (1987). Families as a resource in the rehabilitation of the severely psychiatrically disabled. In A. Hatfield & H. Lefley (Eds.), *Families of the mentally ill: Coping and adaptation* (pp. 167-190). New York: Guilford Press.

Strauss, J. (1989). Meditating processes in schizophrenia. *British Journal of Psychiatry, 155,* 22-28.

A FATHER'S THOUGHTS

Anonymous

THIS ARTICLE ORIGINALLY APPEARED IN THE
Schizophrenia Bulletin, 1983, 9(3), 439-442.

My son Jim has been a paranoid schizophrenic for 9 years. Being retired, I have had time to study the literature about the illness in an attempt to understand it. It is an ambiguous project because each schizophrenic is different and there are many conflicting and overlapping theories. Many endogenous and exogenous factors seem to be involved in the development of schizophrenia, but I believe the evidence points to an endogenous imbalance within the central nervous system. Without such a necessary precondition, I do not believe a person would become schizophrenic whatever his life situation might be.

If so, why Jim should be ill is uncertain. There is no known history of the illness in either parental family, and there are two normal married sisters. The absence of a family history of schizophrenia probably does not rule out a biogenetic factor. Just as certain physically visible "birth defects" can occur in the absence of prior history, possibly an invisible "birth defect" can occur in the central nervous system.

Other factors may be involved in Jim's case. As opposed to his sisters, there was intrauterine complication, arduous birth, postbirth breathing block, and extreme colickiness. From what I have read, it is possible that these factors might be implicated in some way.

Professionals have written of parents remembering their schizophrenic offspring as being normal in childhood, but usually with some question as to parental retrospection or defensive reaction. I do remember Jim as a happy and alert child, and family relationships as being relatively good during his childhood. While I recognize that family life has emotional and attitudinal effects on family members, I do not believe our family life caused Jim's illness. No family is perfect, and it may be that some aspects of family life affect a preschizophrenic in a way that they would not if a biological vulnerability did not exist. I think that before Jim became overtly disturbed, we may have intuitively sensed that something was not quite right, and he in turn may have been negatively affected by our concern.

Possibly a second grade report card has some bearing. It stated as follows:

> Is not working up to ability, does not enter freely into class discussion, does not distinguish between work and play, and has difficulty with attention span.

I have wondered if these characteristics, which are still apparent in adult life, might have been early behavioral markers of a predisposition for poor life adjustment.

Jim showed improvement during grade school because of his mother's coaching and encouragement, but in high school things worsened. While Jim made a fair start the first year, his grades deteriorated the second year and he ultimately was graduated with barely passing grades. I attribute his poor grades not to lack of intelligence but to innate attentional difficulty. Because his sisters and peers received average to excellent grades, I think his scholastic difficulty was a gross blow to his self image and the start of serious self doubt. I had several conferences at the high school; they said Jim was having a difficult adjustment but would grow out of it. Psychiatric treatment was not suggested. We accepted the school's assessment, but in retrospect, Jim's scholastic problems were warning signs.

After high school, Jim obtained a menial job and moved to an apartment with several other boys. Although he had been very much against drugs during high school, he experimented with "uppers" and "downers." After a year, Jim came home and quit taking drugs. His first hospitalization was over a year later. My wife and his sisters say the drugs "did it to him." I would like to believe this but feel Jim's developing illness drove him to experiment with drugs. The drugs may have had an effect on him but I do not believe they were primarily responsible for his illness.

Something must be said about interpersonal relationships. Basically, Jim was a friendly person. He was not a "loner" and was motivated to be with people. He never wanted to upset anybody and did not easily tolerate in himself or others negative affect such as anger, disapproval, or criticism and even positive affect such as joviality. Jim had friends and a girlfriend during high school but over the years he seemed to drift to less desirable associates with whom he probably felt less stressed.

Just after high school, Jim told me he had trouble with people but then would not discuss his problem. He did not mean that he disliked people or was being treated badly. I think he felt unable to cope and sensed his emotional arousal as threatening to himself. At that time Jim blamed himself for his problems and was not alienated from society. As pressures mounted I think he developed a great fear of himself. Later self-blame and fear were rationalized and projected on to family and society in a paranoid way, leading finally to psychosis.

Since his first hospitalization at age 19, Jim has had 11 hospitalizations in 9 years. There was an 11-month stay at a state hospital during the sixth year. Two hospitalizations were by police action and three were by court order. Six times Jim went on his own to the local receiving hospital and was admitted. Jim must have felt an intense feeling of arousal that frightened him and prompted him to seek hospitalization.

Once in the hospital, though, he would not open up to psychiatrists or social workers. Once he did mention fear of loss of self control.

I think that earlier than we realized Jim had an intuition that something was not quite right. Jim told a favored cousin that he thought there was something wrong with himself, but we could not get him to seek help. He had a card on his desk that read, "If you need help, ask for it. If you don't, prove it." Later, I made another effort to get Jim to accept help but it was rejected with hostile agitation. His mind was fighting for survival and the mind will not easily admit to a mental problem. Of course, after becoming psychotic, Jim did not think anything was wrong.

During the first 6 years of Jim's illness, we were unable to establish continuity of treatment or medication because of our lack of knowledge, turnover of psychiatrists at the local receiving hospital, Jim's actions, and other factors. He had two private psychiatrists during this period. There are doctors and doctors, and we had to learn this by harsh experience.

One mental health center psychiatrist took Jim "cold turkey" off the 200 mg Thorazine that had been prescribed by his previous doctor. Jim had been doing pretty well on Thorazine but said it made him tired. While I had been told there would be no withdrawal effects, Jim experienced extreme hyperactivity for 3 sleepless days and nights followed by a 36-hour sleep. After his long sleep Jim emerged a fairly alert and cheerful person. After several days, he became withdrawn and stuporous. A month later, after a minor operation requiring anesthesia Jim became psychotic on the general ward. Transfer to the psychiatric ward and remedication took place but this break marked a turning point for the worse and 2 years later Jim was sent to a state hospital.

State hospitals have unpleasant connotations, but I was pleasantly surprised at the facilities and treatment Jim received. After a period on the receiving ward, he was placed in an open cottage situation. Later he was moved to a "return to the community" program. Although this state hospital had long-term locked wards and a crisis ward, it was still an open place. The staff was very cooperative with the parents.

Jim's progress in the community return program was only fair, but he was placed in a halfway house in our home town. This move put Jim in good spirits, nonhostile, and nondelusionary. He called to tell us of the move and sounded like his old self. This positive change in mood and thought might illustrate a psychological placebo factor. Unfortunately, Jim slipped back into his usual "in-betweenness."

The transitional home was staffed almost entirely by female professionals, some of whom I respect greatly. There was one staff member I could not agree with. She told Jim that if he acted crazy people would think he was crazy. It may be that at a certain stage this approach is workable with some patients. But I don't think a delusional person is conscious of the fact that he is having delusions. Delusions may be deliberate at an unconscious level, but the person does not consciously realize this during an active delusional period.

The home has an "on call" staff psychiatrist, but some patients are under the care of private psychiatrists. There has been antagonism between the home and some private psychiatrists, but the situation is easing now. I don't want to dwell on this friction except to say that some local psychiatrists are not as openminded or pro-

Parents cannot go through years of living with the illness without feeling concern and disappointment.

gressive as they should be. In turn the home staff is suspicious of overmedication and is more therapy minded. I think it is probable also that some patients are undermedicated.

Jim again did not respond well to group therapy. Maybe his lack of response can be related to his school history of not participating in class discussion. He did well in his work duties and was placed in an affiliated work program. He was also moved to a satellite boarding home. I was never sure whether he was moved because he needed less supervision or because of his negative attitude toward group therapy. It is a fact, though, that Jim has improved much more than some of the group therapy-minded patients.

In the work program, Jim does janitorial work 4 hours a day in the community under the supervision of nonprofessional but trained work leaders. The work program has been good for Jim, but he did not like the boarding home and neither did we. After a year he asked if he could come home to live. Against professional advice, we allowed Jim to return home on the condition that he stay in the work program. Parents must sometimes be guided by their own feelings. I'm not sure we really wanted Jim back home, but we felt that rejection would have had a bad effect on Jim and on us. This arrangement has worked out fairly well. But living at home is a second choice. Jim would rather have his own apartment but can't for financial reasons. It is also questionable if he is ready to live by himself.

Considering the nebulous nature of mental illness, I believe the transitional home does a reasonable job. Jim benefited by being there. I was disturbed when the local newspaper published a letter to the editor from a private psychiatrist who was condemnatory of transitional homes. He seemed to feel that if he could not successfully treat a patient in his office, the patient should be in a hospital.

After moving back home, Jim had a relapse requiring a 15-day stay on the psychiatric ward of a general hospital. This was in reaction to being reevaluated for Social Security disability pay. The threat of its loss and phone calls to him by the state representative apparently were too much for him. Perhaps this response illustrates his intolerance for stressful pressure. He was recertified and is back home and in his work program.

As a result of his last hospitalization, Jim came under the care of his present psychiatrist. He was released from the hospital taking Moban and became very hyperactive mentally and physically. A lithium trial had no success. Both medications were stopped and he was put on Haldol, 30 mg per day. In 3 days there was remarkable improvement. In fact, there was some improvement after 1 day. The dosage was reduced after a year to 20 mg. Jim is doing well on Haldol and says it does not bother him as other medications did.

Jim's present psychiatrist seems more progressive than others he has had. The psychiatrist talks to Jim more and is more cooperative with rehabilitation programs. He has expanded his office to include a clinical psychologist and a social counselor. He has even given us his home phone number!

I believe the psychiatrist has been able to make Jim understand his need for medication. Jim is pretty good about his medication but rebels at too many pills or a difficult schedule. Right now he takes his medication at bedtime. I believe the medication is antipsychotic rather than antischizophrenic. The medication seems to reduce arousal, thereby relieving pressure on thinking functions. An adequate single dosage has always seemed to work best with Jim and Haldol seems to have the most favorable results with fewer side effects .

I have read about EE, the expressed emotion factor. No doubt schizophrenics cannot easily handle expressions of concern, anger, disagreement, or disapproval —particularly from parents. Our experience with Jim has been that when he is disturbed by events outside the home, he becomes edgy and seeks assurance from us. It is sometimes difficult to find a middle course that does not support his fear and negative thought and still have him feel we are on his side.

Parents cannot go through years of living with the illness without feeling concern and disappointment. It's not really possible to hide this response. It is intuitively felt by Jim. I once said something to Jim with a smile, and he told me that a smile was no good if it was deceptive. On another occasion, Jim reacted to a smile by asking why I was laughing at him.

Delusions have been a problem. We have had mixed advice about how to deal with delusions and have had to learn by experience. Once when Jim was in a good mood, I tried to reason with him about a delusion. He said, "Dad, don't tell me. I know I started the EPA." This was said in all sincerity and good will. At other times, hostility or withdrawal was the reaction.

Several weeks ago, Jim said he thought he should go into the hospital as he was having hateful thoughts. I told Jim that

In giving support...we have to be realistic...We have had to learn when to stand firm and when to compromise.

since he now realizes he has such thoughts, he can disregard them. Jim told me not to counsel him as I was not a doctor. I then told Jim to call his doctor, which he did, and he did not go to the hospital.

I think UEE, unexpressed emotion, must also be considered. Despite his illness and resentment, Jim still trusts us more than anybody. In giving support to Jim, we have to be realistic even though disagreement may cause resentment, confusion, or withdrawal on his part. We have had to learn when to stand firm and when to compromise. Parents must guard against counter-withdrawal. This can cause resentment, and resentment in a schizophrenic can quickly turn to hostility. Jim may want to talk but is "frozen up." Saying something may "unfreeze" him or not. I have said something to him with no immediate reply and gone back to reading only to have him answer 5 minutes later. Silence can be deadening, and for Jim, probably results in too much brooding. Sometimes a mild display of temper is a steadying cue to him.

I have cited these problems to show that even when parents have an objective orientation to the illness, living with the ill person can be nerve-wrecking and exhausting. I am sure having an ill son has had a negative effect on us. We are probably somewhat affectively blunted now ourselves. But we survive: my wife is back teaching school and I keep busy with two hobbies, studying and trying to write.

Jim is now in his best state of remission ever, but will it last and be improved upon? There is no sure way of telling. As parents, we are frustrated because we are limited in how much we can be of help. So much depends on Jim's own mind. We have concern about his future, particularly after we are gone. We try to guard against Jim's becoming too dependent on us. We can only do the best we can while we are still here. Jim is quite rational now but very moody. He may for the first time be trying to adjust realistically to the conditions of his illness.

Jim mentions his inability to read or keep track of things on TV. But he drives a car very well. Apparently the type of concentration or attention required for driving is not the same as for other types of activity. He listens to music a lot. Music is not stressful to him. I like to play video games on occasion when he and I go out for coffee. He will not play them. One time he said they drive him crazy. I believe the concentration required stresses him. Later, he said he won't play video games because they waste too much electrical energy. This is not an illogical statement, per se, but is it a true belief or a rationalization to cover up his difficulty? I believe the latter and wonder if chronic defensive overrationalization has something to do with causing thought disorder.

While families may be defensive about family history, one must be cautious about what schizophrenics say. Jim once told me that the only people who had ever treated him decently were his sisters, but later when he was hospitalized he said he was having problems because they beat him with frying pans. At other times, it was something his mother or I did. Schizophrenics look for reasons to justify their condition.

Many schizophrenics show resentment toward parents. Some amount of normal resentment develops during the strivings for independence of adolescence and is outgrown later. I observed this in my daughters. We never really restricted independence, but I think normal resentment is magnified in the schizophrenic mind.

I am not positive of my hypothesis in this essay. I see much similarity between myself and Jim, but whatever my faults, I have always had good attentional ability and tolerance for stress. This reinforces my belief that a biological deficiency is the root cause of Jim's illness.

A Mother's View

Gaetana Caldwell-Smith

GAETANA CALDWELL-SMITH WORKS AS AN INSURANCE BROKER, AND IS A WRITER. SHE HAS AN AA IN CLINICAL PSYCHOLOGY AND IS CURRENTLY WORKING ON A BA IN WORLD AND COMPARATIVE LITERATURE WITH A MINOR IN CLINICAL PSYCHOLOGY. SHE IS A CERTIFIED MASTER HYPNOTHERAPIST, GIVING WORKSHOPS ON DREAMS. HER SON CONTINUES TO IMPROVE.

THIS ARTICLE ORIGINALLY APPEARED IN THE *Schizophrenia Bulletin*, 1990, 16(4), 687-690.

My son Mark (he requested that I not use his real name) has registered for the coming college semester. Recently, he sat for the Scholastic Aptitude Test (SAT), a prerequisite for college entry. To some, this might not seem like such a big deal. But to Mark and me, it is a big deal. Four years ago I held faint hope he would be capable of such an undertaking as Mark had been diagnosed as an acute schizophrenic.

Rain beat down incessantly the day I committed Mark to the psychiatric ward at San Francisco General Hospital. We had planned to leave that morning for a brief vacation. I had reserved a primitive cabin for a few days on the ocean just south of the picturesque town of Stinson Beach on the northern California coast. I thought it would be good for Mark to get away from the city, away from city noises and people. I felt it would calm him. That it was the middle of winter did not deter us. We like being near the ocean regardless of the season. I had envisioned the rain pouring down, the ocean thundering against huge boulders a few feet below and sending shivers through our cabin, and Mark and me sitting snugly by the wood stove sipping hot chocolate from heavy mugs.

The previous year Mark had been a student at City College and had been doing well in his art, English, and biology classes. He was older than most students. At 14 he had dropped out of high school. He had become antisocial, rarely seeing his friends. Before long, he had refused to leave his room, except at night when he fixed himself something to eat. At one point he came to me and said he wanted to see a psychiatrist. We went to an outpatient clinic for a while, but it didn't seem to help. He stopped going.

As a lay therapist with a strong background in both Jungian and Gestalt therapy, I conducted daily sessions with Mark. I wore a mask and disguised my voice as a means of obviating subjectivity. At times I remained in his room for an hour and neither of us spoke. Finally, one day he opened up. A few months later he started going for walks. He joined his brothers and me for meals. Soon after, he enrolled in high school courses at the community college and studied diligently every night. Mark graduated in 2 years with a B average. After graduation he passed the tests for the California Conservation Corps. He then worked for a year away from home up north in Calaveras County. The following year, he signed on with the Young Adult Conservation Corps, lived at home, and went to work every day.

Some months later, he quit his job and enrolled at City College. After the first midterm, he complained about the students and he missed days. Most of the time he seemed restless and agitated. He told me men followed him and wanted to kill him. I heard him pacing at night. I would get out of bed three and four times to tell him to be quiet. He played one record repeatedly. He never spoke to me without shouting, and he would shove his fist in my face. When I suggested conducting sessions with him again, he refused, screaming that he was all right; he didn't need them. Sometimes he left the house and didn't return for days, sleeping out, he said, in nearby hills. He didn't speak to his brothers when they came by to talk to him. (They are older and had moved out some time before.) He dropped out of school.

Even as a child, what made people tick had fascinated me. In grammar school I was forever lugging home books on madness and life in insane asylums (as mental institutions were then called). My mother seemed rather proud of my scholarly indulgence. Up until Mark's illness, I had never known anyone diagnosed as mentally ill. I only knew what I had read. I was appalled at how the mentally ill were physically restrained, zapped with electroshock treatments, and drugged into drooling, zombie-like states. I grew to be an idealist, believing, as R. D. Laing once had, that mental illness was a psyche in chaos that would eventually come right again if the illness was left to run its course in a supportive, noninstitutional setting.

During the early stages of Mark's illness, I held to the hope that it would end without the interference of hospitalization, drugs, and physical restraints and that this end would come soon. He reached plateaus of sanity from time to time, which served to nurture my hopes. Then he became self-abusive and physically threatening again. Plateaus came less often. I sensed his torture. I then reconciled myself to go for anything that would put an end to his suffering.

Mark's actions grew more bizarre. He stood naked in the middle of the kitchen floor, raising one arm to the ceiling, screaming gibberish at me when I brought him a blanket to cover himself. He torqued his body into painful contortions. He shouted unintelligible phrases. I could not speak to him. We had no communication. He took several hot showers every day, often leaving the bathroom with the shower going full blast and with clouds of steam rolling through the doorway. Naked, rivulets streaming down skin flushed red, he slogged into the kitchen where he stood glazed-eyed. When I told him to shut off the shower, he yelled at me to leave him alone. A few nights I woke to find him hovering over me.

Somehow, I remained calm. Yet in the refuge of my bedroom I often broke down in tears of sadness, frustration, and fear. Sometimes I cried in front of Mark, who suddenly would break through his madness to assure me he was okay. He wouldn't act "like that anymore."

I managed to keep up with classes, to maintain a social life. When I had friends over, Mark stayed in his room, shouting occasionally. I would go in to him to tell him he was disturbing us. He would apologize, then throw a blanket over his head and stand motionless for hours in the middle of his room.

Living with Mark became like living with wind, or fire, or water, or earth, never knowing when the elements would turn. It helped to think of him as being that unpredictable. I dared not leave him alone overnight. And whenever I went out for a few hours, I would not know what to expect when I got home. I tried to convince him he needed help. He refused to listen. I sought help for him. I had been out of work for several months, working only part time, so I could not afford private care.

I called every public mental health facility I could find in the telephone book. They could do nothing, they said, unless Mark could no longer care for himself or was a threat to himself and others. I finally convinced some caseworkers to come out to evaluate him. I told them I had tried to talk to Mark and he had punched his face until it swelled and turned purple. They would be right over, they said. But when they arrived, Mark got dressed, bolted out the bathroom window, and climbed fences to the street. The caseworkers left. They told me to call when Mark came home. I did, but they couldn't send anyone out. For a couple of days after the aborted evaluation,

Mark skated on another plateau of near sanity. I went ahead with plans for our excursion to the ocean.

We had decided to leave for the cabin very early in the morning. We would catch the first bus to Mill Valley, then hike over Mt. Tamalpais. Then a rainstorm broke during the night (Mark had slept undisturbed), forcing us to change our plans. We would take the bus directly to Stinson Beach, then hike the mile south to the cabins.

I took a shower—my last for a few days since the facilities at the cabin didn't include indoor plumbing or showers. When I emerged from the bathroom, Mark was nowhere to be found. The rain hammered against the windows. I couldn't imagine where he could have gone unless he went down to the garage for the backpacks. I was getting dressed when the doorbell rang. It has to be Mark, I thought. He forgot his key. I opened the door to find Mark, dripping wet, barechested, wearing only one sneaker and a sopping pair of blue jeans. He was handcuffed to a policeman, who explained that he had found Mark running down the median strip of an eight-lane boulevard that parallels our quiet street. It was a weekday morning. Nonstop commuter traffic zoomed along at breakneck speeds. The policeman asked if Mark was all right and if he should take him to General Hospital. "We are going to the ocean in a few minutes," I said. "He'll be fine with me." Mark brushed past the policeman and bounded up the stairs into our flat. The officer asked, "Are you sure?" I said, "Yes."

Overcoming everyday hurdles has more significance for us now than in the past. We no longer take things for granted. And rather than speculate on the future, we accept only what each day brings.

While Mark toweled himself dry, I asked him why he ran out into the rain in such a dangerous place. He said he just wanted to be in the rain. He wanted to feel it wash against his skin. I told him it will be raining where we are going and there won't be policemen or traffic and he can run in the rain all he wants. I went into my room to pack. When I came out, Mark had disappeared again. I had had it. If the police bring him back, I will tell them to take Mark to psychiatric emergency. I went down the back stairs to the garage to get the packs, hoping to find Mark there. I glanced out the rain-streaked and spattered garage window. A dismal scene unfolded in the distance, an impressionist painting in greys and blues. On the boulevard stood a barechested Mark, the patrol car, and the policeman beside it. I trudged up the back stairs. Icy raindrops burned into my scalp and pattered onto my shoulders through my sweatshirt. The view from my bedroom window revealed a now quiet, rain-slicked boulevard bereft of commuter traffic. Mark, the policeman, and the patrol car had vanished. I waited for the officer to bring him home. He never did.

A quarter of an hour later, I got a phone call from the policeman. He said he had taken Mark to psychiatric emergency and that a woman would be calling me soon to get his history. He reassured me that Mark was fine. "He wasn't hurt(!)." The policeman's admission of this surprised me. I wondered if they may have had to physically restrain my son, or rough him up to get him into the patrol car.

Mark had made his choice. By running berserk through commuter traffic in a rainstorm, he had, in effect, run for help. I was relieved. Should he have to remain hospitalized for a while, I would have time to rest and to clean our flat, especially Mark's room. It really needed it.

Thus, began Mark's confinement in Ward 7B of General Hospital. I visited him every day. The atmosphere of the ward and the kindness and concern of the help assuaged my fears. This was no scene from *One Flew Over the Cuckoo's Nest* or *The Snake Pit*. The visiting area was bright, furnished with comfortable couches, bookshelves filled with books and magazines, and a ping pong table. Patients could watch television in a separate section. Most of them were male. While Mark and I visited, others would approach to talk. Some spoke gibberish, others seemed quite lucid. From their rooms in the rear of the ward I could hear moans and screams, which did not disturb me after what I had been through. Among the patients were the pacers, the obsessive-compulsives, the mute, and the frenetic. Some behaved as though they were on a holiday. I witnessed a scene one evening in which parents of one patient dropped off a cardboard box of his belongings, telling the doctors they didn't want their son to come home when he was discharged. I was told this happened a lot. I spoke to Mark's doctors frequently and felt I was given the straight dope about him. His brothers visited, too, and Mark welcomed their attention.

Two months later, his doctors released a heavily medicated Mark to my conservatorship to continue his long haul toward recovery under the National Institute of Mental Health's Schizophrenia Treatment Program (STP). His first week home, I accompanied him to the STP clinic for his medication. After that, Mark insisted on making his weekly visits alone. He traveled by cab for over a year as the chaos of public transportation was more than he could handle. Now he makes the trip every other week.

He and I attended, and still attend to this day, monthly family meetings headed by the psychiatrists and social welfare professionals of the program. Initially, the meetings gave us the education we needed to cope with the illness. They now serve, after more than 4 years, as our major support group. Many of the original families attend. For 2 years, an STP therapist came weekly to our home for an hour of valuable "talk therapy" sessions with both Mark and me. The main thrust of these sessions was to help us solve problems we encounter dealing with schizophrenia on a day-to-day basis. Through the STP clinic, Mark's medication is carefully monitored. Over the years, his intake of antipsychotic drugs has been stabilized, and a dosage of attendant medications (one for a thyroid condition discovered through blood tests) has been prescribed that allows him to function "normally" and gives him motivation.

When I realized the responsibility of caring for Mark at home, my heart sank. A feeling of helplessness overcame me, and for the first few months it would come and go, depending on Mark's behavior and overall ambiance. Though his brothers visited and were loving and supportive of him, for quite some time conversation was strained. I watched Mark carefully for signs of his prolixin injections wearing off. His face took on a haunted look and deep dark circles marked the skin underneath glassy eyes. Then he would sweat profusely a strange acrid odor, an odor I recognized as fear, and he would have to take supplemental prolixin until he received another shot. He argued that he didn't need it, or he insisted that he couldn't take prolixin with cogentin and refused altogether. Although the psychiatrists had warned family members against threatening patients with rehospitalization, I tried to get across to Mark the importance of taking medication as a means of avoiding going back into the hospital. At these times he called the clinic to verify what I had told him. Only when he got a confirmation from the psychiatrist on duty would he agree to take it.

Anguish filled me during his bad days. Fortunately, with the help of extra medication, they never lasted more than 24 hours. Mark's spontaneous remarks, observations, and plain old small talk or sudden smiles were like welcoming beacons into the person we once knew.

A month or so out of the hospital, he got a volunteer job as a maintenance man at a community center. His hours there were not sufficiently organized, however, and he stopped going. He then joined a day treatment center, participating in their programs and activities for over 2 years.

When Mark had been home a year, I felt confident leaving him alone to go on an overnight trip. Since then, I have gone away several times on business or pleasure for as long as a week. I make sure I call Mark every day at a specific time and leave numbers where I can be reached, if I can. The worst thing that can happen when I am away is that he will end up in the hospital; and if it comes to that, I will have to face it at that time. It is foolish to worry.

Though we never made it to the primitive cabin on the coast, 2 years ago Mark did accompany me for a week to Esalen in Big Sur, where I gave a workshop. Since his hospitalization, this was his first encounter with people in this kind of setting. He ate with me, along with strangers, in the huge dining room, serving up his own food cafeteria style. He went on hikes on the trails and down to the beach.

In the past couple of years, he has attended both of his brothers' weddings, and on a small scale he now socializes with friends and relatives. He is the delighted uncle to a daughter of one of his brothers. He has grown comfortable watching PBS channels on television and listening to classical, jazz, and light rock music. And he no longer has qualms about riding public transportation.

A few months ago he told me he wanted to go back to college—only this time it had to be a state college, he said. He took the bus to the admissions office to register. The SAT bulletin came in the mail. He completed the necessary forms and mailed them in. Using workbooks I bought for him, Mark studied for over 2 months. When he returned from taking the test, he said, smiling, "I was the oldest person there, but I didn't care." His eyes sparkled. Whether he passes is immaterial. He has made great progress. Overcoming everyday hurdles has more significance for us now than in the past. We no longer take things for granted. And rather than speculate on the future, we accept only what each day brings.

Looking back over the years of his illness and gradual recovery, I find that what made it, and makes it, easier for me to cope was, and is, continuing with—and recognizing the importance of—my own life, apart from Mark's.

Epilogue: Mark watched the mail every day for the test results. They came a couple of days ago. He passed.

Schizophrenia Through a Sister's Eyes: The Burden of Invisible Baggage

Amy S. Brodoff

AMY S. BRODOFF IS A NOVELIST AND FREELANCE WRITER FOR NATIONAL MAGAZINES SPECIALIZING IN PSYCHOLOGY AND HEALTH.

THIS ARTICLE ORIGINALLY APPEARED IN THE *Schizophrenia Bulletin*, 1988, 14(1), 113-116.

In this essay, I give a detailed account of the impact my older brother's schizophrenia has had on my life, describing our changing relationship from childhood through adolescence and early adulthood. I attempt to analyze and understand the emotional separation from my brother that has been necessary to my survival and personal growth, as well as experiencing the deep sense of loss and sorrow that has accompanied that separation.

About 10 years ago, when I was a sophomore in college and my older brother Andy was a junior at a school nearby, I went to visit him for an extended holiday weekend. On Friday, we attended a party given by a classmate in his dorm. When it was time to leave, Andy opened a door that appeared to lead outside, but instead found himself stepping gingerly inside a closet. "Some people are coming out of the closet, but I'm going back inside," he stated matter of factly. The quip was funny, but in retrospect, it seemed to convey a hidden message: For it was during that weekend that Andy experienced several psychotic episodes and only a short time later that he was diagnosed as schizophrenic.

When I first saw my older brother that weekend, he looked much the same, though perceptibly more troubled and disheveled than usual. His large hazel eyes radiated a gentle green light and had a dash of yellow in the center, subtly changing color depending on what he wore. He was still handsome, but too thin now, unkempt, and a little unsavory. Although he had looked forward to my visit, he had trouble engaging in any sustained conversations and frequently needed to withdraw.

Andy was barely able to sit through the movie he'd chosen for us on Saturday night and jumped up every 10 or 15 minutes to take a walk. On a trip to the ladies room, I found him in a dark corner of the lobby compulsively pacing back and forth. At meals, he was silent and preoccupied, ignoring his food, choosing instead to suck and chew on a mug full of ice cubes as he stared blankly into space.

His behavior was bizarre and troubling, but it didn't prepare me for what happened on the last evening of my stay, shortly before I planned to return to school. Andy had always loved animals, but he loathed and feared insects, particularly spiders. When I returned to the dorm after doing some shopping, I found him wearing a pair of gloves, frantically brushing at his clothes as though trying to rid himself of a swarm of clinging insects. The sight of a spider had convinced him that a vast colony of insects was quietly weaving *his* web. Black ants, beetles, gnats, and fluttering moths had teemed in, he believed fastening themselves to the web—a cage that threatened to imprison him.

My brother was hospitalized, the first in a long series of voluntary and involuntary hospitalizations at institutions around the country as our family embarked on the endless quest for care that might ultimately help him. Although my mother, father, younger brother, two uncles, both grandfathers, and several cousins are all physicians, covering the gamut of specialties including psychiatry, we have yet to find medical care that has led to significant or sustained improvement in Andy's condition.

My brother exists in a subterranean world of fantasy a good deal of the time. Yet, when we were young children, it was I who often created and lived inside an imaginary world complete with a rogue's gallery of characters and a colorful assortment of landscapes, while Andy possessed an unusual hypersensitivity to reality, as though he were perceiving the world through a magnifying glass.

I loved to take long solitary walks in the woods near our home, roaming the meadows beyond our backyard, and exploring the mysterious cemetery and garden that lay hidden behind a stone wall at the corner of our street. In these special secret places, I spun a continuous yarn, a novel in which I was both heroine and author. Just as the sidewalk paintings in *Mary Poppins* were magically transformed into real life worlds, I was able to transform my own world into a storybook, a private pastime I engaged in for amusement or sought as a refuge: whenever my own life seemed especially bleak or chaotic, I could magically invent another.

In contrast to me, Andy didn't transform the world; he perceived life with the painful acuity of one whose mental filtering mechanism has simply melted away, leaving behind only naked nerve fibers. He seemed to have an emotional sixth sense, enabling him to foresee what was going to happen—particularly painful events—long before anyone else was aware of them. When he was only 5, he told me with certainty that our parents were going to get a divorce. I dismissed this notion as nonsense, probably because it was too terrifying to contemplate, and besides, I convinced myself, our parents rarely fought. I refused to worry about things that might never happen—that is, until 6 years later, when Andy's prediction came true: he had perceived the undercurrent of dissonance arid detachment in our parents relationship long before anyone else was willing or able to

acknowledge it, even perhaps, our parents themselves.

Despite the differences in the way we perceived and coped with the world, Andy and I were unusually close as children. His presence in my life, and mine in his, was more constant than that of either of our parents. I adored and emulated my older brother, tagged after him, and vied for his attention; he was my daily companion, my playmate, and so I believed, my protector.

As young children, Andy and I shared a secret language that included a ditty he made up to comfort me when I felt sad or frightened. Whenever I needed consolation, he'd tenderly rub his face against mine and then pat my cheeks with both of his hands while chanting

> Ah sista goah, I love you and
> the pack. I give you milk and
> candy to make the bad go back.

Although the poem would never win a Pulitzer Prize, it was pretty good for a toddler, and the chant became a ritual between us, offering reassurance that Andy would watch over me, as well as our puppy, two cats, turtles, salamanders, and tropical fish, providing nurturance and keeping us all safe from harm.

However, a recent look at old family photos has given my memories a jolt, and made me question who was really protecting whom. Paradoxically, these snapshots belie my memories of Andy as my caretaker. In each and every one, I stand in the foreground with Andy several paces behind me, even though he is older by a year and a half and there are only two of us in the picture. I am sturdy and smiling; Andy is frail, his handsome features scrunched up into a scowl. He holds his body in an odd, concave position, sucking in the center of his body, with his head pitched awkwardly forward. Thin arms, bent at the elbows, hang lank behind his torso as if he holds onto a set of invisible supporting bars. Occasionally, he smiles, but these pictures are the most disturbing of all: My brother's taut, clenched smile, baring most of his upper and lower front teeth, conveys only great tension and pain: it is a frozen, soundless scream.

As Andy and I grew older, our lives took very different directions, and the honeymoon phase of our relationship came to a halt. As my world broadened, Andy's became increasingly constricted. I enjoyed school and was a conscientious student with a widening circle of friends and a schedule brimming with athletics and extracurricular activities. Andy did poorly in school and was frequently on the verge of flunking several of his classes, even though his IQ was within the genius bracket. With few emotional resources or social outlets, my brother was a quiet loner, often scapegoated by peers and teachers alike.

I watched with alarm as Andy became progressively out of touch with his own body, as if it were an alien object belonging to someone else. He began to wear mismatched, ill fitting clothing and neglected basic grooming and hygiene. For several years during high school, his body seemed frighteningly metamorphic, expanding to gross obesity in a matter of months, and then shrinking, just as suddenly, to a haggard thinness bordering on emaciation.

Although I didn't understand what ailed my older brother, it seemed clear that he was on a steady downhill course. Out of a deep fear for my own survival that I scarcely understood, I began to draw rigid boundaries between us, arming myself with evidence that we were nothing alike.

In his eyes, I saw the disturbing reflection of what I feared I might become, and his presence became a daily reminder that the carefully ordered world I had painstakingly created could easily topple down...

My efforts to dissociate myself from Andy were often quite successful: Although we attended the same school for many years, few people were aware that we were brother and sister, despite the evidence of the rather unusual last name we shared. When peers or teachers discovered our relationship, I panicked somehow, I had been found out.

I felt that the part of me that was emotionally fragile, that sensed I didn't quite belong, despite belonging, had magically burst from its boundaries in my inner life and found expression in Andy's illness. What I harbored secretly, he expressed to the outside world. What was to prevent me from deteriorating just like Andy? After all, we shared the same parents, many of the same genes, and the same childhood environment. In his eyes, I saw the disturbing reflection of what I feared I might become, and his presence became a daily reminder that the carefully ordered world I had painstakingly created could easily topple down like an intricate sand castle washed away by a wave.

However, when outsiders recognized that Andy and I were from the same family, I was also painfully reminded of the deep bond I still felt with him. I loved my brother more than I could admit, and my abandonment of him was an abandonment of part of myself. When I witnessed the cruelty Andy endured, I felt the smarting pain of the barbs personally.

Yet, when I attempted to include Andy in my social life, it was an almost predictable fiasco.

Envious of my social acceptance and achievements, enraged by my abandonment of him, and humiliated for being included intermittently out of charity, Andy sabotaged any prospects for an enjoyable time. It was hard to love him when he remained mute and sullen, hurled a boyfriend's hat in front of a passing car, used my silk scarf to clean his ear, or urinated randomly in the park.

As our family privately lurched from one emergency to another involving my brother and the ebb and flow of his moods became the main focus of each day, I began to feel neglected for being healthy. My own concerns were often dwarfed by Andy's larger problems, while my joys and successes seemed even more trivial. I craved more attention and recognition from my parents, but felt guilty about these longings since Andy was obviously so much more needy. In bitter moments, I felt that the only way I could win my parents' affection was by becoming sick too. Yet, I knew that mental illness was far too high a price to pay—even for love.

Some months after Andy was first institutionalized, I went to visit him in the hospital. With a shaved head, a jagged front tooth (a relic of his days rootlessly roaming around Times Square), and gestures that had the diffuse, futile energy characteristic of old men, my brother seemed like a homeless vagabond. His eyes were both vacant and haunted with the naked look of a frightened animal frozen by the beam of approaching headlights. He was pathetically docile, parroting back my words and gestures, as though he didn't know where my identity left off and his own began. The deep sadness I felt at seeing him this way was virtually eclipsed by the welling up within me of panic. His mirroring of my words and gestures had triggered the age old terror that our identities were entwined, that I too might become schizophrenic. When I told Andy that I would have to leave soon, he clutched the scarlet sleeve of my blazer and asked, "Can you see me?"

During these first few years of Andy's illness, the daily rhythms of our family's lives were often turned topsy turvy, since my brother frequently ran away from the hospital, stopped taking his medicine, and aimlessly wandered around the most dangerous sections of cities like New York and New Haven in a psychotic state. More times than I can remember, we had to stop whatever we were doing and chase after him, bring him home, and convince him to return to the hospital— only to have the same cycle repeated in several months' time. These unpredictable upheavals made my family seem like a fragile vessel whirling about in an overpowering eddy. When I was sucked into these emergencies, they threatened to overwhelm me. I couldn't rescue Andy and defuse my parents' conflicts (about how best to care for Andy and who was to blame for his illness) while carrying on with the demands of my own life. I felt the destructive force of the eddy in which our family swirled and knew that if I didn't get some distance, I'd be drawn into the vortex

As our family privately lurched from one emergency to another involving my brother and the ebb and flow of his moods became the main focus of each day, I began to feel neglected for being healthy.

and drowned. To save myself, I decided to jump ship, separating myself from Andy and the family, resolving first to pull together the pieces of my own life.

It is now about a decade since Andy was first diagnosed as schizophrenic. I no longer feel that my brother and I are shadowsides of the same person or that our destinies are entwined. On the deepest level where intellect leaves off and gut emotion begins, I know I am not Andy. Today, I can see him without fear, but not without sorrow. The chronic nature of his illness makes it a problem that is never truly resolved, and the sadness I feel about the bleakness of his life is a burden I still carry around like invisible baggage.

Andy now lives at home with my father and stepmother in Connecticut. On my last visit there, he seemed like a sleepwalker existing in a kind of half-life. He sat for hours, apart from the family, rocking himself. In his hand, he held a glass of ice and was absorbed chewing it. He rolled the blocks around in his mouth until they melted to chips. He let the sharp chips bite his tongue and the cool, melted liquid slide back against his throat. When the glass was empty, he sighed and went back into the kitchen for more. Occasionally, his sighs became deep and rhythmic, building to a crescendo like a heartbeat whose pulse has magically become audible to the outside world. Every few minutes, a strange, inappropriate smile passed his lips as if he could hear something. He gave me the feeling he couldn't speak because he didn't want to be interrupted.

Mourning for a loved one who is alive—in your very presence and yet in vital ways inaccessible to you—has a lonely, unreal quality that is extraordinarily painful.

That day, many days before it, and many days since, I've missed my older brother with the persistent ache and longing usually reserved for a loved one lost through death. Although grieving for someone who has died is painful, some sense of peace and acceptance is ultimately possible. However, mourning for a loved one who is alive—in your very presence and yet in vital ways inaccessible to you—has a lonely, unreal quality that is extraordinarily painful.

When I remember the closeness Andy and I shared as children, the memory often seems dim, almost illusionary, as though it not only happened in another time, but in another realm, to two other people.

MEANWHILE,
BACK ON THE WARD....

Jay Neugeboren

JAY NEUGEBOREN IS THE AUTHOR OF
The Stolen Jew, Before My Life Began,
AND OTHER NOVELS.

THIS ESSAY ORIGINALLY APPEARED IN *American Scholar,*
SUMMER, 1994 AND WILL APPEAR IN SLIGHTLY
DIFFERENT FORM IN *Imagining Robert: My Brother,
Madness, and Survival—A Memoir* (MORROW, 1997).

At 3:00 A.M., on a cool summer night—a few hours after my youngest son has graduated from high school—I find myself cruising the deserted streets of Northampton, Massachusetts searching for the 50-year-old man who is my brother. I have considered calling the police, but I know that, if a policeman actually finds my brother and approaches him, Robert might, as in the past, panic and become violent.

My brother Robert has spent most of his life, since the age of 19, in mental hospitals and psychiatric wards in and around New York City. The list is long: Hillside, Creedmoor, Elmhurst, Gracie Square, Mid-Hudson, Bellevue, Kings County, Rikers Island, South Beach, and others.

Robert had, until the time of his first breakdown in 1962, been a delightful, popular and gifted boy and young man—talented at dancing, acting, and singing, invariably winning the lead in school and camp plays and skits. He'd had a love and talent for tennis, writing, and chess (he was in a chess club with Bobby Fischer at Erasmus Hall High School in Brooklyn, but Fischer refused to play with him; "'With you, Neugeboren, I don't play,' he always said to me," Robert says. Why not? "Because," Robert says, smiling, "I played crazy"). He was a good if erratic student in

high school, won a New York State Regents Scholarship to college, and successfully completed his freshman year at CCNY. He was, in short, a bright and idiosyncratic young man with a sense of life and humor all his own, a person who, until his first breakdown, showed no signs (except for those that, looking back, any of us might find in ourselves) that such a breakdown was at all likely, much less inevitable.

Robert's diagnosis has changed frequently in the past 30 years, depending largely upon which drugs have been successful in keeping him calm, stable, or compliant. He was schizophrenic when enormous doses of Thorazine and Stelazine calmed him; he was manic depressive (bipolar) when lithium worked; he was manic-depressive-with-psychotic-symptoms or hypomanic when Tegretol or Depakote (anti-convulsants), or some new anti-psychotic or anti-depressant—Trilafon, Adapin, Mellaril, Haldol, Risperidone—promised to make him cooperative; and he was schizophrenic (again) when various doctors promised cures through insulin coma therapy or megadose vitamin therapy or gas therapy. At the same time, often in an attempt to minimize side effects, other drugs were poured into him: Artane, Benadryl, Cogentin, Kemadrin, Symmetrel, Prolixin, Pamelor, Navane....

During these years, Robert also participated in a long menu of therapies: group therapy, family therapy, multi-group family therapy, Marxist therapy, Gestalt therapy, psychoanalytically oriented psychotherapy, goal-oriented therapy, art therapy, milieu therapy, et al. Most often, though—the more chronic his condition, the truer this became—he received no therapy at all. It is as if, I often think, the very history of the ways in which our century has dealt with those it calls mentally ill has, for more than 30 years now, been passing through my brother's mind and body.

Robert and I talk with each other almost every day and see each other often, sometimes in New York, sometimes in Massachusetts, and though our visits are not without their difficulties (why should we be different from other brothers?), visits in my home, with my children, have invariably been without incident.

"I've never seen Uncle Robert this way," each of my children said to me, the day before and the day after my son Eli's graduation. "Is he going to be all right? Can I help?" And then: "And what about you, Pop? Are *you* going to be all right?"

My son Eli returned home from his all-night (supervised) graduation party at the local county fairgrounds at about 6:00 A.M., and Robert arrived not long after that and ordered me to put him on a bus for New York immediately. He looked ghastly (he had—inexpertly—given himself a haircut and shaved off his mustache) and seemed altogether disoriented: his hands and arms were flapping uncontrollably, his body was hunched over, his eyeglasses were covered with a milk-white sticky substance ("Scum!" he declared, when I asked), his movements were jagged, and he kept turning on me and screaming things that made no obvious sense. Whether I did or did not reply, he became more and more enraged, telling me again and again that I wasn't *listening* to him, that I never listened to him, and that if I didn't do what he said, he didn't know what he might do.

At the bus stop he scurried around wildly, virtually on all fours, picking up cigarette butts and looking for money. Then he went to each of a half-dozen sidewalk newspaper kiosks and began putting quarters in them, taking out papers, and either stacking them on top of the kiosks, or putting them in a mailbox. He went back and forth to a pay phone, dialing for information about people on Staten Island and yelling at the operator; he walked across the street to a parking lot and shouted questions at me.

I had been in situations like this with Robert before—dozens of times through the past thirty years—and though, as I said to my children, seeing Robert like this was not new for me, each time it happened it took me by surprise, and each time it happened, it seemed unutterably sad and heartbreaking.

How could it be that somebody who was so warm and loving, so charming and happy one moment—one day, one hour—could become so angry and lost moments later? And how could it be that each time it happened—no matter the years gone by—it felt as if it were happening for the first time?

With the years, I've learned to cope with these situations—to be able to help me and Robert get through. Though with the years Robert has actually reversed the path his life had been on (despite the dreadful prognostications, he had come, in recent years, to be able to spend more time out of hospitals than in them, to have made more of a life for himself than most people had dreamt possible), I still found myself going through litanies of familiar questions and doubts: Should I call the local police and have them take him to a hospital and deal with getting him back to New York City? Should I ask Robert where he had been all night, and if he had been drinking, and if he thought he could get back to the city by himself? Should I leave my children and try to drive Robert the 200 miles back to Staten Island?

What could I do that might ease his pain and confusion—that might minimize damage? If he were in free fall, as it were, was there anything I could do to help buffer the fall, so that, instead of plummeting downwards 10 stories before he crashed, he could bounce down gently after, say, only falling a few steps? Should I say anything at all, and was there a right thing or wrong thing to say, and was there anyone I could call on who could help get us through? Or, was it better to say nothing and to just leave him be.

How much of what was going on with Robert was frightening my children or taking away from their celebration and reunion? Was it best to shield them from the worst of Robert's troubles? Or should I inform them more fully of what was happening—of my fears, and of my intentions? In a situation like this, despite the many times I'd been here before, and despite all that I thought I knew about myself and Robert and about how to handle these situations, what I felt most of all was an overwhelming sadness and helplessness. Who knew if there was anything at all that might ease things, or make them less awful? Who knew, really, what to do?

What I did finally—what I found myself doing—was what I've been doing more and more through the years: simply trusting my instincts, and Robert's. I found myself acting on my belief that, despite all, Robert still knew himself, even at a time like this, better than anyone else did, and that if he was determined to get back to Staten Island by himself, he would.

Robert had stayed far away from my children most of the time during his 3 days with us, and—his innate kindness, as ever, at work—had kept both his anger and his confusion hidden, for the most part, when in their presence. Still, each of them noticed what a hard time he

*I*n a realm where the relation of mind to body remains so complex and mysterious, why, I wonder yet again, is so much time and money spent in the search for chemical and organic causes and cures, while back on the ward patients languish and die for the simple lack of human attention to their ordinary, daily needs?

was having, and each came to me and offered sympathy and help.

When, while changing from cap and gown into casual clothes for his graduation party, Eli asked if he could do anything to help with Robert, I told him the best thing he could do was to go off and enjoy the party, that Robert was my responsibility, not his. Eli had replied, "But he's mine, too, Pop."

I smiled. "Maybe, I said. But today is your day. This one's on me, okay?"

My sense of the fear and humiliation (along with the logistical problems) that would result from having local agencies deal with getting Robert from Massachusetts to New York, or my trying to deal with him in a locked car for 4 or 5 hours (a week before his first breakdown in 1962, he had, while we were going 70 miles an hour on a highway, opened the car door and threatened to jump), reinforced my instincts to believe that the best immediate solution was the simplest one: to let Robert get back to his home by himself and as quickly as he could.

So I did what I usually do when things get bad for Robert. I tried, gently and firmly, to be as patient and direct with him as I could. I told him, for example, that I would call ahead to his halfway house to let them know he was on his way and I asked him if he wanted me to drive him to Staten Island.

When he came near to me—and when he walked off and seemed especially lost—I put my arms around him and talked to him and told him I loved him.

While people waiting for the bus stared, or tried not to stare, or moved away, Robert stayed close to me and seemed to be listening. I was glad he'd been able to visit, I said, and I wished he wasn't having such a hard time again, and we'd talk on the phone that evening after he was back at his halfway house, and I was very glad he'd been able to be here for Eli's graduation, and we would see one another again soon.

Robert navigated the long trip home—bus, subway, ferry, and bus—successfully. We spoke that night—he cried a lot, said he hoped he hadn't embarrassed my children, and then he was off on flights of words that, because I knew the reference points (events and people from our childhood, jokes we loved, experiences we'd been through together), seemed more poignant than strange. The following morning, for the first time in a year, and for at least the fiftieth time in his life, he was hospitalized.

When I called the doctor in charge of Robert's ward, he asked what I thought had precipitated Robert's break. I answered by saying that there were some immediate causes that seemed obvious, but that the real precipitant, it seemed to me, was simply the fact of Robert's life—of the last 31 years of his life. If you'd been where Robert had been, and had suffered all the drugs and abuse and incompetence and pain he had suffered, the wonder, it seemed to me, wasn't why he'd broken again, but why he hadn't, like so many others he'd known, died or killed himself or deteriorated completely.

But after I said this, I did name some of the things that had been going on in Robert's life that might have precipitated this break. There was the graduation and being with family (but Robert had been in this situation dozens of times before and had had no difficulties). There were his desires and fantasies about living with me in Massachusetts, now intensified because Eli would be going off to college and I would be living alone. (But I've been the single full-time parent to my three children for many years, and though Robert had often asked about moving in with me, I'd never encouraged him, and he himself had been saying he didn't think it a good idea.) There was the fact that, a few weeks before, Robert's best friend had been moved out of the home in which he and Robert had lived together for 2 years and to which Robert had been hoping to return soon (so where would he live now?). There was also the fact that he had been out of the hospital for 11 months, and the better he became—the more alert, the more himself—the less the make-work activities of the hospital's day center interested him, and the more bored he became.

Though I could, as ever, talk about what I thought had caused Robert's condition, long-term and short-term, the more important question, it seemed to me, wasn't what had caused this breakdown, or any of the others, but what, given his life, had enabled him to survive, and to do more than survive—to retain his generosity, his warmth, his humor, and his sense of self. This, it seemed to me, was the true miracle and mystery.

I had, not long before, asked Robert the same questions the doctor asked me. Did he ever have any sense of what made him go off the way he did sometimes—of what the difference was, of what made things change for him, or in him? He had been silent for a long time and then had said, "No answer."

These were, I said at once, afraid that my questions might have hurt him, questions for which nobody seemed to have the answers.

"So why should I know?" Robert said then. "Am I different from anybody else?"

The doctor concluded that Robert's breakdown had been precipitated by alcohol and substance abuse. Robert had admitted that, on the way up to visit me, he had had a few beers and had inhaled amyl nitrite. The alcohol and substance abuse, the doctor said, had destabilized the parts of Robert's brain that his medications—lithium and Depakote—had stabilized. The problem, therefore, was noncompliance.

I had heard this from doctors many times before, and I responded with the obvious question: Okay, but what was it that had caused the noncompliance? If mental illness was as debilitating and awful a condition as it seemed to be (as surely it had been for Robert), and if the medications alleviated that condition, why would anyone ever stop taking the medications, or do anything to interfere with their beneficial effects? As my father had once put it, to a doctor who refused to continue treating Robert because Robert had stopped taking his pills. "So where, Doctor, is the pill to make him want to take the pills?"

When I visited Robert after his breakdown, on a locked unit at South Beach Psychiatric Center on Staten Island, he was, as he had been before, on isolation: living, day after day, 24-hours a day, in a bare room in which there was nothing but a bed and a dresser. This was called "reduced stimulation."

When I had previously questioned, as gently as I could, whether being on isolation, and on heavy doses of Thorazine (which Robert hated above all drugs), and not being permitted to make or receive calls or visitors, might not feel to Robert like punishment instead of therapy, the staff psychologist had replied that this might temporarily be the case. "But our experience," he said, "is that in retrospect patients come to appreciate the reduction of stimulation—the limits and boundaries that have been set for them."

He had also assured me that Robert was not just locked away in a room—that every hour on the half hour, for 5 minutes, he was taken to the bathroom and for a walk down the hallway. When I asked if Robert had or would be receiving any therapy, the therapist's reply was abrupt: "Robert cannot tolerate therapy."

This seemed to me an absurd statement—Robert couldn't tolerate therapy? You mean *you* can't tolerate trying to work with him, I wanted to scream. Why are you a therapist if you don't want to work with patients, to listen to them? And when will Robert be able to "tolerate" therapy—when he's *well*?

But it was the same old story, and I was in the same old quandary: if I complained too much, or confronted the hospital's staff with their inadequacies, or sent off the letters I composed in my head, I feared they would only talk with me less, care for Robert less.

Robert had been here, in this ward and ones like it, and in even worse places more than once before. (One time at Mid-Hudson, I remembered him telling me, when they had him in a straitjacket for a long period of time, he asked for a smoke so he could let the ashes fall on the jacket and set himself on fire. He succeeded. After the aides got him out of the straitjacket, one of them took him to the basement, beat him up, warned him never to do what he had done again.)

Now, because of my visit, Robert has been granted courtyard privileges, and we sit by ourselves in the small courtyard at a picnic table. He opens the bag of food I've brought him for lunch, but his hands are shaking so badly that when he tries to eat an egg salad sandwich, the egg salad sprays everywhere. He is apologetic and embarrassed. I talk with him easily, we joke back and forth, and after a short while I scoop up pieces of egg, tomato, lettuce, and bread, he takes his false teeth out, and I feed him with my fingers, placing the food directly into his mouth.

When he cannot stand the shaking, he walks away. He calls to me, and I sit next to him on a bench, and we talk about the ward, and the doctors, and my trip down, about Eli's graduation, and the floods in the Midwest, and our cousins. Suddenly Robert turns, leans down, and, with great gentleness, kisses the back of my hand several times, after which he begins weeping.

"Oh, Jay, Jay" he cries softly. "They're barbarians here. Barbarians, barbarians! Pavlovians...."

He presses his mouth to the back of my hand, and I take him to me, hold him close. A few minutes later, we walk around the courtyard. Then he tells me that he likes to walk back and forth, in a diagonal, between two trees—they are about 10 yards apart—and count the number of times. So we walk back and forth together, and I sing to him, and then he joins in—putting his arm around my waist, leaning on my shoulder—and we go back and forth again and again, loudly singing old camp songs we remember from our childhood.

He eats some more, and then we walk again, side by side, our hands clasped behind us, mimicking two diplomats, trading stories and news. He clutches his dentures in one hand, a piece of bread locked in their bite, and when he puts the top bridge back in his mouth, I say something about his being on uppers.

He starts giggling, inserts the lower bridge.

"And now you're on lowers," I say, and add that I don't understand why, since he's on uppers and lowers, which probably balance one another, the hospital has to give him any other medications.

"It's how they make their profit," he says.

When I call Robert from Massachusetts after our visit, he is flying—repeating everything he says twice, rambling on about people living and dead as if they are there with him on the ward, thanking me for visiting him and for the things I brought him, giving me lists of all the foods he has eaten and all the things he wants me to send him, mixing these lists with references to scenes in movies and scenes from our childhood, talking about Adlai Stevenson and Bill Clinton (who is, he says, his son) and how the whole country is in a very big depression—and all the while he keeps telling me he has to hang up, he has to hang up. When he finally takes a breath, and I tell him I love him, his voice suddenly drops and slows down, and he talks to me in a way that is entirely natural. "Oh Jay," he says, "don't you see? There's nothing better in my life than what's happening! You don't know. You don't know, Jay. You don't want to know." He weeps freely, keeps talking. "This life of working here and there in hospitals, or as a volunteer, and being here now, and doing nothing—isn't there ever going to be anything *better* for me? Please get me out of here, Jay. Please, please...."

When, later in our conversation, I tell him that I called him the day before but nobody could find him, he asks me what I called him, and when I say, "I called you my brother," he laughs, says, "That's an old one, Jay. That's an old one—but listen, I'm going to switch the phone to my good ear, all right?"

"There," he says, a few seconds later. "Now can you hear me better?"

Moved as I am by Robert's situation and his life—and his plea for a life different from the one he has —I find, after our visit and our talk, that I am feeling relieved, and, even, mildly exhilarated. Because the truth (I shrug when I realize this, as if to say, to myself: What can I do? That's the way it is.) is that when we're together, whether in my home or on his ward, whether on the West Side of Manhattan (where we lived next door to one another during his first year out of Creedmoor) or in Atlantic City (where, 6 weeks before Eli's graduation, we went together for 2 days at his request to celebrate his fiftieth birthday), we're happy. Not always, and not without a pervasive sense of loss and sadness, but happy to be with each other, no matter the context, because it seems good, simply, in an often frightening and miserable life, to be *known* and to be able to be near the person who knows you and is known by you.

During the weeks that follow Robert's hospitalization, we talk regularly. I visit him and send notes and gifts, and whenever we talk, Robert asks about each of my children, his niece and two nephews. Though our talks sometimes last for less than a minute, and though sometimes he is angry (at doctors, at me, at life) and sometimes sad, and sometimes high—and though sometimes I am nearly swept away by grief, from my sense of all that he senses his life has become and has not become—I find, strangely enough, real pleasure, as ever, in our time spent together.

This happens not only because I know Robert's patterns, if patterns they are, fairly well, but because I know that once his sense of humor returns (and once he begins opening to me in direct ways about his feelings and needs), his recovery will follow, and that he will be back before long in the real world most of us live in. It happens simply because, that is, for better or worse, our lives, in a crucial time for each of us, have once again been joined.

In a few months, Robert will probably, as in the past, get out of his ward and return to his halfway house. If things go well there, he will move from the halfway

The more I know Robert and know about him, the more I'll want to know. And this will only increase, not the sadness of his life, but its wonder.

house into an apartment, and we'll probably go to Atlantic City together again, and we'll see each other more frequently than ever. We'll talk and laugh and trade jokes, argue and complain and become irritable with one another, reminisce and make plans, and go on trips. And he'll gradually tell me, without my asking (as he has already begun to do), about what he did and where he went on the night of Eli's graduation, and that too will become part of the history we share.

The more I know about him, the more I'll wonder about how he came to be who he is. What continues to surprise—but why?—is that the more I know Robert and know about him, the more I'll want to know. And this will only increase, not the sadness of his life, but its wonder.

Several weeks after Eli's graduation, while Robert is still on isolation in his ward at South Beach, I come across a full-page advertisement in the *New York Times* sponsored by NARSAD (the National Alliance for Research on Schizophrenia and Depression), an organization founded by the four most prominent mental health groups in the United States, that talks about the many urgent scientific projects that are paving the way for better treatments and the cure we all hope for. *The* cure? I want to scream. "New hope of a breakthrough cure is on the horizon," the ad proclaims, "as we start to identify the genetic markers that cause depression."

The ad sets forth the current and conventional wisdom about depression and mental illness: its symptoms, the suffering it brings, the numbers of people afflicted.

What the ad says echoes what I've read in most literature put out by mental health professionals and agencies: that mental illness is a "biochemical illness" and a "no-fault biologically based brain disease."

Surely, thinking of mental illness in this way—believing that biology causes mental illness (as it causes diabetes or heart disease, illnesses to which it is compared) and that nobody's to blame—does enormous good: it reduces stigma and guilt, it inspires hope, it allows for increased coverage under insurance plans, it enables useful legislation and research, and so on.

What it does *not* do, however, is deal directly with the major fact of mental illness for those who suffer its larger devastations: its generally long-term, chronic character and how this is experienced, as on Eli's graduation night, by the mentally ill and by those who care for them.

Robert and I have been hearing talk about "breakthrough cures" for more than 30 years now. First it was electroshock, and then it was insulin coma therapy, and then it was family therapy, and then it was the new range of anti-psychotic drugs, and then it was megadose vitamin therapy, and then it was lithium therapy, and then it was anticonvulsant therapy, and then it was Prozac, and then it was clozapine.

What upsets me in the *Times* ad—what upsets me whenever I hear language about breakthrough cures and genetic markers and brain disease—is not the possibility that Robert's condition is chemical, but the belief so many people have in its corollary: that if the condition is chemical, it can be corrected with chemicals. Oh how easy it would be for everybody if there were chemical causes and chemical cures! How free of responsibility we might all be then!

But even if we find cause and cure, what then do we do with the life lived, and the history—and fear, and shame, and doubt, and despair, and sheer misery—that have accompanied that life? If behavior and feel-ings can change the chemistry and patterns of the brain (compare the feelings and physiological changes in athletes, musicians, stockbrokers, writers, artists, and others when in intensely productive periods), just as chemicals can change behavior and feelings, how can we know which is cause and which effect?

The instant I see the words about breakthrough cures, and read about how NARSAD has provided financial support to 315 doctors and scientists in 78 leading universities, medical schools, and research institutions, what I also see, but more vividly, is my brother, in a room by himself, lying in bed hour after hour and day after day, trembling from medications and fear and loneliness.

In a realm where the relation of mind to body remains so complex and mysterious, why, I wonder yet again, so much time and money spent in the search for chemical and organic causes and cures, while back on the ward patients languish and die for the simple lack of human attention to their ordinary, daily needs?

For even if we do one day separate out the gene or the neuron that proves to be the cause of what we decide is this or that species of mental illness, what, then, will we do about the life that has come before and will continue after the moment of diagnosis and medication, and of how the fact of having this condition has affected an individual's history?

Hope and research are fine, and genuine gains have been made. But meanwhile, back on the ward, Robert has to sneak out of his room to telephone me, and his doctors never call me to inform or consult or confer, and the only link to the outside world for 30 or so acutely psychotic patients is a single pay phone. Meanwhile, back on the ward, important messages don't get through. (When Robert, for the first time in his life, threatened suicide, and I informed one of the nurses, and I called back a few days later to speak with Robert's doctor, I discovered that the doctor had never been informed of Robert's threat.) Meanwhile, back on the ward, the major activities are TV and card games, the staff is outnumbered and overworked, the refrigerator is padlocked, and the only time patients can get snacks is when an aide unlocks it twice a day at "refrigerator time."

As it was, for the most part, 30 years ago, so it is now: the little that passes for therapy is simply reward and punishment done up, if at all, in the guise of crude behavior modification programs whose aim is not enhancement, but containment and neutralization. In the world Robert too often lives in, ordinary habits and idiosyncrasies (sloppiness about clothing, loud talking) become psychological deficits for which one receives demerits, and worse. In the world Robert has been living in for too many years, model patients are not very different from model prisoners.

At least, I say to Robert, during one conversation, they don't use straitjackets anymore. When I say this, we both laugh and talk about the time he asked a friend visiting him at Creedmoor if she could take his dirty clothes home for him and get them washed. The friend took Robert's laundry bag to a Chinese laundry, started removing the clothes, only to find that mixed in with the dirty socks and underwear was Robert's straitjacket.

"In the old days it was straitjackets and wet sheets and electricity," Robert says, "and now, I guess, it's isolation and injections."

A few weeks before Eli's graduation, I had asked Robert why he thought it was that he had survived when so many others he knew, from Creedmoor and Mid-Hudson and South Beach and Hillside, never got out, or killed themselves, or deteriorated to the point of no return. Had it ever occurred to him to wonder why, despite all he had been through and all the drugs and therapies that had been poured into him, he had not gone under? Why was he able, more than three decades after his first breakdown (when he tried to kill our father; when he hallucinated extravagantly; when he believed he was being taken, by ambulance, to my funeral; when he tried to chew his tongue out of his mouth; when he was straitjacketed and shot up with large doses of Thorazine; when he had catatonic seizures), to make a life for himself that was so much better than often, during these decades, seemed likely?

"Well," he exclaimed, I had wonderful parents!" He laughed, then was silent for a while. When he spoke again, his voice was warm, thoughtful. "I just wanted to survive and persist," he said. "That's all. And—I don't know—but it's like Faulkner said in the speech he made, for the Nobel, remember?—I wanted to *endure* somehow. I never really wanted to stay on the wards, but I'd get there and then the minute they locked the door on me, I would think, 'Oh my God—I've got to get out of here!' But then I'd throw fits and stuff."

"And also," he added, smiling, "because my brother didn't want to keep visiting me in hospitals."

CONFESSIONS OF THE DAUGHTER OF A SCHIZOPHRENIC

Roxanne Lanquetot

ROXANNE LANQUETOT, M.A., M.S., HAS BEEN TEACHING AT P.S. 106M, BELLEVUE PSYCHIATRIC HOSPITAL FOR THE PAST 13 YEARS. HER STUDENTS ARE COMPOSED OF THE YOUNGEST GROUP OF CHILDREN ON THE INPATIENT CHILDREN'S WARD. SHE HAS BEGUN A PH.D. PROGRAM IN EDUCATIONAL PSYCHOLOGY AT CUNY, AND IS ALSO INTERESTED IN WRITING, ESPECIALLY ABOUT CHILDREN.

THIS ARTICLE ORIGINALLY APPEARED IN THE *Schizophrenia Bulletin*, 1984, 10(3), 467 471.

My mother is a paranoid schizophrenic. In the past I was afraid to admit it, but now that I've put it down on paper, I'll be able to say it again and again: Mother, schizophrenic, Mother, paranoid, shame, guilt, Mother, crazy, different, Mother, schizophrenia.

I have been teaching inpatient children on the children's ward of Bellevue Psychiatric Hospital in New York City for 13 years, and yet I'm still wary of revealing the nature of my mother's illness. When I tell my friends about my mother, even psychiatrist friends, I regret my openness and worry that they will find me peculiar.

My profession is appropriate for the daughter of a schizophrenic; at least psychiatrists will think so. Since I often marveled that I escaped being a disturbed child, I decided to devote my life to helping difficult children. I have been successful in my work, which includes forming relationships with the mothers of my students, especially the schizophrenic ones, whom I visit on the wards during their periods of hospitalization.

I was born in Kansas City, Missouri, in 1933. When I was 5 years old, we moved to the Country Club section of the city, an area as spotlessly bourgeois as any residential area in the United States. The inhabitants of this region composed a homogeneous population of upper middle class citizens, all very similar in their life styles. Not even one unusual person could be found loitering on the streets of this hamlet, let alone a paranoid schizophrenic. If, according to the laws of probability, there were schizophrenics and other crazies scattered about in the population, they were well hidden.

On the outside our house resembled those of our neighbors, but on the inside it was so different that there was no basis of comparison. Our house was a disaster. Everything was a mess. Nothing matched, furniture was broken, dishes were cracked and there were coffee rings and cigarette burns clear across our grand piano. I was ashamed of our house. It was impossible to bring friends home. I never knew what my mother might be doing or how she would look. She was totally unpredictable. At best she was working on a sculpture or practicing the piano, chain smoking and sipping stale coffee, with a dress too ragged to give to charity hanging from her emaciated body. At worst she was screaming at my father, still wearing her nightgown at 6 o'clock in the evening, a wild look on her face. I was never popular as a youngster, and I blamed my lack of popularity on my mother.

My friends had elegant, decorator homes like the ones in *House Beautiful*. Their parents were caring, organized, but traditional. They provided for their children. Nothing was lacking. They were well dressed, and their daughters had the kind of clothes I longed for, the kind that are sold at Saks Fifth Avenue. I attached a great importance to clothes, because I had to manipulate Mother to get them. It was not that we were poor. It was just that my mother didn't care about clothing. She was entirely oblivious to the fact that people wore clothes.

My mother didn't know how to cook. She was never at home to order groceries or plan meals, but she showed concern about proper nutrition for her children and hounded us to eat, or overeat. We dined out at least four times a week at the Fred Harvey restaurant in the Union Station where my grandfather had conveniently opened a charge account, and the rest of the week we ate broiled sirloin. The people who worked in the restaurant were used to us and paid no attention to Mother's idiosyncrasies. We children were allowed to purchase books at the station gift shop, and we read them at the table since no conversation with Mother was possible. Nancy Drew made an excellent dinner companion.

Mother was quite interested in music and ballet, and she took me to every ballet and concert in Kansas City. She always looked terrible when she went out, and more than once she arrived at the theater in her bedroom slippers. I was embarrassed to be seen with her, and before we left home, I would try to convince her to dress properly. She never listened and sometimes became angry, but chic or not, I accompanied her. I loved music and dance as much as she did. I even gave up Saturday afternoons to stay home with her and listen to the Metropolitan Opera broadcasts, and I loved her most and felt closest to her sitting in front of a gas fire, feeling her bony arm around my shoulders as we listened to the music together. Throughout my childhood I was torn between my bizarre, but loving artist mother and the conventional mothers of my friends.

Feelings of shame and fear overwhelmed me in those early years, shame that my friends would find out that my mother was different and fear that I would be different too.

Although Mother was rarely at home during the day, she could be found at the ballet studio. I think that I was probably born at the studio, because I can't imagine that Mother could have gotten to the hospital in time to deliver. Although she continued to take classes until her psychotic break, as soon as I was born she unconsciously decided that I should become the *danseuse étoile* that had been her goal in life. I didn't have the talent to be promoted to such heights, but failing to understand this, she continued to nag me to take more classes and work harder.

Feelings of shame and fear overwhelmed me in those early years, shame that my friends would find out that my mother was different and fear that I would be different too. The fear of being like Mother must have prevented me from studying ballet and piano seriously. My mother played the piano and danced, and she was schizophrenic. If I played the piano and danced, I would be schizophrenic also. I was terrified that if I showed any signs of letting myself go and really working, my mother would close the doors of the studio and fasten them with a heavy, iron bar.

Mother and daughter were competitors in ballet and music. Mother, who had given birth to me when she was just 19 years old, looked young, mother and daughter looked alike, and we were taken for sisters. I didn't think that I could win a music or dance competition with Mother, and I wasn't interested anyway. I wanted to go to college, where I was assured success. Mother had always had trouble in school.

There were other problems in living with a schizophrenic mother. One was the lack of tranquility at home, the commotion, and chaos. My parents were constantly arguing, mainly about money. My mother had no idea of budgeting. She didn't need to learn, because her father was available to supply her with money as needed. My father didn't approve of limitless concert going, dance classes, or book buying. He abhorred eating in restaurants everyday and expected Mother to stay home to take care of the house and prepare supper. I would be awakened at night by screaming and lie in bed pretending to be asleep, morbidly fascinated by my parents' quarrels.

Trying to make up for my mother's shortcomings was one of the major preoccupations of my early years. I was always cleaning and straightening up the house, vainly hoping to restore order, even as early as age 4, according to one of my aunts. I took care of my brothers, but I bitterly resented the fact that no one took care of me. I felt cheated by having to arrange my own birthday parties, ordering the cake, inviting friends, and choosing the present, although I willingly organized parties for my younger brothers. After school I became the little mother who was furious about being deprived of her childhood.

One day, when I was 10, my mother vanished, and as if by magic, my father moved back to the house to take care of us. I resented his return. He had abandoned us, and I must have felt that he was responsible for Mother's problems. We were told that Mother was ill in a hospital in Burbank, California, where my grandfather's sister was a staff physician. I felt very lonely without her and began hanging around the ballet studio. Once the teacher put her arm around me and said, "Poor child, you miss your mother, don't you."

Years later I learned that Mother had run away to New York without telling anyone she was leaving. She was making frenzied visits to the ballet schools there when a friend of the family phoned my grandparents to inform them of their daughter's strange behavior. My grandparents immediately set out for New York to rescue Mother. They brought her to Menninger's Clinic, which had not been in existence very long. At the time the hospital was located in old fashioned red brick buildings that were already on the premises when the Menningers moved in. Equating building height and glass walls with hospital excellence, my grandparents took one look at the hospital and headed for California, where Mother was hospitalized for a year. She regained her physical health, but her mental health was totally ignored. When she was discharged, we joined her in California, where we lived for the next 2 years. Mother was subdued and withdrawn from any human contacts outside of the family. Her withdrawal was less of a bane to our social life than her neurotic existence in Kansas City, but she lost something of the artist, her most interesting self.

When the family returned to the Midwest, we moved into a house in the country next to my grandparents, which made it easier for my grandfather to look after his beloved daughter. Mother was withdrawing more, spending the entire day lying on the bed, sleeping or doing exercises. She rarely left the house except to go next door to rant and rave at my grandmother while my grandfather stood nearby, patting her on the back and saying, "Bonnie, my dear little Bonnie, everything will be all right." Since neither of my grandparents would admit that their dear little Bonnie desperately needed help, we children could say nothing.

At the end of my junior year in high school I was in a serious automobile accident. I tend to think that my mother's consequent decompensation might have been precipitated by my being in a coma for 6 days, but I'm not certain. After I came home from the hospital, she became very strict with me, although she had never interfered in my social life previously. When I protested against her arbitrary, nonsensical restrictions on my dating, we began to have terrible fights. I could not make her accept the fact that a monastic existence was not for me.

Mother and I shared a room with twin beds. When Mother was lying down, she would start to moan as if she were talking in her sleep. "I can't stand that girl. She's evil; she's a bitch. She's just like her father." I was terrorized, but I dared not move. I felt I had to pretend to be asleep, because I didn't want her to know I was listening. I tried to deny the reality of Mother's illness by not acknowledging the outbursts. I used to lie in bed, wishing I were dead, believing that I was the worthless girl she was describing.

My oldest brother was the target of the same kinds of insults, and we comforted each other. We were afraid to talk about Mother's behavior to our grandparents. They wouldn't admit that Mother was mentally ill. She was the chosen one, and my brother and I took second place in the family, the opposite of a child's position in a normal grouping. We were frequently reminded that we would have to replace our grandparents as caretakers when we grew up.

I still remember with horror the night that I came in late from a date and decided to sleep on the couch in the living room in order not to wake Mother. I made an effort to avoid disturbing her, not because I was being considerate, but because I didn't want her to start moaning. As soon as I lay down, she came into the room and stood next to me, calling me a prostitute. When she spat on me, I grabbed her upper arm and bit it as hard as I could. The outline of my teeth etched in black and blue remained visible for over a week, but Mother never mentioned it. Even now when I think of the incident, I feel shame because of my loss of self control and display of aggression toward my poor, defenseless, crazy mother.

Next Mother began to insult strangers on the street. She would stop in front of a well dressed bourgeois of Kansas City, fix her eyes on him for a few seconds, and snap angrily. "What's wrong with you? Why are you looking at me like that? I'm going to tell my lawyer." If my brother or I were with her, we'd be so embarrassed that we'd want to disappear into a crack in the sidewalk. No matter what we did, she wouldn't stop. Once she hit someone over the head with her pocketbook and another time notified the police that the neighbors were spying on her although they'd been gone for 3 months. In the sterile atmosphere of Kansas City, her outbursts upset everyone. In New York she wouldn't have been noticed.

My choice of colleges was based on their distance from Kansas City and Mother. I had to get away before I became crazy. I applied to the University of Chicago, Barnard, and Stanford and was accepted at all three. My grandfather refused to let me attend Chicago U. He said that Chicago was no place for a young girl, but I knew he refused because of Mother, who had attended the Chicago conservatory for 3 months before she returned home to Daddy. I decided against Barnard, because Mother liked New York. I was afraid that she might follow me there. That left Stanford.

Much to my dismay, Mother arrived in San Francisco during my sophomore year at Stanford. She came for a visit and decided to stay. The fantasy about being haunted by the specter of my schizophrenic mother had come true. She moved into a dumpy apartment two blocks from a dance studio and began taking Flamenco dancing from a Spaniard who taught there. She fell in love with her teacher, but he didn't care about her. Although he paid her less attention than he did the other students, she was always hanging around, gazing at him in abject adoration. She never realized how pathetic and absurd she appeared.

After I left Stanford, I went to Europe, distancing myself physically and emotionally from Mother. That same year it had been my oldest brother's turn to escape to college, and Mother was left with only my youngest brother to link her to the real world. This brother had always been her favorite anyway, due to his place in the birth order and the fact that he was born with his hip out of joint and therefore required extra care. He wasn't allowed the freedom of college, because Mother immediately followed him to Saint Louis and remained with him until he failed his courses and was asked to leave. Even a letter from my godmother in Saint Louis pleading with my grandparents to bring Bonnie back to Kansas City was not effective. They could not bring themselves to remove all of Mother's children. My youngest brother had to be the sacrificial lamb. When he became tired of his entrapment, he got married. The marriage was a failure, but it was obviously the only way he could free himself from Mother's stranglehold.

Mother's descent into chronic schizophrenia would take too long to describe. She was finally admitted to Menninger's where she improved during the first year and a half of treatment. Then her father died. She had always been her father's little girl and her universe was shattered without him. The only person in the world she trusted had departed. After the funeral she refused to return to Menninger's. She had learned that no one had the right to send her to an out-of-state hospital against her will.

After school I became the little mother who was furious about being deprived of her childhood.

Two years later she had to return to the hospital. She was driving a car without brakes and insulting black people by loudly declaiming her theories about the inferiority of the black race. By her second admission it was too late. Mother had become a chronic schizophrenic. After the first year of hospitalization we were asked to remove her. The Menningers were only interested in patients whom they could cure. The family, for we remained a close family, rallied its forces to find another hospital, and we transferred her to a Mennonite Hospital in a small town in Western Kansas. We were grieved by the loss of Mother as a functional human being, a bereavement that was finalized by attaching "chronic" to her diagnostic category. I was especially horrified by the necessity of burying my mother in the country. My trepidation was intensified when Mother was moved to a halfway house near the hospital, where the only activity available to patients was filling mattresses.

When Mother began to threaten the doctor at the new hospital to find a lawyer to sue him, the family was forced to make the difficult decision to go to court to have her declared incompetent, to openly admit that she was psychotic. We had to safeguard her trust fund from a shyster lawyer. My grandmother was devastated. Having avoided the truth for the greater part of her daughter s life, she couldn't face the fact that Bonnie was crazy. Since I was in Europe, my brother, my uncle, and the doctor testified that Mother was a danger to herself. Mother was declared "incompetent," and the judge appointed a guardian for her. According to Missouri law, a judge controlled every move made by an "incompetent." Mother lost all liberty, all sense of self. Any step she took had to be authorized by the magistrate.

Once drug therapy came into being, Mother was force fed Haldol against her wishes, and this resulted in a remission of symptoms. Feeling well enough to leave the hospital, she made the decision to go to Menninger's by herself to take an examination that she supposed would disprove her insanity. Of course, her guardian was forced by law to make her return to the hospital. She had not requested the judge's permission to make the journey. Later my brother accompanied her to Menninger's for an evaluation, the results of which showed that she was well enough to leave the halfway house in Kansas and come to New York to be near her children. They specified, however, that she would need to live in a structured environment .

Eventually the family received the authorization to have Mother's guardianship transferred to New York, and a committee was appointed by the New York court. When Mother first joined us in the East, she behaved the way she did when she was discharged from the hospital in California—withdrawn, isolated from everyone but the family, yet able to profit from all the big city had to offer. Listening to music or watching ballet, she came back to life. Vital energy that had been absent for so long returned to her body. The results of changing her habitat were much better than we had ever expected.

Not only did Mother rediscover art and music in New York, but she soon became familiar with the liberal New York laws regarding patients' rights. She refused to continue to take Haldol and slowly began the reverse trip to No Man's Land, where she now dwells. The first sign of her decompensation was a refusal to come to my apartment, and then she rejected me completely. Next the manager of her middle class apartment hotel asked us to remove her. She was annoying the guests

with her outbursts. She had become known to all the shopkeepers on the block as "The Crazy Lady of West 72nd Street." Looking like a zombie, she paraded down West 72nd Street, accusing aunts, uncles, and brother of stealing her father's fortune, screaming at people who frightened her, discernible from her New York counterparts only by a Midwestern accent and an absence of curse words.

Having been told over and over again in our youth that it was our duty to take care of Mother, my brother and I initially resented our burden. We felt that since Mother had not accepted the responsibility of her children, we should not have to be responsible for her. At that time it was difficult to admit that we actually loved our frail, unbalanced mother and wanted to help her. When we grew up, we began to understand why Mother was different, and our resentment lessened. On Haldol, Mother's behavior improved tremendously, and we even harbored false hopes of her return to normal living. We never suspected that she might cease taking medication and regress. Whether or not it's preferable for her to be forcefed Haldol and incarcerated in Kansas or allowed to do as she pleases in liberal New York, as destructive as her life is now, is paradoxical. She was not able to enjoy life and pursue her artistic interests in the former situation, but she is even less able to do so in the latter. Without medication, she can only exist. I believe that basically she is less free in her present life, a prisoner of her delusions and paranoia. My brother, however, disagrees. He thinks that Mother is better off having the choice to live as she wishes, wandering aimlessly in the streets, constructing the world to fit her delusions.

Growing Up With a Psychotic Mother: A Retrospective Study

Bonnie Dunn

THIS ARTICLE ORIGINALLY APPEARED IN THE *American Journal of Orthopsychiatry*, 1993, 63(2), 177-189 AND IS REPRINTED WITH PERMISSION.

Nine adults who had been reared by mothers diagnosed with psychosis reported on their childhood experiences. Analysis of the retrospective data revealed the five common themes of abuse and neglect, isolation, guilt and loyalty, grievances about mental health services, and social supports. The resilience and coping strategies of the participants are examined, and implications for therapeutic interventions with such families are discussed.

People commonly joke about the crazy families in which they grew up, but such families are a grim reality for the many children who grow up with a seriously mentally ill parent. Of patients discharged from mental hospitals in the United States, 65% return to their families every year (Goldman 1982). For the children, living with a psychotic parent can make for a confusing, isolating, and painful childhood. This study presents the childhood experiences, reported retrospectively, of nine adults who grew up with such a parent. It explores their childhood memories in an attempt to discover what it is like to live with a psychotic parent, with the goal of understanding the needs of this group, both as children and as adults.

Literature Review

Being born to a psychotic parent carries both genetic and environmental risks for a child. A large and growing body of research describes the risks of children who have a schizophrenic parent (Gottesman & Shields, 1966; Kety, Rosenthal, Wender, Schulsinger, & Jacobsen, 1978; Tienari et al., 1987), and it is known that children born to a parent with schizophrenia have about a 13% chance of developing schizophrenia themselves, a marked contrast to the estimated 0.5% to 1% chance for the general population (Gortesmun, 1991). Although statistics concerning children of bipolar and psychotically depressed parents are less clear, studies have cited evidence of increased disturbance in these children as well (Billings & Moos, 1983; Rutter & Quinton, 1984).

The environments of children who live with a psychotic parent affect their development. Early childhood studies underline the importance of parental attunement and affect in the development of the growing infant. Psychoses involving disorders of either thought or mood greatly influence an individual's behavior and affect, thus hindering his or her ability to be an effective parent.

Spitz (1965) emphasized the importance to the developing child of the reciprocity of mother-child affectual interactions. Mahler and her colleagues (1975) considered parental attunement to be essential to the child, and they, too, stressed the importance of the interactional nature of the mother-child relationship. Bowlby (1952, 1969) theorized that attachment, beginning in infancy with a warm and continuous relationship with the mother or mother-figure, is the cornerstone of adult mental health. Stern (1985) emphasized the intersubjective nature of the developmental process and assigned critical importance to affective attunement of the parent to the child. He believed that this attunement allows for the sharing and modification of affect between parent and child, gently propels the child's further development, and forms the basis for a sense of self. If parental attunement and appropriate affective response are critical to a child's development, the psychotic symptoms of a parent whose affective range is severely limited or inappropriate, or who is out of touch with reality, would have serious consequences for the child.

Researchers have documented other environmental factors that have an impact on the development of children in families where there is mental illness. Marital difficulties (Merikangas, 1984; Rutter & Quinton, 1984; Weintraub & Neale, 1984; Weissman, 1979), stress and discord among family members (Anthony, 1969; Billings & Moos, 1983; Hatfield, 1978; Noh & Avison, 1988), and social alienation and lack of supports (Hatfield, 1978; Hill & Balk, 1987; Noh & Avison, 1988; Scottish Schizophrenia Research Group, 1987) are common for families of the mentally ill. Family members are afraid of being physically harmed by their psychotic family member (Anthony, 1986; Hatfield, 1978), and these families' economic sources are strained by the illness, leaving the children economically, as well as emotionally and biologically, vulnerable (Hatfield, 1978). While there is much in the research literature that delineates the various possible effects that parental psychosis may have on children in the family, very little is known about the experiences of these children from their own perspectives. There is little in the literature that calls on the experiences of people who have lived with a psychotic parent to explore the unique aspects of such lives, or to inform the development and implementation of interventions designed to help families, specifically the children, in which there is a mentally ill family member.

Method

Subjects

Nine adults who grew up with a psychotic parent participated in this study. Four men and five women, all Caucasian and ranging in age from 21 to 41, were interviewed. One was a journalist, one an engineer, one owned a small business, three were students, one was in human services, one was a market analyst, and one (who had also been diagnosed with schizophrenia) was unemployed.

Study participants comprised a self-selected, purposive sample solicited through classified ads placed in newspapers, notices in newsletters of the Alliance for the Mentally Ill, and referrals by mental health providers. The criteria used to select subjects were that a parent had been diagnosed with psychosis, that the subject lived with that parent during the early childhood years, and that the subject no longer lived with that parent.

Twenty people conforming to the study criteria responded to the notices; 18 had a mother diagnosed with psychosis and two had a psychotic father. In view of the small number with a psychotic father, it was decided to limit the study variables by interviewing only those who had grown up with a psychotic mother. It was also decided to include only those respondents who could be interviewed in a timely manner and were within a 1-hour drive; this reduced the size of the final sample from 18 to 9 subjects.

As a result of having a parent who was often nonfunctioning, these children became caregivers for the parent and younger siblings at an early age.

Although schizophrenia is equally common among men and women, there are many reasons for the significant difference in the number of respondents with a psychotic mother versus those with a psychotic father. The known ratio of schizophrenic mothers to fathers is two to one. Because onset for schizophrenia is generally later in women than in men, and marriage and procreation occur earlier for women, women have a greater chance of finding a mate and bearing children before their first psychotic episode (Gottesrnan, 1991). In addition, children usually remain with the mother when the parents do not live together, even in cases in which the mother is severely mentally ill. Thus, psychotic women are more likely than are psychotic men to be caregiving parents. It would be important to explore, in future studies, more about the consequences of having a father with a psychosis.

Four of the mothers of study participants had been diagnosed with schizophrenia, two with bipolar disorder, and three with multiple disorders that included either schizophrenia or bipolar disorder.

Procedure

Information was obtained through use of a three-part semistructured interview. In Part One, participants were asked about their family structure and history, parental diagnoses, hospitalizations, and treatments, as well as about any mental health treatment they received as children and other contacts with mental health providers. In Part Two, questions addressed participants' childhood relationships with their mentally ill mother and with other family members

> *P*articipants described a childhood in which they received little consistent attention from either parent and where abuse or neglect were common.

and friends. Participants were asked to identify what their needs were at the time and how those needs were or were not met. They were also asked for their opinions about contacts with mental health professionals. In Part Three, subjects discussed their current relationship with their mentally ill mother, with other members of their family, and with mental health providers. Finally, they were encouraged to comment on experiences that had not been specifically addressed by the interview questions; all did so.

Each audiotaped interview was transcribed verbatim. Discrete, important quotes were placed on cards, and sorted into the categories covered by the interview (contacts with mental health services; past and present relationships with family and friends; childhood needs). A subsorting within interview categories (such as expressions of guilt that emerged from a question regarding childhood needs), derived from a content analysis of these quotes, identified themes common to all study participants. These themes, which recurred in all interviews with regularity, became the focus for reporting the study's results.

Results

Five themes characterizing common experiences emerged from these childhood memories, which were striking in their similarity. The themes were abuse and neglect, isolation, guilt and loyalty, grievances with mental health services, and supports. Since the participants' own statements powerfully convey their earlier experiences, representative excerpts from the interviews, organized by the five themes, are presented here.

Abuse and Neglect

All participants spontaneously described the abuse or neglect they experienced due to their mother's mental illness, ranging from maternal withdrawal to extensive physical, and in one case sexual, abuse. The mother's distorted sense of reality had a profound effect on her ability to provide consistently for her child's basic needs. One young man in the study, a college student whose father was a respected professional in his community and whose mother had been diagnosed with paranoid schizophrenia, described this early neglect in the following way:

> I was never bathed. I didn't have clothes. There was a period when I had no friends—easy to understand; I was a ragamuffin.... I didn't understand what bathing was. In fourth grade we used to drink beer before school. There was just a complete lack of supervision.

As a result of having a parent who was often nonfunctioning, these children became caregivers for the parent and younger siblings at an early age. A participant whose mother was diagnosed with paranoid schizophrenia described her situation when, at the age of 15 her mother's delusional and paranoid behavior worsened considerably and the girl supported them both:

> She stopped functioning. It was definitely the biggest trauma of my life. We got evicted from our apartment because she'd scream all night—she'd bother all the tenants. We lived in real dumps, and I

Everybody pretended like nothing was going on. My mother would go off and be hospitalized, and nobody would tell us where she was, nobody would tell us when she'd be back—my father included....

remember living in a hotel with pimps and prostitutes. We finally got an apartment, but it was four subway [changes] from my school. It took me 2 hours to get to school, 2 hours to get home. I had a job that was our only income. I'd get up at 5:00, go to school, go to my job, go to the public library so I didn't have to go home because my mother was so crazy. I'd stay till it closed, and then I'd take my four subways home. She was up all night screaming. The windows were broken.... It was terrible—it was a nightmare.

Three participants were physically abused. One woman recalled her fourth-grade year as being especially difficult. Her mother was in a full-blown paranoid schizophrenic episode, believing that people were planning to kidnap her three children:

> That was a terrible year. She was just in a constant delusion for a full year. She wouldn't let us go to school, we couldn't even leave the house, she used to lock us in our rooms because she was so scared people were gonna get us. And we were really abused....I remember the bruises, and no one ever noticed that....I had this dream that I was going to jump out the window and break my leg, just so they could see what was going on. So many people didn't see, so many people that should've seen.

Another woman who experienced what she called ritualistic abuse by her schizophrenic mother said,

> I was abused with some regularity. I've got multiple fractures, and was out of

school for a good amount of time during my elementary school years with bruises and things like that.

As is evident in these accounts, surprisingly little effort was made to protect the children from the abusiveness of the psychotic parent. Three participants spoke of occasional support from their fathers, and one father won custody of the children from their bipolar mother, but fathers were generally seen by these children as physically or emotionally unavailable to them. Four of the fathers were alcoholics, and three left their families when the children were very young (after the mother had had her first psychotic episode). Participants described a childhood in which they received little consistent attention from either parent and where abuse or neglect were common.

Isolation

Participants spoke of feeling isolated from their peers, their communities, and their own families, and of being confused by these feelings. Eight of the participants reported that their mother's mental illness was not discussed in any real way with them when they were children:

> Everybody pretended like nothing was going on. My mother would go off and be hospitalized, and nobody would tell us where she was, nobody would tell us when she'd be back—my father included....Once, they took my mother off to a mental hospital, and they left my brother and me [aged six and eight] by ourselves. I recall this very vividly. We were alone in the house until the next morning. Nobody ever said anything.

One woman remembered that when her schizophrenic mother received shock treatments, no one explained to her what was happening. Such silence was a common experience among the people in this study. Family members rarely acknowledged or explained to the children anything relating to their mother's illness. Psychotic episodes and behavior, which were confusing and frightening, remained unacknowledged and unexplained, leaving the children with a confused sense of their own reality and a feeling of being isolated within the family:

> My mom [a paranoid schizophrenic] used to always think someone was in the house. She always thought it was my father's mother, and she would send [me and my sister] upstairs to go look...and give us toast and sandwiches to bring up to Grammy. And my sister and I would go up and look, and come back down and say, "Grammy's not here,"—and then we'd get the belt. So we learned to adapt. We'd run upstairs, [eat] the sandwich, come down and say, Grammy said thank you very much"...But my sister and I never talked about it.

Another young woman expressed anger at her family's failure to acknowledge the illness and went on to describe the loneliness and pain it caused her.

> People didn't say what was going on; denial is a form of lying in our family. The way I coped was to be a very good girl—shut down, didn't make waves. So I was always in a good mood—happy; at least other people saw me as happy. I never told anybody. Everybody thought I was easygoing, sweet, and nice ... there was so much pain in my family that I couldn't add to it, so if I was sad I couldn't let anybody know.

In addition to feeling isolated from family members, study participants also described a sense of alienation from the community and their peers. Although most reached out to others at some time, whether it was to a friend, a friend's family, or a teacher, they described feeling different from these other, normal people, almost as if they had two lives, each with its own reality. One man described his awareness of never quite belonging, even while actively seeking the company of a neighborhood family that welcomed him:

> They had a nice home; I was comfortable and terrified at the same time, because I knew I was different—there was always a time when I was going to have to go home....I was always an outsider there, even though I was always very glad to go over. I used to have to limit myself to the times I'd go over, because I was pestering them—I knew I was pestering them.

Another woman described very similar feelings about her connection with a friend's family:

> Even though I was welcomed and the friends and their parents were very nice, I think a lot of them felt bad for me. They always welcomed me, but I felt different. I so much wanted to fit in and be a part of their family that I let that part go.

Six participants recalled their reluctance to invite friends to visit because of their mother's bizarre behavior. Because the mentally ill mother and her family were ostracized by the community, the child's feelings of isolation were further reinforced:

> [Once] I heard some kids talking, they were daring each other to ring her doorbell. You know how neighborhoods have witches? Well, my mother used to be the witch of the neighborhood. I heard people talking about the witch—I wondered who it was—but it was my mother.

Another woman recalled a very similar painful memory:

> People or kids in the neighborhood used to make fun of her, and I used to get really upset, and I would cry, but I also got really angry. I would get angry at my mother, it was easier to get angry at her. I felt different; I felt like there was something wrong with her, and something wrong with us.

Feeling isolated and different was a common experience for the participants in this study. Several individuals described the confusing consequences of having a parent whose reality was different from the one experienced outside the family, and they detailed the feelings of alienation that resulted. One woman described her sense of being different due to her mother's distorted sense of reality:

> I remember being embarrassed because my mother would use words to describe things that I found out later were not what things were. I remember Show and Tell in school, and bringing something that was normal in my house, and the kids really laughed—they thought it was really funny. Kids would laugh; teachers would whisper. I thought it was me—that there was something wrong with me.

Guilt and Loyalty

Guilt and loyalty, though not directly addressed in the interview questionnaire, continually emerged as important themes. Most participants were (and continue to be) quite loyal to their mentally ill mothers, although living with them was extremely difficult and painful. One young college student explained why he returns to live with his mother every summer.

> I want to be there for my mother instead of shipping out and abandoning her. As long as I can stand it, I think it's good for her. It's not good for me—it's pretty bad, actually—sometimes intolerable, and I have to leave.

Another woman left her foster home to return to her mother before she was legally free to do so, knowing that it would be hellish at times but feeling loyal to her mother, who she felt needed her care. Loyalty often contributed to the participants' feelings of isolation:

> I couldn't see my friends because ... I couldn't talk to them about what was going on ... I couldn't tell anybody. It was terrifically humiliating—plus I knew it was totally disloyal.

Difficult loyalty conflicts emerged over issues of child custody. Some of the most emotional responses of these interviews arose when describing those conflicts:

> Social workers came to interview us [during a custody battle between her mother and fathers.] I was in such a bind. I didn't want to hurt her. Now I feel furious about it because the way they did it was so stupid. After the social worker left, [my mother] sat me on her lap and asked me, Don't you love me? Why do you want to leave me?...It was hard, because we wanted to be with [my father].

> [My mother] alienated herself from [family friends who were trying to help]. Then I was *really* alone. [The friends] would come to school with a child welfare worker, call me to the principal's office, and sit down and talk to me about "what's happening with your mother," and I wouldn't talk about it. But the agencies they called should have known that it shouldn't have been up to me to blow the whistle on her—they should not have given me that responsibility! They should have made an adult decision to take me out of the home...I felt my loyalty had to be with her.

Perhaps the most telling expression of the conflict experienced by these children was embodied in this paradoxical statement of one man:

> "The best place for me to be was home. It was bad. A lot of it was sheer hell."

Expressions of guilt were tied to the feelings of loyalty. All but one of the study's participants expressed a belief that they had caused or contributed to their mother's mental illness. "She was sicker after I was born," and "One doctor told us it was our fault," were comments from two participants that revealed this sense of guilt. Many participants described the guilt they felt at being separated from their mentally ill mother. It did not matter if the separation was the result of their own choice or

resulted from decisions made by the adults around them; leaving their mother, while providing relief, also led to feeling guilty. After her father won a custody battle to get the children from their mentally ill mother, one participant recalled:

> My mother always wanted me to visit her, but I didn't want to go: it was depressing. My brothers and sisters wouldn't go....I was the youngest and I would be the one who felt like I had to go, because she was alone if I didn't....I never went because I wanted to go. It was an obligation....It was painful when I lived with my father. I wanted to live with him, but I felt like I'd abandoned my mother.

Many participants expressed guilt that they were healthier and that their accomplishments exceeded those of their mother or other family members. One woman, describing her considerable personal and professional achievements, said, "All the things I've managed to accomplish—none of it kept her from being crazy." One young woman, concerned for the older sister who was very protective of her during their tumultuous childhoods, said,

> I feel bad...[my sister] gave me all her strength and had none left for herself. Now she's having all the problems....I feel guilty....I just want to make her better.

Another expressed guilt at going away to college, thus "abandoning" his schizophrenic mother, and described his feeling that his father (who remains married to his mentally ill wife),

> Sacrificed his life....It's been good for my mother, it's been good for us [kids]. But it's important to have a life, and to have somebody love you, and he's totally sacrificed that.

Contacts With Mental Health Services

All but one study participant found childhood contacts with mental health services to be negative. (The exception was a young woman who, as an adolescent, went into a psychoeducational treatment with her mother and learned different ways to deal with schizophrenia. However, an earlier experience with therapy had left this same girl terrified when the therapist encouraged her mother to describe her delusions, which seriously frightened her young daughter.) As children, they often witnessed their mother being taken away to be hospitalized, but rarely received explanations of what had happened or what to expect. Visits with their hospitalized mother were recalled as terrifying experiences that caused them much pain and guilt. Often these children felt that they were to blame for their mother's hospitalization. Many suspect that their mother was mistreated or abused while hospitalized:

> It felt like animals. The smells, the sounds, the screams, the cold, sterile beds that barely had covers on them. I couldn't imagine anything worse—to see your parent in a place like that was terrible.

> Don't ever throw your mother in a state institution. That's one of the hardest periods I ever went through. It was a cruel place. I think my mother was sexually abused there ... when she came out, she was very, very frightened.

While contacts with the mental health system in general were perceived negatively by study participants, direct contacts with mental health providers were described even more strongly as unpleasant, guilt-

I had been saved... helped a great deal by being "adopted" by this family...they had a healthy home, you could tell when you went in there. They had regular meals; it was homey. But I used to have to limit myself to the times I'd go over.

provoking, or even harmful. One young man recalled a family therapy session when he was in seventh grade in which the therapist told the family that his schizophrenic mother's bizarre behavior was the family's fault. His initial feeling of guilt was later expressed with anger:

> They try to peg what is a medical problem as something else...it's just reprehensible to tell a bunch of kids it's their fault, but it's still going on....It's like treating a cancer in the Stone Age.

Another participant recalled being told by a social worker that she needed to be more understanding of her mother. This young woman, who described herself as a child who had hidden her real feelings for the sake of her family, remembered how devastated she was to hear that she was not doing enough. Still another participant, who had had her bones broken on several occasions during her mother's frightening psychotic attacks, was coerced at the age of 18 by her mother's psychiatrist into staying with her delusional mother when no one else would:

> Her psychiatrist appealed to me to stay. He guilt-tripped me into staying in the household for another 18 months.... These crazy psychiatrists! What was most frustrating is that the psychiatrists would violate her confidentiality by hooking family members in when it was useful, but wouldn't respond to family members when it wasn't convenient for them.

These direct contacts with mental health professionals though possibly having some value to the mother as patient, are remembered by the children as personally hurtful and damaging.

Despite their negative views of their childhood contacts with mental health services and professionals, eight of the nine participants in this study had entered individual therapy as adults. This information was imparted spontaneously during the interviews. With the exception of two participants (both male), their reasons for seeking treatment—whether they were symptomatic or had received a diagnosis—are not known. The participant who had been diagnosed with schizophrenia entered treatment when he became delusional. Another man entered treatment when he had a "breakdown" several years ago.

All eight found therapy helpful in understanding the impact of their mother's mental illness on the family and on them as individuals. One young woman recalled finally being told by a therapist what was wrong with her mother

That was one of the greatest days, when someone said, "Your mother is a paranoid schizophrenic." They gave it a name, they explained it to me, and I said, "Thank you! Now I know." That just meant the world to me. It's so much easier to deal with something concrete.

In therapy, participants were able to discuss their fears for their own sanity, very common among children of psychotic parents, and reported working on setting limits, both emotional and physical, with their mother. Some emphasized the relative safety of the therapeutic setting; it was a place where they could begin to explore their relationship with their mother, who had so often seemed omnipresent and omnipotent to them:

The biggest help is finding a place where you know you won't get hurt if you tell the secrets. What's easy is finding a place to tell your own secrets....What's more difficult is if you tell your mother's secrets....if you report her behavior it still feels dangerous.

I was in therapy with a wonderful therapist for about 8 years. It's sort of a reparenting. I would actually think of it as critical to getting on with life. I think that many of us who live through that kind of stuff don't ever let ourselves feel anything about it because it doesn't feel safe...[you have to] create a safe space. But it made a big difference to me—it really changed the course of my life.

Social Supports

All nine of the study participants identified one or more people whom they saw as supportive and helpful when they were children. In some cases it was the grandparents; often it was neighbors, family friends, teachers, or coaches. These people were available to the children on a somewhat regular basis. The children rarely, if ever, talked to them about their family situations, but they saw these people as safe and saw their homes or places of work as places in which they were welcome. In retrospect, these supportive others were viewed as lifelines to the world outside the chaotic and bizarre family situation and as providing them with care, attention, and a certain amount of reality testing. Many participants described these people as having made a very big difference in their lives:

*A*ll but one of the study's participants expressed a belief that they had caused or contributed to their mother's mental illness.

I sometimes wonder why I'm not crazy.... That's the only thing I can think of, that my grandmother took care of me—really me. I was the youngest. I was her pet. She was very attentive and I felt very taken care of by her. She paid a lot of attention to me, just loved me.

I had been saved—well, not saved, but helped a great deal by being "adopted" by this family...they had a healthy home, you could tell when you went in there. They had regular meals; it was homey. But I used to have to limit myself to the times I'd go over.

I connected with a teacher I had...she's a friend to this day. She used to have her [classroom] open during lunch...ultimately some of us got incorporated into her family. We used to go over to her house [for] family dinners, and it's the first regular family I ever saw.... She was a major changing point for me.

These connections were often initiated by the adults, but in many instances participants described actively seeking certain people out, targeting people with whom they knew they could feel comfortable and accepted. The women in the study were more likely to describe themselves as having actively sought out certain people, while the men took a more passive role as children in accepting the support or companionship of others. These supportive relationships were not without difficulty. Many participants described feeling that they didn't quite belong with these families or friends, and many experienced loyalty conflicts, even while pursuing these friendships.

Although all the participants clearly articulated pain-filled relationships with their psychotic mother, five recalled a special, if inconsistent, loving relationship with her. This love and support varied with the intensity and duration of their mother's psychotic episodes:

She was extremely indulgent in some ways, and even though we were poor there was a way in which I was treated to think highly of myself....I was the apple of her eye, I had a sense of myself....What I learned to do was to connect real strongly with people. I learned some of that from my mom who—when she's not crazy—is a very connected person. What I learned from her did me well.

Discussion

These extensive, first-person accounts of daily life with a psychotic parent corroborate previous findings and contribute new information that can add to our understanding of the experiences and needs of children of mentally ill parents. It must be remembered, however, that the small size of the study sample limits the generalizability of its findings, however informative.

The burden described by many families of the mentally ill (Anthony, 1969; Hatfield, 1978) was experienced by all the participants in this study, particularly the neglect and the fear of physical harm they lived with as a child of a psychotic mother. The pervasiveness of the neglect is an indication of the devastating effect that the mental illness of one family member has on the entire family.

Resistance of Mental Health Professionals to Working With People With Serious Mental Illness

Kenneth Minkoff

KENNETH MINKOFF, M.D., IS MEDICAL DIRECTOR OF CHOATE INTEGRATED BEHAVIORAL CARE, WOBURN, MA.

THIS ARTICLE WAS ORIGINALLY PUBLISHED IN *New Directions for Mental Health Services,* 1987, 33 (SPRING), 3-20 AND IS REPRINTED WITH PERMISSION. LANGUAGE USAGE HAS BEEN UPDATED BY THE AUTHOR.

Among mental health professionals, the prevailing attitude is that working with people with serious mental illness is unrewarding, nonprestigious, and hopeless. Consequently, our efforts to overcome barriers to the care of people with serious mental illness will never be successful unless we focus on professionals' resistances to working with these patients.

Nearly 10 years ago, the American Psychiatric Association Task Force on the Chronic Mental Patient recognized that "among professionals such as ourselves, and among paraprofessionals, there are prevailing attitudes—that working with these patients is unrewarding and dull, that outcome is hopeless—[and] that prestige is not available for working in [seriously mentally ill] programs" (Meyerson, 1978). Unfortunately, as I note later, these negative attitudes are no less prevalent today, and undoubtedly contribute significantly to the difficulty of providing people with serious mental illness with quality mental health services regardless of setting or system of care.

Other chapters in this sourcebook explore the roles of the "difficult" patient population, the poorly integrated mental health service delivery system, and the discriminatory mental health reimbursement system in creating obstacles to the care of people with serious mental illness. It must be emphasized, however, that problems in each of these areas are magnified significantly by the caregivers' own negative attitudes. Because of their underlying resistance to working with people with serious mental illness, mental health professionals often do not assertively seek to overcome these barriers, and choose instead to consider the problems insurmountable. At the same time, highly motivated professionals will often overcome far greater barriers to pursue areas of genuine interest.

Thus, "difficult" patients with serious mental illness may be regarded as burdensome, while those in psychoanalytic treatment for narcissistic personality disorder are regarded as challenging. Similarly, while some community mental health centers meet the challenge of serving people with serious mental illness by developing model programs (Bachrach, 1980), many others subvert this mandate by diverting resources to healthier and more interesting patients. Finally, many psychiatrists may avoid working with chronic patients because of low pay or poor insurance reimbursement, while actively pursuing equally low-paying jobs in prestigious academic settings or struggling to practice equally poorly reimbursed psychoanalytic psychotherapy in highly competitive urban environments.

It should be clear, therefore, that professional efforts to overcome barriers to the care of people with serious mental illness will never be successful if we focus only on people, places, and things outside of ourselves. No solution can be considered comprehensive if it fails to address the significant resistances of professionals themselves to working with this patient population. Consequently, in this article I will attempt to analyze the problem of professional resistance to working people with serious mental illness, delineate some of the reasons for this resistance, and describe some possible solutions. I will begin by analyzing the available data to determine the extent of the problem.

Studies of Professional Attitudes

It may be that one of the manifestations of professional resistance to working people with serious mental illness is that the problem itself has been studied so little. Among numerous studies of public attitudes toward mental illness reviewed by Rabkin (1974), only one was concerned with the attitudes of mental health professionals (Schroder & Ehrlich, 1968). In this study, psychiatric nurses acted no differently than the general public in displaying increased social distance and rejection toward people with serious mental illness. A recent study by Pines and Maslach (1978) related staff burnout and job dissatisfaction to working with more severely ill (for example, schizophrenic) patients. Creden and Casarego (1975) found that 53% of psychiatric residents were opposed to a state hospital rotation in the residency, while 57% declared themselves to be psychoanalytically oriented, and less than 10% were interested in integrating biological and psychosocial aspects of psychiatry.

Only one recent study specifically measures professional attitudes toward people with serious mental illness. In this study, 85% of the respondents agreed that people with serious mental illness are not a preferred population to treat, 55% believed that most clinicians prefer to avoid them, and 65% believed that there were no satisfying professional rewards in treating this population (Mirabi et al., 1985). In summary, these alarming figures suggest that the extent of the problem of professional resistance to working with people with serious mental illness is indeed substantial.

Where does this extensive resistance come from? Review of the literature suggests that avoidance of people with serious mental illness by mental health profession-

als is related to: 1) avoidance of people with serious mental illness by society at large, 2) avoidance of chronically ill patients by the medical profession in general, and 3) failure of mental health professionals to provide adequate training and peer support to overcome the specific affective and attitudinal barriers to psychotherapeutic work with people with serious mental illness. I will address each point in turn. I will cover the first two briefly, since they have been discussed in more depth elsewhere; the balance of this article will focus on problems within the mental health profession itself.

Societal Attitudes Toward Mental Illness

Rabkin's comprehensive review (1974) of the literature on public attitudes toward people with serious mental illness reveals the extent to which they are excluded and rejected by society at large. Studies of social distance indicate that of the four major "unacceptable" groups in society—exconvicts, alcoholics, the mentally retarded, and people with serious mental illness—people with serious mental illness are rated the most unacceptable (Tringo, 1970). Schroder and Ehrlich (1968) demonstrate that mental health professionals share these attitudes. It is a common misconception that more enlightened professionals will have less exclusionary attitudes than the general public.

However, while education may facilitate identification and labeling of mental illness, it does not prevent rejection. "The public is less quick than mental health professionals to label odd or deviant behavior as mental illness, but once the label [is] assigned—the response [is] characteristically negative and rejecting" (Rabkin, 1974; Phillips, 1967). As a result of education, people may believe that they should regard mental illness as "just another illness," but they still feel that mental illness is more repellent to most people than other illnesses (Elinson & Padella, 1967). In fact, more education about and awareness of the seriousness of mental illness may actually increase avoidance of this population. Rabkin (1974) found that "more contact [with chronic patients] is not a sufficient condition for attitude change" unless the patients are observed—as they so rarely are—in "normal routine assignments [where they] seem human like you and me." Segal and Aviram (1978) observed that, as a result of deinstitutionalization, "a new system of exclusion" has emerged in the community to replace the old pattern of exclusion in the institution. Clearly, mental health professionals and community mental health centers are a part of this new exclusionary system. By excluding people with serious mental illness from treatment, they merely reflect the prevailing prejudices of the community they serve.

Physicians' Attitudes Toward People With Serious Mental Illness

An ideal norm of the medical profession is that physicians should not prefer one type of patient over another, but the real norm is that the most rewarding experience is with patients who respond well to treatment (Merton, 1957). Thus, negative attitudes toward people with serious mental illness are endemic to all aspects of medicine, not just psychiatry. Jeffery's study of emergency room patients reveals that patients are identified as "rubbish" when they break the "rule" that the medical staff must be capable of treating their illness (Jeffery, 1979). Other studies indicate that medical training inculcates medical students with the belief that "where the physician's work does not afford...the possibility of...restoring health through skillful practice...[thus] those patients who can be cured are better than those who cannot" (Becker, 1961). While acute patients are "interesting and educational," chronicity "produces no new increments of information or clinical experience" (Becker, 1961). Short-term rotations encourage this belief and provide little

incentive for medical students to appreciate the slower, smaller gains that rehabilitative medicine can produce for people with serious mental illness. Kutner (1978) concludes that there is "little indication that our system of medical education has as yet begun to turn significant attention to producing a greater number of 'management-oriented' as opposed to 'diagnosis-oriented' physicians who are interested in following patients over the course of a chronic illness."

It is reasonable to conclude that all helping professions—psychology and social work as well as psychiatry—share many of the same basic negative attitudes toward chronicity. Moreover, it is also likely that, as in the medical profession, these attitudes are firmly inculcated during professional training, and are very difficult to change over time. Thus, the avoidance of people with serious mental illness by the mental health professions reflects in part a pervasive avoidance of chronicity by all helping professions. As such, it may be more difficult to condemn, and even more difficult to change.

Problems Within the Mental Health Professions

Working with people with serious mental illness creates a number of special difficulties for mental health professionals beyond the more general problems already discussed. First, clinicians react to people with serious mental illness with a broad range of powerful (and often negative) feelings that may create barriers to effective intervention. Second, adequate training in the special skills required to overcome these affective barriers—and to work effectively with people with serious mental illness—is often not provided in professional training programs. Third, clinicians who treat people with serious mental illness often lack the peer support and validation they need to persevere in their work.

Affective barriers. The importance of overcoming affective barriers to working with people with serious mental illness cannot be overstated. As Minkoff and Stern (1985) point out, "Regardless of how the clinician conceptualizes treatment, making empathic connection with [a person with serious mental illness] is crucial to the success of any therapeutic intervention." Unfortunately, however, clinicians often find that making empathic connection with [a person with serious mental illness] creates an emotional challenge they are unable to meet. "Schizophrenia…is a terrifying disease for the patient and clinician alike. The devastation, shame, and despair of the experience of…psychosis make empathy very difficult for even the most experienced clinician…not only may it be difficult for the [clinician] to even connect with the person behind the bizarre symptomatology, but once the connection is made, the patient's daily struggle with the shame and stigma of being 'crazy' and the despair of being chronic may be more than [the clinician] can bear" (Minkoff & Stern, 1985). Thus, many clinicians find that to work with people with serious mental illness—or their families—they need to distance themselves intellectually and emotionally; consequently, their ability to provide effective treatment becomes severely limited.

There are a complex variety of attitudes, feelings, stresses, and "paradoxes" that confront clinicians working with people with serious mental illness (Lamb, 1982; Stern & Minkoff, 1969; White & Bennett, 1981; Minkoff & Stern, 1985). These can be organized into four major categories.

Feelings of hopelessness and despair. Clinicians have enormous difficulty when confronted with incurability and the need to work with patients on adaptation to illness and adjusting to lower expectations for success. "Chronicity challenges our 'wish to cure' and our sense of competence and control. Recognizing the poor prognosis for

some of our patients' illnesses means acknowledging our own helplessness—sometimes we may need improvement to satisfy our own sense of success, and, unfortunately, we may blame the patient when he fails to improve" (Group for the Advancement of Psychiatry, 1987). Clinicians, faced with chronicity, generally experience unbearable feelings of despair. They may then need to deny the reality of the patient's disability to protect themselves from pain. They "maintain the fantasy [usually consciously denied] that they will be able to cure the patient . . . [becoming] frustrated and disappointed when their best efforts fail" (White & Bennett, 1981). The most difficult challenge of all is to simply acknowledge the patient's despair, to bear it with him or her, and to put it into a hopeful perspective.

Similarly, clinicians' "intense need to be actively changing and improving people" (Neilsen et al., 1981) results in an expectation of "too much progress in too little time" (White & Bennett, 1981). "We are not surprised when intensive psychotherapy with persons of character ego strength takes years to achieve character change. Yet we are frequently dismayed when the long-term severely disabled take years to progress in social and vocational rehabilitation" (Lamb, 1979).

The resulting frustration and impatience lead to staff burnout and avoidance of working with people with serious mental illness. Clinicians also have difficulty setting appropriate goals for people with serious mental illness. Successful outcome for all patients has been traditionally measured according to normative standards, which include absence of symptoms, avoidance of relapse, full employment, and full social interaction (Strauss & Carpenter, 1977). Because these normative goals are unattainable for most people with serious mental illness, clinicians may feel that "treatment is doomed to fail before it even begins"

(Minkoff & Stern, 1985). Paradoxically, the more invested the [clinician] becomes in the client's progress, the more discouraged and burned out he or she becomes when the patient's limitations become apparent (Stern & Minkoff, 1979; Minkoff & Stern, 1985). To resolve this paradox, clinicians must learn to develop individualized outcome criteria and attainable treatment goals that are based on the patient's own history and baseline, through a life-course perspective of the patient's career of mental illness. Failure to learn this new value system for measuring therapeutic success with people with serious mental illness results in the continuing perception that they are impossible to treat and should be avoided (Minkoff & Stern, 1985).

Feelings of helplessness and inadequacy. In Mirabi's study (Mirabi et al., 1985), 83% of respondents agreed that burnout, associated with feelings of helplessness and frustration, was common when treating people with serious mental illness. "Most clinicians are not optimistic that current therapeutic regimens relieve symptoms or can stabilize the chronically mentally ill," and are particularly frustrated by a lack of resources and repeated treatment failures (Mirabi et al., 1985).

A significant majority of clinicians believe that their training has not prepared them adequately to feel successful with people with serious mental illness and thereby to prevent burnout (Mirabi et al., 1985; Lamb, 1982; Stern & Minkoff, 1979). Thus, presumably well-trained clinicians are confronted with "unaccustomed feelings of failure when their skills do not work with chronic patients" (Stern & Minkoff, 1979). The resulting assumption that these patients cannot be helped becomes a self-fulfilling prophecy when clinicians resist learning the special skills they need to overcome their helplessness because they believe they will feel ineffective with people with serious mental illness no matter what they do

(Minkoff & Stern 1985 White & Bennett, 1981; Fink, 1975; Sabin & Sharfstein, 1975. This vicious cycle creates a substantial barrier to the development of a cadre of mental health professionals who can become patients' experts and provide people with serious mental illness with the high-quality treatment they need.

Feelings of dislike or disgust toward patients. As noted previously, mental health professionals are not immune to the feelings of repugnance toward people with serious mental illness characteristic of society at large. Clinicians who enjoy working with attractive, verbal, insightful clients may be repelled by people with serious mental illness who are unkempt, uncooperative, bizarre, and crazy.

Patients' manipulative behavior and lack of compliance with medication are particularly infuriating for many clinicians (Mirabi et al., 1985). Many clinicians may displace these negative feelings by saying that their "healthier" patients would feel uncomfortable or frightened if they saw "sicker" patients in the waiting room; the "sicker" patients are then excluded, although they are the ones most in need.

It is characteristic of many training programs that such feelings are not dealt with aggressively as countertransference issues to be resolved. Rather, because such attitudes are syntonic with the negative attitudes of the majority of clinicians (Mirabi et al., 1985), these negative views receive a subtle but pervasive reinforcement.

In addition to disgust for the bizarreness of people with serious mental illness, clinicians also often experience "distaste for their passivity and dependency" and feelings of being "drained." "Patients often do not appear to be trying to improve and thus repeatedly violate social norms concerning the obligations of sick people" (Neilsen et al., 1985). As Lamb (1979) points out, mental health professionals share "the basic moral disapproval in our society of dependency, of a passive, inactive lifestyle, and of acceptance of public support instead of working." However, such a lifestyle is necessary for many people with serious mental illness to reduce stress and prevent exacerbation of their symptoms. This value system leads to a paradox for many clinicians, who feel that if they provide the caretaking patients need they are being "bad" therapists by fostering dependency (Minkoff & Stern, 1985). Clinicians may then tend to underestimate the strength of the patient's dependency and primitive transference attachment (White & Bennett, 1981), and precipitate relapse and regression by pushing for independence that the patient cannot manage. The patient may then be blamed—and rejected—for failing to improve.

Feelings of discomfort. Clinical work with people with serious mental illness is often more demanding than work with moderately ill patients in that it requires more activity and case management (Lamb, 1982), a multiaxial psychosocial approach (Minkoff & Stern, 1985; Group for the Advancement of Psychiatry, 1987; Neilsen et al., 1981), individualized treatment strategies (Minkoff & Stern, 1985; White & Bennett, 1981), family education and involvement (Group for the Advancement of Psychiatry, 1987), and increased role flexibility and variability over time (White & Bennett, 1981). Clinicians who "must learn how to adapt their therapeutic stance to fit the needs of the patient rather than take the same stance with all patients . . . may feel exposed and uncomfortable with this new therapeutic posture (White & Bennett, 1981). Similarly, clinicians may need to function as case managers or primary physicians; perform home visits and fill out disability forms; and provide didactic teaching, medication, and hospitalization rather than simply remain in the comfortable but limited role of psychotherapist (Lamb, 1982; White & Bennett, 1981).

Further, clinicians may resent the fact that their work with people with serious mental illness rarely involves psychodynamic psychotherapy, which many view as the only true psychotherapy. Psychotherapy with people with serious mental illness can be psychodynamic psychotherapy, but it usually is not. Clinicians "are often discouraged when their efforts to do psychodynamic psychotherapy are unsuccessful…[and] disappointed that the psychosocial approach they need for success is not psychotherapy as they envisioned it" (Minkoff & Stern, 1985). This conflict often results in the decision to avoid treating people with serious mental illness altogether.

It is probable that these feelings are experienced to some degree by all clinicians who work with people with serious mental illness. Because these feelings are so widespread, they contribute greatly to the pervasive negative attitude toward chronic patients found throughout the mental health profession. This, in turn, creates a significant barrier to good care. Although clinicians who have adequate training and support in working with chronic patients can often learn to overcome these negative attitudes, such training and support is often not available. This will be discussed in the following sections.

Training deficits. In their extensive review of the characteristics of successful programs for training mental health professionals to work with people with serious mental illness, Neilsen et al. (1981) expressed their hope and belief that "residency education in chronic psychiatric care can expose residents to the real rewards of treating severely disturbed patients, and that, as a result, residents will be more likely to continue such work after graduation."

Unfortunately, as they and many other authors have observed, this hope is rarely realized (Lamb, 1982; Minkoff & Stern, 1985; White & Bennett, 1981; Fink, 1975;

Sabin & Sharfstein, 1975; Neilsen et al., 1981). Sixty-eight percent of respondents in a survey conducted by Mirabi and others (1985) believe that most clinicians do not receive adequate training in caring for people with serious mental illness. Training programs in all mental health disciplines commonly fall short in their ability to address the specific—and extensive—educational needs of trainees working with people with serious mental illness, even when providing quality service to people with serious mental illness is a major clinical objective of the training program.

Neilsen and others (1981) observed that a successful training program must develop a positive feedback loop involving three components: "1) knowledge, 2) skills, and 3) attitudes; and supervision and role models. The interplay of these components is crucial. Proper skills, knowledge, and attitudes turn mere exposure into successful experiences, and the feedback loop continues as successful experiences lead to more and more refined skills, knowledge, and attitudes that make further success and exposure more likely." In reality, however, this feedback loop breaks down at every juncture: Clinical exposure is not adequate, necessary skills are not taught, and truly competent supervision (for people with serious mental illness) is not available. This breakdown is due in part to inadequate resources, limitations in the mental health system, and the inability of most training directors to understand and give priority to the needs of trainees working with people with serious mental illness. Regardless of the cause, however, the failure of training programs to provide adequate training experiences with people with serious mental illness not only results in a failure to overcome trainees' negative attitudes toward these patients, but also subtly confirms and encourages these attitudes. In short, the feedback loop described above does not occur. Unsuccessful experiences and lacklus-ter supervision result in less refined skills and more negative attitudes, which result in even less success and less motivation to learn. In such a context, avoidance of working with people with serious mental illness may seem like a blessing for all those concerned. To understand how the feedback loop breaks down, I will examine each of the three components in return.

Lack of adequate clinical exposure. Adequate clinical exposure to people with serious mental illness in a training program is hard to define specifically, but generally requires:

• Exposure to a sufficient *number* of patients to be able to observe the variety of clinical presentations that people with serious mental illness make.

• Encouragement to follow some patients in *depth,* to go beyond medication or case management to become familiar with the patient and his family, to become closely involved with them, and to understand their pain and their struggle.

• Ability to follow patients "for enough *time,* generally the length of the residency, so that a variety of interventions and approaches can be attempted, integrated, and evaluated for each patient" (Minkoff & Stern, 1985), so that the pattern of the patient's life course with mental illness is clear.

• Exposure to the treatment of people with serious mental illness in a *setting* where good care is provided—where there is an appropriate range of treatment modalities, where there are competent and committed role models, and where colleagues are observed caring about their patients and feeling positively about their work.

Unfortunately, in most training programs, these conditions are not met. Exposure to people with serious mental illness often occurs in overburdened community programs with staff who are "overextended, undersupervised, and unable to provide the highest quality of treatment" (Group for the Advancement of Psychiatry, 1987). Trainees may be led to believe that they should avoid people with serious mental illness in these settings because they are not "good" teaching cases. Further, because of the short-term nature of the placement, there is often not enough time for trainees to truly engage people with serious mental illness and to observe the pattern of their long-term slow adaptation to their illness. Moreover, the patients themselves may be unwilling to invest heavily in a relationship with a therapist who will treat them for a relatively short time. Thus, both patient and trainee may find it easier to remain in a superficial relationship that does not challenge or reward either party. This relationship will often seem boring to the trainee in contrast to the more intense psychotherapeutic relationships formed with the more acute and less ill clients in the bulk of his or her caseload. The nature of the work with these healthier patients often is more conducive to producing demonstrable rewards for trainees in the relatively short period of their placement. Thus, the nature of the training system itself subtly discriminates against people with serious mental illness.

Lack of specific training in necessary skills. There is a lack of formal curriculum. Discrimination against people with serious mental illness in training programs extends to the curriculum as well. Most training programs provide extensive reading, teaching, and supervision on psychoanalytic psychotherapy of nonpsychotic patients and psychopharmacologic therapy for acute psychiatric illnesses, as well as formal exposure to family therapy, group therapy, behavior therapy, and so on. However, there is little established literature and no formal curriculum for teaching a comprehensive clinical approach to the assessment and treatment of people with serious mental illness. Thus trainees often struggle to apply theory and practice more suited to moderately ill patients to their work with people with serious mental illness, usually with disappointing results.

Then there is a lack of training in an integrated biopsychosocial approach. Because of the absence of a formal curriculum, trainees often learn about people with serious mental illness in a haphazard fashion, which contributes to their sense of confusion and fragmentation. Many authors have emphasized the importance of teaching an integrated biopsychosocial approach for conceptualizing the assessment and treatment of people with serious mental illness (Lamb, 1982; Minkoff & Stern, 1985; Group for the Advancement of Psychiatry, 1987; Neilsen et al., 1981). This requires understanding the use of biological interventions to treat symptoms of mental illness, combined with a wide range of psychosocial and family interventions to facilitate adaptation and rehabilitation, perhaps over the course of a lifetime. Unfortunately, this integrated approach is very difficult to teach, and is rarely taught (Creden & Casarego, 1975).

> *Trainees do not know how to treat people with serious mental illness successfully, and do not know that they do not know. As a result, they blame the patients—as a group—for treatment failure.*

Trainees "who are exposed to these multiple biological, psychological, familial, and social variables, and their associated and at times conflicting therapeutic approaches, often feel like a jack-of-all trades and a master of none" (Minkoff & Stem, 1985). Efforts by trainees to find one "correct" approach for people with serious mental illness only leads to further frustration because each patient's needs are so different. Trainees often avoid this issue by seeking to develop narrow areas of expertise and restricting those interventions to these specialty areas (for example, psychopharmacology, behavior therapy, and psychodynamic psychotherapy). However, in the long run, as they focus their clinical efforts more on the limited number of patients who are most responsive to their particular skills, they become increasingly convinced that the majority of people with serious mental illness are indeed too difficult and frustrating to treat. The study by Mirabi and others (1988) found that 73% of respondents believed that people with serious mental illness were too often treated with one modality when they needed multiple approaches. Unfortunately, most training programs encourage this process of specialization because the teachers are often specialists themselves. Thus, the failure to provide an integrated teaching approach for people with serious mental illness is perpetuated from one generation of professionals to the next.

There is also a lack of training in specific treatment techniques with people with serious mental illness. In a similar position, most training programs fail to teach the full range of specific skills and attitudes necessary to implement successful treatment interventions for these patients. These skills include: 1) the ability to empathize with patients facing the hopelessness and despair of their chronic illness; 2) the ability to develop specific management strategies for problems such as denial, noncompliance with medication, and bizarre behavior; 3) the ability to conceptualize attainable treatment goals and develop individualized treatment plans; 4) the ability to work as part of a multidisciplinary treatment team within a complex mental health system; and 5) the ability to assume a variety of roles within the context of a single therapeutic relationship—therapist, case manager, consultant, teacher, doctor, and friend (Lamb, 1982; Minkoff & Stern, 1988; White & Bennett, 1981; Group for the Advancement of Psychiatry, 1987; Neilsen et al., 1981). These skills are teachable, but like most psychotherapeutic skills they are not easy to learn. Trainees must have opportunities to practice, under supervision, a wide variety of treatment techniques and styles. In addition, they must have the emotional support, from supervision, to work through the significant stresses and paradoxes encountered in the process of learning these new approaches, which often challenge the trainees' previous beliefs about the nature of treatment and mental illness (Minkoff & Stern, 1985). It is rare, however, for training programs to devote the necessary energy and intensity to this type of training. It is common for trainees to work intensively on their countertransference with psychotherapy cases, but uncommon to work as intensively on their feelings about working with people with serious mental illness. Trainees are exposed to obscure psychoanalytic techniques and highly unusual psychopharmacologic interventions before learning to apply the broad range of elegant therapeutic interventions for people with serious mental illness. In addition, trainees are rarely even aware of what they are missing. As a result of the absence of a formal curriculum, trainees do not know how to treat these patients successfully, and do not know that they do not know. As a result, they blame the patients—as a group—for treatment failure. Their negative expectations about work with this population are confirmed, and their avoidance of further work with seriously mentally ill patients becomes inevitable.

Lack of competent supervision. For trainees to resolve negative attitudes, overcome affective barriers, and develop appropriate skills for working with people with serious mental illness, the availability of competent supervision in the treatment of chronic patients is essential. Unfortunately, supervisors who are competent in this area are hard to find. In most training programs, competent supervision is readily available only in psychodynamic psychotherapy, psychopharmacology, family therapy, and other distinct therapeutic entities, usually as applied to nonchronic, nonpsychotic patients. Thus trainees often must present their work with people with serious mental illness to supervisors who are neither skilled nor interested in working with this population. For the most part, these supervisors have only a narrow range of expertise and consequently little facility in the application of the complex biopsychosocial approach required for working with seriously mentally ill patients. In fact, most supervisors do not work at all with seriously mentally ill patients, and therefore have limited skills of any kind with these individuals. The supervisors' own training in working with people with serious mental illness has usually been limited and often predates the biopsychosocial "era," and consequently may be outdated. Supervisors may therefore have firm but erroneous beliefs concerning the etiology and treatment of major mental illness, ranging from beliefs in a predominantly psychodynamic causation of mental illness to a belief in the complete inefficacy of all nonpharmacologic interventions. Moreover, most supervisors share the strong negative attitudes toward patients with serious mental illness characteristic of the profession in general, and experience strong feelings of helplessness, hopelessness, and inadequacy in relation to the treatment of the population.

Thus with regard to seriously mentally ill patients, supervision is more likely to result in the conveyance of misinformation and pessimism than in the transmission of positive attitudes, comprehensive skills, and successful treatment experiences. The trainees' own pre-existing negative attitudes toward seriously mentally ill patients are reinforced, not corrected. Rather than learning to consider themselves skilled in their work with seriously mentally ill patients, trainees learn from their supervisors that it is acceptable to feel helpless, and their avoidance of working with these patients is once again encouraged.

The previous discussion indicates the extent to which current mental health training programs fail to overcome trainees' negative attitudes toward people with serious mental illness. Inadequate clinical exposure, lack of comprehensive curriculum, and absence of competent supervision combine instead to perpetuate and reinforce these negative attitudes. In such a context, the positive feedback loop envisioned by Neilsen and others (1981) seems more like a vain hope than a possible reality. Trainees are in fact often taught, more or less explicitly, how not to work with seriously mentally ill patients. This reflects a pervasive lack of support for working with these patients that extends beyond training into every aspect of professional life. This will be discussed further in the following section.

Lack of peer support and validation. Other chapters in this book [reference to original publication (*New Directions for Mental Health Services,* 1987)] describe at length the tremendous difficulty of working with people with serious mental illness—the mental health system provides inadequate support, the legal system interferes with clinical decision-making, the families require and increasingly demand extensive involvement in treatment, and the patients themselves are frequently uncooperative and resistant. Clearly, mental health professionals who do work with these patients, who try to persevere in the face of all these difficulties, require and deserve extensive peer support and professional appreciation for their valiant efforts. Unfortunately, this support and validation are often lacking. As a result, clinicians who work with seriously mentally ill patients often feel that they are outside the mainstream of their professions, and frequently find that they must avoid these patients to advance their professional status, their salary, and their reputation. In the study by Mirabi and others (1985) 63% of respondents believed that satisfying professional rewards for working with seriously mentally ill patients were lacking, and in a similar study by Schwartz and others (1981), therapists working with seriously mentally ill patients reported that the least satisfying aspect of their work was being devalued by their professional peers.

The so-called helping professions subtly encourage professional value systems that downgrade the efforts of those who treat patients who need help most.

What is the cause of this lack of peer support? Its roots begin in Kubie's (1971) description of "a disease without a name whose presenting symptom is a retreat from patients...practiced, defended, and approved by many eminent psychiatrists.... Intensive clinical involvement with patients is the activity least likely to be rewarded by peers."

Kubie was of course not referring only to seriously mentally ill patients, but clearly the "retreat" from these patients is even more profound. The affective barriers and training deficits already noted combine to leave clinicians feeling helpless and hopeless with these patients. To protect themselves from this assault on their collective profes-

sional pride, mental health professionals devalue the work rather than confront their own lack of skill. The Group for the Advancement of Psychiatry (1987) reports that "despite the fact that the chronic mentally ill are the sickest, neediest, and most difficult patients, clinicians usually get little credit, status, or prestige from developing clinical expertise with this population.... [T]he most esteemed clinicians concentrate their private office practices on the 'less ill,' and academic status derives from research (usually psychopharmacologic), not from clinical expertise." In addition, according to Stern and Minkoff (1979), "few clinicians, therefore, develop special interest or expertise in treating the chronically ill, because such interest would be inconsistent with their professional values and their own ego ideals. The irony is that...the so-called helping professions subtly encourage professional value systems that downgrade the efforts of those who treat patients who need help most."

In addition to this lack of support from professional peers, there is often a lack of support from other mental health professions. Borus (1978) points out that psychiatrists in community mental health settings often feel unappreciated and undervalued by nonmedical colleagues, who in turn feel that psychiatrists are often arrogant, undertrained, and unhelpful (especially with seriously mentally ill patients). These interdisciplinary tensions create an unsupportive atmosphere that undermines the morale of the entire treatment team.

Thus mental health professionals who do work with seriously mentally ill patients do not receive peer support as a matter of course. The development of a support system of colleagues becomes a necessary task, and is an additional barrier to overcome. Where this support system is absent or inadequate—as it often is—burnout is inevitable (Lamb, 1979).

The preceding discussion illustrates how affective barriers, deficient training, and lack of peer support contribute to the resistance of mental health professionals to working with people with serious mental illness. Thus, the mental health profession is little different from other helping professions—and from society as a whole—in its avoidance of chronicity in general and chronic mental illness in particular.

The picture is bleak, and, if nothing else, chronic. Is there any hope? Can anything be done? As with other chronic conditions, a hopeful perspective requires that we look for specific practical solutions that address step-by-step attainable goals. In the final section of this article, I will discuss possible approaches that might begin to address these issues.

Recommendations

"Psychiatry must recognize its primary obligation to serve first those patients with the most serious and debilitating illnesses whom the public sees as most distressed and distressing" (Borus, 1978).

The need to make this noble sentiment a reality is at the heart of this problem. However, to approach working with seriously mentally ill patients as an obligation is in the long run self-defeating because it continues to suggest that clinicians work with these patients because they have to, not because they want to. In the positive feedback loop described earlier, proper skills, proper attitudes, successful experiences, and a desire to work with these patients are all integrated. Affective issues,

training issues, and peer support issues all must be ad-dressed simultaneously to focus maximum energy on overcoming the significant resistances discussed elsewhere in this chapter. I will discuss how this can be done.

First, focus on training. It is easier to develop positive attitudes in trainees who are more open to learning new ideas than to try to teach established professionals to unlearn" the negative attitudes they already have.

Second, identify and organize a cadre of established professionals who are specialists in working with people with serious mental illness. Despite the predominant negative attitudes toward serious mental illness within the mental health professions, there does exist a small but significant number of established clinicians who are dedicated specialists in the care of people with serious mental illness (Lamb, 1982; Stern & Minkoff, 1979; Neilsen et al., 1981; and Schwartz et al., 1981).

Unfortunately, unlike psychoanalysts and psychopharmacologists, these specialists have not identified and organized themselves to establish their visibility and leadership as a recognized subspecialty with a definable area of experience and expertise. If a nationwide institute for the biopsychosocial treatment of serious mental illness were established with recognized leadership and clear criteria for membership, it would significantly facilitate the wide dissemination within the mental health professions of a heightened awareness of the value, challenge, and complexity of working with this population. This would then create an atmosphere more conducive to validating the efforts of trainees to learn the specific skills they need to pursue this work successfully.

Third, establish a formal curriculum for training in the biopsychosocial treatment of people with serious mental illness. The lack of a specific curriculum, as noted earlier, contributes both to the difficulty of training for work with the chronic mentally ill and to the view that working with this population has less professional rigor and merit. The material to develop such a curriculum is available but has never been organized into a coherent framework with the imprimatur of a representative group of recognized chronic patient specialists (Lamb, 1982; Minkoff & Stern, 1985; White & Bennett, 1981; Group for the Advancement of Psychiatry, 1987; Neilsen et al., 1981). One of the first functions of an institute as described above might be to establish, validate, and disseminate a training format that can be duplicated throughout the country, both in established training programs and new training institutes developed specifically for working with the chronic mentally ill. These training institutes could provide a wide assortment of programs ranging from introductory workshops for paraprofessionals to formal postgraduate subspecialty training, complete with official recognition and certification for those who graduate.

Fourth, identify and emphasize in training those aspects of working with chronic patients that are most rewarding. As noted earlier, work with chronic patients is too often presented as an obligation and a burden. The enjoyment, excitement, and satisfaction of working with this population is rarely sufficiently emphasized. In a recent survey (Schwartz et al., 1981), therapists who chose to work with people with chronic mental illness stressed the satisfaction they derived from maintaining the patient, achieving small-step goals, developing a long-term alliance, and working with the patient's entire family. To achieve this sense of satisfaction, they stressed the need for long-term work with these patients, a biopsychosocial approach. In the context of a community support system, realistic goals, and acceptance of the patient as a person. This positive orientation can be used as a cornerstone for the development of the formal training curriculum discussed above.

Most important, training must emphasize the relationship of working with people with serious mental illness to the therapist's own personal development. For most clinicians, the deepest reward and excitement of working in the mental health profession is the opportunity to involve oneself as a person on an emotional level in the intensely human process of helping others. True enthusiasm for working with people with serious mental illness can only occur for clinicians who can bring this intense emotional involvement into their work. As Beels (1975) indicates, "people who are really effective in this work [with seriously mentally ill patients] are able to keep going because they see it as part of their own personal development." To "make contact with the person behind the diagnostic label" (Neilsen et al., 1981) of serious mental illness, the clinician must confront his own "private understanding of human hope and despair—as reflected in his own life" (Beels, 1975). Few aspects of human experience raise these questions so deeply and so poignantly as does the experience of living with serious mental illness. Psychiatrists have tended to turn their backs on the intensity of this pain and despair. However, those clinicians who can find the personal inner resource to face this despair with the patients and their families, and learn to maintain a hopeful perspective in spite of it, open the door to a depth and richness of personal involvement that is truly unique in clinical work. To the extent that the richness of experience can be successfully conveyed in training, much of the resistance to working with people with serious mental illness can be overcome.

References

Bachrach, L. L. (1980). Overview: Model programs for chronic mental patients. *American Journal of Psychiatry, 137,* 1023-1031.

Becker, H. S., et al. (1961). *Boys in white, student culture in medical school.* Chicago: University of Chicago Press.

Beels, C. C. (1975). Family and social management of schizophrenia. *Schizophrenia Bulletin, 13,* 97-118.

Borus, J. F. (1978). Issues critical to the survival of community mental health. *American Journal of Psychiatry, 135,* 1029-1035.

Creden, J. R. & Casarego, J. I. (1975). Controversies in psychiatric education: A survey of residents' attitudes. *American Journal of Psychiatry, 32,* 270-274.

Elinson, J., & Padella, E. (1967). *Public image of mental health services.* New York: Mental Health Study Center.

Fink, P. J. (1975). Problems of providing community psychiatry training to residents. *Hospital and Community Psychiatry, 26,* 292-295.

Group for the Advancement of Psychiatry. (1987). *A family affair: Helping families cope with mental illness: A guide for the professionals.* New York: Brunner/Mazel.

Jeffery, R. (1979). Normal rubbish: Deviant patients in casualty departments. *Sociology of Health and Illness, 1,* 90-107.

Kubie, L. (1971). The retreat from patients. *Archives of General Psychiatry, 24,* 98-106.

Kutner, N. G. (1978). Medical student's orientation toward the chronically ill. *Journal of Medical Education, 53,* 111-118.

Lamb, H. R. (1979). Staff burn-out in work with long-term patients. *Hospital and Community Psychiatry, 30,* 396-398.

Lamb, H. R. (1982). *Treating the long-term mentally ill.* San Francisco: Jossey-Bass, 1982.

Merton, R. K. (1957). Some preliminaries to a sociology of medical education. In R. K. Merton, G. G. Reader, and P. L. Kendall (Eds.), *The student physician.* Cambridge, MA: Harvard University Press.

Meyerson, A. T. (1978). What are the barriers or obstacles to treatment and care of the chronically disabled mentally ill? In J. Talbott (Ed.), *The chronic mental patient.* Washington, D.C.: American Psychiatric Association.

Minkoff, K., & Stern, R. (1985). Paradoxes faced by residents being trained in the psychosocial treatment of people with chronic schizophrenia. *Hospital and Community Psychiatry, 36,* 859-864.

Mirabi, M., Weinman, M.L., et al. (1985). Professional attitudes toward the chronic mentally ill. *Hospital and Community Psychiatry, 36,* 404-405.

Neilsen, A. C., III, Stein, L. I., Talbott, J. A., et al. (1985). Encouraging psychiatrists to work with chronic patients: Opportunities and limitations of residency education. *Hospital and Community Psychiatry, 32,* 767-775.

Phillips, D. L. (1967). Identification of mental illness: Its consequences for rejection. *Community Mental Health Journal, 3,* 262-266.

Pines, A., & Maslach, C. (1978). Characteristics of staff burnout in mental health settings. *Hospital and Community Psychiatry, 29,* 233-237.

Rabkin, J. (1974). Public attitudes toward mental illness: A review of the literature. *Schizophrenia Bulletin, 10,* 9-33.

Sabin, J. E., & Sharfstein, S. S. (1975). Integrating community psychiatry into residency training. *Hospital and Community Psychiatry, 26,* 289-292.

Schroder, D., & Ehrlich, D. (1968). Rejection by mental health professionals: A possible consequence of not seeking appropriate help for emotional disorders. *Journal of Health and Social Behavior, 9,* 222-232.

Schwartz, S., Krieger, M., & Sorenson, J. (1981). Preliminary survey of therapists who work with chronic patients: Implications for training. *Hospital and Community Psychiatry, 32,* 799-800.

Segal, S. P., & Aviram, U. (1978). *The mentally ill in community based sheltered care.* New York: Wiley.

Stern, R., & Minkoff, K. (1979). Paradoxes in programming for chronic patients in a community clinic. *Hospital and Community Psychiatry, 30,* 613-617.

Strauss, J. S., & Carpenter, E. T. (1977). Prediction of outcome in schizophrenia. *Archives of General Psychiatry, 43,* 159-163.

Tringo, J. L. (1970). The hierarchy of preference toward disability groups. *Journal of Special Education, 4,* 295-306.

White, H. S., & Bennett, M. B. (1981). Training psychiatric residents in chronic care. *Hospital and Community Psychiatry, 32,* 339-343.

Spirit Breaking: When the Helping Professions Hurt

Patricia E. Deegan

PATRICIA E. DEEGAN, PH.D., IS DIRECTOR OF TRAINING, NATIONAL EMPOWERMENT CENTER, LAWRENCE, MA.

THIS ARTICLE ORIGINALLY APPEARED IN THE *Humanistic Psychologist*, 1990, 18(3), 301-313 AND IS REPRINTED WITH PERMISSION.

Too often the human services dehumanize and depersonalize those who come to receive services, as well as those professionals who provide services. Through exploration of subjective accounts of how people with physical disabilities and people with psychiatric disabilities are frequently hurt by helping professionals, the phenomenon of spirit breaking is introduced. Suggestions for re-humanizing the human services are made, including new models for clinical interaction that serve to empower rather than disempower service recipients, and the contributions that people with disabilities are making in their own state and national movements for social justice and the right to humane treatment and rehabilitation services.

Recently I was asked to speak with a group of graduate students in clinical psychology. In preparing my talk I reflected on what the most important message was I could share with these young people who would soon enter professional practice. The message I felt called to share was rather simple: *People with disabilities are people.* When we forget that people with disabilities share a common humanity with us, then the human is stripped from the human services and the stage is set for the emergence of the inhuman and the inhumane. The inhuman and the inhumane emerge from that rupture which occurs when one human being fails to recognize and reverence the humanity and the fundamental sanctity, sovereignty and dignity of another person. Such a rupture in mutual relatedness occurs often in the helping professions and for this reason helping professionals sometimes hurt rather than help people with disabilities. Too often the human services dehumanize and depersonalize. Many people with disabilities refer to this special kind of hurt as spirit breaking or how the system tries to break your spirit.

I think we can all learn from the paper I shared with those graduate students. It went like this:

Being a student is very important work. Beyond merely mastering a finite content area of study and becoming proficient in clinical practice, we also have the obligation to develop and articulate our values and the ideals which form the foundation of our clinical praxis. We must take the latter aspect of our work very seriously, because when we leave the university setting and enter the day-to-day business of clinical psychology it is very easy to become compromised in our values and ideals. It is easy to lose sight of our humanity as the common ground we share with those who come to us for help.

When we make the transition from being a student to being a professional clinician, our culture and human service institutions grant us a broad range of power over the lives of people who are in distress. With that power comes enormous responsibility and great risk. Our responsibility is to never lose sight of the fundamental sanctity, dignity, and sovereignty of another human being no matter what their diagnosis may be, no matter how "regressed" or "poor" their prognosis may be, and no matter what their disability may be. The risk is that the power which is granted and which we also assume as clinicians, can begin to eat away at our values and ideals such that we fail to safeguard and uphold the fundamental sanctity, dignity, and sovereignty of those whom we seek to serve. The danger is that we can overidentify with the professional roles we play and forget the people we are. The danger is that our minds can become severed from our hearts such that our human hearts no longer guide, inform, and shape our work with people.

In my years of experience working as a clinician in public sector mental health, as well as my experience as a recipient of mental health services, I have found myself needing to ask some difficult questions about the power granted to clinicians: about the way we assume this power as privilege; about how our use of this power can erode our values and ideals; about how our use of this power can systematically disempower those we are supposed to be serving; and about how it can oppress and sometimes hurt the people who come to us for help. These are some of the questions I find myself asking: Is there room for the human heart in the human services? Why does working in human services sometimes feel so dehumanizing? Why does receiving human services sometimes feel so dehumanizing? Why do we use the language of war rather than the language of love in the human services? For instance we talk about sending staff out into the *field* to provide *front line* services to *target populations* for whom we develop and implement treatment strategies, whether or not they want them.

There are no easy answers to these questions. However, I am confident that the only way to overcome the forces of dehumanization is to be bold and daring and brave enough to be fully human in the places where we work and to always recognize that we work with people and not with disabilities or diagnoses. This may seem self evident, and yet this simple ethic is routinely ignored. For instance in Rosenhan's (1973) now classic study entitled *Being Sane In Insane Places* he exclaims:

Neither anecdotal nor "hard" data can convey the overwhelming sense of powerlessness which invades the individual as he is continually exposed to the depersonalization of the psychiatric hospital. (p. 256)

I too have experienced the effects of depersonalization and dehumanization. Below is an account of one such experience:

It was nighttime. Nighttime in a mental hospital. If I looked out the wire mesh windows I could see the stars assuming their winter formations in the bitter cold December sky. To me the stars were beautiful. To me they were like beacons of light from another time and another place. It was good to see those stars breaking through all that darkness. And though they gave no warmth the stars shone through that darkness as a promise, as a hope. But all that was on the outside. On the inside of the mental hospital, things were very different.

In some ways nighttime in a mental hospital is the hardest time. It's hard because you have to stay still long enough to fall asleep. You have to be with yourself, alone and in the dark, with the sound of your own heart beating lonely and scared and in pain and so far away from the people you love. So far away and all alone.

And as you lie there at night, sounds amplify and echo down the great empty corridors. Some sounds you get used to real quickly, like the jangle of keys locking and unlocking doors and bathrooms and elevators and nurses stations. You get used to the sound of the keys that separate those who can leave and those who have to stay, those keys that separate those who get to go home and those many who have no home to go to. You get used to the sound of keys jangling and echoing down empty nighttime corridors real fast. But there are some sounds you can never get used to. Like the sound of a man strapped down in restraint and crying out "Help. Help me. Someone please help me."

When I first heard him crying out I jumped out of bed and hurried down the hallway. What I found amazed me. There, outside the door of the seclusion room was a mental health worker sitting with his legs swung casually over the side of a soft lounge chair. He had parked the lounge chair outside of the open door from which the cry was emanating. The mental health worker was flipping through a magazine. He appeared to not hear the cry of the man in the seclusion room. Actually, it was as if he didn't even recognize that the patient in that room was a person who was in great distress.

Quietly, I slipped past the mental health worker and looked inside the seclusion room. An old man, probably about 60 or so, with white hair and very thin, was strapped down on a green rubber mattress. Heavy leather cuffs lashed his wrists and ankles to the cold steel of a metal bed frame. He was stripped naked except for his underwear.

When I saw that mental health worker sitting in casual comfort outside of the room in which a man was restrained, humiliated and crying out for help, I froze in terror and disbelief. For a moment I could not move. I felt numb. Then I felt a tearing inside my heart.

You see, if you are a patient in a mental hospital and you hear a fellow patient who is in restraint and who is crying out for help, you are not allowed to answer the cry. You are not allowed to be fully human, to be whole and therefore able to respond to another human being compassionately. You are not allowed to go into that room next to the old man and talk softly to him. You are not allowed to bring him a drink of water or to wipe his brow or to just sit there with him so that he will not feel so abandoned. In fact, if you respond humanly and with compassion, you get punished. That is, if you are a patient in a mental hospital and you try to go in and comfort a person who is crying out from the seclusion room, you get an initial warning from the staff and, if you repeat the violation, you get your "privileges" revoked for the day.

There is such a great irony in the fact that mental patients get punished for responding from the fullness of their human hearts to the cry of another person who is in distress.[1] That is, there is an anguished feeling of having "fallen to pieces," or of being "shattered," or "fragmented" that often is a part of the experience of mental illness. To respond as a whole person, as a wholly human being, to the cry of another patient, is actually a response that could be healing. Indeed, the word "whole" or "wholeness" has the same etymological root as the word "healing." To respond as a whole person to the cry of another would be healing. But such a response is punished. Thus an opportunity for healing is lost, while brokenness, fragmentation, and dehumanization are reinforced as prescribed roles for staff as well as patients.

I knew that to stand for too long in front of that seclusion room was dangerous. And so I turned quickly away and returned to my bed. But I could not sleep. Instead, I lay in bed, my eyes open, staring into the darkness and listening.

The old man kept crying out all night long. He kept saying "Help me. Help me..." Sometimes his voice was strong, like a lion. At these times I would hear his voice crying out loud and strong and insistent. At other times, I could hear his voice weaken and quaver, like the sound of a lost and broken child. And as the night wore on, his voice grew hoarse and dry and weary and

---

[1] Thanks to my colleague Deborah Anderson for helping me understand how health and wholeness are thwarted when mental patients are punished for responding as whole empathic human beings to the cry of another person in distress. Ms. Anderson and I continue to research the spirit breaking consequences of these and other routine procedures practices and policies within the mental health system.

drugged. By dawn, his voice became more of a whisper haunting down the empty corridors.

It was a terrible thing to hear that man's struggle. All night I heard that man crying out in an effort to save the last vestiges of his dignity. I heard that man struggling against overwhelming odds to assert his humanity in an environment which was utterly dehumanizing. I heard his voice rising up like a blaze in the darkness, trying to leave a mark or a streak or some trace of dignity, before being swallowed up in the darkness and oblivion of chemical restraint. The voice I heard was a human voice. His message was perfectly clear: "Help me". But the staff did not hear that simply human voice. Perhaps they thought they were hearing a symptom?

But it was not just the man in restraint who got hurt that night. I, too, was very deeply wounded. Something inside of me started to break that night. In my heart I felt a deep aching and a profound sense of outrage. My anger was not a symptom of mental illness. Anger is never a symptom of mental illness. The anger and outrage I felt were human responses to an inhuman situation.

During the course of that dark night a kind of numbness settled into my soul. I felt powerless, helpless, and trapped in a situation over which I had almost no control. I did not intend for my heart to close up tight and numb. It happened almost like a reflex, like a way of surviving in a place that is not good for the human heart.

Our responsibility is to never lose sight of the fundamental sanctity, dignity, and sovereignty of another human being no matter what their diagnosis may be, no matter how "regressed" or "poor" their prognosis may be, and no matter what their disability may be.

It is so important we understand that I am not describing an isolated, "merely personal," experience here. In fact, I would argue that a majority of people with disabilities have experienced what I am speaking about. In clinical language we might refer to this as an experience of trauma, with subsequent emotional constriction or numbing (van der Kolk 1987). Sociologists who study the impact of institutionalization might help us understand the impact of dehumanization and depersonalization on people in total institutions (Goffman 1961). However to fully understand this experience, we must look further than clinical explanations.

In many respects people with disabilities who have lived the experiences of dehumanization, trauma, and depersonalization are the real experts. When those of us with psychiatric disabilities come together and talk among ourselves, we don't use clinical language. Instead, we talk about the experience of "spirit breaking," or we refer to times when "they almost broke my spirit," or times when "they broke my spirit." We use our own language and discover our own words in order to reclaim our experiences and validate them. As Paulo Freire (1989) helps us understand, overcoming the effects of dehumanization and oppression means "each man wins back his right to say his own word, to name the world" (p. 13). Indeed, the first step in overcoming oppression is expression. That is why it is so important to listen to people and allow them to find their own words in order to name their own world.

The experience of spirit breaking occurs as a result of those cumulative experiences in which we are humiliated and made to feel less than human, in which our will to live is deeply shaken or broken, in which our hopes are shattered and in which giving up, apathy, and indifference become a way of surviving and protecting the last vestiges of the wounded self. This experience is not confined to any one disability group. It can and does happen to people with mental retardation, people with physical disabilities, people with head injuries, people who are blind, members of the deaf community, and people with psychiatric disabilities. For instance, I work with a man who has a spinal cord injury. He tells of a time his spirit was very nearly broken and a deep, reflexive numbness settled over his heart. His story goes like this:

The experience of spirit breaking occurs as a result of those cumulative experiences in which we are humiliated and made to feel less than human, in which our will to live is deeply shaken or broken, in which our hopes are shattered and in which giving up, apathy, and indifference become a way of surviving and protecting the last vestiges of the wounded self.

Just like the old man in restraints, that outraged scream was the desperate assertion of the boy's dignity. Dignity safeguards that sacred, inviolate place within the human heart wherein dwells the very integrity of the human spirit. It was this deepest sense of spirit, of self and/or dignity, that had been violated. The boy gave witness to that violation in his screams (Des Press, 1976).

But the doctors failed to hear the humanness of the boy's cry. Instead they ordered that he be given tranquilizing drugs. And it was at that point when he had been rendered powerless and helpless, when no one would listen to him or embrace and acknowledge his humanity, that a numbness began to settle into my friend's heart. That was when he experienced his spirit as being deeply wounded and beginning to break.

It is clear those doctors did not respond humanly and with compassion to the cry of a real person. Just like the mental health worker, who sat in comfortable indifference outside the door of the seclusion room, those doctors failed to realize the patient was a real person. I would argue that because both the mental health worker and the doctors failed to see patients as people, they became a little bit less human themselves. As Paulo Freire (1989) puts it, dehumanization "marks not only those

At 15 years old he had been recently paralyzed from the neck down. He was lying naked, under a sheet, on his hospital bed. A group of interns came into his room, led by a chief resident who was conducting rounds. Without asking permission, the chief resident ripped the sheet off the fifteen year old boy and exposed his naked body for all to see. The boy began to scream and scream and scream.

whose humanity has been stolen, but also (in a different way) those who have stolen it" (p. 28). That is how the terrible cycle of dehumanization works. When helpers fail to see and hear the personhood of the people they work with, and when we see diagnoses and disabilities rather than human beings, then we as helpers become a little less human ourselves. We become a little less able to respond from the fullness of our human hearts to the cry of another person who may be in distress. And it is precisely in situations and relationships which are dehumanizing, that people with disabilities suffer the experience of spirit breaking.

The experience of spirit breaking is not confined to specific places. In other words it does not just happen in mental hospitals or state schools or rehabilitation hospitals. It can and does happen in community residences, outpatient medication clinics, vocational rehabilitation programs, private practice, homeless shelters, clubhouses, and respite centers. For instance, I know a man with a psychiatric disability who approached his community case manager and stated that he "wanted help making friends and getting a girlfriend." The case manager responded: "What? You can't expect me to pimp for you!" My friend was deeply hurt and humiliated by this comment. He says the cumulative impact for this and many other humiliating experiences at the hands of helping professionals, nearly broke his spirit.

Spirit breaking can and does happen in any environment in which there are people who have power and people who have been stripped of their power to direct their own lives and make their own choices. It can happen in any environment in which there are those in a position of dominance and those who are deemed to be subordinate. It can happen in environments where there are people who are considered by implication to be superior, because they are surrounded by people who are labeled as infe-

rior. Simply put, it occurs when we relate to people as if they are disabilities, as if their personhood is disabled, and as if somehow, they are not real people at all.

But the point is, people with disabilities are real people. The man in restraint was not a "madman." First and foremost, he was a human being. The teenage boy in the hospital bed was not "a quadriplegic." He was a human being. We are not disabled people. We are people with disabilities. Our personhood must always come first. It is offensive to refer to us as "the mentally ill" or to refer to people with physical disabilities as "the disabled." We are people with mental illness, people with psychiatric disabilities, people with physical disabilities, etc. If our personhood does not come first, that is, if we are perceived as disabilities and diagnoses rather than as human beings, then the relational foundations which result in dehumanization and spirit breaking are laid in place.

Striving to be as fully human as possible is, in the final analysis, the only way to overcome the forces of dehumanization. Humanizing the human services is a task which begins with you and with me. Jean Baker Miller (1976), Janet Surrey (1987), and the other women of the Stone Center at Wellesley College in Massachusetts are pioneering a new and exciting theory and praxis of clinical work, which suggest how we might enter into therapeutic relationships that avoid the pitfalls of dehumanization and depersonalization.

The Stone Center scholars note that traditionally and culturally we have come to understand power as signifying domination, control, and mastery. In other words, we equate power with "having power over someone or something." Human service institutions grant clinicians power in this sense of the word. In fact, the "sicker" a person is perceived to be the more power and control we are expected to exercise over nearly every detail of their life.

The theorists at the Stone Center argue that these traditional, institutionalized power relationships are dehumanizing, precisely because they lack the possibility of true mutuality. These are hierarchical relationships in which clinicians have most, if not all, of the power and patients have little if any power to control their own lives, destinies and the resources effecting their lives. These hierarchical and paternalistic relationships not only set the stage for dehumanization to occur, but also prescribe a role of passivity, dependence and learned helplessness for the patient (Seligman, 1975). Esso Leete (1988), a woman who has been diagnosed and treated for schizophrenia and is a nationally recognized spokesperson in the consumer/ex-patient/psychiatric survivor movement, captures the essence of the effects of such disempowering and dehumanizing relationships when she says:

> I can talk, but I may not be heard. I can make suggestions, but they may not be taken seriously. I can voice my thoughts, but they may be seen as delusions. I can recite experiences, but they may be interpreted as fantasies. To be a patient or even an ex-client is to be discounted. (Leete, 1988)

There is an alternative to such hierarchical, dehumanizing, and disempowering relationships. Again following the lead of the Stone Center theorists we find that by definition "power" can also mean the capacity to move or produce change. Surrey (1987) helps us to understand that power need not mean "having power over" but can mean "having power with" or "having power together" (p. 4). She urges us to enter into relationships that are mutually empowering for both the clinician and the client. Relationships between professionals and clients are empowering when both parties are available to be "moved by" the thoughts, perceptions, and feelings of the other:

In such empowering interaction, both people feel able to have an *impact* on each other (Stiver, 1985) and on the movement or "flow" of the interaction. Each feels "heard" and "responded to" and able to "hear," "validate," and respond to the other. Each feels empowered through creating and sustaining a context which leads to increased awareness and understanding. Further, through this process, each participant feels enlarged, able to "see" more clearly, and energized to move into action. The capacity to be "moved," and to respond, and to "move" the other, represents the fundamental core of relational empowerment. (p. 6-7)

Because power is often related to the ability to control another person, Surrey (1987) and the other Stone Center theorists recognize that relational empowerment means learning new ways to relate to clients. It means learning how to have power *with*, rather than power *over*, those who come to us in distress. It means learning how to work with another person such that neither the clinician nor the client is in control. Rather, both can learn to experience themselves as being heard and responded to as well as being moved and moving the other. Clearly, this model holds promise for helping us understand how to re-humanize the human services. However, it remains to be seen how (and even if) these insights and values can be incorporated into human services institutions, which seem almost by definition to operate on the hierarchical principles of having power and control over patients/inmates. Certainly clinicians can help re-humanize the human services but my real hope for achieving this goal rests with the community of people with disabilities. There are over 43 million people with disabilities in this country. We are the largest minority group in America. Slowly but surely we are becoming organized and empowered to act. The recent passage of the Americans With Disabilities Act (ADA) is a landmark piece of civil rights legislation for us. The ADA confirms what we have known for a long time. That is, whereas clinicians usually insist the disability resides "within us," we understand that what is truly disabling to us are the barriers in our environment preventing us from living out the full range of our human interests and gifts and preventing us from living, loving, worshipping, and working in the community of our choice. What is truly disabling to us is stigma which, though rampant in the general population, is also widespread in the helping professions. In human service institutions, policies and clinical/rehabilitation praxis, stigma often disguises itself as a kind of benevolent paternalism or the sympathy of "false charity" which Freire (1989) characterizes as follows:

> False charity constrains the fearful and subdued, the "rejects of life" to extend their trembling hands. True generosity lies in striving so that these hands—whether of individuals or entire peoples—need to be extended less and less in supplication, so that more and more they become human hands which work and, working, transform the world. (p. 29)

These stigmatizing and infantilizing attitudes are disabling to us. In addition to stigma, we find discrimination in employment, housing, and education disabling. Poverty, oppression, segregation, and unemployment are conditions we find disabling. Staff attitudes characterized by low expectations, prophecies, and prognoses of doom, as well as policies, procedures, and practices which teach us to be passive, helpless, dependent, and irresponsible are also disabling to us.

Finally, those aspects of the human services which dehumanize and break (or try to break) our spirit are disabling to us. These wounds "numb" or at times "break" our will to live, rob us of hope, and instill a deep sense of apathy, despair, personal worthlessness, and self hatred. Many of us experience these wounds as more disabling than the mental illness or physical injury/syndrome we may have been diagnosed with. It is these wounds that take a long, long time to heal.

My real hope for re-humanizing the human services rests with people with disabilities as we begin learning that we can organize, that we have power in our numbers, and that we can overcome oppression through expression. The days of silence are over. As professionals and as fellow human beings, we have a great deal to learn from the people we seek to serve. It is important to listen to people with disabilities. For instance, Bill LaLime is a member of a Massachusetts grassroots organization made up entirely of people with psychiatric disabilities. The organization is called M*POWER (Massachusetts People/Patients Organized for Wellness, Empowerment, and Rights). Mr. Lalime (1990) has written about his struggle to remain human while receiving what, at times, can only be characterized as "inhuman services." He also suggests what we can do to help bring about change:

> I want to have my story written down so I can remember where I've been and so I don't forget what I've been through. If I have it on paper, I know it's not a lie, it's something I've been through.

> If people read our stories, they know what we've been through. People who haven't been through what we've been through need to hear our stories so they'd know what we experience. The system sucks. I've been through the whole nine yards. The system has to change. One way we can help it to change is by telling our stories.

> I couldn't fight the system by myself, it was really hard. They tried to break me to a point where I lost my values. There were things happening that could have broken my spirit. But I still had enough of myself to keep going, even though I got sick and tired of being locked up. When I

went in the hospital, I lost my values, my intellectual thoughts, my thinking, my self-esteem. I know it's my values that I lost. Values means my morals. They force you to do things against your will, against your values.

When I was at [a well known private hospital] they drugged me with medication and when I got up in the middle of the night, I didn't know where I was and I fell against a metal hinge with my back and had a big black and blue mark and it was bleeding. I told the nurse and asked her to look at it and she did, but she wouldn't do anything about it. She said, "What happened to you?" and I told her, she and the other staff said "Just lay down in bed and rest and it will go away." But it didn't go away.

I kept complaining to the staff. I asked for aspirin but they wouldn't give me anything for the pain because there were no doctors on call. They kept telling me to wait till the next shift and they wouldn't do anything about it. And then she next shift would tell me to wait for the next shift, and on and on. Finally, on Sunday morning, I told a mental health aide I'd been trying to get help for my hurt back for 3 days and the aide told me to wait until it goes away. I said I couldn't wait anymore and threw the aide against the window. They finally took me to the hospital to get some treatment for my back.

At [an inpatient community mental health center], they took my cheese away from me. I was eating too much food that day, and at night they took my cheese away from me and I got violent. I threw a chair at them and they locked me up, and I swallowed money to aggravate them while I was in seclusion. They were watching me through the window. I'd say, "Here's a coin, I'm eating it," and I'd swallow it. They'd laugh at me, and they'd say "swallow another one." And so I'd do it again. I'd swallowed 13 coins in all. I stopped because they lost interest, they weren't amused anymore, and they went away.

When I was in the hospital, the loneliness in there and no one to talk to, the only ones to talk to were the other patients. It was a horrible thing. Other patients meant a lot to me. It was beautiful. They helped me a lot. The patients kept me going. The way they felt, too. We talked about our problems outside the hospital. I got very discouraged, because when I left the hospital, I couldn't visit my friends, because I was a former patient and there was a rule against my visiting I felt lonely after I got out of the hospital.

At [...] and other hospitals, they took my rights away, I wrote letters, but I never got any back because the staff wouldn't give them to me or, if they did, they opened them first and read them. I didn't have that much privacy. I couldn't bring my girlfriend in my room. Or every five minutes they came in my room to check on me. Without privacy, you feel you can't trust anyone. I lost my freedom. The locked doors, I couldn't leave. I was very scared by that. I didn't have many visitors, because they didn't like where I was. They were scared to come visit because of where I was. I was very lonely.

Talking on the phone to my teacher and minister kept me going because they knew what I was going through. I'd tell my minister and my teacher and they could see how I was. For example, Thorazine made me slur my words. They were concerned about me, but the staff weren't concerned. They didn't care.

I was in [a state hospital]. I was in the shower and four men—patients—came in and raped me, and the guard, who was watching, laughed about it. I remember and I don't forget about it. You're in a daze in there. There's nothing to do there. Visitors stare at you. Once they gave me Haldol and I was screwed up for 7 hours. My neck muscles were all tightened up and my legs were all locked up. I was on the floor for 7 hours, because of this reaction to Haldol. They gave me two shots of Benadryl, but it took two or three hours to work. I didn't know what happened to me. My mouth tightened up and I tried to tell them I was having a bad reaction, but I couldn't talk well, and they just told me I was fine, there was nothing wrong with me. But I wasn't fine.

The stuff I've been through was like a nightmare. Sometimes I go back into the nightmare. I cry every night about it. Remembering it is like being in the nightmare again. But I'm going to remember it till the day I die. It will be with me for the rest of my life. Sometimes I scream at night because I've dreamed about [the hospital I was raped in] or some other hospital I've been in.

When I came home from [the hospital I was raped in], I went to a lake where I could listen to the birds chirping in the sky and I could watch the waves on the water, and it gave me peace of mind, and if I wanted to scream, I could and no one would hear me. I was all alone and it was really beautiful. If I'm up in my room by myself, I can think about my own problems. It isn't easy, but I can deal with it. Today, I don't have to think about it so often.

We need better doctors, people who care and can help people. We need to say what we want, what the problems are. If they can't listen the first time, we go back again and again until they'll listen to us. Things might not change overnight. But if we can come together as a group to work towards change, it gives us something to look forward to.

Bill LaLime is right. We need better doctors. We need people who care and who can help people. We need people who will listen to us, and if they don't listen the first time, we need to keep going back until they do listen.

References

Des Pres, T. (1976). *The survivor: An anatomy of life in the death camps.* New York: Pocket Books.

Freire, P. (1989). *Pedagogy of the oppressed* (M. B. Ramos Trans.). New York: Continuum.

Goffman, E. 91961). *Asylums: Essays on the social situations of mental patients and other inmates.* New York: Anchor Books.

LaLime, W. (1990). Untitled speech used as part of Lowell M*POWER's AntiStigma workshop, Lowell, Massachusetts.

Leete, E. (1989). *The role of the consumer movement and persons with mental illness.* Presentation at the Twelfth Mary Switzer Memorial Seminar in Rehabilitation, Washington, DC, June 15-16.

Miller, J. B. (1976). *Toward a new psychology of women.* Boston: Beacon Press.

Rosenhan, D. L. (1973) On being sane in insane places. *Science, 178,* 250-258.

Seligman, M. E. P. (1975). *Helplessness: On depression, development and death.* San Francisco: Freeman.

Stiver, I. (1985). The meaning of care: Reframing treatment models. *Work in Progress #20.* Wellesley, MA: Stone Center Working Papers Series.

Surrey, J. (1987). Relationship and empowerment. *Work in Progress #30.* Wellesley, MA: Stone Center Working Papers Series.

van der Kolk, B. A. (1987). *Psychological trauma.* Washington DC: American Psychiatric Press.

A Person-Driven System: Implications for Theory, Research, and Practice

Diane T. Marsh, Randi D. Koeske, Pamela A. Schmidt, Daniel P. Martz, and William B. Redpath

DIANE T. MARSH, PH.D., AND RANDI D. KOESKE, PH.D., ARE PROFESSORS OF PSYCHOLOGY AT UNIVERSITY OF PITTSBURGH AT GREENSBURG.

PAMELA SCHMIDT WAS AN UNDERGRADUATE STUDENT AT THE TIME OF THE STUDY.

DANIEL MARTZ AND WILLIAM REDPATH ARE CONSUMER ADVOCATES IN WESTMORELAND COUNTY.

APPRECIATION IS EXPRESSED TO FREDERICK J. FRESE, PH.D., AND J. ROCK JOHNSON, J.D., WHOSE VISION HAS SIGNIFICANTLY INFLUENCED OUR CONCEPTION OF A PERSON-DRIVEN SYSTEM.

Truly revolutionary changes are currently under way for people with mental illness. For the first time in history they are advocating for themselves as individuals and in groups comprised only of consumers of mental health services. Both nationally and locally, consumers are moving into central roles in the design, implementation, and evaluation of service delivery systems and in their own treatment and rehabilitation (e.g., Campbell, 1991; Chamberlin & Rogers, 1990).

These developments are in distinct contrast to the earlier institutional era, which offered individuals with mental illness only one option: segregation and asylum. That era ended roughly in the 1970s and was followed by an era of deinstitutionalization and community development, with emphasis on the central role of the community mental health system. Beginning in the mid-1980s, we have witnessed the emergence of a new era of full community participation and integration (e.g., Carling, 1990; Hannum et al., 1994).

In the present era we are committed to developing a person-driven system that can meet the essential needs of people with mental illness—as they perceive them—in their communities. We will discuss the prerequisites for a person-driven system and examine the implications of such a system for theory, research, and practice.

Prerequisites for a Person-Driven System

As indicated in Table 1, there are eight prerequisites for a person-driven system. These include: a) new conceptions of people with mental illness; b) new models for professional practice; c) new collaborative modes of working with consumers; d) new roles for consumers and professionals; e) greater understanding of the experiences, needs, and recovery of people with mental illness; f) more effective intervention strategies; g) better training of professionals; and h) more responsive systems of care. Initially, we will focus on the theoretical prerequisites for a person-driven system, turning then to the implications for research and practice.

Theoretical Implications of a Person-Driven System

There are four theoretical cornerstones of a person-driven system: new conceptions, new models, new modes, and new roles.

New Conceptions of People With Mental Illness

People with mental illness are first and foremost human beings who are not synonymous with their disabilities (see Hunter & Marsh, 1994). Indeed, they have the potential for growth and recovery; have capacities, talents, and gifts; and have expertise regarding their own experiences, needs, and goals. Accordingly, we need to focus on the person beyond the symptoms, to underscore the potential for a positive outcome, to encourage the contributions of consumers, and to acknowledge their expertise. For example, a recent study documented the contributions of people with mental illness to their families (Greenberg, Greenley, & Benedict, 1994).

TABLE 1.
PREREQUISITES FOR A PERSON-DRIVEN SYSTEM

New conceptions of people with mental illness

New models of professional practice

New collaborative modes

New roles for consumers and professionals

Greater understanding of experiences and needs

More effective intervention strategies

Better training of professionals

More responsive systems of care

We also need a comprehensive biopsychosocial perspective that can encompass the biological substrate of mental illness, the psychosocial aspects of the illness, and its social context (e.g., Bachrach, 1993; Cacioppo & Bernston, 1992). As Fink (1988) has discussed, such a model provides a foundation for examining relationships among the mind, brain, body, and world at large; and for incorporating important scientific, technological, and humanistic developments. Similarly, Levy and Nemeroff (1993) point out that each disorder has a genetics, a neurobiology, a psychology, a psychopharmacology, and a sociology.

In addition, our reconceptualization of people with mental illness recognizes their potential for a resilient response to a catastrophic event. In the words of J. Rock Johnson, "Like the phoenix, I rose again and again from my own ashes" (1993, p. 6). Emerging from the cauldron of mental illness, they may develop some exceptional personal qualities: new strengths, insights, and expertise; increased tolerance and compassion; impressive coping ability; and courage and tenacity in their quest to reclaim their lives.

New Models for Professional Practice
Many traditional models of help-giving behavior have fostered passivity, dependency, learned helplessness, and lowered self-esteem (Deegan, 1990; Dunst, Trivette, & Deal, 1994). Moreover, traditional models have focused almost exclusively on the pathology of people with mental illness and on the alleviation of psychotic symptoms. As we relinquish such disempowering models, we are shifting to competency-based models that encourage assertiveness and independence, promote feelings of mastery and self-confidence, enhance self-esteem, acknowledge strengths and resources, and foster feelings of hopefulness.

A competence paradigm offers a constructive alternative to the traditional pathology paradigm (see Marsh, 1992; Masterpasqua, 1989). As presented in Table 2, a competence paradigm assumes a developmental model, views consumers as people with disabilities, emphasizes their positive attributes, fosters collaborative partnerships, enhances coping effectiveness, and proposes recovery as the goal of intervention.

New Modes of Working With Consumers
Reflecting these conceptual developments, professionals and other service providers are implementing new modes of working with people who have mental illness (see Frese, 1994). These new modes are essentially collaborative partnerships that build on the strengths, resources, and expertise of all parties; that promote an atmosphere of mutual respect; that consider the needs, desires, concerns, and priorities of consumers; that involve consumers in deci-

TABLE 2.
A PARADIGM SHIFT IN PROFESSIONAL PRACTICE

		Pathology Paradigm	Competence Paradigm
Nature of Paradigm	→	Disease-based medical model	Health-based developmental model
View of Person	→	Mentally ill	Person with a disability
Emphasis on	→	Pathology and limitations	Strengths and resources
Role of Professionals	→	Practitioners	Consultants
Role of Consumers	→	Patients	Collaborators
Assessment Based on	→	Clinical typologies	Competencies and deficits
Goal of Intervention	→	Treatment of mental illness	Recovery
Modus Operanti	→	Providing psychotherapy	Enhancing coping effectiveness
Systemic Perspective	→	Individual or family system	Ecological system
Services Model	→	Authoritarian model	Educational model

Adapted from Hunter and Marsh (1994).

sions that affect them; and that develop mutual goals for treatment and rehabilitation. When families are involved in primary caregiving or informal case management, their inclusion in the collaborative partnership is also essential.

New Roles for Consumers and Professionals

Consistent with these new conceptions, new models, and new modes, both people with mental illness and their professional caregivers are assuming new roles in the mental health system and in society. Emerging roles for consumers include those of consultants, treatment team members, providers, and advocates. In these roles, people with mental illness offer their expertise regarding the subjective experience of mental illness and the requirements of systems of care. They also take a more informed and assertive role in their own treatment and rehabilitation. Programs run by consumers, such as support groups and drop-in centers, complement the programs offered by professionals and meet different—and equally important—needs.

Professionals are moving into new roles as consultants to consumer-run programs and as educators of consumers regarding

mental illness and its management (e.g., Freund, 1993). They also work with consumers in skills-oriented programs that offer training in a range of personal, interpersonal, educational, and vocational areas (e.g., Liberman, Kopelowicz, & Young, 1994). In the larger society, consumers and professionals are increasingly joining forces as advocates for a more humane and responsive system of care. Professionals and consumers may also work as a team to offer recovery workshops to self-help groups (Spaniol, Koehler, & Hutchinson, 1994).

Research Implications of a Person-Driven System

There are a number of research implications of a person-driven system. First, in accordance with the new conceptions of people with mental illness we have discussed, researchers are focusing attention on the human beings who happen to have mental illness and on their experiences, needs, capacities, and recovery. We are learning more about the "inner world of madness" (Torrey, 1988), and about the subjective experience of mental illness. As Hatfield and Lefley (1993) have discussed, relevant issues include the loss of a sense of self among people who are sometimes fully engulfed by their psychosis, the central role of acceptance of the illness, and the importance of identity issues among people who are often defined in terms of their illness.

Second, consonant with the new models we have described, researchers need to assess the biological, psychosocial, and sociocultural dimensions of mental illness, and to emphasize strengths as well as limitations. Finally, as the new modes and roles are translated into practice, research will be conducted in collaboration with consumers, who can contribute significantly to experimental design, data collection, and analysis of results (e.g., Everett & Boydell, 1994).

The involvement of consumers in research is likely to increase our understanding of their experience of mental illness, of their essential needs, and of the relative value of various coping resources (e.g., Tanzman, 1993). We can discover the rich tapestry of their lives, their hopes and dreams, their joys and sorrows, their fears and anxieties, and their daily struggle to gain control over their lives. In addition, we can learn about their universal needs for survival, for safety and security, for love and belonging, for self-esteem, for meaningful activity, and for self-actualization. This human context provides an essential foundation for designing, implementing, and evaluating services.

We can also learn about the process of recovery and the many variables that can mediate this process (e.g., Anthony, 1993;

Reflecting their assertion that their personal qualities and strengths are their most valuable resource in coping with mental illness, a majority of respondents emphasized the importance of personal responsibility.

Spaniol & Koehler, 1993; Weisburd, 1994). For instance, we can determine the signs of impending relapse; the environmental events that serve as mediators, protectors, or exacerbators; the intervention strategies that are most effective; the strengths and limitations of the current service delivery system; and the changes that are needed.

A Collaborative Research Project

Researchers are increasingly working collaboratively with consumers in their investigations (e.g., Rappaport. 1993). We will describe one collaborative research project, which included two consumer advocates (D. M. and W. R.) as members of the research team and coauthors of this article. The project was undertaken in conjunction with "empowerment workshops" that were held for people with mental illness at a university campus. Workshop participants were receiving mental health services in a seven-county area of Western Pennsylvania. Using a survey administered to participants, we collected demographic data and assessed the relative importance of their needs and coping resources. In open-ended questions, we also explored their experience of mental illness and requested their suggestions for other consumers, professionals, and families.

Description of Participants
Participants consisted of 78 people who attended the workshops. Some of the surveys had missing data, which is reflected in

the following results. Respondents ranged in age from 19 to 65 (mean age = 39) and included 31 males and 47 females. A majority resided with others (n = 43, 61%); over one third (28, 39%) lived alone. Approximately one third (26, 34%) reported they were married or in a stable relationship. When asked about the highest grade in school completed, 11 respondents (15%) indicated they had not completed high school; 33 (43%) had finished high school; and 32 (42%) had completed at least some college work. Some (9, 12%) reported they were currently in school.

Participants were diagnosed with the most severe and persistent forms of mental illness. They reported their current diagnoses as schizophrenia or other psychosis (21, 37%); depression (13, 23%); bipolar disorder (9, 16%); borderline personality disorder (5, 9%); and anxiety disorders (e.g., obsessive-compulsive disorder, panic disorder) (3, 5%). Thus, 90% of participants received primary diagnoses of serious mental illness, which is generally defined to include these diagnostic categories. Many respondents (23, 29%) indicated they had received more than one diagnosis. Many (29, 40%) also reported problems with alcohol, drugs, food, or other addictions.

The age of participants at the time they became aware of their problem ranged from 3 to 56 (mean age = 24). The largest group (28, 44%) was under 18 at the time of initial awareness; 14 (22%) were between 19 and 25; and 22 (34%) were over age 25. Their age at the time of their current diagnosis ranged from 4 to 56 (mean age = 30). Eleven respondents (19%) were under 18; 12 (21%) were between 19 and 25; and 35 (60%) were over 25. Thus, participants waited an average of 6 years before obtaining an accurate diagnosis of their mental illness.

Respondents had received a wide range of interventions. These included (in rank order): medication (63, 83%); hospitaliza-

tion (54, 71%); group therapy (53, 70%); individual psychotherapy (45, 59%); a support group (33, 43%); and other treatment (12, 16%). A majority of participants were currently in treatment (65, 89%) and taking medication (63, 86%). A few (4, 5%) indicated they had received no treatment.

In responding to questions regarding their financial status, participants reported the following current sources of income (in rank order): Supplemental Security Income (SSI) (34, 47%); Social Security Disability Insurance (SSDI) (23, 32%); part-time job (14, 19%); welfare (12, 16%); savings (10, 14%); family (9, 12%); full-time job (3, 4%); and other income (7, 10%). Over three fourths (49, 77%) reported their total annual income from these sources was under $10,000. Almost one fifth (12, 19%) indicated their income was between $10 and $15,000. Thus, fewer than 5% of respondents had an income greater than $15,000. In describing how they paid for treatment, participants listed the following financial resources (in rank order): Medicaid (48, 69%); insurance (21, 30%); County assistance (20, 29%); personal income (10, 14%); family income (4, 6%); and other resources (5, 7%).

Experience of Mental Illness

A majority of participants (n = 62) answered the open-ended question regarding the impact of mental illness on their lives. Six themes emerged from their responses, with the number of participants mentioning each theme noted parenthetically: a) limitations (24, 39%); b) loss (21, 34%); c) altered self-concept (17, 27%); d) altered family relationships (17, 27%); e) isolation (12, 19%); and f) spirituality (9, 15%). We will briefly discuss each of these themes.

First, many limitations were noted as a consequence of the mental illness, including interpersonal, academic, vocational, and financial limitations. Second, loss appears to be a central component of the experience of mental illness, including loss of relationships, jobs, and money, as well as of hopes, dreams, and expectations. Third, self-concept was inevitably altered by the mental illness, both negatively (e.g., lower self-esteem at the onset of their illness) and positively (e.g., improved self-esteem as they learned to cope with their illness). Fourth, family relationships were also affected, with the potential for both negative changes (e.g., stress, disruption, disengagement) and positive changes (e.g., closer family ties). Fifth, isolation was also fundamental to the experience, with emphasis on the presence of loneliness and social stigma. Finally, spirituality was affected both in negative ways (e.g., loss or questioning of faith) and in positive ways (e.g., stronger faith).

Although the impact of mental illness on their lives was predominantly negative, particularly during the initial years of the illness, it is noteworthy that many participants also reported positive changes in their self-concept, their spirituality, and their family relationships.

The following excerpts from the surveys capture many of the central themes:

> I can do many parts of a job well but get bogged down and confused with details. I cannot work fast enough to earn much money. I've often felt discriminated against because of symptoms of my illness. People often don't take my suggestions or actions seriously.

> At first I hit rock bottom in almost every area in my life and began to vegetate. But with good therapy, good doctors, and my help from within and God's grace, I am at a wonderful point in life now. I have regained my self-respect.

> My relationship with my family is not as close. My jobs have been affected. I can't handle stress as much. I have low self-esteem, feel alone and very lonely.

> I became unable to continue my senior year in college. I am also unable to work because I need the daily support of partial hospitalization. I've lost all of my friends except one because of the stigma associated with mental illness. My relationship with my mother has improved and become more open.

> My self-image is very poor. I feel isolated from people, have low self-esteem. I have poor coping abilities with stress.

> The illness itself has not had any good effects, but the process of getting healthier has, especially on my spirituality, my self-image, and my character and personal qualities. Now I have a greater sense of serenity, self-liking, wonder at the world, and caring for myself and others.

Needs and Coping Resources

Participants were asked to rate the importance of a range of essential needs. As presented in Table 3, all of these needs were rated as significant, consistent with the tenets and scope of a community support system (CSS) (National Institute of Mental Health, 1981). The needs with the highest ratings were an adequate income, a comfortable and safe place to live, and satisfactory insurance coverage. The remainder of their needs fell into three general areas: mental health services (treatment, crisis intervention, accurate diagnosis, treatment choices); education and support (suggestions for coping, information about mental disorders, support and understanding); educational and vocational opportunities (opportunity to work, chance to attend school or learn skills); transportation; and social life.

Respondents were also asked to evaluate the relative value of various coping resources. Again, they rated many resources as helpful, consistent with a multimodal approach to intervention with this population (e.g., Breslin, 1992). As indicated in Table 4, they identified their personal qualities and strengths as their most important resource. Professional resources also received high ratings, including medication and individual therapy, as did consumer advocacy and support groups. Participants also rated the following as helpful: their friends, other people with mental disorders, group therapy, a case manager, hospitalization, and clergy.

TABLE 3.
NEEDS OF PEOPLE WITH MENTAL DISORDERS

(*N*= 78)

Need	Mean	SD
Adequate income	4.76	.77
Comfortable and safe place to live	4.63	.91
Adequate insurance coverage	4.58	.88
Treatment	4.54	.88
A safe and supportive place during crises	4.54	.89
Opportunity to work	4.50	.99
Practical suggestions for coping	4.50	.87
Accurate diagnosis	4.48	.99
Information about mental disorders	4.48	.93
Support and understanding	4.44	.91
Treatment choices	4.44	1.05
Transportation	4.41	1.04
Chance to attend school or learn skills	4.18	1.13
Contact with people different from myself	4.11	1.02
Contact with people like myself	3.99	1.17

Note. Rating scale: 1 = not at all important, 2 = slightly important, 3 = somewhat important, 4 = quite important, 5 = very important.

Lowest ratings of helpfulness were assigned to their own family, a family advocacy group, and family therapy. Perhaps these relatively low ratings of family resources are not surprising among individuals who often experience mental illness just as they are poised for adulthood. It is normative in our society for young adults to separate from their families and to move into independent lives in their communities. The limitations imposed by the mental illness (and by society) may result in unwelcome dependence on their families and in resentment on both sides. On the other hand, mean ratings obscure individual differences in the ratings of coping resources. For example, over one third of respondents (27, 37%) rated their own families as quite or very helpful.

TABLE 4.
COPING RESOURCES OF PEOPLE WITH MENTAL DISORDERS

(*N* = 78)

Resource	Mean	SD
Personal qualities and strengths	3.93	1.14
Professionals	3.75	.98
Medication	3.74	1.26
Consumer advocacy group	3.55	1.24
Individual therapy	3.54	1.28
Support group	3.54	1.24
Friends	3.44	1.09
Other people with mental disorders	3.42	1.27
Group therapy	3.18	1.29
Case manager	3.13	1.65
Hospitalization	3.02	1.37
Clergy	3.00	1.50
Family	2.90	1.51
Family advocacy group	2.75	1.43
Family therapy	2.46	1.48

Note. Rating scale: 1 = not at all helpful, 2 = slightly helpful, 3 = somewhat helpful, 4 = quite helpful, 5 = very helpful.

Suggestions for Consumers, Professionals, and Families

Participants offered many suggestions for other people with mental illness, for professionals, and for families.

Suggestions for consumers. Most participants (*n* = 57) offered suggestions for other people with mental illness. These suggestions fell into three general areas: personal resources (37, 65%); community resources (24, 42%); and professional resources (12, 21%). Reflecting their assertion that their personal qualities and strengths are their most valuable resource in coping with mental illness, a majority of respondents emphasized the importance of personal responsibility. Specific suggestions included accepting the illness, learning about the illness and about their rights as consumers, trusting their instincts, being persistent and working hard, and avoiding drugs and alcohol.

Participants also recommended that other people with mental illness seek out community resources, including supportive relationships and satisfying activities. Finally, they recommended that consumers seek out good professionals and follow their advice.

The following survey excerpts illustrate some of these suggestions:

> Treatment works—seek professional help. Trust your instincts. If you are not comfortable with your psychiatrist, social worker, or case manager, get someone else. You have rights. Learn them and exercise them. Learn everything you can about your illness, medication, and treatment.

> Believe in yourself. Have courage, be determined not to give up.

> Stay strong. If people don't understand your illness, don't worry about it. Just go on. Get in a support group and make friends with people with similar problems.

Suggestions for professionals. A majority of participants (*n* = 56) also offered suggestions for professionals. Their strongest recommendations fell into two general areas: empowerment and recovery (36, 64%); and compassion and respect (35, 63%). They emphasized the potential of professionals to enhance the empowerment and recovery of people with mental illness, recommending that professionals listen to their concerns, explain about mental illness and its treat-

ment, answer their questions, encourage their independence, offer treatment choices, and assist them in meeting their actual needs (rather than those that professionals assume they have).

In addition, participants underscored the importance of the therapeutic alliance, asking professionals for understanding and consideration, for respect, and for sufficient time. A smaller number (5, 9%) focused on competent practice, recommending that professionals keep abreast of current developments in the area of mental illness and that they act professionally (e.g., keep their personal problems at home).

The following survey excerpts illustrate these recommendations:

> *Listen.* We are people first, not illnesses. Treat us as such. Work with us. Help us to become as independent, self-actualized, and healthy as we can be.

> Don't act like God. Be more compassionate and understanding.

> Treat us as individuals with good and bad qualities. Don't focus so much on the bad qualities.

Suggestions for families. Finally, many participants (*n* = 52) offered suggestions for families. Their suggestions focused on the following areas: acceptance and support (39, 75%); a constructive family environment (18, 35%); and family education and support (16, 31%). Three fourths emphasized their need for acceptance and support from their families, noting their needs for love, patience, understanding, encouragement, and contact. They also asked to be treated as adult members of the family who are not synonymous with their mental illness.

Second, participants emphasized the importance of a constructive family environment that enhances their prospects for recovery and reduces their risk of relapse. They recommended that their families minimize criticism, communicate openly and nonjudgmentally, and provide a secure and structured environment. Finally, they suggested that families meet their own needs for education about the mental illness and for support for themselves. Consumers are well aware that mental illness is a calamitous event for all members of the family. As the needs of families are met, they will be better able to offer support to the member with mental illness.

The following survey excerpts illustrate some of these recommendations:

> Learn everything you can about the illness and medication, etc. Get help for yourself. Don't nag or push or patronize. But set rules and hold people accountable whether or not they have an illness. In setting rules, just be flexible because of people's illnesses.

> Listen, understand, and love. Offer moral support. Don't judge or expect we can do everything you can do.

> Educate yourselves about mental illness. Attend support groups to make the consumer feel less shame about the illness.

Summary
Our collaborative research project generated a number of interesting findings. First, participants portrayed the devastating impact of mental illness on all aspects of their lives, including their self-concept, their relationships, and their potential for rewarding work. They described the intense feelings of loss that accompanied the diminished lives many of them led as a result of their illness. They also documented the potential of people with mental illness for a resilient response to a catastrophic event, emphasizing the positive personal qualities that have emerged from their encounter with the illness.

Second, people with mental illness have a wide range of needs that must be met to ensure that they can lead meaningful and productive lives in their communities.

Congruent with the CSS concept, they underscored their needs for an adequate income, for satisfactory housing, for treatment and rehabilitation, for support, for education about mental illness, for skills to cope with the illness, for transportation, and for social life. Respondents also identified the resources that had been most helpful in coping with mental illness. Their most important resources were their personal qualities, professional treatment, and consumer advocacy and support groups. Finally, participants offered many suggestions for other people with mental illness (e.g., make use of personal, community, and professional resources); for professionals (e.g., foster empowerment, be compassionate and respectful); and for families (e.g., offer acceptance and support).

Practice Implications of a Person-Driven System

A person-driven system has important implications for professional practice in the area of mental illness. For example, we need to employ effective intervention strategies, improve professional training programs, and develop comprehensive and responsive systems of care.

Effective Intervention Strategies
The tenets of a person-driven system suggest a number of guidelines for intervention (see Hunter & Marsh, 1994). It is important to separate the person from the mental illness, to design services to meet individual needs, and to focus on strengths as well as limitations. Additionally, intervention should offer both treatment and rehabilitation, target quality of life as well as symptom alleviation, and aim for enhanced functioning in all areas. The overarching objective of intervention is to offer the optimal mix of services for each individual.

Professionals are assuming a more hopeful attitude in light of new evidence regarding positive outcomes among people with mental illness. Long-term follow-up studies suggest a life process open to multiple influences and characterized by many outcomes, a majority of them positive (Wasylenki, 1992). In one 10-year study of over 1300 subjects, for example, researchers found that one half to two thirds achieved recovery or significant improvement (Harding, Zubin, & Strauss, 1987). Thus, it is essential to identify the personal, environmental, and treatment variables that can foster these positive outcomes and to offer a more realistic and positive appraisal to consumers and their families.

Our reconceptualization of people with mental illness recognizes their potential for a resilient response to a catastrophic event.

Based on the competence paradigm presented earlier, a new generation of professionals is offering competency-based interventions that aim to empower through self-determination (Hunter & Marsh, 1994). Specific components of such interventions include education about mental illness, acquisition of new skills, and development of new self-concepts. Competency-oriented practitioners are developing multimodal interventions, modeling adaptive behavior, and attending to the social and human context. They are also establishing treatment coalitions among professionals, consumers, and family caregivers.

Better Professional Training

It is generally agreed that most professionals are relatively poorly prepared to offer services to people with mental illness (Brown et al., 1993; Johnson, 1990). Essential components of preprofessional training programs include relevant curricula concerned with mental illness and its treatment, supervised internships that provide

contact with people with mental illness and their family members, and experience in the public sector (see Coursey, 1994). For example, recovered consumers can share their experiences and expertise with graduate students as part of the formal curriculum, which offers an essential experiential database for practitioners in training. In the words of one consumer, "We live what you only read about."

Professionals need expertise in treatment and rehabilitation, so that they can both decrease pathology and maximize health; they also need training in psychotherapeutic techniques that are effective in the treatment of mental illness (e.g., Weiden & Havens, 1994). In addition to these formal components of training, it is essential for professionals to be open to new competency-based models of professional practice and to new collaborative modes of working with consumers.

Comprehensive Systems of Care

Finally, we must advocate for more effective and responsive systems of care, with recovery as the benchmark for system evaluation. At the level of the service delivery system, a person-driven system will include a full array of services, supports, and opportunities needed by people with mental illness to function in their communities (e.g., Baker, 1993; Brekke, 1992). As specified in the CSS concept, these include mental health, health, educational, rehabilitation, social, recreational, residential, and family support services.

Services need to be delivered in an individualized, assertive, and continuous manner, with emphasis on outreach, case management, skills training, and community support systems (e.g., Test et al., 1991). For example, the individualized service plan should be designed to meet the needs of consumers as they perceive them rather than the needs of professionals or the system. At the social level, essential elements of a person-driven system include sufficient resources and funding in the area of mental illness, enhanced status for professionals who work in this area, and improved attitudes and reduced stigma.

Conclusion

The concept of a person-driven system offers a guiding vision that is gradually being translated into reality in communities throughout the country. Although there are local variations, all of these systems of care:

- Welcome consumers as full partners in the treatment and rehabilitation enterprise;

- Are driven by the goals of consumers rather than the goals of professionals or the system;

- Offer assistance without loss of dignity;

- View consumers first and foremost as human beings with the same needs as everyone else;

- Recognize their strengths and talents;

- Maximize opportunities for their contributions; and

- Foster meaningful and productive lives.

As we succeed in developing a person-driven system of care, we are also building a society that respects and values all of its members and that is enriched by their diverse contributions.

References

Anthony, W. A. (1993). Recovery from mental illness: The guiding vision of the mental health service system in the 1990s. *Psychosocial Rehabilitation Journal, 16,* 11-23.

Bachrach, L. L. (1993). The biopsychosocial legacy of deinstitutionalization. Hospital and *Community Psychiatry, 44,* 523-24.

Baker, F., Jodrey, D., Intagliata, J. & Straus, H. (1993). Community support services and functioning of the seriously mentally ill. *Community Mental Health Journal, 29,* 321-331.

Brekke, J. S. & Test, M. A. (1992). A model for measuring the implementation of community support programs: Results from three sites. *Community Mental Health Journal, 28,* 227-247.

Breslin, N. A. (1992). Treatment of schizophrenia: Current practice and future promise. *Hospital and Community Psychiatry, 43,* 877-885.

Brown, D. B., Goldman, C. R., Thompson, K. S., Cutler, D. L., Karno, M., Diamond, R. J., Factor, R. M. & Stein, L. I. (1993). Training residents for community psychiatric practice: Guidelines for curriculum development. *Community Mental Health Journal, 29,* 271-296.

Cacioppo, J. T. & Berntson, G. G. (1992). Social psychological contributions to the decade of the brain: Doctrine of multilevel analysis. *American Psychologist, 47,* 1019-1028.

Campbell, J. F. (1991). The consumer movement and implications for vocational rehabilitation services. *Journal of Vocational Rehabilitation, 1,* 67-75.

Carling, P. J. (1990). Major mental illness, housing, and supports: The promise of community integration. *American Psychologist, 45,* 969-975.

Chamberlin, J. & Rogers, J. A. (1990). Planning a community-based mental health system: Perspective of service recipients. *American Psychologist, 45,* 1241-1244.

Coursey, R. D. (1994). Serious mental illness: The paradigm shift involved in providing services and training students. In D. T. Marsh (Ed.), *New directions in the psychological treatment of serious mental illness* (pp. 123-140). Westport, CT: Praeger.

Deegan, P. E. (1990). Spirit breaking: When the helping professionals hurt. *Humanistic Psychologist, 18*, 301-313.

Dunst, C. J., Trivette, C. M., & Deal, A. G. (Eds.). (1994). *Strengthening and supporting families. Volume 1: Methods, strategies and practices.* Cambridge, MA: Brookline.

Everett, B. & Boydell, K. (1994). A methodology for including consumers' opinions in mental health evaluation research. *Hospital and Community Psychiatry, 45,* 76-78.

Fink, P. J. (1988). Response to the Presidential Address: Is "biopsychosocial" the psychiatric shibboleth? *American Journal of Psychiatry, 145,* 1061-1067.

Frese, F. J. (1994). Psychology's role in a consumer-driven system. In D. T. Marsh (Ed.), *New directions in the psychological treatment of serious mental illness* (pp. 79-98). Westport, CT: Praeger.

Freund, P. D. (1993). Professional role(s) in the empowerment process: "Working with" mental health consumers. *Psychosocial Rehabilitation Journal, 16,* 65-73.

Greenberg, J. S., Greenley, J. R. & Benedict, P. (1994). Contributions of persons with serious mental illness to their families. *Hospital and Community Psychiatry, 45,* 475-480.

Hannum, R., Myers-Parrelli, A., Schoenfeld, P., Cameron, C., Campbell, H. & Chrismer, L. (1994). Promoting social integration among people with psychiatric disabilities. *Innovations & Research, 3*(1), 17-23.

Harding, C. M., Zubin, J. & Strauss, J. S. (1987). Chronicity in schizophrenia: Fact, partial fact, or artifact? *Hospital and Community Psychiatry, 38,* 477-486.

Hatfield, A. B. & Lefley, H. P. (1993). *Surviving mental illness.* New York: Guilford.

Hunter, R. H. & Marsh, D. T. (1994). Mining giftedness: A challenge for psychologists. In D. T. Marsh (Ed.), *New directions in the psychological treatment of serious mental illness* (pp. 99-122). Westport, CT: Praeger.

Johnson, D. L. (Ed.). (1990). *Service needs of the seriously mentally ill: Training implications for psychology.* Washington, DC: American Psychological Association.

Johnson, J. R. (1993). J. Rock Johnson. *NAMI Advocate, 14*(5), 5-6.

Levy, S. T. & Nemeroff, C. B. (1993). From psychoanalysis to neurobiology. *National Forum, 73*(1), 18-21.

Liberman, R. P., Kopelowicz, A. & Young, A. S. (1994). Biobehavioral treatment and rehabilitation of schizophrenia. *Behavior Therapy, 25,* 89-107.

Marsh, D. T. (1992). *Families and mental illness: New directions in professional practice.* New York: Praeger.

Masterpasqua, F. (1989). A competence paradigm for psychological practice. *American Psychologist, 44,* 1366-1371.

National Institute of Mental Health. (1981). *A network of caring: The Community Support Program of the National Institute of Mental Health* (DHHS Publication No. ADM 81-1063). Washington, DC: U. S. Government Printing Office.

Rappaport, J. (1993). Narrative studies, personal stories, and identity transformation in the mutual help context. *Journal of Applied Behavioral Science, 29,* 239-256.

Spaniol, L., & Koehler, M. (Eds.). (1993). *The experience of recovery.* Boston: Center for Psychiatric Rehabilitation.

Spaniol, L., Koehler, M., & Hutchinson, D. (1994). *The recovery workbook.* Boston: Center for Psychiatric Rehabilitation.

Tanzman, B. (1993). An overview of surveys of mental health consumers' preferences for housing and support activities. *Hospital and Community Psychiatry, 44,* 450-455.

Test, M. A., Knoedler, W. H., Allness, D. J., Burke, S. S., Brown, R. L. & Wallisch, L. S. (1991). Longer-term community care through an assertive continuous treatment team. In C. A. Tamminga & S. C. Schultz (Eds.), *Advances in neuropsychiatry and psychopharmacology. Volume 1: Schizophrenia research* (pp. 239-246). New York: Raven Press.

Torrey, E. F. (1988). *Surviving schizophrenia: A family manual* (rev. ed.). New York: Harper & Row.

Wasylenki, D. A. (1992). Psychotherapy of schizophrenia revisited. *Hospital and Community Psychiatry, 43,* 123-127.

Weiden, P. & Havens, L. (1994). Psychotherapeutic management techniques in the treatment of outpatients with schizophrenia. *Hospital and Community Psychiatry, 45,* 549-555.

Weisburd, D. E. (Ed.). (1994). Recovery. *The Journal of the California Alliance for the Mentally Ill [Special issue], 5*(3).

RECOVERING OUR SENSE OF VALUE AFTER BEING LABELED

Patricia E. Deegan

PATRICIA E. DEEGAN, PH.D., IS DIRECTOR OF TRAINING, NATIONAL EMPOWERMENT CENTER, LAWRENCE, MA.

THIS ARTICLE WAS ORIGINALLY PRESENTED AT A CONFERENCE "REHABILITATION OF CHILDREN, YOUTH, AND ADULTS WITH PSYCHIATRIC DISABILITIES: ACHIEVING VALUED ROLES," IN TAMPA, FLORIDA IN JANUARY 1993 AND WAS PUBLISHED IN THE *Journal of Psychosocial Nursing*, 1993, 31(4) AND IS REPRINTED WITH PERMISSION OF THE PUBLISHER.

In the final decade of this millennium, after centuries of being so fundamentally and brutally devalued by our culture, there is a glimmer of hope that people who have been labeled with mental illness can reclaim their dignity, can be viewed by others as being people of worth, and can begin to achieve valued roles. There is no doubt that the landmark piece of civil rights legislation, the Americans with Disabilities Act, will help to remove many of the barriers that have historically prevented those of us with psychiatric disabilities from achieving valued roles in this society. We are all charged with the valued role of carrying a new message of hope, of healing, and of recovery back into the communities where we live, love, work, and worship.

A Retrospect

As I was preparing this article, I found myself wondering how those of us who have experienced being profoundly devalued as a result of being labeled with a mental illness move from thinking we have little or no value, to discovering our own unique value. How do we reclaim and recover our sense of worth and value when we have been devalued and dehumanized? In the course of my reflections I found myself thinking back to the days when I was an adolescent and was first diagnosed with major mental illness. I was thinking about my first two hospitalizations and how I was labeled with schizophrenia and 3 months later, at my second hospital admission, I was labeled with chronic schizophrenia.

I was told I had a disease that was like diabetes, and if I continued to take neuroleptic medications for the rest of my life and avoided stress, I might be able to cope. I remember that as these words were spoken to me by my psychiatrist it felt as if my whole teenage world—in which I aspired to dreams of being a valued person in valued roles, of playing lacrosse for the US Women's Team or maybe joining the Peace Corps—began to crumble and shatter. It felt as if these parts of my identity were being stripped from me. I was beginning to undergo that radically dehumanizing and devaluing transformation from being a person to being an illness; from being Pat Deegan to being "a schizophrenic."

As I look back on those days I am struck by how all alone I was. This profound sense of being all alone only served to compound my sense of feeling worthless and of having no value. Granted, people gave me medications, people monitored my blood pressure, people did art therapy, psychotherapy, occupational therapy, and recreational therapy with me. But in a very fundamental way I experienced myself as being all alone, adrift on a nameless sea without compass or bearing. And that deep sense of loneliness came from the fact that although many people were talking to me about my symptoms, no one was talking to me about how I was doing. No one came to me and said, "Hey, I know you're going through hell right now. I know you feel totally lost in some nightmare. I know you can't see a way out right now. But I've been where you are today. I got labeled with schizophrenia and a whole bunch of other things too. And I'm here to tell you that there is a way out and that your life doesn't have to be about being in mental institutions. I'm around if you want to talk."

No one ever came to me and said those words. All I knew were the stereotypes I had seen on television or in the movies. To me, mental illness meant Dr. Jekyll and Mr. Hyde, psychopathic serial killers, loony bins, morons, schizos, fruitcakes, nuts, straight jackets, and raving lunatics. They were all I knew about mental illness, and what terrified me was that professionals were saying I was one of them. It would have greatly helped to have had someone come and talk to me about surviving mental illness—as well as the possibility of recovering, of healing, and of building a new life for myself. It would have been good to have role models—people I could look up to who had experienced what I was going through—people who had found a good job, or who were in love, or who had an apartment or a house on their own, or who were making a valuable contribution to society. But as I said, this did not happen for me in those early years.

So today I want to take the opportunity to say the things that no one ever said to me back then. I want to talk with the 17-year-old girl that I once was. I want to talk to her about what I know now but didn't know then. I want to talk to her, and in so doing, speak to all of us who have been labeled with mental illness, who have suffered deeply, who have known despair, who have been told that we have no value and who have felt alone, abandoned, and adrift on a dead and silent sea.

A Bleak, Monotonous Existence

I turn my gaze back over the 21-year span of time that separates me from that 17-year-old girl. I am trying to see her...it's difficult to look at her. I can see the yellow, nicotine-stained fingers. I can see her shuffled, stiff, drugged walk. Her eyes do not dance. The dancer has collapsed and her eyes are dark and they stare endlessly into nowhere. It is the time between the first and second hospitalization and she is back living at her parents' home. She forces herself out of bed at 8 o'clock in the morning. In a drugged haze she sits in a chair, the same chair every day. She is smoking cigarettes. Cigarette after cigarette. Cigarettes mark the passing of time. Cigarettes are proof that time is passing and that fact, at least, is a relief. From 9 A.M. to noon she sits and smokes and stares. Then she has lunch. At 1 P.M. she goes back to bed to sleep until 3 P.M. At that time she returns to the chair and sits and smokes and stares. Then she has dinner. She returns to the chair at 6 PM. Finally, it is 8 o'clock in the evening, the long awaited hour, the time to go back to bed and to collapse into a drugged and dreamless sleep.

This same scenario unfolds the next day, and then the next, and then the next, until the months pass by in numbing succession, marked only by the next cigarette and then the next...

And as I watch her, I know it is not so much mental illness that I am observing. I am witnessing the flame of a human spirit faltering. She is losing the will to live. She is not suicidal—but she wants to die because nothing seems worth living for. Her hopes, her dreams, and her aspirations have been shattered. She sees no way to achieve the valued roles she had once dreamed of. Her future has been reduced to the prognosis of doom she had been given. Her past is slipping away like a dream that belonged to someone else. Her present is empty but for the pungent cigarette smoke that fills the void like a veiled specter. No, this is not mental illness I am seeing. I am seeing a young woman whose hope for living a full and valuable life has been shattered. She feels herself to be among the living dead and her spirit is wavering under the weight of it all.

What I Wish I Could Tell Her

I walk into the room and sit near her. I want to talk to her. Just the thought of it makes me want to start to cry. What should I say to her? I lean towards her as she sits smoking in her chair.

"Patricia…I'm worried about you. I can see that you are suffering deeply. Your suffering is not invisible to me. I know that the professionals have been very busy observing you, treating your symptoms, and trying to rehabilitate you; but no one has addressed the way you are suffering. The fact that you have felt so alone in your suffering doesn't mean there's something bad or shameful about you. Try to understand that most professionals—in fact most people—are afraid to sit quietly and to be with a person who is suffering. It's the same sort of thing that happens at a funeral—when people line up to console the person who is bereaved, they get all anxious and awkward and don't know what to say.

"People find it frightening to just spend time with people who are in great pain. You see, a person who is in great anguish is crying out. Even if they are totally silent like you are, way down deep I can hear you crying out. And that cry, the cry of an anguished person, has the power to awaken the cry, the wound, the brokenness that exists inside every person. Every person, no matter how high up the social ladder they have climbed or no matter how valued their role is in our society, every person has a cry, a wound, a brokenness down deep inside of them. Thus, to be with a person who is anguished is to risk experiencing the cry that is way down deep inside each of us. That is why the professionals have been so busy doing things to you, rather than being with you. Granted, it's their job, but it's also true that staying busy by doing things to you helps keep their anxiety under control, which in turn helps to distance them from the cry that your suffering might evoke in them.

"I also hear anger in your suffering. You are angry because you have been diagnosed with a major mental illness. You feel angry because all your friends are doing normal stuff like going to school, going on dates, and dreaming their dreams. You feel, 'Why me. Why has this happened to me?' I don't know the answer to that question. I don't know why you were dealt this hand of cards. But what I do know is this: You may have been diagnosed with a mental illness, but you are not an illness. You are a human being whose life is precious and is of infinite value.

"You are at a critical juncture, a very important time. The professionals are telling you that you are a schizophrenic. Your family and friends are beginning to refer to you as 'a schizophrenic.' It is as if the whole world has put on a pair of warped glasses that blind them to the person you are and leaves them seeing you as an illness. It seems that everything you do gets interpreted through the lenses of these warped glasses. If you don't laugh, that is worrisome and, if you laugh too much, that is also worrisome. If you don't move, they get alarmed, and if you move around too much, they get alarmed. The range of behaviors and feelings you are allowed has been dramatically narrowed as a result of the blinders that those around you have put on.

"Almost everything you do gets understood in reference to your illness. You used to have days when you had 'ants in your pants,' but now they say you are agitated. You used to feel sad sometimes, but now you are said to be depressed. You used to disagree sometimes, but now you are told you lack insight. You used to act independently, but now you are told that your independence means you are uncooperative, noncompliant, and treatment resistant. You used to take risks. You learned from your failures as you were growing and learning. But now that you have been labeled with a mental illness the dignity of risk and the right to failure have been taken from you. No wonder you get angry. Normal people get to make many stupid choices over and over again in their lives. Nobody tells them that they need a case manager. How many times has Elizabeth Taylor been married? At last count it was seven or eight times, I think. The poor woman lacks insight! She exercises poor judgment! She is failing to learn from past experiences! She is making the same dumb choice again! How come they don't get her a case manager?

"But this is a critical time for you because there is the great danger that you might succumb to the messages you are being given. You might slowly find yourself putting on those same warped glasses and viewing yourself as others are seeing you. The great danger is that you might undergo that radically devaluing and dehumanizing transformation from being a person to being an illness, from being Patricia to being 'a schizophrenic' (or 'a bipolar' or 'a multiple'). The reason this is so dangerous is because once a person comes to believe that he or she is an illness, there is no one left inside to take a stand toward the illness. Once you and the illness become one, then there is no one left inside of you to take on the work of recovering, of healing, of rebuilding the life you want to live. Once you come to believe that you are a mental illness, you give away all your power—and others take responsibility for you and for your life.

"That is why I say that this is a critical and dangerous time. It is important that you resist the efforts, however unintentional they might be, to transform you into an illness. In this regard let your anger, especially your angry indignation, be your guide. See how your anger flares up into angry indignation each time you get referred to as an illness. You are not an illness, and that angry indignation is like a fiery shield that blazes up to protect you and your dignity.

Some people will try to tell you that your anger is a symptom of mental illness. Don't believe them. Anger is not a symptom of mental illness. Some people may even try to medicate you in order to make your anger go away. This can be dangerous—by extinguishing someone's anger through the use of medications we run the risk of breaking their spirit and of wounding their dignity. Many of us know that recovering from the effects of such spirit-breaking practices is far more difficult than recovering from mental illness.

"Your anger is not a symptom of mental illness. Your angry indignation is a sane response to the situation that you are facing. You are resisting the messages you are being given. In and through your fiery indignation your dignity is saying, 'No, I am not an illness. I am first and foremost a human being. I will not be reduced to being an illness or a thing. I will keep my power and save a part of myself that will, in time, be able to take a stand toward my distress and begin the process of recovery and healing.

"What really needs to happen is that people must understand that it's going to take you a while to figure out what is going on with you. You need to find a way of making sense of what is happening to you that you can live with. For many of us, this takes time and even some trial and error. You may want to talk with professionals, other people who have been diagnosed, clergy, and/or friends. You might decide to read up on the subject to learn more about it. Maybe you'll get a second or third opinion from other professionals. Make sure to think things over for yourself. Know that as you grow you can develop, change, and modify your understanding of what is going on with you and/or your life situation. I'm not saying that nothing is going on. Something happened that caused you to end up in a mental hospital. You need to start defining for yourself what that something is and what you can do to change it.

"As for me, after years of trying to sort this out and, like most of us, having received all sorts of diagnoses, I've settled on trying to keep it simple. The way I see it is that I have some pretty uncomfortable experiences like hearing voices that put me down and strong urges to hurt myself and sometimes my thoughts get all jumbled and I can't communicate well. I don't care what they want to call it. All I know is that sometimes these experiences can get so overwhelming that I find it difficult to work or go to school or have friends. I've decided that I have a disability. To me it's important to say that I have a disability but that I am not a disabled person. You see, the great thing is that I have learned that it is possible to live a whole and healthy life and still have a disability. People don't usually think of these words going together but it's true: I live a whole and healthy life and I have a psychiatric disability. The reason I can do this is because the most valued and important thing I do in my life is work on my recovery. The most valued role I fulfill every day is to remain faithful to my journey of recovery. My journey of recovery and healing is my work. If I do that work, everything else falls into place.

"One of the biggest lessons I have had to accept is that recovery is not the same thing as being cured. After 21 years of living with this thing it still hasn't gone away. So I figure I'm never going to be cured but I can be in recovery. Recovery is a process, not an endpoint or a destination. Recovery is an attitude, a way of approaching the day and the challenges I face. Being in recovery means I know I have certain limitations and things I can't do. But rather than letting

You may have been diagnosed with a mental illness, but you are not an illness. You are a human being whose life is precious and is of infinite value.

these limitations be an occasion for despair and giving up, I have learned that in knowing what I can't do, I also open up the possibilities of all I can do.

"To me recovery means I try to stay in the driver's seat of my life. I don't let my illness run me. Over the years I have worked hard to become an expert in my own self-care. For me, being in recovery means I don't just take medications. Just taking medications is a passive stance. Rather, I use medications as part of my recovery process. In the same way I don't just go to the hospital. Just 'going to the hospital' is a passive stance. Rather, I use the hospital when I need to. Over the years I have learned different ways of helping myself. Sometimes I use medications, therapy, self-help and mutual support groups, friends, my relationship with God, work, exercise, spending time in nature—all these measures help me remain whole and healthy, even though I have a disability.

"Being in recovery is not a panacea. It doesn't mean the pain or suffering is over. Every day I have to get up and reaffirm my intention to stay whole and healthy and to work on my recovery. I still have relapses but I try to understand that having a relapse is not a failure on my part. I find that when I relapse in recovery, it is because I am breaking through into some new and scary and wonderful part of living.

"I have found that although my symptoms may seem the same or even worse, relapsing while in recovery is not the same thing as 'having a breakdown.' When I relapse in recovery I'm not breaking down; rather, I am breaking out or breaking through. It may mean I am breaking out of some prison or fear-filled place where I have been trapped inside of myself. It may mean I am breaking through to new ways of trusting people and myself. So you see, when I have a relapse within the context of my recovery, I try not to see it as a failure. It means I am growing, breaking out of old fears, and breaking through into new worlds—like learning to make friends and keep them, to trust people, and to love people.

"I find it important to choose to work with professionals who understand the difference between breaking down and breaking through/breaking out. The symptoms may appear identical, but if you examine my life, if you look at life from the standpoint of my journey of recovery, there's a big difference between breaking down and breaking through/breaking out. If you choose to work with professionals in your recovery, it is important to find ones who understand this distinction.

"Everyone's journey of recovery is unique. Each of us must find our own way and no one can do it for us. However, talking with other people with psychiatric disabilities who are in recovery can be very helpful, perhaps even the most helpful thing of all.

"It is important to understand that we are faced with recovering not just from mental illness, but also from the effects of being labeled mentally ill. I believe many of us emerge from mental institutions with full-blown post-traumatic stress disorders that are a direct result of the trauma and abuse we may have experienced or witnessed in mental institutions or in community based programs. We are also faced with recovering from the process of internalizing the stigma we are surrounded with, as well as the effects of discrimination, poverty, and second-class citizenship. Indeed, there's no doubt that the label of mental illness comes as a 'package plan' that too often includes poverty, trauma, dehumanization, degrada-

tion, being disenfranchised, and being unemployed. Many of us find that the recovery process goes hand in hand with the empowerment process. We find that recovery means becoming politicized and aware of the social, economic, and human injustices we have had to endure. We find that empowerment and recovery means finding our collective voice, our collective pride, and our collective power, and challenging and changing the injustices we face.

"Finally, Patricia, I want to mention one other thing that can happen and that you must guard against during these early years of being in the mental health system. You might hear professionals referring to you or other people as being 'high functioning' or 'low functioning.' Whether you get labeled high functioning or low functioning, don't fall into the trap of believing it. These are not attributes that exist inside a person. They are value judgments that are put on a person. All those words really mean is that there are those people whose actions or talents or gifts we value and there are those people in which we find no value. There are no high-functioning or low-functioning people. There are people whose contribution we are able to see and value and there are those whose gifts we have failed to see and have failed to value. When you hear a mental health worker say that someone is low functioning, say to yourself, 'That person is not low functioning. It's just that the mental health worker has failed to see and value the gifts and special talents of that person.'

"The real challenge in all this is to somehow learn to value yourself. That can seem like such an impossible task because you get bombarded with messages and images that are so negative and degrading. How is it, when we are surrounded by such messages of despair, that we can begin to value ourselves? That's a difficult question to answer. I am 21 years older and I am still working on really valuing myself. But somehow when I look back at you, Patricia, as I watch you smoking and staring, when I see the way you are suffering and are all alone, somehow, despite all they have said about you, I see you and a tenderness fills my heart. You are precious and good. You are not trash to be discarded or a broken object that must be fixed. You are not insane. You do not belong in institutions for the rest of your life. You don't belong on the streets. And even though they tie us down in four-point restraints and though they lock us up against our will like animals, you are not an animal. You are a human being. You carry within you a precious flame, a spark of the divine.

"Patricia, if I could reach back through the years I would hold you. I would say you are beautiful. I would say don't listen to the prognosis of doom. You are more than all their words. There is a place for you. There is a reason. This is not suffering for the sake of just more pain. A new life can be born of this labor. A water that is life giving can be found in this desert. Don't give up, although there is no magic answer, no magic drug, and no magic cure. I would hold you now. I would tell you I love you. I would want to protect you. I would want to rescue you, but I know that I couldn't. It's not about being rescued. It's about taking up your journey of recovery, finding good people who will accompany you on that journey and then following your journey to wherever it leads you.

"They may tell you that your goal should be to become normal and to achieve valued roles. But a role is empty and valueless

When I have a relapse within the context of my recovery, I try not to see it as a failure. It means I am growing, breaking out of old fears, and breaking through into new worlds.

unless you fill it with your meaning and your purpose. Don't become normal. Our task is not to become normal. You have the wondrously terrifying task of becoming who you are called to be. And you are not called to be an inhuman thing. You are not called to be a mental illness. You were born into this world for a reason and only you can discover what that reason is. You were born into this world to grow and it is possible to grow into a whole, healthy person who also has a psychiatric disability. Your life and your dreams may have been shattered—but from such ruins you can build a new life full of value and purpose.

"The task is not to become normal. The task is to take up your journey of recovery and to become who you are called to be. You were born to love and to be loved. That's your birthright. Mental illness cannot take that from you. Nobody can take that from you. Patricia, become who you are called to be. Do what you do with love. Loving and being loved is what matters. That is the value."

A Pit of Confusion

Anonymous

THIS ARTICLE ORIGINALLY APPEARED IN THE
Schizophrenia Bulletin, 1990, 16(2), 355-359.

A white-coated attendant strapped me to a hard table and injected me with a sedative. The bright lights and shining metal apparatus in the emergency room swam before my eyes, and a confusion of echoing voices hummed in my ears, but I did not fall asleep.

I closed my eyes tightly to rest in the blackness. Soon the blackness began to manufacture shapes, images, and entire scenarios from my life. Far away I heard my father's voice; it comforted me, even though he was in another room and talking to someone else. It droned on and on. I thought he was making arrangements for someone to take me to visit my older brother, whom I had set out to visit that morning at 3 A.M.—before the police and the ambulance had come for me.

The best thing I could do was to keep my eyes on the cross; it symbolized so much; it represented my only hope now, in this pit of confusion, so I pictured in my mind a brilliant white cross of light, and to this cross, I clung, blocking everything else from my mind.

My mother rode in the ambulance with me from the local hospital to the nearest state hospital. I, however, thought the ride would bring me to my brother; my mind was far too groggy and bewildered to realize that my parents made arrangements to admit me to a mental institution.

"She seems to be sleeping peacefully." My mother's voice sounded far away, like an airplane droning off in the distance. Soon I would be with my brother, I thought.

The attendants carried me into the dark corridor. A jumble of voices bounced off the walls—harsh bellows, still murmurs, and authoritative orders—but to me the sounds blended together in a common senselessness.

The next thing I knew, I was lying on a bed, and my mother was leaning over me, fixing the crisp starchy-smelling draw sheet and fluffing the pillow. "You're going to stay here a few days, dear," she said. "It's for your own good." My mother kissed me and left me alone.

I was 22 years old and was experiencing a schizophrenic psychotic episode. The trouble started 5 weeks before I was to graduate from college. I lost the ability to concentrate on my class work, I lost weight, and I began having difficulty sleeping.

I had recently been converted to born-again Christianity, and suddenly I was obsessed with my religion, so that it crowded everything else out of my mind. Reality departed from me, as I imagined the end of the world had come and that I was living in the Millennial Kingdom with a resurrected body. I had kept these delusions well hidden, so that only my family and closest friends had suspected something might be wrong.

The delusions seemed to fade away gradually in the course of the next week, but my parents insisted that I visit a special brain clinic, where a psychologist placed me on megavitamin therapy. I was supposed to swallow about 30 pills a day, a program that struck me as unnecessary, since I no longer suffered from delusions at that time. Therefore, I was negligent about taking the pills; I took them only sporadically, if at all.

I awoke to the seriousness of what had befallen me and withdrew from college. I spent the last part of the spring term taking it easy, and dreaming of the time my parents trusted I was well enough to travel to visit my older brother, who lived near a seaside resort. I was close to my brother and felt it would do me wonders to be near him.

But the delusions crept back. At 3 A.M. I took an ice-cold shower and began singing church hymns at the top of my lungs. Then I walked naked through the dark hall to my bedroom, dressed, and packed my blue canvas flight bag with a beach towel and a Bible. The time had come to visit my brother.

As I headed for the front door with my bag, I met an obstacle. It was my father. Where do you think you're going? he asked. "I'm going to visit my brother," I said boldly, and I stepped past my father, opened the door, and walked out into the night. I think my father was too stunned to try to stop me.

I can't explain the complex twisted thoughts that went through my head outside in the dark. A part of me was sure that somehow by pure faith I would be whisked off to my brother's place. But another part of me was petrified with fear, and suddenly I began to shout.

In that confusing hour the police came, caught me in the wheat field across the street from my house, and wrestled me to an ambulance that waited in our driveway. I remember yelling that I wasn't "insane." I was sane enough to realize that someone thought I wasn't.

I opened my eyes. My mother was gone. Where was I? I sat up and looked out the window by my bed. I looked down onto a row of parked cars in a gravel lot, and my eyes scanned a compound of yellow brick buildings that ascended a steep hill. It must be a prison. I thought I was a prisoner in a state prison.

The pieces to the puzzle were not falling together the way they should be. Where was the key? What must I do to unlock the prison doors? What must I do to break through the barrier that separated me from my brother?

I went to the door of my small room and peered into the hall. Men and women with unstylish clothes and expressionless eyes paraded back and forth past my door. "Where do I know you from?" I asked a hefty woman with a tiny face. The woman's short curly hair circled her pudgy face in ringlets. I thought I knew her.

"In a cottage by the sea," said the woman squinting austerely at me, "I was you and you were me."

This enigmatic message must be a piece to the puzzle. I pondered it. Grandma, before she had died, had lived by the sea. Suddenly I knew the woman was my grandma.

Somehow Grandma was alive again, in this large rather brutal looking woman's body. How much more bearable this person would be, now that Grandma was with me.

"Are you my Grandma?"

The woman's thin lips parted in a guarded smile. "Never tell a soul what you learn from me. You want the answers, and I have the key."

There was no doubt about it. This woman was my grandma.

The next morning when I awoke I found myself staring into the face of a matronly looking woman wearing a white uniform. The woman shifted a wad of gum to the side of her mouth and smiled confrontingly at me.

"Hi," she said. "I'm the head nurse, and I'll bet you're pretty confused this morning, aren't you? I'll bet you don't even know where you are."

"I'm in prison," I said. "I remember. My mother brought me here."

"No, dear, it isn't a prison. It's a hospital. This is a state hospital." She giggled and shook her finger at me. "Doesn't it make you feel better to know you're not in a prison?"

"Why am I here?' "

"I can't answer that," said the nurse. "When you come back from breakfast, you'd see our staff psychiatrist. You can discuss your case with him. He's a wonderful doctor; we all like him very much."

Psychiatrists were for crazy people. So it was that kind of hospital.

"Why am I here?"

I repeated the question to the psychiatrist. His short brown hair waved frizzily over his forehead. A carefully trimmed moustache highlighted the sensitive features of his face. He peered at me through thick glasses.

"You're here for a 10-day evaluation period," he said. "Tell me a little about yourself." His pen was ready.

l don't remember what I told him. I guess whatever I said was enough for him to diagnose my ailment as schizophrenia. I later learned that schizophrenia was a kind of wastebasket term encompassing a broad range of combinations of symptoms including delusions and hallucinations, an inability to synthesize and sort incoming stimuli, an altered sense of self, an unusual change in emotions (such as the absence of anger feelings when they would be expected), etc. I learned that the common notion that schizophrenia is a split personality is an error that impedes understanding of the disease among the public.

Schizophrenia is more common than people realize. It occurs in approximately 1 out of every 100 Americans at some time during their lifetime. But because of its stigma, it is a topic that remains in the closet even in the 1980s.

The doctor told me that there were new drugs called neuroleptics that had proved remarkably successful in cases like mine. He was going to administer initially high doses and hope for the best.

I had heard someone use the term chronic wards in reference to those buildings. It didn't sound like a nice term, and when I had asked what it meant, someone had said patients on the chronic wards never recover.

"When am I going to visit my brother?" I asked him at the close of the session.

"If you've ever heard a lion roar, then break down the door," the woman I thought was my grandma advised me, when I told her how urgently I wanted to visit my brother.

A scene from the *Wizard of Oz* film flashed into my mind. The frightened lion crashing head first through a glass window to escape the terrible wizard's presence.

If you've ever heard a lion roar, then break down the door. It made perfect sense. It was a piece to the puzzle. What a gold mine of wisdom my grandma was! I charged at the door! The lower portion of the door was solid wood, the upper portion glass. The impact knocked my breath from me, and I rubbed my side. Grandma trotted to my side. She rapped the glass partition with an angry fist, "Come and give this girl a hand. You ought to help her out." Inside the nurse's station, which was a buffer between my ward and the outside exit to the building, the staff waved grandma away. One of the aides held up a newly printed notice that said I was to be restricted to the ward. "Someone here deserves a clout," Grandma muttered. That night before I dropped off to sleep in my musty little room, I heard grandma wailing like a wounded lamb in the next room. "It doesn't matter if I'm brave! You're going to send me to my grave!"

It was morning. A square patch of sunlight shimmered on the hospital bedspread. Suddenly it dawned on me. There would be no trip to see my brother. Everything seemed clear to me. It was as if a fog had lifted, and I could again think rationally.

The doctor had mentioned a 10-day evaluation period. Did this mean I could go home at the end of the 10 days? I wanted to talk to the person in charge of my case.

I was introduced to a social worker. She was a petite woman with freckles. We went in an office to talk. "Can I go home at the end of my 10 days?" I asked. The social worker smiled and poured two cups of coffee, one for each of us. "I want us to talk first," she said.

So we proceeded to talk. My condition was one that still puzzles the experts to some extent. No one can be sure just what caused it. Theories conflict with each other, some claiming inherited factors, some claiming environmental factors, and others suggesting that both factors contribute in an integral fashion.

We talked generally about my personality. I admitted I was a loner and was probably somewhat backward socially. I had never had a boyfriend, rarely even dated, and my friendships with girls were limited and superficial. I spent most of my time studying or doing things alone.

"You have to make some social adjustments," she said. "I know," I said. "I have to learn to interact with people."

I convinced her that I had remarkable insight into my life and its needs. Indeed, I more than anything wanted to get out of there after my 10-day period. Finally the social worker promised that she would recommend to the team meeting that I be discharged at the end of the 10 days.

The dining hall was crowded, I noticed that most of the patients straddled a middle-aged mark; there were only a few younger ones in their twenties or thirties.

Many had come from the buildings on the hill that I had viewed from my window. My ward, the admissions ward, was located at the base of the hill, but many of these other patients who converged on the dining hall had come from the other buildings.

I had heard someone use the term chronic wards in reference to those buildings. It didn't sound like a nice term, and when I had asked what it meant, someone had said patients on the chronic wards never recover.

I tried not to stare impolitely at the idiosyncratic behaviors these individuals displayed, the tongues that hung from their mouths, the heads that bobbed from side to side, and the occasional drooling of saliva down the chins. I said a silent prayer of thanks that I would be going home in a few days.

A cheerful red-haired boy about my age befriended me in the dining hall. He offered to escort me around the hospital grounds after lunch, and I agreed. He brought me a bouquet of wild flowers when he came to my room. "Thank you," I said. It was the first time a guy had ever given me flowers. Yet, the farthest thought from my mind was the notion of striking up a romance. My big concern was the anticipation of going home.

He showed me the road that wound through the complex of brick buildings; the dairy barn, where we stopped to lure the lowing cows to the fence with handfuls of dry grass; and a baseball field adjoining an adolescent unit.

As we strolled, the boy put his arm around me. I pulled away. "You already have a sweetheart, or what?" He plucked a blade of grass and stuck it between his teeth. "No," I said. "I just don't know you well enough." I wasn't ready to be involved with anyone.

The next day the social worker brought news from the team meeting. In the team meetings the hospital staff, including the doctor, the nurses, aides, and social workers, all got together and discussed the progress of the patients; the team meeting had to approve all discharges.

"Congratulations," she said to me. "The team approved your discharge." I breathed a great sigh of joy. I had been fairly sure the team would approve the discharge. But it was good to hear the official verdict just the same.

I was going home tomorrow. It was great to think of going home. I walked outside and found a spot on the hospital lawn where the May sun beat down on the cool grass. I lay down and peered up at the sky.

A lanky young man with long brown hair approached me. He stood in front of me. "I'm so fed up with this place," he said bitterly. "1 don't belong here with all the crazy old hags. I'm only 19."

I wanted to extend my friendship to the guy. He was young, wearing a T-shirt and blue jeans, and hated this place. That was already more than enough grounds for a friendship to exist; I instantly felt a rapport with him.

"Mind if I sit down with you," he asked, "I'm dying to talk to somebody sane." I liked him more and more all the time. I just came in last night, he said. I thought I was in a torture chamber, and I yelled my head off. They finally gave me a shot.

"I was just here for 10 days," I told him. "I'm going home tomorrow." Then I told him about some of the delusions and strange ideas. "A lot of the delusions were religious," I said, "and some were about me thinking I was going to visit my brother."

"Why do you think God would let something like this happen to you," my new friend asked. It was a question I'd thought hard about myself.

"I don't know," I admitted. "I guess I'll never know."

I knew I would still try to trust God. I would simply accept what had happened and be thankful that my prognosis was good with the availability of the new drugs and the increased exploration and study of conditions such as mine. All I could do was hope in God and be optimistic.

My friend told me a little about some of his own delusions. He had thought that he and his girlfriend were Adam and Eve, for one thing. But he was over that now. "It's ridiculous for me to be here," he said. "You'll get out soon," I assured him.

Then we walked to the administration building. It housed a recreation room and a canteen. We bought cokes and candy bars at the canteen, and then played several games of pool. "You're not a bad pool player for a girl." "Thanks," I said. Today I was going home! I went outside for a walk. Another sunny day. I walked along the drive that circled the hospital grounds and climbed the hill past the chronic wards.

They that wait on the Lord shall renew their strength, I thought to myself. They shall mount up with wings as eagles; they shall run and not be weary; they shall walk and not faint. I would need strength to face the world after my experience.

When I circled back to the admissions ward, my father's car was parked in front. My parents had come!

A few moments later I stood with my suitcase, while my mother talked with the social worker about followup therapy for me. I would receive outpatient psychiatric therapy at a mental health facility in my own county.

I was numb with joy. The pieces to the puzzle had finally come together.

Note: Problems arose after my discharge that required a more lengthy hospitalization. Through a combination of neuroleptic medication and intense psychotherapy, I battled to the point where the illness remitted; I now lead a normal life as a librarian in a busy city public library.

A Consumer Perspective on Psychosocial Treatment

Esso Leete

ESSO LEETE HAS SPENT OVER TWENTY YEARS IN BOTH THE PUBLIC AND THE PRIVATE MENTAL HEALTH SYSTEMS, RECEIVING A VARIETY OF TREATMENTS FOR HER CHRONIC SCHIZOPHRENIA. AFTER TREATMENT AT A RESIDENTIAL PSYCHIATRIC FACILITY IN THE COMMUNITY AND BEING STABILIZED ON MEDICATIONS, SHE HAS SUBSTANTIALLY RECOVERED AND NOW RUNS A SELF-HELP SUPPORT GROUP, SPEAKS NATIONALLY, AND IS EMPLOYED FULL-TIME AS A MEDICAL RECORDS TRANSCRIBER AT A STATE HOSPITAL IN DENVER, A FACILITY TO WHICH SHE WAS ONCE INVOLUNTARILY COMMITTED.

THIS ARTICLE ORIGINALLY APPEARED IN THE *Psychosocial Rehabilitation Journal*, 1988, 12(2).

The author begins by providing a brief history of her illness, chronic schizophrenia. The article then describes what she understands psychosocial rehabilitation to be and what she sees as its mission in terms of a viable treatment for psychiatric patients, particularly the seriously mentally ill. The author identifies elements of an effective psychosocial treatment program, specifically describing her treatment at a residential halfway house in Denver. The article also highlights how important it is for clients to understand their illness, to have choices, and to exercise as much control as possible over their own lives. The importance of staff attitudes is stressed, as well as the necessity for both professional and primary consumer to work together as partners in the recovery process.

More than by any other one thing, my life has been changed by schizophrenia. For the past 20 years I have lived with it and in spite of it, struggling to come to terms with it, without giving in to it.

Although I have fought a daily battle, it is only now that I have some sense of confidence that I will survive.

Let me give you some background on myself—my credentials, if you will. I am the eldest of three children. My father was in the Army and we moved every 2 or 3 years, including a move to Germany. I was shy and slow to make friends and these frequent uprootings were extremely difficult for me; I sorely missed the predictable routines, stable friendships, consistent schools, and familiar houses that others enjoyed.

We returned to the United States for my senior year of high school, which is when I became ill. I didn't know it at the time (and I think others denied it), but looking back I can see the changes. Except for participation in sports I had always been more comfortable by myself, and in my senior year I became increasingly withdrawn and sullen. I felt alienated and lonely. Everybody was so distant from me; there seemed to be a huge gap between me and the rest of the world, including my family. I watched dispassionately as my two younger sisters matured, dated, shopped and shaped their lives, while I seemed stuck in a totally different dimension.

I graduated as a National Honor Society member from high school. It was expected that I would get a scholarship and I did; When I reluctantly went off to college I was alone for the first time and totally unprepared for life away from home. I was isolated; I had no close friends and as time went on, I spoke to virtually no one. Increasingly, I found myself in classes drawing pictures of Van Gogh and writing poetry instead of taking notes. I forgot to eat and began sleeping in my clothes. Even routine things like taking a shower rarely occurred to me.

Towards the end of the first semester I had my first acute psychotic episode. At the time, I did not understand what was happening, and it was extremely frightening. One night, walking alone on a beach, my perceptions suddenly shifted. The intensifying wind became an omen of something terrible, trees and bushes bent threateningly towards me, and tumbleweeds chased me. I was running, but making no progress. When I finally reached my dormitory, after what seemed like hours, I was exhausted, confused, and hearing voices for the first time. Later that week, I had similar experiences, still not comprehending that I was out of touch with reality as others knew it. That reality had given way to the multiple realities with which I would now live.

One day soon thereafter, I returned from classes and was surprised to find my father in my dormitory room, my packed bags waiting at the door. Someone must have notified him of my condition, for he had come to take me away. He had been advised to admit me to a hospital; this was my first psychiatric hospitalization. Diagnosis: schizophrenia. I was treated with medications and released after a few months. I have now been hospitalized 15 times, the longest being for a year. I have had twice as many doctors. I have had 10 diagnoses (most of them variants of schizophrenia), been tried on nearly 20 medications, and had almost every kind of therapy imaginable, including four-point restraint and seclusion therapy, as well as insulin coma therapy concomitant with E.C.T. In other words I have been treated *with* everything *for* everything.

Although I do not have formal educational credentials, I have become somewhat of an expert in the area of my illness. Having lived with it these many years, I now have a personal understanding of it that could not really have come from books. I have found that there are a variety of problems people with long-term mental illness face, both in the world at large and within ourselves, that contribute to our difficulties. I see comprehensive psychosocial rehabilitation as one means by which we can improve our lives, by providing assistance with problems that are social, psycho-

logical, educational, financial, residential, and vocational. I use the term *psychosocial rehabilitation* to refer to this comprehensive array of ongoing services offered to people with mental illness to develop or enhance independent living skills to the maximum extent possible. These services should incorporate continuity of care, provide interpersonal support, and encourage individual growth in all areas of life. Specifically, I feel the focus of treatment should be our adjustment in the present through control of our symptoms. To this end we need an environment with structure. We need illness education, skill enhancement, practical advice, problem-solving techniques, and improved reality-testing. And this must be furnished in an atmosphere of support, reassurance, and encouragement.

Unfortunately, as is often the case, it was many years into my psychiatric difficulties before I was offered any serious or meaningful psychosocial treatment for the deficits deposited by my mental illness. Of course, all hospitals and treatment programs have their own conception of what psychosocial rehab is and what services they feel they can and should provide. There were hospitalizations, especially in the distant past, that provided virtually no psychosocial rehabilitation. In fact, I feel psychiatric hospitals are often counterproductive, because a successful hospital patient may only be able to function in an institutional setting; adaptive hospital behavior bears absolutely no relationship to effective functioning in the community. A regimented hospital setting where you make few decisions and exercise little control over your daily life cannot possibly prepare you for reintegration and independent living. Only by actually living in our communities can we successfully adapt and normalize our lives.

To this end, I see psychosocial rehab as essential for people with long-term mental illness. There is no question in my mind that it affects the long-term course of our disease and influences the degree to which we will recover. We may have an inherited predisposition which makes us more vulnerable to stress and psychosis, we may have a cerebral dysfunction that alters our thought processes, but there are, fortunately, ways to overcome these handicaps. Psychosocial rehabilitation can teach us some of these.

Psychosocial treatment works because it is both individualized and comprehensive. A good program views psychiatric patients as having a variety of needs, interests, and capabilities and treats us as individuals, offering a wide variety of skills training geared towards successful community adaptation. This may be accomplished in a residential care facility in the community (which is my first choice), a hospital day program or partial hospitalization program, a clubhouse model treatment program, an assigned case manager, or aftercare treatment with assertive outreach to the patient. Included in this should be medication management (if applicable), individual and family therapy, residential and vocational assistance, social skills acquisition, and an accessible means of crisis intervention and stabilization. I will address each of these components.

Medication (although not for everyone and not without risks) can be extremely helpful. Like many, I have continuing difficulty coping with stress, but I find taking my medication makes it easier for me to function day to day. Before I reached this important realization, I was caught in a vicious circle. When I was off the medication I couldn't remember how much better I had felt on it, and when I was taking the medication I felt so good that I was convinced I did not need It. Fortunately, I was finally able to make the connection between taking the medication and feeling better. Individual psychotherapy has also been extremely helpful to me. Even though my meds may stabilize me, because my illness influences every area of my life I need ongoing supportive therapy to help me understand and successfully live with a serious illness. It is, of course, also important for the family or other support systems to become informed of my disorder. We must all understand what we are dealing with, thereby learning problem-solving techniques and to communicate openly with each other, without fear or blame. In addition, I think both family members and consumers can benefit greatly from self-help support groups, a form of psychosocial rehabilitation often overlooked. Let me speak from the patient's perspective about this, since that is what I know best.

As you are aware, in addition to handicaps imposed by our illnesses, we must constantly deal with barriers erected by society as well, leaving us often feeling alienated, helpless, and hopeless. A peer-run support group can help us immensely to overcome these obstacles. I know, because about 3 years ago I began such a support group, and I have benefitted as much as anyone from the experience. Our support group offers each member support, friendship, and hope for the future. We as primary consumers need to meet socially with others who have experienced what we have, to exchange information about coping skills, and to take responsibility for ourselves, because mental patients are kind of an esoteric group. We have been ostracized from society, yet we need a group to which we can belong. Even more important, I feel we must meet with others like us in order to see firsthand what we have accomplished and what we can achieve. We will draw strength and hope from each other in this way. We have gradually liberated our minds from dehumanizing stereotypes we have learned to internalize. We have seen that we are one in the struggle, the pain, and the disappointments, but that we can also share the dreams, the aspirations, and the triumphs of our peers.

We have all suffered and many have overcome their illness and the stigma surrounding it. It is not easy, it is not quick. The realization that it can be done is one of the most useful and personally gratifying aspects of my support group, for success will never be realized if it cannot be imagined. We did not choose to be ill, but we can choose to deal with it and learn to live with it. A peer-run support group can help us understand our disease and learn to function in spite of it, to overcome our illness by compensating for our disabilities. By choosing to participate in such a group, we have been able to take some control over our lives, and we feel both a sense of ownership and empowerment. A support group can give us the personal strength and commitment to overcome the stigma, prejudice, discrimination, and rejection we have experienced and to reclaim our personal validity, our dignity as individuals, and our autonomy. And we can do this with pride, in a group founded by us, shared among us, sustained by us, and enriched by us.

In addition, we can benefit from very specific social skills training as part of a psychosocial rehab program. My social skill development seems to have been basically arrested in my late teens, when I first became ill. It is possible, however, to learn appropriate social responses and interactions. For example, I have found that I am much more accepted in social situations now that I no longer wear my hat everywhere, wash my hair more frequently, have

Although I do not have formal educational credentials, I have become somewhat of an expert in the area of my illness. Having lived with it these many years, I now have a personal understanding of it that could not really have come from books.

activities in my life to share with others, and do not talk to myself or to my voices in public. I have slowly learned to monitor my symptoms and to develop some self-control over them.

Developing problem-solving techniques is important because otherwise troubles and anxieties, even small ones, will overwhelm me to the point where I become totally stressed out, can no longer cope effectively, and may even become psychotic. I have found that many psychiatric patients have this problem. We do not seem able to deal with life events, uncertainty, worry or frustration as well as others and at a certain point it becomes too much and we may relapse. Learning strategies to deal with these problems is therefore crucial, and there are some very effective cognitive and behavioral modifications that can be learned through psychosocial rehab to help with this.

Goal-setting can also be taught via psychosocial treatment, as well as setting realistic expectations so that we do not set ourselves up for repeated failure. One area affected by this is vocational rehabilitation. The only two occupations of "meaningful" activity sanctioned by our society are school and full-time employment, and we are acutely aware of this. Most of us know that a job will structure our time, provide a more acceptable lifestyle, in-crease our social contacts, and enhance our self-confidence, self-image, and self-esteem. Yet we are fearful of employment. If we fail, our self-esteem will be damaged. Perhaps we will even relapse. Also, we hesitate because of the work disincentive currently a part of the income support programs; if we attempt work, even if we do not succeed, our benefits may be terminated or cut.

Contrary to popular belief, many persons with mental illness do want to work. Unfortunately, as one of the members of my support group stated regarding employment, "People in mental health have to choose between kindergarten and college." We can either be employed in an unchallenging sheltered workshop setting or risk full-time competitive employment —something that is often initially too stressful for us. If we are lucky, we may find part-time employment, but this may be stress-provoking because of low pay or the temporary nature of much of it. One possible solution to this dilemma is the clubhouse model, where members participate actively in all aspects of running the program and also take paid positions in transitional employment, then move on to a regular job after appropriate training.

Most of my experiences come from my involvement with Community Care Corporation a private residential program in Denver. I refer to their program because I am most familiar with it and also because I feel it is among the best. They solve this problem of job experience in a very creative way. They speak to the residents and find out where their interests lie, then contact local businesses specializing in these areas.

A support group can give us the personal strength and commitment to overcome the stigma, prejudice, discrimination, and rejection we have experienced and to reclaim our personal validity, our dignity as individuals, and our autonomy.

They make an agreement with the employer that he will hire an individual for 6 months, during which time Community Care pays half the salary. The business is obligated to put the person on the payroll on a permanent basis at the end of this time if his work is satisfactory. In addition, this program is successful because staff members at the halfway house meet regularly with both employer and employee to deal with any job-related problems. It's a great way to gain experience and get into the work force.

I would like to say a bit more about the psychosocial program at Community Care, which by the way, recently helped me through a partial relapse. To understand why this program has been so helpful to many people with serious mental illness, let me quote their identified treatment philosophy from a doctoral paper written by Alan Melinger, Psy.D., one of the founders and directors of the program, now deceased at age 38. He wrote of their treatment philosophy: Community Care is committed to the treatment of emotionally disturbed individuals in the least restrictive setting possible. Another major philosophical commitment lies in the belief that it is beneficial to address independent living skill building in the treatment process. A third major philosophical commitment lies in the belief that community support services must be ongoing and that supportive links to the system must be available even for those patients who have achieved independent living and competitive employment. Finally, Community Care is committed to providing service to the patient's family and including family members in the treatment whenever possible.

I think this philosophy, shared by all staff members, contributes to the program's continued success. It is implemented very consistently in all phases of the Community Care program in ways that I would like to describe so that you can see what is possible in psychosocial rehabilitation for people with mental illness. The structuring of their program to their philosophy of participation I feel is the key to their success, which is approximately 90 to 95%.

First of all, services are personally designed and highly individualized. Therefore, there is flexibility in the format and content of their day program classes to adjust to the changing needs of the population. In fact, Community Care has established an advisory board composed of individuals who have successfully completed the program and are living independently. One of the tasks of this board is to periodically evaluate the program. Input from current residents is encouraged as well. This illustrates one way in which shared involvement in decision-making processes is accomplished between residents and staff. There is a clear expectation that all members of the community, including the residents, will assume the social responsibilities within the community. The staff makes it clear from the beginning that they are there to guide or assist the client rather than direct him, thus avoiding the issue of control that is so large for many patients. Nor do they continually confront from imagined positions of power, resulting in those inevitable power struggles. Instead, input regarding our treatment and environment is encouraged, indeed sometimes demanded. Although the program is both structured and supervised, residents do not feel imprisoned and at the

mercy of an arbitrary staff, as we usually do in hospitals. A trusting alliance develops between the clients and staff members, which contrasts remarkably with the repression and alienation we usually feel. Staff members give support, reassurance, nurturance, and a healthy—although sometimes confrontational—dose of reality-testing.

Residents are accepted and always treated with dignity and respect, thereby gaining in self-respect. We believed in staff members at Community Care because they believed in us—a new feeling. Interactions were nonthreatening; we always knew staff members were on our side. Staff members perceived the residents first and foremost as human beings and they were available to us for assistance in overcoming the problems in our lives. To help with this, treatment focused on the healthy and adaptive aspects of residents. There was strong staff orientation towards success and an expectation from the beginning that we would all leave and become independent through the continuing process of building on our strengths. However, we also knew that support would be ongoing, even when out of the program, and therefore we did not feel anxious or threatened in our attempts at independence. This is because Community Care has a policy that if a client out in the community has a relapse, he or she is welcome to come back into the program for stabilization. This knowledge eliminates our fear of abandonment and allows us to test our wings without fear.

Clients were viewed as partners in the recovery process which increased our self-esteem and promoted our personal growth. All residents were equally responsible for daily maintenance of the facility, meal preparation, etc. We were also expected to take an active role in community government, including disciplinary decisions. In addition, each of us was placed in the unique position of team leader at our weekly Individual Treatment Planning session where we would schedule our daily class attendance, outside activities, and specific, individual goals for that week, as well as arrange our individual and family therapy sessions. In this way a real sense of ownership in the system and in our improvement was fostered.

Effective psychosocial rehabilitation such as I have described can help us learn to accept our mental illness and manage medications and side effects, available social services, problems with loved ones, vocational endeavors, residential options, and symptoms. In addition, we can learn to take control of our lives and to live independently. However, in spite of successful programs like Community Care, we rarely even hear recovery mentioned as a possibility for psychiatric patients. Professionals continue to measure our progress with concepts like consent and cooperate and comply instead of choose, insinuating that we have no control over our illnesses. This is completely erroneous. We can and should be an active agent in managing our own illnesses, as well as partners in the design and implementation of our own treatment. The patient is most familiar with his disease and has a valid point of view even expert point of view. We are perfectly capable of studying, understanding, accepting and dealing with our illness and its symptoms.

Indeed, I have found it imperative to understand my illness. I have now learned what my own sources of stress are and I mentally prepare for these situations by anticipating problems. In other words, I realize my particular limitations and plan in advance. I find my vulnerability to stress and accompanying symptoms decreases the more I am in control of my own life. I try to recognize my personal warning signs of relapse, though not always, successfully. I realize that because I have gone through what I have—and continue to—I have a certain strength and persistence that others may not have. In short, I have had to develop a new perspective and philosophy about myself and my life in response to the challenge of schizophrenia.

Unfortunately, I know of no magic answer that will eliminate the tragedy of mental illness; but let me briefly summarize what helped me in my own recovery process. And I emphasize, I progressed via a community-based psychosocial treatment program. Finding professionals who recognized and respected my differences and individual needs was crucial to my recovery. Being treated with dignity, as an individual with strengths and weaknesses, instead of a mental patient who could never improve, was important. Having some hope is crucial to recovery; none of us would strive if we believed it a futile effort. I found acceptance and reassurance more helpful than confrontation. Social skills acquisition enabled me to successfully reintegrate with my community. Vocational skills led me to employment. Continuing support and encouragement for my efforts gave me the strength and faith in myself to battle against my disabilities, minimize my vulnerabilities, and work effectively with my individual assets. I believe that if we confront our illnesses with courage and struggle with our symptoms persistently, we can overcome our handicaps to live independently, learn skills, and contribute to society, the society that has traditionally abandoned us.

Self-Help and Mental Health

Audrey J. Gartner and Frank Riessman

AUDREY J. GARTNER IS EDITOR, *The Self-Help Reporter*,
NATIONAL SELF-HELP CLEARINGHOUSE, GRADUATE
SCHOOL AND UNIVERSITY CENTER,
CITY UNIVERSITY OF NEW YORK.

FRANK RIESSMAN, PH.D., IS PROFESSOR OF SOCIOLOGY,
GRADUATE SCHOOL AND UNIVERSITY CENTER,
CITY UNIVERSITY OF NEW YORK.

THIS ARTICLE ORIGINALLY APPEARED IN
Hospital and Community Psychiatry, 1982, 33(8), 631-635
AND IS REPRINTED WITH PERMISSION.

Over the past decade self-help groups have become an important way of helping people cope with various life crises. Groups have organized to help individual members deal with a wide range of health related and other problems. The authors define the meaning of self-help in such groups and describe the range of groups now available, including a number of mental health related groups. The part self-help groups play in providing social support, preventing illness and death, and reducing the need for hospitalization is discussed. The authors also examine the role of professionals in initiating and working with such groups. They point to self-help groups as one means of meeting the increasing demands placed on health and mental health service systems during the 1980s.

Over the past 10 years, self-help groups (also called mutual-aid group or mutual-support groups) have spread from coast to coast and have ballooned to a total of about 500,000; they now involve more than 15 million people). The U.S. Department of Health and Human Services (1980) predicts that the number of persons reached by mutual-support or self-help groups should double by 1990 to reduce the gap in mental health services.

Not only has there been growth in numbers, but also in the range of problems addressed by the groups. There are self-help groups for nearly every disease category listed by the World Health Organization as well as groups concerned with a wide variety of psychosocial problems. Self-help groups have arisen to help people through literally the whole range of life crises, from birth to death. Groups have developed for couples who are infertile, parents of newborns, parents whose child has died, single parents, divorced persons, adolescents and their parents, older persons having difficulties with their children, and the widowed. There are groups for parents who abuse their children, isolated older people, the handicapped, drug abusers, suicide-prone people, smokers, drinkers, overeaters, and patients discharged from mental institutions.

Self-help groups are also developing among those with caretaking responsibilities for others—parents of children with handicaps, parents or relatives of individuals who have been institutionalized, those taking care of sick or older parents, and spouses of those who have had strokes or other disabling conditions. There are also self-help food cooperatives, job-finding groups, energy conservation groups, and housing and community groups. Extensive lists of self-help groups are available in the literature (Evans, 1979; Gartner & Riessman, 1980).

What is a Self-Help Group?

Self-help groups have been defined as "voluntary small group structures for mutual aid in the accomplishment of a specific purpose. They are usually formed by peers who have come together for mutual assistance in satisfying a common need, overcoming a common handicap or life-disrupting problem, and bringing about desired social and/or personal change" (Katz & Bender, 1976).

The following can be added to this description:

• Self-help groups always involve face-to-face interactions.

• Personal participation is extremely important, since bureaucratization is the enemy of the self-help organization.

• The members agree on and engage in some actions.

• Typically the groups start from a condition of powerlessness.

• The groups fill needs for a reference group, a point of connection and identification with others, a base for activity, and a source of ego reinforcement.

There are groups addressed to particular mental health conditions, such as Depressives Anonymous, Manic-Depressives Anonymous, Neurotics Anonymous, and Schizophrenics Anonymous. Recovery, Inc., begun as an ex-patient group, is now the largest group for persons with nervous disorders, including former inpatients and those who have never been hospitalized.

Other groups have formed to deal with the various forms of addiction. Here self-help groups have played an important role and frequently are recommended as the treatment of choice by traditional mental health agencies: for alcoholics, Alcoholics Anonymous, of course, but also more specialized groups such as the Calix Society for Catholics, the National Association of Recovered Alcoholics in the Professions and Women for Sobriety; for the drug-dependent, the Delancy Street Foundation, Narcotics Anonymous, and Pills Anonymous.

There are also groups addressed to the mental health needs of various populations:

for children who have problems with an alcoholic parent, Alateen; for abusive parents, Parents Anonymous, or for the consequences of parents' sexual molestation of their children, Daughters and Sons United; for minority group members, Sisterhood of Black Single Mothers; for the mentally retarded, National Association for Retarded Citizens; for the chronically disabled, Center for Independent Living; for older persons, Senior Actualization and Growth Encounter; and for women, thousands of groups ranging from local organizations such as Abused Women's Aid in Crisis and the long-established national La Leche League to those focusing on particular life crises such as divorce or widowhood.

Indeed, one of the most important expressions of self-help is found in the feminist perspective. The feminist focus on health and body issues, fostered by the shared experiences of consciousness-raising groups has broadened until today it encompasses self-help and know-your-body courses, alternative health care services, women's centers and clinics, and a distinguished body of literature, including books (*Our Bodies, Our Selves,* [1971], is the best-known example), pamphlets, and movies (Marieskind & Ehrenreich, 1975). Among the self-help groups dealing with specific health issues are DES-Action, Reach to Recovery (for women who have had mastectomies), and Womanpause.

The specific goals of any woman's self-help group vary, but two are always central. One is to provide health education for women; the second is to aid a woman in self-fulfillment. A study examining alternative self-help support systems (The women and mental health project, 1976) documents the existence of many women-to-women mental health and related services that are meeting a vast array of emotional and physical needs which many women feel are best understood by other women.

Prevention and Self-Help

The role of prevention in human services has taken on new relevance recently, since Richard Schweiker, Secretary of the Department of Health and Human Services, singled out prevention as a major concern. Self-help groups have two unique preventive features: they provide social support to their members through the creation of a caring community, and they increase members' coping skills through the provision of information and the sharing of experiences and solutions to problems.

The importance of social support in preventing mental illness is seen in a prevention equation, adapted from George Albee (1981), former chair of the task force on prevention of the President's Commission on Mental Health:

$$\text{Incidence of dysfunction} = \frac{\text{Stress + Constitutional vulnerabilities}}{\text{Social supports + Coping skills + Competence}}$$

The equation suggests two major strategies for preventing dysfunction: decreasing stress, constitutional vulnerabilities, or both, or increasing social supports, coping skills, and competence. While stress appears to be a major factor contributing to the development of dysfunction, we cannot always control the stressors in our lives. Many stressors—illness or death of a loved one, accidents, and economic setbacks—cannot be eliminated or reduced by the individual. It is difficult, then, to have an impact on the numerator of the prevention equation. The bottom line, literally, lies in strengthening social supports, coping skills, and competence.

The scientific community and popular culture have both hailed social support as a vital component in health and survival. Research data from psychiatric, psychological, and sociological studies point to the effectiveness of social-support groups in protecting members from the emotionally and physically deleterious effects of illness and in improving the quality of their lives.

One such study assessed the relationship between social and community ties and the mortality rates of a sample of 4,725 residents in the San Francisco Bay area over a 9-year period (Berkman & Syms, 1979). The authors examined the impact of various social ties—marriage, family and friends, membership in a religious group, and informal and formal group associations—on mortality from all causes. The findings showed that people with the most social ties had lower mortality rates over the period than those without such ties, even taking into consideration self-reported physical status, socioeconomic status, health practices, and use of preventive health services. It was only in the presence of mounting social disconnection, when individuals failed to have links in several different spheres of interaction, that mortality rates rose sharply.

Self-help groups have developed to replace the natural support networks that have been lost or have become disconnected as society has changed. Disintegration of the traditional extended kinship system and the isolation of mobile nuclear families have made families particularly vulnerable to stress. While the stresses placed on new mothers or on the newly widowed once were addressed in the family setting, in contemporary America support groups have come to play an important role in the lives of many.

A study of factors in postpartum emotional adjustment sheds light on the effectiveness of mutual aid in helping new mothers improve their coping skills (Gordon, Kapostins & Gordon, 1965). A total of 298 new mothers who belonged to mutual support education groups experienced less emotional distress in the 6 months after childbirth than did 362 control subjects, and their infants were healthier. Follow-up studies 4 to 6 years later showed that, compared with the control subjects, the new mothers in the experimental self-help group had maintained their emotional gains, had subsequently given birth to greater numbers of healthier children, and had suffered fewer physical illnesses, marital conflicts, sexual problems, and divorces. The data showed that although preparing for problems of postpartum adjustment is helpful to new mothers, developing a network of supportive friends and family is more important.

Programs for widows involve a variety of relationships between those who have successfully adapted to their widowhood and the newly widowed, through individual widow-to-widow programs, mutual-support groups, and services such as "widow hotlines" staffed by the widowed. A 2-year study of postbereavement adaptation by 162 widows showed that although participants in an experimental widow-to-widow program followed the same course of adjustment to bereavement as those in a control group, those receiving intervention adjusted more rapidly (Vachon, Lyal, Rogers, et al., 1980). Lieberman and Borman reported that active participation in THEOS, a self-help group for the widowed, positively affects the mental health status of the members (Lieberman & Borman, 1981). Both current and former THEOS members who helped each other through their social network consistently showed better outcome on seven variables: depression, anxiety, somatic symptoms, use of psychotropic drugs, self-esteem, coping mastery, and well-being.

Despite the benefits shown in these and other studies, the great majority of widowed persons do not participate in self-help groups. And, as a recent report shows, the need for social support may be particularly great among widowers (Greenberg, 1981). Researchers at the Johns Hopkins University School of Hygiene and Public Health conducted a 12-year survey of more than 4,000 widowed persons age 18 and over. They found that the death of a spouse appears to be much more devastating to men. Very little difference in death rates was found between persons who had lost a husband or wife in the past year and married persons of the same age, sex, and background. In the ensuing years, however, the survey found that widowed men as a group had a mortality rate 28% higher than that of their married counterparts. Moreover, widowed men between the ages of 55 and 65, who made up more than one fourth of the people in the study, had a mortality rate 60% higher than that of married men of the same age.

Many more people might join a self-help group if one suitable to their needs existed, if they were made aware of the group, and if they were encouraged to join by mental health practitioners, physicians, funeral directors, friends, or others familiar with their needs.

Deinstitutionalization

While the preceding studies have dealt with acute mental health needs, the following project demonstrates a self-help approach to a chronic condition. With the growth of deinstitutionalization, self-help groups are bridging the gap between hospitalization and community living for ex-patients.

The Community Network Development Project at the Florida Mental Health Institute illustrates how the creation of a mutual-aid network can be an effective method for reducing hospital recidivism among mental health clients (Gordon, Edmunson & Bedell, 1982). The project's development was guided by the belief that a self-help program for aftercare clients should strengthen the members' abilities to take an active part not only in their own rehabilitation, but in the rehabilitation of their peers as well.

The project consisted of the establishment of a mutual-aid network of self-help groups for aftercare clients. Members of the support groups were trained in leadership and given responsibilities ranging from teaching some psychoeducational classes to telephoning members to remind them of the next group meeting, driving members to meetings, baking cakes for the group, and arranging outings. Not only did this program help individuals improve their personal functioning, but it also contributed to the survival of the group.

Eighty patients who were being discharged from a 9-week intensive treatment unit were randomly assigned to the project or to a control group for traditional aftercare services. Both groups received equivalent discharge planning, including appropriate referrals to a local mental health center for follow-up treatment if necessary. The groups did not differ significantly according to age, sex, race, marital status, diagnosis, previous hospitalization, or length of follow-up time. At an average follow-up interval of 10 months, only half as many project members as control subjects had required rehospitalization (17.5% to 35%), and their average length of stay was less than a third as long as that of the controls (7 days vs. 24.6 days). Finally, twice as many project members were able to function without any contact with a mental health system(52.5% vs. 26%).

How Do Groups Work?

The power of self-help groups derives from their combining a number of very important properties—the helper-therapy principle, group reinforcement, continuous

Self-help groups have developed to replace the natural support networks that have been lost or have become disconnected as society has changed.

intervention, an ideological perspective, and the implicit demand that the individual do something for himself. They enable their members to feel and use their own strengths and power and to exert control over their own lives.

The helper-therapy principle, in its simplest form, states that those who help are helped most (Riessman, 1965). Thus, an alcoholic in AA who is providing help and support to another AA member may be the one who benefits most. Since all members of the group play this giving role at one time or another, they all benefit from the helping process. While all help-givers themselves may be helped in a nonspecific way by playing the helping role, people who have a particular problem may be helped in much more specific ways by providing help to others who have the same problem, whether it be alcoholism, drug addiction, smoking, or underachieving.

Dewar (1976) said, "It feels good to be the helper. It increases our sense of control, of being valued, of being capable." Part of this feeling comes from the self-persuasion and positive role-playing that occurs. In the process of influencing others with the same problem, the helper must play the "well" role—the sober alcoholic, the coping single parent, the controlled schizophrenic—and, in doing so, persuades or influences himself. Further, playing the helper role achieves special benefits. In helping another struggle with a similar problem, the helper has a chance to observe how the other addresses the problem, and may gain insight and a feeling of social usefulness.

Of course, in self-help the participant is not an isolated individual, but part of a group that provides support, reinforcement, a safe haven, feedback, sanctions, and norms. Many of the groups also provide an ideology—a perspective on one's problems, others' attitudes, and the ways one may respond.

While the range of self-help groups is broad, and the particular factors involved vary, Durman (1976) identifies as common themes their response to the "need for human interaction, available quickly in crisis, at all hours, for potentially long periods of time, in which the focus is not basic change in the outlook or personality, but in sustaining the ability to cope with a difficult situation."

Self-Help and Professionals

The new models of service delivery to be developed in the 1980s will incorporate an increasingly strong relationship between professionals and self-help groups. An ongoing concern in the self-help movement has been the nature and extent of professionals' involvement in the functioning of the groups. Alternative self-help models of practice stress mutual aid, intimacy with others, and personal caring and involvement, while professional caregiving has been seen by some critics as more detached and distant. Independence from professional intervention has been part of the self-help rhetoric from the beginning of the movement, and concern has often been expressed about the potential hazards of involving professionals, such as their usurping control of the group.

Controversy over professional involvement with self-help groups should not obscure the fact that professionals have been involved for a long time with many self-help activities. Professional participation has ranged from following a relative hands-off policy through facilitating the establishment of groups or intervening for a limited time and then ending involvement (as in the case of many widows' groups) to maintaining an ongoing leadership role.

However, professionals typically have not been trained to perceive a need, help establish a self-help group to fill the need, and then disengage from the group. Special training is required to overcome some of these "trained incapacities." The professional could be trained to help lay individuals who want to start a self-help group or who need assistance in relating to groups that already exist. Training would reduce the danger of the professional usurping control, developing or maintaining member dependence, or professionalizing a nonprofessional movement.

The kind of assistance provided could range from instilling group development and process skills to developing public relations skills. The professional might help the group acquire needed resources and improve linkages with the formal caregiving system. Direct consultation to the group might be provided occasionally, as needed. Professional practitioners can bring to self-help groups the values of a systematic approach, particular skills, and access to resources. In return, there is much that self-help groups can bring to traditional human service practice—vitality, a new perspective, an energy and involvement too often lacking, and a potential constituency.

We do not hold the view that self-help is so precious and tenuous an arrangement that involvement with professionals will co-opt or corrupt it. At the least, there can be a complementary relationship. Sometimes, as with postsurgical groups, one can follow the other, or, as with Recovery, Inc., individuals can be involved simultaneously with both a self-help group and professional care. Beyond this, we envision the potential for a new synthesis that relates self-help approaches to professional practice and vice-versa.

Self-Help and Health

In the new health-related self-help groups, professionals may play a role that differs somewhat from their roles in other support groups. In most self-help groups, the professional generally is peripheral. However, in the health-related self-help groups, the professional may become somewhat more involved because the members recognize that relevant medical information and advice are essential. Thus, in arthritis self-help groups, members typically want professional information on the latest developments in treatment, on current research findings, and on new approaches to ameliorating the effects of the illness. They also want advice on ideas and interventions that they hear about through sources such as the media and their friends. Often the professional can play an important role in correcting misinformation.

Hypertension groups, multiple sclerosis groups, and other such groups follow a similar pattern. Sometimes group members will be interested in using approaches that have a professional technical basis such as biofeedback, meditation, and other relaxation techniques, and here again the professional may advise about these approaches and facilitate their use.

In some ways the professional's role in health groups is similar to that of the sponsor in Parents Anonymous. In the latter case the professional, usually a social worker, contributes to the understanding of the group's process and other group related issues, but in no way leads the group, or makes decisions for the group. The basic autonomy of the group prevails, but there is a special role for the professional that the group recognizes and typically requests.

The basic experiential effect of the self-help group, particularly as it functions to help members deal with problems of living related to the illness or health problem, should not be overlooked. In the case of most chronic illnesses, the basic issue is care rather than cure, and the mutual-support group can play a powerful role in helping individuals cope with their illness and with life problems related to family, job, and life style. The group can also reduce the isolation that often accompanies the illness and can provide the basic support that a large body of research has shown to be critical in reducing the effects of illness and stress.

In essence, then, this "mixed" type of self-help group maintains the two fundamental characteristics of all mutual-support groups—the group's autonomy and decision making power, and its experiential input in dealing with problems or needs—while adding professional expertise.

Converting Needs Into Resources

The human service needs of contemporary society are great, but the realities of the present are such that there will not be sufficient professional resources to meet them. In the United States, there are 32 million arthritics, 20 million people with high blood pressure, 5 million diabetics, 10 million alcoholics, 4 million drug addicts, and millions suffering from other physical and mental ailments. It is impossible for the professional caregiving system to provide all the services needed by these people. Thus the self-help strategy takes on enormous meaning. Self-help converts problems or needs into resources. Instead of seeing 32 million people with arthritis as a problem, it is possible to see them as resources and caregivers who will be active in dealing with the everyday concerns of the arthritic.

Mutual-aid groups are inexpensive, highly responsive, and accessible to the consumer, who himself is a caregiver as well as receiver. They can expand infinitely to deal with the ever-expanding need; as the need arises, so does the potential for response. What we see now is only the tip of a very large iceberg. An extensive study by the California Department of Mental Health's Office of Prevention shows that although 75% of those queried felt that getting together with persons with similar health and mental health problems was a good idea, only 9% had done so (Office, 1979). There is, it seems, a considerable market for further growth of self-help activities.

Few developments in recent years have as far-reaching potential for mental health services as does the self-help phenomenon. The mental health services network is strained by growing and more diverse demands for services at a time of limited fiscal resources. Now, too, there is increasing questioning of the nature and efficacy of traditional professional services. Self-help becomes a way to expand human services quantitatively by reaching more people, and qualitatively by making people more independent and interdependent. At the same time, self-help groups provide a personalized and energetic approach to human services.

References

Albee, G. (1981). Remarks made at conference: an ounce of prevention: reorienting mental health priorities, January 16. *Self-Help Reporter, 5,* 1-2, 1981.

Berkman, L.F. & Syms, S.L. (1979). Social networks, host resistance, and mortality: a nine-year follow-up study of Alameda County residents. *American Journal of Epidemiology, 109,* 186-204.

The Boston Women's Health Book Collective. (1971). *Our bodies, ourselves.* New York: Simon & Schuster.

Dewar, T. (1976). *Professionalized clients as self-helpers: Self-help and health: A report.* New York, City University of New York, Queens College, New Human Services Institute.

Durman, E.C. (1976). The role of self-help in service provision. *Journal of Applied Behavioral Science, 12,* 433-443.

Evans, G. (1979). *The family circle guide to self-help.* New York: Ballantine Books.

Gartner, A. & Riessman, F. (1980). *Help: A working guide to self-help groups.* New York: New Viewpoints-Vision Books.

Gordon, R.D., Kapostins, E.E. & Gordon, K.K. (1965). Factors in postpartum emotional adjustment. *Obstetrical Gynecology, 25,* 156-166.

Gordon, R.E., Edmunson, E., Bedel, J. et al. (1982). Reducing rehospitalization of state mental patients: Peer management and support. In A. Yaeger & R. Slotkin (Eds.) *Community mental health.* New York: Plenum.

Greenberg, J. (1981). Researchers find widowers die earlier than widows do. *New York Times,* July 30, p 1.

Katz, A. & Bender, E. (Eds.). (1976). *The strength in us: Self-help groups in the modern world.* New York: Franklin Watts.

Lieberman, M.A. & Borman, L.D. (1981). The impact of self-help groups on widows' mental health. *National Reporter, 4,* 2-6.

Marieskind, H.I. & Ehrenreich, B. (1975). Toward socialist medicine: the women's health movement. *Social Policy, 6,* 34-42.

Office of Prevention, California Department of Mental Health. (1979). A study of California public attitudes and beliefs regarding mental health and physical health. *Pursuit of Wellness, 1,* 1-65.

Riessman, F. (1965). The "helper therapy" principle. *Social Work, 10,* 27-32.

US Department of Health and Human Services. (1980). *Promoting health, preventing disease: Objectives for the nation.* Washington, DC: Author.

Vachon, M.L.S., Lyall, W.A.L., Rogers J, et al. (1980). A controlled study of self-help intervention for widows. *American Journal of Psychiatry, 137,* 1380-1384.

The women and mental health project: Women to women services. (1976). *Social Policy, 7,* 21-27.

Consumer-Run Housing in the Bronx

Eva Conrad

EVA CONRAD IS CO-DIRECTOR OF INCA SUPPORTED HOUSING, BRONX, NEW YORK.

THIS ARTICLE ORIGINALLY APPEARED IN *Innovations and Research*, 1993, 2(3), 53-55 AND IS REPRINTED WITH PERMISSION.

Need for Program

For several years a very exciting brew has been bubbling around Bronx Psychiatric Center stirred by a blend of "consumers," "survivors," "professionals," and "family members" that includes Celia Brown, O'Neil Daniels, Karl Gaddy, Dick Gelman, Marlene Lopez, Pauline Magnetti, Bernadette and Peter Masiello, and Peter Stastny. The first organization to emerge from this brew was INCube, Inc., lead by management wizard and roving charismatic Miriam Kravitz, Esq. INCube is a not-for-profit umbrella organization to "incubate" consumer-started and -run businesses and nonprofit service organizations. Inca Supported Housing was one of the first entities INCube birthed. Three conditions converged to hasten Inca's emergence:

1) Two pioneering, consumer-run programs that are part of Bronx Psychiatric Center prepared the way: The Department of Peer Support Services, directed by Celia Brown, is a successful, ongoing peer counseling program at Bronx Psychiatric Center. Celia has trained peer workers throughout the Bronx and started a peer worker support group. The Co-Op Center, founded by Karl Gaddy, is a consumer-operated work program with a track record of developing cooperation, goal-directed decision making, a solid work ethic, and raised aspirations among participants.

2) There is widespread desperation for housing among consumers. Open-market housing for people on SSI no longer exists in New York City, forcing people to remain in hospitals, shelters for homeless people, community residences, adult foster care or with their families longer than necessary. Living in institutional settings for years on end is not normal living. What happens to a person who has all privacy stripped away, every responsibility and choice stripped away? What happens when an unwarranted diagnosis during crisis leads to high doses of the most damaging drugs, which then act to mask the person's true condition? What happens when crises are met with physical abuse, when periods of poor judgment are occasions for exploitation, sexual and otherwise? When a person who is capable of forming friendships and doing daily activities for himself never has the opportunity to develop these capacities, what happens? The conditions in most institutions lead to environmentally-induced social disabilities. In the absence of low-cost housing, and fearing psychiatric institutions, many have chosen to live in shelters or nomadically, in constant fear, more often sleepless than not, with little access to medical care, good nutrition, clothes, showers or laundries, but surrounded by a panoply of violence and drugs. This is too high a price to pay for freedom and leads to more death and physical disability than we could possibly know. Even living at home can deny people opportunities to achieve skills and independence needed to survive when the family unit is not available.

3) The Regional Office of the New York State Office of Mental Health responded to the housing crisis by funding subsidized housing, and they were willing to fund peer-run projects, such as Inca.

Description of Program-Client Demographics

In it's first year Inca placed 17 clients in 15 apartments. Before living in Inca supported apartments, three clients were homeless; four came from long-term or crisis wards of mental hospitals, including one who came to the crisis ward from a shelter; two clients were able to leave adult foster care; three left their family's apartments. One couple was in danger of being evicted and living without adequate furniture. Another family lived in circumstances unsuitable for raising children. One client came from a community residence and married when she got her apartment. Over half of our clients have experienced a period of homelessness within the last 3 years. Right now, several Inca clients have open-market part-time or freelance jobs, several are applying for vocational training, and most presently work part time in sheltered employment. Four clients have had brief hospitalizations and returned to their apartments since their involvement with Inca. No one has given up his or her apartment.

Selection

Over 100 people wanted to be interviewed for the first 15 apartments. We used a lottery system to determine who would be interviewed: Those choosing number 1 through 15 were given an application immediately. People with higher numbers were called in order. As the year went on, some people in the lottery obtained other housing. Nonetheless, people with very high numbers were not offered applications. Those who entered our first lottery had a one in four chance of being offered an application.

Interviews were conducted by three staff members. Sometimes a second interview was scheduled.

The applicant was given a "yes" or "no" answer almost immediately. We were evaluating whether each randomly-chosen applicant had a good chance of succeeding, not looking for "ideal" candidates Criteria were: 1) 6 months during which the candidate was free to come and go in the community, which could include that part of a

hospital stay during which the applicant was free to leave the hospital grounds; 2) 6 months or freedom from substance abuse and a commitment to remaining substance free; 3) financial need and the willingness to apply for benefits when earned income was less than the SSI level; 4) the interview committee's belief that the applicant would succeed at living independently with the help available from our program, combined with that available from family, long-time friends, counselors, and rehab programs.

Inca Evolves

With the help of Celia Brown, we designed an independent living course for tenants-to-be. Experts from the community taught sessions on maintaining benefits, managing money, and meeting building owners. Celia conducted sessions on what it would be like to live on your own, and she coached Inca workers on how to lead sessions. As people began moving into apartments, we heard about the Sunday afternoon blues. People were occupied during the week, but many got a familiar empty feeling as the weekend turned into "another week." Bronx Independent Living Services, a community-based advocacy and resource center for people with any disability who live in the Bronx. offered the support group space to meet one Sunday afternoon a month. Right now, the support group sees its needs as social and practical networking and systems advocacy. We are very happy to be associated with the feisty people at Bronx Independent Living Services.

What Inca Clients Want From Inca

We call our first round of clients "Inca Pioneers." They have experienced Inca's birth and growing pains, and we count on them to help us find solutions to problems all agencies and clients face, without reverting to invasions of privacy or limitations on freedom to choose. For most people, the promise of "permanent housing in the community" meant they would have the opportunity to take their place alongside everyone else, in a decent apartment with a lease like anyone else's. Many people mentioned the need for "a quiet neighborhood." People did not want to be in a building where many people received services from a social service office on the premises. Such a planned ghetto was seen as stigmatizing. Inca clients have pleasant, well-equipped apartments in buildings throughout the North Bronx where their neighbors have no way of identifying them as "mental patients." They appreciate the opportunity to live in quiet neighborhoods near parks, good shopping, and transportation. Inca clients also wanted to live in their apartments with the same freedom as other tenants. If they wanted to live with a roommate, lover, common law spouse, their children, or other relatives, they wanted it to be considered a question of legal occupancy, not "morality" or "appropriateness." Inca clients wanted the right to reject a particular apartment without risking bureaucratic wrath, and to negotiate an apartment change with the same freedom any other tenant has. All this seems reasonable to Inca workers, and has posed no problems. Many clients wanted the opportunity to choose furnishings that reflect their personal taste and individual needs, from stores of their choice. Inca tries to oblige. We have found

Inca clients ...wanted to live in their apartments with the same freedom as other tenants. If they wanted to live with a roommate, lover, common law spouse, their children, or other relatives, they wanted it to be considered a question of legal occupancy, not "morality" or "appropriateness."

individualized shopping rather time-consuming and therefore plan to develop a buying club in which clients are issued positive-balance-only cards, recognized by stores with which Inca has established relationships.

Future Plans

Inca will provide services to an additional 15 clients who will have scattered-site apartments in the North Bronx, funded by the New York State Office of Mental Health. Inca has also submitted a proposal to the U.S. Department of Housing and Urban Development which would increase our ability to reach out to and serve homeless people. This proposal has special features designed to help victims of domestic violence and families.

Summary

Inca clients feel comfortable with counselors who have been where they have been, and experienced what they have experienced. Inca workers continue to be committed to making independent housing with respectful, non-coercive support services available to an increasingly wide range of expatients.

Comparison of Self-Help Groups for Mental Health

Linda Farris Kurtz and Adrienne Chambon

LINDA FARRIS KURTZ, PH.D., IS PROFESSOR, SCHOOL OF SOCIAL WORK, EASTERN MICHIGAN UNIVERSITY, YPSILANTI, MI.

ADRIENNE CHAMBON, PH.D., IS ASSOCIATE PROFESSOR, FACULTY OF SOCIAL WORK, THE UNIVERSITY OF TORONTO, TORONTO, ONTARIO.

THIS ARTICLE ORIGINALLY APPEARED IN *Health & Social Work*, FALL 1987, 12(4), 275-283 AND IS REPRINTED WITH PERMISSION.

This study examines and compares three international mental health self-help organizations: Recovery, Inc., Emotions Anonymous, and GROW International. The authors investigated membership characteristics, ideologies, meeting procedures, and the organizational characteristics of degree of centralization and formalization, roles of professionals, and sources of funding. The findings suggest differences in what types of clients benefit from participation in each of the three organizations, and counter criticisms of self-help groups.

Social workers always have played a significant role in the development and use of mutual-help groups in all fields of practice (Whittaker, 1983; Shulman, 1983). However, there is little evidence that social workers in the psychiatric field make optimal use of such groups. Mental health organizations, for example, do not promote self-help referrals with the same commitment as those in the alcoholism field. (Kurtz, 1984). Differences in referral patterns probably stem from the diverse treatment approaches to alcoholism and mental illness that date back to the early part of the twentieth century. Current needs for community care, however, have resulted in increased interest in self-help for psychiatric clients; however, professionals often lack the information about self-help approaches necessary to make appropriate referrals (Black & Drachman, 1985; Toseland & Hacker, 1895). This article provides some of that information by comparing three associations: Recovery, Inc., Emotions Anonymous (EA), and GROW International.

In 1978, the *Report of the President's Commission on Mental Health* emphasized the importance of improving community supports for the mentally ill, and thus contributed to the growing enthusiasm for self-help groups as a resource for former mental patients and others with chronic health problems (President's Commission on Mental Health, 1978). Professionals' early efforts to establish and evaluate mutual helping systems for mental patients have shown that participation in such groups reduces hospital stays and rehospitalization (Fairweather et al., 1984; Grosz, 1973). Studies of mental patients in community care indicate that aftercare and support programs are effective, but must be maintained; relapse occurs when support is withdrawn (Test, 1981). Self-help groups are a valuable resource because they are ongoing, and are relatively low-cost to both member and society.

Professionals are believed to harbor overly cautious or negative attitudes toward self-help groups, but repeated surveys of professionals have found that this is not so. (Levy, 1978; Todres, 1982; Toseland & Hacker, 1985; Black & Drachman, 1985; Kurtz, 1985; and Hermalin et al., 1979). While a minority of professionals hold negative attitudes, they are not prevalent enough to explain underutilization of self-help groups. Lack of information has been found to be the most important factor in low referrals to self-help groups, and, in fact, may contribute to negative attitudes as well as to underutilization (Black & Drachman, 1985; Hermalin et al., 1979; Todres, 1982; and Toseland & Hacker, 1985).

The authors surveyed 120 psychiatric social workers in 24 agencies about their use of, attitudes toward, and experiences with self-help groups, in general, and the three groups reported on here in particular (Kurtz, Mann, & Chambon, 1987). Eighty-four percent of the social workers surveyed had made referrals to a wide range of groups, the largest percentage (67%) to alcoholism groups. Moreover, 72% held positive attitudes toward self help, but only 66 (56%) had referred to the three groups reported on here. The majority (73%) of the 44 who had not referred to self-help groups reported that they did not make such referrals because they were unaware of the organizations or did not know enough about them to make a referral. The finding is salient especially in view of the fact that the social workers surveyed were chosen because of their agencies' close proximity to the meeting places of one or more self-help association. The preliminary data suggest that social workers are more reluctant to refer to mental health-oriented self-help groups than to more well-known groups, such as Alcoholics Anonymous (AA).

Thus, mental health workers need more information about self-help groups that address mental health needs. While it is the associations' responsibility to make their goals and activities more accessible and understandable to professionals, researchers within the professions should make independent assessments of the associations to enable mental health workers to make appropriate referrals. Such assessments can inform professionals about the role self-help groups can play in both prevention and intervention within the broader network of community services to the mentally ill. The authors focused on the three largest independent, international associations that together serve several thousand individuals who have diverse kinds of mental health problems.

Methods

The authors relied on three qualitative data collection methods for the investigation: 1) observation of and participation in meetings of the three organizations' groups in the Chicago area; 2) interviews of group leaders, staff, and members; and 3) a reading of the groups' literature. The authors observed at least two of each associations' local groups (for a total of eight groups) and conducted eight interviews to complement the study of organizational literature. The observations and interviews revealed how members use the ideas expressed in the literature and also presented a concrete picture of membership characteristics. The researchers, however, did not attempt to observe or to interview representative samples of all Chicago area groups and members, and thus the findings cannot be generalized to all affiliated groups in Chicago or elsewhere.

History and Overview

Psychiatrist Abraham Low founded Recovery, Inc., the oldest and largest of the three organizations, in Chicago in 1937 for his patients, most of whom had been hospitalized. The organization today admits to meetings any person who identifies him or herself as "nervous" or as a former mental patient, and comprises 922 groups in six countries. The vast majority of Recovery members are referred by professionals, particularly psychiatrists, psychologists, and general medical practitioners (*Directory of Group Meeting Information,* 1978). Only 18% of the total membership is referred by social service agencies.

Emotions Anonymous (EA) was begun in St. Paul, Minnesota, in 1971 by individuals who, even though they had no problems with alcohol, had attended AA meetings *(Emotions Anonymous,* 1973). The group eventually split from AA and adopted AA's Twelve Steps and Twelve Traditions. EA is open to anyone who wants to achieve emotional well-being, and has more than 800 groups in 14 countries (Letter from EA headquarters, 1984). Although EA has no survey data on its membership, it was the researchers' impression that fewer EA members are referred by professionals than are Recovery members. Members reported hearing about the group from other members, from members of other Twelve Step Programs (such as AA or Overeaters Anonymous), or having read about EA meetings in church bulletins or community newspapers.

GROW was founded in Sydney, Australia, in 1957 by a Roman Catholic priest, Father Cornelius Keogh, and other anonymous members who had attended AA meetings. GROW has spread to seven countries and reports about 600 affiliated groups (Personal communication from C. Keough, March 1985). Its presence in the United States is confined largely to Illinois, where there are about 100 groups. GROW is open to anyone who wants to join; however, it specifically targets hospital patients and those recently hospitalized. GROW has received state funds from the Department of Mental Health to conduct outreach and recruitment efforts and it is the only one of the three organizations that employs field workers to organize groups. Professionals are a major source of new members for GROW: referrals to GROW result from field staff efforts to recruit members from inpatient settings and from contacts with social agencies.

Membership Characteristics

Demographic characteristics vary from group to group within each organization.

The authors' observations generally support earlier research on membership characteristics of Recovery and GROW (Grosz, 1985; Rappaport et al., 1985). The majority of Recovery's and EA's members are white, female, and middle class. Twenty-two of Recovery's 36 Chicago-area groups, are located in the suburbs. Three of EA's 20 local groups meet in the inner city and 17 in the suburbs. GROW's members in Chicago are less affluent and more evenly divided between men and women. Moreover, GROW recently has organized groups in Chicago's black neighborhoods. At the time of the study, all of GROW's seven groups in Chicago were located in the inner city and one nearby suburb.

The organizations address similar problems. Diagnostic labels are not used, nor is anyone rejected because of the nature of identified problems. Members reveal histories of every kind of mental health difficulty, including depression, schizophrenic episodes, bi-polar mood disorders, anxieties, and phobias. Many members report periods of inpatient psychiatric care. Because GROW targets state hospital patients for membership, its participants appear to have more serious difficulties with community adjustment and more recent inpatient experience. The organizations do not address directly the problems of family members of the participants.

Goals and Beliefs

Recovery members' goals are to control symptoms and tension arising from angry and fearful "temper" and to achieve "averageness." Founder Low defined *temper* as a set of defeatist thoughts that produce tension, which in turn leads to symptomatic behavior. Defeatist thoughts are reinforced by use of the "symptomatic idiom" and "temperamental lingo" (Low, 1978, p. 17–20). Individuals who experience angry temper tell themselves that wrongs have

been done to them, thus provoking indignation, impatience, and similar reactions.
When experiencing fearful temper, the individuals think they may do wrong, which in
turn results in feelings such as fear, shame,
and inadequacy. Temper reinforces or inten-
sifies symptoms and a temperamental reaction follows. To accept oneself as average is
to avoid the illusion of exceptionality and
to embrace reality.

The Recovery method is called "will
training." Members train the will to replace
cognitive and emotional habits. Members
also use Recovery language to resist self-
diagnosis and prognosis, and thus stop sabotaging the physician's authority. The
Recovery language replaces the symptomatic idiom with a more precise vocabulary
that accurately describes the situation. For
example, an event may be termed (and
therefore thought to be) unbearable, when
it simply is uncomfortable. To change
behavior, Recovery members are urged to
"move the muscles." Moving the muscles to
do what one believes is impossible can be
undertaken in small steps or "part acts"
rather than faced as one overwhelming task.
The method is cognitive and behavioral; it
discourages responses based on feeling, as
exemplified in the Recovery slogan "feelings
are not facts." Recovery meetings focus on
the simple, daily reactions that can have disastrous results. By changing reactions and
tracing them to their temperamental source,
participants gradually begin to change the
defeatist beliefs that seem to govern a nervous person's life (Low, 1978).

EA members' goals are serenity and
peace of mind. EA views emotional ill
health as a chronic and progressive physical, mental, and spiritual illness. Just as an
alcoholic "hits bottom" by chronic inebria-
tion, the emotional sufferer allows negative
aspects of life to dominate until minor
problems become complete despair. The
person experiencing his or her emotional
bottom achieves serenity by following the

Twelve Steps, beginning with admission
that one is powerless and that life has
become unmanageable. EA members come
to believe that there is a higher power and
become willing to accept help. In the fourth
step, the member takes a personal inventory
in which both positive and negative attributes are listed. The member shares with
another person and, when ready, asks God
to remove the shortcomings on the list.
Next, members list those to whom they owe
amends for harm done and make direct
amends wherever possible. The last three
steps suggest continuing to take inventory,
meditating and praying for knowledge of
God's will, and carrying the EA message to
others (Emotions, Anonymous, 1973).

EA's concept of will differs from that of
Recovery. EA members reflect the sentiment
expressed in AA that troubles originate from
"self will run riot" (Alcoholics Anonymous,
1976; Emotions, Anonymous, 1973).

EA members achieve serenity, in part, by
abandoning futile attempts to force their
will on others and to change themselves
without help from a higher power. In EA,
surrender to a higher power does not mean
complete passivity. Instead, such surrender
reflects an acceptance of reality as it exists
and a cessation of efforts to "play God."

GROW's objective is to assist members
to attain mental, social, and spiritual maturity. GROW's roots in AA are apparent in
GROW's similarity to EA. Some years after
its beginning, GROW became aware of
Recovery and incorporated Recovery methods into its program. GROW members are
told that emotional illness comes about in
"The Twelve Stages of Decline," which
begin with self-centeredness. When one is
unable to separate reality from fiction, one
has "hit bottom" in GROW terms.
GROW's Twelve Steps of Personal Growth
blend AA and Recovery methods. Steps 1
through 5 and 12 are similar to those of
EA. Steps 6 through 11 reflect Recovery
principles. For example, step 9 states "We

trained our wills to govern our feelings." Help comes to members through self-activation, mutual help, and surrender to God: GROW thus has combined the concepts of will found in the other two programs. In response to irrationality, one trains the will to govern feelings. In response to self-centeredness, one "surrenders to the healing power of God" (Grow, 1982, p. 5).

Meetings

Recovery meetings are based on panel presentations. After a reading from Low's (1978) book, *Mental Health Through Will Training*, or listening to one of several audiotapes made before his death, three or four volunteers form a panel. Panel members, following the prescribed format, tell of events in their lives during which the method helped them. Each presentation incorporates four stages: 1) describe the event, 2) describe the symptoms that began as a result of the event, 3) describe how the method was used, and 4) describe what used to happen in similar situations before using the method. After each presentation, participants give the presenter feedback. At the end of the meeting, new members, visitors, and others may ask questions.

Each group holds meetings once a week and members may attend more than one group. Most of those observed in meetings were experienced members, although one or two newcomers were observed in most meetings the researchers attended. Members appear to attend at least weekly. Between-meeting support primarily consists of 5-minute phone calls from one member to another. Low encouraged Recovery members to limit contacts between meetings to 5 minutes, during which time a member reminds the caller of the Recovery principles needed to handle the situation.

EA members take turns reading from the group's literature at the start of each meeting. Next, one member introduces a step for consideration by telling how he or she has worked on or experienced that principle in daily life, termed "telling one's story." The format for telling one's story resembles the format in Recovery, except that EA members do not differentiate feelings, thoughts, and physical responses. First the speaker tells what happened during the event that triggered the willingness to change and to enter the EA program. Next, the speaker tells how life was before entering EA and finally, what it is like now. Following the first speaker, other members take turns telling shorter versions of their experiences. The meeting ends with a closing statement and also a prayer.

EA, like AA, allows each group autonomy in determining how meetings should be structured. Groups observed for this study followed the above format, which is suggested by the EA brochure "Why Is This a Step Meeting?" (Emotions Anonymous, undated). However, not all groups follow this pattern. A group may be more loosely structured and discuss a topic other than one of the Twelve Steps and may allow more interaction during the discussion. In the meetings observed, members took turns with no exchanges following presentations.

The preliminary data suggest that social workers are more reluctant to refer to mental health-oriented self-help groups than to more well-known groups, such as Alcoholics Anonymous.

Interaction took place only during the short periods before and after meeting and during a 15-minute break.

Each EA group met once a week and, as in Recovery, members can and do attend more than one group each week. Members choose a sponsor whom they telephone or meet with individually between meetings. In addition, members are provided with telephone numbers of other members whom they may call outside of group meetings. Groups arrange socials occasionally or, more frequently, all group members in the metropolitan area are invited to a retreat for 1or 2 days. Members also are invited to attend retreats in other parts of the United States.

EA members' utilization of the association can be illustrated best by one group, which was observed weekly for more than 7 months. During this time, approximately 50 individuals attend at least one meeting; of those, 30 (60%) attended more than once, and 19 (38%) attended regularly during the 7 months.

GROW meetings follow a prescribed sequence: the meetings begin with a reading of the GROW Memento followed by "group interaction." During group interaction, members report progress, tell problems, and give personal testimony to their recovery in GROW. Participants then read GROW literature out loud and members then are given practical tasks and quizzed on their understanding of the GROW program. The meeting ends with an evaluation of the meeting and a closing prayer.

GROW meetings also are held weekly and members may attend more than one meeting each week. In addition to meetings, field staff and organizers for GROW organize social activities between meetings in an effort to provide a supportive community to members. GROW membership attendance patterns are similar to those described for EA: about one third of those who attend one meeting of GROW do not return, one third attend several meetings before dropping out, and one third attend regularly over a lengthy period (Rappaport, Seidman, & Toro, 1986).

Organizational Structure and Funding

Key structural aspects of the organizations include group size, degree of formalization of leadership roles, and degree of centralization of administrative decisions. Funding and the role of professionals also will be discussed. The three organizations differ considerably on all dimensions except professionalism.

Group size is limited in Recovery and in GROW but not in EA. Recovery literature states that there should be a maximum of 30 members in each group; the groups observed ranged from fewer than 5 to more than 30 members present. GROW groups are limited to 15 members, and most observed were smaller than 15. EA has no meeting or group size limit; in practice, EA meetings range anywhere from 5 to 30 participants.

In all three organizations, with some exception in GROW, group leadership is limited to members. In Recovery, group leaders must receive training designed by national headquarters before being eligible for leadership. The leadership role is least formalized in EA, where any participant may direct a meeting. The facilitator role rotates so that one person seldom retains the position, however, there is no regulation that prevents a group from having a permanent leader. GROW is the only one of the three that hires and pays members to act as group leader. GROW employees in the United States are fieldworkers who organize new groups and assist in developing group leadership. Until such leadership has matured, the fieldworkers lead the newly-formed groups. GROW also allows professionals to serve as temporary leaders in rare instances when a member-leader is not available.

The three self-help associations differ in the extent to which they allow group autonomy. Recovery's organizational control is the most centralized. Recovery groups are led by a member who has received training and follows a printed meeting format. EA groups follow the tradition of autonomy established by AA: "Each group should be autonomous except in matters affecting other groups or EA as a whole" (Emotions Anonymous, undated, p. 243). Further, EA has no prescribed leader training or meeting format. EA administrative staff and Board of Trustees offer guidance but do not control group activities. In the United States, GROW's paid field workers maintain control of affiliated groups by organizing new groups, training new leaders, and serving as group leaders in the groups' early stages.

The organizations accept funds from nonmembers at the risk of losing autonomy. Nevertheless, GROW has accepted government funds and private grants. Recovery accepts small grants and outside donations. EA, following the AA tradition, accepts nothing but small donations from members and payment for literature. Recovery and GROW also collect small donations from members. Recovery requests that members pay dues, but does not require them to do so. None of the organizations charges fees for attendance at group meetings.

Philosophically and structurally, professionals have no formal role in any of the three organizations. Because GROW has an arrangement with the Illinois Department of Mental Health, the relationship with mental health workers in the state's mental health facilities is closer than are those between professionals and the other two organizations. For example, GROW workers form groups in state hospitals for patients before discharge. Recovery maintains close informal ties with professionals who, because of experience with and commitment to the method, frequently refer to the organization. EA has the fewest associations with professionals.

Interviews with members and observation of groups show little evidence of antagonism toward professionals within any of the three organizations. Many, if not most, of the members had received or are receiving professional therapy. Recovery is the only organization that holds an official position on psychiatry: Low (1978) instructed that patients must not question the recommendations and opinions of their physicians: to do so is to exhibit temper and to sabotage treatments. GROW leaders, however, resist the medical treatment model and the practices of hospitalization and drug therapy. Although they do not criticize specific professionals, they do believe that medical practices improperly ignore the spiritual aspect of recovery and rely too heavily on chemical treatments. GROW leaders also believe that some professionals encourage clients to express their feelings excessively in treatment sessions. (Personal communication from C. Keough, March 1985).

Philosophically and structurally, professionals have no formal role in any of the three organizations.

Comparative Analysis

The three organizations are similar in a number of ways. None has specific membership qualifications; all maintain structured meeting formats that convey clear ideologies for recovery and growth. All three programs employ personal narratives that demonstrate how to use the program and encourage identification with successful efforts. None of the organizations believes in including professional group facilitators, although GROW makes some exceptions to this rule. All of the associations allow members to attend more than one group, which gives members additional support if needed. All develop informal support networks through phone calls and sponsorship of various kinds.

The three organizations also differ in significant ways. GROW's members are on average less affluent and more disturbed. EA and GROW emphasize spiritual growth; Recovery is completely secular. Recovery's method emphasizes more active efforts to control one's situation, EA encourages surrender of control, and GROW combines the two perspectives. During meetings, Recovery and GROW provide more opportunities for feedback among members. Organizational structures differ in that Recovery centralizes and formalizes policy for all affiliated groups, GROW maintains slightly looser control of affiliates, and EA has no centralized policy for group leadership and exactly how the meeting process must be structured. Recovery and GROW identify and train group leaders; EA does not. GROW accepts government funds, Recovery accepts small grants and donations from external sources, and EA only accepts donations from members. GROW allows professionals to take an active role in group development and to act as temporary leaders; professionals do not have roles in meetings of the other two groups. GROW leaders are more critical of professional methods than are Recovery and EA members.

The observations address some of the criticisms of self-help groups occasionally expressed by professionals. Social work practitioners and authors have criticized self-help groups for being too rigid or too unstructured, being hostile to professionals, encouraging inappropriate dependency,

reinforcing stigmatized identities, and failing to communicate with professionals (Wechsler, 1960). The authors observed that the three organizations provide structure that avoids unproductive interaction and allows for individual needs and differences. Taking into account the lack of professional expertise, the high attendance turnover, and the large size of some groups, the structured approaches appear highly effective. Little hostility was expressed toward professionals in or outside of meetings; GROW leaders' criticism of professionals is targeted to specific professional practices and was not discussed in meetings. The groups do allow members to depend on them for support and acceptance, but also encourage members to take independent action such as reading literature, writing personal inventories, and helping others. The dependency did not appear to be inappropriate, nor was it as hierarchial as is dependency on a professional. Association with others in similar situations may encourage the acquisition of stigmatized identities, and this possibility requires further study. The degree of acquisition of stigmatized identities clearly varies from group to group. Unlike groups that directly engage in public education, these three focus on assisting members to redefine identities in ways that are tolerable and that provide direction for change. For more severely ill members, stigma already has been acquired through professional labels and the member's own deviance from social norms. The group can reduce the shame of those by transforming them into qualifications for membership, and once overcome, forming the basis on which to help others.

Lack of communication with professionals is perhaps the most salient criticism, because increased information is the most important factor in promoting use of self-help groups. All of the organizations respond to requests for information by selling literature or speaking before professional groups. GROW is most effective in this area because it has government funds to promote its organization. Because they are low budget, volunteer-run associations, Recovery and EA do not have adequate resources to make the outreach efforts professionals may want. Thus, professionals may need to initiate such communications.

A Viable Resource

Implications for practice emerge based on these observations. Referrals to the three organizations should be based on recognition of their differing goals and beliefs. Recovery encourages those who feel helpless to control feelings that dominate behavior and to take positive action. EA's philosophy of turning control over to a higher power should assist those who are prone to chronic worry, tension, and compulsive but ineffective efforts at control. Individuals who respond to a spiritual or religious approach will find that philosophy in EA and in GROW. Although nonreligious people are welcome in EA and GROW, they may be more comfortable in the secular atmosphere of Recovery. For individuals who need structure and want to depend on a leader, Recovery and GROW are more appropriate. Although GROW targets the least advantaged individuals, its complex blend of both AA and Recovery principles may make it more difficult to learn and to apply. On the other hand, less privileged and less emotionally stable people may find themselves more accepted and supported in GROW groups. All three associations provided structured, cognitively-based programs to support individual change, support for coping with life problems, and monitored interactions between group members.

Finally, further research should be conducted on self-help groups for psychiatric clients. A more representative sample of groups should be studied to ascertain membership characteristics, group processes, and attitudes toward professionals.

Outcome of membership in the three organizations could be compared by random referrals to the three organizations and follow-up inquiries about the experience. Such studies might determine more precisely which kinds of people benefit most from which organization, and how well the groups actually inculcate their beliefs about emotional recovery.

The authors found both in their own research and in reviewing the literature that most social workers have positive attitudes toward self-help methods and that social workers only need more information about, and more communication with, self-help organizations. Kurtz, Mann, & Chambon, 1987). The findings suggest that the three organizations are viable resources for a large percentage of those who attend their meetings. The organizations have long histories of independent and consistent group services in most large metropolitan areas and in some smaller communities. More detailed information should make it possible for social workers to decide who should be referred, to support their referrals with information to the client, and to differentiate between groups. In regions of the country where choices between groups are not possible, information about these international organizations may prompt social workers to help groups get started in new locations.[1] Appropriate referrals and assistance in expanding self-help networks will bring additional community support services to people who need them.

---

[1] Contact Recovery, Inc. at 802 N. Dearborn, Chicago, IL 60610; Emotions Anonymous at Box 4245, St. Paul, MN 55104; GROW at 403 W. Springfield Avenue, Champaign, IL 61820.

References

Alcoholics Anonymous. (1976). *The Story of how many thousands of men and women have recovered from alcoholism, Third Edition*. New York: A.A. World Services.

Black, R.B. & Drachman, D. (1985). Hospital social workers and self-help groups. *Health and Social Work, 10* (Spring), 95- 112.

Recovery, Inc. (1985). *1985 Directory of Group Meeting Information*. Chicago, IL: Author.

Edmunson, E.D., Bedell, J.R. & Gordon, R.E. (1984). The Community network development project: Bridging the gap between professional, aftercare and self-help. In A. Gartner and F. Riessman, (Eds.), *The Self-help revolution*, pp. 184–195, New York: Human Sciences Press

Emotions Anonymous. (1973). St. Paul, MN: Emotions Anonymous International.

Emotions Anonymous. (Undated). *Why Is This a Step Meeting?* St. Paul, MN: Emotions Anonymous International.

Fairweather, G.W. et al. (1969). *Community life for the mentally ill: An alternative to institutional care*. Chicago: Aldine Publishing Co.

Grosz, H. (1973). *Recovery, Inc.: A Survey*. Chicago, IL: Recovery, Inc.

GROW. (1992). *The program of health to maturity*. Sydney: Author.

Hermalin, J., et al. (1979). Enhancing primary prevention: The marriage of self-help groups and formal health care delivery systems. *Journal of Clinical Child Psychology, 8* (Summer), 125-129.

Kurtz, L.F. (1984). Linking treatment centers with alcoholics anonymous. *Social Work in Health Care, 9* (Summer), 85-94.

Kurtz, L.F. (1985). Cooperation and rivalry between helping professionals and members of AA. *Health and Social Work, 10* (Spring), 104- 112

Kurtz, L.F., Mann, K.B. & Chambon, A. Linking between social workers and mental health mutual-aid groups. *Social Work in Health Care, 13* (Fall), 69-78.

Levy, L. (1978). Self-help groups viewed by mental health professionals: A survey and comments. *American Journal of Community Psychology, 6* (July), 305-313.

Low, A. (1978). *Mental health through will training* (reprint), Winnetka, IL: Willett Publishing Co., 17-20.

Lurie, A. & Shulman, L. (1983). The professional connection with self-help groups in health care settings. *Social Work in Health Care, 8* (Summer), 69-77.

President's Commission on Mental Health. (1978). *Report of the Task Panel on Community Support Systems, Vol. 11* (Washington, D.C.: U.S. Government Printing Office).

Raiff, N.R. (1978). *Recovery, Inc.: A study of a self-help organization in mental health*. p. 45. Unpublished PhD dissertation, University of Pittsburgh. Available on microfilm (#7917492; Ann Arbor, Mich.: University Microfilms International, 1979).

Rappaport, J. et al. (1985). Finishing the unfinished business: Collaborative research with a mutual help organization. *Social Policy, 15* (Winter), 12-24.

Rappaport, J., Seidman, E. & Toro, P.A. (1986). *Self-help and serious psychopathology*. (Unpublished report to the National Institute of Mental Health). (Photocopied.)

Test, M.A. (1981). Effective community treatment of the chronically mentally ill: What is necessary? *Journal of Social Issues, 37* (Summer), 71-86.

Todres, R. (1982). Professional attitudes, awareness and use of self-help groups. *Prevention in Human Services, I* (Spring), 91-98

Toseland, R.W. & Hacker, L. (1985). Social workers' use of self-help groups as a resource for clients. *Social Work, 30* (May-June), 232-239.

Wechsler. (1960). The self-help organization in the mental health field: Recovery, Inc., a case study. *Journal of Nervous and Mental Disease, 130* (April), 297-314.

Whittaker, J.K. (1983). Mutual helping in human service practice. In J.K. Whittaker and J. Garbarino, *Social support networks: Informal helping in the human services*, pp. 29-67, Hawthorne, NY: Aldine Publishing.

SELF-HELP PROGRAMS: A DESCRIPTION OF THEIR CHARACTERISTICS AND THEIR MEMBERS

Judi Chamberlin, E. Sally Rogers, and Marsha Langer Ellison

JUDI CHAMBERLIN IS A PROJECT DIRECTOR AT THE CENTER FOR PSYCHIATRIC REHABILITATION, BOSTON UNIVERSITY.

E. SALLY ROGERS, SC.D., IS DIRECTOR OF RESEARCH AT THE CENTER FOR PSYCHIATRIC REHABILITATION AND RESEARCH ASSOCIATE PROFESSOR, DEPARTMENT OF REHABILITATION COUNSELING, BOSTON UNIVERSITY.

MARSHA LANGER ELLISON, PH.D., IS A RESEARCH ASSOCIATE AT THE CENTER FOR PSYCHIATRIC REHABILITATION, BOSTON UNIVERSITY.

THIS ARTICLE ORIGINALLY APPEARED IN THE *Psychiatric Rehabilitation Journal,* 1996, 19(3), 33-42 AND IS REPRINTED WITH PERMISSION.

User-run programs have proliferated in the past 10 years, yet there are few empirically-based studies about them. A survey of self-help programs was undertaken to increase our understanding about the users of such programs, their demographics, and their perceptions of how such programs have affected the quality of their lives. Respondents were also asked about their satisfaction with user-run programs. The study was conducted using a Participatory Action Research paradigm (Whyte, 1991), using an advisory committee of persons who have used such programs, and with the intention of developing an evaluation methodology that could be replicated in future studies of user-run programs. Despite limitations in representativeness, these survey results are useful in understanding the perceptions of self-help members. Results of the survey and the methodology are discussed.

Introduction

The value of self-help groups is being discussed with increasing frequency, and as more client-run programs are funded by state, local, and national mental health authorities, it becomes increasingly more important to acquire reliable information about them. While some descriptive information about user-run programs does exist (Chamberlin, Rogers, & Sneed, 1991; Chester, 1991; Emerick, 1988; Kaufman, Freund & Wilson, 1989; Mowbray, Chamberlain, Jennings, & Reed, 1988; Mowbray, Wellwood, & Chamberlain, 1988; Roberts, Salem, Stein, & Zimmerman, 1985; Zinman, 1982; Zinman, Harp, & Budd, 1987), there are few studies examining the effect of such programs. One exception is the work of Rappaport and his colleagues who have studied self and mutual help organizations rather extensively, including both descriptive and theoretical examinations (e.g., Salem, Seidman, & Rappaport, 1988; McFadden, Seidman & Rappaport, 1992) and empirical studies (e.g., Toro, Reischl, Zimmerman, & Rappaport, 1988; Roberts, Luke, Rappaport, Seidman, et al., 1991). Preliminary data indicate that, compared with recent self-help members, longer-term members had "larger social networks, a higher rate of current employment, and lower levels of psychopathology" (Rappaport, et al., 1985, p. 18).

Another recent study was conducted by Segal, Silverman, and Temkin (1995) at two self-help agencies in California. These authors found that the two agencies surveyed served a largely male, African American and homeless population, many of whom had substance abuse problems. These members were primarily interested in obtaining food, shelter, clothing, or other practical necessities, rather than counseling or other traditional mental health services.

Some consumers involved in the provision of self-help services have recognized both the need for more evaluation studies of self-help programs and the unique problems such evaluation poses (Rogers, 1988; Zinman, 1988). For example, as Zinman (1988) has asserted, in order to study self-help groups, members must be involved in the development of the evaluation methodology, with professionals serving as technical experts or consultants. Without this involvement many consumers and programs will simply refuse to be studied, in part because of anti-professional sentiment, as documented by Emerick (1990). Hatfield also notes that evaluation might differ if implemented by consumers, because the questions themselves may differ from what professionals would ask (1988). Furthermore, self-help programs for persons with mental illness are informal organizations with fluid membership, much like other self-help programs such as Alcoholics Anonymous. These programs pose special methodological problems for survey research and in terms of obtaining representative samples.

Because there are few studies examining self-help programs, it is difficult to draw conclusions about the effect such programs have on members' lives, or to discuss the relative effectiveness of traditional mental health services vis-à-vis self-help programs. This study was an innovative step designed to develop evaluation methods by users of such programs and to acquire empirically-based data on the effect of user-run programs as perceived by members. Though consumer or user-run programs represent a small portion of the universe of self-help programs, our focus was on user-run programs because we wanted to study in particular those programs that are directed by consumers and whose activities are self-determined.

Methodology

This study was designed with the assistance of a consumer research advisory board, under the direction of the senior author. At the onset of the project, the senior author selected ten individuals whom she believed could represent the diverse opinions of the self-help movement nationally. Three research planning meetings were held with this research advisory board to design and plan the study and to develop survey questions. The use of a research advisory committee such as this is encouraged by proponents of Participatory Action Research (Whyte, 1991; Rogers & Palmer-Erbs, 1994), who assert that for evaluation to be meaningful and credible, constituents of that research must be involved.

Subjects

The Research Advisory Board decided to sample members of six self-help programs in various parts of the country. Six programs were chosen primarily because of the limited fiscal resources of the study. With the assistance of the Research Advisory Board, a list of potential self-help programs nationally was developed and letters were sent to these programs requesting their participation. From that initial recruitment letter, 64 programs expressed interest and met the criteria of being a consumer-run program, as defined by the Research Advisory Board.[1] For example, programs had to be run by consumers who had control of their own budget, staff, and activities.

The advisory board reviewed all 64 programs in the final group during the summer of 1991 and decided to select programs that afforded diversity in geography, racial and ethnic makeup, and program type. Because many advisory board members were familiar with the various programs, they had available a great deal of information about the programs under consideration. After several hours of discussion, six programs were selected that were thought to represent the broad scope of consumer run self-help programs. The six self-help programs were in the following states: New Hampshire, New Jersey, Indiana, Arkansas, Washington, and California. The senior author visited all but one site to discuss the project further, to discuss the logistics of project implementation, to meet members, and to secure final agreement for participation.

Overall, respondents indicated that being involved in self-help had a salutary effect on their quality of life, including their general life satisfaction.

Advisory Board decided to avoid standardized, psychological instruments in favor of survey questions that were potentially less threatening to members. All ratings of quality of life, self-esteem, social supports, and demographics were based upon self-report. A separate survey instrument was developed to obtain descriptive information about the programs themselves. This nine-page questionnaire described the mission, funding, structure, activities, and physical facilities of the program. Additional questions were used to verify that the program met the definition of a self-help organization described earlier.

Instrumentation

Instruments for the study were also developed in conjunction with the advisory board. Instruments were developed to collect information about the members' demographics, including the length of time they had been involved in self-help programs; their perceived quality of life, self-esteem, and social supports since participating in self-help; and their satisfaction with their current program. Standard guidelines for developing paper and pencil survey instruments were followed (Dillman, 1978; Fink & Kosecoff, 1985).

Questions were developed using concepts from existing scales (e.g. quality of life and self-esteem); however, the Research

The final instruments were pilot tested during the winter of 1991 with a local self-help program that was not scheduled to participate in the study to insure that the instruments were unambiguous and formatted in an easy-to-use manner.[2]

Survey Implementation

Data collection with the six selected programs began in March 1992 and concluded in August 1992. Detailed written instructions about member recruitment and data collection were provided to each site liaison requesting that they attempt to get as many members as possible to complete the survey.

---

[1]Self-help programs were defined as having to meet the following criteria: 1) Groups are local and grass roots (although they may be affiliated regionally, statewide, or nationally). 2) The group controls its own budget, staffing, and governing body. 3) The group's philosophy is developed by the group members and not imposed from outside. 4) Membership and participation are voluntary. 5) The group is flexible and doesn't have a set program that everyone must follow. 6) Membership is open to past or present "mental patients" (in-patients or out-patients) and usually to people who consider themselves "at risk." Members self-define themselves as mental health clients (or whatever term they may use, e.g., ex-patient, consumer, survivor, etc.). 7) The group is participatory. 8)The group focuses on a people-to-people non-clinical approach. Note: This definition was made for the purposes of the project only, and may not describe all self-help groups.

[2] Copies of the instruments are available from the senior author.

Each site was receiving a small stipend for participation ($250) and liaisons were advised to inform members that their program would benefit as a result of their participation in the survey.

The senior author had frequent contact with the sites to monitor the data collection. A total of 271 usable questionnaires (California, n = 111; New Jersey, n = 77; Arkansas, n = 36; Indiana, n = 21; Washington, n =14; New Hampshire, n = 12) were returned. Response rates were calculated using each site's number of active members; they ranged from a low of 10% in New Jersey to a high of 55% in Arkansas. However, no attempt was made to have each site monitor refusals (or the reasons for members' refusal) nor is it possible to calculate what the exact number of active users is, given the way that self-help programs operate. Therefore a more precise response rate cannot be calculated.

Results

Program Description
Descriptive data from each of the self-help programs were synthesized to gain an understanding of the operation of the self-help programs participating in this study.

Mission, funding, and staffing. As part of the survey, we asked each site liaison to provide us with information about the program's mission statement and how that mission statement was developed. All programs reported that their mission statement was developed solely by members of their organization, without collaboration with professionals or input from funding bodies. Keywords in the mission statements were content analyzed, and, not surprisingly, the programs seek to: promote empowerment and independence among members, promote choice and self-determination, provide peer support, provide education, information, advocacy, and assistance to access services. Other mission statements referred to improving the quality of life of members, eliminating stigma, and promoting respect for persons with mental illness.

Several of the programs have received support from the National Institute of Mental Health, the Center for Mental Health Services, their state department of mental health, or their office of vocational rehabilitation. County health or government boards were the source of support for two programs, and charitable foundations provided support for several programs as well. One program mentioned the receipt of funds from the U. S. Department of Housing and Urban Development. Total operating budgets range from a low of $47,000 per year, to a high of $2.9 million per year. Programs reported a fair amount of autonomy in how they expend their operating funds.

Programs were asked about their staffing patterns: the number of full-time equivalent staff ranged from a low of 1.5 to a high of 12.5. Several programs reported having a significant contingent of volunteers to supplement their paid staff. The most common job titles reported by the programs were: advocates, peer support persons, resource coordinators, employment and education specialists, and residential support persons. Programs also report having administrative, managerial, and business support staff (i.e., clerical workers, managers and directors, bookkeepers, and the like).

Activities. Table 1 contains a checklist of services that each program provides. Programs were asked to indicate whether each activity was an official and routine service of their organization. The only service provided by all programs participating in this study was assistance with legal problems. Assistance with employment and general advocacy efforts were next most common. Social/recreational services and temporary shelter were provided by only half the responding programs. The "other activities" provided by programs included

TABLE 1.
TYPE OF ACTIVITIES AND SERVICES PROVIDED BY PROGRAMS

Type of Activities and Services	% of Programs Providing Services
Social/Recreational Activities	50%
Protection or Advocacy for Individual Members	66%
Advocacy Efforts on Behalf of all Persons with Psychiatric Disabilities	83%
Assistance with Housing	66%
Assistance with Legal Problems	100%
Assistance with Employment	83%
Transportation	50%
Food Assistance	66%
Temporary Shelter	50%
Assistance with Activities of Daily Living	66%
Other	100%

services such as an emergency hotline, peer counselor training, technical assistance to start other self-help groups, publishing a newsletter, educating the community about mental illness, developing permanent housing, and so forth.

Membership information. Programs were asked about the procedures that prospective members must follow to participate in their program. Only one of the responding programs indicated that members must provide evidence that they had received mental health services in order to attend the program. Programs identified their services as being open to "ex-patients," "consumers of mental health services," and "psychiatric survivors." One program followed a more traditional approach and required that the individual have a "diagnosis of mental illness;" one program required that potential members have "experienced mental illness." Programs indicated that they had from 40 to 750 "active users," with a mean of 199. The one program having 750 active users greatly skewed the mean. The median number of active users was 65.

Programs were asked whether participation in their self-help program is ever required by treatment professionals, to which two of the six programs responded

affirmatively. All programs stated that they give members an opportunity to choose to participate in some activities and not in others. Finally, programs were asked whether they were involved in monitoring the treatment or services of individual members. Only one program responded yes to that question, stating that they provide consumer case management services, and peer support for participants of certain mental health programs.

Demographics of Self-Help Members
Gender, age, race, and marital status. There was a greater percentage of male respondents (59.8%) than female (40.2%). The average age was 40.4 years. Racially, the sample consisted of 56.4% whites, 36% African Americans, and 7.6% others. Most participants reported being either single (54.1%) or divorced/separated (31.3%). Only 14.6% reported that they were married. More than half of the participants reported having children (52.8%).

Psychiatric involvement. Respondents were asked a number of questions about their psychiatric history and involvement. (A decision was made not to ask about psychiatric diagnosis, since we believed that many people either did not know their diagnosis, or had multiple diagnoses and would not know which to report. The Research Advisory Board also expressed concern about the implicit labeling such a question would connote.) The average age at first reported psychiatric contact was 23 years. Fifty percent of respondents reported currently taking psychiatric medication and, on average, respondents took psychiatric medication for 8.8 years. The majority of respondents (67.5%) reported having been hospitalized for psychiatric reasons at least once in their lifetime. The average total number of psychiatric hospitalizations was 4.8; the average number of years spent as an inpatient was 1.2.

Education, employment, and income. The sample group was fairly well educated with the majority having a high school degree (46.2%) or higher educational attainment, (19.7% associates/technical degree; 11.4% college degree; and 8.3% graduate degree). However, most respondents were not competitively employed. A "regular job" was held by 16.2% of respondents; 34.5% of respondents were currently unemployed; 12.6% reported having a "sheltered/supported job." Others held "volunteer jobs" or reported being "in school, not working" or classified themselves as "housewife/husband." Those working averaged 24.5 hours per week.

The median monthly income for respondents was $575 (range $0 to $4,500; the median is reported because a few high monthly incomes appeared to skew the mean). Sources of income reported were Social Security (55.7%); employment income (22.1%); welfare (22.1%); other sources (18.8%); vocational program (4.1%); and "no income" (5.9%).

Housing. In terms of living arrangements, most respondents lived in private homes or apartments (48.1%), and the next most frequent response was homelessness (15.2%). Some respondents lived in a "rooming house/apartment" (12.9%), in "other supervised living" (11.7%), or

"other" arrangements (12.1%). When asked about with whom they reside: 38.7% reported living alone; 26.9% reported living with other non-related persons; 16.2% of respondents stated they lived with a spouse or live-in partner; 9.2% live with their children; 5.2% live with parents; and 4.4% report living with "other family members."

Demographics of self-help sample members and other populations with mental illness. Contrasting the demographics of the self-help sample with data from a national sample of community support clients surveyed in 1984 (Mulkern & Manderscheid, 1989), we found some consistencies and some disparities. The self-help sample has a higher proportion of males (59.8% vs. 51% of community support clients), a much higher proportion of African-Americans (36% vs. 11%); and the self-help sample had much higher educational attainment (14.4% had less than a high school diploma vs. 46% for the community support sample). The two groups were close in age (average of 40.4 years vs. 44 years respectively) and had similar rates of marriage with 54.1% of the self-help group reporting being single in contrast with 53% of the community support group.

Data on psychiatric involvement showed a much lower proportion of people who had ever been psychiatrically hospitalized in the self-help sample (67.5% vs. 91%) and a much lower average number of months hospitalized (12 months vs. 46 months). However, these data should be read keeping the nearly 10-year discrepancy in mind and the concurrent social policy to reduce hospital admissions and lengths of stay. Half of the self-help sample reported currently using medication, whereas 87% of the community support sample did so.

The above data could support contentions that self-help groups tend to reach people who are less psychiatrically involved. However, further elucidation of the self-help sample is necessary prior to drawing conclusions. Although all six program sites varied in some significant ways from one another, one of the sites is consistently different from the others. The California site, which comprises 41% of the whole sample, includes a drop-in center that largely serves the homeless population of Oakland. This particular group, when separated from the rest of the sample shows a characteristically different population than those served by the other five sites. The following demographics are statistically different for the California site versus the other five sites. California has significantly more males, far greater numbers of African Americans, more unmarried people, greater numbers of unemployed people, less receipt of Social Security income, greater homelessness; fewer people using medications, fewer ever hospitalized, fewer total number of psychiatric hospitalizations, and a lower average number of months spent as an inpatient. These findings are similar to Segal and his colleagues (1995).

Excluding the California sample, we found that the psychiatric involvement of the remaining subjects in this sample were similar to the community support sample. For the remaining five sites, 87% had ever been psychiatrically hospitalized; they had been hospitalized on average 6.6 times; 67.5% were currently taking psychotropic medication, and they were taking medications on average for 11.7 years. Racially, the other five sites also resembled the community support sample (87% white, 9% African American). The difference in educational attainment remains consistent whether or not the California site is excluded.

Service Utilization

Respondents were queried about the number and types of mental health services they used in the past year. From a list of 22 possible services, respondents had used, on average, 7 services in the past year. The most frequently used services were: counseling (71.7%), medication (61.5%), general support (54.7%), transportation (45.7%), emergency services (44.5%), day activities (40.0%), and psychiatric hospital (38.5%). The California site did not differ significantly from the other sites regarding service utilization.

Involvement in Program

Respondents were very involved in their user-run programs spending an average of 15.3 hours a week at the program. A sizeable minority (39.5%) held a formal position or title within the program. Of these positions, 63% were paid positions and the average number of hours worked per week was 16.4. The average amount of time participants had been involved with their current self-help program was 2.9 years. The average amount of time participants had been involved with any self-help program was 4.7 years.

Quality of Life, Self-Esteem, and Social Supports

Respondents were queried about their perceived quality of life, particularly satisfaction with their housing, finances, social situation, work, and physical well-being. More respondents were satisfied with their housing (59%); social situation (61.4%); and physical well-being (66.2%) than dissatisfied. Conversely members were dissatisfied or very dissatisfied with their work (58.0%) and their finances (59.8%). Other items on this instrument asked respondents to rate the effect of participation in the self-help program on their quality of life. Respondents reported positive or highly positive effects of self-help on their general satisfaction with life (78.4%) and on how successful their life has been (72.1%). Self-help participation increased positive feelings by "a fair amount" or "a great deal" for 88.1% of respondents and it helped 88.1% of respondents "get the things they want out of life" by a "fair amount or great deal." When asked what effect self-help had on their housing, financial and social situations, 77% of participants said it had some or highly positive effect.

There was a significant difference among the six sites with respect to quality of life scores. (F (5,266) = 6.8, p < .00009). The California site showed lower quality of life scores. This was attributed to the population served who were more likely to be homeless and had lower incomes.

In regard to self-esteem, respondents were asked how self-help involvement had affected their feelings about themselves. Respondents reported feeling more positive about themselves as a result of self-help involvement (92%), having more respect for themselves (87.5%), feeling more productive and capable (86.8%), feeling better about themselves and able to recognize their strengths (89.4%). Furthermore, 87.5% reported that being involved in self-help provided the opportunity to help others.

Finally, respondents were asked about the impact self-help involvement has had on their social life. Respondents were asked to indicate whether the quality and the frequency of contact with family and friends has: "Changed in a way I like"; "Changed in a way I do not like"; or "Not changed." Forty-six percent of participants indicated that self-help involvement had changed the amount of contact they had with their family in a way they liked. Forty-three percent of respondents indicated no change in the amount of contact, and 11% stated that the amount of contact they had changed in a way they did not like. Fifty percent of respondents indicated that self-help involvement had changed the quality of their family contact in a way they like and 41% stated their contact had not changed qualitatively. Similar results were found on the questions regarding contact with friends: 53% indicated the amount of contact had changed in a way that they liked; 38% reported no change. Fifty-eight percent of respondents reported that the quality of their contact with friends had changed in a way that they liked and 34% reported no change. When respondents were asked, overall, whether self-help involvement affected the number of family, friends, or others with whom they had regular contact, 60% stated it had, in a way that they liked. Thirty-two percent reported no change in frequency of regular contact with family and friends. Sites differed with respect to their reports of how self-help had affected their self-esteem and quality of life (see Table 2).

TABLE 2.
RESULTS OF ANALYSES OF VARIANCE EXAMINING THE DIFFERENCES
AMONG SELF-HELP PROGRAMS ON THE MAJOR MEASURES

Measure	F	Significance Level
Quality of Life	6.8	.00009**
Satisfaction with Program	1.67	.14NS
Community Activities	2.58	.03*
Self-Esteem	2.37	.04*
Service Utilization	1.29	.27NS
Social Supports	2.65	.023*

Note: NS = Not significant; *Significant at p < .05 level; **Significant at p < .001 level

Satisfaction with Participation in Program

A 19-item questionnaire using a four-point Likert scale was administered to respondents to gather information about their satisfaction with their self-help program. Overall, programs received very positive ratings of satisfaction. For example, the majority of respondents found that participation helped them to solve problems (59.4%), and helped them to feel more in control of their lives (64.2%). The majority found that the self-help program was easy to get to, had convenient hours, and was in a comfortable building. Most felt treated as an equal by other members (81.2%) and that they were treated with courtesy and respect (82.3%). Nearly all (91.5%) would recommend the program to a friend. Most find that they get the kind of help they are looking for (69.7%). Nearly all respondents rated the overall quality of their program as good or excellent (48.7% and 35.3% respectively). There were no significant differences in satisfaction with program across the six sites.

Satisfaction with program also varied significantly with two demographic variables. Using an analysis of variance, there was an overall significant difference in satisfaction by educational attainment (F (4, 267) = 2.5, p = .02), with those having the lowest educational attainment and those having the highest educational attainment showing the highest satisfaction scores. Another significant difference arose when satisfaction was analyzed by living arrangement for the respondent (F (4, 267) = 3.1, p = .01). Satisfaction scores were highest for people living in various kinds of supervised arrangements, for those living in private domiciles, or in unsupervised co-operative apartments. Homeless people and people living in rooms or other arrangements had relatively lower scores. One might speculate whether individuals

who are homeless were less satisfied because they expected the program to assist them to obtain suitable housing and did not receive that assistance. Analyses by all other demographic variables showed no significant differences in relation to satisfaction with self-help including extent of psychiatric involvement and extent of involvement in this or other self-help program, age, race, sex, or employment status.

Community Activity

Respondents were given a checklist of community activities (Rappaport, 1985) and asked to indicate which of these activities they had engaged in during the last year. Activities included items such as voting in an election, writing to a political official, boycotting a product, and so forth. Table 3 contains the percentages of individuals stating they performed each activity. Over 90% of the respondents indicated they participated in at least one of those community activities; almost 40% indicated they participated in five or more community activities.

Discussion and Conclusions

Prior to a discussion of the findings, it is important to note that these results must be interpreted cautiously for two reasons. First, they represent only 6 out of 64 self-help programs that expressed a willingness to participate in this study. The programs chosen for this study were selected deliberately, and with the intention of getting geographical representativeness and organizational variety. Secondly, the researchers did not have the ability to systematically track response rates within each of the six programs. That level of monitoring was considered too burdensome for the sites and very difficult given the informal "drop-in" structure of all the programs surveyed. It is possible that the data presented here is therefore biased, and not representative of all

TABLE 3.
PERCENT OF VARIOUS COMMUNITY ACTIVITIES IN WHICH RESPONDENTS
INDICATED THEY HAD PARTICIPATED WITHIN THE LAST YEAR

Type of Community Activity	Percent
Joined an organization to benefit the community	37%
Joined a church	40%
Boycotted a product	11%
Attended meetings of a community organization regularly	39%
Wrote to a public official	20%
Volunteered time or money to community organization	48%
Ran for office of community organization	8%
Contributed time or money to political campaign	12%
Attended a demonstration	37%
Collected signatures in a petition drive	16%
Introduced a friend to a community organization	41%
Signed a petition	44%
Voted in an election (city, state, or national)	55%
Wrote a letter to an editor of a newspaper	9%
Phoned a public official to express feelings on issues	21%
Helped with fundraising on a project	32%

self-help members. On the other hand, all members were encouraged to respond to the survey, and we received no reports from the site liaisons that obvious selection biases occurred. Given the dearth of information available on self-help programs, we believe that these data have value in understanding self-help programs and their members despite these methodological limitations. Aside from selection or sampling bias, it is also important to note that these results are all based upon self-report. No attempts were made to verify or validate the effects of self-help on members' lives through other source of information.

The self-help programs that participated in this study receive support from traditional funding sources such as the Center for Mental Health Services, state and local mental health authorities, and the Department of Housing and Urban Development. Despite this, the programs do not appear to be beholden to those sources, and are able to develop their missions and operate their programs quite autonomously.

In contrast to traditional mental health programs, these user-run programs describe themselves as interested in advocating for empowerment, choice, and self-determination for their members. Two of the programs we surveyed operated with a very significant budget and paid staff, suggesting that while self-help programs may have started as small, informal organizations who survived on a "shoestring," they are growing into formidable operations. Programs report offering assistance with residential, employment, and education services; service coordination; legal help; general advocacy; and social and recreational services. Results suggest that, at least to some extent, the role of the self-help programs has been both to fill gaps in the present system of care and to help members get what they need from existing services. However, some self-help programs actually provide what might be considered traditional mental health services.

Results of the analyses of demographic characteristics of self-help members was somewhat confounded by the California site. It might be concluded that some self-help programs, particularly those in poor, urban areas serve individuals who are less involved in the traditional mental health system than do other similar programs. The California site serves far more individuals who are homeless, African American, and with proportionately fewer having a history of being hospitalized for psychiatric reasons. Given the lack of resources for poor, urban individuals, self-help programs may be appealing to them whether or not they strongly identify with the mission of the self-help movement. These findings are consistent with those of Segal and his colleagues who surveyed two self-help programs in the San Francisco area and found demographics similar to ours, and that members were attracted to the social supports and material assistance offered by self-help programs.

Results of data on service utilization suggest that respondents do not rely only upon services available to them through their self-help organization, but also on services that might be considered traditional, such as counseling, day services, and inpatient hospitals. Respondents seem able to meld services from traditional sources with those offered by the self-help program.

Judging by the amount of time respondents spend in their programs (an average of 15 hours per week), these organizations seem to fill various gaps for respondents and thus possibly reducing the need for other, more costly services. It appears from the data regarding the number holding positions within their program, that members belong to self-help programs not only to receive help, but also to give help, which is the essence of a mutual help organization. These respondents were also fairly seasoned users of self-help, having spent an average of almost 5 years involved in such programs. When the data were compared to

the national UCDI data, it would appear that users of the programs we surveyed are more educated on average than those surveyed in the UCDI study. This finding was apparent when the data were analyzed with and without the California sample. The possibility of self-selection needs to be investigated further. It is possible that individuals with higher levels of education feel more comfortable in self-help organizations, or perhaps that individuals with higher levels of education were more willing to participate in this survey.

Overall, respondents indicated that being involved in self-help had a salutary effect on their quality of life, including their general life satisfaction. Members were relatively more dissatisfied with their work and financial situation than their housing, social situation, and physical health, a not surprising finding given the low employment rates and the abysmally low incomes reported. California respondents reported a lower perceived quality of life, also not surprising given the high degree of homelessness and the low incomes among that group. Self-help involvement also positively affected members' self-esteem and social lives, according to their self-reports. It might be concluded from the satisfaction with self-help programs that the programs surveyed are achieving their mission: members overwhelmingly reported being satisfied with the services and personal interactions within the self-help programs.

These results are consistent with the findings of Mowbray and Tan (1992) and Carpinello, Knight, and Jatulis (1992), both of whom evaluated consumer drop-in centers. In the Mowbray and Tan study, members expressed satisfaction with their program and positive effects as a result of participation. Carpinello and associates discussed the positive effects afforded by self-help involvement in the areas of self-concept, well-being, social functioning, decision-making, and achieving educational and career goals.

Though this study has made an attempt to answer questions about who uses self-help programs, much investigation remains to be done. First the methodological limitations of this study limit the certainty with which conclusions can be drawn. However, for a variety of reasons, it is doubtful that a truly representative survey of self-help members can be conducted. Furthermore, there are questions that require a prospective, longitudinal research design, or an in-depth sociological perspective, such as whether participation in self-help positively affects hospitalization and rehabilitation outcomes, the structure of self-help programs and how they operate, or how self-help programs differ from traditional mental health services. Obviously, questions such as these were beyond the scope of the current study, and suggest the need for further research. Because this study did not involve systematic, representative sampling methods, the results must be interpreted cautiously. For example, it is difficult to generalize these results with certainty to all user-run programs, or more broadly to self-help programs in general. However, our deliberate selection of a geographic and organizational range of programs allows us to generalize with some confidence.

The level of community involvement for respondents deserves further investigation. For example, community involvement appears very high (e.g., 19.6% reported writing a letter to a public official within the last year; 55% reported having voted in a city, state, or national election) that they raise questions about the reputation for apathy and lack of affiliation frequently attributed to persons with severe mental illness. Are these respondents a unique group, or does membership in such programs raise the political conscience of its participants? These data give reason to believe that at least some consumers are more like the general public in terms of their community or political activism, and less like the popular stereotypes, than many investigators would lead us to believe.

As self-help groups and programs continue to proliferate, and as they affect larger and larger segments of the community mental health population, it becomes increasingly important to learn more about them. In order to best study this population, a participatory approach is essential, since many such programs will simply refuse to be studied otherwise. As we learn more about self-help programs and their participants, we may learn about different and non-traditional ways that quality of life and community tenure can be improved.

References

Carpinello, S., Knight, E., & Jatulis, L. (1992). *A study of the meaning of self-help, self-help group processes, and outcomes.* National Association of State Mental Health Program Directors, Proceedings of the 3rd Annual National Conference of State Mental Health Agency Services Research.

Chamberlin, J., Rogers, J., & Sneed, C. (1989). Consumers, families and community support systems. *Psychosocial Rehabilitation Journal, 12*(3), 93-106.

Chester, M. (1991). Mobilizing consumer activism in health care: The role of self-help groups. *Research in Social Movements, Conflict and Change, 13,* 275-305.

Dillman, D. (1978). *Mail and telephone surveys: The total design method.* New York: Wiley.

Emerick, R. (1988). *The mental patient movement: Toward a typology of groups.* Unpublished manuscript, San Diego State University.

Emerick, R. (1990). Self-help groups for former patients: Relations with mental health professionals. *Hospital and Community Psychiatry, 41,* 401-406.

Fink, A., & Kosecoff, J. (1985). *How to conduct surveys.* Beverly Hills, CA: Sage Publications.

Hatfield, A. (1988, May). *Report of research meeting on community support and rehabilitation services.* Presentation at the Joint NIMH/CSP-NIDRR Conference. Bethesda, MD.

Kaufman, C., Freund, P., & Wilson, J. (1989). Self-help in the mental health system: A model for consumer-provider collaboration. *Psychosocial Rehabilitation Journal, 13*(1), 6-21.

McFadden, L., Seidman, E., Rappaport, J. (1992). A comparison of espoused theories of self and mutual help: Implications for mental health professionals. *Professional Psychology Research and Practice, 23*(6), 515-520.

Mowbray, C., Chamberlain, P., Jennings, M., & Reed, C. (1988). Consumer-run mental health services: Results from five demonstration projects. *Community Mental Health Journal, 24*(2), 151-156.

Mowbray, C., & Tan, C. (1992). Evaluation of an innovative consumer-run service model: The drop-in center. *Innovation & Research, 1*(2), 19-24.

Mowbray, C., Wellwood, R., & Chamberlain, P. (1988). Project stay: A consumer-run support service. *Psychosocial Rehabilitation Journal, 12*(1), 33-42.

Mulkern, V. M., & Manderscheid, R. W. (1989). Characteristics of community support program clients in 1980 and 1984. *Hospital and Community Psychiatry, 40*, 165-172.

Rappaport, J., Seidman, E., Toro, P. A., McFadden, L. S., Reischl, T. M., Roberts, L. J., Salem, D. A., Stein, C. H., & Zimmerman, M. A. (1985). Collaborative research with a mutual help organization. *Social Policy*, Winter, 12-24.

Salem, D. A., Stein, C. H., & Zimmerman, M. A. (1985, Winter). Collaborative research with a mutual help organization. *Social Policy*, 12-24.

Reissman, F. (1985, Winter). New dimensions in self-help. *Social Policy*, 2-4.

Roberts, L., Luke, D., Rappaport, J., Seidman, E., et al. (1991). Charting uncharted terrain: A behavioral observation system for mutual help groups. Special Issue, *American Journal of Community Psychology, 19*(5), 715-737.

Rogers, J. A. (1988, May). *Report of research meeting on community support and rehabilitation services*. Presentation at the Joint NIMH/CSP-NIDRR Conference. Bethesda, MD.

Rogers, E. S., & Palmer-Erbs, V. (1994). Participatory action research: Implications for researchers in psychiatric rehabilitation. *Psychosocial Rehabilitation Journal 18*(2), 3-12.

Salem, D. A., Seidman, E., & Rappaport, J. (1988). Community treatment of the mentally ill: The promise of mutual-help organizations. *Social Work, 33*(5), 403-408.

Segal, S., Silverman, C., & Temkin, T. (1995). Characteristics and service use of long-term members of self-help agencies for mental health clients. *Psychiatric Services* (formerly *Hospital and Community Psychiatry), 46*, 269-274.

Toro, P., Reischl, T., Zimmerman, M., Rappaport, J., et al. (1988). Professionals in mutual help groups: Impact on social climate and members' behavior. *Journal of Consulting and Clinical Psychology, 56*(4), 631-632.

Whyte, W. F. (Ed.) (1991). *Participatory Action Research*. Newbury Park, CA: Sage Publications.

Zimmerman, M., & Rappaport, J. (1988). Citizen participation, perceived control and psychological empowerment. *American Journal of Community Psychology, 16*(5), 725-750.

Zinman, S. (1982). A patient-run residence. *Psychosocial Rehabilitation Journal, 6*(1), 3-11.

Zinman, S. (1988, May). *Report of research meeting on community support and rehabilitation services*. Presentation at the Joint NIMH/CSP-NIDRR Conference. Bethesda, MD.

Zinman, S., Harp, H., & Budd, S. (Eds.). (1987). *Reaching across: Mental health clients helping each other*. Riverside, CA: California Network of Mental Health Clients.

FOSTERING SELF-HELP ON AN INPATIENT UNIT

Kathleen M. Kelly, Frederick Sautter, Karen Tugrul, and Michael D. Weaver

THIS ARTICLE ORIGINALLY APPEARED IN THE *Archives of Psychiatric Nursing*, 1990, 4(3), 161-165 AND IS REPRINTED WITH PERMISSION. COPYRIGHT BY W.B. SAUNDERS COMPANY.

A self-help movement for people with chronic mental illness is growing but is not as advanced as the system of self-help for the chemically dependent. Barriers to organized self-help among those with chronic mental illness include stigma, denial, and the debilitating effects of the illnesses themselves. The authors developed a coping group on a 12-bed psychiatric unit to address these problems. The group was designed to strengthen ties with a local self-help club and to foster the idea that people with chronic mental illness can have a positive impact on the course of their illness. Mental health consumers who were successful coping with their illnesses were guest speakers and role models for group members. The coping group, which was well received by participants, stimulated research questions and suggested potential modifications of clinical practice. In recent years, a mental health consumer movement has gathered momentum. Individuals who have been receiving psychiatric services are now clamoring for a more active role. There are currently several national consumer organizations that are growing in power and visibility. Some self-help groups, like Recovery Inc., are primarily therapy groups concerned with personal growth. Others, like the National Mental Health Consumers Association, are involved in supporting research and empowerment through political action as well as focusing on mutual-aid groups.

The prototypical self-help group is Alcoholics Anonymous (AA), which is the cornerstone of alcoholism treatment, and whose meetings are an integral part of inpatient programs. In fact, self-help and peer assistance are highly valued within the chemical dependency system of care. A glance at a newspaper's classified advertising section reveals that status as a recovering alcoholic is an asset when seeking a job in chemical dependency treatment. However, the formal linkages that exist between self-help groups and professional treatment programs for alcoholism are not generally in place for persons suffering from chronic mental illness. Professionals and consumer groups often have an uneasy relationship with both groups, fearing invasion of their turf (Gartner & Riessman, 1977).

Two years ago, one of the authors (K.M.K.) had the privilege of hearing a most intelligent and articulate mental health consumer speak to a group of psychiatric professionals about his battle with schizophrenia. Although almost all of the members of the audience had had significant experience and contact with people with psychotic illness, they listened and responded to the speaker as if they were hearing about the experience of mental illness for the first time. A psychiatrist who had made his reputation treating the chronically mentally ill asked in an awed whisper, "What is it like to be psychotic?" The speaker was not only a recovering schizophrenic, as he referred to himself, but also a student of social work who could both speak the language of professionals and use his obvious talents to enable listeners to comfortably identify with him. During the discussion, the room was charged with an excitement and optimism unusual for the group.

The speaker further extended his use of an alcoholism model. He spoke of 10 years of denial and then of finally hitting "rock bottom" after 13 hospitalizations. He also described the laborious process of retraining himself to concentrate well enough to study. Listeners were left with the idea that perhaps schizophrenia was not so hopeless an illness after all and that maybe denial and noncompliance were time-limited problems. His description of his life as a recovering schizophrenic was inspirational in the tradition of the former alcoholic who gives hope to the struggling newcomer.

Hearing the consumer describe his experience with mental illness in the model and language of chemical dependency caused this author to speculate about ways in which the chemical dependency model might be useful in the care of those with chronic mental illness. Certainly, there are some obvious similarities. As with addictions, one may be "recovering," i.e., successfully coping with the illness, without the expectation of ever being cured. In addition, the chronically mentally ill, like the chemically dependent, are vulnerable to relapse and have a need for strategies to cope with and manage the illness. Further, the stigma attached to both chronic mental illnesses and addictions encourages sufferers to deny their memberships in the shunned groups.

Recovering alcoholics are supported by the vast network of self-help groups that AA provides. In addition, prominent people have shared their problem with the public and helped to destigmatize the disease of alcoholism. In contrast, people with a major mental illness, particularly psychotic illness, have few role models or opportunities to meet those who have successfully coped with serious mental illnesses.

Barriers to Effective Self-Help

There are several reasons for the lack of role models for people with chronic mental illness. First, studies consistently have shown that the mentally ill are one of the most stigmatized groups in society (Krauss

& Slavinsky, 1982, p. 27). In fact, mentally ill people have more negative attitudes toward others who are mentally ill than any other handicapped group does toward others who share its suffering (Krauss & Slavinsky, 1982, p. 27; O'Mahoney, 1982). Second, the denial of mental illness is a well-known phenomenon that often interferes with the ability of the consumer to cope with his or her own illness.

Denial and stigma are related. O'Mahoney (1982) found that both mentally ill patients and psychiatric staff members shared a negative stereotypic view of the mentally ill. The patients did not characterize themselves in terms of the stereotype, but they were able to distinguish differences between their current self and usual self. O'Mahoney (1982) concluded that denial in mental illness is a normal process and that rejection of a negative self-stereotype serves a protective function. It is not surprising that mental health consumers avoid joining a stigmatized group.

A third barrier to linking patients to role models who are coping successfully with their illnesses is found in the nature of the illnesses themselves. Many mental health consumers are fearful and anxious in situations where they are required to speak. They often underestimate their abilities and are reluctant to hold themselves up as examples for others. In addition, many have difficulty with social skills and have trouble forming relationships.

The Nurse's Role in Self-Help

The authors believe that self-help concepts should be part of all treatment programs for the chronically mentally ill. Orem (1985) maintains that a nurse's role is twofold and involves both the giving of care and the promotion of self-care. Estroff (1982, p. 609) stated that "organized self-help has not, on the whole, been taken seriously in psychiatric treatment except, of course, in the ever-present muttering about patients having to motivate themselves to change." In the authors' opinion, nothing has changed in this regard. A review of the professional literature revealed large numbers of articles describing self-help groups for a multitude of problems but very few for individuals with a major mental illness.

Psychiatric nurses can foster self-care on inpatient units by helping consumers to identify and share effective coping strategies. Giving the consistent message that people with a chronic mental illness can gain some mastery over the illness instills self-esteem and promotes hope. Plum (1987), in a study of patients' perceptions of helping and hindering factors in recovery from mental illness, found that hope was one of the most useful variables in the process of recovery. Psychiatric nurses, as patient advocates and coordinators of care, are also in a good position to forge links between organized self-help groups and the professional mental health system.

Self-Help in a Coping Group

In an attempt to strengthen ties with a self-help social club in our community and to foster the idea that consumers with chronic mental illness can have a positive impact on the course of their illness, the authors developed a coping group on a 12-bed university hospital psychiatric unit. The group focused on learning to cope with and self-manage mental illness. That is not to say that consumers were given the message that they could care for their illnesses without assistance; instead, they were encouraged to find ways in which they could control their illnesses and collaborate with professionals in their own care.

The population of this large, Midwestern inner-city university hospital was generally poor, with roughly 68% falling below the poverty line. Approximately 50% of the patients were black and a large number

were of Appalachian origin. Since many of the patients on the unit were screened for inclusion in a research study, there tended to be a greater number of people with a diagnosis of schizophrenia or bipolar affective disorder than would generally be found on similar adult general psychiatric units. At any given point in time at least half of the patients on the unit were psychotic. Most had severe forms of mental illness and could expect some degree of residual disability after discharge. As is true in most hospitals today, the patient turnover was very rapid. In addition, the unit was an active, "intensive care" environment with many demands placed on the patients in terms of participation in therapy.

The size of the group varied, but generally was composed of between five and nine members per individual session. Criteria for admission to the group was either inpatient or ex-patient status on the 12-bed psychiatric unit. Psychotic members were welcome. Eligible members were excluded, temporarily, only if they were judged to be acutely agitated. If asked to leave, the agitated member was told that he or she was welcome to come back to a future session. Although the authors recognized that the rapid turnover made it optimal for the group to meet daily (Yalom, 1983), it was not possible to fit more than two groups per week into the patients' busy schedule. The group met on Mondays and Thursdays for 40-minute sessions. Leadership of the group rotated among three of the authors, with two people co-leading and one functioning as observer/process recorder for an individual session.

The format of the group was flexible and depended on the wishes and abilities of the current group. Since one of the purposes of the group was to empower consumers, it was important that the group members feel that the group was truly theirs. On the other hand, as Yalom (1983, p.107) points out, there is "no place in inpatient group psychotherapy for the nondirective leader." Hospitalized consumers are in crisis and have little excess energy available to deal with the anxiety generated by a group without structure.

The authors dealt with this conflict by preparing several topics and exercises that would provide structure to the group and that the patients had identified as being of particular concern. Some of the prepared topics included strategies for coping 1) with symptoms, 2) with taking medication, and 3) with family. An exercise that was particularly helpful in stimulating discussion was the presentation of written scenarios of situations commonly experienced by mental health consumers. The group members were asked to share their handling of a similar situation. The authors felt that it would be easier to discuss difficulties in the third person, and in fact, the scenarios usually generated a lively discussion. At the beginning of each group, members were offered the choice of selecting their own topic or choosing from among the prepared subjects. The ability and desire to choose the group topic varied with the composition of the group, but even the groups with the lowest functional ability were given this option. Thus, the leadership style ranged from structured and directive to facilitative pending on the functional ability of the group.

Role Models for Effective Coping

Every third week (or sixth session) a guest speaker from a local self-help club came to speak to the group about his or her own experiences and successful coping strategies. In addition, the speaker briefly would describe the self-help club and encourage patients to come for a visit. Two of the mental health consumers who had organized the club agreed to come periodically. They also agreed to ask other suitable club members to speak. The criteria for being invited to be a special guest speaker

were that the person have a mental illness that 1) required daily medication, 2) had considerable impact on his or her current life, or 3) had caused disability at some point in his or her life and from which the person was not totally symptom-free. Speakers were also required to express the conviction that they had gotten considerably better or stabilized and that at least part of their improvement was through their own efforts. All of the speakers had attractive qualities.

The authors hoped that having a positive role model with which to identify would decrease the group members' need to deny the fact of their mental illness. Although denial serves a protective function and may be viewed as a positive coping mechanism (Forchuk & Westwell, 1987), it becomes a maladaptive defense when it interferes with successful self-management of mental illness.

The groups featuring a guest speaker were consistently the ones best attended. Schizophrenic group members with prominent negative symptoms frequently showed an unusual range of affect during guest speaker groups. Many chronically passive group members seemed to come alive and take a more active role. Patients who rarely spoke asked the guest speaker detailed questions about how he or she coped with interfering voices or forestalled a relapse.

The group, unlike others on the unit, was not mandatory. Perhaps it always attracted a good percentage of patients because it gave them a sense of autonomy during a time (hospitalization) during which they were definitely not in control. Former patients who had been discharged were encouraged to return for group meetings and most frequently attended guest speaker sessions.

At times, discharged patients came to the group because they were just barely hanging on in the community and needed additional support. Some of these ex-patients said that they came to hear (from the guest speaker) that it was possible to make it and that the session had enabled them to return to the community for another try. Some of the unit staff had feared that allowing former patients to return for groups would create a situation in which decompensating patients would return to the unit in lieu of contacting their therapist or going to the psychiatric emergency room. This did not turn out to be a problem. In the one case where an ex-patient (with a diagnosis of borderline personality disorder) came to the group seeking admission to the hospital, the group helped her to identify that hospitalization had been of limited benefit for her in the past. This patient left for home with a list of coping strategies generated by the group and plans to see her therapist.

Some of the ex-patients who were fairly regular in attendance functioned as role models for hospitalized group members. They described coping strategies that had been effective, gave advice, and provided examples of stability that acutely ill patients could strive for and emulate. One element that is crucial to self-help groups is the helper-therapy principle (Gartner & Riessman, 1982, p. 633), which states that "those who help are helped most." When a patient plays the "well" role, she or he influences herself or himself as well as those she or he is trying to help (Gartner & Riessman, 1982). One guest speaker emphasized to the group that she still often felt very shaky inside but that she knew that she must get herself out of bed and down to the social club. This woman, who trained and coordinated the staff at the local self-help club, had learned from experience that helping others was the only thing that kept her from sinking into despondency.

Observations

Several themes have emerged consistently across almost all patient groups. Discussions about medication have been more affectively charged than most other topics. Although side effects were a concern, it was the necessity of taking medication at all that disturbed patients the most. Several patients stated that the daily act of taking pills was a reminder that they were defective. Group members overwhelmingly preferred to view their illness as stress-induced rather than of a biological origin (the authors explained that it was "like a cold"). Perhaps the concept of illness is rejected by patients because, like taking medication, it implies a defect, whereas having problems with extraordinary stress can be viewed as a temporary problem having to do with the environment and not the individual.

Most patients with a chronic psychotic illness had developed at least one effective coping strategy for decreasing auditory hallucinations. A frequent strategy that group members found to be effective was that of verbally commanding the voices to go away. This was consistent with Field's (1985) finding that auditory hallucinations can be controlled with verbal interventions. Psychotic group members often expressed astonishment that they were not the only ones who heard voices. For many, the group was their first opportunity for frank discussion of psychotic symptoms. The isolation of these patients in the midst of a busy psychiatric ward was striking.

At times, the leaders found it to be a delicate balancing act to meet the needs of both the lower and the higher functioning group members. Yalom (1983) recommends splitting inpatient groups into two levels based on functional ability. However, given the small size of the unit and the group's goal of using more stable patients as role models, the authors decided to offer only one group.

For example, when several group members wanted to talk about dealing with hallucinations, the leaders reframed the topic to be that of dealing with unwanted interference from so-called bad thoughts, voices, or noise. Thus, nonpsychotic members were drawn into the discussion because most had had experience with unpleasant, intrusive thoughts. The coping strategies for both were essentially the same and nonpsychotic members often had excellent suggestions. These suggestions would have been lost to a part of the group under a level system.

Implications for Clinical Practice and Research

Formal outcome measures were not used to evaluate the coping group. However, group members' comments were enthusiastic, and as previously mentioned, although the group was not mandatory, it was well attended. In the future, the authors plan formally to study the effectiveness of this type of group. It would be useful to know if a coping group could indeed decrease denial and if less denial would lead to better compliance with professional treatment plans. One of the authors (K.M.K.) is currently participating in a research group that is testing a denial rating scale. When completed, the scale will be a useful tool for evaluating the coping group. Another question raised by the group was: What sort of self-care strategies work for consumers? This is an important area for study. An intriguing observation was the consumers' preface for viewing their illnesses as stress-related rather than biological in nature. Research is needed to ascertain whether this observation is one that is generally held. If so, it would be interesting to know why consumers prefer to view their illnesses in that way. Knowledge of what type of illness model is acceptable to consumers could guide educational programs designed to teach them about their illnesses. The coping group is fertile ground for both research and direct practice.

Acknowledgement
The coping group described in this paper was developed on the Psychobiology Unit at University Hospital, 234 Goodman Street, Cincinnati, Ohio.

References

Estroff, S. E. (1982). The next step: Self-help. *Hospital and Community Psychiatry, 33*(8), 609.

Field, W. E. (1985). Hearing voices. *Journal of Psychosocial Nursing, 23*(1), 9-14.

Forchuk, C. & Westwell, J. (1987) Denial. *Journal of Psychosocial Nursing, 25*(6), 9-13.

Gartner, A. J. & Riessman, F. (1977). *Self-help in the human services.* San Francisco, CA: Jossey-Bass.

Gartner, A. J. & Riessman, F. (1982). Self-help and mental health. *Hospital and Community Psychiatry. 33*(8), 631 -635.

Krauss, J. B. & Slavinsky, A. T. (1982). *The chronically ill psychiatric patient and the community.* Boston, MA: Blackwell.

O'Mahoney, P. D. (1982). Psychiatric patient denial of mental illness as a normal process. *British Journal of Medical Psychology, 55,* 109-118.

Orem, D. (1985). *Nursing: Concepts of practice* (3rd ed). New York, NY: McGraw-Hill.

Plum, K. C. (1987). How parents view recovery: What helps, what hinders. *Archives of Psychiatric Nursing, 1*(4), 285-293.

Yalom, I. D. (1983). *Inpatient group psychotherapy.* New York, NY: Basic.

CHARACTERISTICS AND SERVICE USE OF LONG-TERM MEMBERS OF SELF-HELP AGENCIES FOR MENTAL HEALTH CLIENTS

Steven P. Segal, Carol Silverman, and Tanya Temkin

DR. SEGAL IS DIRECTOR, DR. SILVERMAN IS PROGRAM DIRECTOR, AND MS. TEMKIN IS RESEARCH ASSOCIATE AT THE CENTER FOR SELF-HELP RESEARCH, 1918 UNIVERSITY AVENUE, SUITE 3D, BERKELEY, CALIFORNIA 94612. DR. SEGAL IS ALSO PROFESSOR IN THE SCHOOL OF SOCIAL WELFARE AT THE UNIVERSITY OF CALIFORNIA, BERKELEY.

AN EARLIER VERSION OF THIS PAPER WAS PRESENTED AT THE ANNUAL MEETING OF THE AMERICAN PUBLIC HEALTH ASSOCIATION HELD OCTOBER 24-28, 1993, IN SAN FRANCISCO.

THIS ARTICLE ORIGINALLY APPEARED IN *Psychiatric Services*, MARCH 1995, 46(3), 269-274 AND IS REPRINTED WITH PERMISSION.

Objective: This study examined the characteristics of long-term members of self-help agencies managed and staffed by mental health clients, why they sought help from the agencies, and how they differed from clients of community mental health agencies. Methods: A survey and assessment instruments were used to obtain information on the service utilization of 310 long-term agency members as well as on their resources, history of disability, functional status, psychological disability, health problems, and DSM-III-R diagnosis. Data from management information systems of the self-help and community mental health agencies were used to compare service populations. Results: The self-help agencies served a primarily African American population (64%), many of whom were homeless (46%). Eighty-seven percent had confirmed DSM-III-R diagnoses, and 50% had dual diagnoses with moderate to severe substance or alcohol abuse or dependence. They had sought help from the self-help agencies primarily for resources such as food or clothing, for "a place to be," or because they were homeless. Obtaining counseling or help for substance or alcohol abuse was a less important reason for coming to the self-help agencies. Conclusions: A high proportion of the persons served by the self-help agencies in the study were homeless and had a dual diagnosis of mental disorder and substance abuse. The self-help agencies provided their clients with material resources while community mental health agencies provided psychotherapeutic and medical care.

During the past 10 years, growth in the number of self-help agencies has constituted a major development in mental health services. Self-help agencies are often incorporated as voluntary organizations and are independently managed and staffed by former patients (Levy, 1984). Clients usually refer to themselves as members of the organization. These organizations are defined as agencies because they provide mutual assistance (euphemistically called self-help) such as help in locating housing and obtaining disability benefits and other entitlements, as well as offer peer support groups. Self-help agencies have established goals and technologies that they and others believe are effective in improving the lives of their members (Shore, 1992). These agencies further claim to serve individuals who are less well served by traditional mental health services.

We know very little about self-help agencies and their place in the mental health service system. Existing research, well summarized by Thomas Powell (1987), has concentrated on self-help groups such as Recovery or Emotions Anonymous, which are generally not formal voluntary service organizations. Thus the literature on self-help groups does not address self-help agencies' practices of offering a spectrum of services reputedly comparable in scope to those offered by professional organizations.

Despite a lack of knowledge about the activities of self-help agencies, mental health professionals regard these organizations as service providers. As self-help agencies have proliferated, support for their activities by state legislatures, local mental health systems, and foundations has increased (Zinman, 1987; Emerick, 1989a). A 1993 collaborative survey conducted by the Center for Self-Help Research and the National Association of State Mental Health Program Directors showed that 46 states funded 567 self-help groups and agencies for persons with mental disabilities and their family members (National Association of Program Directors, 1993). Self-help, or more accurately mutual assistance, is a key component of the services system and one of the few components of the system that will grow in the immediate future.

It is thus surprising that there are few empirical data describing the basic characteristics of members of self-help agencies. This paper uses data from a survey of members of four self-help agencies in the San Francisco Bay Area to address four questions. First, what are the demographic, diagnostic, and social characteristics of long-term members of self-help agencies? Second, how do members learn about the self-help agencies and what services do members use? Third, are the characteristics of members of self-help agencies comparable to those of persons who use community

mental health agencies located nearby? Fourth, are the demographic characteristics of members of self-help agencies in the San Francisco Bay Area comparable to those of members of self-help agencies outside of California?

Description of Agencies

Self-help agencies run by mental health clients vary widely in program philosophy, mission, and range of activities (Emerick, 1989a; Katz & Bender, 1976; Emerick, 1989b; and Emerick 1992). The self-help agencies we studied are concerned with improving members' lives and helping them gain skills and resources to achieve stability, but they also place the responsibility to make the necessary changes on the members themselves. At the same time, the agencies believe that societal inequities contribute to members' problems and that these inequities must be changed through collective action.

Zinman (1987) developed a typology of self-help organizations based on program activities. The four self-help agencies we studied fit the model of the drop-in or community center. They provide a place for members to socialize, to build a support network, and to receive advocacy and a gamut of services to assist in independent living. Three of the four agencies target their services to individuals who are homeless or at risk of homelessness. The fourth targets services to all seriously mentally disabled individuals and has many homeless

The self-help agencies we studied are concerned with improving members' lives and helping them gain skills and resources to achieve stability, but they also place the responsibility to make the necessary changes on the members themselves.

individuals among its membership. All provide mutual support groups, drop-in space, resources for survival in the community, and direct services. All have members who are active in state and national consumer-led organizations.

The services provided by the agencies include assistance in getting food and finding temporary shelter and permanent housing, counseling and advocacy concerning financial benefits, job counseling, substance abuse counseling and support groups, counseling about money management, payeeship services, case management, peer counseling, and information and referral. All provide coffee, snacks, clothing, food vouchers, free use of a telephone, and special-interest support groups. All have paid staff and volunteers, but vary in the extent to which staff functions are specialized and their volunteer programs formalized. Finally, staff, volunteers, and members at all agencies are engaged in a variety of adhoc political activities, including demonstrating to protest proposed cuts in welfare and mental health funding, testifying at city council hearings, gaining appointments to task forces and local commissions, and holding press conferences.

The differences between the populations served by self-help agencies and those served by community mental health agencies suggest a division of labor between the two types of agencies that has not yet been formalized or validated. Self-help agencies provide psychosocial and material assistance, while community mental health agencies provide medical and psychotherapeutic care.

Methods

In 1992 and 1993 we surveyed 310 long-term members of four self-help agencies in two counties in the San Francisco Bay Area. The agencies were the only consumer-run organizations in the area that had achieved agency status. Each agency was independently incorporated, had a governing board, and offered a wide spectrum of services.

We attempted to interview all staff and volunteers, who were themselves mental health clients and members of the self-help organization, as well as a sample of other long-term members. Respondents were categorized as staff or volunteers if they worked at least 10 hours a week at the self-help agency.

We selected long-term members randomly from people who fit our eligibility criteria and who were present in the drop-in center when an interviewer was available. Persons who had been members of the agency for at least 3 months and who had attended the agency at least twice a week during that period were eligible to be interviewed. Interviewers went to the self-help agencies at different times and on different days with no consistent schedule. All interviewers were trained by the Center for Self-Help Research. Interviewers included former mental health clients and mental health professionals with experience in interacting with people with serious mental disabilities.

Only 3 of 25 staff and 10 of 236 long-term users who were approached to participate in the survey refused to participate. All active volunteers participated. The total response rate was 96%.

Respondents were asked questions about service utilization, resource availability, history of disability, and experiences in the agency. Functional status, psychological disability, and health problems were assessed using the Brief Psychiatric Rating Scale (BPRS) (Overall & Gorham, 1962); the Langner Scale (Langer, 1962), which screens for psychiatric symptoms indicating impairment; and the Health Problems Checklist (Segal, VanderVoort, & Liese, 1995). The interviewers also administered the Diagnostic Interview Schedule (DIS), excluding modules for diagnoses believed to be either uncommon in this population (for example, bulimia) or to have a less critical effect on daily coping (for example, tobacco dependence).

Data were also drawn from a management information system we developed for one of the four self-help agencies as well as from the management information systems of two community mental health agencies located near two of the self-help agencies. We also used information from one self-help agency's fiscal reports to obtain data on the demographic characteristics of the total client population of that agency.

Results

Findings are presented in four sections: characteristics of respondents data about referral and services, comparisons of people who use community mental health agencies and self-help agencies, and data about several self-help organizations outside California.

TABLE 1.
DEMOGRAPHIC CHARACTERISTICS OF LONG-TERM CLIENTS OF FOUR SELF-HELP AGENCIES IN THE SAN FRANCISCO BAY AREA

(N= 310)

Characteristic	%
Gender	
Male	72
Female	28
Ethnicity	
African American	64
White	17
Latino or black Latino	7
Native American	5
Asian	1
Other, declined to answer	6
Primary diagnosis	
None	13
Drug or alcohol abuse	20
Antisocial personality disorder	12
Panic disorder, posttraumatic stress disorder, anxiety disorder, dysthymia	24
Affective disorder	19
Schizophrenia	13
Homeless or living in shelter	46
Marital status	
Never married	49
Ever married	51
Never married or lived with partner for more than a year	14
Ever married or lived with partner for more than a year	86
Age (years)	
18 to 24	5
25 to 44	76
45 to 64	19
Over 65	<1
Education	
Less than high school	27
High school	30
Technical	3
Some college	31
Bachelor's degree or more	8

Client Characteristics
Demographic characteristics. Table 1 shows data on the demographic characteristics of the 310 survey respondents. The mean age was 37 years, and the median age was 38 years. Particularly noteworthy was

the high proportion of African American and homeless individuals in the survey sample.

Twenty-seven percent of respondents were staff or volunteers (members who worked 10 or more hours a week at the agency). There were no significant differences between staff and volunteers and other respondents in gender or ethnicity. Staff and volunteers had more education than other respondents: 18% of the staff and volunteers had a bachelor's degree or more education, compared with 4% of other respondents (χ^2 = 7.27, df = 6, $p<$ .0006).

Housing status. Forty-six percent of respondents were literally homeless, that is, they lived on the streets or in a shelter. Many of the remaining respondents were precariously housed: 18.5% of them had to vacate their residences within 2 months, and almost half within 2 weeks. Of those who had to leave within 2 months, 62% had no idea of where they would live next. If the percentage of precariously housed respondents with no prospects for housing were added to the percentage who are literally homeless, a total of 59% of the respondents could be considered homeless.

In addition, 78% of respondents had been homeless at least once in the past 5 years, often for considerable periods of time. The median amount of time they had been homeless was a little more than 2 years. Ten percent had been homeless for the entire 5 years.

Staff and volunteers were less likely than other respondents to be literally homeless at the time of the interview (29% vs. 52%; χ^2 = 12.34, df = 1, p = .0004). However, they did not differ from other members in likelihood of being precariously housed or of having been homeless during the past 5 years.

Disabilities. Respondents had multiple disabilities. Eighty-seven percent had confirmed *DSM-III-R* diagnoses, as indicated by the DIS. Half of the respondents had a dual diagnosis of mental illness and moderate or severe substance abuse or dependence. An additional 20% had a diagnosis of only substance abuse or dependence. No differences were found between staff and volunteers and other respondents in diagnostic characteristics, although staff and volunteers were more likely to have a diagnosis of an affective disorder (25% vs. 16%; χ^2 = 4.80, df = 1, p = .028).

Fifty-nine percent had a score of 4 or higher on the Langner Scale, indicating serious psychological disability (Langer, 1962). Staff and volunteers were slightly less likely than other respondents to have a score of 4 or higher, but the difference only approached significance (p = .06).

The BPRS rates respondents on 24 items using a scale from 1 to 7, on which scores of 6 and 7 indicate clinically significant symptoms occurring in the past month (Overall & Gorham, 1962). Ratings are based on self-report and interviewer observations. BPRS interrater reliabilities were in the .9 range in this study. Twenty-four percent of respondents had at least one clinically significant symptom. Staff and volunteers were less likely than others to have clinically significant symptoms, as measured by the BPRS (16.5% vs. 27.6%; χ^2 = 4.096, df = 1, p =.04).

Taken together, the DIS, Langner, and BPRS scores support the claim that self-help agencies serve a population with severe mental disabilities, which justifies their support by public mental health systems.

Many respondents also had physical disabilities. Respondents were asked about the occurrence of 34 heath problems during the previous 6 months, including those often found among homeless individuals such as swollen ankles, arthritis and rheumatism, and frequent severe chest colds. Only 10% had no health problems; 25% listed eight or more problems. Twenty-two percent mentioned arthritis or rheumatism, 7% fits or seizures, and 5% tuberculosis. No differences in health problems were observed between staff and volunteers and other respondents.

Income and employment. Although 98% of respondents had held paid jobs in the past, only 24% did so at the time of the interview. Many of those who were employed had low-paying, undependable jobs. Respondents worked a median of 19 hours per week, and 52% of those who worked held temporary jobs. Of respondents who were working, 19% were unable to find at least some work every week. Median monthly wages were $550. Those who were not employed by the self-help agencies typically performed low-skilled manual labor.

Many respondents received government support. Thirty-six percent received Supplemental Security Income or Social Security Disability Income, and 36% received general assistance. Nine percent of respondents had children who stayed with them; 5% received Aid to Families With Dependent Children.

A caveat in interpreting these figures is that many respondents made at least some income from panhandling or "hustling"—combinations of legal and illegal activities. Interviewers asked for details from respondents who said they engaged in these activities, but respondents varied in their willingness to discuss them. In many cases, respondents did not view hustling as work, and the reimbursement they received for these activities was not in cash.

Life stressors. Eighty-seven percent of respondents had experienced at least one of 16 major stressors shown in Table 2 in the past year, and 60% had experienced such stressors in the past month. Given the high percentage who were homeless, the num-

TABLE 2.
STRESSFUL LIFE EVENTS IN THE PAST YEAR AMONG LONG-TERM CLIENTS OF SELF-HELP AGENCIES
AND SAMPLES OF COMMUNITY RESIDENTS AND PSYCHIATRIC OUTPATIENTS,
IN PERCENTAGES

Event	Long-Term Clients (N = 310)	Community Sample (N = 275)[1]	Outpatients (N = 118)[1]
Thrown out of or lost place where staying	44	—	—
Lost job	23	6.3	8.7
Lost other source of income	20	—	—
Separated from spouse or significant other	32	0.8	8.8
Lost or had stolen a valuable possession	47	—	—
Lost or used up money saved	48	—	—
Turned down for entitlements	21	—	—
Spent time in jail or prison	29	—	—
Involuntary hospitalization	8	—	—
Serious accident	15	2.0	4.4
Sick or disabled	18	14.2	16.7
Someone close died	39	15.7	16.7
Someone close very sick or hurt	30	10.7	11.4
Lost custody of child	8	—	—
Beaten, mugged, stabbed, or raped	24	—	—
Attempted suicide	8	—	—

From Dohrenwend and Dohrenwend (1974)

bers who lost housing or a job is not surprising. However, respondents were also likely to have experienced disruption through separation, death, or illness of significant others and to have themselves been ill or injured. Eight percent attempted suicide in the past year.

For comparison of respondents' life stressors with those of other populations, Table 2 also shows data from earlier studies of life stressors in a community sample and a sample of psychiatric outpatients (Dohrenwend & Dohrenwend, 1974). Although the data for the two comparison groups are old, the large differences between the percentages shown for the comparison groups and those for the respondents are disturbing.

Referral and Services

Two raters coded responses to an open-ended question about ways in which respondents had heard about the self-help agency. Responses were classified with a 95% rate of agreement into seven categories. Pathways to the agency primarily depended on informal referrals. Most respondents (46.1%) were referred by friends or relatives. One fifth were referred by a mental health or social service agency. Twenty percent heard about the agency by word of mouth on the street, and 10% saw the agency when they happened to be walking by.

Responses to an open-ended question about what initially brought respondents to the self-help agency suggested the importance of basic resources. Two raters classified responses to this question with 78% agreement into eight categories. Most respondents came to the agency for resources such as food or clothing (31.6%). Others came for a "place to be" (22%), because they were homeless and needed help (12.8%), or because they sought "to be with people" (10.2%) or to see what was available (8.1%). Obtaining counseling (8.4%) or help for substance or alcohol

abuse (4.9%) or participating in self-help or helping others (4.3%) were less important reasons for first coming to the agencies.

During a 6-month assessment period, basic resources from the self-help agency were received by the following percentages of respondents: food (26.3%), bus pass (28.5%), place to shower (21.2%), clothing (36.9%), mailing address (42.3%), personal items (18.6%), temporary housing (34.3%), storage (23.4%), supported employment (22%), help in finding a job (24.7%), help with rent (17.9%), and service information (38.85%).

A total of 41.8% of respondents received counseling. Forty-five percent of those respondents received counseling only for psychiatric problems, 25% only for substance abuse problems, 22% for both types of problems, and 8% for some other problem. The median duration of counseling was 42 weeks for psychiatric problems and 20 weeks for substance abuse counseling. Psychological counseling was primarily provided by mental health professionals affiliated with the community mental health agency; substance abuse counseling was provided by equal proportions of professionals and nonprofessionals.

Fifty-two percent of respondents had a history of psychiatric hospitalization, and 75% of that group had been hospitalized within the past 10 years. Of the respondents hospitalized in the past 10 years, 71% had been held involuntarily at least one time.

The management information system at one of the self-help agencies we studied showed that over a 1-year period the agency provided about 239 service hours in an average week. The average daily attendance for drop-in and service activities was 162, with a range from 100 to 283. An individual who was highly active in the agency's activities received about 11 hours of service a week, and a less active individual about 1.5 hours. For persons at both levels of activity, primary services included training

TABLE 3.
CHARACTERISTICS OF CLIENTELE AT TWO SELF-HELP AGENCIES AND TWO CLINICS
OPERATED BY A COMMUNITY MENTAL HEALTH AGENCY (CMHA) IN THE
SAN FRANCISCO BAY AREA, IN PERCENTAGES

| Characteristic | Self-Help Agencies | | CMHA Clinics | |
	Agency 1 (N= 1,456)	Agency 2 ((N=987)	Clinic 1 ((N=2,650)	Clinic 2 ((N=735)
Gender				
Male	61.0	71	51	51.0
Female	39.0	29	49	49.0
Ethnicity				
African American	76.0	78	57	38.7
White	18.0	17	26	46.5
Latino or black Latino	4.0	1	4	3.7
Native American	1.0	1	1	1.0
Asian	0.5	1	9	1.7
Other, declined go answer	0.5	2	3	1.4
Primary diagnosis[2]				
None	9.0	13	1	na
Drug or alcohol abuse	16.0	21	3	12.5
Antisocial personality disorder	8.0	15	0	na
Panic disorder, posttraumatic stress disorder, anxiety disorder, dysthymia	25.0	27	6	6.1
Affective disorder	24.0	16	21	37.4
Schizophrenia	18.0	8	35	19.0
Other nonorganic disorder	na	na	33	na
Other organic disorder	na	na	2	na
Homeless	55.0	62	11	20.0

[1] Median ages of the four client groups were 40 years at self-help agency 1, 35 years at self-help agency 2, 40 years at CMHA Clinic 1, and 38 years at CMHA clinic 2.

[2] Primary diagnoses for clients of the self-help agencies were estimated from data on the sample of long-term members.

in independent living skills, peer counseling, access to telephones, and assistance in obtaining clothing. Both groups of individuals used the drop-in center more than 20 hours a week.

Comparing Users of Two Types of Agencies

Table 3 shows demographic and clinical characteristics of all members—not just our long-term sample—at two of the self-help agencies we studied and characteristics of clients of two clinics operated by a community mental health agency serving the area

in which the self-help agencies are located.

The two self-help agencies are partly funded by the community mental health agency and are intended to serve homeless individuals with mental disabilities. A much higher percentage of persons served by the self-help agencies are homeless compared with those served by the clinics operated by the community mental health agency, even though the clinics are located near the self-help agencies. Thus the self-help agencies are able to attract and retain precisely the individuals they claim to serve and are intended to serve by one of their funding sources.

The extent to which the self-help agencies reach the homeless mentally disabled population in the area is impossible to determine. However, data gathered by Robertson and associates (Robertson, Zlotnick, & Westerfelt et al., 1993) in the county where this study was done and during the same time period show that the ethnic distribution of homeless individuals with *DSM-III-R* diagnoses matches exactly that among the homeless individuals in our sample.

The populations served by the self-help agencies and by the clinics operated by the community mental health agency overlap—28% of respondents to our survey currently received psychiatric counseling, and an additional 26% had done so in the past. Eighty-seven percent of the survey respondents had a confirmed *DSM-III-R* diagnosis. Of those who currently received psychiatric counseling, 66% began counseling after they became members of the self-help agency. The data suggest that the self-help agency is able to reach individuals through informal referral and then to connect those who wish additional services with community mental health agencies.

The *DSM-III-R* diagnoses derived from the DIS may underrepresent the actual number of disorders present in the survey sample. The DIS screening criteria for symptom severity include consultation with professionals, use of medication, and interference with daily life activities. An unknown proportion of the individuals we interviewed avoided professionals, took illegal rather than legal drugs to alleviate symptoms, and denied that psychological problems interfered with their daily activities, even though the interviewer suspected that they were a cause of the respondents' homelessness.

Given selection procedures that traditionally have reduced use of outpatient mental health services by African Americans (Neighbors, 1985), especially those with dual diagnoses or substance abuse problems, these data are extremely important because they include many individuals from these less-well-served groups. About 64% of the persons served by the self-help agencies in our sample are African Americans; at least 50% of the members of these agencies have been diagnosed with moderate to severe substance or alcohol abuse or dependence in addition to their mental disorder.

A National Perspective

To our knowledge, no data on a nationwide sample of clients of self-help agencies exist. However, information on 160 clients of five self-help agencies outside of California were gathered by Judi Chamberlin at the Center for Psychiatric Rehabilitation in Boston (Chamberlin J. personal communication, 1993).

Although no diagnostic data are available for this sample, notable demographic differences were found between the members of the self-help agencies in our study and of those studied by Chamberlin. The agencies in our study served more males (72% vs. 55%) and emphasized services to African Americans (64% vs. 9%) and homeless persons (46% vs. 15%). The agencies in our study also served a higher proportion of persons with at least some college education (39% vs. 15%) and a higher proportion of persons with less than an high school education (27% vs. 15%).

Current information provided by leaders in the self-help movement indicates that programs with high percentages of members who are African American and other people of color are beginning to develop throughout the country (D'Asaro, 1994; D'Asaro, A., personal communication, 1995).

Discussions and Conclusions

The self-help agencies in the San Francisco Bay Area that we surveyed, along with local community mental health agencies, serve a highly needy population with mental disorders and substance abuse diagnoses. The demographic characteristics of the population served by the self-help agencies were similar to those of mentally disabled homeless people in the San Francisco Bay Area and in other urban areas (Robertson, Zlotnick, & Westerfeld, 1992; Robertson, Zlotnick, & Westerfeld, 1993; Rossi, 1989). The demographic data suggest that self-help agencies, in combination with community mental health agencies, can serve a poor, primarily African American and often homeless population—subgroups that are traditionally less well served by the mental health system.

The differences between the populations served by self-help agencies and those served by community mental health agencies suggest a division of labor between the two types of agencies that has not yet been formalized or validated. Self-help agencies provide psychosocial and material assistance, while community mental health agencies provide medical and psychotherapeutic care. Evidence for this division of labor includes, first, the importance of self-referrals to self-help agencies among long-term members of such organizations, and, second, the high proportion of long-term clients receiving professional counseling primarily at local community mental health agencies who started such counseling after coming to the self-help agency. How well this division of labor works for clients remains unclear.

The comprehensive social supports, material assistance, and advocacy services required by poor, homeless, and seriously mentally disabled individuals are available in self-help agencies. Members are first attracted to self-help agencies by the material and social assistance offered, less so by counseling services. This finding is consistent with the expressed needs of homeless mentally disabled persons (Ball & Havassy, 1984; Tessler, 1989). Clients' use of counseling services develops with time.

Clients of self-help agencies who become staff and volunteers are in some ways better off than other long-term clients, but not so much so as to make them a separate or unique group. Although staff and volunteers are more educated and are more likely than other members to have an affective disorder, the majority of members filling these positions have neither a bachelor's degree nor an affective disorder. Staff and volunteers may be less symptomatic than other members, but they still show considerable symptoms. They are more likely than other members to have housing, but they are equally as likely to be housed precariously and to have experienced homelessness in the past 5 years.

Acknowledgments
This research is supported by grant MH-47487 from the National Institute of Mental Health and by grants from the Zellerbach Family Fund and the San Francisco Foundation.

References

Ball, J., & Havassy, B. E. (1984). A survey of the problems and needs of homeless consumers of acute psychiatric services. *Hospital and Community Psychiatry, 15,* 917-921.

D'Asaro, A. (1994). Consumers of color organize. *The Key, 2,* 3, 1-11.

Dohrenwend, B. C., & Dohrenwend, B. P. (1974). *Stressful life events.* New York: Wiley.

Emerick, R. E., (1989a). Group demographics in the mental patient movement: Group location, age, and size as structural factors. *Community Mental Health Journal, 25,* 277-300.

Emerick, R. E. (1989b). *Group structure and group dynamics in the mental health self-help movement: Toward a typology of groups.* Paper presented at a symposium on the Impact of Life-Threatening Conditions: Self-Help Groups and Health Care. Providers in Partnership, Chicago, March 31, 1989.

Emerick, R. E., (1992). *Group structure and group dynamics for ex-mental patients.* In A. F. Katz (Ed.), Self-help: Concepts and applications. Philadelphia:Charles Press.

Katz, A., & Bender, E. (1976.) *The strength in us: Self-help groups in the modem world.* New York: New Viewpoints.

Langner, T. S. (1962). A 22-item screening score for psychiatric symptoms indicating impairment. *Journal of Health and Human Behavior, 3,* 269-276.

Levy, L. H. (1984). Issues in research and evaluation. In A. Gartnet & E. T. Reissman (Eds.),*The self-help revolution.* New York: Human Sciences.

National Association of State Mental Health Program Directors. (1993). *Putting their money where their mouths are: SMHA support of consumer- and family-run programs.* Alexandria, VA: Author.

Neighbors, H. N. (1985). Seeking professional help for personal problems: Black Americans' use of health and mental health services. *Community Mental Health Journal 21,* 156-166.

Overall J. E., & Gorham, D. R. (1962). The Brief Psychiatric Rating Scale. *Psychosocial Reports 10,* 799-812.

Powell, T. (1987). *Self-help organizations and professional practice.* Silver Spring, MD: National Association of Social Workers.

Robertson, M., Zlotnick, S., & Westerfeld, A. (1992). *Homeless adults: mental health statistics and service utilization patterns.* Paper presented at the annual meeting of the American Public Health Association, Washington, DC, Nov 1992.

Robertson M, Zlotnick C, Westerfelt A, et al. (1993). *Health status and access to health services among homeless adults in Alameda County.* Paper presented at a meeting of the Society for Behavioral Medicine, San Francisco, March 11, 1993.

Rossi, P. (1989). *Down and out in America.* Chicago: University of Chicago Press.

Segal, S. P., VanderVoort, D. J., & Liese, L. H. (1995). *Health and a residential care population.* Working paper. Berkeley, CA: University of California Mental Health and Social Welfare Research Group.

Shorc, M. F. (1992). What is new in consumer-operated mental health services? *Harvard Mental Health Letter, 9*(2), 1.

Tessler, R. (1989). What have we learned to date? Assessing the first generation of NIMH supported research studies on the homeless mentally ill. In J. Morrissey & D. Dennis (Eds.), *Homelessness and mental illness: Toward the next generation of research studies,* Rockville, MD: National Institute of Mental Health.

Zinman, S. (1987). Definition of self-help groups. In S. Zinman, H. Harp, & S. Budd (Eds.), *Reaching across: Mental health clients helping each other.* Riverside CA: California Network of Mental Health Clients.

Zinman, S., Harp, H. T., & Budd, S. (Eds.). (1987). *Reaching across: Mental health clients helping each other.* Riverside, Calif, California Network of Mental Health Clients.

Professional Underutilization of Recovery, Inc.

Donald T. Lee

DONALD T. LEE, MSW, ACSW, IS A MENTAL HEALTH CONSULTANT IN JULIAN, CA.

THIS ARTICLE ORIGINALLY APPEARED IN THE
Psychiatric Rehabilitation Journal, 1995, 19(1), 63-69
AND IS REPRINTED WITH PERMISSION.

Professional literature since 1960 often reflects extreme misinterpretations of the self-help group, Recovery, Inc., developed by A. A. Low, a psychiatrist. The literature is reviewed, misinterpretations identified, corrections and clarification presented. There are 4 types of distortions: Language, meeting structure, ascribing religious parallels and the nature of self-help groups. Recovery, Inc. is seldom used by mental health professionals. This seems to be due to lack of information about the group and distortions from the literature and brief observations. Failure of therapists to collaborate results in losing critical treatment advantages not found and duplicated in professional services alone.

Introduction

Recovery, Inc. is an enigma among self-help groups. Few, if any other self-help groups, have been as misunderstood by their supporters, as well as their detractors, and as ignored or undiscovered by so many professionals. This paper will explore from the literature some misunderstandings by professionals about Recovery, Inc. and will cite one study by the author. It will point out certain reasons this self-help organization, the second oldest in age to Alcoholics Anonymous among self-help groups, is not yet more fully utilized.

Before looking at the literature on Recovery, Inc. it will be helpful to gain a wider perspective on professional attitudes towards self-help groups. The emergence of self-help groups presented a quandary for professionals, would they utilize these new entities and work with them or reject them (Dumont, 1974; Levy, 1976; Powell, 1979; Black & Drachman, 1985)? This question has not been settled today with any uniformity.

Katz (1965) pointed out quite early, "it seems clear that there are powerful restraining psychological influences at work and it will be some time before the self-help approach will be more widely understood and utilized." Although he was addressing social workers when he wrote this he could have been describing any of the mental health professions.

Generally there have been strong recommendations by academics and some clinicians to integrate professional treatment and self-help groups to improve mental health services (Huey, 1977; Gottlieb & Schroter, 1978; Hermalin, Melendez, Kamarck, Levans, Ballen, & Gordon, 1979; Powell, 1979; Todres, 1982; Lurie & Schulman, 1983; Coplan & Strull, 1983; Toseland & Hacker, 1985; Black & Drachman, 1985; Kurtz & Chambon, 1987; and Kerson, 1990).

Toseland and Hacker (1983) found that social workers held "positive or very positive views about self-help groups." Powell (1987) pointed out that while professionals may hold positive attitudes this did not necessarily mean they referred patients to self-help groups.

Kurtz, Mann, and Chambon (1987) did an extensive study of professional utilization of self-help groups finding that professionals are less willing to use self-help groups when the self-help group is offering services that more closely resemble professional services. They found they can work together if the differences between their work are clearly established.

Katz (1993), taking a wary view, points out, "that there is still a long way to go before professionals broadly accept these groups" and he likens the process to that of industrial workers faced with learning "new skills when their plants begin making different products."

In 1973, Grosz found only 37% of Recovery members had been referred by professionals. Psychiatrists accounted for 20% and the remainder were family physicians, social workers, and religious advisers. In 1978, Raiff found that 30% of Recovery members had been referred by physicians and 9% by other professionals and semiprofessionals. Levy's (1979) study of 748 mental health agencies' utilization of self-help groups showed Recovery, Inc. as being well above average in the view of professionals referring patients compared to 20 other self-help groups (S. Sachs, personal communication, re: letter from L. H. Levy, June 29, 1993). Galanter in 1990 found only 12% of Recovery members referred by psychiatrists.

At best this is a meager percentage of referrals coming from the professional sector. These declining percentages also may point to a reduction in professional referrals over the 16 years covered by these studies.

The author completed a project in 1989 to introduce Recovery, Inc. to a number of forensic programs. A study was made subsequently of forensic mental health professionals to learn usage patterns of self-help groups and in particular, Recovery, Inc. (Lee, 1993).

Ninety-four percent of these 47 professionals referred patients to Alcoholics Anonymous or Narcotics Anonymous. These forensic professionals utilized nine other self-help groups. In spite of extensive use of other self-help groups only 2% of these therapists had used Recovery, Inc. and 38% reported they had never heard of Recovery, Inc. or had heard only of the name (Lee, 1993).

History of Recovery Inc.

Abraham A. Low, a psychiatrist with psychoanalytic training, began formulating the Recovery method in 1937 when he was the assistant director of the Illinois Psychiatric Institute (Low, 1950). Low was treating in a group, patients diagnosed psychotic who now were ready to return to the community. Later he combined neurotic patients he was treating in the community with his hospital patients (T. Rice, personal communication, January 1994).

During the 1940s he continued refining the method and expanding his concepts. He published *Mental Health Through Will Training* for his patients' use in learning the method through case examples and lectures (Low, 1950). Low began in 1952, 2 years before he died, teaching patients how to run the meetings themselves and how to employ the method's self-help aspects (Low, 1950; Rau & Rau, 1971).

Recovery, Inc. has been a self-help group since that time with members conducting meetings and training the leaders. Groups spread throughout the United States, Canada, the Caribbean (See Low's book, *Mental Health Through Will Training,* Spanish language edition [Low, 1976]) as well as England, Wales, and Ireland (C. Jungheim, personal communication, January 1994).

Summary of Recovery Inc. Method

When Low pioneered his treatment method it was some years before Beck and Meichenbaum applied the term cognitive to this treatment approach (Cormier & Cormier, 1985). Low taught his patients a blend of Recovery and self-help methods that were most harmonious. However, this congruence occurred so early that many professionals, especially those firmly entrenched in psychoanalytic theory, had a difficult time accepting Recovery, Inc.

Low also was a semanticist (Collier, 1991; Lee, 1991) who created a special language for his method to reach his patients more effectively. He recognized that language was of utmost importance (Rau & Rau, 1971) for it was fundamental to the cognitive treatment process. Patients would become alarmed by symptoms and would self diagnose their condition in extreme terms (intolerable, uncontrollable, terrible, etc. or of dangerous organic etiology). When Low found that patients were angry towards themselves (fearful temper) or others (angry temper) this brought on tenseness that triggered symptoms. Low described how patients entered a vicious cycle accompanied by defeatism. Symptoms meant danger [the fear of a permanent handicap] and defeatism derived from the belief that the patient had a permanent handicap. Thus more symptoms ensued (Low, 1950). Low (1950) emphasized that each person has a *will* that is always available. By systematically applying the cognitive behavioral concepts he developed, (for example, controlling thoughts, moving or controlling muscles, averageness [lowering expectations] and objectivity [describing symptoms factually]) patients could use their will to take responsibility for their lives and control the tenseness leading to symptoms.

Low (1950) carefully developed his treatment language to be free of alarmist associations and fully understandable to his patients. He knew it was essential to have a non-psychiatric vocabulary since he did not want patients in a self-help mode getting in over their heads with psychiatric terminology they didn't understand.

He taught his patients ways to resolve their problems of distressful symptoms and physical sensations through a variety of cognitive-behavioral techniques. Recovery, Inc. in gaining acceptance among professionals was faced with two problems: 1) The term *cognitive behavioral therapy* was not applied for some years, and 2) cognitive behavioral therapy also suffered from lack of general acceptance among professionals; in large part because the supporting research for cognitive behavioral therapy was not yet available (Cormier & Cormier, 1985).

How Recovery, Inc. Meetings Function

Low established the self-help component of his approach to enable mentally disordered people, with systematic training, to lead meetings and use the method. He knew they needed firm structure to achieve a secure setting. Meetings, therefore, follow a formal pattern. Everyone sits around a table and takes turns reading aloud a chapter from Low's book, *Mental Health Through Will Training*. Members can participate in a variety of ways according to their level of functioning. Some may sit and listen, while others read, give an example, "spot" (describe what Recovery terms apply to an example presented), and ask questions in the mutual-aid period at the end of the meeting.

Structured meetings permit less functional members, or those lacking confidence, to participate flexibly and just to the degree they are capable. New members are asked

Few, if any other self-help groups, have been as misunderstood by their supporters, as well as their detractors, and as ignored or undiscovered by so many professionals.

not to give examples or try to "spot" at meetings until they become familiar with the method through reading part of Low's book. They are encouraged to ask questions and participate in the mutual-aid period. When the members are through reading aloud the leader asks for four volunteers to give examples.

An assistant leader will begin by reading aloud the questions outlining how examples should be presented. Panel members then follow this outline for giving their examples about a triviality of everyday life showing when and where the event took place, who was there and what was said or done. The member then describes the working up process of what nervous or mental symptoms developed and what Recovery methods were used to handle them. As Low taught, all members must relate how they have endorsed the effort they made in using the Recovery method. The member completes the example by describing the differences experienced in their life before Recovery training compared to now. This comparison serves to remind members how much progress they have made and to show other members how systematic practice can help.

The leader asks each experienced member to "spot" or to identify in Recovery terms what methods were employed or should have been used by the person presenting. The member giving the example may accept or reject what is said by others, but it must be done silently.

Low emphasized a vital treatment approach when he told his patients to focus

Although cognitive behavioral treatment is widely accepted now, Low's methods were not identified with it until recently; in part because the language Low devised for his patients was unfamiliar to most professionals.

only on trivialities of everyday life. First, it relabels and reduces the problem to a manageable size so as not to overwhelm the patient. Second, it was an astute way Low had of dealing with some extraordinarily complex problems. A triviality of everyday life will often condense and represent the patient's basic life problem. People generally are not threatened by discussing trivialities of everyday life; they are seen as inconsequential events. Focusing on trivialities makes it possible to discuss coping mechanisms that otherwise might be too threatening.

Low gave his patients a diverse range of techniques to handle their problems. He taught patients how they can control their thoughts because they can only think one thought at a time. Therefore, when the patient has an insecure thought this can be replaced by a secure thought. Low taught patients why they cannot change their feelings nor their sensations directly. However, if they systematically change their thoughts this will change feelings and sensations.

Recovery members are taught to use their will to command their muscles to either move or to be controlled depending on the problem they are suffering. Again, the patients' use of will enables them to say yes or no to thoughts and impulses thereby placing them in better control of their own lives (T. Rice, personal communication, January 1994).

Members augment the above Recovery methods when they reinforce their good mental health practices by self-endorsement of effort, not accomplishment.

Analysis of Critical Literature

There have been numerous misunderstandings about Recovery, Inc. by professionals in the literature. Critics and some supporters did not recognize that Low was a pioneer in utilizing cognitive behavioral treatment methods. Most professionals, regardless of whether they supported the organization or criticized it, failed to recognize the importance of Low's treatment method.

Although cognitive behavioral treatment is widely accepted now, Low's methods were not identified with it until recently; in part because the language Low devised for his patients was unfamiliar to most professionals.

These problems have caused a rift between professionals, who have been so influenced, and this self-help group. These problems fall into four areas:

1.) Unfamiliarity with cognitive behavioral therapy leading to objections to Recovery language and terms.

2.) Lack of appreciation of patients' needs for security and uniformity leading to objections about structure and methods of the organization.

3.) Ascribing religious parallels to the structure of meetings and the enthusiasm of members.

4.) Holding unrealistic expectations due to confusing self-help groups with social or medical agencies.

Some critics (Antze, 1976; Omark, 1982; Powell, 1992) were unable to accept the language Low used as a necessary condition for cognitive therapy. They did not appreciate that Low was writing for his patients' use and not for other professionals. While some have referred to his work as cognitive, (Wechsler, 1960; Levy, 1976; Kurtz & Chambon, 1987) most, including a support-

er, (Dean, 1971), did not understand that Low had worked out a comprehensive system enabling his patients to understand and overcome their difficulties.

Critics (Wechsler, 1960; Levy, 1976; Omark, 1982) also complained that Recovery meetings are too structured. These authors did not appreciate that mentally disordered people, who usually need more structure, attend Recovery, Inc. meetings. Structure promotes learning through repetition and uniformity thereby providing substantial emotional security.

Great misunderstandings occurred about Low's dictum that patients should keep from sabotaging their mental health by refraining from self-diagnosis. Wechsler (1960) and Antze (1976) so misunderstood Low's prohibitions about self-diagnosis that they asserted that Low was telling his patients that they were all well! Low wanted his patients to accept his diagnosis that their condition was not a hopeless, incurable organic disorder. Low particularly emphasized the somatic symptoms of both psychosis and neurosis from the patient's viewpoint. He was keenly aware how somatic symptoms spelled danger of the permanent handicap to his patients. The critics could not understand why Low's patients needed to know that they had no organic pathology. This is far different from telling patients that they were all well.

Reinforcement is an important aspect of cognitive behavioral therapy. Cognitive behavioral therapists have found that when patients reward themselves for exhibiting healthy behavior (reinforcement) this promotes their continued use of such healthy behavior (Cormier & Cormier, 1985). Reinforcement is most effective the closer it occurs to the desired event (Cormier & Cormier, 1985). Low's approach was unique because he put an emphasis on endorsing effort and control, not accomplishment. Low (1950) insisted patients only endorse effort and not accomplishment because everyone can make an effort, but average people may or may not succeed in every attempt to change. Low's distinction is uniquely important for it puts the focus on self-effort and the use of will. It also removes the tendency for patients to seek approval from others. He wanted them to incorporate their own system of self reward and not become dependent on outside approval.

One of Low's bitterest critics, Wechsler (1960), so misunderstood self-endorsement that he distorted what Low said. For example, he wrote, "The emphasis on the power of positive thinking and on inspiration is also analogous to some religious tenets." Nowhere in Low's writings does one find anything about the power of positive thinking. Furthermore, Wechsler (1960) mistakenly thought patients were seeking praise from other members. What he heard was Low's admonition that leaders should remind members to endorse themselves when in giving an example they fail to state they endorsed themselves.

Other critics (Wechsler, 1960; Antze, 1976) have charged quite mistakenly that Low's method devaluates feelings. Lieberman and Bond (1979) similarly describe Recovery, Inc. as a method that "encourages 'denial-like' mechanisms." Low (1950) makes it quite clear that people should cultivate feelings and express them. Too many critics have mistaken temper for feelings, as did Low's patients. Low (1950) said, Feelings call for expression, temper for suppression. The assertion of

Cognitive behavioral therapists today relabel many of their patient's distorted views into different terms, thereby enabling the patient to cope more effectively. Low's approach was good cognitive behavioral therapy—not devaluating feelings.

temper blocks the expression of true feelings (Low, 1950). Low was most insistent that his patients learn how to express their genuine feelings for this is how best to communicate with other people (Low, 1950). Low had an opportunity to correct his patients' misperceptions, but not his critics.

Low was working with both post psychotic and seriously ill neurotic patients and he knew they tended to misinterpret both feelings and sensations. He said a person could not change either one directly. However, by changing one's thoughts, feelings and sensations can be altered. For example, if a patient told Low that he felt people were staring at him, Low might have said the patient must change his insecure thoughts for secure thoughts.

Cognitive behavioral therapists today relabel many of their patient's distorted views into different terms, thereby enabling the patient to cope more effectively. Low's approach was good cognitive behavioral therapy—not devaluating feelings. Many of Low's critics jumped to almost bizarre conclusions about his method seemingly without checking their impressions against what Low wrote.

Wechsler (1960) and Omark (1982) deplored Recovery's lack of a procedure by which patients were discharged or graduated. Both authors seemed to believe that a self-help group should have an admissions service, records, and formal discharge procedures. They thought Recovery, Inc. trapped patients into becoming forever dependent because there were no discharge procedures. Most mental health professionals are more concerned with their chronically disordered mental patients avoiding treatment, discontinuing their medication, and other noncompliant behavior. The author knows of no self-help group that sets a time limit on membership. It is inconceivable for an Alcoholics Anonymous group, for example, to terminate a member upon achieving sobriety. Older members assert how many years of sobriety they have attained precisely to forcefully influence new members as well as to reinforce their own progress. Displaying well role models is one of the special attributes of Recovery, Inc. (Lee, 1966).

One critic (Gartner, 1976) feared long-term attendance at Recovery meetings would promote dependency. Dean (1970), Raiff (1982), and Suler (1984) refute this. The author's experience has been that long-term membership promotes independence and autonomy. Recovery members who stay in the organization for a number of years take on greater responsibilities and become more self-sufficient over time. Independence building should not be surprising since the Recovery method emphasizes asserting one's will and becoming self-led versus symptom-led.

Several critics of Recovery, (Wechsler, 1960; Antze, 1976; Spiegel, 1977), have likened Recovery meetings to a religious ceremony. They also thought Recovery members used Low's book as a Bible. These pejorative comments may well have prejudiced professionals unacquainted with the reality.

Suler (1984) said, "Overly dependent members may almost deify the founders of the teaching, as some critics have construed Recovery's reverence for Abraham Low." Hurvitz, (1970) writing about Alcoholics Anonymous and Recovery, Inc., came up with a far different conclusion. He saw Alcoholics Anonymous "as following a religious tradition emphasizing guilt, estrangement, penance and reunion; while Recovery has a secular tradition emphasizing will and responsibility."

Galanter (1990) saw Recovery, Inc. as being a zealous cult. What Galanter failed to appreciate was the history of Recovery, Inc. since Low died. First, many of Low's original patients have actively trained leaders and administered the organization. They were keenly aware, when Low was alive, of the many attacks on his method. They grasped the problem he faced with other psychiatrists wanting to take over and manipulate his method. Recovery patients knew Low's method helped them and they wanted to preserve the method he had devised. Newer members have all learned this history. Recovery members had good reason to be apprehensive when there have been so many misunderstandings about the Recovery method.

Frustration in many Recovery members led to an attempt to sell Recovery to professionals by some over-enthusiastic supporters. What Galanter thought was zealousness was an expression of frustration. Members of Recovery, Inc. find the method works and are unable to see why so many professionals cannot see it, too.

Many of the Recovery members the author has talked to over 28 years have expressed disappointment that more professionals have not collaborated with Recovery for their patients. Patients report how helpful close

Low wanted his patients to accept his diagnosis that their condition was not a hopeless, incurable organic disorder.

affiliation has been when it occurs, not only for them but for the therapist too, as Dean (1971) reported.

Possibly all of the above factors contributed to the lack of understanding about Recovery, Inc. The central issue is that so many professionals have overlooked Recovery, Inc. as a vital established community resource while others have rejected it. In a time when we especially need all of our mental health assets this is a serious loss.

Recommendations

Due to the cognitive behavioral basis in Recovery methods it is valuable for a therapist to use these concepts with their patients. The therapist can count on the other members of Recovery, Inc. to support the authority of the patient's own therapist. A wide range of patients with different diagnoses are able to benefit from a joint or collaborative program (Lee, 1971). As Barter (1993) points out, "Many psychiatrists and mental health professionals unfamiliar with Recovery, Inc. assume that Dr. Low's techniques work only for the neurotic and the 'worried well.' In fact, severely mentally ill individuals have been involved with Recovery's method and have been helped by it."

One major advantage for patients under professional treatment is to have an ongoing support group focused on a similar approach to help augment professional sessions. The Recovery group reinforces individual therapy and provides many opportunities for patients to increase their coping skills. Recovery, Inc. uniquely supports the therapist even when the therapist's approach differs from Recovery methods.

Katz (1993) said, "professional services cannot [provide]: the powerful element of peer support, the effects of individual role models in the group, and the interactions occasioned by the giving and receiving of help." Therapists referring patients to Recovery, Inc. can work in unison to furnish those critical factors not found in professional services alone. This will enrich the present mental health system by giving it the best of both professional and self-help resources.

Conclusions

Mental health professionals underutilize Recovery, Inc. for four reasons:

1.) Some of the earliest literature on Recovery, Inc. was highly prejudicial against this self-help group due to gross misunderstandings of Low's method. Some of Low's critics were unable to understand cognitive behavioral therapy as a treatment system. Subsequently, many professionals have been influenced by strong anti-Recovery biases in the literature.

2.) The four types of misapprehensions identified from the critical literature may reveal that other professionals have followed a parallel process and formed erroneous opinions about this self-help group just as did the authors cited.

3.) Many professionals are unaware of Recovery, Inc. They lack basic information about the second oldest self-help group in the mental health field.

4.) The dynamism and longevity of self-help groups has demonstrated for five decades that they are an integral part of the mental health arena. Nevertheless, many professionals, possibly due to their own unclear professional role definitions, have looked on this self-help group as a rival rather than a vital collaborative resource for their patients.

References

Antze, P. (1976). The role of ideologies in peer psychotherapy organizations: Some theoretical considerations and three case studies. *Journal of Applied Behavioral Science, 12,* 323-346.

Barter, J. T. (1993). *Uniqueness of Recovery, Inc.* Newsletter, Abraham A. Low Institute. p.3.

Black, R.B., & Drachman, D. (1985). Hospital social workers and self-help groups. *Health & Social Work, 10,* 95-103.

Collier, G. (1991, May 16). The essential role of language in the Recovery method. In P. L. Berning (Chair), *Conference on mental illness, stigma and self-help, Recovery, Inc., and the pioneering work of Abraham A. Low.* Chicago, IL.

Coplon, J. & Strull, J. (1983). Roles of the professional in mutual aid groups. Social Casework: *Journal of Contemporary Social Work, 64,* 259-266.

Cormier, W. H., & Cormier, L. S. (1985). *Interviewing strategies for helpers.* (2nd ed.). Monterey, CA: Brooks/Cole.

Dean, S. R. (1970/71). Self-help group psychotherapy: Mental patients rediscover will power. *International Journal of Psychiatry, 17,* 72-78.

Dean, S. R. (1971). The role of self-conducted group therapy in psychorehabilitation: A look at Recovery, Inc. *American Journal of Psychiatry, 127,* 934-937.

Dumont, M. P. (1974). Self-help treatment programs. *American Journal of Psychiatry, 131,* 631-635.

Galanter, M. (1990). Cults and zealous self-help movements: A psychiatric perspective. *American Journal of Psychiatry, 147,* 543-551.

Gartner, A. (1977). Self-help and mental health. *Social Policy, 7* (2), 28-40.

Gottlieb, B. H., & Schroter, C. (1978). Collaboration and resource exchange between professionals and natural support systems. *Professional Psychology, 9,* 614-622.

Grosz, H. J. (1973, June 20). Professionals found referring patients to self-help groups. *Psychiatric News,* p.20.

Hermalin, J., Melendez, L., Kamarck, T., Levans, F., Ballen, E., & Gordon, M. (1979). Enhancing primary prevention: The marriage of self-help groups and formal health care delivery systems. *Journal of Clinical Child Psychology, 8,* 125-129.

Huey, K. (1977). Developing effective links between human-services provider and the self-help system. *Hospital & Community Psychiatry, 28,* 767-770.

Hurvitz, N. (1970). Peer self-help psychotherapy groups and their implications for psychotherapy. *Psychotherapy: Theory, Research and Practice, 7,* 41-49.

Katz, A. H. (1965). Application of self-help concepts in current social welfare. *Social Work, 10* (3), 68-74.

Katz, A. H. (1993). *Self-help in America: A social movement perspective.* NJ: Twane.

Kerson, T. S. (1990). Lending a vision: Ways in which self-help efforts promote practice creativity. In H.H. Weissman (Ed.) *Serious play: Innovations & creativity in social work.* Silver Springs, MD: NASW.

Kurtz, L. F., Mann, K. B., & Chambon, A. (1987). Linking between social workers and mental health mutual-aid groups. *Social Work in Health Care, 13,* 69-77.

Kurtz, L. F., & Chambon, A. (1987). Comparison of self-help groups for mental health. *Health and Social Work, 12,* 275-283.

Lee, D. T. (1966). Recovery, Inc: A well role model. *Quarterly of Camarillo, 2,* 35-36.

Lee, D. T. (1971). Recovery, Inc.: Aid in the transition from hospital to community. *Mental Hygiene, 55,* 194-198.

Lee, D. T. (1991, May 16). Abraham A. Low: pioneer in cognitive behavioral therapy. In P.L. Berning (Chair), *Conference on mental illness, stigma and self-help, Recovery, Inc., and the pioneering work of Abraham A. Low.* Chicago, IL.

Lee, D. T. (1993). *Follow-up report on 1989 Recovery project.* Sacramento, CA: State Department of Mental Health, Forensic Services Branch.

Levy, L. H. (1976). Self-help groups: Types and psychological processes. *Journal of Applied Behavioral Science, 12,* 310-322.

Lieberman, M. A., & Bond, G. R. (1979). Problems in studying outcomes. In M. A. Lieberman & L. D. Borman (Eds.), *Self-help groups for coping with crisis.* (p.289). San Francisco: Jossey-Bass.

Low, A. A. (1950). *Mental health through will training.* (15th ed.) 1967. Boston: Christopher.

Low. A. A. (1976). *Mental health through will training.* (Spanish language ed.). Glenco, IL: Willett.

Lurie, A., & Schulman, L. (1983). The professional connections with self-help groups in health care settings. *Social Work in Health Care, 6,* 69-77.

Omark, R. C. (1982). Cycles and balances: personality change versus organizational maintenance. *Psychiatric Quarterly, 54,* 109-122.

Powell, T. J. (1979). Comparisons between self-help groups and professional services. *Social Casework, 60,* 561-585.

Powell, T. J., & Cameron, M.J. (1991). Self-help research and the public mental health system. *American Journal of Community Psychology, 19,* 797-805.

Raiff, N. R. (1978). *Recovery, Inc.: A study of a self-help organization in mental health.* (Doctoral dissertation, University of Pittsburgh, 1978). University Microfilms International, 1979, Ann Arbor, MI (#7917492:170).

Rau, N., & Rau, M. (1971). *My dear ones.* NJ: Prentice-Hall.

Spiegel, D. (1977). The psychiatrist as a consultant to a self-help group. *Hospital & Community Psychiatry, 28,* 771-772.

Suler, J. (1984). The role of ideology in self-help groups. *Social Policy, 14* (3), 29-36.

Todres, R. (1982). Professional attitudes, awareness and use of self-help groups. *Prevention in Human Services, 1,* 91-98.

Toseland, R. W. & Hacker, L. (1985). Social workers' use of self-help groups as a resource for clients. *Social Work, 30,* 232-237.

Wechsler, H. (1960). The self-help organization in the mental health field: Recovery, Inc. a case study. *Journal of Nervous and Mental Diseases, 130,* 297-314.

Public Attitudes Toward Persons with Mental Illness

Andrew B. Borinstein

ANDREW BORINSTEIN IS A VICE-PRESIDENT OF DYG, INC., A SOCIAL AND MARKET RESEARCH FIRM IN ELMSFORD, NEW YORK.

THIS ARTICLE ORIGINALLY APPEARED IN *Health Affairs,* 1992 (FALL), 186-196 AND IS REPRINTED WITH PERMISSION.

Historically, the study of public attitudes toward mental illness and persons with mental illness has mostly been the domain of mental health professionals—namely psychiatrists, psychologists, psychiatric social workers, academics in those related fields, and psychiatric program directors and administrators (e.g., Baron, 1981; Bord, 1971; Elinson, Padilla, & Perkins, 1967; Rabkin, 1974; Segal, 1978; and Steadman, 1981). This area of research was of finite interest to public opinion analysts, largely because the issue had little political or public resonance until quite recently. Before the late 1960s and early 1970s, a period when many patients in mental institutions were deinstitutionalized, the topics of mental health in general and persons with mental illness in particular also were of limited concern to the public. Mental illness was a topic most often treated by individuals and families as a "private matter" that was more or less off-limits to outsiders, except perhaps, medical professionals and other family members.

Deinstitutionalization and the problems associated with the implementation of community-based mental health care brought mental illness into the public sphere. What had been a very real but mostly hidden social issue had become a more visible social problem confronting a larger public. Lack of planning, social services, psychotropic medicines, medical facilities, and housing for this newly deinstitutionalized population combined to strain the already reduced public and voluntary social and human service delivery networks. The end result was that many of the newly deinstitutionalized ended up homeless and on the streets of America's cities, becoming a greater part of the American urban landscape and grabbing the attention of the news media.

Other societal changes have contributed to greater public awareness of mental health issues as well. The media, with the creation of magazine and newspaper health and science sections, health-related television programming, and specialty magazines such as *Psychology Today,* have helped to demystify many psychological and mental health issues for millions of Americans. New psychotropic medicines have been developed in the past two decades to help persons with mental illness. Also, the stigma associated with seeing a psychiatrist or psychologist has lessened. Americans, in casual conversations with friends, family, and even strangers, are much more likely now than perhaps at any other time in this country's history, to admit that "they are seeing someone" to help sort out emotional or psychological problems. In addition, many employers, recognizing the need for employee mental health care, now have health insurance plans to cover some costs associated with psychiatric care.[1] Finally, the American public has benefited from public education programs conducted by various mental health organizations.

Thus, as the issues of mental illness have become demystified, yet more complex, other groups of professionals—journalists,

---

[1] According to data from an August 1988 survey by Riter Research, nearly six in ten Americans (57%) who have health insurance said that the coverage they possess provides mental health benefits.

geographers, urban planners, and public opinion analysts—have been attracted to the study of Americans' attitudes toward issues involving mental health and mental illness. In the summer of 1989 the Robert Wood Johnson Foundation Program on Chronic Mental Illness approached Daniel Yankelovich and DYG, Inc., to conduct a major research project on Americans' attitudes toward locating housing for people with chronic mental illness in residential neighborhoods.[2] The foundation recognized that many communities have resisted the location of all types of facilities in various neighborhoods—the "Not-in-My-Back-Yard" (NIMBY) phenomenon. The foundation wanted to provide the nine cities in its program as well as the American public with an in-depth understanding of the resistance to and acceptance of housing facilities for persons with mental illness. The intention was that with a greater understanding of the issues, these nine programs would be better equipped to address and overcome the NIMBY phenomenon.

Moreover, with virtually no recent national opinion data available on Americans' attitudes toward mental illness, the foundation wanted to explore general public attitudes and perceptions on this important issue.[3] This article reports some of the major findings from this survey, using descriptive statistics.

The study's findings are based on a telephone survey of approximately 1,326 Americans, representative of the total population of adults age 21 and older. The interviews were conducted between December 1–11, 1989. The typical interview required approximately 29 minutes to complete. Interviewers followed a specific selection procedure so that women would comprise 52% of the sample and men, 48%. In total, approximately 3,016 individuals were contacted to reach the quota of 1,326 completed interviews. This represents a response rate of nearly 44%.[4]

Public Perceptions Of Mental Illness

Incidence. According to the survey results, a majority of Americans believe that the number of people with mental illness has increased over the past 20 years (69%) and that mental illness is a serious health problem in the United States (89%) (Table 1). Forty-five percent of respondents said it is a very serious problem (ranking ahead of mental retardation [28%] but behind drug

---

[2] Additional research project funding was provided by the American Psychiatric Association, the National Institute of Mental Health, and the Pew Charitable Trusts.

[3] Prior to this study, there appear to be only two other publicly released surveys in the late 1970s and 1980s that queried Americans on aspects of mental illness. The first survey, entitled, "Family Health in the Era of Stress," which was conducted in October 1978 by Yankelovich, Skelly, and White for the General Mills corporation, focused in part on the attitudes and opinions of family members about personal health, mental health, and mental illness. The second survey, entitled "Teenagers at Risk: Adult Perspective," which was conducted in August 1988 by Riter Research for the National Association of Private Psychiatric Hospitals, mostly focused on American attitudes toward children and teenagers with mental illness.

[4] The survey results have been sample-balanced to reflect the proper age, sex, race, income, and geographical region of all individuals age 21 and older throughout the United States. In theory, in 19 cases out of 20, the findings based upon the samples will differ by no more than three percentage points from what would have been obtained by interviewing all individuals age 21 and older throughout the country. Two versions of the questionnaire were employed in this study. Questionnaire Versions A and B are identical except for questions 5, 12, and 13. These questions tested different "names" for facilities for persons with mental illness (question 5) and descriptions for persons with mental illness (questions 12 and 13). The two versions were alternated across representative half-samples of respondents. In conducting interviewing for the telephone survey, surveyors chose respondents from all U.S. households on the basis of random probability sampling procedures, which took into account unlisted telephone numbers. The sample was stratified according to census regions, states within regions, and cities/towns/rural areas within states.

abuse [85%], acquired immunodeficiency syndrome [AIDS] [81%], alcoholism [73%], cancer [69%], and heart disease [58%]).

TABLE 1.
AMERICANS' PERCEPTIONS OF THE NUMBER OF PEOPLE WITH MENTAL ILLNESS OVER THE PAST 20 YEARS

Survey Response	Percent Responding
Number has increased a lot	41%
Number has increased a little	28%
Number has stayed the same	19%
Number has decreased a little	4%
Number has decreased a lot	2%
Not sure	6%

Source: The Robert Wood Johnson Foundation Program on Chronic Mental Illness, survey of the general public, December, 1989.

Note: N = 1,326.

An impressive number of Americans report personal experience with mental illness and mental health professionals. Approximately 16% of all survey respondents said that they have sought the professional services of a psychiatrist, psychologist, or other mental health professional, and 24% said that someone in their family or household has sought professional help. Overall, three in ten survey respondents reported that they or someone in their family has sought the help of a mental health professional at some time in their lives.

Causes. Americans believe that mental illness is caused by physical disturbances (such as a chemical imbalance in the brain) or environmental conditions (such as the stress of daily life or alcoholism/drug abuse); over nine in ten respondents cited these factors as overall causes of mental illness (Figure 1.). When asked to choose the single most common cause of mental illness, nearly 27% named both chemical imbal-

FIGURE 1.
PUBLIC'S PERCEPTION OF CAUSES OF MENTAL ILLNESS

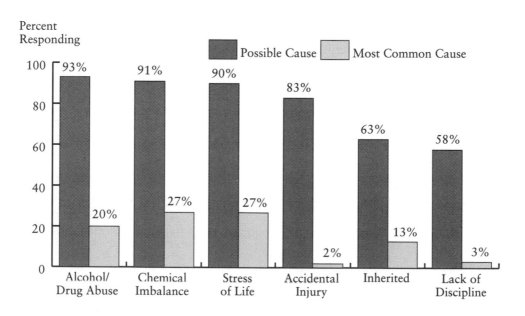

ances in the brain and stress of daily life, and 20% cited alcohol or drug abuse.

Knowledge about mental illness. In sum, Americans do not consider themselves well informed about mental illness but do think they should know much more. Only one in four respondents said they are very well informed about mental illness, and nearly half, fairly well informed. More importantly, one in four said they are not at all well informed about mental illness. Respondents felt better informed about all other health problems we inquired about—alcoholism (47%), cancer (43%), drug abuse (38%), heart disease (37%), and AIDS (30%)—except mental retardation (24%). However, six in ten respondents said, in response to another question, that they should know a good deal more about mental illness.

Sources of information. According to the survey, Americans are more likely to receive information about mental illness from the mass media than from mental health professionals. For example, 87% of respondents said that they had seen something about mental illness on television in the past several years. Other sources were newspapers (76%), magazines (74%), radio (73%), family or friends (51%), and books (50%). Only about three in ten said that they had received information from a mental health professional such as a psychiatrist or psychologist (31%) or a physician (29%).

Americans may be receiving most of their information about mental illness from the news media, but whether they believe what they hear or see from those sources is another issue. When asked how believable they thought such reports were, only 5% of respondents said they were "extremely believable"; 29% found them "very believable"; 61% said the stories were only "somewhat believable"; and 2%, "not at all believable."

Attitudes toward mental illness. Respondents were also asked to agree or disagree with a series of attitudinal statements about mental illness. These statements covered a wide range of issues, including stigma, the likelihood of becoming mentally ill, and the possibility of cure and medical treatment for persons with mental illness. Despite the apparent knowledge gap that many have about mental illness, the study found that Americans have the following perceptions about mental illness and persons with mental illness (Table 2).

First, Americans do not believe that mental illness affects only a certain group of people. Nearly three out of four respondents agreed with the statement, "Virtually anyone can become mentally ill." And importantly, despite the relatively high degree of contact with mental health professionals reported earlier, nearly two thirds of respondents agreed with the statement, "There is still a lot of stigma attached to mental illness." Also, over six in ten said that it is not easy to recognize someone who once had a serious mental illness; over four in ten agreed with the statement, "Having a mental illness is no different from having any other kind of illness." (However, nearly three in ten disagreed with this statement, perhaps an indication of some of the stigma associated with having a mental illness.) Fewer than two in ten agreed that most of today's homeless people are mentally ill; nearly half of all respondents disagreed with that statement.

Survey responses reveal that a majority of Americans agree that maintaining a normal life in the community will help a person with mental illness get better and that with treatment, most people with serious mental illness can get well and return to productive lives. In addition, a plurality of Americans do not agree that mental health facilities should be kept out of residential neighborhoods (although more than two in ten respondents said they should be kept out, and another one in three neither agreed or

TABLE 2.
PUBLIC'S VIEWS ON STATEMENTS ABOUT MENTAL ILLNESS
AND PEOPLE WITH MENTAL ILLNESS

Survey Item	Agree[a]	Disagree[b]	Neutral[c]	Not sure
Virtually anyone can become mentally ill.	74%	8%	17%	1%
There is still a lot of stigma attached to mental illness.	65%	6%	26%	3%
Most people with serious mental illness can, with treatment, get well and return to productive lives.	54%	8%	37%	1%
In most cases, keeping up a normal life in the community will help a person with mental illness get better.	53%	12%	34%	1%
The mentally ill are far less of a danger than most people believe.	48%	15%	35%	2%
Having a mental illness is no different from having any other kind of illness.	43%	28%	27%	2%
Locating a group home or apartments for people with mental illness in residential neighborhoods does not endanger local residents.	41%	18%	39%	2%
Locating a group home or apartments for people with mental illness in a residential area will not harm property values.	29%	33%	35%	3%
I don't believe mental illness can ever really be cured.	26%	46%	26%	2%
People with chronic mental illness are, by far, more dangerous than the general population.	24%	34%	38%	4%
Mental health facilities should be kept out of residential neighborhoods.	22%	44%	33%	1%
Even if they seem OK, people with chronic mental illness always have the potential to commit violent acts.	21%	41%	36%	2%
Most of the homeless today are, in fact, mentally ill.	18%	48%	31%	3%
It is easy to recognize someone who once had a serious mental illness.	13%	63%	22%	2%
The best way to handle the mentally ill is to keep them behind locked doors.	6%	81%	11%	2%

Source: The Robert Wood Johnson Foundation Program on Chronic Mental Illness, survey of the general public, December 1989.

Note: N = 1,326.

[a] Rating of "5" or "6" on a six-point scale.
[b] Rating of "1" or "2" on a six-point scale.
[c] Rating of "3" or "4" on a six-point scale.

disagreed with the statement) or that mental illness can never be cured. Furthermore, the vast majority of Americans do not agree that "the best way to handle the mentally ill is to keep them behind locked doors."

While a plurality of Americans do not perceive persons with mental illness as excessively violent or particularly danger-ous, 15 to 24% of respondents, depending on the question asked, were concerned

TABLE 3.
ACCEPTABILITY OF NEIGHBORHOOD FACILITIES

Type of Neighborhood Facility	Would Welcome[a]	Would Not Welcome[b]	Neutral[c]	Not sure
School	68%	15%	16%	1%
Day care center	65%	12%	22%	1%
Nursing home for the elderly	63%	11%	25%	1%
Hospital	58%	18%	23%	1%
Medical clinic (e.g., eye or allergy clinic)	57%	15%	27%	1%
Group home for the mentally retarded	45%	21%	33%	1%
Homeless shelter	43%	28%	28%	1%
Alcohol rehabilitation center	42%	25%	32%	1%
Drug treatment center	40%	31%	28%	1%
Shopping mall	36%	40%	24%	—
Group home for AIDS[d] patients	29%	37%	33%	1%
Factory	24%	57%	18%	1%
Garbage landfill	8%	85%	6%	1%
Prison	7%	79%	14%	—

Source: The Robert Wood Johnson Foundation Program on Chronic Mental Illness, survey of the general public, December 1989.

Note: N = 1,326.

[a] Rating of "5" or "6" on a six-point scale.
[b] Rating of "1" or "2" on a six-point scale.
[c] Rating of "3" or "4" on a six-point scale.

about the potential violence and dangerousness of persons with mental illness.

Finally, we discovered a mixed reaction to the single statement about property values. One in three respondents thought that property values would be harmed if a group home or apartments for people with mental illness were located in a residential neighborhood; about three in ten thought that property values would not be endangered; and over one in three provided responses falling between the belief that "harm" and "no harm" to property values would occur.

The NIMBY Phenomenon

Despite the lack of overwhelmingly negative attitudes about persons with mental illness, Americans are reluctant to welcome a wide variety of mental health facilities into their communities. In fact, the NIMBY phenomenon may exist as a real barrier to opportunities for people with mental illness.

Overall, opposition to the location of any type of facility appears to be somewhat commonplace. For example, 14% said that their neighborhood had opposed some type of facility (ranging from a school or hospital to a drug treatment center or garbage dump) in the past 5 years; half of these indicated that this opposition was successful in stopping plans for locating these facilities in their neighborhood.

Respondents were asked to use a six-point scale to rate the acceptability of 18 types of facilities (including both mental health and other facilities) that could be placed in their neighborhood (Table 3). Results indicate that all facilities are not perceived similarly and that three distinct tiers of acceptability exist. The first tier consists of several facilities that are most welcome by community residents: a school, a day care center, a nursing home, a hospital, and a medical clinic. Perhaps these are viewed as facilities that would be useful to all neighborhood residents. The second tier is composed of facilities that received a mixed review: a group home for the mentally retarded, a homeless shelter, an alcohol rehabilitation center, and a drug treatment center. These facilities may be perceived as serving the needs of a special population while at the same time not posing a threat to neighborhood property values or danger to its inhabitants. The third tier consists of facilities that most residents absolutely do not want in their community: a shopping mall, a group home for people with AIDS, a factory, a garbage landfill, and a prison. Perhaps these facilities are perceived as attracting excess automobile traffic and a potentially dangerous population that is truly unwanted, or posing a serious threat to property values because of environmental damage.

Facilities for people with mental illness are not among the more acceptable facilities. Eight different descriptions of facilities or homes for persons with mental illness were examined in this study, and the ratings for most of these fell at the second tier of acceptable facilities (Table 4).

While acceptance and support of locating facilities in neighborhoods vary according to demographic groups, income appears to be an important indicator of opposition. Those opposed to neighborhood facilities are more likely to live in affluent neighborhoods. As noted earlier, over one in ten of all respondents said that their neighborhood had acted to oppose a facility in the past 5 years. However, over two in ten of those with an annual household income of $50,000 and over said that their neighborhood had been involved in opposing a facility during the past five years. A similar pattern emerges when the acceptability level of the facilities is examined: the acceptability of neighborhood facilities decreases as income increases. That is, lower (under $15,000 annually) and moderate ($15,000–$24,999 annually) household income groups are more accepting than are affluent households (annual household income of $50,000 or more) of all types of neighborhood facilities.

Furthermore, nearly half of all respondents (48%) would not "welcome" any of the mental health facilities into their neighborhoods. That is, they would not give a rating of "6" or "5" on the six-point scale ranging from "would welcome" to "absolutely would not welcome" to any of the mental health facilities tested. Demographically, these respondents tend to be affluent, male, well-educated, professional, married, homeowners, and living in large cities or suburbs. Attitudinally, "nonwelcomers" of mental health facilities appear to be pessimistic about the future, fearful of taking chances (risk averse), competitive, Darwinistic, and less tolerant of different types of lifestyles. Finally, their beliefs about mental illness are less hopeful than are those of the general population. "Nonwelcomers" are less likely to believe that anyone can become mentally ill and that most people with mental illness can get well and return to productive lives.

Explaining the phenomenon. During the 1960s and 1970s, when deinstitutionalization of persons diagnosed with chronic mental illness was both an acceptable practice and social policy, most Americans embraced a different set of social values than those prevalent in the late 1980s and early 1990s. During the 1960s and 1970s Americans were more accepting of different lifestyles; values of pluralism, diversity, and egalitarianism were strongly held during that era, along with the civil rights of individuals—particularly those of racial minorities, prisoners, and patients with mental illness. Perhaps most importantly, federal funds were available to experiment with different types of social and health-related programs to help the economically and medically disadvantaged. In sum, the underlying

TABLE 4.
PUBLIC'S ACCEPTANCE OF NEIGHBORHOOD MENTAL HEALTH FACILITIES

Type of Mental Health Facility	Would Welcome[a]	Would Not Welcome[b]	Neutral[c]	Not sure
Group home for people with mental illness (*n* = 642)	37%	28%	33%	2%
Group home for people with depression (*n* = 642)	31%	27%	41%	1%
Outpatient facility for people with emotional problems (n = 684)	31%	24%	44%	1%
Group home for former mental patients (*n* = 684)	31%	1%	37%	1%
Mental health outpatient facility (*n*= 642)	31%	34%	34%	1%
Independent apartments for people with mental disabilities (*n*= 642)	30%	30%	39%	1%
People who are recuperating from mental illness (*n*= 642)	27%	25%	46%	2%
Independent apartments for people with mental illness (*n*= 684)	27%	35%	38%	—

Source: The Robert Wood Johnson Foundation Program on Chronic Mental Illness, survey of the general public, December 1989.

[a] Rating of "5" or "6" on a six-point scale.
[b] Rating of "1" or "2" on a six-point scale.
[c] Rating of "3" or "4" on a six-point scale.

values structure of the 1960s and 1970s helped to create a social climate in which Americans were more accepting of and willing to assist (through individual action or via taxation) those who could not help themselves.

However, beginning in the late 1980s Americans adopted a different set of social values that reflect changed attitudes and beliefs. First, Americans began to question a belief that had been central to the concept of continual social mobility—the belief that economic well-being for current and future generations is a given. The belief that each generation will enjoy a higher standard of living than the one before it served as the underpinning for the values revolution of the 1960s and 1970s. By the early 1980s this principle had been replaced by the belief that individual success, based on hard work, self-reliance, mastery, and the willingness to accept risk, was still possible for those who strove for it, but it was not automatic and not necessarily available to everyone.

Furthermore, growing concern among Americans of all economic and social classes about their future economic well-being has increased overall insecurity and contributed to the current NIMBY-like social climate. Along with this declining sense of affluence, Americans have become less concerned about the civil rights of individuals, less tolerant than in the 1960s and 1970s of diverse lifestyles, and more risk averse and pessimistic about community life.

Unless these attitudes soften and the corresponding desire to keep housing for persons with mental illness out of various communities abates, the prospect of allowing persons with mental illness the opportunity to become an accepted part of a neighborhood or community remains tenuous at best.

Future Research Directions

This research only touches the surface regarding American attitudes toward mental illness and persons with mental illness. Future research could further examine the underlying attitudes that contribute to the phenomenon of not welcoming mental health facilities and persons with mental illness into neighborhoods. For example, given today's social climate, to what extent do the public's perceptions of fear, physical violence, and harm to property values (as well as other factors) contribute to the rejection of persons with mental illness? Does the public have differing perceptions and degrees of tolerance for individuals with different types of mental illness? Does it matter what sex or age the individual is? Who does the public perceive to be persons with mental illness? What role does the news and entertainment media play in shaping public attitudes and contributing to stereotypes about mental illness and persons with mental illness? Further research into these areas could increase the level of understanding about an important social issue with nationwide ramifications.

References

Baron, R. C., (1981). Changing public attitudes about the mentally ill in the community. *Hospital and Community Psychiatry,* March, 173-178.

Bord, R. J. (1971). Rejection of the mentally ill: Continuities and further developments. *Social Problems,* Spring, 496-509.

Rabkin, J. (1974). Public attitudes toward mental illness: A review of the literature. *Schizophrenia Review,* Fall, 9-33.

Segal, S. P. (1978). Attitudes toward the mentally ill: A review. *Social Work,* May, 211-217.

Steadman, H. J. (1981). Critically reassessing the accuracy of public perceptions of the dangerous of the mentally ill. *Journal of Health and Social Behavior,* September, 310-316.

These data are from the DYG SCAN, an annual tracking study of American social values that identifies trends in public lifestyles and values. For further information, contact the author at DYG, Inc., 555 Taxter Road, suite 475, Elmsford, New York, 10523.

THE QUIET DISCRIMINATION

Anonymous

THIS ARTICLE ORIGINALLY APPEARED IN THE *Schizophrenia Bulletin*, 1981, 7(4), 736-738.

On November 28, 1976, an editorial entitled "Miracles for What?" appeared in the *New York Times*. It discussed discrimination in employment against the recovered cancer patient as well as the person who has undergone psychiatric treatment.

The editorial gave a brief but accurate picture of the discrimination that is faced by people who were once ill but are either in remission or undergoing treatment. The fact that the physical or emotional problem has been stabilized and that this person is now able and eager to regain a former position or is seeking a job is not taken into consideration. The discrimination is subtle and quiet.

I write from personal experience. My emotional difficulties continued from earlier years and "blossomed" out in adulthood. Interestingly enough, I somehow was able to function relatively well if only in regard to being employable. Finally, the stress came to a head and my outpatient counseling was not enough. After a suicidal action, I ended up hospitalized on a psychiatric unit. I now not only had to deal with this trauma but upon release the distress of losing my job. The stress I was under led me—perhaps foolishly—to "confide" in my employer. I was at work only a few days when I was politely fired but "assured" that I would receive good references. The fact that I had been there for nearly 4 years and a good worker did not matter. My lack of self-esteem and self-confidence increased along with my anxiety. The days passed into weeks, the weeks into months. I sat home depressed, on medication, and collected unemployment compensation. In my few moments of self-confidence, I would go out looking for a job. This more often than not added a great deal of stress. I now found that I had to contend with explaining an obvious time lapse from my last job. I also noticed that many job applications would inquire about medical and psychological stability. For example: "Have you ever been medically or psychiatrically hospitalized?" "Are you now or have you ever consulted a therapist?" I found myself caught in a trap. If I were to be honest, as I naively was in the beginning, most assuredly I would never (and did not) hear from that interviewer again. If I discreetly manipulated my work history and possibly obtained the position, I might risk a future discovery and be liable for automatic termination.

I eventually did gain employment but only through fixing up my work history on the application. I learned that honesty is not always the best policy. Unfortunately there were more hospitalizations, but upon discharge my self-confidence was greater and, though I did not get a job quickly, a job would develop—again, only through doctoring my work history. In the past several years I have managed for the most part to be gainfully employed, off medication, and to earn a college degree with the continuous help of outpatient therapy.

There is much discrimination against people who seek or have obtained psychiatric treatment (inpatient or outpatient). No matter how productive and functioning they are, the stigma is still there. It not only exists in employment. I am considering graduate school, and there too, questions about past and present psychiatric treatment confront me. This is especially true for professional schools for mental health clinicians, a field in which I am interested. The admission forms often request a biographical sketch describing how the student became interested in the field and any personal experiences with psychiatry. This, too, obviously is a Catch-22 position. To admit my personal experiences is to court possible and realistic rejection, (I have spoken off the record with an instructor in a well-known school of social work about my situation, and his advice was: I do not think discussing your hospital experiences would be a plus. General outpatient therapy might be a positive point, but hospitalization would make the admissions committee wary, no matter how far in the past it was.) If I do not discuss it, I would in a way be compromising my principles. These experiences have had a very deep and intense effect on my life and interest in the field. If anything, I believe I am especially sensitive and aware as no one who has not gone through these experiences could be.

How many thousands of people who need help do not seek it out of fear of what others will think, the fear of loss of employment or admission/readmission to a professional school, as well as possibly in the case of adoption?

We have made extensive gains in efforts to rid ourselves of discrimination based upon sex, age, religion, and race. We have "affirmative action" programs, yet when will society at large rid itself of its prejudices and fears regarding the stabilized and functioning person who has undergone or is undergoing psychotherapy?

The media has not helped in this matter. It has in fact often hindered the cause. Hardly a month goes by that we do not read a lurid news story of "man goes berserk and kills neighbor" or "former mental patient kills wife." Those headlines are remembered. We do *not* remember or pay attention, because it never is reported, to the fact that thousands of individuals who have undergone treatment, are undergoing counseling, or are stabilized on medication are able to go about their daily lives without harming or frightening others.

The evidence is overwhelming that the majority of mental patients and former mental patients are, as a class, less dangerous than the "average" citizen. Witness the New York study showing that over a 5-year period the arrest rate for 5,000 former patients, all adult males, was less than one twelfth the rate for the community at large; the rate for serious crime was even lower. Those former patients who did brush against the law usually were guilty of no more than loitering, vagrancy, or public intoxication. Other studies of patients and prospective patients have reached the same conclusions: mental illness does not cause dangerous behavior. Mental patients may plot and scheme, they may threaten injury to themselves or others, but rarely do they follow through. The most common characteristic of mental patients is an inability to organize their lives and assert themselves. And that characteristic makes them less dangerous than people who are more aggressive, hence, more "normal" (Ennis, 1972, p. 225).

Recovered cancer patients, recovered alcoholics, the handicapped, and those who have undergone or are undergoing psychotherapy (and/or hospitalization as well) are eager to be productive members of society. They want to regain their place in the work force. They want nothing more and nothing less than to be given that opportunity! I would hazard to guess that they as a whole are more loyal and far less likely to take advantage of an employer than otherwise might be the case.

Chemotherapy has vastly improved, lengthened, and saved the lives of cancer patients. Psychotherapy and psychotropic drugs have helped thousands of people to continue to go about their daily lives, in the work force as well as the home and community. Medical and psychiatric treatment has been a boon to many, but at times I am sure they painfully wonder, for what?

Reference

Ennis, B.J. (1972). *Prisoners of psychiatry.* New York: Harcourt Brace Jovanovich.

Educating The Public About Mental Illness: What Will It Take to Get the Job Done?

Mary E. Fraser

MARY E. FRASER, D.S.W., IS A CONSULTANT WITH THE MENTAL HEALTH RESOURCE PROGRAM, GRADUATE SCHOOL OF SOCIAL WORK, UNIVERSITY OF NORTH CAROLINA-CHAPEL HILL. AT THE TIME OF THIS STUDY, SHE WAS ASSOCIATE DIRECTOR OF THE UTAH STATE DIVISION OF MENTAL HEALTH.

SPECIAL THANKS TO DAVE TOMB, MD, WHO PROVIDED HELPFUL COMMENTS ON EARLY DRAFTS OF THIS MANUSCRIPT.

THIS ARTICLE ORIGINALLY APPEARED IN
Innovations and Research, 1994, 3(3), 29-31.

Negative public attitudes toward people with mental illness have been broadly documented since the 1950s. Misinformation about mental illness and those who suffer from it is widespread. This article describes the efforts one state has taken to identify the degree and extent of misunderstanding among its citizenry and the efforts it has taken to remedy it. Based on the results of two public opinion surveys conducted 4 years apart, negative attitudes toward people with serious mental illness will be difficult to change unless focused and coordinated public education efforts are undertaken.

The community mental health movement, begun nearly 30 years ago, has been fueled by a vision of people with mental illness living, freely integrated, as accepted members of local communities. Unfortunately, this vision has not yet become a reality for a large percentage of Americans with mental illness. The stigma of mental illness is one of the primary barriers to the achievement of this goal (*Community Support Network News,* 1990). For as long as people with mental illness are feared and shunned, they will not be truly integrated into community living.

Public Opinion Prior to Study

The stigma of mental illness has been broadly documented since the early 1950s. For years, people with mental illness have been regarded with more distaste and less sympathy than virtually any other group of people with disabilities in our society (Rabkin, 1974). Studies examining public attitudes toward people with mental illness at that time unambiguously established that they were negatively viewed by the general public.

Studies conducted since 1960, however, have shown mixed results. Some show improvement in public attitudes; however, many show little change. The results of the more negative studies suggest that people with mental illnesses are still heavily stigmatized (Tringo, 1970); that educational programs have only minimally affected public knowledge about mental illness (Sabin & Mancuso, 1972); and that when people encounter any form of mental illness, they respond with fear, dislike, and aversion (Rabkin, 1974; Wahl & Roth, 1982). This stigmatization extends even to family members of people with serious mental illness (Main et al., 1993) and has clearly resulted in significant discrimination in the health care coverage of psychiatric disorders (Domenici, 1993).

Over the past decade, a number of organizations, both public and private, have sponsored public education efforts designed to combat the effects of negative attitudes toward people with mental illness. Little has been published about their content and effect. This article describes the efforts undertaken by the state of Utah to uncover sources of misunderstanding about mental illness among its citizenry and the state's attempts to right them.

The Study

Two surveys were conducted, one in 1988 and another in 1992, to find out what Utahns knew and did not know about mental illness and to see if the original level of misunderstanding could be improved over time. Both surveys, conducted by the University of Utah Survey Research Center, were based on telephone interviews with approximately 500 randomly selected adults throughout the state. All respondents were screened to be 18 years or older and the identical questionnaire was administered in full to every respondent.

Results of the First Survey

The results of the first survey suggested that Utahns, like many other Americans, experience serious gaps and misconceptions in their understanding of serious mental illness. A sampling of the findings showed that:

- 89% felt that serious mental illness is caused by alcohol and drug use.

- 87% felt that serious mental illness is caused by stress.

- 80% felt that serious mental illness is caused by lack of coping skills.

- 74% felt that "schizophrenia" is equivalent to "split-personality."

- 71% felt that serious mental illness is caused by emotional weakness.

- 65% felt that serious mental illness is caused by bad parenting.

- 44% felt that people with serious mental illness choose to be ill.

- 41% felt that people with serious mental illness should be treated in an institution.

- 38% felt that people with serious mental illness are more dangerous than the rest of society.

- 35% felt that serious mental illness is caused by sinful behavior.

Despite these poor responses, the public seemed to be rather well-informed on some issues. For example:

- 90% recommended treatment from a community mental health center.

- 89% felt that people with serious mental illness can be helped by psychotherapy or counseling.

- 89% felt that people with serious mental illness don't seek treatment because of social stigma.

- 89% felt that serious mental illness is caused by a chemical imbalance.

- 85% felt that serious mental illness is caused by genetic factors.

Survey results also showed that certain sectors of the population were more misinformed than others. For instance, people over 65 years tended to believe that people with serious mental illnesses were incurable, hopelessly disabled, dangerous, sinful, and willingly ill. They also tended to believe that people with serious mental illness should be hospitalized at the state hospital for long periods of time and that medication should be used to "tranquilize" them.

High school graduates and those with less education were poorly informed. But so were people with a graduate education. Professionals had some peculiar, moralistic ideas about the causes and cures of mental illness. Overall, the best informed individuals were those with some college education.

Church-affiliated persons (65% Mormon, 9% Protestant, 7% Catholic, and 5% other) tended to believe in religious causes for serious mental illness (e.g., sinful behavior), seek religious cures, and adopt a more harsh and moralistic attitude toward people with serious mental illness. Church affiliated persons did, in most cases however, have the same knowledge of the "facts" of mental illness as the nonchurch affiliated group.

Urban dwellers were slightly better informed about serious mental illness than those who lived in rural areas. Rural respondents tended to reflect conservative religious views and were more likely to recommend treatment for serious mental illness from non-mental health professionals.

The fact that most people continue to be poorly informed about serious mental illness was recently corroborated by the Robert Wood Johnson Founda-tion Survey conducted in 1989 (Borenstein, 1992). This survey found that only 25% of respondents described themselves as very well informed about mental illness. Respondents felt better informed about all other health problems mentioned— alcoholism (47%), cancer (43%), drug abuse (35%), heart disease (37%), and AIDS (30%). Six in ten (60%) said that they should know more about mental illness.

Over 60% of the population still believes that emotional weakness, bad parenting, and stress cause severe mental illness.

Intervening Factors

Between 1988 and 1992 a number of efforts were undertaken in Utah to educate the public about mental illness, by a variety of agencies and organizations. For example, the Division of Mental Health organized a campaign to inform the public about schizophrenia and provided training to Community Mental Health Center staff and advocacy group members on methods of public education. Private psychiatric hospital corporations advertised aggressively throughout the state during this period. These advertisements often provided valuable information about depression, sub-stance abuse, and childhood emotional disorders. Commercial and public TV covered and dramatized stories about mental illness. Local newspapers featured special series on people who are homeless and mentally ill, Clozaril, and innovative mental health treatment programs.

Results of the Second Survey

Did any of this make a difference? Did Utahns learn more about mental illness? Were harmful misconceptions reinforcing negative attitudes about people with mental illness corrected?

Unfortunately, based on the 1992 survey results, the answer is no. Although the level of misconception was lessened in some instances, almost no change in the public's perception of people with mental illness was found over the 4-year period. Misinformation and negative attitudes continue to be the rule. Over 60% of the population still believes that emotional weakness, bad parenting, and stress cause severe mental illness.

Agency Response

Because of these discouraging results, Utah's Division of Mental Health has now developed a more targeted and organized public education effort. School-aged children have become the first target. Information packets are now distributed to all junior and senior high school classrooms; displays are designed for school libraries. Bookmarks with information about identifying and getting help for mental health problems are made available to all students. Curricula supplements for teachers are being developed.

Providing up-to-date information about mental illness to religious leaders has also been prioritized. In many communities, religious leaders are a major source of authority and information. This is especially true in small, rural communities where a high degree of misinformation about and negative attitudes toward people with mental illness still exist.

Conclusion

Stigma continues to be a major deterrent to the provision of proper care and the availability of community support to people with serious mental illness. More attempts to educate the public about mental illness need to be described and evaluated. The effects of a variety of public education strategies need to be examined. Until the costs associated with negative public attitudes are well understood and effective means developed to change them, the terrible price extracted from the people who suffer from mental illnesses by a misinformed public is unlikely to change.

References

Borenstein, A.B. (1992). Data watch: Public attitudes toward persons with mental illness. *Health Affairs, 11*(4), 186-196.

Community Support Network News, May 1990.

Domenici, P.V. (1993). Mental health care policy in the 1990s: discrimination in health care coverage of the seriously mentally ill. *Journal of Clinical Psychiatry, 54,* Suppl: 5-6.

Main, M.C., Gerace, L.M. & Camilleri, D. (1993). Information sharing concerning schizophrenia in a family member: Adult siblings' perspectives. *Archives of Psychiatric Nursing, 7,* 147-153.

Rabkin, J. (1974). Public attitudes toward mental illness: A review of the literature, *Schizophrenia Bulletin, 10,* 9-33.

Sarbin, T.R. & Mancuso, J.C. (1972). Paradigms and moral judgments: Improper conduct is not disease. *Journal of Consulting and Clinical Psychology, 39,* 6-8.

Tringo, J.L. (1970) The hierarchy of preference toward disability groups. *Journal of Special Education, 4,* 295-306.

Wahl, O. & Roth, R. (1982). Television images of mental illness: Results of a metropolitan Washington media watch. *Journal of Broadcasting, 26,* 599-605.

Barriers to Recovery and Empowerment for People with Psychiatric Disabilities

Pamela J. Kramer and Cheryl Gagne

CHERYL GAGNE, M.S., IS A SENIOR TRAINING ASSOCIATE AT THE CENTER FOR PSYCHIATRIC REHABILITATION. HER AREAS OF INTEREST INCLUDE RECOVERY AND EMPOWERMENT FOR PEOPLE WITH PSYCHIATRIC DISABILITIES.

PAMELA KRAMER, M.S., HAS A MASTER'S DEGREE IN REHABILITATION COUNSELING FROM BOSTON UNIVERSITY AND IS CURRENTLY EMPLOYED AT THE HUMAN SERVICES RESEARCH INSTITUTE. SHE ALSO WORKS AS AN INDEPENDENT CONSULTANT SPECIALIZING IN PSYCHIATRIC DISABILITY.

MS. GAGNE AND MS. KRAMER ARE BOTH PSYCHIATRIC SURVIVORS.

THE AUTHORS WISH TO ACKNOWLEDGE THE DOZENS OF SURVIVOR/EX-PATIENTS WHO SPENT TIME TALKING WITH US ABOUT THE BARRIERS TO RECOVERY AND EMPOWERMENT IN THEIR LIVES.

Introduction

People who have experienced psychiatric disability, and who have survived psychiatric treatment, have been writing and talking about recovery and empowerment for decades—and professionals are beginning to pay attention. Increasingly, recovery and empowerment are being linked with the experience of psychiatric disability and are being considered as valuable outcomes for mental health service delivery. Researchers and clinicians are beginning to embrace the concepts of recovery and empowerment as new and exciting tools for clinical practice and research. This new interest by professionals has been fueled by the strength of the survivor/ex-patient movement and its members' convincing testimony that recovery can be achieved through personal and collective empowerment.

The Psychiatric Survivors Movement: A Brief History

The survivor/ex-patient movement began in the early 1970s, but its roots can be traced back to earlier survivor/ex-patients in the late nineteenth and early twentieth centuries, who wrote of their mental hospital experiences and who attempted to change laws and public policies concerning the "insane" (Chamberlin, 1989). During the 1970s, mental patients began organizing and taking lessons from other civil rights movements. Patient-controlled organizations were formed across the nation, many identifying themselves with the "Mental Patients' Liberation Front." A national newsletter, *Madness Network News,* emerged as a voice for the movement until it ceased publication in the mid 1980s. Throughout the 1970s and 1980s the annual International Conference on Human Rights and Psychiatric Oppression served as a gathering place where those in the movement could share ideas and experiences. Early struggles were fought over commitment laws, forced drugging, human rights violations, and abuse in mental hospital and other treatment facilities.

Today, the psychiatric survivor/ex-patient movement continues to face formidable obstacles. Unfortunately many of the battles remain the same. The increased strength of the biopsychiatric model of mental illness, which views psychiatric disability as a chronic biochemical disorder, minimizes the importance of psychological, social, and spiritual aspects of psychiatric disability. Changing government priorities and policies, such as managed care, are having powerful effects on existing programs and services, limiting access and choice. Self-help alternatives are still rare and those that do exist are severely underfunded. However, there are some hopeful signs, one of which is the emerging alliance between the disability rights and psychiatric survivors movements. Members of both movements stress the lack of civil rights—not the individual—as the central problem. The Independent Living Movement emphasizes *consumer control;* focuses on advocacy as well as services; and believes strongly that any person, no matter how disabled, can make choices and take control of his or her life. The Psychiatric Survivor/Ex-patient Movement works to establish linkages with other oppressed groups who are fighting for common concerns such as healthcare, safe and affordable housing, and civil rights.

Definitions of Empowerment and Recovery

Recovery and empowerment are powerful constructs charged with personal meaning about which much has been written during the last 10 years. Fisher (1994) defines empowerment as "connecting with a community of peers and caregivers on a mutually respectful level and fully participating in the decisions affecting one's life." Vanderslice (1985) defines it as "a developmental process through which people become more able to influence those people and organizations that effect their lives and the lives of those they care about." She also details some of the beliefs and requisite steps vital to the empowerment process: "First, people, individually or in groups, must develop a greater sense of self-worth and self-confidence. Second, there must be a change in people's perceptions of their relations with other people and with institutions that define their social world." And finally, she emphasizes that "implicit in this definition is the belief that individuals know what is best for themselves and their families."

We often internalize myths and stereotypes of people with psychiatric disabilities and become as we are portrayed.

Recovery is defined as a process by which people with psychiatric disabilities rebuild and further develop personal, social, environmental, and spiritual connections in their lives. It is a process of adjusting one's attitude, feelings, perceptions, and goals in life and a process of self-discovery, self-renewal, and transformation (Spaniol et al., 1993).

The Decade of Recovery

Anthony (1990) proposed that the 1990s be the "decade of recovery" for people with severe psychiatric disabilities. This shared vision of recovery for persons with psychiatric disabilities between professionals and survivor/ex-patients has fostered unprecedented collaboration and new thinking about psychiatric disability.

Survivors and ex-patients have organized to advance the cause of people with psychiatric disabilities. They have expressed dissatisfaction with mere maintenance in the community and have called for services, supports, and opportunities that will help them to lead more fulfilling lives. This dissatisfaction has fueled the activism of the survivor/ex-patient movement and has generated dialogue with providers about the concepts of empowerment and recovery.

Fundamental beliefs about the course of psychiatric disabilities are changing. Survivor/ex-patients, practitioners, and researchers are challenging the concept of chronicity in schizophrenia and other severe mental illnesses. Long-term outcome studies support an optimistic view about the prognosis of schizophrenia (Harding, 1987; Ciompi, 1980) and more recent data suggest that rehabilitation interventions and work opportunities can significantly improve recovery outcomes (DeSisto & Harding, 1995).

Professional interest in recovery and psychiatric disability has been stimulated by new developments in psychopharmacology that hold the promise of further reducing psychiatric symptomatology. Professionals are excited about these new medications but equating symptom reduction with recovery does not address the iatrogenic disability and stigma, nor the issue of personal and collective empowerment. The recovery vision transcends the debate over the causes of severe psychiatric disability and can be adopted by most of the groups concerned with the treatment of those with psychiatric labels (Anthony, 1990).

Barriers to Recovery and Empowerment

Barriers are obstacles that impede, delay, or interfere with the recovery and empowerment process for people with psychiatric disabilities. There are two types of barriers, i.e., those imposed by the individual with psychiatric disability upon his- or herself, and those imposed by society or an outside force. For the purpose of this paper we will refer to these two distinct types of barriers as *internal* and *external* barriers.

When the word *barrier* is used in relation to disability, it is usually assumed to mean a physical or architectural obstacle that blocks or limits access. This could include obstacles such as an unramped flight of stairs, an inaccessible bathroom or phone booth, an obstacle undectable to a person using a cane, or a narrow space that makes accessibility to an area or a service impossible for a person with a disability. Barriers in relation to psychiatric disability are less concrete. Many of these narrow spaces and obstacles exist only in the mind—these are referred to as *attitudinal barriers.*

Attitudinal barriers are beliefs and assumptions based on prejudicial or stereotypical images of people with disabilities;

for example, assuming that a person with a physical disability who uses a wheelchair is helpless and dependent, or thinking that a person who has a speech disability is stupid or less intelligent. False assumptions about people with disabilities create barriers that are difficult to penetrate. There is a pervasive belief that people with psychiatric or physical disabilities cannot or should not work, marry, reproduce, vacation, shop, and so on.

People with disabilities have been viewed historically as a burden on family and society, objects of pity, and even thought to have been possessed by evil spirits (Goffman, 1963). The media often portrays a paradoxical image of people with disabilities, including portrayals as "special" or "exceptional," or dangerous and violent, just to name a few. Disability needs to be viewed as a natural part of the human experience along with birth, aging, and death (World Institute on Disability, 1992). In fact, statistics show that one in five people (20% of the U.S. population) will experience a psychiatric condition some time in their lives.

Chamberlin (1990) refers to a concept known as "mentalism," i.e., a set of assumptions that most people seem to hold about mental patients: that they are incompetent, unable to do things for themselves, constantly in need of supervision and assistance, unpredictable, and likely to be violent or irrational. Not only does the general public express mentalist ideas, so do ex-patients themselves. These crippling attitudes and stereotypes become a form of internalized oppression. They have devastating effects on individuals to whom they are applied, and on society as a whole. "Unfortunately, societal stereotyping stands as the most potent systems barrier to employment for persons with psychiatric disabilities" (Noble et al., 1987). These attitudes are pervasive in our society which devalues difference and confers status in relation to personal or professional achievement. Many people with disabilities have not had the supports, resources, and opportunities to achieve to their fullest potential.

In some ways, architectural barriers are easier to address. Once the need has been established and the funds secured (which we know is never easy), a contractor or architect can be called in and the obstacle removed or replaced with a ramp or other feature that provides access for people with disabilities. Attitudinal barriers are much more insidious. In today's era of "political correctness" attitudinal barriers are difficult to confront. People are very careful to watch what they say but often fail to examine or challenge their own fears, values, or beliefs about people with disabilities. Most people understand that it is impolite to refer to that "poor crippled girl," or that "crazed lunatic schizoid," but these same individuals may feel perfectly justified in speaking out against a group home in their neighborhood, expressing concern for the safety of their children or the character of their neighborhood. Until these attitudes change, attitudinal barriers will remain as one of the greatest obstacles to equal rights and full societal participation for people with disabilities.

The most common obstacles to recovery and empowerment for people with psychiatric disabilities are:

- Lack of accurate information and access to resources.

- Poverty, isolation, and segregation.

- Medication side-effects and other chronic health conditions.

- Issues related to physical/sexual abuse and trauma.

- Lack of positive role models.

- Discrimination in the workplace.

- Financial disincentives in government benefit programs.

- Lack of choice and of alternative services.

- Absence of civil rights.

- Mistreatment and abuse by providers.

- Lack of involvement and participation in treatment planning and policy decisions.

Internal Barriers: "Barriers Within"

For many people with psychiatric disabilities, "I am my own worst enemy" is a statement that resonates with painful accuracy. Many of us, over the years, have gotten in the way of our own recovery. Negative beliefs that we have internalized often produce the greatest barriers, often in the form of immobilizing self-hatred and self-criticism. The sources of these negative beliefs about ourselves may be our families, popular culture, or the mental health system. Although many external attitudinal and systemic obstacles confront survivor/ex-patients today, many of the people we spoke with identified internal barriers as the most difficult obstacle to recovery and empowerment.

> In my recovery process, the barriers that I find most difficult are the internal barriers. I've been told that I am much harder on myself than anyone else could think of being. I finally had to admit it to myself. My intelligence is fairly high and I am able to do most jobs quite capably, however when I cannot reach them, I put myself down miserably. "I am a failure, I am stupid." These are the things that I end up telling myself even if they aren't true. If I put myself down enough, then there won't be anything that others can tell me that would hurt me more that I do myself. (L.K., consumer/survivor)

Often the toughest barriers exist in our own minds. Many survivor/ex-patients received strong negative messages from early childhood, "You'll never succeed in life," "You're too stupid," "You're not smart enough," or "Why can't you be more like your sister/brother?" Negative feelings about our inferiority or "badness" were later confirmed by the mental health system. Many of us still hear haunting echoes from our pasts, "Work is much too stressful with your illness," "You'll always need medication and treatment," and "You'll never be able to do the kind of work you used to do." Such statements, whether spoken or implied, are still pervasive and contribute to immobilizing negative images and lack of self-worth.

> One astonishing day several years ago, I realized that I was the only person who could interrupt the internalized oppression in my heart and mind. Stopping other people from acting oppressively was challenging, but stopping myself from believing that I was nothing but a "useless eater," a drain on society, was so much more difficult." (Bureau, 1993)

A common phenomenon reported among survivor/ex-patients is the fear of losing all supports as we get better at managing our lives. Often services and support end when they are needed the most. All people, including people without disabilities, need support to make the transition to increased independence. These disincentives create a sense of loss and may even feel like punishment: "Why should I get better if that means I'll be all alone and have no one to help me?" These are systemic issues that need to be addressed. Support needs to be flexible and on-going for as long as needed or desired.

A common phenomenon reported among survivor/ex-patients is the fear of losing all supports as we get better at managing our lives. Often services and support end when they are needed the most.

Many of us have become experts in seeing only our weaknesses, having been told that our goals are unrealistic and that we don't know what is best for ourselves. With our own inner wisdom and confidence stripped away, many of us have become afraid to succeed, to fail, or to even try. These internalized beliefs about ourselves are often the result of years or decades of dealing with providers whose focus is solely on symptoms and pathology with little or no focus on skills or strengths. Many of us have also endured well-meaning but over-protective staff members who, in their desire to insulate us from failure, never gave us a chance to succeed or to learn from life experience. This often leads to a self-fulfilling prophecy of failure or underachievement.

Internalized oppression and learned helplessness are well-documented phenomena that are significant internal barriers to recovery and empowerment for individuals who have experienced psychiatric disability or psychiatric treatment (Bishop, 1994; Bureau, 1993; Chamberlin, 1978; Lovejoy, 1982; Weingarten, 1994). "Oppressed people usually come to believe the negative things that are said about them and to act them out. No other form of liberation can get very far unless the participants in the struggle are also freeing themselves from internalized oppression" (Bishop, 1994). "Learned helplessness grew out of the despair I experienced in the initial years of my illness, and from over-reliance on therapists and medication. Another contributing factor was the atrophy of social skills and some learned behaviors as a result of the reclusive and isolating life style that I adopted once I became ill" (Weingarten, 1994). In terms of our collective recovery and empowerment, we often internalize myths and stereotypes of people with psychiatric disabilities and become as we are portrayed. First the oppressors do it to us, then we become experts in doing it to ourselves.

Learned helplessness and internalized oppression can be overcome, if recognized and aggressively addressed as a community. "We have worked to eliminate internal discrimination by discussion with our peers, reading survivor/ex-patient literature, creative expression, self-exploration, setting our own goals, and playing an active role in our own treatment" (Fisher, 1992). "The struggle against internalized oppression and mentalism generally was seen as best accomplished in groups composed exclusively of patients, through the process of consciousness-raising borrowed from the women's movement" (Chamberlin, 1990). Internalized oppression and learned helplessness contribute to many people becoming stuck and immobilized within the mental health system. As psychiatric survivors, ex-patients, consumers, and people with psychiatric disabilities, we have to break free of our past and learn to create ourselves anew. Until, we are able to make needed changes in our self-perceptions, we will remain trapped as prisoners of our pasts.

External Barriers: "Barriers Imposed by Outside Forces"

External barriers are obstacles that are imposed by forces outside of, and greater than, the self. External barriers include conditions that make it difficult or impossible for persons with psychiatric disabilities to maintain their independence and live with dignity in the community. These include: discrimination in housing, employment, and public accommodations, as well as stigma, poverty and segregation.

The director of volunteers was very gracious when I first visited the nursing home. He stated that he was thrilled that someone as young as myself would want to donate time and talent to work with people in his nursing home. We set up a schedule that met both our needs. Then he had fill out an application "as a formality." My honest responses on the application made it clear that I had not been employed or in school for 6 years and that I was receiving psychiatric care. The day before I was to start, the director phoned to say that he would not be needing my services because the occupational therapist would not have time to supervise me and they wouldn't be taking any more volunteers. I felt devastated and couldn't speak except to thank him for his time. I couldn't help but feel that the rejection was the result of my psychiatric history and care. It was a very long time before I felt confident enough to try for another volunteer job.

The marginalization and vilification of people who are poor (which includes most people with disabilities) is leading to increased isolation and despair. Coupled with the lack of adequate resources and access to supports that enable people with disabilities to live more independently (e.g., alternative self-help or survivor/ex-patient-run programs, safe housing, non-medicalized supports, financial assistance, personal assistance services, and assistive technologies), many people with disabilities are finding it difficult just to survive on a daily basis.

After working for all of my life, I was unable to work for almost a year. I didn't qualify for SSDI because I was still working a little bit and I wasn't so sure that I wanted to receive a check anyway. I needed just a little financial support until I could get back on my feet—but I was unable to secure any. I ended up losing my apartment and moving back in with my parents which was a disaster for me. I was hospitalized eight times in the year that I lived with my parents. All I could think about was all that I had lost. After my eighth hospitalization, I reluctantly moved into a halfway house. I want to return to work and support myself.

Many people with psychiatric disabilities are forced to live in situations that make it nearly impossible to survive with spirit or sense of self intact, much less to thrive or grow. These situations include: living in undesirable and unsafe housing, living in poverty, violations of privacy and confidentiality, never having money to do "normal" things like go to a movie or concert, lack of access to transportation, coupled with a lack of opportunity or fulfilling work.

> There have been many external and internal barriers to my recovery with a psychiatric disability. One of the biggest external barriers has been the lack of adequate treatment options. At times I have needed to be in a safe, contained environment in order to deal with particularly intense and difficult issues. What has been available has been hospitalization.

> What has happened when I feel I need extra support, however, is that I have to threaten to hurt myself so I can get hospitalized, even when self-injury is not the real issue. I have been labeled with throwaway diagnoses, like "borderline," which effectively means the hospital staff can ignore and dismiss me and my needs.

> Another part of the problem is that I am beyond the initial stages of healing. I have a handle on my process and know what I need. Even when I have been on a hospital unit where the staff understands sexual abuse, they are usually only well-versed in the first stages of healing, and therefore don't know how best to assist me. A big problem is psychiatrists who think they know better than I do what my problem is, and what I need. They *don't* know better that I do.

Other external barriers are fueled by societal norms and attitudes, particularly by those who work in the helping professions.

Helpers often become part of the problem by perpetuating myths about people with disabilities and by seeing "their clients" as sick, in need of pity and constant "care." These biases can translate into beliefs and behaviors that create impenetrable barriers. These attitudes include a fear of letting go; trying to protect clients from failure; not encouraging clients to take risks due to the helper's own fears; feeling that client outcomes, success, or failure will reflect on the helper's capabilities; and the most damaging one, having little or no expectations, not believing in the (innate) potential inside every human being.

> The biggest barrier to my recovery was listening to all those professionals. Always telling me what I couldn't do instead of believing in me and encouraging me. They would say things like "You shouldn't try to work, it's too stressful," and "You'll always need to be on medication." They told me that my goals where unrealistic. They might as well have told me to just give up! Once I stopped listening to them I started my recovery. I've done pretty well for myself. I've been able to hold a job for five years and I don't take medication anymore.

Many of these attitudes are rooted in a belief in chronicity that has been perpetuated by the medical model. The medical model itself contributes to the intractability of barriers facing persons with psychiatric disabilities. Even with the current focus on rehabilitation, the influence of the medical model is still very powerful in most rehabilitation programs and clinical settings. A model that focuses on illness, chronicity, stabilization, and symptom management creates and trains helpers who are often unable to help the people they work with realize their full potential—consequently contributing to the hopelessness and despair of people with psychiatric disabilities.

> They told me I would be sick for the rest of my life and would always need to take

medication. A friend of mine said to me one day, "You don't have to believe your diagnosis, it's only a label." I thought I'd been given a death sentence from the medical "experts" which I had no choice but to accept. That single moment was the one that changed my life forever. I spent the next several years using self-help and holistic alternatives. From time to time I still do individual therapy with a progressive therapist. Nine years later, I'm working full time, living on my own and I'm starting my own business.

The medical model creates a climate of "us" and "them." Whereas professionals are able to rest comfortably together as a group behind a facade of "us" normalcy, and see the people they work with as "them" or "other," "sick" and not normal. This creates conditions that are oppressive both for the worker and the person receiving services. Many professionals are afraid to share or disclose relevant personal experiences that may be very helpful for fear of being labeled, losing credibility, or being seen as unprofessional.

> I was at a real crucial point in my recovery. I had been through lots of "treatment" and still didn't feel much better. I had just gotten out of the hospital after a major suicidal overdose. I was confused and overwhelmed with my life. I felt ashamed about the overdose and everyone knowing and all. I thought I was sick for having those kind of thoughts. Until one day, I'll never forget it, a staff person at my halfway house, who I really respected, told me that she too had felt suicidal in her life and that it was possible to survive and get through those feelings." I was so happy that day. I finally had hope that I was a normal person and that I could make it through this struggle.

The medical model creates and maintains an imbalance of power by putting the individual receiving help in a subordinate and/or devalued position, having to rely on the "experts" in order to get better. Professionals and programs who maintain a strict "no disclosure" policy do a great disservice to the people they work with and themselves. Personal disclosure with discretion can be a very powerful tool in the healing process. The medical model fails to acknowledge or nurture the role of the participant in his or her own treatment, or the ability of helpers to use their own humanness as a healing tool in the recovery and empowerment process. These attitudes, albeit well-meaning yet misguided, can create a serious barrier to recovery and empowerment for people with psychiatric disabilities. It is crucial that helpers examine the subtle yet powerful messages conveyed though their actions and interactions.

> I remember when I was living in a halfway house. A number of the women decided they wanted to adopt a stray abandoned kitten. The issue was brought up with the director, who stated emphatically "You people can't even take care of yourselves, how do you think you can take care of a kitten." I remember feeling like the wind had just been knocked out of me. It was a time when I was really struggling to feel OK about myself and my situation. Her comments refueled my anger and commitment to go back to school and get my degree in psychiatric rehabilitation and to do advocacy work. I still believe that some of the greatest barriers and destructiveness exists within our own profession.

Implications
Consider the following scenarios:

> My therapist kept confronting me on why I didn't seem to want to get "well." She would always say what a nice person I was and how lots of people would want to hire me for a job—if only I wanted to work. What she didn't help me with was the fact that I had no means of support, financial or emotional, I often had no place to live and bounced from place to place, I had no money to buy work

clothes, I was sometimes on the street, had no phone and did not live a "normal" life, so how could she expect me to do "normal" things like getting a job?

Living in the halfway house and going to the workshop during the day was not a life. Every minute was scheduled with appointments, groups, and chores. I never had any time to myself to think or deal with what I was feeling inside. And every time I tried to talk to staff about my feelings, all they would do was ask me if I needed to go to the hospital or if I should take a PRN. There was no place in my life to process the feelings that were keeping me stuck in this vicious cycle of hospitalizations, medications, and halfway houses. I asked many times for an individual therapist and each time they would talk me out of it or just plain say "no," and always I listened because I thought they knew best.

The service provider in the first scenario focused solely on the emotional or internal barriers, a trap that psychotherapists often fall into, and was unable to see the impact of the external barriers in her client's life that kept her from being able to go back to work. In the second situation, the service provider's focus is completely focused on the external barriers, which often happens in residential programs, and does not support the individual in developing the emotional skills necessary to live more independently. Helpers must remember the following:

• Internal and external barriers are *equally* important to address.

• One cannot be addressed without addressing the other.

Helpers need to consider both environmental and emotional obstacles and seek to address both internal and external barriers. If not, they will do a great disservice in their attempts to assist individuals in their recovery and empowerment process.

Conclusions

Recovery is possible for people with severe psychiatric disability. Personal and collective empowerment is a critical element in recovery from psychiatric disability. Even though there are significant barriers to recovery and empowerment in mental health programs and policies, and in interactions with mental health personnel; professionals have the capacity to support recovery. Psychiatric survivors report that mental health professionals can be instrumental in their recovery by providing support, linking them to other psychiatric survivors, and helping them navigate through the barriers in the mental health system.

References

Anthony, W.A. & Spaniol, L. (Eds.) (1994) *Readings in psychiatric rehabilitation.* Center for Psychiatric Rehabilitation. Boston University Sargent College of Allied Health. Boston, MA.

Anthony, W.A. (1993) Recovery from mental illness: The guiding vision of the mental health service system in the 1990s. *Psychosocial Rehabilitation Journal, 16*(4), 11-23.

Anthony, W.A., Cohen, M.R., & Farkas, M.D. (1990). *Psychiatric rehabilitation.* Center For Psychiatric Rehabilitation. Boston University. Sargent College of Allied Health. Boston, MA.

Bishop, Anne. (1994). *Becoming an ally: Breaking the cycle of oppression.* Fernwood Publishing. Halifax.

Bureau, Bob. (1993, August) *Empowerment is more than a buzzword, it's a way of life.* The National Empowerment Center, Lawrence, MA. August 1993.

Bureau, Bob. (1993, September). *Interrupting internalized oppression.* The National Empowerment Center, Lawrence, MA.

Carling, P.J. & Ridgeway, P.A. (1988). Overview of psychiatric rehabilitation approach to housing. In W.A. Anthony and M. Farkas, (eds.). *Psychiatric rehabilitation: Putting theory into practice.* Baltimore. Johns Hopkins University Press.

Chamberlin, J. (1978). *On our own: Patient-controlled alternatives to the mental health system*. McGraw Hill. New York.

Chamberlin, J. (1990). The Ex-patients movement: Where we've been and where we're going. *The Journal of Mind and Behavior, 11* (3&4), p. 323-336

Chamberlin, J. (1995). Psychiatric survivors: *Are we part of the disability movement? The Disability Rag and Resource*. Avacado Press. April/May 1995.

Danley, K.S. & Mellen, V. (1987). Training & personnel issues for supported employment programs which serve persons who are severely mentally ill. *Psychosocial Rehabilitation Journal. 10*(3), 11-19.

Deegan, P. (1988) Recovery: The lived experience of rehabilitation. *Psychosocial Rehabilitation Journal, 11*(4), 11-19.

Fisher, D. *How community psychiatrists and survivor/ex-patients can promote mutual empowerment*. The National Empowerment Center. 20 Ballard Road. Lawrence, MA 01843.

Freeman, J. (Ed.) (1983) *Social movements of the sixties and seventies*. Longman Books. New York.

Goffman, E. (1963) *Stigma: Notes on the management of spoiled identity*. Prentice Hall. New Jersey.

Harding, C.M., Brooks, G.W., Ashikaga, T., Strauss, J.S., & Breier, A. (1987). The vermont longitudinal study of persons with severe mental illness, II: Long-term outcome of subjects who retrospectively met *DSM-III* criteria for schizophrenia. *American Journal of Psychiatry, 144*, 718-726

Leete, E. (1989). How I perceive and manage my illness. *Schizophrenia Bulletin. 15,* (2).

Lovejoy, M. (1982). Expectations and the recovery process. *Schizophrenia Bulletin*. Vol. 8, No. 4.

New York State Office of Advocate for the Disabled. (1986). *What makes disabled people disabled: Attitudes & barriers*. Empire State Plaza, Agency Bldg 1, 10th Floor, Albany, NY 12223. phone 1-800-522-4369 v/tty.

Noble, J., Jr., & Collignon, F. (1987). Systems barriers to supported employment for persons with chronic mental illness. *Psychosocial Rehabilitation Journal, 11*(2).

Unzicker, R. (1989, July). On my own: A personal journey through madness and re-emergence. *Psychosocial Rehabilitation Journal, 13*(1), 71-77.

Vanderslice, V.J. (1985). Empowerment: A definition in progress. *Human Ecology Forum*.

Weingarten, R. (1994). Despair, learned helplessness and recovery. *Innovations & Research, 3* (2), 31-32.

World Institute on Disability. (1992). *Just like everyone else: The changing image of disability—Spotlight on the independent living movement and the Americans with Disabilities Act*. Oakland, CA.

The Power of Language in the Helping Relationship

Susan Spaniol and Mariagnese Cattaneo

SUSAN SPANIOL, ED.D., A.T.R., LMHC, IS ASSISTANT PROFESSOR, EXPRESSIVE THERAPIES PROGRAM, LESLEY COLLEGE GRADUATE SCHOOL, CAMBRIDGE, MASSACHUSETTS.

MARIAGNESE CATTANEO, PH.D., A.T.R., LMHC, IS PROFESSOR, EXPRESSIVE THERAPIES PROGRAM, LESLEY COLLEGE GRADUATE SCHOOL, CAMBRIDGE, MASSACHUSETTS.

THIS ARTICLE IS BASED ON THE ARTICLE "THE POWER OF LANGUAGE IN THE ART THERAPEUTIC RELATIONSHIP," WHICH WAS PUBLISHED IN *Art Therapy: Journal of the American Art Therapy Association,* 11(4), 266-270.

The purpose of this article is to examine the use of language and its impact on the helping relationship. It is intended to raise critical awareness of how biases become imbedded in language, how language usage maintains differences in power, and how to monitor language use in professional practice. The article begins by looking at the cognitive, social, and cultural roots of language development. It then looks at how verbal interactions affect helping relationships, and it raises awareness of the impact of language usage when talking and writing about people with psychiatric disabilities. Finally, it offers specific suggestions for improving written and verbal communications for professionals.

As competent speakers we are aware of the many ways in which linguistic exchanges can express relations of power. We are sensitive to the variations in accent, intonation and vocabulary which reflect different positions in the social hierarchy. We are aware that individuals speak with differing degrees of authority, that words are loaded with unequal weights, depending on who utters them and how they are said, such that some words uttered in certain circumstances have a force and a conviction that they would not have elsewhere. We are experts in the innumerable and subtle strategies by which words can be used as instruments of coercion and constraint, as tools of intimidation and abuse, signs of politeness, condescension and contempt. In short, we are aware that language is an integral part of social life, with all its ruses and iniquities, and that a good part of our social life consists of the routine exchange of linguistic expression in the day-to-day flow of social interaction. (Thompson, 1991, p. 1)

Introduction

Language is a dynamic social instrument that absorbs and reflects all aspects of human experience. Because language is molded by people's experiences, cultural characteristics of groups become imbedded in its syntax and meaning. And since language reflects cultural differences, its standard, "acceptable" usage is determined by the language habits of the dominant culture. It is especially important for people in psychiatric rehabilitation roles to be aware of the language they use when communicating with and about people they help because the relationship between helper and helpee is traditionally based on an imbalance of power.

Language Development

Speech is a uniquely human social event. The development of speech helps children adapt to their social worlds because it enables them to communicate their feelings, needs, and thoughts to others. Infants' early cries, coos, and babblings motivate their caretakers to tend to their needs. Over time, young children gain control of their speech.

Their vocabulary and grammar expand exponentially until, by around age three or four, they have usually mastered the profoundly complex skill of language communication.

Despite the universals of human development, each child's use and understanding of language is also determined by their personal and individual history. Language is dynamic, not static, changing its form over time and place. Similarly, the meaning of words is relative, not fixed, varying with individual circumstances. How children learn to speak and how they understand what they hear is influenced by their families, their neighborhoods, and their schools. Likewise, how adults comprehend and use language is affected by a complex mosaic of factors that include education, economics, class, occupation, age, gender, and politics.

Language usage is a critical issue because it shapes how people feel, think, and act. It is the basis for people's sense of existence and identity because it is a tool for developing self-awareness and self-concepts. The words people hear early in life become their first units of thoughts, and children's structures of speech shape the pattern of their thoughts (Vygotsky, 1972). Language enables people to name, define, and organize inner worlds of feelings, sensations, and thoughts. It allows them to externalize these interior phenomena by translating them into signs and symbols that communicate meaning to others. It also directs their actions because language is integral to anticipating, planning, and problem-solving.

Professionals need to remember that scientific terminology derives from a medical model that diagnoses pathology rather than describing functioning.

Language and Culture

Power is a social fact that exists whenever a person's role allows him or her to exert control, influence, or authority over someone else. Language is a social instrument that is *shaped by* culture and also *shapes* culture. Its "proper" usage reflects the speech and writing of those in power. It is the domain of the dominant culture.

In the United States, for example, standard English reflects the speech and writing habits of educated people. White middle- and upper-class professionals shape, define and name ideas, feelings, things and people. People who are disenfranchised in our culture due to race, ethnicity, class, gender or disability often have language habits that are not considered standard English. Therefore people in nondominant cultures are shaped, defined, and named by the dominant culture; they are silenced because they do not speak or write the language of privilege.

People in our society are seen and heard when they use the words and syntax of the dominant culture. If they do not use standard language, they remain silenced and invisible whether they speak or not (Freire, 1989). When Hegel examined the dialectic relationship between the consciousness of the "master," who does the naming, and that of the "oppressed," who is named, he wrote, "The one is independent, and its essential nature is to be for itself; the other is dependent, and its essence in life or existence is for another" (Hegel, pp. 236-237). Members of a nondominant culture can become trapped in their own silent world. If they choose to speak the language of the dominant culture, they risk disavowing their own identity in the process. According to Adrienne Rich (1977), "In a world where language and naming are power, silence is oppression, is violence" (p. xv) .

Standard English is an idiom of the privileged class. It is inclusive of values of the dominant culture and exclusive of those outside the circle of power. It contains overt and subliminal messages that exclude those who are disenfranchised. This use of language can cause people in the disempowered group to feel unworthy, inadequate, and/or inferior. The growing awareness of the politics of language focuses attention on its latent and overt sexism and racism.

While fine distinctions about language usage may sound blandly academic, their effects can be deep, tragic, and enraging. In her book, *Lost in Translation* (1989), Hoffman observes:

> Linguistic dispossession is a sufficient motive for violence, for it is close to the dispossession of one's self. Blind rage, helpless rage or rage that has no words— rage that overwhelms one with darkness. And if one is perpetually without words, if one exists in the entropy of inarticulateness, that condition itself is bound to be an enraging frustration. (p.124)

The Use of Language in Psychiatric Rehabilitation

The role of the psychiatric rehabilitation professional is an artificial construct that is inherently unequal, even when consumers initiate the search for services. When they are referred for services, it is not uncommon for professionals to assume that they have a serious disability and conduct initial interviews with the intention of identifying symptoms and other areas of weakness. It is a human tendency to notice information that confirms initial assumptions, and therefore ignore contradictory or paradoxical evidence. Therefore the person's disabilities, rather than his or her abilities, may become the focus of consultation and future planning.

Distinctions of roles are emphasized from the beginning of treatment in order to "set the frame." Professionals are sometimes trained to be relatively reticent while encouraging the person with the disability to disclose as much as possible. It is not uncommon for the person to attribute counselors with magical qualities such as omniscience and healing powers, or to feel strong regressive tugs in their presence. Professionals need to sensitize themselves to how the quantity, as well as the quality, of the language they use may create an imbalance of power.

Most professionals are aware that mental illness can produce a sense of disempowerment in people with psychiatric disabilities. However, a more subtle and pernicious peril to people with mental illness is the harmful effect of disempowerment itself. Mack (1994), a Harvard psychiatrist who has treated people in diverse populations for several decades, warns of the iatrogenic effects of the imbalance of power often caused by mental health treatment. He believes that many of the disorders professionals encounter in people with psychiatric disabilities actually result from the sense of powerlessness and helplessness engendered by their treatment. Mack explains:

> The feeling of possessing some form of personal power, the sense that one is to a degree the creator of one's own life, is essential to the sense of self.... Conversely, the experience of being overwhelmed or helpless may threaten or fragment the sense of self, leading to fears of dissolution or death. (p. 178)

Talking and Writing About People With Mental Illness

The foundation of any interaction is shared meaning. This is especially true in the helping relationship because empathy, support, and trust are essential to building and maintaining an alliance. Language exerts power over consumers when it includes technical terminology unfamiliar to lay people. Technical and scientific expressions can be useful among professionals because they create an interdisciplinary vocabulary, but they are usually alienating in conversing with the person they are helping. Using exclusive language is a way of talking above people, even while talking to them; it tends to make them feel anxious, intimidated, and inferior. Coleman (1983) insightfully states:

> At the heart of the matter lies a struggle for control—the use of symbols to guide, manage, dominate, direct or regulate the perceptions of others. (p. 401)

Professionals should take care to remain sensitive to words that could "type" or label someone. Like scientific terminology, accurate diagnoses can be useful in the proper context. They organize quantities of complex information in a form that can be understood by the various disciplines of a team. They may help determine appropriate mental health and treatment goals, as well as medication, and they are a "necessary evil" in applying for reimbursement from insurance companies. However, professionals need to remember that scientific terminology derives from a medical model that diagnoses pathology rather than describing functioning. Therefore, it should be reserved only for those occasions when it is required, and even then scientific terminology should be used sparingly.

There is potential risk in labeling people. The risk is that those who label others will cease to see them as individuals and will identify them with their illness instead. When people are labeled and categorized by people in the helping professions, those helpers may interact with them on the basis of a category instead of providing individualized care based on individual needs. Rather than *working with* a person who happens to have a disability called schizophrenia, for example, they *treat* "a schizophrenic."

Deegan (1993), a clinical psychologist and a former psychiatric patient, describes the perils of being labeled by an illness. She cautions that when people identify with their illnesses they often give up control of their lives, passing the responsibility on to their helpers. Remembering when she was first labeled with chronic schizophrenia, she recalls her deep sense of loneliness and worthlessness. In an imaginary conversation with herself as a young woman, Deegan underscores the negative language used to reinterpret normal human behavior when someone becomes labeled with a mental illness.

> Almost everything you do gets understood in reference to your illness. You used to have days when you had "ants in your pants" but now they say you are agitated. You used to feel sad sometimes but now you are said to be depressed. You used to disagree sometimes but now you are told you lack insight. You used to act independently but now you are told that your independence means you are uncooperative, noncompliant, and treatment resistant. You used to take risks. You learned from your failures as you were growing and learning. But now that you have been labeled with a mental illness the dignity of risk and right to failure have been taken from you. No wonder you get angry. Normal people get to make many stupid choices over and over again in their lives. Nobody tells them that they need a case manager. (p. 9)

Just as language is culturally relative, so are concepts of mental illness. People are most apt to label those they know least well. Szasz (1970) cautions against "manufacturing madness" and notes that what is identified as mental illness may actually be problems of everyday living. Giving psychiatric labels to those who are unconventional or different from the dominant culture may be a way of trying to control those whom we fear or do not understand.

In a pluralistic society, professionals need to be aware that all aspects of their relationships with people with psychiatric disabilities are influenced by cultural assumptions about wellness and illness, and abilities and disabilities. Before rushing in to label a person's illness or disability, professionals need to remind themselves that each society has different notions of the causes, diagnoses, course, and cures of mental illness. Professionals need to try to familiarize themselves with the cultural beliefs, practices, and perspectives of people they help so they can understand how these people experience their worlds.

Professionals may also consider the possibility that eagerness to label people with mental illness is a form of xenophobia. It is commonly accepted that we feel threatened by people who are *different* from us. However, it is also possible that what some professionals fear most about people they are helping are their *similarities*. Labeling people may be a means by which some professionals reassure themselves that they are indeed different from people who have a mental illness. It is important for professionals to remind themselves that what separates them from people with psychiatric disabilities are merely accidents of time, place or circumstances.

Suggestions and Recommendations

Before exploring and modifying their language usage, professionals need to take time to examine whether aspects of their personal biases, professional assumptions, and clinical theories interfere with their ability to perceive the words and behavior of people with psychiatric disabilities. They can examine their assumptions about mental illness. They can reflect on the influence of the medical profession's disease model of mental illness, which focuses on pathology rather than strengths and transformation. They can wonder under what conditions

diagnoses advance treatment, and when they become stigmatizing, disenfranchising, or dehumanizing. And they can wonder if they ever make assumptions about chronicity, unemployability, and dangerousness based on their fears or preconceived attitudes of people with mental illness.

An Ethnographic Approach to Language Usage

What people do, say, think, know, make, and use constitutes culture, and attempts to describe culture, or aspects of culture, are called ethnography (Bogdan & Biklen, 1982). Ethnographers believe that reality is a social construction. One way therapists can avoid using culture-bound language is to adopt the attitude of an ethnographer, or anthropologist, who seeks a subjective understanding of the lives and behavior of other peoples.

Before actually writing or talking about people with psychiatric disabilities, it is useful to try to gather a generous amount of data over an extended period of time. Professionals can try to approach people with psychiatric disabilities with as few preconceptions and judgments as possible, listening to them attentively, observing their behavior closely, and interacting with them respectfully. Like anthropologists studying an unfamiliar culture, they can try to spend time listening to the language people with psychiatric disabilities use when they talk about themselves and with each other.

During, or immediately after each consultation, professionals can record their clients' words as accurately as possible. In this way, the records kept by professionals will enable people with psychiatric disabilities to "speak for themselves," in their own words and syntax, through verbal and written rehabilitation reports. Professionals can also consider consulting with the person for corroboration or corrections of their written reports before presenting them to members of the team.

Nonjudgmental Language

It takes vigilance to use language that conveys meanings accurately and objectively. Many words and phrases commonly used in the mental health field imply judgment and too often become disparaging labels. When counselors communicate about consumers, many use terms that imply polarities, such as low functioning and high functioning, appropriate and inappropriate, and normal and abnormal. But human behavior is rarely so dichotomous. Rather than describe people in such contrasting terms, it is often more accurate and less judgmental to use more specific words to represent the gray area that lies in between.

Another language habit that encourages labeling is the use of words that indicate facts rather than inferences. This occurs most often when the communicator uses a variation of the verb "to be" (Hatfield, 1986). Facts have objective reality that can be verified, while inferences are, at best, educated guesses. When professionals make statements, it is important to use qualifying terms, such as "perhaps," "might be," "possibly" or "seems to be." For example, consider the difference between stating, "He is anxious about working with others," and remarking, "He seems to be anxious about working with others," and then quoting the person's own words about this subject or describing observed behavior.

Sometimes mental health professionals use language that has negative or fatalistic implications.

When counselors communicate about consumers, many use terms that imply polarities, such as low functioning and high functioning, appropriate and inappropriate, and normal and abnormal. But human behavior is rarely so dichotomous.

For example, a term used frequently is the adjective "chronic," which implies that a person can never recover. It is more accurate and less harmful to use words such as "prolonged," "persistent," "serious," or "severe" because no one can predict the certain course for any individual. Several long-term studies of the course of psychiatric disorder show that one half to two thirds of people with severe mental illness recover sufficiently to function well in the community (Frances, 1990; Harding, Zubin, & Straus, 1987; Huber, Gross, Schuttler, & Linz, 1980). Similarly, when communicating about people with psychiatric disabilities, professionals can choose to emphasize strengths rather than weaknesses and abilities rather than disabilities, because negative characterizations can become self-fulfilling prophecies.

One of the best resources for language describing a non-dominant culture is the group itself. Just as most professionals try to identify racial and gender groups by names they prefer, they can also identify those they help by terms chosen by these people. Chamberlin, a vocal advocate for people with mental illness who has lectured worldwide and advised President Clinton, refers to "former patients, psychiatric survivors, mental health consumers, and consumers." She asks her audience to "note the multiplicity of terms...[as] there is no single term we are all comfortable with. We choose to call ourselves by many different names. I prefer to call myself a psychiatric survivor'" (Bachrach, 1992,

p. 867). Survivor is the most radical term used by people with serious mental illness. Writing for a publication called *The Disability Rag* (1991), Rosen describes the rationale for this term:

> Those of us who are involved in the struggle to end our oppression are, simply, survivors. There is no better word to define the reality that belongs uniquely to us.... Until we define our existence, in a word we ourselves have chosen, we will never be free. (pp. 6-7)

"People First Language"

Although there is no universal agreement on terminology, the consensus favors what is called "people first language." *Guidelines for Reporting and Writing about People with Disabilities*[1] (1993) is a pamphlet published by the University of Kansas to inform professionals from various fields about preferred language usage and to suggest straightforward terminology for portraying people with disabilities. These guidelines were endorsed by over 100 national disability organizations and are used by the Associated Press. The updated American Psychological Association's *Publication Manual* (1994) has added a new chapter on language bias to help authors avoid "perpetuating demeaning attitudes and biased assumptions about people." It emphasizes the importance of using language that maintains the integrity of people as human beings.

As the term suggests, "people first language" puts people first, not their disability. For example, according to the guidelines people should refer to "a person with schizophrenia" or "a person who has experienced schizophrenia," rather than give someone a generic label such as "a schizophrenic." This way, the person, rather than their functional limitations, becomes the subject of the sentence and focus of the statement. Preferred terms for talking about people with mental illness include "people with emotional disorders, psychiatric illness, or psychiatric disabilities." The guidelines also suggest that diagnostic terms, such as psychotic and schizophrenic, be used only when medically and legally accurate, and should never be used out of context.

Conclusion

Using respectful but accurate language when speaking and writing about people with psychiatric disabilities can have a favorable impact on the outcome of psychiatric rehabilitation. Language can be empowering. Just as attitudes become imbedded in language, language can also precipitate attitudinal change. It is possible that addressing and discussing people in respectful terms will increase their self-esteem and help build a more positive sense of identity. It may be that hearing themselves talked about in respectful language causes a shift in self-perception from one who is stigmatized, disenfranchised, and disempowered to one who is valued, respected, and empowered. It is worth considering.

A small newsletter called *Pathways to Promise: Interfaith Ministries and Prolonged Mental Illness* (1994) recently published the poem "Beyond Programs: A Parable," which gives voice to some of the sentiments this article seeks to convey:

> *I don't want* to be a client, I want to be a person.
>
> *I don't want* a label, I want a name.
>
> *I don't want* services, I want support and help.

---

[1] For free copies of the guidelines, or a 14 x 20 poster about disability writing style, contact: Research and Training Center on Independent Living, 4089 Dole Bldg., University of Kansas, Lawrence, KS 66045, or phone: 913/864-4095 (voice/TDD) or fax (864-5063).]

I don't want residential placement, I want a home.

I don't want a day program, I want meaningful, productive things to do.

I don't want to be programmed all my life.

I want to learn to do things I like and go where I want to go.

I want to have fun, to enjoy life and have friends.

I want the same opportunities as all of you. (p. 2)

References

American Psychological Association. (1994). *Publication manual.* (4th ed.). Washington, DC: Author.

Bachrach, L. (1992). The chronic patient: In search of a title. *Hospital and Community Psychiatry, 43* (9), 867-868.

Bogdan, R., & Biklen, S. (1892). *Qualitative research for education.* Boston: Allyn and Bacon.

Coleman, W. (1983). The struggle for control in health care settings: Political implications of language usage. *Et Cetera, 40,* 401-409.

Deegan, P. (1993). Recovering our sense of value after being labeled. *Journal of Psychiatric Nursing, 31*(4), 7-11.

Freire, P. (1989). *Pedagogy of the oppressed.* (M. B. Ramos Trans.). New York: Continuum.

Harding, M., Zubin, J., & Strauss, J. (1987). Chronicity in schizophrenia: Fact, partial fact, or artifact? *Hospital and Community Psychiatry, 38*(5), 477-486.

Hegel, G. (1964). *The phenomonology of mind.* New York: Humanities Press.

Hoffman, E. (1980). *Lost in translation: A life in a new language.* New York: Penguin Books.

Huber, G., Gross, G., Schuttler, R., & Linz, M. (1980). Longitudinal studies of schizophrenic patients. *Schizophrenia Bulletin, 6*(4), 592-605.

Interfaith Ministries and Prolonged Mental Illness. (1994). *Pathways to promise.* St. Louis.

Mack, J. (1994). Psychotherapy and society: Power, powerlessness and empowerment in psychotherapy. *Psychiatry, 57,* May, 178-198.

Research and Training Center on Independent Living. (1993). *Guidelines for reporting and writing about people with disabilities.* (3rd ed.). Lawrence, KS: University of Kansas.

Rich, A. (1977). Introduction. S. In Ruddick, & P. Daniels, (Eds.), *Working it out.* (p. xv). New York: Pantheon Books.

Stone, S. (1991). Survivor. *The Disability Rag,* May/June, 1-7.

Szasz, T. (1970). *The manufacture of madness.* New York: Harper and Rowe.

Thompson, J. B. (1991). Editors introduction. In P. Bourdieu, *Language and symbolic power.* Cambridge, MA: Harvard University Press.

Vygotsky, L. (1972). *Thought and language.* Cambridge: Massachusetts Institute of Technology Press.

STUDENT PERCEPTIONS OF PERSONS WITH PSYCHIATRIC AND OTHER DISORDERS

Mike Lyons and Robyn Hayes

MIKE LYONS, B. OCC. THY., MS, IS LECTURER, DEPARTMENT OF OCCUPATIONAL THERAPY, UNIVERSITY OF QUEENSLAND, QUEENSLAND, 4072 AUSTRALIA.

ROBYN HAYES, B. OCC. THY., IS SENIOR TUTOR, DEPARTMENT OF OCCUPATIONAL THERAPY, UNIVERSITY OF QUEENSLAND, QUEENSLAND, AUSTRALIA.

THIS ARTICLE ORIGINALLY APPEARED IN THE *American Journal of Occupational Therapy,* 1992, 47(6), 541-548, AND IS REPRINTED WITH PERMISSION.

Policy shifts toward fostering community inclusion of persons with disabilities have brought community attitudes (including attitudes of professionals) into sharper focus as a cause for concern. Using a social distance scale, this study examined the attitudes of cohorts of occupational therapy and business students toward persons with psychiatric and other disorders. Contrary to expectations, occupational therapy seniors did not demonstrate significantly different attitudes from occupational therapy freshmen. Although freshman occupational therapy students expressed a desire to maintain less social distance from persons with various disabilities than did freshman business students, there was nonetheless a hierarchy of preference for persons with certain disabilities over others. This order of preference had only weak stability between cohorts, with persons with psychiatric disabilities consistently ranking among the least favored. It is proposed that occupational therapy curricula attend to students' attitudes toward persons with psychiatric and other disabilities. To this end, certain strategies to enrich students' education are suggested.

The stigma of mental illness, like a dark shadow....As long as schizophrenia is treated like some evil and frightening nemesis, not as just an illness, we shall continue to spurn those who are afflicted, and to abandon their families. (Deveson, 1991, p. 259)

It has been suggested that "the true challenge for rehabilitation...is not the development of new technology and miracle drugs but to overcome attitudinal barriers to interaction and relationships [with persons with disabilities] through understanding and acceptance" (Roush, 1986, p. 1551). This paper is concerned with the attitudes of health professionals toward the persons they serve. We have chosen to focus on occupational therapy students' attitudes toward persons with psychiatric disorders as a microcosm of the broader issues surrounding professional attitudes.

Why the Concern With Professionals' Attitudes?

Health professionals have been described as "gatekeepers of information and services [for persons with disabilities]" (Altman, 1981, p. 322). As such, their attitudes are important in shaping life-style opportunities for persons with disabilities and roles they are encouraged to adopt in society (Benham, 1988). Furthermore, the attitudes manifested by health professionals may greatly affect a person's response to professional intervention (Potts & Brandt, 1986).

Why the Focus on Attitudes Toward Persons With Psychiatric Disorders?

Gibson (1984) expressed concern about the dearth of research by occupational therapists in psychiatry. Furthermore, there have been problems with the recruitment and retention of occupational therapists in psychiatric practice (Bonder, 1987; Haiman, 1990; Scott, 1990). One reason advanced for this declining presence has been concern over the stigma associated with psychiatric illness (Burnett-Beaulieu, 1982; Ezersky, Havazelet, Scott, & Zettler, 1989; Hargrove, Fox & Goldman, 1991). Without research into such issues as occupational therapists' attitudes, the quality of our services to persons with psychiatric disorders will be less than they have a right to expect.

Why the Interest in Students' Attitudes?

Understanding more about the socialization process of students into the occupational therapy profession, including the acquisition of values and attitudes, has been identified as important to improving the quality of education and practice (Sabari, 1985). Indeed, concern has been expressed about the disparity between educational preparation of occupational therapists and the expectations they must meet in practice (Wittman, 1990). Questions have been raised about the adequacy of undergraduate education in psychiatry, in particular, and about its effect on the attitudes of occupational therapists and other health professionals (Kelly, Raphael & Byrne, 1991; Scott, 1990).

Literature Review

Community Placement

Shifts in public policy over the last three decades have seen large scale deinstitutionalization of residents of psychiatric institutions. The deinstitutionalization movement has proceeded in the face of a number of major obstacles including inadequate provision of community support services (Deveson, 1991; Peterson, 1982) and adverse community reaction to persons with psychiatric disorders (Best, 1985; O'Sullivan & Brody, 1986).

There is a lack of appropriately trained rehabilitation and support staff to assist people in dealing with the problems they confront in their daily lives (Duckmanton,

1987; Mechanic, 1986). Occupational therapists, with their focus on performance of daily occupations in work, leisure, home, and community domains, are a necessary part of the network of services for persons with psychiatric disabilities who wish to return to or remain in the community (Hayes, 1989).

Within a general climate of negative community attitudes toward persons with any type of disability, it appears that the greatest stigma is attached to those conditions in which the person's behavior is perceived as unpredictable (Schneider & Anderson, 1980) or potentially dangerous (Torrey, 1988). The lack of resources devoted to tackling the widespread misinformation, suspicion, and fear in the community has contributed to the social rejection, isolation, and abuse of persons with psychiatric disabilities (Deveson, 1991).

Professional and Student Attitudes

There has been a growing recognition that negative community attitudes toward persons with disabilities may be shared by some rehabilitation professionals (Chubon, 1982; Roush, 1986). Tringo (1970) found that, in his sample, rehabilitation students and practitioners did not differ significantly from nonrehabilitation students in their attitudes toward persons with a range of disabling conditions including psychiatric disabilities. A study of attitudes held by student health professionals' (physical therapy, nursing, and medicine) about arthritis found that, although persons with arthritis were judged as being slightly less normal than persons without disabilities, they were judged to be significantly more normal than persons with a history of alcohol abuse or persons with psychiatric disabilities (Potts & Brandt, 1986).

Studies of occupational therapy practitioners' and students' attitudes toward persons with disabilities have yielded conflicting results. Benham identified "a very positive attitude" (1988, p. 307) among delegates at an American Occupational Therapy Association (AOTA) conference (based on a 33% response rate). Estes, Deyer, Hansen, and Russell (1991) found that occupational therapy students held more positive attitudes toward persons with disabilities than did students in a medical technology program. It has been suggested that occupational therapy students' attitudes become more positive as they progress through their studies (Estes et al., 1991; Westbrook & Adamson, 1989). On the other hand, a study by Lyons (1991) of occupational therapy and business students showed no difference between these two groups in their attitudes toward persons with disabilities. Furthermore, occupational therapy students' attitudes did not vary with years of undergraduate education completed. Westbrook and Adamson have expressed concern "that occupational therapy students tend to underestimate the normalcy of lives that handicapped people are managing to live in a relatively prejudiced society" (1989, p. 130).

None of these studies has considered differential attitudes to various types of disability, in particular psychiatric disability. Only one study (Gordon, Minnes, & Holden, 1990) was located concerning occupational therapists' attitudes to persons with specific disabilities (amputation, blindness, epilepsy, and cerebral palsy). It found that the attitudes of student health professionals (occupational therapy, physical therapy, medicine, nursing, clinical psychology) varied according to the social context. For example, students were more favorably disposed toward working with than toward dating or marrying someone with a disability. Of the four groups, persons with epilepsy were most preferred by students.

Prompted by the declining occupational therapy presence in psychiatry, Scott (1990) identified the need for research into various issues, including students' attitudes toward persons with psychiatric disabilities. It could be that more adverse attitudes held by occupational therapy students about persons with psychiatric disorders, relative to their attitudes to persons with other disabilities, contributes to a preference by graduates not to work or conduct research with persons with psychiatric disability.

Attitude Measurement

A variety of methods has been used to measure attitudes toward persons with disabilities. From a substantial body of literature, Altman (1981) identified and critiqued three general methodological approaches: a) picture ranking, in which photographs or videotapes are ranked to measure individual reaction to the visual effect of disabling conditions; b) sociometric methods that measure subjects' behavioral responses in situations that may involve contact with persons with disabilities; and c) paper-and-pencil survey methods that require subjects to respond in oral or written form to a series of questions about persons with disabilities or other anomalous conditions. Survey methods have been the most commonly used (Altman, 1981)—most notably, various forms of the Attitude Toward Disabled Persons scale (ATDP) (Yuker & Block, 1986) and measures of social distance (e.g., Bowman, 1987). One advantage of the latter is that

As practitioners or academics…it is important that we create a culture that is conducive to the development of positive attitudes in students.

they attempt to explore differential attitudes toward persons with various disabilities, whereas the ATDP makes no such distinction among types of disability.

The concept of *social distance* was defined by Bogardus (1925, cited in Tringo, 1970) as "the degree of sympathetic understanding that exists between persons" (p. 296). Bogardus devised a Social Distance Scale from which Tringo (1970) developed his Disability Social Distance Scale (DSDS). The DSDS contains nine categories of social distance that are scaled with Thurstone and Chave's (1929) method of successive intervals. Disability Social Distance Scale respondents are presented with a taxonomy representing degrees of social intimacy, from which they indicate their preference for social contact with persons with various anomalous conditions.

Using preferred social distance as an indicator of attitudes, studies have found that those anomalous groups regarded as least acceptable/most rejected are persons with psychiatric disorders, along with those with mental retardation, a criminal record or a history of alcohol or substance abuse (Bowman, 1987; Goldstein & Blackman, 1975, cited in Schneider & Anderson, 1980; Shears & Jensema, 1969; Tringo, 1970). Tringo (1970) maintained that consistent findings of prejudice against these groups reflect a firmly fixed hierarchy of preference in relation to a range of disability groups. He found that the six most preferred groups of persons were those identified by various physical disabilities.

Research Questions

The presumed relationship between attitudes held by students toward persons with psychiatric disorders and the quality of occupational therapy services in psychiatry has prompted this study. Our purpose was to investigate the attitudes of occupational therapy students toward persons identified by different disability labels, in particular toward persons with psychiatric disorders. Our five guiding questions were:

1. Do freshman occupational therapy students express a desire for significantly less social distance from persons with disabilities than do freshman business students?

2. Do senior occupational therapy students express a desire for significantly less social distance from persons with disabilities than do freshman occupational therapy students?

3. Do students express a preference for persons with certain disabilities over others in terms of desired social distance?

4. If there is a hierarchy of preference, is this stable across all cohorts of students?

5. If there is a hierarchy of preference, where are persons with psychiatric disorders placed on it?

Furthermore, because we were aware before we commenced the study that the gender profile of the business students (52% male) was dramatically different from that of the predominantly female occupational therapy group (8% male), we judged it important to compare male and female responses overall before investigating the above questions.

Method

Subjects

The study participants were 223 undergraduate occupational therapy students (freshmen through seniors) and 326 freshmen in a business studies program at an Australian University. The business studies students provided a comparison group outside the rehabilitation field. Despite the difference in gender profiles, both programs have a large number of female students and both require a similar academic entry level. Demographic data on the participant subsets are shown in Table 1.

TABLE 1.
SUBJECTS' COURSE, YEAR OF STUDY, AND AGE

Group	Women	Men	Total	Age (mean)
Business (Year 1)	126	200	326	18.4
Occupational therapy (Year 1)	62	4	67[a]	18.4
Occupational therapy (Year 2)	51	6	57	19.0
Occupational therapy (Year 3)	50	3	53	20.6
Occupational therapy (Year 4)	41	5	46	21.1
Total	330	218	549[a]	

[a] One respondent failed to specify gender.

At the time of the study, the freshman occupational therapy students had had no course contact with persons with disabilities. Senior occupational therapy students had completed three full-time, supervised fieldwork affiliations, each of 6 weeks' duration. For the majority of these students, one such affiliation would have been within a psychiatric setting.

Instrument and Procedure

A questionnaire containing both the Disability Social Distance Scale (DSDS) (Tringo, 1970) and questions on respondents' gender and age was administered to subjects at the end of a scheduled class period, before or within the first week of the academic year. The DSDS is a measure of a person's feelings about how closely he or she would choose to be associated with persons with various disabilities. The scale's list of 21 disabilities and anomalous conditions "represents the major types...in the United States in the terms by which they are most commonly known" (Tringo, 1970, p. 297). For the purpose of this study, one term that is not commonly used in Australia, ex-convict, was changed to a more commonly used term, person with a criminal record. Respondents were required to rate persons with each of the conditions on a scale from 1 to 9, with 1 (would marry) being the most intimate and 9 (would put to death) the most extreme. Each rating was converted to

a Thurstone-type scale value as follows: would marry (0.33), would accept as a close kin by marriage (0.57), would have as a next door neighbor (0.85), would accept as a casual friend (1.06), would accept as a fellow employee (1.21), would keep away from (2.95), would keep in an institution (3.14), would send out of my country (3.65), and would put to death (4.69) (Tringo, 1970).

Results

The statistical analysis of data took three forms: a) analyses of variance of the DSDS scores of different groups (males and females, female business and occupational therapy students, and female freshman and senior occupational therapy students), b) rank ordering of the mean score of each disability variable for three subgroups of subjects, and c) correlation coefficients of all disability variables for three subgroups of subjects.

Variability in Students' Attitudes

An analysis of variance revealed a highly significant difference in attitudes between male and female subjects. The males chose much greater social distance from persons with disabilities, $F(1,499) = 92.31$, $p < .001$.

The close association between gender and attitude led us to exclude males from comparative analysis between occupational therapy and business students because the substantial difference in the proportion of males in the business and occupational therapy groups would have been a confounding variable, and because the small numbers of male occupational therapy students spread across 4-year cohorts would have meant that they could not provide meaningful data as a separate group.

However, the male business students were included in the rank ordering and correlation coefficient analyses as a separate cohort. It was felt that their group had sufficient numbers (200) to contribute useful data to the examination of attitudes toward persons with disabilities, particularly in relation to the stability of hierarchy.

The DSDS scores of female freshman occupational therapy and business students were significantly different, $F(1,171) = 33.23$, $p < .001$. The occupational therapy students expressed a desire for much less social distance than did the business students. However, there was no significant difference in desired social distance between female freshman and senior occupational therapy students.

Students' Hierarchy of Preference

To assess whether the relative position of persons with a certain disability on a hierarchy of preference is stable across groups, Pearson's correlation coefficients were determined between female freshman occupational therapy students and female freshman business students and between female and male business students. Correlation coefficients of 0.39 and 0.22 respectively suggest that the order of preference is weak; therefore, the rank ordering of disability variables was considered separately for each subject group. The mean score of each disability variable was calculated to give a hierarchy of preference for each of three subgroups: female occupational therapy students, female business students, and male business students. The most and least preferred on these hierarchies are presented in Table 2.

TABLE 2.
STUDENTS' PREFERENCES ON DISABILITY VARIABLES: MOST AND LEAST PREFERRED DISABILITY

Disability	Female Occupational Therapy Students Mean Score/Rank		Female Business Students Mean Score/Rank		Male Business Students Mean Score/Rank	
Most preferred						
Asthma	0.345	1	0.452	1	0.525	1
Diabetes	0.374	2	0.516	2	0.618	2
Arthritis	0.399	3	0.543	3	0.653	3
Ulcer	0.434	5	0.564	4	0.693	4
Amputation	0.415	4	0.587	5	0.735	5
Heart disease	0.442	6	0.632	6	0.745	6
Least preferred						
Hunchback	0.630	16	0.922	16	1.201	16
Cerebral palsy	0.682	17	1.111	17	1.592	18
Mental retardation	0.780	18	1.269	18	1.777	20
Mental illness	0.843	19	1.366	19	1.763	19
Alcoholism	1.262	20	1.513	20	1.589	17
Criminal record	1.301	21	1.726	21	1.828	21

Note: Other conditions incorporated in the Disability Social Distance Scale but omitted from this table are blindness, cancer, deafness, dwarfism, epilepsy, old age, paraplegia, stroke, and tuberculosis.

Despite only weak correlation between overall group preferences, the choice and order of disability groups at both ends of the different hierarchies are relatively uniform. For all groups, the same six conditions were most acceptable, namely asthma, diabetes, arthritis, ulcer, amputation, and heart disease, with just one variation between occupational therapy and business students in the ranking of these. Similarly, all groups identified the same six least acceptable conditions, namely criminal record, alcoholism, mental illness, mental retardation, cerebral palsy, and hunchback, with several variations between male business students and female occupational therapy and business students in the ranking.

Clusters of Preference

Further analysis was conducted to help interpret the thinking behind the social distance rankings of persons with various disabilities, in particular the low ranking of persons with psychiatric disorders. Pearson correlation coefficients were calculated for all disability variables for the three subgroups of subjects in an attempt to identify clusters of disabilities perceived similarly by students.

The only disability group that correlated highly with the mental illness variable was the mental retardation variable and this was so only for business students (for both male and female business students, $r = 0.77$). There was insufficient variation in the correlation coefficients to warrant factor analysis.

Discussion

Comparisons With Other Studies

The result that females expressed significantly greater acceptance (that is, desired less social distance) toward persons with various disabilities than did males is consistent with findings from other studies revealing more positive attitudes among females (e.g., Tringo, 1970). The finding that, among female freshman students, those in occupational therapy expressed significantly more positive attitudes toward persons with various disabilities than did those in business was gratifying but surprising to us. In a concurrent study conducted with the same sample of students and using the Attitudes Toward Disabled Persons Scale-Form A (ATDP-A) Rebuker & Block, 1986), Lyons (1991) identified no difference in attitudes between freshman occupational therapy students and business students. Two factors that may account for the difference in findings from the two instruments are that a) in framing questions for respondents, the DSDS differentiates among disabling conditions rather than using the generic term disabled people as the ATDP-A does and b) the DSDS asks respondents for their personal preferences regarding their degree of social contact with, as opposed to their beliefs about various characteristics of, persons with disabilities.

Regard for Persons With Psychiatric Disorders

Overall, the correlation between hierarchies of preference for different conditions identified by occupational therapy and business students is weak. However, it is notable that occupational therapy students do not differ from business students in their ranking of the relative social undesirability of persons with psychiatric disorders (expressed as mental illness on the scale). There is a consistent preference for persons with physical disorders and, in particular, those with physical disorders that are largely invisible, namely asthma, diabetes, arthritis, stomach ulcer, and heart disease. The same consistency of ranking at the bottom of the hierarchy is apparent for persons with what might be considered as disorders of the mind, namely mental retardation, psychiatric disorders, alcoholism, and criminality.

Although occupational therapy students expressed more positive attitudes than business students, they still resemble them in their poorer regard of persons with psychiatric disorders relative to other conditions (Potts & Brandt, 1986). Female occupational therapy students' social distance scores on the mental illness variable ($n = 202$, with 2 missing cases) were mean = 0.843, SD = 0.520, min = 0.330, max = 3.140. We must ask: Is it good enough that occupational therapy students score significantly better than business students in their attitudes toward persons with psychiatric disorders? Is it important that some occupational therapy students near the end of their course would choose to avoid all social contact with any person in their community labeled as mentally ill, that they, in fact, would seek to exclude any such persons from their neighborhood and, at best, would confine them to an institution? In a profession that espouses a proactive stance in support of the rights as citizens of all persons, no matter how severe their disability (Yerxa, 1983), the harboring of such views by some of its future practitioners is of grave concern. Can the best interests of persons with whom we work be served by therapists holding such beliefs? Would we countenance employing a civil rights worker who believed that segregation was the best option for all nonwhite Americans?

Socialization of Students

It is notable that these occupational therapy students did not manifest a difference in attitudes between freshman and senior cohorts. This is consistent with the findings of Lyons (1991) that used the ATDP-A, and at variance with suggestions from other cross-sectional studies that occupational therapy students' attitudes change in a positive direction as they proceed through their undergraduate training (e.g., Estes et al., 1991). These findings raise the question of whether the socialization process of under-graduate training has any appreciable effect on students' initial attitudes toward persons with psychiatric disorders. In other words, students' knowledge and therapeutic skills may be developed, but not their beliefs and feelings toward such persons.

Yerxa (1983) articulated certain values she identified as being fundamental to occupational therapy, including a deep sense of every person's essential human worth and dignity and a belief in every person's potential regardless of the nature or severity of his or her disability. Our findings prompt the question: Do current educational practices pay sufficient attention to students' attitudes and values and to conveying effectively the fundamental principles of occupational therapy and how they will be applied in good practice? A study by DePoy and Merrill (1988) found that occupational therapy students learned to articulate the values described by Yerxa as they progressed through their education. However, the students perceived a discrepancy between the values their teachers espoused and the values their teachers actually operated on in practice, including values exercised in their interactions with students. The net result was that many graduating students believed it was neither relevant nor possible to base their own practice on these values.

This leads us to question what attitudes toward persons with psychiatric disorders students encounter in their training. Are the attitudes of the academics and clinicians with whom they come in contact different from those attitudes prevailing in the community? As practitioners or academics, we are agents of professional socialization. It is important that we create a culture that is conducive to the development of positive attitudes in students. To do so we must examine our own attitudes concerning persons with psychiatric and other disabilities (Mitchell, 1990).

Effect of Contact on Attitudes

Contact with persons with disabilities has also been recognized as a powerful influence on attitude formation (Donaldson, 1980). However, as this study found, contact per se is not automatically beneficial. In a number of studies, unguided contact with persons with disabilities has resulted in either no change or change toward more negative attitudes (Gething, 1982). For example, subjects who experienced simulated physical disabilities reported almost exclusively negative insights into the feelings of persons with disabilities. Such contact, which highlights what persons with disabilities cannot do, presents them as "passive victims of fate, devastated by difficulties" (Wright, 1980, p. 275) evoking aversion and fear and reinforcing negative stereotypes. In our view, much of students' clinical contact with persons with psychiatric disabilities occurs only in situations where, as patients, their problems, deficiencies, or distress are highlighted.

We consider that such a climate for contact will do little to engender positive attitudes in students, a viewpoint shared by Roush (1986). We believe that students could benefit from an occupational therapy curriculum that provides opportunities for them to have contact with persons with psychiatric disorders beyond the clinical setting, for example, in recreational and other social settings.

When contact with persons with disabilities is voluntary and enjoyable and between persons of equal status, positive change can be expected (Gething, 1982). In accordance with the principles of social role valorization (Wolfensberger, 1983), Lyons (1991) found that students who had had contact with persons with disabilities in the context of a valued social role (e.g., co-worker, friend) had significantly more positive attitudes than students whose contact had been, for example, only in a service role (e.g., patient) or who reported that they had had no contact with persons with disabilities.

Gething (1984) devised and implemented a program that has successfully fostered positive attitudes toward persons with disabilities. Her program comprises accurate information to challenge negative myths and stereotypes about disability, carefully controlled disability simulation exercises, personal contact with persons with disabilities who "can talk about life experiences in a frank manner" (p. 48), and discussion.

Future Directions

The content of occupational therapy curricula (and possibly even the recruitment process for students) needs to attend more to the attitudes and values that shape the complexion of our future professionals (Sabari, 1985). This is the case if occupational therapists are to meet the challenges of future psychiatric practice in roles such as forming alliances with consumer groups to a) fight the stigma and oppression associated with psychiatric disability, and b) advocate for improved mental health services, training, and research (Council on Long Range Planning & Development, 1990). Also, for dealing most effectively with professional and community attitudes, further research is needed regarding conditions in the social and physical environment that lead to the development of certain attitudes toward persons with psychiatric disorders.

We believe that psychiatric occupational therapy could benefit qualitatively and quantitatively from a proactive approach to fostering positive attitudes among graduating students toward persons with psychiatric disability. Some areas of curricular innovation that could be evaluated include the following:

• The opportunity and the requirement for students to have guided contact over an extended period (to allow for development of relationships) with persons with psychiatric disorders, within the context of nonclinical roles.

• Facilitation of student reflection on their feelings and what they have learned through such contact, by means such as diary keeping and discussion with their teachers and other students (Smith & Delahaye, 1987).

• Complementing professional experience with educational input from persons with psychiatric disorders and their families for more of the insider's view of living with a disability (Hargrove et al., 1991). Students have much to learn from these persons as they talk about their lives, their needs, their perspectives, and their reactions to professional intervention (Deveson, 1991). This contact can occur in a variety of ways, such as lecture and tutorial presentations by persons with disabilities and family members and audiovisual and written first person accounts.

Methodological Issues

Attitudinal research, in general, is controversial as there are often marked discrepancies between the attitudes persons express and their overt behavior (Rabkin, 1972). Other personal and situational factors apart from attitudes must account for the variation in people's behavior. For example, MacNeil, Hawkins, Barber, and Winslow (1990) surveyed therapeutic recreation majors' preferences for working with persons from five different disability groups across three different age bands, youth (0–20 years), adult (21–54 years) and senior (more than 55 years). Although preference for working with most groups declined as the group's age increased, the relative attractiveness of each disability group varied for the different age bands.

Of the youth group, persons with a psychiatric disorder were least preferred; in the adult group, they were ranked third, and in the senior group, they were rated second to those with chemical dependency as the least preferred group.

Another variable found to influence attitudes toward persons with mental illness is the perception of dangerousness associated with psychiatric hospitalization. Link, Cullen, Frank, and Wozniak (1990) found a desire for a great social distance by a subgroup of respondents who perceived psychiatric patients as dangerous. Conversely, respondents who did not see the patients as a danger chose a small social distance.

It appears that the term mental illness evokes different perceptions for different persons. Gove (1990) suggested that the stereotype that laypersons associate with mental illness is one of a severe disorder with bizarre behavior, quite different from the behavior of most people with a history of mental illness. Once discharged from psychiatric hospital, persons are perceived as ex-mental patients. Being labeled a former mental patient has been found not to bear the same stigmatizing and exclusionary reaction as the label mentally ill (Olmsted & Durham, 1976).

Future research needs to consider the more complex equation of how variables such as the age and perceived dangerousness of persons with mental illness, when combined with attitudes of laypersons and health care providers, affect others' behavior toward persons with mental illness.

Summary

In this paper, we have explored the attitudes of under graduate occupational therapy students and their peers. Our results suggest that, although occupational therapy students begin their course with more favorable attitudes toward persons with disabilities than do business students, some still view persons with disabilities unfavorably, especially those with disorders of the mind. Evidence that these attitudes do not improve through the duration of the occupational therapy course raises concern about the socialization of students through their academic and clinical experiences. Given the general plight of persons with psychiatric disorders and the problems of staff recruitment and retention in psychiatric occupational therapy, we need to explore innovations in occupational therapy curricula that will enhance student attitudes toward persons with psychiatric and other disabilities.

References

Altman, B. (1981). Studies of attitudes toward the handicapped: The need for a new direction. *Social Problems, 28*, 321-337.

Best, J. (1985). Mental health—potholes in the road from Richmond. *Medical Journal of Australia, 142*, 270-272.

Benham, P. (1988). Attitudes of occupational therapy personnel toward persons with disabilities. *American Journal of Occupational Therapy, 42*, 305-311.

Bonder, B. (1987). Occupational therapy in mental health: Crisis or opportunity? *American Journal of Occupational Therapy, 41*, 495-499.

Bowman, J. (1987). Attitudes toward disabled persons: Social distance and work competence. *Journal of Rehabilitation, 53*, 41-44.

Burnett-Beaulieu, S. (1982). Occupational therapy profession dropouts: Escape from the grief process. *Occupational Therapy in Mental Health, 2*, 45-55.

Chubon, R. (1982). An analysis of research dealing with the attitudes of professionals toward disability. *Journal of Rehabilitation, 48*(1), 25-30.

Council on Long Range Planning & Development. (1990). The future of psychiatry. *Journal of the American Medical Association, 264*, 2542-2548.

DePoy, E. & Merrill, S. (1988). Value acquisition in an occupational therapy curriculum. *Occupational Therapy Journal of Research, 8*, 259-274.

Deveson, A. (1991). *Tell me I'm here.* Melbourne: Penguin.

Donaldson, J. (1980). Changing attitudes towards handicapped persons: A review and analysis of research. *Exceptional Children, 46*, 504-515.

Duckmanton, R. (1987). *Study of the role of community support systems in the rehabilitation of the chronically mentally ill.* Unpublished report to National Health and Medical Research Council, Australia.

Estes, J., Deyer, C., Hansen, R. & Russell, J. (1991). Influence of occupational therapy curricula on students' attitudes toward persons with disabilities. *American Journal of Occupational Therapy, 45*, 156-159.

Ezersky, S., Havazelet, L., Scott, A. & Zettler, C. (1989). Specialty choice in occupational therapy. *American Journal of Occupational Therapy, 43*, 227-233.

Gething, L. (1982). A preliminary report on the Cumberland Disability Program. *Australian Rehabilitation Review, 6*(2), 58-62.

Gething, L. (1984) . Cumberland's strategy for changing attitudes towards disabled people. *Australian Disability Review, 1*, 44-52.

Gibson, D. (1984). The dearth of mental health research in occupational therapy. *Occupational Therapy Journal of Research, 4*, 131-149.

Gordon, E., Minnes, P. & Holden, R. (1990). The structure of attitudes toward persons with a disability, when specific disability and context are considered. *Rehabilitation Psychology, 35*, 79-90

Gove, W. (1990). Labelling theory's explanation of mental illness: An update of recent evidence. In M. Nagler (Ed.) *Perspectives on disability*. Palo Alto, CA: Health Markets Research.

Haiman, S. (1990). Education and enticement: A recruitment strategy. *Occupational Therapy in Mental Health, 10*(1), ix-xvi.

Hargrove, D., Fox, J. & Goldman, C. (1991). Recruitment, motivation, and reinforcement of preprofessionals for public sector mental health careers. *Community Mental Health Journal, 27*, 199-207.

Hayes, R. (1989). Occupational therapy in the treatment of schizophrenia. *Occupational Therapy in Mental Health, 9*(3), 51-68.

Kelly, B., Raphael, B., & Byrne, G. (1991). The evaluation of teaching in undergraduate psychiatric education: Students' attitudes to psychiatry and the evaluation of clinical psychiatry. *Medical Teacher,* 13(1), 77-87.

Link, B., Cullen, F., Frank, J., & Wozniak, J. (1990). The social rejection of former mental patients: Understanding why labels matter. In M. Nagler (Ed.) *Perspectives on disability.* Palo Alto, CA: Health Markets Research.

Lyons, M. (1991). Enabling or disabling? Students' attitudes toward persons with disabilities. *American Journal of Occupational Therapy,* 45, 311-316.

MacNeil, R., Hawkins, D., Barber, E. & Winslow R. (1990). The effect of a client's age upon the employment preferences of therapeutic recreation majors. *Journal of Leisure Research,* 22, 329-340.

Mechanic, D. (1986). The challenge of chronic mental illness: A retrospective and prospective view. *Hospital and Community Psychiatry,* 37, 891-896.

Mitchell, R. (1990). A liberation model for disability services. *Australian Disability Review,* 3, 31-36.

Olmsted, D. W. & Durham, K. (1976). Stability of mental health attitudes: A semantic differential study. *Journal of Health and Social Behavior,* 17, 35-44.

O'Sullivan, A. & Brody, M. (1986). Discharge planning for the mentally disabled. *Quarterly Review Bulletin,* 12(2), 55-67.

Peterson, R. (1982). What are the needs of chronic mental patients? *Schizophrenia Bulletin,* 8, 610-616.

Potts, M. & Brandt, K. (1986). Various health professions groups' beliefs about people with arthritis. *Journal of Allied Health,* 15, 245-256.

Rabkin, J. G. (1972). Options about mental illness. *Psychological Bulletin,* 77, 153-171.

Roush, S. (1986). Health professionals as contributors to attitudes toward persons with disabilities. A special communication. *Physical Therapy,* 66, 1551-1554.

Sabari, J. (1985). Professional socialization: Implications for occupational therapy education. *American Journal of Occupational Therapy,* 39, 96-102.

Schneider, C. & Anderson, W. (1980). Attitudes toward the stigmatized: Some insights from recent research. *Rehabilitation Counseling Bulletin,* 23, 299-313.

Scott, A. (1990). A review, reflections and recommendations: Specialty preference of mental health in occupational therapy. *Occupational Therapy in Mental Health,* 10(1), 128.

Shears, L. & Jensema, C. (1969). Social acceptability of anomalous persons. *Exceptional Children,* 35, 91-96.

Smith, B. & Delahaye, B. (1987). *How to be an effective trainer* (2nd ed.). Sydney: Wiley.

Thurstone, L. L. & Chave, E.J. (1929). *The measurement of attitude.* Chicago: University of Chicago Press.

Torrey, E. F. (1988). *Surviving schizophrenia: A family manual.* New York: Harper & Row.

Tringo, J. (1970). The hierarchy of preference toward disability groups. *The Journal of Special Education,* 4, 295-305.

Westbrook, M. & Adamson, B. (1989). Knowledge and attitudes: Aspects of occupational therapy students' perceptions of the handicapped. *Australian Occupational Therapy Journal,* 36, 120-130.

Wittman, P. (1990). The disparity between educational preparation and the expectations of practice. *American Journal of Occupational Therapy,* 44, 1130-1131.

Wolfensberger, W. (1983). Social role valorization: A proposed new term for the principle of normalization. *Mental Retardation,* 21, 234-239.

Wright, B. (1980). Developing constructive views of life with a disability. *Rehabilitation Literature,* 41, 274-279.

Yerxa, E. (1983). Audacious values: The energy source for occupational therapy practice. In G. Kielhofner (Ed.) *Health through occupation: Theory and practice in occupational therapy.* Philadelphia: F. A. Davis.

Yuker, H., & Block, J. (1986). *Research with the Attitudes Toward Disabled Persons scales (ATDP) 1960-1985.* Hempstead, NY: Center for the Study of Attitudes Toward Persons with Disabilities.

The Multiple Effects of Culture and Ethnicity on Psychiatric Disability

Laurene Finley

LAURENE FINLEY, PH.D., IS ASSISTANT PROFESSOR, DEPARTMENT OF PSYCHIATRY, MEDICAL COLLEGE OF PENNSYLVANIA AND HAHNEMANN UNIVERSITY, PHILADELPHIA, PA.

Introduction

The National Institute of Mental Health (NIMH) reports that nearly a third of those it serves are persons from different ethnic and cultural groups (NIMH, 1990). Even though this is a sizable subgroup, there has been consistent concern about the provision of accessible, adequate, equal, and responsive care to persons in the publicly funded mental health system (Solomon, 1988). Non-white admission rates to psychiatric institutions, for example, are usually higher than for whites (Snowden and Cheung, 1990). Non-white rates for involuntary commitments are nearly 2.5 times higher (Rosenstein, Milazzo-Sayre, MacAskill, & Mandescheid, 1987). Non-whites, notably African Americans, do have higher utilization rates in partial hospital programs (Wade, 1993). Solomon (1988), however, found in a county-wide study that though a higher percentage of blacks made contact with a community mental health center within 1 year after discharge, whites tended to remain in treatment somewhat longer. Consumers who were white also received a significantly higher number of service hours and were more likely to receive residential and social rehabilitation services.

Though efforts have been made to more clearly identify the criteria that define the population of those who have severe and persistent mental illness, the fact remains that the criteria barely hint at the socioeconomic, ethnic, and cultural heterogeneity of these individuals and their families (Liberman, 1988). Current psychiatric rehabilitation literature fails to provide the necessary information to help providers understand the importance, role, and function of culture on psychiatric disability, as well as the type of approaches and services required in the rehabilitation of these persons.

Understanding the Cultural Context

Defined as people having a common origin, customs, experiences, and styles of living; culture shapes a group's values, beliefs, goals, expectations, and perceptions. It is a major form of group identification, a source shaping one's personal identity, and a major determinant of family patterns (McGoldrick, Pearce, & Giordano, 1982). Cultural membership may include participation in one or more different groups, including but not limited to ethnicity, social class, religion, sexual orientation, gender, and disabilities. There is also evidence that ethno-cultural values and identification not only help shape personal development but can predict and explain behaviors that are retained for many generations after immigration to this country (Greeley, 1974).

Ethno-cultural group membership may have a two-fold impact on individuals and families. Each group has had its own history of oppression and discrimination upon entering this country and consequently each group harbors, to some degree, both positive and negative attitudes towards its heritage (Devore & Schlesinger, 1981). On one hand it functions as a "psychological" buffer, providing safety and protection, and fostering cohesion, pride, and a sense of identity. Embedded within culture are potential sources of strength that may be utilized by individuals and families as resources for recovery and a sense of psychological well-being. When persons or families are facing stress, crisis, loss, or disability, they will rely inherently on those strengths, coping skills, and solutions that have been learned in the family and cultural context.

On the other hand, consumers from different cultural groups and family members interact with other groups within the larger society, and they *acculturate* or *assimilate*. Acculturation is the process by which one variously accepts or rejects the more pervasive norms of American behavior. The degree to which these norms are accepted is directly related to the amount and kind of exposure to the dominant American culture (Randall-David, 1989). Members within the same family may experience acculturation at different rates and with varying styles. Sometimes these variations contribute to intrafamilial, intergenerational stress or conflict.

Assimilation denotes the complex processes by which one relinquishes cultural values, behaviors, or traits, and acquires new ones through gradual interaction with others (Randall-David, 1989). When interacting with other cultures, particularly the mainstream culture, it is difficult not to encounter the psychosocial stressors involved in the acculturation and assimilation processes. Abandoning one's subtle but characteristic speech patterns, changing one's last name, having plastic surgery in order to anglicize one's features, looking for the "right" schools, learning the norms of the new culture while struggling not to abandon one's group—all are examples of the types of stressors that might be encountered by members of cultural groups.

Liberman (1988) has described a multifactorial model to assist rehabilitation practitioners in understanding the complex interaction of psychobiological vulnerability, socioenvironmental stress, and protective, coping factors as they effect the heterogeneity in the course and outcomes of those with severe and persistent mental illness.

Though not adequately described in the psychiatric rehabilitation literature, "socioenvironmental" factors can contribute to even greater social deficits and handicaps for consumers and family members.

Socioenvironmental handicaps, according to Pinderhughes (1982), result from continual adaptations and responses to a circular feedback process, referred to as the "victim system"—a by-product of racism, poverty, and oppression. Barred from the opportunity structure and subjected to daily insults or "microaggressions" accumulated over time, individuals are caught in a system which limits achievement and skill attainment (Pinderhughes, 1982; Boyd-Franklin, 1982; Chestang, 1972; Pierce, 1970). These limitations produce poverty, and in turn, poverty places undue stress on familial relationships. Over time, the family becomes less able to adequately perform its social roles. Individual growth is restricted and an inability to support and maintain the community, of which the family is a part, results. Communities, in turn, are produced that are too disorganized to adequately support its members (Pinderhughes, 1982).

Consumers and families from different cultures in the public care system may be caught in the "victim system." They come for services with their unique sociocultural histories, sometimes viewing the world as a hostile, dangerous, and unpredictable place. Suspicious of providers and lacking familiarity with dominant cultural institutions, they may be wary of receiving help from "outsiders." Perceived intrusiveness of "outsiders," or fear of being considered weak, may explain their reluctance to work with persons outside the nuclear and extended family. Often, because it is perceived as being easier and less humiliating, they rely consistently and heavily upon their family members for resolving problems.

Managing the multiplicative effects of mental illness with the co-occurring, socioenvironmental factors of discrimination, poverty, and cultural demands to adapt may create major stress and pose considerable challenges to consumers and their families. The socioenvironmental variables are risk factors that may precipitate or exacerbate episodes of psychiatric symptoms, or contribute to the effects of long-term social disabilities. Wade (1993) suggests that differences between long-term social disabilities and mental illness are all too often ignored in the provision of rehabilitative services.

Family Structure

Working with the unique worldviews of consumers and family members requires that providers be able to articulate the social norms, rules, expectations, and guidelines used by cultural group members to interpret the general blueprint of the dominant, Western culture. One of the first tasks for the provider is to be able to define "who is considered family?"

Family structures differ cross-culturally. Extended family and kinship networks consisting of "blood" and "nonblood" related persons are extremely important. These persons may be counted upon for moral support, financial aid, and help in crises. They also may have considerable power in decision-making, often expressing views as to whether the family member should follow the provider's recommendations or treatment regimen.

In the African American community, for example, one may find "play aunts," "play uncles," "play brothers and sisters," close friends, neighbors, boyfriends or girlfriends of the parents, or baby-sitters who are "family." In addition, the "church family" members such as ministers, deacons, deaconesses, and "sisters" or "brothers" of the church, may also be interested and involved in the family (Boyd-Franklin, 1989). This rich fabric of kinship relationships is a source of considerable strength in many African American families and can be utilized in the formation of important social networks for persons having a psychiatric disability.

Other ethno-cultural groups have a similar fabric of familial relationships. Some Asian American families define the basic family unit as extended with often three or four generations living together. Puerto Rican families may maintain close ties to relatives in Puerto Rico. Despite the distance, family members might be highly involved in the rehabilitation of a mentally ill family member.

The extended family may play a central role in all aspects of the Italian American family life as well. The family is seen as a great resource and protector against difficulties. So highly involved are family members, particularly in decision making, that they may be perceived by providers as "enmeshed" and "interfering" (Rotunno & McGoldrick, 1982). Separation from the family is not desired, expected, or easily accepted. In this regard, problems may emerge when this cultural value of strong family ties conflicts with a professional's value of individuation and separation, for example, when consumers are encouraged to separate from families and live in group homes or other supported housing options.

Gaining access to the family, so as to engage them, requires an understanding of how culture affects the structure, decision-making, and problem-solving styles of ethnic families. Determining who is the significant decision maker and addressing him or her first is an important first step in forming an alliance. Asking permission to speak with or to access other family members would be considered a sign of respect. Gathering information regarding the family's perceptions of their problems also facilitates the engagement process. Randall-David (1989), for example, suggests asking other important questions such as: What do you think is your problem? What do you think caused your problem? What do you think that your sickness does to your body? How severe is it? What type of treatment do your think you should receive?

Attitudes Toward Illness and Help-Seeking

Persons with a psychiatric disability and their families may perceive mental illness, and the role of religion and the supernatural in understanding and treating the illness, in ways that may appear quite foreign to providers. Clear demarcations between physical and emotional illness and spiritual problems, for example, typically are not made by ethnic consumers. Illness is approached as a mixture of psychological, somatic, and spiritual complaints. Symptoms may be conveyed through a somatic or supernatural idiom that tends to generate less social rejection and self-devaluation. The illness may be attributed to bad luck, evil spirits, the evil eye, punishment by God, or the result of impaired relationships with others. Western cultural beliefs, in contrast, are focused on the individual's ability to determine his or her fate. Mental illness is distinguished from physical illness, and spiritual problems are not considered within the purview of the provider (Flaskerud, 1984; Snow, 1974).

Each ethno-cultural group may seek out culturally compatible healers either in place of, or in addition to, Western methods and approaches. African Americans, for example, may use ministers, root workers, the family doctor; Southeast Asian Americans may seek out herbalists, family and friends, or diviners; and Puerto Ricans may use, Espiritistas, Santerios, a priest, a minister, or family (Randall-David, 1989). Folk healers speak the same language, live in the community, are sanctioned by community members, and may use cultural remedies both familiar and compatible with the extended family's religious and spiritual beliefs.

Providers may be expected by ethnic group members to function as experts, directly asking questions and providing authoritative guidance and explanations. It may also be expected that the response to somatic complaints be followed by a physical examination and a prescription for medication. Providers who ignore the expectations of ethnic group consumers may be perceived as insensitive, rude, or rejecting. Noncompliance issues and dissatisfaction with care may also result.

The impact of unique worldviews on perceptions and management of problematic behavior was investigated by Flaskerud (1984). Responses of six different ethnic groups, Mexican American, Chinese American, Filipino American, Native American, African American, and Appalachians, were compared with those of mental health professionals. Significant differences were found between the two groups in the type of labels used to describe behavior, whether the "problem" warranted professional treatment or not, and recommendations for management of the behaviors. In one example, a middle-aged woman saw visions of religious figures, believed that she had healing powers, and went into a trance-like state. Some of the ethnic group members labeled her behavior as religious, a gift from God, loneliness, or simply "protestant." They recommended the need for friends, travel, recreation, and keeping busy. Mental health providers, on the other hand, labeled the woman's behavior as psychotic and recommended psychiatric treatment, most often psychotropic drugs.

The importance of taking time to understand the beliefs and attitudes of consumers cannot be overestimated. Rehabilitation efforts with persons from different cultural groups who also have a psychiatric disability, may be thwarted because of the lack of congruence between provider and consumer regarding the nature of the problem, its source, and strategies required to address the effects of the disability.

Differences In How Problems May Be Presented and Discussed

Interviewing and engagement of consumers can be confounded by class, cultural factors, language, psycholinguistics, and conversational style differences. Providers assume that certain behaviors or rules of speaking are universal and have the same meaning for all ethno-cultural groups. Assumptions of this nature may increase the social distance between the provider and the consumer.

A classic, qualitative study involving Jewish, Italian, Irish, and White Anglo Saxon Protestant (WASP) patients investigated the extent to which one's ethnic roots might effect the symptom expression of pain (Zborowski, 1969). Jewish and Italian patients, for example, were both verbally and nonverbally expressive, emphasizing the intolerable severity of their pain experience. The Irish and WASP patients, however, were more reserved, preferring to hide and to rationalize their pain. Jewish patients expressed more anxiety and worry, concerned more about long range effects of pain while Italians were more present oriented, describing their pain as constant and present all the time (Zborowski, 1969). The study suggests that symptom expression, management, and clarity of presentation may all be affected by culture.

Emotional expressiveness of symptomatic behavior, however, might be misinterpreted by providers because the dominant American culture tends to value a more reserved presentation style. African Americans, for example, may be misunderstood when they demonstrate emotional expressiveness and intensity, prolonged eye contact, and greater bodily movements when speaking. Their styles of communication are often high-keyed, animated, heated, interpersonal, and may appear confrontational or argumentative when testing out ideas (Kochman, 1981; Sue & Sue, 1990).

Incorrect motives have been attributed to African American expressive behavior, i.e., that the person is irrational, abrasive, aggressive, out of control, too emotional, hostile, and prone to violence (Kochman, 1981).

Cultures also dictate different norms about distances in personal space. For Latinos and African Americans, conversing with a person may require a closer proximity than what is normally comfortable for Anglos (Jensen, 1985). Providers may be prone to back away because of the close proximity or make a behavioral attribution that the consumer is inappropriately intimate, aggressive, or otherwise lacking in social skills. Conversely, consumers and family members may perceive the provider as aloof, cold, distant, unfriendly, or unhelpful.

Kinesics, the meaning of different bodily movements, also appears to be culturally determined. Behavioral assessments of a consumer's social skills, for example, may be based on observations of facial expressions when interacting with others, and the presence or absence of such expressions perceived as reflecting the degree of the consumer's emotional responsiveness or involvement. Smiling, for example, is an expression believed to indicate liking or positive affect. People are perceived to be more intelligent and have a good personality if they smile (Lau, 1982). However, smiling to an Asian American, for whom outward emotional expressions are discouraged except in extreme situations (Yamamoto & Kubota, 1983), may convey other meanings such as shyness, embarrassment, or weakness.

Providers designing rehabilitation strategies for Asian Americans to improve a social skill disability, for example, might need to: 1) assess the consumer's behavior according to cultural and American mainstream norms; 2) identify the cultural context in which the social skill will be needed;

3) insure that strategies are compatible with cultural norms and expectations; and 4) when preparing the consumer for different cultural milieus, teach the consumer the rules and norms of the new culture while retaining behaviors required in his or her native culture.

Eye contact, silence, frankness, and directness in communication are all conversational cues mediated by culture and subject to potential assessment and misunderstanding by providers. For example, in Asian cultures, silence is a sign of politeness and respect. Rushing in to fill the void in a conversation might prevent an Asian family member from elaborating further. Providers who would do so might be perceived as rude, brash, immodest, and disrespectful (Jensen, 1985).

Requiring consumers and family members to converse in a second language might present certain difficulties. Facts can usually be related in an acquired language. Affect, however, is much more difficult to relate unless the second language has been used for a length of time at home, school, or the workplace. The consumer and family may exhibit difficulties with vocabulary, grammar, syntax, and use of idioms in the second language (Westermeyer, 1987).

Misreading verbal and nonverbal cues is often a reflection of our biases and our fears about difference. Consumers and their families may question providers' trustworthiness. They may be concerned about the openness and honesty of the provider and the degree to which perceived biases may impede service provision. How providers meet these challenges will most likely diminish or enhance their credibility (Sue & Sue, 1990).

Diagnosis and Assessment

More accurate interpretations of communication styles and conversational conventions will contribute to more accurate diagnosis and assessment practices. One of the first steps in psychiatric rehabilitation begins with a comprehensive medical-psychiatric diagnosis and a functional assessment so that clarity in identifying impairments and disabilities might be achieved (Westermeyer, 1987; Liberman, 1988). Comprehensive treatment and rehabilitation strategies also require an accurate diagnosis so that psychopharmacological agents and treatments can be matched to consumer need (Liberman, 1988).

The achievement of diagnostic and assessment objectivity, however, continues to be a major issue for persons from different cultures. It has been suggested that historically, cultural bias in diagnosis is often linked to the sociopolitical tenor of the times. For example, during the slavery period, African American slaves were diagnosed as having "drapetomania," a disease causing slaves to run away (Smith, 1981)! "Dysaethesia aethiopica" is another example of a disease thought to cause slaves to waste and destroy everything they handle (Smith, 1981)! Canino and Spurlock (1994) found that in the past, psychiatrists often failed to diagnose depression in African Americans because it was believed they were too impoverished or too happy-go-lucky to be depressed.

Loring and Powell (1988), found that the race and sex of the patient and provider influenced the diagnosis even though clear *DSM III* clinical criteria were used. Culture-specific expressive patterns and behavioral profiles in psychotic patients from different ethnic groups with the same diagnosis have been reported (Katz, Marsella, & Dube, 1988). Studies report that African Americans and Hispanics are frequently diagnosed as schizophrenic when in fact they may actually be suffering from depression (Adebimpe, 1984; Jones & Gray, 1986).

Affective disorders may appear differently for African Americans and Hispanics when compared to whites, such that more hallucinations and delusions are frequently observed (Mukherjee, 1983; Jones, Gray & Parsons, 1981; Jones, Gray & Parsons, 1983). Block (1986) suggests that there appears to be a relationship between expressive communication styles and symptom expression and intensity. For example, African American expressive style may be related to a tendency to express sadness and depression through agitation, anger, or acting out. Canino and Spurlock (1994) suggest that the acting out behaviors observed in many inner cities could, in fact, be depression that has gone undetected. Such behaviors may be a reaction to the loss of one's peers due to violent deaths. We also find that for Asians the incidence of depression might also go undetected or be underestimated because of the rather subdued verbal and nonverbal communication styles exhibited.

Socioenvironmental factors that may contribute to long-term social disabilities also require accurate assessments and must be differentiated from impairments that are a result of the illness (Wade, 1993). Adaptive, defensive behavioral patterns may be adopted by consumers from different cultural groups as a means of coping with the harshness of their environment. These adaptive responses, referred to as "getting by" or "survival" behaviors, have had a functional value in the consumer's natural community but may be mistaken by providers as symptoms of the mental illness. For example, "frontin," a behavioral, nonverbal, presentation style utilized by some African Americans, is an image, a "front" worn to mask one's true intentions and emotions. The person is keenly observant of the environment yet appears to be withdrawn or uncommunicative to others. This defensive style might be utilized in interactions with persons in the dominant culture when a lack of psychological safety is perceived.

Latinos receiving treatment or rehabilitative services may also exhibit adaptive behaviors that are often found to be frustrating for providers. Acquiescing to persons in authority yet failing to follow through on what has been agreed upon, happens frequently. The agreement, in these instances, protects the individual from being perceived as disrespectful to those in an authority role. It is a manifestation of not wanting to offend. Providers, however, may view such behavior as noncompliant or manipulative.

Mirowsky (1985) described "cultural paranoia" as mistrust that is an adaptive, "survival" response found where opportunities and resources are scarce, where protection by societal institutions is scarce, and where exploitation and victimization are common. It is not uncommon for paranoid beliefs to be rooted in socioeconomic quality of life issues rather than in individual psychopathology (Mirowsky, 1985). These beliefs might be present under particular stressors such as immigration, acculturation, assimilation, or prejudice, and must be differentiated from those symptoms of functional paranoia.

In an investigation of significant, self-reported, racially discriminatory experiences, Sanders Thompson (1990) describes the socioenvironmental impact of these experiences on survey participants. She found that two of the most commonly noted responses to discriminatory, stressful life events were intrusion and avoidance reactions. Intrusion symptoms involve recollections, nightmares, flashbacks, and thoughts about the incidences. Avoidance symptoms occur when individuals attempt to defend against the unpleasant reactions they have in response to recollections of the event. They reflect a refusal to accept what has happened and an attempt to avoid reminders that would generate strong emotions. In her study, these symptoms reached clinical levels 30 days after the stressful event and were still at clinical levels at 90 days.

Persons with psychiatric disabilities, who are also members of different cultural groups, are all too often at risk from the labeling, stigmatizing, and discriminatory practices in the very system purported to provide them services. Improved accuracy of diagnoses, combined with functional and environmental assessments would facilitate better rehabilitation planning and transitions to different cultural milieus in the community.

Setting Appropriate Goals

Consumer goals, and the processes used to meet these goals, need to be compatible with the consumer's worldview in order to maximize attainment. It is important for providers to recognize that the group or family goals may take precedence over those of the individual consumer. For example, rather than help a consumer from a different cultural group achieve independence by separating from his family and living in a supportive housing option, it may be more beneficial to the family that the individual consumer begin to address the performance of roles and tasks expected of him as a family member.

Sue (1981) and Sue and Sue (1990) outline three major conditions that may occur when goals and processes are incongruent: 1) goals are appropriate to the culture but the strategies needed to help consumers meet their goals are incompatible with the consumer's life experiences; 2) goals are questionable but methods or approaches are compatible; and 3) both the selected goals and methods are inappropriately matched to the consumer's ethnic background. Consider, for example, an African American inner-city, male, young adult consumer with a dual diagnosis of mental illness and substance abuse who consistently gets into fights with others. Using behavioral, structural approaches to eliminate "fighting" behaviors may be a culturally compatible strategy, yet, trying to stop "fighting behaviors" may be incompatible with defensive coping behaviors needed for survival and self-protection in his neighborhood or community.

The ability to adapt and to function effectively in both mainstream and ethnic communities is a goal that must be integrated into program services. Cook and Roussel (1988) conducted a research study to examine the vocational outcomes for persons with a psychiatric disability who were also members of different cultural groups. Nonwhites had a lower probability of achieving competitive employment. Their results suggested that many of the same factors influencing participation in the general labor force also had an impact on the non-white subgroup receiving rehabilitation services. The authors suggested that specialized programs be developed to assist subgroups of consumers having difficulty obtaining employment or transitioning to other cultural milieus. Learning to adequately differentiate norms, rules, expectations, and behaviors in both their own cultural environments and others will facilitate and enhance intercultural movement.

Overcoming the deleterious effects of long-term social disabilities resulting from multiple stigmas, and discrimination emanating from racism, sexism, and other "isms," is a much needed goal for all consumers—and particularly for those from different ethnic communities. Patterned after the social learning theory and stress inoculation training (Meichenbaum, 1985), inoculation against stigma and discrimination is a proposed model of intentional, planned interventions aimed at strengthening resistance to potential internalized, discriminatory experiences in different social and vocational contexts (Finley, 1992; 1995). The outcome is stress reduction; the enhancement of one's personal resources; and improved coping and problem-solving skills for more effective management of cross cultural encounters (Finley, 1995). A variety of self-instructional, self-management, cognitive-behavioral procedures are utilized to develop a repertoire of coping skills (Meichenbaum, 1985).

Stress inoculation training has been applied to a variety of mental health and medical populations. On a limited basis, it has been applied to "victim" populations (Meichenbaum & Jaremko, 1983). Meichenbaum (1985) speculates that this model would be useful with persons who have been victimized or experienced cataclysmic life events, or those who have experience a delayed response syndrome. The generalization of a stress inoculation model for ethnic consumers may be quite useful in anticipating and managing difficult cross cultural encounters. Recently, a structured, experiential, highly interactive model based on cognitive-behavioral approaches has been developed for ethnic consumers attempting to resist the internalization of negative stereotypes (Finley & Pernell-Arnold, 1992).

Group Approaches

Considerable controversy exists over the effectiveness of current treatment approaches for ethnic clients. Increasingly, there is recognition of the need for therapeutic and rehabilitative approaches that are consistent with the lifestyles and values of ethnic group persons.

Several examples of different types of group approaches, organized around the factor of racial homogeneity, are described in the literature (Primm, 1990; Finley, 1976). Racial or ethnic homogeneity provides a sense of safety for those who otherwise lack familiarity with majority group cultural norms. Activities and aspects of the surface culture, i.e., art, poetry, music, food, are utilized as material for the group. In response to finding that African American consumers were being under-served in their program, a psychosocial rehabilitation agency conducted an exploratory study where a racially homogeneous group was established for these consumers and matched with another group of African American consumers who were not group participants. One finding from the study suggested that utilization of the group model may have helped to increase program participation of black consumers (Stillman, 1973).

Same-culture groups have also been designed to raise the self esteem of African American men, and African American and Jewish mixed gender groups (Primm, 1990; Weinstein-Kline, 1980; Finley, 1976). Employing elements of the surface culture, these groups have been described as promising avenues to decrease isolation through intragroup similarity, as well as to increase socialization and activities compatible with cultural needs. A culturally-familiar and stimulating environment is created that allows for greater exploration of cultural identity and enhanced feelings about oneself and one's ethnic group.

Kinzie, Leung, Bui, Ben, Keopraseuth, Riley, Flelck, & Ades (1988) describe a group designed for South East Asian refugees. The goals of the group are to increase socialization, develop practical living skills, improve adaptation to America, and educate about psychiatric illness and the role of medication. Socialization activities, such as preparing and cooking ethnic food and telling traditional stories, are used to promote group cohesion and cultural identity while allowing group members to discuss psychological and personal issues. Three major themes typically addressed in these groups include: generational and cultural conflicts, persistent psychosomatic symptoms; and the loss of relatives, family, country, language, and social position.

Program or service orientation strategies have been recommended by Acosta, Yamamoto and Evans (1982) and Smith and Hunt (1975). A structured orientation for black and Hispanic students in an urban setting was developed to prepare them for a psychoeducational group experience. Use of music popular in each of the cultures was used to identify concerns and themes that might parallel the students' own experiences. Goals and misconceptions about the perspective group program, as well as norms and expectations for member behavior, were clarified in order to maximize the use of the program activity. This approach has applicability for persons who experience psychiatric disability who are members of nondominant ethnic groups.

Family Approaches

Increasingly, family education is recognized as being critically important in working with consumers who have psychiatric disabilities. Families as well as close family associates, i.e., "non-blood" kin, need to be intricately involved in the treatment and rehabilitation process. Though research is emerging on the role of family involvement with mental health services, there is little data on the specific needs of ethnic families coping with a member who has severe mental illness (Vandiver, Jordan, Keopraseuth, & Yu, 1996). If the needs of dominant-culture families fail to be addressed, it is quite likely that the needs of culturally and ethnically diverse families have also been neglected (Solomon, 1988; Spaniol & Zipple, 1988).

Providers need to develop a therapeutic role for the family that is consistent with its cultural style. A supportive network for the consumer could be developed within the family structure using novel ways of working with families either in agency settings, home, or other community settings. Family network approaches, which include family members, neighbors, extended kin, and mental health and other providers, may serve as innovative forums for collective problem solving and conflict resolution (Speck & Attneave, 1983). Home-based intervention approaches, as described by Falloon (1984), may be particularly appropriate for urban, ethnic group families. Pragmatic, educational, on-site approaches are utilized and 24-hour crisis intervention is provided.

Chapters of National Association for the Mentally Ill (NAMI) have sometimes found it difficult to attract ethnic families. Pernell-Arnold and Finley (1992) identify several strategies to both attract and retain members. Long-term linkages with churches and local community groups are recommended. Considerable outreach and personal contacts with family members, between meetings, in the early stages of psychoeducational group development are required. Personal approaches may be helpful in addressing the affiliation needs of ethnic families. Obstacles to participation need to be anticipated and resolved. Providing opportunities for achievement and recognition by giving certificates or other methods of reinforcement for attendance and special contributions can help foster group development, so that a family member's voluntarism might not be perceived as exploitation.

Consumer Involvement

Just as the role and importance of culture has posed special challenges for professionals and family members, so too is the consumer movement posed with these same challenges. Large-scale ethnic involvement in the consumer movement has been minimal at best. Little attention seems to have been devoted to this issue in the research literature.

There are any one of several different reasons why ethnic group members seem to lack visibility in the consumer, self-help movement. First, the same class, cultural worldview, and language barriers that pose significant barriers with other dominant culture institutions are also barriers with consumer-run organizations (Hikmah Gardiner, personal communication, February, 1996). In some instances, ethnic biases may not be transcended. Other situations may be characterized by denial as issues of discrimination are ignored. Ethnic consumers may experience difficulty in feeling comfortable and finding their "place" in more monocultural arenas. There is some evidence, for example, that African Americans are most comfortable in racially mixed group settings when the proportion or number of members of a different racial group relative to their own group is 50% to 50% (Davis, 1979, 1981).

It may be well advised for some ethnic group members to first work through various issues related to their ethnicity, self-help, and advocacy within more ethnically homogeneous group settings before venturing into heterogeneous ones (Shipp, 1983). Environments that tend to be more ethnically homogeneous, such as those which exist as part of indigenous, social networks, may be perceived as having less conflict, being more cohesive, and better attended in contrast with more heterogeneous group settings (Merta, 1995).

Second, the multiplicative effects of the victim system combined with psychiatric disability and/or other "isms" magnifies the sense of learned helplessness for ethnic consumers. Consumers may well believe the "hype," i.e., they may internalize the compounded, negative stereotypes that they are not capable because of their various group memberships. Their willingness to participate in advocacy efforts is thereby greatly limited. Additionally, the agenda of the self-help movement fails to address or to develop strategies to impact the effects of discrimination emanating from multiple sources.

Third, some ethnic consumers may feel uncomfortable in organizing their identity around their illness or disability. Lefley (1990), in discussing the role of culture in the etiology, duration, and curability of mental illness, suggests that traditional cultures might be less stigmatizing because mental illness is often viewed as external to the consumer. Persons tend not to fuse their core identity with the illness. Strengths are derived from their worldview, religion, and family system. Persons with severe mental illness may appear to be less socially isolated, often encouraged to assume "normal" social roles that benefit both the family and the community at large. Some ethnic consumers could tend not to participate in group activities where their mental illness is promulgated as the primary basis and justification for the group's purpose, role, and function.

Finally, in more traditional cultures, distinctions between "primary" consumers (i.e., families) and "secondary" consumers (i.e., persons with severe mental illness) are artificial. Families are naturally viewed as allies and integral components of the treatment process (Lefley, 1990). So, for example, a primarily African American mental health agency in Cleveland, Ohio, utilized a ethnically homogeneous, group format to develop member leadership. Families of these consumers were invited to events in which their family members were observed functioning in more responsible, social roles. The families became excited and committed to organizing themselves in ways which would support the continued growth and development of their family members (A. Pernell-Arnold, February 29, 1996). The advocacy and self-help approaches for both families and consumers were inextricably linked.

Conclusion

Considerable cultural variability exists among persons who also have a psychiatric disability. This group is not monolithic. Continuing to ignore the ethno-cultural factor will only perpetuate glaring service inequities. Significant gaps in the research, theory, knowledge, and innovative methods for dealing effectively with diverse consumers and families remains. There is an obvious need to develop approaches that can integrate the ethno-cultural factor into all aspects of mental health and rehabilitative practices.

References

Acosta, F., Yamamoto, J., & Evans, L. (1981). *Effective psychotherapy for low income and minority patients.* New York: Plenum Press.

Adebimpe, V.R. (1984). American blacks and psychiatry. *Transcultural Psychiatric Research Review, 21,* 81-111.

Armstead, C., Lawler, K., Gordon, G., Cross, J., & Gibbons, J. (1989). Relationship of racial stressors to blood pressure responses and anger expression in Black college students. *Health Psychology, 8,* 541-556.

Block, C. (1981). Black Americans and the cross-cultural counseling experience. In A.M. Marsella & P.B. Peterson (Eds.), *Cross-cultural counseling and psychotherapy.* New York: Pergamon.

Boyd-Franklin, N. (1989). *Black families in therapy: A multisystems approach.* New York: Guilford Press.

Canino, L.A. & Spurlock, J. (1994). Culturally diverse children and adolescents: Assessment, diagnoses and treatment. New York: Guilford Press.

Chestang, L. (1972). *Character development in a hostile environment (occasional paper No. 3).* Chicago: University of Chicago School of Social Service Administration.

Cheung, F. & Snowden, L. (1990). Community mental health and ethnic minority populations. *Community Mental Health Journal, 26*(3), 277-291.

Chu, C. Sallach, H.S., Zakeria, S.A. (1985). Differences in psychopathology between black and white schizophrenics. *International Journal of Social Psychiatry, 31,* 252-257.

Cook, J. & Roussel, A. (1988, October). Who works and what works: Effects of race, class, age and gender on employment among the psychiatrically disabled. *Community Network News.* Boston: Boston University, Center for Psychiatric Rehabilitation.

Davis, L. (1979). Racial competition of groups. *Social Work, 24,* 208-213.

Davis, L. (1981). Racial issues in the training of group workers. *Journal for Specialists in Group Work, 6,* 155-159.

Devore, W. & Schlesinger, E. (1981). *Ethnic sensitive social work practice.* St. Louis, MI: C.V. Mosley Company.

Falloon, I.R.H., Boyd, J.L., & McGill, C.W. (1984). *Family care of schizophrenia.* New York: Guilford Press.

Finley, L. (1978). The black experience group: A therapeutic group activity model for the black schizophrenic. In *Innovations in Counseling Services.* Washington, D.C.: American Personnel and Guidance Association.

Finley, L. (1992, June). *When cultures meet.* Presentation at the Medical College of Pennsylvania and the National Alliance for the Mentally Ill Conference: Treating the seriously mentally ill, educating professionals for the 21st century. Philadelphia, PA.

Finley, L. (1995, January). Inoculation workshop against racism and discrimination. Workshop conducted for the Multicultural Research and Training Institute, Temple, University, Philadelphia, PA.

Finley, L. & Pernell-Arnold, A. (1992). *Inoculation workshop against racism and discrimination.* Unpublished.

Flaskerad, J.H. (1984). A comparison of perceptions of problematic behavior by six minority groups and mental health professionals. *Nursing Research, 33*(4), 190-197.

Frieberg, P. (1991). Studies look at Blacks' health behavior. *The Monitor, 22*(7), p. 34.

Gardiner, H. (1996, February). Personal communication with president of Do Drop-In, a consumer drop-in center.

Greenley, A.M. (1974). *Ethnicity in the United States.* New York: John Wiley and Sons, Inc.

Hines, P. & Boyd-Franklin, N. (1982). Black families. In M. McGoldrick, J. Pearce & J. Giordano (Eds.), *Ethnicity and family therapy* (pp. 84-107). New York: Guilford Press.

Jensen, J.V. (1985). Perspective on non-verbal intercultural communication. In L.A. Samovar & R.E. Porter (Eds.), *Intercultural communication: A reader.* Belmont, CA: Wadsworth.

Jones, B.E., Gray, B.A., & Parsons, E.B. (1983). Manic-depressive illness in a hospital unit. *American Journal of Psychiatry, 138,* 654-657.

Jones, B.E. & Gray, B.A. (1986). Problems in diagnosing schizophrenia and affective disorders among blacks. *Hospital and Community Psychiatry, 137,* 61-65.

Jones, B. & Gray, B. (1986). Problems in diagnoses schizophrenia and affective disorders among blacks. *Hospital and Community Psychiatry, 37*(1), 61-63.

Karno, M. (1966). The enigma of ethnicity in a psychiatric clinic. *Archives of General Psychiatry, 14,* 515-520.

Katz, K.M., Marsella, A., & Duke, K.C. (1988). On the expression of psychosis in different cultures: Schizophrenia in an Indian and in a Nigerian community. Culture, *Medicine and Psychiatry, 12,* 331-335.

Kinzie, J., Leung, P., Bui, A., Ben, R., Keopraseuth, K., Riley, C., Fileck, J., & Ades (1988). Group therapy with Southeast Asian refugees. *Community Mental Health Journal,* 24(2), 157-166.

Kochman, T. (1981). *Black and white styles in conflict.* Chicago, Ill: The University of Chicago Press.

Lefley, H.P. (1985). Families of the mentally ill in cross-cultural perspective. *Psychosocial Rehabilitation Journal, 8,* 57-75.

Lefley, H.P. (1987). Culture and mental illness: The family role. In A.B. Hatfield and H.P. Lefley (Eds.), *Families of the mentally ill: Coping and Adaptation.* New York: Guilford Press.

Lefley, H.P. (1990). Culture and chronic mental illness. *Hospital and Community Psychiatry,* 41(3), 277-286.

Liberman, R.P. (Ed.) (1988). *Psychiatric rehabilitation of chronic mental patients.* Washington, D.C.: American Psychiatric Press.

Loring, M., Power, B. (1988). Gender, race and *DSM-III*; A study of the objectivity of psychiatric diagnostic behavior. *Journal of Health and Social Behavior, 29,* 1-22.

Lou, S. (1982). The effect of smiling on person perception. *The Journal of Social Psychology,* 117, 63-67.

Lukoff, D. & Ventura, J. (1988). Psychiatric diagnostic. In R.P. Liberman (Ed.), *Psychiatric rehabilitation of chronic mental patients* (pp. 29-58). Washington, D.C.: 1988.

McGoldrick, M., Pearce, J., & Giordano, J. (1982). *Ethnicity and family therapy.* New York: Guilford Press.

Meichenbaum, D. & Jaremko, M. (1983). *Stress reduction and prevention.* New York: Plenum.

Meichenbaum, D. (1985). *Stress Inoculation Training.* Needham Heights, MA: Allyn & Bacon.

Merta, R.J. (1995). Group Work: Multicultural perspectives. In J.G. Ponterotto, J.M. Casas, L.A. Suzuki, & C.M. Alexander (Eds.) *Handbook of multicultural counseling* (pp. 567-585). Thousand Oaks, CA: Sage Publications, Inc.

Mirowsky, J. (1985). Disorder and its context: Paranoid beliefs as thematic elements of thought problems, hallucinations and delusions under threatening social conditions. *Research In Community and Mental Health,* 5, 185-204.

Mukherjee, S. Shukla, S., & Woodle, J. (1983). Misdiagnoses of schizophrenic in bi-polar patients: A multiethnic comparison. *American Journal of Psychiatry, 140,* 1571-1574.

National Institute of Mental Health (1990). *Mental health, United States, 1990* (DHHS Pub. No. ADM 90-1708). Washington, DC: U.S. Government Printing Office.

Pearson, J.C. (1985). *Gender and communication.* Dubuque, IA: W.C. Brown.

Pernell-Arnold, A. & Finley L. (1992). *Psychosocial rehabilitation services in action: principles and strategies that result in rehabilitation.* Contract Bid #P09-07-09-92-DP). Columbia, S.C.: South Carolina Department of Mental Health.

Pierce, C. (1970). Offensive mechanisms. In F. Barbour (Ed.), *The black seventies.* Boston, MA: Sargent.

Pinderhughes, E. (1982). Afro-American families and the victim system. In M. McGoldrick, J. Pearse & J. Giordano (Eds.), *Ethnicity and family therapy* (pp. 108-122). New York: Guilford Press.

Poussant, A.F. (1972). *Why blacks kill blacks.* New York: Emerson Hall.

Primm, A.B. (1990, February). Group psychotherapy can raise self-esteem in mentally ill black men. *The Psychiatric Times: Medicine and Behavior,* pp. 24-25.

Puig, A. (Fall-Winger 1991). Racism as a traumatic stressor. *Delaware Valley of Black Psychologists Newsletter,* pp. 6-10. Philadelphia, PA: Delaware Valley Association of Black Psychologists.

Randall-David, E. (1989). *Strategies for working with culturally diverse communities and clients* (Report No. MCH 113793). Washington, D.C.: The Association for the Care of Children's Health.

Rosenstein, M. & Milazzo-Sayre, L., MacAskill, R. & Manderscheid, R. (1987). *Use of inpatient services by special populations.* In R.W. Manderscheid and S.A. Barrett (Eds.), Mental Health, United States. (DHHS No: ADM87-1518). Washington, D.C.: U.S. Government Printing Office.

Rotunno, M. & McGoldrick, M. (1982). Italian Families. In M. McGoldrick, J. Pearce and J. Giordano (Eds.), *Ethnicity and family therapy,* (pp. 340-363). New York: Guilford Press.

Sanders-Thompson, V.L. (1990). Factors affecting the level of African American identification. *Journal of Black Psychology, 17,* 19-35.

Sanders-Thompson, V.L. (1994). A preliminary outline of treatment strategies with African Americans coping with racism. *Psych Discourse, 25*(6), 6-9.

Shipp, P.L. (1983). Counseling Blacks: a group approach. *Personnel and Guidance Journal, 62,* 108-111.

Smith, J.E. (1981). Cultural and historical perspectives in counseling blacks. In D.W. Sue (Ed.), *Counseling the culturally different* (pp. 141-185). New York: John Wiley and Sons.

Smith, J. & Hunt, P. (1975). Involving the culturally different in group counseling. Unpublished manuscript.

Snow, L.F. (1974). Folk beliefs and their implications for care of patients. *Annals of Internal Medicine, 81,* 82-96.

Snowden, L. & Cheung, F. (1990). Use of inpatient mental health services by members of ethnic minority groups. *American Psychologist, 45*(3), 101-115.

Solomon, P. (1988). Racial factors in mental health service utilization. *Psychosocial Rehabilitation Journal, 11,* 3-12.

Solomon, P. & Marcenko, M. (1992). Families of adults with severe mental illness: Their satisfaction with inpatient and outpatient treatment. *Psychosocial Rehabilitation Journal, 16*(1), 121-134.

Spaniol, L. & Zipple, A. (1988). Family and professional perceptions of family needs and coping strengths. *Rehabilitation Psychology, 33,* 37-45.

Speck, R. & Attneave, C. (1973). *Family networks.* New York: Vintage Books.

Stillman, S. (1973). Increasing black client participation in a community social service agency. *Program Evaluation Report Series—No. 6,* pp. 1-6. Cleveland, Ohio: Hill House Rehabilitation and Research.

Sue, D.W. & Sue, D. (1990). Counseling the culturally different: *Theory and practice.* New York: John Wiley & Sons.

Tsvi, P. & Schultz, G. (1988). Ethnic factors in group process: Cultural dynamics in multi-ethnic therapy group. *American Journal of Orthopsychiatry, 58*(1), 136-142.

Wade, J.C. (1993). Institutional Racism: An analysis of the mental health system. *American Journal of Orthopsychiatry, 63*(4), 536-544.

Weinstein-Klien, J. (1980). *Jewish identity and self-esteem: Healing wounds through ethnotherapy.* New York: Institute on Pluralism and Group Identity of the American Jewish Committee.

Westermayer, J. (1987). Clinical considerations in cross-cultural diagnoses. *Hospital and Community Psychiatry, 38*(2), 160-165.

Yamamoto, J., & Kubota, M. (1983). The Japanese American family. In J. Yamamoto, A. Romero, & A. Morales (Eds.), *The psychosocial development of minority group children.* New York: Brunner/Mazel.

Zborowski, M. (1969). *People in pain.* San Francisco: Jossey-Bass.

Rites of Passage Bibliography

Hill, P. (1992). *Coming of Age: African American male rites-of-passage.* Chicago, Ill: African American Images.

Lewis, M. (1988). *Her story: Black female rites of passage.* Chicago, Ill: African American Images.

Warfield-Coppock, N. & Harvey, A. (1989). *A rites of passage resource manual.* New York, NY: United Church of Christ, Commission for Racial Justice.

EMPIRICAL CORRECTION OF SEVEN MYTHS ABOUT SCHIZOPHRENIA WITH IMPLICATIONS FOR TREATMENT

Courtenay M. Harding and James H. Zahniser

COURTENAY M. HARDING, PH.D., IS WITH THE WESTERN INTERSTATE COMMISSION FOR HIGHER EDUCATION, MENTAL HEALTH PROGRAM AND THE SCHOOL OF MEDICINE, UNIVERSITY OF COLORADO.

JAMES H. ZAHNISER, PH.D., IS WITH THE MENTAL HEALTH CORPORATION OF DENVER.

THIS ARTICLE ORIGINALLY APPEARED IN *Acta Psychiatrica Scandanavica*, 1994, 90 (SUPPL 384), 140-146 AND IS REPRINTED WITH PERMISSION.

This paper presents empirical evidence accumulated across the last 2 decades to challenge seven long-held myths in psychiatry about schizophrenia which impinge upon the perception and thus the treatment of patients. Such myths have been perpetuated across generations of trainees in each of the mental health disciplines. These myths limit the scope and effectiveness of treatments offered. These myths maintain the pessimism about outcome for these patients thus significantly reducing their opportunities for improvement and/or recovery. Counter evidence is provided with implications for new treatment strategies.

There are at least seven prevalent myths about schizophrenia that often discourage clinicians and significantly impact the perception, and thus the treatment, of patients. All of these myths have been challenged by research data, yet they persist in training and practice across mental health disciplines. This paper endeavors to contribute a more balanced and contemporary view of the person with schizophrenia in order to reenergize clinicians and revitalize treatment approaches.

Myth: Once a schizophrenic always a schizophrenic.

Reality: There is ever widening heterogeneity of outcome across time.

Kraepelin (1902) initiated the myth by categorically splitting mental illness into either good outcome (manic depression) or poor outcome (dementia praecox). Diagnosis was verified or invalidated by the outcome. Even Eugene Bleuler (1908), who was originally more optimistic about the outcome of schizophrenia, later decided that there was never "full *restitutio ad integrum.*" Harding and associates (1987; 1992) explained that these two pivotal investigators suffered from "the clinician's illusion" (Cohen & Cohen, 1984). The "illusion" occurs when clinicians repeatedly see the few most severely ill in their caseloads as "typical" when, in fact, such patients represent a small proportion of the actual possible spectrum. The Scandinavians have generally held a broader view as evidenced by their use of the category "reactive psychosis" (Angst, 1986). However, even in Scandinavia, pessimism has remained about patients who were unable to fit these criteria or patients who fit these criteria, but failed to improve quickly.

Evidence. Recent worldwide studies have investigated the assumption of downward course and all have found wide heterogeneity in the very long-term outcome (over 2 decades) for schizophrenia, despite differences in diagnostic criteria used (Ciompi & Muller, 1976; Huber, Gross & Schuttler, 1979; Tsuang, Woolson & Fleming, 1979; Bleuler, 1978; Harding et al., 1987a; Harding et al., 1987b; DeSisto et al., 1995a; Desisto et al., 1995b). The European studies have often been dismissed in the U.S. because of the perception that their criteria were not equivalent and because of sheer ethnocentricity. However, notwithstanding the criticisms of diagnostic differences (valid or not), all of these studies have come to the same conclusions. The longer investigators followed an identified intact cohort (whether probands were in or out of treatment), the more pronounced the picture of increasing heterogeneity and improvement in function. These studies have consistently found that one half to two thirds of patients significantly improved or recovered, including some cohorts of very chronic cases. The universal criteria for recovery have been defined as no current signs and symptoms of any mental illness, no current medications, working, relating well to family and friends, integrated into the community, and behaving in such a way as to not being able to detect having ever been hospitalized for any kind of psychiatric problems. All of these investigators of long-term studies were trained in the older, more pessimistic conceptual models and were surprised by their own findings. Because the myths had been repeated so often, they had become reified. The strong belief systems and resistance, encountered by these investigators, were caused by many factors and were not easily altered by one study (Harding, Zubin & Strauss, 1987; Harding, Zubin & Strauss, 1992). However, there is now a confluence of results.

Suggested treatment strategies. Slowly, these investigators have all persisted. The beliefs about course and outcome are changing. Clinical practices and programs are being restructured (Test & Stein, 1978; Rotelli & Dell'Aqua, 1991; Liberman, Mueser & Wallace, 1986; Ciompi, 1980; Mosher & Burti, 1989). The mental health disciplines are getting the message. Given the evidence, it is suggested that treatment programs be constructed "as if" everyone will turn the corner toward significant improvement and/or recovery. This suggestion is made because the state of the art does *not* permit clinicians to triage patients on the basis of prognostic factors. In schizophrenia, particularly the multiple episodic

types, the display of early symptom severity and dysfunction in illness trajectories may persist for many years. Then, as the illness lifts, the patient's energy returns, thinking clears, coping strategies for stressors improves, and he or she inches the way toward improvement in both function and symptom reduction. This is the opposite picture of a relentless downhill course for most patients as described by Kraepelin. This long process of recovery implies a revision of what the clinician tells patients and their families about prognosis ("You have a very serious illness which takes some time to work itself through. However, worldwide data shows over more than 50% of patients significantly improve or even recover. We will be there to walk with you on this journey toward recovery"). This new message keeps a small spark of hope alive. Hope promotes the self-healing capacity inherent in any recovery process for any illness (Cousins, 1979; Siegel, 1986; Herth, 1990). Treatment also means a cohesive, comprehensive biopsychosocial approach to the whole person (Moyers, 1993; Engel, 1980), and a collaborative effort between the patient, the family, the clinical team, other community agencies, and natural networks. Treatment means celebrating the small moves forward, and learning from the steps backward, in a manner which does not blame the patient, the team, or the family. Treatment means environmental engineering to reduce the stressors. Important to remember is the need to re-evaluate repeatedly because the same structured environment that enables a patient to organize a disorganized brain can become psychotogenic later when a now organized brain faces a much too organized environment (Strauss et al., 1985).

Myth: A schizophrenic is a schizophrenic is a schizophrenic.

Reality: There is wide individual heterogeneity within the diagnostic category.

Paraphrasing "Rose is a rose is a rose" (Stein, 1934), there is a tendency in the field to lump everyone with the same diagnosis together for treatment and research.

Evidence. In reality, every group of patients has substantial heterogeneity. In addition to the major impact of gender (Seeman & Lang, 1990), there are considerable differences in age, developmental tasks, education levels, job histories, symptom presentation, coping skills and other personality strengths and weaknesses, meaning systems, and response to stress in general and to stress of particular situations (Harding et al., 1987). Further, it should be noted that the field has forgotten the heterogeneity of schizophrenia, itself. When E. Bleuler renamed dementia praecox, he called it "the group of schizophrenia" (Bleuler, 1911). Recently, Kendler (1986) has developed several models of genetic-environmental interaction and weighting in the etiology of schizophrenia. His models make a great deal of sense given the wide heterogeneity of our patients.

Suggested treatment strategies. The heterogeneity, described above, requires a comprehensive, biopsychosocial assessment of each patient's unique status, the place in his or her own course trajectory, and ecological niche. Individual differences require individualized treatment planning, an appreciation of developmental achievements or strivings, and a recognition of the "person behind the disorder" (Bleuler, 1978). In order for clinicians to achieve this level of understanding, they must consider the task as a genuinely collaborative enterprise with both the patient and others who know him or her well. Continued assessment of changing, ongoing status is especially important after years of severe psychopathology and dysfunction, given the longitudinal nature of these disorders. The use of "timeliness"or "life charts" is recommended in this endeavor by collecting data in a chronological comprehensive life history, as well for setting a collaborative tone for treatment (Vaillant, 1980; Meyer, 1951). Attention to individual differences, life histories, and developmental steps, will encourage patients to perceive themselves, not as "schizophrenics," but rather as people, who happen to have schizophrenia. Consumers repeatedly note that this recognition of their "personhood" plays a critical role in their recovery and rc-acquisition of their sense of well being (Campbell & Schraiber, 1989; Lovejoy, 1982).

Myth: Rehabilitation can be provided only after stabilization.

Reality: Rehabilitation should begin on day one.

This myth has been deeply embedded within a narrow but popular version of the medical model. "Real treatment" in today's managed care climate consists of assessment, diagnosis, and medication. Anything else, such as rehabilitation, must wait until stabilization and is often considered to be an ancillary service. But stabilization usually leads just to "maintenance" and not to rehabilitation.

Evidence. "Real treatment" has been only modestly successful in reducing symptoms, and in helping the patient by increasing the levels of functioning in self care, work, interpersonal relationships, and integration back to the community. However, there is a burgeoning field of psychiatric rehabilitation that combines with medical treatments to significantly improve the patient's level of functioning (Adler, 1981; Anthony, Cohen & Cohen, 1983). The problem has been a paucity of integrated models proposed to incorporate all of these facets of care. The notable exceptions have been Engel's "biopsychosocial model" (Engel, 1980) and Adler and associates' paper (Adler, 1981) which set forth an expanded medical model as a task for psychiatry. Adler's model delineates the tasks for psychiatry to be legal, societal-rehabilitative, educative-developmental, as well as medical. Anthony (Anthony, Cohen & Cohen, 1983) has proposed a rehabilitation model but left out most of the illness factors.

Suggested treatment strategies. Rehabilitation is accruing an honored place in the treatment of patients as a key modality in partnership with psychopharmacology. Skill building (e.g., how to manage one's symptoms, managing one's medication, learning how to manage a budget, acquiring a job skill, conducting social conversation), all raise a patient's self-esteem and lower symptoms. Anything that lowers symptoms and improves function deserves to be called and reimbursed as "treatment" (Liberman, Mueser & Wallace, 1986; Anthony, Cohen & Cohen, 1983; Breier & Strauss, 1983; Diamond, 1984).

Myth: Why bother with psychotherapy for schizophrenia?

Reality: Supportive psychotherapy is crucial for integrating the experience and enhancing continued adult development.

Research findings, regarding the ineffectiveness of psychotherapy in curing schizophrenia, have led to widespread discouragement in this area and to a relative lack of innovation and research. Heinrichs (1986) concluded from his review that "The kindest interpretation of controlled studies to date is that the benefit of psychotherapy with schizophrenia has not yet been demonstrated." However, instead of abandoning psychotherapy altogether, the challenge is for clinicians to use psychotherapy appropriately for maximum benefit.

Evidence. Two main lines of evidence support the judicious use of psychotherapy. First, surveys and personal accounts of consumers have indicated that they value psychotherapy and find it to be beneficial in various ways (Coursey, Keller & Farrell, 1995; Legatt, 1986; Ruocchio, 1989; Coursey, Farrell & Zahniser, 1991). Second, several different types of psychosocial interventions have demonstrated positive impact on the lives of persons with schizophrenia including family interventions (see below), group therapies tailored to the needs of persons with schizophrenia (Kanas, 1986; Kanas, 1991), and very specific, targeted cognitive remediation (Chadwick & Lowe, 1990; Green, 1993).

Suggested treatment strategies. To accept that psychotherapy cannot help persons with schizophrenia reinforces the dangerous and erroneous message that such persons are separate, distinct, and deficient relative to others. On the other hand, a realistic and appropriate approach to the use of psychotherapy in the overall treatment plan can facilitate patients' recovery by integrating their experiences of a life interrupted by severe illness and by helping them learn coping strategies. Coursey (1989) clarified the basis of a sound psychotherapy for persons suffering from schizophrenia: 1) psychotherapy should not be seen as competing with medication but, rather, as complementary to it; 2) psychotherapy can and should address the personal, human issues raised by having a serious mental illness; 3) psychotherapy must be practical, thus making use of educational as well as experiential approaches to help individuals learn to manage the disorder; and 4) psychotherapy should address the "normal problems of living that people with schizophrenia have to deal with just as anyone else does" (p. 351).

Neligh and Kinzie (1983) have identified ten practical approaches to accomplish the goals mentioned above. These authors suggest the following: 1) accepting the current level of functioning without pressure to change, 2) determining the appropriate frequency of contact for each patient, 3) selecting a comfortable style of relating, 4) modeling desirable social attitudes, 5) facilitating problem-solving skills, 6) providing a safe place for patients to express emotions, 7) managing dependence, 8) effecting changes in the patient's environment, 9) setting limits and discussing consequences of actions, as well as, 10) establishing rules for confidentiality and the need to share information across systems of care. These authors propose a respectful, humane approach that emphasizes positive social behaviors, upbeat emotional tone, the provision of advice, information sharing, compliments, jokes, and companionship, as well as sharing in the triumphs and tragedies of life. Such supportive psychotherapy may increase self-esteem, facilitate awareness of limitations, avoid deterioration and/or hospitalization, prevent undue dependence, and improve levels of function.

Myth: Patients must be on medication all their lives.

Reality: It may be a small percentage who need medication indefinitely.

This myth has been generated by physicians for a wide variety of reasons. First, it is an attempt to underscore the importance of taking medication in a power struggle with the patient. Secondly, if a physician believes in Myth #1 "once a schizophrenic always a schizophrenic" or its corollary "once a broken brain always a broken brain," then the physician believes that medication is the key to maintenance of life-long stabilization.

Evidence. There are no data existing which support this myth. When analyzing the results from the long term studies, it was clear that a surprising number (at least 25–50%), were completely off their medica-

tions, suffered no further signs and symptoms of schizophrenia, and were functioning well. Over time, most patients altered their dosages and schedules. These behaviors often resulted in relapses early on in their illness trajectories when the illness was raging. The physicians in charge often felt justified and the patients felt defeated. Part of the trouble lay in human nature since there is usually only a 40 to 50%, compliance rate for any kind of prescription taking in the U.S. by any kind of patient (Diamond, 1984). Other problems involved: 1) the patient's lack of understanding about having an illness, 2) becoming disoriented enough not to manage taking medication, 3) the lack of clear knowledge about the reasons for and the skills needed in taking medication, 4) the frequent increase of covert and overt side effects that are unpleasant or undesirable (e.g. dyskinesia, dystonia akinesia, akathisia, obesity, impotence, dry mouth, weight gain), and 5) the lack of engineering to reduce environmental stressors. Such high stressors have been shown to increase relapse rates in some patients even if medicated intramuscularly. However, even though patients experimented with their medications and learned to use them more regularly, the long-term studies found that more subjects than not eventually discovered through trial, error, and time, that they were able to function without medication later on in their illness trajectories.

Suggested treatment strategies. Most successful approaches involve the following: a strong patient-physician collaboration (Neligh & Kinzie, 1983), targeted psychoeducational and skill-building strategies aimed at prodromal and chronic symptom recognition and medication management (Liberman, Mueser & Wallace, 1986), as well as built-in re-assessment strategies and standardized side effects monitoring techniques (Neligh & Kinzie, 1983).

Myth: People with schizophrenia cannot do anything except low-level jobs.

Reality: People with schizophrenia can and do perform at every level of work.

The idea that persons with schizophrenia are unable to work or can only achieve a low level of function because of their illness has had long standing credence especially in the United States. Anthony and associates (1984) reported in their review of the literature that only 10 to 30% of patients worked full time throughout a year or at follow-up. This finding has reinforced this perception.

Evidence. The early vocational approach consisted primarily of sheltered workshops designed originally for the developmentally disabled (Ciardello, 1981). Until recently, little thought was given about whether or not these workshops were appropriate settings for these patients or for those with serious mental illnesses. In addition, there has been minimal appreciation about the power of stigma, the low priority in the vocational rehabilitation ladder, distinct systems problems at the interface (such as rigidity, isolation, compensatory ad hoc operations, and narrow frames of reference [Harding et al., 1987; Anthony et al., 1984]). However, in their 1974 follow-up study, Strauss and Carpenter (1974) found that symptoms and levels of functioning, such as work, were only loosely related to one another in an "open-linked" fashion. The Vermont Longitudinal Research Project (Harding et al., 1987) also found that, in their "improved but not recovered group," wide heterogeneity existed within the same person with some cohort members working well despite ongoing and persistent hallucinations and/or delusions. These patients had learned not to tell anyone because it "upset"others. For other patients work

became the primary treatment strategy to reduce symptomatology (Strauss et al., 1985; Breier & Strauss, 1983; McCrory, 1988).

Across time, clinicians have appreciated the interactive therapeutic effects of work on illness (e.g. Galen [172 AD] "Employment is nature's best physician and is essential to human happiness"[see Strauss, 1968, p. 663]). Harding, Strauss, Hafez, and Lieberman (1987) discovered that "Despite this basic understanding of human functioning, the integration of work into systems that treat severe mental illness is limited, sporadic, and inadequately addressed" (p. 317). When a rehabilitation program has a strong emphasis and a cohesive approach for clients, the long-term trajectory is significantly enhanced and the work histories greatly altered (Harding et al., 1987; Desisto et al., 1995b).

Suggested treatment strategies. At the current time, vocational and other forms of rehabilitation are accomplished by "persistent, energetic personnel inventing ingenious solutions to the roadblocks set up at the system interfaces" (Harding et al., 1987). To treat the patient first means to "treat" the system of care in order to encourage flexibility, collaboration, database training, and a unified theoretical framework. Other approaches have been laid out such as the vocational strategies of "choose-get-keep" job model from the Boston group headed by Anthony and associates (1984). They formulate a rehabilitation diagnosis, develop a rehabilitation plan (which incorporates resources available and needed), and devise individually constructed interventions. This collaboration involves career counseling, skills training, placement, and work training to keep the job once the person has one (such as getting to work on time and dressing neatly and maintaining appropriate social interaction [Anthony et al., 1984]).

Myth: Families are the
etiological agents.

Reality: Families as collaborators
can provide critical information and
provide environments to lower a
relative's vulnerability to episodes.

The myth, that families cause schizophrenia, flourished prior to the most recent biological revolution in psychiatry. Proponents
of this myth targeted the family's severe
dysfunctions, especially in the area of communication, as the cause of schizophrenia.
For example, after observing communication difficulties in persons with schizophrenia, many theorists (Bateson et al., 1956;
Lidz, 1973; Wynne & Zinger, 1977) rea-
soned that the dysfunctions were learned
through interaction with disturbed family
members. Although many investigators
have since discarded this myth, it has survived even in the current biological era,
such that numbers of clinicians and academics, who train students in the different
mental health disciplines, still believe it
(Lefley, 1992).

Evidence. Although family researchers
have demonstrated that the emotional and
interactional climate of families can help
precipitate relapses in their relatives
(Brown, Birley & Wing, 1972) as well as
the efficacy of enhanced family communication in lowering vulnerability to relapse
(Goldstein & Doane, 1982), they have
failed to show that family factors are necessary and sufficient causes of schizophrenia
(Falloon, 1988; Zubin & Spring, 1977). No
evidence exists that a family's psychosocial
climate, communication patterns, or parenting practices are primary causes of schizophrenia. In fact, despite the finding that vulnerable individuals from families high in
expressed emotion are more likely to
relapse, the majority of families are not
rated high on this factor (Lefley, 1992).
Many families, who are low in EE, may

very well represent a biologic protective factor (Falloon, 1988). Family researchers now
recognize that it is the co-occurrence of an
ill individual's behaviors and the various
emotional/interactional characteristics of a
family's response that often precipitates
symptoms. The available evidence suggests
that schizophrenia is an episodic disorder
which, not unlike many other episodic disorders (e.g., asthma, Crohn's Disease,
arthritis), is often vulnerable to environmental stresses and triggers. Stressors, such
as family environment, are now not considered to be sufficient in and of themselves to
be considered etiological agents of the
underlying disorder.

Suggested treatment strategies. The optimal roles of families in treatment, and the
appropriate relationships between clinicians
and families are now well established, if not
widely realized. Families need, and want,
education, information, coping and communication skills, emotional support, and to be
treated as collaborators (Bernheim, 1982).
As many authors have noted (Beels &
McFarlane, 1982), scientific theories of family causation contributed to the alienation
between professionals and families, as well
as to the guilt and burden that families feel.
For this reason, clinicians need to make a
special effort to solicit the collaboration and
involvement of family members. In some
cases it may even be necessary to entice families into collaboration by acknowledging
the difficulties they have experienced and
apologizing for the way they have been
treated by the mental health system. Once a
relationship is established, clinician, patient,
and family can work together to identify
needs and appropriate interventions. Many
families benefit from communication training, psychoeducation about the illness, and
coping strategies. Fortunately, several effective models exist (Leff, et al., 1982; Kanter,
Lamb & Loeper, 1987; Huber, et al., 1980).
In addition to assisting families in the acquisition of skills and knowledge, it is impor-

tant for the clinician to encourage families to develop realistic, yet optimistic expectations about their relatives' chances for improvement (see above discussion of Myth #1), and about their own ability to contribute to the recovery process, thus helping to relieve family burden.

Conclusion

This paper has reviewed seven prevailing myths about the group of schizophrenias. The authors have proposed counterevidence to each myth. Some treatment strategies were suggested to enhance the possibility of improvement and recovery through reduction of symptoms and the increase of levels of functioning for patients. It is hoped that this paper will encourage clinicians, program designers, policy makers, patients and their families to deal more effectively with these difficult and often prolonged disorders. A longitudinal perspective about schizophrenia should imbue everyone with a renewed sense of hope and optimism. After studying 508 patients across 22 years, Huber and colleagues (1980) stated that "schizophrenia does not seem to be a disease of slow, progressive deterioration. Even in the second and third decades of illness, there is still potential for full or partial recovery." All of the recent long-term follow-up investigators have recorded the same findings (Ciompi & Muller, 1976; Huber, Gross & Schuttler, 1979; Tsuang, Woolson & Fleming, 1979; Bleuler, 1978; Harding et al., 1987a; Harding et al., 1987b; DeSisto et al., submitted, a; Desisto et. al., submitted, b).

References

Adler, D. (1981). The medical model and psychiatry's tasks. *Hospital and Community Psychiatry, 32,* 387-392.

Angst, J. (1986). European long-term followup studies of schizophrenia. *Schizophrenia Bulletin,* 14 (4), 501-513.

Anthony, W.A., Howell, J. & Danley, K.S. (1984). Chap. 13. Vocational Rehabilitation of the psychiatrically disabled. In M. Mirabi (Ed.), *The chronically mentally ill. Research and services,* 215-237.

Anthony, W.A., Cohen, M.R. & Cohen, B.F. (1983). The philosophy, treatment process, and principles of the psychiatric rehabilitation approach. *New Directions in Mental Health,* 67-69.

Bateson, G., Jackson, D.D., Haley, J. & Weakland, J.H. (1956). Toward a theory of schizophrenia. *Behavioral Science, 1,* 251-264.

Beels, C.C. & McFarlane, W.R. (1982). Family treatment of schizophrenia: Background and state of the art. *Hospital and Community Psychiatry, 33*(7), 541-550.

Bernheim, K.F. (1982). Supportive family counseling. Schiz Bull., 8, 634-640.

Bleuler E. (1908). Die Prognose der Dementia praecox (Schizophrenien Gruppe) *Allg. Z. Psychiat., 65,* 436.

Bleuher, E. (1911). Dementia Praecox oder Die Gruppe der Schizophrenien. In hrsg. von G. Aschaffenburg, *Hanbuch der Psychiatrie,* Leipzig, Deuticke.

Bleuler, M. (1978). Die Schizophrenen Geistesstorungen im Lichte langjahriger Kranken—und Familiengeschicten Stuttgart: George Thieme Verlag 1972: (New York: Intercontinental Medical Book Corp, *The Schizophrenic Disorders: Long-Term Patient and Family Studies.* Translated by Clemens SM. New Haven: Yale University Press.

Breier, A. & Strauss, J.S. (1983). Self-control of psychotic disorders. *Archives of General Psychiatry, 40,* 1141-1145.

Brown, G.W., Birley, J.L.T. & Wing, J.K. (1972). Influence of family life on the course of schizophrenic disorder: A replication. *British Journal of Psychiatry, 121,* 241-258.

Campbell, J. & Schraiber, R. (1989). *The wellbeing project: Mental health consumers speak for themselves.* Sacramento, CA: California Dept. of Mental Health.

Chadwick, P.D.J. & Lowe, C.F. (1990). Measurement and modification of delusional beliefs. *Journal of Consulting and Clinical Psychology, 58*(2), 225-232.

Ciardello, J.A. (1981). Job placement success Of schizophrenic clients in sheltered workshop programs. *Vocational Evaluation and Work Adjustment Bulletin, Fall,* 125-128.

Ciompi, L. (1980). Catamnestic Long-term study on the course of life and aging of schizophrenics. *Schizophrenia Bulletin, 6,* 606-618.

Ciompi, L. & Muller, C. (1976). *Lebensweg und Alter der Scizophrenenen: Eine katamnestische Lonzeitstudies bis ins senium.* Berlin: Springer Verlag.

Cohen, P. & Cohen, J. (1984). The clinicians illusion. *Archives of General Psychiatry, 41,* 1178-1182.

Coursey, R.D., Keller, A.B. & Farrell, E.W. (1995). Individual psychotherapy and persons with serious mental illness: The client's perspective. *Schizophrenia Bulletin, 21(2),* 283-301.

Coursey, R.D., Farrell, E.W. & Zahniser, J.H. (1991). Consumers attitudes toward psychotherapy, hospitalization. and aftercare. *Health and Social Work,* 16(3), 155-161.

Coursey, R.D. (1989). Psychotherapy with persons suffering from schizophrenia. *Schizophrenia Bulletin, 15,* 349-353.

Cousins, N. (1979). *Anatomy of an illness as perceived by the patient: Reflections on healing and regeneration.* New York, Norton.

Desisto, M.J., Harding, C.M., McCormick R.V., Ashikaga, T. & Gautum, S. (1995a). The Maine-Vermont three decades studies of serious mental illness: Matched comparison of cross-sectional outcome. *British Journal of Psychiatry, 167,* 331-338.

Desisto, M.J., Harding, C.M., McCormick R.V., Ashikaga, T. & Gautum, S. (1995b). The Maine-Vermont three decades studies of serious mental illness: Longitudinal course of comparisons. *British Journal of Psychiatry, 167,* 338-342.

Diamond, R.J. (1984). Increasing medication compliance n young adult chronic psychiatric patients. *New Directions in Mental Health Services, 21,* 59-69.

Engel, G. (1980). The clinical application of the biopsychosocial model. *American Journal of Psychiatry, 137,* 535-544.

Falloon, I.R.H. (1988). Prevention of morbidity in schizophrenia. In I.R.H. Falloon (Ed.), *Handbook of behavioral family therapy.* New York: Guilford.

Falloon, I.R.H., Boyd, J.L. & McGill, C.W. (1985). *Family management of schizophrenia.* Baltimore: Johns Hopkins University Press.

Goldstein, M. & Doane, J.A. (1982). Family factors in the onset, course, and treatment of schizophrenic spectrum disorders: An update on current research. *Journal of Nervous and Mental Disability, 170,* 692-700.

Green, M.F. (1993). Cognitive remediation in schizophrenia Is it time yet? *American Journal of Psychiatry, 150*(2), 178-187.

Harding, C.M., Zubin, J. & Straus, J.S. (1992). Chronicity in schizophrenia revisited. *British Journal of Psychiatry, 161* (Suppl. IX), 27-37.

Harding, C.M., Brooks, G.W., Ashikaga, T., Strauss, J.S. & Breier, A. (1987a). The Vermont longitudinal study of persons with severe mental illness: 1. Methodology, study sample, and overall status 32 years later. *American Journal of Psychiatry, 144* (6), 718-726.

Harding, C.M., Brooks, G.W., Ashikaga, T., Strauss, J.S. & Breier, A. (1987b). The Vermont longitudinal study II. Long-term outcome of subjects who retrospectively met *DSM III* criteria for schizophrenia. *American Journal of Psychiatry, 144* (6), 727-725.

Harding, C.M., Strauss, J.S., Hafez, H. & Lieberman, P. (1987). Work and mental illness: I. Toward an integration of the rehabilitation process. *Journal of Nervous and Mental Disability, 175*(6), 317-327.

Harding, C.M., Zubin, J. & Strauss, J.S. (1987). Chronicity in schizophrenia: Fact, partial fact, or artifact? *Hospital and Community Psychiatry, 38*(5), 477-486.

Heinrichs, D.W. (1986). The psychotherapy of schizophrenia. In G. D. Burrows, T. R. Norman, G. Rubenstein (Eds.), *Handbook of studies in schizophrenia—Part 2.* New York: Elsevier.

Herth, K. (1990). Fostering hope in terminally ill people. *Journal of Adv Nursing, 15,* 1250-1259.

Huber, G., Gross, G. Schuttler, R. & Linz, M. (1980). Longitudinal studies of schizophrenic patients. *Schizophrenia Bulletin, 6,* 592-605.

Huber, G., Gross, G. & Schuttler, R. (1979). Schizophrenie: Verlaufs und sozialpsychiatrische Langzeituntersuchungen an den 1945 bis 1959 in Bonn hospitalisierten schizophrenen Kranken: *Monographien aus dem Gesametgebiete der Psychiatrie.* BD 21. Berlin Springer Verlag.

Kanas, N. (1991). Group therapy with schizophrenic patients: A short-term, homogenous approach. *International Journal of Group Psychotherapy, 41,* 33-48.

Kanas, N. (1986). Group therapy with schizophrenics. *International Journal of Group Psychotherapy*, 36, 339-351.

Kanter, J., Lamb, H.R. & Loeper, C. (1987). Expressed emotion in families: A critical review. *Hospital and Community Psychiatry*, 38, 374-380.

Kendler, K.S. & Eaves, L.J. (1986). Models for the joint effect of genotype and environment on reliability to psychiatric illness. *American Journal of Psychiatry*, 143(3), 279-89.

Krapelin. (1902). *Dementia praecox, in clinical psychiatry: A textbook for students and physicians*. 6th ed. Translated by Diefendorf AR. New York: Macmillan.

Legatt, M. (1986). Schizophrenia: The consumer's viewpoint. In G. D. Burrows, T. R. Norman, G. Rubinstein, *Handbook of studies in schizophrenia—Part 2*. New York: Elsevier.

Leff, J., Kuipers, L. Berkowitz, R. et al. (1982). A controlled trial of social intervention in the families of schizophrenic patients. *British Journal of Psychiatry*, 141, 121-134.

Lefley, H.P. (1992). Expressed emotion: Conceptual, clinical, and social policy issues. *Hospital and Community Psychiatry*, 43(6), 591-598.

Liberman, R.P., Mueser, K.T. & Wallace, C.J. (1986). Social skills training for schizophrenic individuals at risk for relapse. *American Journal of Psychiatry*, 143, 523-526.

Lidz, T. (1973). *The origin and treatment of schizophrenic disorders*. New York: Basic Books.

Lovejoy, M. (1982). Expectations and the recovery process. *Schizophrenia Bulletin*, 8 (4), 605-609.

McCrory, D.J. (1988). The human dimension of the vocational rehabilitation process In M. D. Bell & J. A. Ciardello (Eds.), *Vocational rehabilitation of persons with prolonged psychiatric disorders,* p 208-218, Baltimore: Johns Hopkins University Press.

Meyer, A. (1951). The life chart and the obligation of specifying positive data in the psychopathological diagnosis. In: *Contributions to medical and biological research*. Vol. 2, Hoeber. 1919. Reprinted in E.E. Winters (Ed.), *The collected papers of Adolf Meyer*. Baltimore: Johns Hopkins Press.

Mosher, L.R. & Burti, L. (1989). *Community mental health: Principles and practice*. New York, W. W. Norton & Co.

Moyers, B. (1993). *Healing and the mind*. New York, Doubleday.

Neligh, G.L. & Kinzie, J.D. (1983). Therapeutic relationships with the chronic patient. In D. L. Culture (Ed.), Effective aftercare for the 1980s. *New Directions for Mental Health Services*. San Francisco: Jossey-Bass.

Rotelli, F. & Dell Aqua, G. (1991). La storia della psichiatria Triestina. *Il Lanternino, XVI* (4) Prog. 92: 1-36.

Ruocchio, P.J. (1989). How psychotherapy can help the schizophrenic patient. *Hospital and Community Psychiatry*, 40, 180-190.

Seeman, M.V. & Lang, M. (1990). The role of estrogens in schizophrenia: gender differences. *Schizophrenia Bulletin*, 16(2), 185-194.

Siegel, B. (1986). *Love, medicine, and miracles*. New York; Harper & Row.

Stein, G. (1934). *Sacred Emily in portraits in prayer*. New York, Random House.

Strauss, J.S., Hafez, H., Lieberman, P. & Harding, C.M. (1985). The course of psychiatric disorder: III. Longitudinal principles. (special article). *American Journal of Psychiatry*, 142(3), 289-296.

Strauss, J.S. & Carpenter, W.T. (1974). Characteristic symptoms and outcome in schizophrenia. *Archives of General Psychiatry*, 30 (30), 429-434.

Strauss, M.B. (1968). (Ed.) *Familiar medical quotations*. Boston: Little Brown, 663.

Test, M.A. & Stein, L.L. (1978). Community treatment of the chronic patient: research overview. *Schizophrenia Bulletin*, 4 (3), 350-364.

Tsuang, M.T., Woolson, R.F. & Fleming, J.A. (1979). Long-term outcome of major psychoses. 1: Schizophrenia and affective disorders compared with psychiatrically symptom-free surgical conditions. *Archives of General Psychiatry*, 36, 1295-1301.

Vaillant, G. (1980). Adolf Meyer was right: Dynamic psychiatry needs the life chart. *Journal of the National Association of Private Psychiatric Hospitals*, 11, 4-14.

Wynne, L.C. & Singer, M. (1977). Thought disorder and family relations. *Archives of General Psychiatry*, 9, 199-206.

Zubin, J. & Spring, B. (1977). Vulnerability—A new view of schizophrenia. *Journal of Abnormal Psychology*, 86, 103-126.

Rehabilitating Ourselves: The Psychiatric Survivor Movement

Judi Chamberlin

JUDI CHAMBERLIN IS ASSOCIATED WITH THE CENTER FOR PSYCHIATRIC REHABILITATION, BOSTON UNIVERSITY AND IS A FOUNDER OF THE RUBY ROGERS CENTER, SOMERVILLE, MA.

THIS ARTICLE ORIGINALLY APPEARED IN THE *International Journal of Mental Health*, 1995, 24(1), 39-46, AND IS REPRINTED WITH PERMISSION.

My task, a very difficult one, is to present the views of users of psychiatric services with respect to psychiatric rehabilitation. Organizations of former patients/ psychiatric survivors/mental health clients/ consumers exist throughout the United States and in many other countries around the world—no one person can represent them all. And note the multiplicity of terms: there is no single term we are all comfortable with. I prefer to call myself a psychiatric survivor; my organization is the U.S. National Association of Psychiatric Survivors.[1]

When I first became involved, 20 years ago, in what we then called the mental patients' liberation movement, we saw very clearly that what we were organizing was a civil rights movement. We were an oppressed group—oppressed by laws and public attitudes, relegated to legalized second-class citizenship. In the early 1970s, our movement was small and unfunded. People joined because they wanted a voice, because they saw coming together and organizing as a way to fight back against a system that had taken away their power and their control over their own lives. It was only with other former patients that we could express our anger, our pain, our outrage, without being dismissed as "delusion-al" or "paranoid." Although much has changed in 20 years, the basic fact remains that we are still oppressed, and that our movement is primarily a political one, a struggle for our rights.

Our movement is, at the same time, developing innovative self-help/mutual support alternative services, because we have learned, through having undergone similar experiences, that we have much to give one another. We are not afraid of one another's pain. Whereas mental health professionals often want to drug our pain out of existence, or isolate us so that they will not have to deal with that pain, we know how to offer comfort based on shared experience. It is simply a matter of common sense (but so much of psychiatric practice seems to be the antithesis of common sense) that when we are hurting, we want human contact, we want to know that we are not alone, we want comfort and caring. As peers, we can offer this support, knowing that although we may be the ones giving help today, tomorrow we may need that help, and the people we comfort today may then be our comforters.

Twenty-five years ago, I was diagnosed as a chronic schizophrenic. I was told what a limited life I could expect to lead. I originally entered a mental hospital voluntarily, seeking help for the overwhelming pain of depression that had followed a miscarriage. I expected to find help and understanding; instead, I found that no one listened to me or took me seriously. Heavy doses of psychiatric drugs were the "treatment." When I protested that I did not find them helpful, my opinions were simply dismissed. I soon found myself committed to a state hospital, where I remained for several months. It was the worst period of my life. My struggle to overcome the effects of this experience was what led me to become involved in an ex-patient group.

---

[1] This organization went out of existence in 1995.

Our self-help/mutual support activities and our political activism are two aspects of the same endeavor, working together in our quest for decent lives. Our members distressingly often report the routine disrespect to which they are subjected in the psychiatric system: not being listened to, not being believed, infantilized, losing control of their own money, being told where to live, how to spend their time, being denied a normal sexual life—I could go on and on. These are not isolated complaints, but are an integral part of the operation of a system based on the presumption that mental illness equals incompetence equals the need for professionals to make decisions ostensibly "in our best interests."

In 20 years of organizing, I have personally spoken to literally thousands of current and former patients. I hear these stories again and again; and I also hear, over and over, the excitement and enthusiasm when people discover that there is a movement, that they can become a part of it, and that we are articulating their interests. I have been fortunate in getting to travel; and wherever I go, all over the United States, in Canada, in Britain, in Iceland, in the Netherlands, in Italy, Portugal, Australia, or New Zealand, it is remarkable how similar the stories are. But, in fact, this is not really surprising. The psychiatric system is international, so our movement must be as well.

The key issue is forced treatment. This is something psychiatrists and other mental health professionals do not like to talk about, or else brush aside quickly, reassuring themselves that they are acting, reluctantly, "in our best interests," or claiming, disingenuously, that it is not organized psychiatry, but the state that administers involuntary commitment. But we who have been the recipients of involuntary commitment, of forced treatment, cannot brush it aside so lightly. We are the ones who, at a time in our lives when we were already feeling vulnerable, had whatever remained of our control, our decision-making power, taken away from us.

It is not surprising that this process makes us feel, quite accurately, even more powerless, even more out of control. Yet we learn quickly not to speak of our feelings. Talk about power, talk about being locked up, being in what to all intents and purposes is a prison, will only get us into more trouble, will get us further labeled. To be a good patient is to be grateful, to say, "Thank you, Doctor; I appreciate what you have done for me," while inside one's head a voice screams otherwise (and that voice is not a psychiatric symptom). To be a good patient is to learn to play the game, to lie convincingly, and worst of all, to lie to ourselves until we no longer know what we believe.

When I talk to audiences of psychiatric survivors about playing the game, I see heads nodding, smiles of recognition—we know what it means to play the game: we have done it, we have lived it. And I should remind you, your patients also know how to play the game. You may want to believe that your hospital, your institution, your program is different, that you deal with your patients in a forthright manner; but so long as you work within a system based on coercion, patients and professionals are prevented from being honest with one another. If you do not believe me, I should say that it is you who are delusional.

So long as forced treatment exists, patients will continue to be angry, psychiatrists will continue to diagnose our anger as a symptom, and we shall be stuck in the same tangle. And our movement is going to continue to organize around the issue of forced treatment, because it is the key issue from which all else flows. We simply cannot talk about working together for good treatment so long as we know that you have the power to determine that we will be treated whether we wish it or not. Professionals often want us to work together in partnership, but it is hard to be partners when there is such a huge and genuine power differential, especially when it is considered bad form even to point out that it exists.

If you want us to work in partnership with you, many things will have to change. You will have to open up the process so that we can enter into honest dialogue together. That means making it possible for us to attend your meetings and your conferences. And this process of inclusion must go far beyond conferences. We need to be involved in the planning, delivery, and evaluation of services. We need to be actively recruited into professional training and into professional positions. And we ask your support as we apply for funding for our own client-run alternative programs.

Good models exist. Mental health professionals should become familiar with our many successful client-run programs in the United States, and with models of user involvement in planning in Britain and the Netherlands.

As part of my work at the Center for Psychiatric Rehabilitation at Boston University, I am directing a study of the efficacy of client-run programs. In order to do meaningful research on self-help, program participants must be involved in a consultative, collaborative role, not be merely passive subjects of a research process controlled by others. In our study, an advisory board of 12 people involved in self-help programs by and for former psychiatric patients worked with me to figure out what were the important questions to ask about self-help, and professional researchers acted as consultants to help us put those questions into usable form. Participants in six different self-help programs around the United States were surveyed in terms of measures of self-esteem, friendship networks, empowerment, and satisfaction with participation in self-help programs. [2]

The process of developing and administering client-directed needs assessments is in its infancy, but it is essential if services are to meet our self-defined needs. It is amazing how differently clients and professionals look at needs. Whereas professionals tend to take a purely clinical view, we talk about far more basic needs: a decent place to live, an adequate income, friends, something productive to do with our time. We value programs that help us meet these needs; we do not think much of programs that continue to infantilize us, that continue to control our lives. People do participate in such programs, and they sometimes rate them well in client-evaluation studies; but often that is because they have little or no choice. If a program controls your money, for example, and your housing, and you know that your basic necessities depend on pleasing staff members, it is not surprising that, when asked, you will tell those same workers what a good program it is. And, I submit to you, this is how client satisfaction is measured in many, many programs.

Let me tell you about an alternative, client-run service, and how different it is. I shall use as a model the Ruby Rogers Center in Cambridge, Massachusetts, [3] which I helped to start. Our center is funded by the Massachusetts Department of Mental Health, but it is totally run and controlled by its members, all of whom have long-standing, ongoing involvement with traditional mental health services. In our center the basic decision-making is done by the members at our weekly business meeting. We decide how to allocate our funds, which members will get the paid jobs within the center, how to deal with people who break our rules, and how to keep our center comfortable and supportive. Our center is open 7 days a week, and it is a place where members come to socialize, to see their

---

[2] The completed study showed that participants in self-help programs gained in all of these dimensions. Results of the study are currently (i.e., in 1995) in the process of analysis.

[3] In 1994, the program moved to Somerville, MA.

friends, to participate in activities, to get information about the mental health system and about their rights, and to join together to work for better lives.

There are many centers like ours around the United States, and we are demonstrating that we can be effective in breaking the cycle of frequent rehospitalization and chronic difficulties in maintaining ourselves in the community. This is what we mean when we speak of client-run projects, not merely doing the menial work in programs run and directed by others.

Another client-run program is the Oakland Independence Support Center in Oakland, California. This is a program run by and for people who have been homeless and who have received psychiatric services. Although people with these two labels are often considered unable to help themselves and to need highly structured and supervised programs, the Oakland Independence Support Center has proven this not to be the case. The program works directly with homeless people, helping them to get benefits, to find shelter, and, eventually, to move into decent, affordable, permanent housing. All the counselors have successfully made this transition themselves, and they are powerful role models for others.

Sue Estroff (1995) has pointed out an important truth, one we psychiatric survivors are well aware of, but one mental health professionals seldom, if ever, mention: the major thing we psychiatric patients produce is your job—and there are many well paying, prestigious jobs among them. In contrast, many of us live on tiny disability pensions. How many mental health professionals appreciate how difficult it is to make a few hundred dollars last all month and give us credit for doing so month after month, year after year? Instead, we are frequently further diagnosed when we do not have enough money for rent or food, when we "squander" our money on a few simple pleasures, when we

do not budget "properly." And the solution, all too often, is for professionals to take control of our money, to dole it out a few dollars at a time, rather than join with us to demand that our benefits be raised to a decent, livable level.

So, again, in the end it all comes down to rights. We could say, "Let us learn how to live decently on our benefits" (as if that were possible); or we could, instead, struggle for a better benefit system, one that pays enough so we really could live decently, one that does not penalize us when we try to return to work. We could say, "Let us work to improve the existing services, even when they do not meet our needs"; or we could, instead, work to change the system so that it will provide the services we want, services we have a role in operating, and/or client-run alternative services. We could say, "Let us work for the right to decent treatment"; or we could, instead, work for all our rights as citizens, as human beings, including the right to refuse unwanted psychiatric interventions.

It is particularly important that we not settle for "rights" that are not rights at all. The first draft of the United Nations declaration on our rights spoke about the "rights of persons detained on grounds of mental ill health." In the later draft, that language disappeared, and the document is now simply a listing of our "treatment rights." I think we shall be worse off with this document than with no United Nations declaration at all, and I believe our movement will work to change this document and to ensure that we have a voice, our own voice, as part of the United Nations process to develop an appropriate document.

At the World Congress for Mental Health in Mexico City, the clients and survivors present (who constituted a very small number) laid the groundwork for the establishment of the World Federation of Psychiatric Users, with plans to circulate a newsletter internationally. In the

Netherlands, a European Users' Network has been established, with delegates from most European countries and financial support from the European Community and the Dutch government.[4] Linkages between groups in the USA and Canada are being strengthened, so we can speak with a united North American voice. And all this is being done with very little funding, out of our determination to work together on the issues that affect our lives.

In Burlington, Vermont, White Light Communications, a survivor-run video production business, is making and marketing videotapes about our movement. It is one of 14 client-run programs around the United States originally funded as demonstration projects by the Community Support Program of the National Institute of Mental Health (NIMH).[5] The NIMH has begun to involve ex-patients, survivors, and consumers in planning and evaluation meetings. In 1990 it sponsored a meeting on client views of alternatives to involuntary treatment. Sadly, NIMH has been criticized for this involvement, as if it were somehow improper for us to have any role at all other than being passive recipients of services. Despite these pressures, the Community Support Program has been a good friend of our movement, respecting our positions and recognizing that although we might not always agree, ours is a voice that deserves to be heard.

What does this all mean for psychiatric rehabilitation? I urge you to look at rehabilitation in its broadest sense. It is not merely that we are broken and need to be fixed. We exist in a society that is broken and that affects our functioning and our well-being. We are damaged by racism, by sexism, by classism, by heterosexism, by poverty and oppression. If our functioning is viewed in a vacuum, these factors are ignored, and we are seen as defective. If, instead, we are seen within the context of these factors, then efforts to help us will be much more meaningful and much less focused on our individual defects and pathologies. It makes little sense to ignore the society in which we all must live.

Rehabilitation, in its truest sense, must mean not only assisting our readaptation to society but recognizing the ways in which social practices prevent that readaptation. Stigma and discrimination must be honestly faced and fought. Inadequate incomes and housing must be changed, or we can never live decent and comfortable lives. And unless the questions of power and powerlessness are dealt with in an open and frank way, we shall never be accorded our basic human dignity and our fundamental human and citizenship rights.

With or without the assistance of the mental health professions, we clients/consumers/psychiatric survivors, in the USA and elsewhere, will define for ourselves what our needs are and what are the best ways for us to assume our rightful place in society.

Reference

Estroff, S. E., (1995). *International Journal of Mental Health, 24* (1), pp39-46.

---

[4] The European Network of Users and Ex-Users in Mental Health held its second meeting in Helsingor, Denmark, in April 1994.

[5] Now the Center for Mental Health Services.

The Independent Living Movement and People with Psychiatric Disabilities: Taking Back Control Over Our Own Lives

Patricia E. Deegan

PATRICIA E. DEEGAN, PH.D., IS THE DIRECTOR OF TRAINING AT THE NATIONAL EMPOWERMENT CENTER, LAWRENCE MA.

THIS ARTICLE ORIGINALLY APPEARED IN THE *Psychosocial Rehabilitation Journal*, 1992, 15(3), 3-19 AND IS REPRINTED WITH PERMISSION.

In this paper, the question as to what the Independent Living Movement could mean for people with psychiatric disabilities is explored. Using the life story of a young man's efforts to move out of a chronic care institution to his own apartment, the author shows independent living to be a grassroots movement of people with disabilities, a "lived philosophy" that grew out of the experience of people learning to take back control over their lives and the resources that affect their lives, and consumer controlled service delivery and advocacy centers. It is argued that although Independent Living was first developed for and by people with physical disabilities, the principles of Independent Living can work for people with psychiatric disabilities who are seeking to regain control over their own lives. Specific suggestions for developing programs for people with psychiatric disabilities are given and have been piloted through a program at the Northeast Independent Living Program in Lawrence, Massachusetts.

Betty, I have to go and do a training for all of the case managers in the state. You have had lots of case managers. What is the most important thing I should tell them? "Tell them that no matter what they say, compliance is not the road to independence."

During the spring of 1989, I was asked to conceptualize and pilot a completely consumer-controlled and consumer-run program for people with psychiatric disabilities through the Northeast Independent Living Program in Lawrence, Massachusetts. The question put to me was this: "What, if anything, could Independent Living mean for people with psychiatric disabilities?" Immediately the phrase "independent living" sent shivers up my spine. It conjured up images of people living in group homes, learning skills such as how to cook spaghetti for 20 people so that eventually they could "graduate to independent living," live in a single room, and eat meals-for-one at the local coffee shop. Despite my reservations, I accepted the challenge. However, before trying to figure out what Independent Living could mean for people with psychiatric disabilities, my first task was to figure out what it meant for those with physical disabilities.

What Is Independent Living?

Independent Living (I.L.) is actually three things. First, it is a national grassroots movement for social justice and civil rights made up of people with disabilities. Second, Independent Living is a philosophy developed by people with disabilities. Finally, Independent Living Centers are service delivery and advocacy centers that are controlled by, and are largely run by, people with disabilities (DeJong, 1979). Although today Independent Living Centers are largely "cross-disability centers," meaning that they seek to involve people with all types of disabilities, in its earliest years I.L. was pioneered primarily by people with physical disabilities.

One of the best ways to understand what I.L. is is to talk with people who have been involved in it. Charles Carr, executive director of the Northeast Independent Living Program, was a pioneer in the I.L. movement on the East Coast. I interviewed Charlie and his story helps us to understand what I.L. means in the context of the life of a person with a disability.

Charlie's Story

Charlie first became spinal-cord injured when he was 14 years old. After being medically stabilized, he was transferred to a hospital and finished high school. Like many young people, he had a desire to go to college and, although his grades were good, there were no laws protecting him from discrimination in 1970. Thus, he was not accepted at any of the colleges to which he initially applied.

> I remember going to Boston University for my interview. I never said anything on my application about having a disability. So I went in to the Dean, who was clearly taken aback by me.... He was embarrassed because he couldn't shake my hand. So he plops down to look at my records and he has no eye contact with me and he says, "Well, you did well in high school and your S.A.T.s look good and I'm curious, um, what do you think you can do here?" And I said, "Well, I think I can get a good education. I have a scholarship from the state and I think I can be a good student here." And he said, "My personal feeling is that I don't think you can handle it." And I said, "I think I can handle it!" And he said, "How will you get to classes?" So after I told him the whole story about my plans on how I would take notes and stuff, he said, "But what about the emotional pressure?" I

said, "Sounds great! I'm ready for it! I want to see people. I want to get out and do things and make friends." And so the interview ended. I got a letter back that basically said I was not accepted because I couldn't handle it.

Having been rejected from the colleges to which he applied, Charlie had no choice but to live in a chronic care hospital. At the age of 18, he lived in an institution for the dying.

> After seeing the name tags on lunch trays disappear over the course of the first 3 months, it dawned on me, it really hit me—*this was my life*. I was in this place and I was so young that I was going to see people die the rest of my life until I died. That really shook me up quite a bit.

Rather than resigning himself to these and other injustices, Charlie found that he was angry and was able to use that angry indignation to begin to move into action to change the injustice he faced.

> It really shook me up quite a bit to know that I was expected to do my living among the dying. That *this was my life!* But then I said, "This is not my life! It's not gonna be my life! No way, no how." I was too young, too energetic, and too hopeful to settle for this.

> And so my friend David and I began to work with this young, progressive administrator at the county hospital named John Noble. He was a guy with vision, a guy with compassion, and a guy who was willing to listen to me and David. And we said, "John, can you get us out of here somehow? Can you let us go to school?" And he scratched his head and said, "Well, tell me why." And I swear, we gave him both barrels! So he listened and walked away scratching his head, and about a week later he came back beaming. He said, "Charlie and David, I want to talk to you. You guys are going next door in 2 months. We're gonna fix up an empty wing for young adults with disabil-

ities who want to go to school." And this was the beginning!

Shortly after that, David and I got accepted at Mass Bay Community College. There was a progressive dean there and none of the buildings were ramped. And this dean says, "If you guys can get a 3.0 grade point in two classes for two consecutive semesters here, we'll let you into this school." Well, of course we aced those two courses and so room by room, building by building, they put these wooden ramps in for us. And all of a sudden there was a waiting list of literally hundreds of young people at Wellington Hall (the empty wing that was designed for us). It filled up in 3 months and Mass Bay Community College became a haven for students with disabilities.

And my life began to change during that summer of '71 because I got to integrate into a real school. I mean it took courage. For 7 years I had been told my life was gonna be nothing more than living in a nursing home. They had been chipping away at my spirit and slowly I was starting to believe them, no matter how hard I tried not to. But I was proving them wrong, a little bit at a time.

Eventually Charlie and his friends graduated from Mass Bay Community College and wished to continue on for their bachelor's degree. Although they had been living in the wing of Wellington Hall and even though they had private rooms with doors (but no locks from the inside), they still knew that they were institutionalized. Their next step, following the lead of some students with disabilities at the University of Illinois at Champaign-Urbana, was to get the authorities at Boston University to provide them with a residential "dormitory" for students with disabilities. Eventually they achieved the goal of living on campus, but the facility was still run by medical professionals and a board made up of people who did not have disabilities. And so Charlie and his friends began to organize the residents

and, through a block vote of the residents, succeeded in voting in a board comprised completely of people with disabilities. They called this facility the Boston Center for Independent Living, established in 1974. It was the second I.L. Center in the country.

Although living on a university campus was better than living at Wellington Hall, it still fell short of living independently. And so the group explored the possibility of getting independent, subsidized apartments within elderly housing complexes. They eventually succeeded in this, yet Charlie could not at first bring himself to move out of the college "dormitory." He watched a couple of his friends move out on their own, but for the time being he waited.

> I had my chance to go but I was so nervous. I was so, so nervous about failing and having to come back to the institution. And I think if I had failed then it would have crushed me. I just wasn't ready. But I was torn. I wanted to be able to have my own place. I wanted the control. I was sick of thinking about when the next time a nurse would bust into my room unannounced.

Eventually, some more apartments became available. I was ready. I got a ride over there. By this time, it's November of 1974. We had been negotiating for a long time with the Department of Public Welfare to do this very unheard-of thing called "personal care attendants." It was completely unheard-of at the time. So I went over to the new apartment complex with this orderly from the place I had been living in. He had already agreed to be one of my personal care attendants if I got in. I began to fill out the applications ... and I got the place!

When I first opened the door of that apartment, it reminds me now of that scene from the *Wizard of Oz*. You know the scene, where the house comes crashing down, and after Dorothy wakes up she opens the door and there's Oz outside, in color, after her whole world was black and white. It was like I was looking at something that could never be mine!...It was like I was reluctant at first to go in. Like I was going into a place I shouldn't be. It had a glorious living room, carpet, two huge bedrooms, huge kitchen, and a bathroom I could actually turn around in. Incredible!

But the truth is I was still scared. So this nurse did this wonderful, wonderful thing for me. She said, "Charlie, if you don't make it after your first couple of months, I promise you I'll hold your bed for you here. You don't have to come back here embarrassed or upset. You come back here and hold your head high. You tried. You can do it. You can try for as long as you want."

In January of 1975, Charlie spent his first night living outside of an institution since he was 14 years old. Here's how he describes that turning point in his life:

That first night I slept like a log. I woke up the next morning and I heard Michael snoring in the next room and I said, "I must be in heaven!" I just knew from that moment on I would never go back to Wellington Hall. I had made it through my first night! And we got up and had ourselves one hell of a victory breakfast.

Now, it wasn't all easy from there. Michael, my personal care attendant, worked days and I was on semester break. And I didn't know the limits of my independence at all. I have to say that I fell out of my wheelchair a lot of times and spent countless hours on the rug, and some very nasty things happened to me. But not for one minute did I think about going back. I mean, I was in awe!

Charlie defines the essence of Independent Living as regaining control over one's life. By reclaiming the dignity of risk and the right to failure, as well as the right to try and succeed, people can leave institutions, make their own choices, and live independently.

Now for me, that was the beginning of regaining control. It was not easy to gain control over my life again. It was very difficult. Some things came very naturally but some things didn't. One of the things I had to learn is that with control comes sacrifice. In order to be in control you still have to depend on people. I guess at that point I hadn't thought that through very much. But I did have to rely on people and I still do. I also got to realize that everybody relies on somebody, somehow, for something. Even though I had been relying on nurses and attendants and staff for years, they really had all the power and all the control over me. But now it was different. I still relied on people but now I decided who I depended on. I decided what I wanted to do, what I wanted to eat, etc. I had no choices when I was institutionalized.

Regaining control over your life. That's the key. That's what Independent Living is all about. And between 1974 and 1977, Independent Living blossomed. We weren't going to rely on visiting nurses to come to dress us, feed us, and put us to bed at times that were convenient for *them*. So we began to expand greatly on this service idea we came up with. We called it personal care attendants (PCAs). We learned to hire, interview, and train our own PCAs to do what we wanted, on the schedule we wanted it done. And we got the Department of Public Welfare to pay for our PCA services. I mean, between 1974 and 1979 we went from 10 people using PCAs to probably close to 200 people using them. Before you knew it, Independent Living had gone from a concept to a practice. There was no turning back.

As I listened to Charlie's story, and the stories of many other people with disabilities, it became apparent that the themes of being institutionalized, losing control over one's life, having few if any options with regard to choosing where and how to live, and having professionals essentially run our lives for us—all these were themes that crossed the artificial barriers that separate groups of people with disabilities. Here were themes and common experiences that anyone who has been labeled with a disability could immediately relate to, including people with psychiatric disabilities.

What Can Independent Living Mean for People with Psychiatric Disabilities?

As mentioned earlier, Independent Living is actually three interrelated things. First, it is a grassroots movement for social justice and civil rights made up of people with disabilities. Second, it is a philosophy or, better yet, a "lived philosophy" that grew out of the day-to-day experience of people who were struggling to regain control over their lives and the resources that affected their lives. And finally, Independent Living is also a national network of nonprofit agencies that provide services and advocacy. These Independent Living Centers (ILCs) are run and staffed primarily by people with disabilities. At this point I would like to examine each of these three aspects in relation to their relevance for people with psychiatric disabilities.

Independent Living Is a Grassroots Movement for Social Justice and Civil Rights Made Up of People With Disabilities.

Charlie's story helps us to understand that those of us with disabilities live in environments which are oppressive, which rob us of our right to self-determination, and which create and nourish dependency on people who have great power to determine the course of our lives. Charlie's response to being institutionalized was to become angry. His angry indignation was a vital, strong, positive response in the face of injustice. He was able to mobilize his anger and use it as a motivating force to bring about change. But he did not achieve these changes all by himself. He achieved change by joining with other people with disabilities who also found themselves in situations of oppression. Together they found power in their numbers and the pathway to independence.

People with psychiatric disabilities also live in oppressive environments that thwart us in our efforts to regain control over our lives and the resources that affect our lives. However, unlike people with physical disabilities whose angry indignation is seen as an appropriate response to unjust situations, our anger is often viewed as but one more symptom of our psychopathology. Indeed, many of us have learned that we get punished for expressing our anger, i.e., our medications may be increased if we are perceived as being angry, we may be asked to leave a program, we get told we are "decompensating" and many times are rehospitalized, and we are told we are "agitated" and are restrained and/or put in seclusion "for our own good."

Learning that it is O.K. to be angry, that we have a lot to be angry about, that we do not have to view our anger as a symptom of mental illness, and that we do not have to accept punishment for being angry is a fundamental task that faces each of us who have been labeled with a major mental illness. Our anger is a powerful motivating force because at the heart of our angry indignation is the core of self-affirmation. In anger we reclaim our right to say:

> The injustice, the abuse, the degradation, and the discrimination that I have suffered is wrong. I am a valuable human being. I do not accept the conditions of oppression to which I am expected to "adjust." By daring to express our angry indignation and joining with other people with psychiatric disabilities who can validate and affirm our anger, we discover that we have power in our numbers and can begin to work toward social justice and our own liberation. (Shaw, 1989)

In my opinion, the first task in developing programs in Independent Living Centers for people with psychiatric disabilities is to begin to do grassroots organizing with that community of people. We must avoid the pitfall of forcing people with psychiatric disabilities into the same mold that worked for people with physical disabilities. Likewise, we must avoid the temptation to pressure people into immediately offering services and viewing I.L. Centers as instant alternatives to traditional mental health services. Independent Living began as a grassroots movement of people with disabilities. Those of us with psychiatric disabilities must have the same opportunity to build upon our own grassroots movement, which has its own history (Chamberlin, 1971, 1984), and to therefore forge the path of our own liberation.

At the Northeast Independent Living Program we have found it imperative to work closely with other local grassroots organizations made up of people with psychiatric disabilities and to stay in touch with our national organizations. We have also hired a skilled grassroots, direct-action community organizer and an organizing trainee to provide technical assistance to member-controlled groups that are organizing to change the mental health system. Finally, we have developed a model for running completely consumer-run and controlled conferences. These conferences serve as excellent tools for developing leadership within our local community of people with psychiatric disabilities, for conducting outreach, and for providing a forum for expression, consciousness raising, and role modeling the use of anger as a motivating force without danger of being punished. We conduct these conferences in the community as well as inside state mental hospitals.

As we develop our own grassroots movement for social justice, we also begin to discover that there are many issues that face all people with disabilities. Stigma, lack of affordable housing, work disincentives, inferior health care, poverty, unemployment, and segregation are barriers to self-determination and independent living that face all people with disabilities. The great promise of developing Independent Living Centers into true cross-disability centers is that of developing strong alliances between the groups that represent the 43 million Americans with disabilities. "Cross disability" means to acknowledge the autonomy and celebrate the diversity of each culture of people with disabilities, while also rejecting the artificial barriers that are forced upon us due to our respective labels. When we join together we are the largest minority group in the country and, as the passage of the Americans With Disabilities Act proves, within our numbers we have the collective power to overcome oppression.

Independent Living is a Philosophy.

From its origin as a grassroots movement for social justice and civil rights, Independent Living also evolved into a "lived philosophy" whereby people with disabilities began to understand themselves and their world in new ways. In his paper, "Independent Living: From Social Movement to Analytic Paradigm," Gerben DeJong (1979) captured the emerging philosophy of the I.L. movement. The hallmarks of the Independent Living philosophy as described by DeJong include 1) the notion that the problem does not reside inside of an individual but rather exists as barriers in our environment; 2) that we have the right to failure and the dignity of risk; 3) that consumers must be sovereign and have a major voice in the development of programs they use; 4) that we can become experts in our own self-care and learn to demedicalize our lives; and 5) that self-help can offer us many things that professional help cannot. These principles of the philosophy of Independent Living can apply to people with psychiatric disabilities in the following ways:

The hallmark of the I.L. philosophy is the recognition that the problem does not reside inside of an individual. For instance, Charlie was taught by well-meaning professionals that the problem was his limited range of motion and mobility due to his spinal cord injury, and that it was located inside of Charlie. However, in time, Charlie and his peers began to understand that with the proper adaptive equipment, skills and support, they could achieve the mobility necessary to move through environments. They learned that having a disability was a given, not a problem. The real problem existed in the form of barriers in the environment that prevented them from living, working, and learning in environments of their choice. The problem was the stairs that blocked them from accessing educational opportunities. The problem was attitudinal barriers such as ignorance and fear that led to discrimination in opportunities for employment. The problem was the uncut curbstones that blocked them from exercising their right to vote because they could not access voting booths. From this new vantage point, the focus changed from trying to change individuals to identifying and removing environmental barriers to independence and self-determination. The task became to confront, challenge, and change those barriers and to make environments accessible.

People with psychiatric disabilities are also taught that the problem exists inside of us, particularly inside of our heads. Just like people with physical disabilities, we are taught that since the problem exists inside of us, the focus must be to change us.

The more the system takes control of our lives and choices, the more helpless, disempowered, irresponsible, and dependent we learn to become...

However, if we begin to think about it, having a psychiatric disability is, for many of us, simply a given. The problem comes when we seek treatment and either cannot afford it or it is not relevant to our needs as we see them. The problem comes when we wish to live in the community and find that there is no housing that we can afford. The problem comes when we seek rehabilitation programs but there are no options or programs that are relevant to our needs. The problem comes when we try to get into school but are denied admission because we are known to have been diagnosed with mental illness. The problem comes when we want to work and are ready to work but encounter discrimination in the workplace.

If we remember that environments are not just physical places, but also include social and interpersonal environments, then it is clear that those of us with psychiatric disabilities face many environmental barriers that impede and thwart our efforts to live independently and to regain control over our lives and the resources that affect our lives. Some of the environmental barriers that we face include poverty, stigma, and prejudice; fear and ignorance; discrimination in opportunities for housing, education, training, socializing, employment, and medical care; segregation in mental health "ghettos; lack of treatment options from which to choose; lack of the opportunity to get a second opinion when desired; lack of options from which to choose a rehabilitation program; and lack of peer support/self-help groups and completely consumer-controlled alternatives to traditional mental health programs. Some of the environmen-

FIGURE 1.
THE CYCLE OF DISEMPOWERMENT AND DESPAIR

The Central Attitudinal Barrier

People with psychiatric disabilities cannot be self-determining because to be mentally ill means to have lost the capacity for sound reasoning. It means one is irrational and crazy. Thus all of the thoughts, choices, expressions, etc., of persons who have been diagnosed with mental illness can be ignored...

The System Takes Control

Therefore professionals within the system must take responsibility for us and our life choices...

The Prophecy Is Fulfilled

As we become experts in being helpless patients, the central barrier is reinforced...

Learned Helplessness

The more the system takes control of our lives and choices, the more helpless, disempowered, irresponsible, and dependent we learn to become...

tal barriers we face may not be as concrete as an uncut curbstone, but they are just as real and equally devastating in terms of the unnecessary dependency and helplessness they create in us.

At the Northeast Independent Living Program, we have identified what we believe to be the central attitudinal barrier that people with psychiatric disabilities face. This central attitudinal barrier, conceptualized in Figure 1, is the cornerstone of the cycle of despair and disempowerment that is so familiar to us.

Of course, the result of this fundamental attitudinal barrier and cycle of disempowerment and despair is that the locus of control and responsibility for our own lives is taken away from us and transferred onto mental health and judicial systems. When we lose

control over our lives in this way, then a profound sense of helplessness and hopelessness begins to pervade our lives. Esso Leete (1989) captures this sense of helplessness when she writes:

> I can talk, but I may not be heard. I can make suggestions, but they may not be taken seriously. I can voice my thoughts, but they may be seen as delusions. I can recite my experiences, but they may be interpreted as fantasies. To be a patient or even an ex-client is to be discounted. (p. 1)

Seligman (1975) has empirically demonstrated the profound impact that loss of control over one's life situation can have. He calls the phenomenon "learned helplessness." One learns to become helpless in situations in which one has no control and, no matter what one does, it doesn't really matter. The syndrome of learned helplessness creates deficits in three important spheres of human functioning, including motivation (i.e., I don't care because what I do doesn't matter anyway); cognition (i.e., my actions fail to have an impact here and everywhere else, too); and emotion (i.e., I give up trying and experience apathy/ depression/ anxiety). The symptoms of learned helplessness include apathy, resignation, anger, submissiveness, depression, anxiety, withdrawal, and compliance. These symptoms are often mistaken by mental health professionals to be the so-called "negative symptoms" of psychotic disorders. However, no amount of medication or psychotherapy can put these symptoms into remission. The antidote to learned helplessness is choice, taking back our power and learning to take control over our own lives.

We believe that the central attitudinal barrier permeates mental health policies, procedures, programs (environments), and the training that mental health professionals receive. Because the consequence of this attitudinal barrier is to create learned helplessness and unnecessary dependency in people with psychiatric disabilities, we now understand that we are faced with recovering not only from mental illness, but also from the effects of learned helplessness (Deegan, 1988, 1990). For many of us, the effects of learned helplessness and what we call "spirit breaking" (i.e., "how the system tries to break your spirit"), can be more damaging than the original illness. Thus the central attitudinal barrier, i.e., the assumption that people with psychiatric disabilities cannot become self-determining, must be understood as a barrier that pervades and permeates mental health policy, procedures, and

For many of us, the effects of learned helplessness...can be more damaging than the original illness.

programs. It is a barrier that is as real and as disabling as an uncut curbstone is to a person using a wheelchair. Our task is to identify that central attitudinal barrier in all its guises, to challenge it, and to change it wherever we might find it.

The philosophy of Independent Living is also founded on the observation that nondisabled people are allowed to make all sorts of mistakes and to take risks in their lives. For example, we all know people who repeatedly fall in love with the same type of person, only to find that within a short time their relationship shatters on the rocks and they are once again heartbroken. Then our friends go out and repeat the same scenario all over again! Clearly our friends are making what we might consider to be some pretty dumb choices. They seem to lack insight into their situation. They are failing to learn from past experiences. Should our friends be assigned a case manager? Wouldn't that be in their best interest? The answer is of course not. You see, people who have not been labeled with a disability are allowed to make all sorts of dumb choices over and over and over again in their lives and nobody intervenes on their behalf. People who have not been labeled with a disability are expected to take risks in their lives. That is how human beings grow and learn. However, once we are perceived as *being* disabled, then it is assumed we are fragile and need protection, and we suddenly find that we are not allowed the dignity of risk and the right to failure.

Reclaiming the dignity of risk and the right to failure is an essential part of the philosophy of Independent Living. Recall Charlie telling of how he had to learn the limits of his independence. Recall how he fell out of his wheelchair and spent countless hours on the living room rug until his personal care attendant returned. In all of these ways Charlie was shedding the myth of being crippled and frail, which is so often associated with physical disabilities. He was winning back his dignity as well as his right to take risks and grow.

Those of us with psychiatric disabilities also find ourselves robbed of the dignity of risk and the right to failure. Often the attitudes that give rise to the notion that we are fragile and need to be protected from risk and failure are glazed in a sugary sweet benevolence. We are told that decisions are being made for us because they are clinically in our best interest and that they are for our own good. However, we find that such benevolent attitudes are frequently a sign of "mentalism" (Chamberlin, 1971). Just as racism, sexism, heterosexism, and able-ism devalue, stereotype, and make second-class citizens out of entire groups of people, so, too, does mentalism. Mentalism is characterized by the following assumptions:

1. Mentalism is the assumption that people who have been diagnosed with mental illness are dangerous, unpredictable, and to be feared.

2. Mentalism is the assumption that we are less than human, more like children than adults.

3. Mentalism is the assumption that we are fundamentally different from other people.

4. Mentalism is the assumption that we do not know what we need.

5. Mentalism is the assumption that what we say is crazy and can be ignored.

6. Mentalism is the assumption that we must have others make choices for us.

7. Mentalism is the assumption that we should not take risks and should be protected from failures.

8. Mentalism is the assumption that others must decide what is in our best interest.

9. Mentalism is the assumption that we should strive to be normal.

10. Mentalism is the assumption that we are disabled people rather than people with disabilities.

Mentalism is rampant in the training we receive as mental health professionals. Mentalism becomes institutionalized as the policies, procedures, theories, and programs that continue to force those of us with psychiatric disabilities into positions of dependence. I believe that mentalism is ultimately disabling to mental health professionals as well. Mentalistic assumptions disable mental health professionals in their efforts to be of help. At the Northeast Independent Living Program we have conducted workshops to help rehabilitate mental health professionals who are disabled by mentalistic assumptions in their efforts to help.

Finally, it should be noted that, although at times it is seemingly benevolent, mentalism is ultimately dehumanizing. It is what Paulo Freire (1989) calls "false charity" as opposed to "true generosity":

> True generosity consists precisely in fighting to destroy the causes which nourish false charity. False charity constrains the fearful and subdued, the "rejects of life," to extend their trembling hands. True generosity lies in striving so that these hands—whether of individuals or entire peoples—need be extended less and less in supplication, so that more and more they become human hands which work and, working, transform the world. (p. 29)

Thus, part of the work that faces us in our journey toward independent living is to learn to identify, challenge, and change mentalism and the false charity that robs us of our right to failure and the dignity of risk. We are learning that we are not fragile cripples that need to be protected. We are discovering our pride and our dignity. We are discovering that we are a strong people with fiercely tenacious spirits (Deegan 1990; Anderson & Deegan, 1991). We would challenge anyone to try to live on $400 a month (SSI) and survive! It is not protection that we need. It is choice, opportunity, control, and, as Charlie put it, learning the limits of our independence and deciding on whom we will choose to rely for support.

A third principle of the philosophy of Independent Living is that of consumer sovereignty. This principle "asserts that because disabled persons are the best judges of their own interests, they should have the larger voice in determining what services are provided in the disability services market" (DeJong, 1979, p. 439). We saw this principle emerging in Charlie's story when people organized a block vote and succeeded in voting in a board of directors that was comprised entirely of people with physical disabilities.

Today there is a growing awareness of the importance of including people with psychiatric disabilities on agency boards and planning committees. However, all too often we do not hold a majority vote on these committees and at times we are merely a token presence. We are rarely invited to participate on committees that have true decision-making power. In contrast, Independent Living Centers are completely consumer controlled with at least 51% of the board of directors being comprised of people with disabilities.

In an excellent article entitled "Mental Health Consumer Participation on Boards and Committees: Barriers and Strategies," Valentine and Capponi (1989) outline six barriers that people with psychiatric disabilities face when attempting to participate on boards. These barriers include 1) the incongruence between an agency's stated ideal of consumer participation and its actual practice of it; 2) tokenism, or the tendency to invite only one or two consumers onto the committee and to assign them perfunctory responsibilities; 3) lack of representativeness whereby only "reasonable" consumers are asked to join committees; 4) role strain defined as "the tendency for roles and functions learned outside of the committee context to interfere with the appropriate performance of roles within the committee" (p. 10); 5) poor communication characterized by the use of mental health jargon that serves to mystify the consumer and leave us speechless in the same way we might have nothing to contribute to a meeting in which the primary language used was Russian; and, finally, 6) economic factors that act as barriers to participation, especially if we remember that, although most committee members are there on work time, are getting paid to participate, and have private transportation, people living on fixed incomes are expected to participate during their own leisure time, to participate without pay, and to assume the cost of transportation to and from the meetings. These barriers must be addressed and removed if people with psychiatric disabilities are to

> *Unlike people with physical disabilities whose angry indignation is seen as an appropriate response to unjust situations, our anger is often viewed as but one more symptom of our psychopathology.*

move toward true consumer sovereignty and gain control over the resources that are affecting our lives.

Integral to the philosophy of Independent Living is the notion that people with disabilities can become experts in their own self-care. To live independently means to demedicalize our lives by learning self-care techniques that minimize medical presence in our daily life. Learning to enter into partnership with physicians and nurses, learning when to use hospitals, and learning how to stay in charge of our own lives are important skills for us to learn.

Additionally, many of us find it important to accept the fact of our disability while simultaneously rejecting the disability package plan. The disability package plan can be characterized as learning to become compliant; resigning ourselves to the prognoses of doom that surround us; internalizing the overt and covert messages that our very *personhood* is disabled; surrendering control of our lives to medical authorities; becoming experts in being dependent, passive patients and regressing into the sick role; and progressing onto the lifelong "impaired role" described by Siegler and Osmond (1973) as having "a lower status than the sick role, but in return for this childlike status, they are allowed to spend their days as children do, playing card games, taking up hobbies, having meals served to them, 'playing' with each other, or, most often, doing nothing at all" (p. 441).

Many people with psychiatric disabilities refuse to accept their diagnoses and we are told that this "lack of insight" is but one more sign of our psychopathology. However, we believe that, while some people choose (most rightfully) to reject the entire notion of being diagnosed with a mental illness, many others are rejecting the package plan that comes with such a diagnosis. They are rejecting the prescribed roles of helplessness described above, as well as the poverty, homelessness, discrimination,

segregation, and stigma that are also frequently part of the disability package plan. But the message contained within the philosophy of Independent Living is that we can accept that we have a disability while simultaneously rejecting the disability package plan. Implicit in this notion is the idea that it is possible to take a stand in relation to our disability. It is possible to be a whole, healthy person and still have a disability. Disability is not synonymous with being a passive victim who is broken and needs to be fixed (Anderson & Deegan, 1991).

Finally, the philosophy of Independent Living is founded on the concept of self-help and peer support. We need not turn to professionals for all of our answers. In fact, there are many things that we know by virtue of living with a disability that professionals simply cannot know because they have not experienced it. People with disabilities helping others with disabilities is a hallmark of Independent Living.

Independent Living Centers Are Service Delivery and Advocacy Centers that Are Consumer Controlled.

Just as the "lived philosophy" of Independent Living grew out of the struggle for social justice and civil rights, so too did the creation of Independent Living Centers grow out of people's developing sense of what they needed in order to live independently in the environments of their choice. Professionals did not sit back and assess what people needed and then developed I.L.C.s for them. Rather, as Charlie's story so beautifully illustrates, as people with physical disabilities began to take steps toward regaining control over their lives and the resources that affect their lives, they slowly began to define unique services to meet their needs *as they defined their needs*. Hence, I.L.C.s did not attempt to become parallel service delivery systems, nor did they seek to duplicate existing services. Beginning with the revolutionary concept of training people to acquire personal care attendants, I.L.C.s also became places where people with physical disabilities did peer counseling, shared their expertise in self-care, and learned the skills to work the system to get what they needed. Individual advocacy as well as organized lobbying efforts to remove environmental barriers, to monitor access laws, and to advocate for the interests of people with disabilities also became a part of what I.L.C.s were, and are, all about.

*B*y *reclaiming the dignity of risk and the right to failure, as well as the right to try and succeed, people can leave institutions, make their own choices, and live independently.*

I believe that the community of people with psychiatric disabilities must be allowed the time to grow and develop in its own way. As stated earlier, our first task is to continue to organize our community on local, statewide, and national levels. As we organize and raise our consciousness, we are developing a lived philosophy that is similar in spirit to that which people with physical disabilities discovered for themselves. In the same way, I believe that with time we will begin to discover entirely new types of services that will neither duplicate existing mental health services nor seek to provide a parallel service delivery system. But I stress that these new services will grow out of our emerging sense of what it is we need to regain control over our own lives. We will not and should not be expected to come into I.L.C.s and immediately begin to provide the same services that have worked for people with physical disabilities. We need time to organize our movement, to develop our "lived philosophy" and to let our vision of truly unique services emerge from our experience of taking back control over our own lives.

We have been developing a pilot project run by and for people with psychiatric disabilities at the Northeast Independent Living Program for nearly 3 years now. In that time we have begun to organize our local movement for social justice, and from that is emerging our lived philosophy and an understanding of the environmental barriers that we find disabling. After 3 years we are just now beginning to understand what some of our service needs are and how we can go about addressing them through I.L.C.s. For instance, we are understanding that one of the most central issues in our lives is the issue of psychotropic medications. We are beginning to see that I.L.C.s could provide peer-run skills training groups on how to talk to a psychiatrist and get what you want. We also see a tremendous need for getting into state hospitals to do skills training and personal advocacy with people regarding how to go to a treatment team and get what you want. Finally, we are beginning to consider developing a skills training group so that people can write a type of modified psychiatric living will called a health care proxy. In this unique service, people could come to the I.L.C. (or we could get out to them) and learn the skills to write their own personal psychiatric living will. Such a document, written while a person is out of the hospital, would allow him or her the opportunity to designate a proxy or special friend or confidant. This proxy or designated person would agree to see that one's stated treatment preferences were respected and followed out in the event that one was rehospitalized and deemed incompetent. This service is truly in the spirit of the philosophy of Independent Living because it helps us extend control over our own lives even during periods when the system would seek to strip us of that control.

Conclusion

Independent Living holds great promise for the community of people with psychiatric disabilities. Regaining control over our lives and the resources that affect our lives is a theme that crosses artificial barriers between groups of people with disabilities and unites us in a common experience and common goal. As Independent Living Centers become increasingly focused on cross-disability and the inclusion of all groups of people with disabilities, there are certain precautions that must be exercised. For instance, as people with psychiatric disabilities begin to develop programs in I.L.C.s, we must not be expected simply to jump in and start providing services that have historically worked for people with physical disabilities. Cross-disability means to respect the autonomy of each group, to celebrate our diversity while remaining conscious of the issues that we share in common. It means to give us time to organize our movement, raise our consciousness, develop our own lived philosophy, and discover and develop the services that we need in order to live independently.

References

Anderson, D. & Deegan, P. (1991). *Recovery and the empowerment of people with psychiatric disabilities.* Unpublished manuscript.

Chamberlin, J. (1978). *On our own: Patient controlled alternatives to the mental health system.* New York: McGraw-Hill.

Chamberlin, J. (1984). Speaking for ourselves: An overview of the ex-psychiatric inmates movement. *Psychosocial Rehabilitation Journal, 8*(2), 56-64.

Deegan, P. (1988). Recovery: The lived experience of rehabilitation. *Psychosocial Rehabilitation Journal, 11*(4), 11-19.

Deegan, P. (1990). Spirit breaking: When the helping professions hurt. *The Humanistic Psychologist, 18*(3), 301-313.

DeJong, G. (1979). Independent living: From social movement to analytic paradigm. *Archives of Physical Medicine and Rehabilitation, 60,* 435-446.

Freire, P. (1989). *Pedagogy of the oppressed* (M. B. Ramos, Trans.). New York: Continuum.

Leete, E. (1989). *The role of the consumer movement and persons with mental illness.* Presentation at the Twelfth Mary Switzer Memorial Seminar in Rehabilitation, Washington, DC, June 15-16.

Seligman, M. E. P. (1975). *Helplessness: On depression, development and death.* San Francisco: Freeman .

Shaw, J. (1989). *Anger as a motivating force.* Unpublished speech presented at the No Surrender Conference, June.

Siegler, M. & Osmond, H. (1973). *The sick role revisiting.* Hasting Center Studies, 1(3).

Valentine, M. B. & Capponi, P. (1989). *Mental health consumer participation on boards and committees: Barriers and strategies.* Canada's Mental Health, June, 8-12.

THE EX-PATIENTS' MOVEMENT: WHERE WE'VE BEEN AND WHERE WE'RE GOING

Judi Chamberlin

JUDI CHAMBERLIN IS ASSOCIATED WITH THE CENTER FOR PSYCHIATRIC REHABILITATION, BOSTON UNIVERSITY AND IS A FOUNDER OF THE RUBY ROGERS CENTER, SOMERVILLE, MA.

THIS ARTICLE ORIGINALLY APPEARED IN THE *Journal of Mind and Behavior*, 1990, 11(3&4), 323(77)-336(90) AND IS REPRINTED WITH PERMISSION.

The mental patients' liberation movement, which started in the early 1970s, is a political movement comprised of people who have experienced psychiatric treatment and hospitalization. Its two main goals are developing self-help alternatives to medically-based psychiatric treatment and securing full citizenship rights for people labeled "mentally ill." The movement questions the medical model of "mental illness," and insists that people who have been labeled as "mentally ill" speak on their own behalf and not be represented by others who claim to speak "for" them. The movement has developed its own philosophy, and operates a variety of self-help and mutual support programs in which ex-patients themselves control the services that are offered. Despite obstacles, the movement continues to grow and develop.

A complete history of the mental patients' liberation movement is still to be written. Like other liberation struggles of oppressed people, the activism of former psychiatric patients has been frequently ignored or discredited. Only when a group begins to emerge from subjugation can it begin to reclaim its own history. This process has been most fully developed in the black movement and the women's move-

ment; it is in a less developed stage in the gay movement and the disability movement (of which the ex-patients' movement may be considered a part).

The "madman," as defined by others, is part of society's cultural heritage. Whether "madness" is explained by religious authorities (as demonic possession, for example), by secular authorities (as disturbance of the public order), or by medical authorities (as "mental illness"), the mad themselves have remained largely voiceless. The movement of people who call themselves variously, ex-patients, psychiatric inmates, and psychiatric survivors is an attempt to give voice to individuals who have been assumed to be irrational—to be "out of their minds."

The ex-patients' movement began approximately in 1970, but we can trace its history back to many earlier former patients, in the late nineteenth and early twentieth centuries, who wrote stories of their mental hospital experiences and who attempted to change laws and public policies concerning the "insane." Thus, in 1868, Mrs. Elizabeth Packard published the first of several books and pamphlets in which she detailed her forced commitment by her husband in the Jacksonville (Illinois) Insane Asylum. She also founded the Anti-Insane Asylum Society, which apparently never became a viable organization (Dain, 1989). Similarly, in Massachusetts at about the same time, Elizabeth Stone, also committed by her husband, tried to rally public opinion to the cause of stopping the unjust incarceration of the "insane."

In the early part of this century, Clifford Beers, a wealthy young businessman, experienced several episodes of confused thinking and agitation which caused him to be placed in a mental hospital. Following his recovery, Beers (1953) wrote a book, *A Mind that Found Itself,* which went through numerous editions and which led to the formation of the influential National Committee on Mental Hygiene (later the

National Association for Mental Health). Dain (1989) states that:

> Beers was outspoken about abuse of mental patients and passionate in defending their rights and damning psychiatrists for tolerating mistreatment of patients. But he eventually toned down his hostility to psychiatry as it became obvious that for his reform movement to gain the support he sought at the highest levels of society it would have to include leading psychiatrists. Although he envisioned that eventually former mental patients and their families would be recruited into the movement, the public's persistent prejudice against mentally disturbed people and Beers' own doubts and inclinations, plus pressures from psychiatrists, drew him away from this goal. (pp. 9-10)

Dain also notes, in passing, the formation of the Alleged Lunatics' Friend Society in 1845 by former patients in England. On the whole, however, this early history is obscure, and the development of modern ex-patient groups in the United States at the beginning of the 1970s occurred primarily without any knowledge of these historical roots.

Although the terms have often been used interchangeably, "mental patients' liberation" (or "psychiatric inmates' liberation") and "anti-psychiatry" are not the same thing. "Anti-psychiatry" is largely an intellectual exercise of academics and dissident mental health professionals. There has been little attempt within anti-psychiatry to reach out to struggling ex-patients or to include their perspective. The focus in this paper is on ex-patient (or ex-inmate) groups. I identify the major principles that have guided the development of the ex-patients' movement, sketch the recent history of this movement, describe its major goals and accomplishments, and discuss the challenges facing it in this decade.

Stigma and discrimination still make it difficult for people to identify themselves as ex-mental patients if they could otherwise pass as "normal," reinforcing public perceptions that the "bag lady" and the homeless drifter are representative of all former patients. Like the exemplary black persons of a generation or two ago—who were held to be "a credit to their race" and, by definition, atypical of black people generally—so the former mental patient who is successfully managing his or her life is widely seen as the exception that proves the rule.

Guiding Principles of the Movement

Exclusion of Non-Patients

In the United States, former patients have found that they work best when they exclude mental health professionals (and other non-patients) from their organizations (Chamberlin, 1987). There are several reasons why the movement has grown in this direction—a direction which began to develop in the early 1970s, influenced by the black, women's, and gay liberation movements. Among the major organizing principles of these movements were self-definition and self-determination. Black people felt that white people could not truly understand their experiences; women felt similarly about men; homosexuals similarly about heterosexuals. As these groups evolved, they moved from defining themselves to setting their own priorities. To mental patients who began to organize, these principles seemed equally valid. Their own perceptions about "mental illness" were diametrically opposed to those of the general public, and even more so to those of mental health professionals. It seemed sensible, therefore, not to let non-patients into ex-patient organizations or to permit them to dictate an organization's goals.

There were also practical reasons for excluding non-patients. Those groups that did not exclude non-patients from membership almost always quickly dropped their liberation aspects and became reformist. In addition, such groups rapidly moved away from ex-patient control, with the tiny minority of non-patient members taking on leadership roles and setting future goals and directions. These experiences served as powerful examples to newly-forming ex-patient organizations that mixed membership was indeed destructive.

In attempting to solve these organizational problems, group members began to recognize a pattern they referred to as "mentalism" and "sane chauvinism," a set of assumptions which most people seemed to hold about mental patients: that they were incompetent, unable to do things for themselves, constantly in need of supervision and assistance, unpredictable, likely to be violent or irrational, and so forth. Not only did the general public express mentalist ideas; so did ex-patients themselves. These crippling stereotypes became recognized as a form of internalized oppression. The struggle against internalized oppression and mentalism generally was seen as best accomplished in groups composed exclusively of patients, through the process of consciousness-raising (borrowed from the women's movement).

Consciousness-Raising

The consciousness-raising process is one in which people share and examine their own experiences to learn about the contexts in which their lives are embedded. As used by the women's movement, consciousness-raising helped women to understand that matters of sexuality, marriage, divorce, job discrimination, roles, and so forth were not individual personal problems, but were instead indicators of society's systematic oppression of women. Similarly, as mental patients began to share their life stories, it became clear that distinct patterns of oppression existed and that our problems and difficulties were not solely internal and personal, as we had been told they were. The consciousness-raising process may be

hampered by the presence of those who do not share common experiences (e.g., as women or as mental patients). As the necessity for consciousness-raising became more evident, it provided still another reason for limiting group membership.

Consciousness-raising is an ongoing process, with people and groups constantly recognizing deeper levels of oppression. Within an ex-patient group, various activities often lead to further consciousness-raising experiences. For example, a group may approach a local newspaper or television reporter to write a story about the group's work or to give its viewpoint on a current mental health issue. If the group's representatives are treated respectfully and their opinions listened to, no consciousness-raising issue arises. If, however, the reporter is unwilling to listen to the group's representatives or seems to disbelieve them or makes comments about their mental status, it can become an occasion for further consciousness-raising. Whereas, before the advent of the patients' liberation movement, the group might have altered its strategy or even disbanded after such a discouraging incident, armed with the knowledge that they have run into systematic discrimination they can decide how to proceed. They may complain to the reporter's superior. They may raise questions about discrimination against mental patients. Because of consciousness-raising, they will have a clear idea of what they are facing.

Historical Development of the Movement

Like many new developments in the United States, mental patients' liberation groups began primarily on the east and west coasts and then spread inland. Among the earliest groups were the Insane Liberation Front in Portland, Oregon (founded in 1970), the Mental Patients' Liberation Project in New York City, the Mental

Patients' Liberation Front in Boston (both founded in 1971), and the Network Against Psychiatric Assault in San Francisco (founded in 1972). Local groups took a long time to establish ongoing communications, because they were not funded and membership consisted mostly of low income individuals. The development of two major means of communication, the annual Conference on Human Rights and Psychiatric Oppression, and the San Francisco-based publication, *Madness Network News,* helped the movement to grow. Interestingly, both the Conference and *Madness Network News* began as mixed groups but later were operated and controlled solely by ex-patients (see below).

The first Conference on Human Rights and Psychiatric Oppression was held in 1973 at the University of Detroit, jointly sponsored by a sympathetic (non-patient) psychology professor and the New York City-based Mental Patients' Liberation Project (MPLP). Approximately 50 people from across the United States (and Canadian representatives) met for several days to discuss the developing philosophy and goals of mental patients' liberation. The leadership role of ex-patients was acknowledged; for example, the original name proposed by the sponsoring professor for the conference ("The Rights of the Mentally Disabled") was roundly rejected as stigmatizing. Although no plan was made in Detroit to continue the conference, the practice later developed of designating an attending group to sponsor the next year's conference. The confer-

By its very nature, self-help combats stigma, because the negative images of mental patients ultimately must give way to the reality of clients managing their own lives and their own programs.

ence became limited to patients and ex-patients only in 1976. Conferences were held annually through 1985 (see below for later developments).

Madness Network News began as a San Francisco-area newsletter in 1972 and gradually evolved into a newspaper format covering the ex-patients' movement in North America as well as worldwide. *Madness Network News'* original core group included both self-styled "radical" mental health professionals and ex-patients, but within a few years a major struggle ensued and the paper was published solely by ex-patients. There were also struggles between women and men ex-patients resulting in special women's issues edited by all-women, all-ex-patient staffs. *Madness Network News* existed solely on subscription income, which was sufficient to cover printing and mailing costs, but did not allow for salaries. For many years this publication was the voice of the American ex-patients' movement, a journal which published personal experiences, creative writing, art, political theory, and factual reporting, all from the ex-patient point of view. *Madness Network News* ceased publication in 1986.

The heart of the movement, however, continued to be the individual local group. Although some groups existed for only short periods, the overall number of groups continued to grow. Most groups were started by a small number of people coalescing out of a shared anger and a sense that through organization they could bring about change. Groups were independent, loosely linked through Madness Network News and the annual Conference. Each group developed its own ideologies, terminology, styles, and goals. Groups were known by an astonishing variety of names, from the straightforward (Mental Patients' Alliance; Network Against Psychiatric Assault) to the euphemistic (Project Acceptance; Reclamation, Inc.). Some groups were organized as traditional hierarchies with officers, and held formal meetings, while other groups moved toward more egalitarian structures with shared decision-making and no formal leadership. Groups were united by certain rules and principles: mental health terminology was considered suspect; attitudes that limited opportunities for mental patients were to be discouraged and changed; and members' feelings—particularly feelings of anger toward the mental health system —were considered real and legitimate, not "symptoms of illness."

The activities of various groups included organizing support groups, advocating for hospitalized patients, lobbying for changes in laws, public speaking, publishing newsletters, developing creative and artistic ways of dealing with the mental patient experience, etc. The two primary thrusts were advocacy and self-help alternatives to the psychiatric system, as it quickly became clear to each group that its own membership's needs largely fell into these two areas.

Different groups developed different terminologies to describe themselves and their work. "Ex-patient" was a controversial term because it appeared to embrace the medical model; *Madness Network News* promoted the use of "ex-psychiatric inmate," which became widespread. Other groups referred to themselves as "clients," "consumers," or "psychiatric survivors." Differences in terminology stressed differing emphases and priorities; clearly the individuals labelling themselves "inmates" or "survivors" took the more militant stance.

Because most groups existed with little or no outside funding they were limited in their accomplishments. The question of funding generated numerous controversies, as did the question of reimbursement for organizational labor. Even if the group decided it had no objection in principle to receiving outside funding, obtaining such funding was difficult. Potential funding sources tended to look askance on ex-patient groups—especially groups that rejected psychiatric ideology and terminology. Moreover, foundations which funded community organizing efforts did not view ex-patient groups as falling within their purview. Finally, state departments of mental health were seldom approached because of their role in running the very institutions in which group members had been oppressed. And those mental health departments that were approached were highly skeptical of the ability of ex-patient groups to run their own projects.

Gradually, however, inroads were made. Members of ex-patient groups demanded involvement in the various forums from which they were excluded—conferences, legislative hearings, boards, committees and the like. Although at first in only the most token numbers, ex-patients were slowly invited to take part in such forums. Often groups had to insist on being invited, however.

Once involved in such meetings, ex-patients could move in two different tactical directions: cooperation or confrontation. Clearly, much was said in these forums which directly contradicted the movement's developing ideology. While most such meetings featured a reliance on psychiatric terminology and diagnosis, and on the assumption that patients existed in a lifetime dependency relationship, the patients' movement stood in opposition to the medical model and in support of self-reliance and self-determination. Although ex-patients' objections to such mentalist assumptions were often used as a reason to exclude ex-patients from future meetings, it is to the movement's credit that the ex-patients did speak up and object to much of what was being said. Frequently-heard objections from professional participants were that the expatients "polarized the discussion" or were "disruptive." Professionals sometimes chose to work with non-movement identified ex-patients who were much more likely to be compliant. For example, the most publicly visible post to go to an ex-patient in the 1970s—as one of the twenty-member President's Commission on Mental Health—went to a woman who had never worked with an ex-patient group but who had written about her patienthood experience in professional journals.

However, from this forum, as from others, the movement refused to be excluded. Movement activists packed many of the Commission's public hearings, testifying eloquently about the harmfulness of the psychiatric treatments they had experienced while pleading for enforcement of patients' rights and funding of patient-run alternatives to traditional treatment. The Commission's final report acknowledged the role of alternative treatments, stating that many of the latter "are wary of being classified as mental health services, convinced that such a classification entails a medical perspective and implies authoritarian relationships and derogatory labeling" ("Report," 1978, p. 14). The report went on to note that "groups composed of individuals with mental or emotional problems are in existence or are being formed all over the United States" (pp. 14-15).

The movement also demanded its inclusion in a series of conferences organized by the Community Support Program (CSP), a small division of the National Institute of Mental Health (NIMH). CSP, which began in the late 1970s, focused on providing assistance to programs in community set-tings. However, in the movement's view, these programs often perpetuated many of the worst features of institutionalization, including labeling, forced drugging, and paternalistic control. The participation of ex-patients in CSP conferences (even though the movement activists were vastly outnumbered by mental health professionals) forced CSP to acknowledge the importance of funding patient-run programs as a part of community support. Such recommendations would not have been made—indeed, would not even have been considered—without the tenacity of movement activists who insisted on being heard.

Participation in professionally-sponsored conferences and meetings produced an additional unintended benefit. It enabled ex-patients to meet each other and learn from one another. Such contacts, especially by people from different geographical areas, were previously difficult but later became a source of inspiration and support during the exercise of an otherwise thankless task—to present the patient viewpoint to audiences that were often indifferent or even hostile toward that view.

Self Help and Empowerment

Gradually, the movement began to put some of its principles into action in the operation of self-help programs as alternatives to professional treatment. Although the Mental Patients' Association (MPA) in Vancouver, Canada, began operating its drop-in center and residences within months of its founding in 1971, the first such projects did not appear in the United States until the late 1970s, largely because funding was unavailable.

Programs that developed out of the ex-patients' movement tend to be skeptical about the value of the mental health system and traditional psychiatric treatment (Chamberlin, Rogers, & Sneed, 1989). Members usually gravitate to these groups because they have had negative experiences in the system. Often, members are angry, and their anger is seen by the group as a healthy reaction to their experiences of abuse by the mental health system. At the same time, members, despite their distrust of the system, may simultaneously be involved in professionally-run programs. Members of user-run services are free to combine their participation in self-help groups with professionally-run services, in whatever proportion and combination each member determines.

Through successes experienced in self-help groups, members are enabled to take a stronger role in advocating for their own needs within the larger mental health system. Empowerment means that members have a voice in mental health matters generally—they reject the role of passive service recipient. Group members found themselves moving naturally into the role of advocate, representing the needs of clients on panels, boards, and committees. This may require accommodation on the part of other groups and group members such as administrators, policy makers, legislators, and family members, who typically have listened to everyone but the client about client needs.

Self-help groups do not exist in a vacuum. Even a group that sees itself as totally separate from the mental health system will, of necessity, have some interactions with it, while groups that have been aided or brought into existence by mental health professionals will need to devise their own ways of making themselves autonomous from the larger system. By taking on a role other than that of the passive, needy client, self-help group members can change the systems with which they interact, as these systems adjust to respond to clients in their new roles as advocates and service providers.

Self-help is a concept, not a single program model. The concept is a means by which people become empowered and begin to think of themselves as competent individuals as they present themselves in new ways to the world. By its very nature, self-help combats stigma, because the negative images of mental patients ultimately must give way to the reality of clients managing their own lives and their own programs. The successes of self-help groups have been striking. Groups are handling annual budgets that may be in the hundreds of thousands of dollars; producing newsletters, books, and pamphlets; educating other clients and professionals about group work; influencing legislation and public policy; publicizing and advocating on their own behalf in the media; and, in general, challenging stereotypes and creating new realities. At the same time, individual group members may still be battling the particular manifestations that led to their being psychiatrically labeled in the first place. Self-help is not a miracle nor a cure-all, but it is a powerful confirmation that people, despite problems and disabilities, can achieve more than others (or they themselves) may have ever thought possible.

Advocacy

Self-help is one of two co-equal aspects of the ex-patients' movement; the other is advocacy, or working for political change. Unlike groups such as Recovery Inc. or Schizophrenics Anonymous, patient liberation groups tend to address problems that go beyond the individual. The basic principle of the movement is that all laws and practices which induce discrimination toward individuals who have been labeled "mentally ill" need to be changed, so that a psychiatric diagnosis has no more impact on a person's citizenship rights and responsibilities than does a diagnosis of diabetes or heart disease. To that end, all commitment laws, forced treatment laws, insanity defenses, and other similar practices should be abolished.

Ending involuntary treatment is a long-term goal of the patients' liberation movement. Meanwhile, movement activists work to improve conditions of people subjected to forced treatment, and to see that their existing rights are respected, keeping in mind that these are interim steps within a basically unjust system.

Existing laws have the power to compel people to receive treatment for mental illness. This almost never occurs in the case of physical illness, except in the rare instances when courts overrule parents who refuse medical treatment for a child. The courts in these instances assume the *parens patriae* role, acting in lieu of parents in what the court defines as the child's best interest. When a person of whatever age is ordered by a court to undergo psychiatric treatment, this same *parens patriae* power comes into effect. This connection between the legal and medical systems places the mental patient at a disadvantage that is not faced by patients with physical illnesses.

In addition to the *parens patriae* doctrine, which assumes that a mentally ill individual is incapable of determining his or her own best interest, an additional doctrine, the police power of the state, is used to justify the involuntary confinement of individuals labeled mentally ill. This doctrine is based on the assumption that mentally ill people are dangerous and may do harm to themselves or to others if they are not confined. The belief in the dangerousness of the mentally ill is firmly rooted in our culture. It is especially promoted by the mass media, which frequently run stories in which crimes of violence are attributed to mental illness. If the alleged criminal has been previously hospitalized, the fact is prominently mentioned; if not, frequently a police officer or other authority figure will be quoted to the effect that the accused is "a mental case" or "a nut." In addition, unsolved crimes are often similarly attributed. Both the *parens patriae* power and the police power relate to the stereotyped view of the prospective patient—that he or she is sick, unpredictable, dangerous, unable to care for himself or herself, and unable to judge his or her own best interest.

The movement's advocacy has focused on the right of the individual not to be a patient, rather than on mere procedural safeguards before involuntary treatment can be instituted. A major lawsuit testing this right was filed by seven patients at Boston State Hospital in 1975, many of whom had been members of a patients' rights group that met weekly in the hospital with the aid of the Mental Patients' Liberation Front. The suit, originally known as *Rogers v. Macht,* was called, in later stages, *Rogers v. Okin* and *Rogers v. Commissioner of Mental Health* (1982). It established a limited right-to-refuse-treatment (i.e., psychiatric drugs) for Massachusetts patients.

Since *Rogers v. Commissioner,* right-to-refuse-treatment cases have been decided in a number of states, including New York (*Rivers v. Katz,* 1986) and California (*Reise v. St. Mary's Hospital,* 1987), and the right has been established administratively in some other states. While the movement first greeted these decisions as victories, it has become clear that, in practice, these reforms do little to change the power relationship between patient and psychiatrist. Each procedure (varying from state to state) provides one or more methods to override the patient's decision to refuse drugs; and whether the procedure is administrative or judicial, the end result is that most drug-refusing patients whose cases are heard are forced, ultimately, to take the drugs, despite the ostensible right to refuse them (Appelbaum, 1988). Many movement activists have become discouraged and no longer believe that the courts will help people avoid involuntary patienthood through the mechanism of the right to refuse treatment.

Many individuals in the ex-patients' movement first encountered a critique of the mental health system—a critique which confirmed their feelings—in the works of Thomas Szasz. In such books as *The Myth of Mental Illness* (1961) and *The Manufacture of Madness* (1970), in a career spanning more than 30 years, Szasz has always spoken powerfully about the essential wrongness of forced psychiatric treatment, and the fallacy of defining social and behavioral problems as illnesses. In a recent paper, Szasz (1989) provides a devastating critique of the mental patients' "rights" movement, which has been guided largely by lawyers and non-patients.

> Rallying to the battle cry of "civil rights for mental patients," professional civil libertarians, special-interest-mongering attorneys, and the relatives of mental patients joined conventional psychiatrists demanding rights for mental patient—*qua* mental patients. The result has been a perverse sort of affirmative action program: since mental patients are ill, they have a right to treatment; since many are homeless, they have a right to housing; and so it goes, generating even a special right to reject treatment (a right every non-mental patient has without special dispensation). In short, the phrase "rights of mental patients" has meant everything but according persons called "mental patients" the same rights (and duties) as are accorded all adults qua citizens or persons. (p. 19)

The National Association of Psychiatric Survivors (NAPS), founded in 1985 as the National Alliance of Mental Patients, promotes the same ideals Szasz espouses. The first item in its Goals and Philosophy Statement reads:

> To promote the human and civil rights of people in and out of psychiatric treatment situations, with special attention to their absolute right to freedom of choice. To work towards the end of involuntary psychiatric intervention, including civil commitment and forced procedures such as electroshock, psychosurgery, forced drugging, restraint and seclusion, holding that such intervention against one's will is not a form of treatment, but a violation of liberty and the right to control one's own body and mind. We emphasize freedom of choice for people wanting to receive psychiatric services through true informed consent to treatment which includes the right to refuse any unwanted treatments. We will also work to assure the rights of all people who have been psychiatrically labeled including but not limited to people in halfway houses, day treatment, residential facilities, vocational rehabilitation, nursing homes, psycho-social rehabilitation clubs as well as psychiatric institutions. (NAPS, no date, p. 1)

This is the essence of "mental patients'" liberation. NAPS was formed specifically to counter the trend toward reformist "consumerism," which developed as the psychiatric establishment began to fund ex-patient self-help. Ironically, the same developments which led to the movement's growth and to the operation of increasing numbers of ex-patient-run alternative programs, also weakened the radical voices within the movement and promoted the views of far more cooperative "consumers." The very term "consumer" implies an equality of power which simply does not exist; mental health "consumers" are still subject to involuntary commitment and treatment, and the defining of their experience by others.

It is not surprising that once the Community Support Program at NIMH began funding "consumer" conferences, the International Conference on Human Rights and Psychiatric Oppression disbanded. The first CSP-funded conference, "Alternatives '85," was held in Baltimore in June, 1985; the last International Conference in Burlington, Vermont, in August of that year. The dissolution was aided by a group of "consumers" who may have seen the liberation perspective as a threat. At the same time, some extreme radicals opposed any form of organization as oppressive, believing that a totally decentralized and unstructured movement could accomplish its goals.

Madness Network News disintegrated the next year. Its all-volunteer staff became exhausted by the effort of putting out the newspaper with no funds but member subscriptions, and they were succeeded by a very small group of extreme radicals who published only one issue—critical of anyone attempting to develop organizational structure or sources of funding for movement activities. The paper then ceased publication, leaving a gap in movement communication that went unfilled for several years. Although *Dendron,* a newsletter published by the Clearinghouse on Human Rights and Psychiatry in Eugene, Oregon, began publishing shortly thereafter, only recently has it become as visible within the movement as had been *Madness Network News.*

Where the Movement Stands Now

At present, many groups exist that claim to speak "for" patients, that is, to be patients' advocates. Even the American Psychiatric Association claims this role, as does the National Alliance for the Mentally Ill (NAMI), a group primarily composed of relatives of patients, which enthusiastically embraces the medical model and promotes the expansion of involuntary commitment and the lifetime control of people labeled "mentally ill." However, a basic liberation principle is that people must speak for themselves.

Former patients recognize numerous currents of opinion within their community (which, after all, numbers in the millions). There are groups whose members promote the illness metaphor (e.g., National Depressive and Manic-Depressive Association); groups whose members pro-

mote self-help in conjunction with treatment for illness (e.g., Recovery, Inc.); groups whose members see themselves as consumers (e.g., the National Mental Health Consumers' Association); and groups whose members see themselves as liberationists (e.g., National Association of Psychiatric Survivors). However, it is safe to say that by far the largest number of patients and ex-patients are those who identify with none of these organizations—indeed most patients and ex-patients have probably never even heard of these groups.

The movement continues to face formidable obstacles. The psychiatric/medical model of "mental illness" is widely accepted by the general public. Indeed, new psychiatric "illnesses" are being "discovered" all the time, and psychiatry now claims that social deviants—from rapists to repetitive gamblers—are suffering from a variety of newly defined "mental illnesses." Psychiatry is entrenched, as well, in the courts, the prisons, the schools, and all major institutions of society.

At the same time, there are many hopeful signs for the movement. The ex-patients' movement is developing alliances with the physically disabled, with the poor, and with ex-patients in other countries. Physically disabled people have organized their own self-help programs, using the model of independent living. According to the principles of independent living, any person—no matter how physically disabled he or she may be—can live independently if provided with the proper supports. Such supports must be individualized—a person may need special equipment, personal care attendants, modified transportation vehicles, and so forth. The particular mix of supports is determined by the individual, in consultation with an independent living specialist (who is also a physically disabled person). As the disability rights movement has grown, it has become a powerful force for legal change as well. For more than 10 years, this movement has lobbied in favor of the Americans with Disabilities Act, the so-called civil rights bill for the disabled. The bill was signed into law on July 26, 1990. Although the ex-patients' movement entered that struggle late, the final version of the Act does include persons with "psychiatric disabilities" under its protections.

Linkages of the ex-patients' movement with the impoverished include efforts at affordable housing, campaigns for universal medical insurance, and involvement in the Rainbow Coalition. It has proved extremely useful for ex-patient activists to become involved in these activities—not only do ex-patients require the services being advocated but demystification in the eyes of one's allies can serve an invaluable purpose. When labeled as "mentally ill"—a nameless, faceless person—the "mental patient" may be seen as the enemy; as a co-worker and a colleague, facing the same problems and struggling for the same solutions, the ex-patient becomes an individual: knowable and understandable.

The growing internationalization of the ex-patients' movement is another sign of the movement's growth and strength. As groups exchange newsletters, and attend meetings and conferences, a shared ideology is developing. Although the lack of a solidifying terminology continues to be troubling, such variety does not necessarily indicate wide variations in viewpoints and activities. Whether group members call themselves clients, consumers, ex-patients, users, or psychiatric survivors, groups throughout the world are united by the goals of self-determination and full citizenship rights for their members.

It is true that the vast majority of former patients remain unorganized, but this challenge is being met. As groups become more visible, they recruit more members. This occurs because ex-patient groups speak to a truth of the patienthood experience: that people's anger and frustration are real and valid, and that only by speaking out can individuals who have been harmed by the entrenched power of psychiatry mount a challenge against it.

References

Appelbaum, D. (1988). The right to refuse treatment with antipsychotic drugs: Retrospect and prospect. *American Journal of Psychiatry, 145,* 413-419.

Beers, C. (1953). *A mind that found itself.* Garden City, New York: Doubleday.

Chamberlin, J. (1979). *On our own: Patient-controlled alternatives to the mental health system.* New York: McGraw-Hill.

Chamberlin, J. (1987). The case for separatism. In I. Barker and E. Peck (Eds.), *Power in strange places* (pp. 24-26). London, England: Good Practices in Mental Health.

Chamberlin, J., Rogers, J.A. & Sneed, C.S. (1989). Consumers, families, and community support systems. *Psychosocial Rehabilitation Journal, 12,* 93-106.

Dain, N. (1989). Critics and dissenters: Reflections on 'anti-psychiatry' in the United States. *Journal of the History of the Behavioral Sciences, 25,* 3-25.

National Association of Psychiatric Survivors. (No date). *Goals and philosophy statement.* Unpublished manuscript.

Report to the President for the President's Commission on Mental Health. (1978). Volume 1. Washington D.C.: United States Government Printing Office.

Riese v. St. Mary's Hospital, 209 Cal. App. 3rd, 1303, 1987.

Rivers v. Katz, 67 N.Y., 2nd, 485, 1986.

Rogers v. Commissioner of Mental Health, 390 Mass. 498, 1982.

Szasz, T. (1961). *The myth of mental illness.* New York: Hoeber-Harper.

Szasz, T. (1970). *The manufacture of madness.* New York: Dell.

Szasz, T. (1989, July). The myth of the rights of mental patients. *Liberty,* pp. 19-26.

Professional Training for Consumers and Family Members: One Road to Empowerment

Robert I. Paulson

ROBERT I. PAULSON, PH.D., WAS PROFESSOR AND FORMER DIRECTOR, SPECIALIZED MENTAL HEALTH TRAINING PROGRAM, SCHOOL OF SOCIAL WORK, UNIVERSITY OF CINCINNATI, CINCINNATI, OHIO. HE IS CURRENTLY PROFESSOR AND DIRECTOR, SOCIAL WORK RESEARCH DEVELOPMENT CENTER, GRADUATE SCHOOL OF SOCIAL WORK, PORTLAND STATE UNIVERSITY, PORTLAND, OREGON.

THE AUTHOR WOULD LIKE TO ACKNOWLEDGE THE ASSISTANCE OF DR. JOYCE BORKIN, CO-DIRECTOR OF THE SMHTP, IN THE IMPLEMENTATION OF THE PROGRAM.

THIS ARTICLE ORIGINALLY APPEARED IN THE *Psychosocial Rehabilitation Journal*, 1991, 14(3), 69-80.

This article describes the experience of an innovative MSW Specialized Mental Health Training Program in training consumers and family members as mental health professionals to work with persons with major mental illness and their families. The paper focuses on the issues and problems in successfully integrating consumers and family members into traditional academic programs and mental health settings. The unique contributions of consumers and family members as mental health professionals as well as the methods employed in securing the participation of family and consumer groups in the program planning, design, and implementation are presented.

Introduction

The professional training of consumers and family members is somewhat controversial. Clearly, professional training is just one of many options which should be available to consumers to enrich their lives and fulfill their wishes and potential.

There is also a caveat to recognize, which is the very real danger that in becoming professionals, consumers and family members risk co-optation, or loss of some skill and sensitivity which make them effective as natural helpers.

Nonetheless, the doors to professional training should remain open to consumers and family members. The reality is that all too often professional programs have a negative bias against consumers and family members. The programs deliberately attempt to exclude them, or to "socialize" them out of their consumer perspectives. It is critical that professional training programs are sensitive to these issues and utilize consumer experiences as strengths, to be preserved and reinforced.

Furthermore, the argument put forth is that the special strengths and perspectives that consumers and family members possess is of vital importance to the mental health professions. Indisputably, the perspectives of consumers and family members enhance the learning of other professional colleagues. Specifically, for consumers who entertain this route, professional status can provide additional legitimacy to bring about positive changes in mental health service delivery.

These caveats notwithstanding, professional training must be available to those consumers and family members who choose to exercise this option. Mental health professional training programs, which are designed to train professionals to work with persons who have long-term mental illness, must incorporate these special concerns, attributes, and abilities. This article describes one such program, The Specialized Mental Health Training Program (SMHTP) at the University of Cincinnati School of Social Work.

The SMHTP, which trains social workers to work with persons with major mental illness, has completed its third year of implementation. It is the only social work program of its kind in Ohio, and one of only ten nationally, that are funded by the National Institute of Mental Health (NIMH). Two student cohorts have graduated from the program. There were two mental health consumers in the first year and two family members. In the second graduating year there was one consumer and one family member.

This program is unique in recruiting primary consumers and family members as students. Of the first year graduating class, both consumers are employed as case managers, one of the family members is employed in an inpatient setting, and the second was employed as director of a day treatment program. The consumer and family member who have most recently graduated have both been offered jobs working with persons with major mental illness in well-established agencies.

This paper will discuss the broad involvement of families and consumers in the SMHTP, but will focus primarily on issues related to training family members and consumers for roles as mental health professionals. The decision to recruit family members and consumers was based on the strong philosophical belief that training consumers and family members as mental health professionals would facilitate their empowerment. Important questions have been raised based on such a philosophy and experience. For example, has the experience so far supported this initial belief? Is there a down-side to this approach? What are the special considerations that academic programs must address in providing professional training to consumers and family members? How have the consumers and family members viewed their training experience? These are some of the pertinent questions that will be addressed in this paper. To place these questions in context, a brief description of the SMHTP is necessary.

The SMHTP consists of a number of additions to the regular MSW program in the School of Social Work. The SMHTP students participate in a specialized field placement experience, a lecture series, and four specialized courses that replace the regular elective options. In the first year, student placements are in an inpatient setting, and, in the second year, a variety of community support system agencies comprise the placement sites. The lecture series provides beginning exposure to the three major areas of psychiatric rehabilitation, symptom management including psychopharmacology and non-medical alternatives, and community support programs with an emphasis on case management and assertive community treatment. The four specialized courses are Introduction to the Characteristics and Treatment of Persons with Major Mental Illness and their Families, Psychiatric Rehabilitation, Community Support Programs and Assertive Community Treatment, and Strategies for Working with Families and Consumers.

Philosophically, the program design incorporates the basic tenets and beliefs that are inherent in the community support program (CSP) framework (Stroul, 1986), assertive community treatment (Stein & Test, 1985), and psychiatric rehabilitation approaches (Anthony; Anthony, Cohen & Cohen, 1984). Of the 12 principles incorporated into the SMHTP curriculum design (Paulson, 1990), three directly relate to consumer and family member involvement in the caregiving process. These principles include:

1. Consumer and family involvement is essential in treatment planning and service delivery. A collaborative approach enables the wishes and needs of the consumer and family member to be seriously and respectfully addressed.

2. Programs should be responsive to consumer needs rather than forcing consumers to conform to existing program structures.

3. Programs based on continuum designs, which traditionally are practitioner-driven, should be replaced with consumer-driven choices such as supported work and housing.

Family and Consumer Involvement in the Program

This philosophy was implemented with the development of the SMHTP. Building relationships with family members and consumers has been a major effort from the initial stages of the program design and process, and these relationships continue as an important and essential presence. The program design was shared with the board of directors of the local Alliance for the Mentally Ill (AMI) group and the executive director of AMI of Ohio. The president of the WE CARE Network, which is the state consumer caucus, and the coordinator of the National Consumer Caucus, which was held in Cincinnati in 1987, were also asked to review the initial program design. Their input led to substantive changes which were incorporated into both the Ohio Department of Mental Health (ODMH) and NIMH grant proposals.

The grant proposals were also shared with these consumers and family members, and, upon funding, an advisory committee was formed which included key mental health professionals, consumers and family members. This committee met throughout the initial year, and was incorporated into the advisory committee of the Multidisciplinary Training Program Consortium (MTPC) when the SMHTP became a participant in the multidisciplinary project.

As part of the MTPC, an Importance Rating Sheet of potential content areas was administered to staff members of local agencies, state associations, and members of local family and consumer groups asking them to rank the content areas in terms of perceived importance. Interviews were also conducted with local consumer and AMI groups and with a special group of mental health professionals who were also consumers, to elicit their views regarding the knowledge and skills needed by mental health professionals to work with persons with major mental illness.

Consumers and family members are regularly invited as presenters early in the academic year for the lecture series, and for some of the regular classes as well. This year a family member taught the course on "Strategies for Working with Families and Consumers." Students also attend major events such as state-wide meetings of primary and secondary consumers, and where appropriate, programs and meetings of local consumer and family groups. Interaction with family groups is considered to be an important aspect of field placement experiences.

Consumers and Family Members as Students

Because of the historical unresponsiveness of professional schools to the needs of this population, the SMHTP has taken the unique step of recruiting consumers and family members as students in the program. Their involvement has served to "keep the program honest," and has fulfilled a philosophical commitment to train qualified consumers and family members for whom the program was appropriate. Leaders in the consumer movement across the state were contacted directly or referred by ODMH, which assisted with recruitment for the program. Family members were recruited through direct contact at local AMI chapter meetings.

The decision to include primary consumers and family members as students was considered very seriously. There was a clear realization that such an effort would require added resources. Some of the issues which surfaced during implementation were anticipated, others were not. Some of the issues apply to both consumers and family members while others are exclusive to only consumers, or family members. The training issues which relate to consumers and family members will be discussed first.

Reliving the Past/Returning to Old Haunts

The participation of consumers and family members posed some particularly sensitive situations with respect to field placements. As expected, placement in a public inpatient setting could be particularly provocative and disturbing to a person or a family member who had prior negative experiences in such settings. On the one hand, the purpose of the dual hospital-community placement model was to provide an understanding of how the hospital and community systems operate. Unless the student was to be involved in a purely administrative capacity, it would be important to learn to function as a direct service provider in these settings. For example, consumers were particularly vulnerable to feelings of rage when placed in these settings, which they successfully learned to control and channel in constructive ways. This was an important issue that required a case-by-case consideration, particularly in relation to consumers.

In or Out of the Closet

A more subtle issue results with students who are not known in the community as mental health consumers, and have not chosen to openly identify themselves as con-

Consumer/ professionals are likely to be more accurate and comprehensive in educating consumers about the side effects of medication and to help the client sort out which symptoms are related to the illness, and which to the effects of medication.

sumers. While family members might be reluctant to share the fact that they have an ill family member, this is more problematic with respect to consumers themselves. Where students do not wish to identify themselves, it presents certain difficulties and challenges. For example, the behaviors that may result from the illness may alienate colleagues. Sensitizing students to this person's needs and building a support system for the consumer/student is a much greater challenge when the issues cannot be openly discussed.

Great care must be taken to protect the anonymity of the consumer's status while working with other students and to be supportive and responsive to the strengths of mental health consumers in general and that of their consumer/ colleague in particular. In those situations where students sense unusual reactions and behaviors, which they find confusing, potential tensions can be created in the group. These issues are more difficult to resolve than those in which the consumer status is known. Nonetheless, in some ways this provides the ultimate test of the program's ability to transmit to students an appreciation and respect for the consumer or family member's need/right to maintain the confidentiality of his or her status. This also presents an excellent, although challenging, opportunity to develop the skills and attitudes of the other students to support persons with a major mental illness.

In some situations, where the consumer

prefers not to be identified, the program is faced with the responsibility of protecting the confidentiality of the student and at the same time sharing potentially important information with a field agency. The question to be dealt with is what are the liabilities of the program regarding occurrences related to the student's psychiatric condition. On the surface the answers may appear simple, but legally and ethically they become extremely complicated and at times leave the program on the horns of a dilemma. It should be noted that this dilemma is no different from those that may arise when students with many other potentially serious chronic diseases such as diabetes or epilepsy are present. The program's current response is to discuss the situation thoroughly with the student and negotiate an agreement regarding what will be shared with the placement agency.

A similar dilemma occurs upon graduation when the consumer/professional wishes a reference. The program cannot totally ignore the student's illness and maintain its credibility with the prospective employer. At the same time, one cannot violate the student's confidentiality. Furthermore, unless one knows the attitude of the interviewer toward consumer/professionals, the program would certainly want to avoid biasing the agency against the consumer's candidacy. In these cases it seems that the best solution is to be straightforward regarding the person's abilities, including a discussion of development needs around non-illness related issues while encouraging the consumer to share pertinent information related to the illness. The training program must explore with the student how much and under what circumstances information should be shared about the student in order to protect the student's opportunities and respect the agency's requirement for certain information.

Professional Roles

One of the reasons for training consumers and family members as mental health professionals is the belief that their special experiences with mental illness will result in bringing special sensitivities and competencies to their professional roles. However, these experiences can simultaneously present difficulties and disadvantages. The training program needs to be responsive to these issues in order to develop these students' special potential in a positive way. Considerably more support and supervision were necessary to enable these students to sort out their own agendas, past experiences, and mixed feelings about working in the system in a professional capacity.

To the extent that these students have been active in advocacy roles, special attention is needed to help them integrate their advocacy styles into their professional roles. They need to learn new techniques and strategies that will be equally effective but also acceptable to their employers and colleagues. For example, as president of the statewide consumer network, one student had been accustomed to contacting top policy makers by telephone, including the Director of the Ohio Department of Mental Health, regarding problems and issues. Helping the student realize that this approach as an employee of an agency would not be permissible proved to be a difficult task to accomplish.

To assume that consumers and family members will adopt the same professional roles as other students is to deny both the strengths and disadvantages of their experience with mental illness. Considerably more experience is required with consumer and family member/professionals to systematically delineate the strengths and limitations so that they can be used to develop new and modify existing professional roles.

This raises the more general issue of the responsibility of the program to help define meaningful roles for consumers who are students without altering the requirements of the MSW program. Certainly, there was no problem with the intellectual capacity of any of the consumers. However, issues of appropriate role behavior in direct practice contexts were more generally the problem. Finding meaningful administrative and planning roles for these students, which would build on their strengths and allow them to make contributions in a new role is a goal the program still struggles with. The problem is exacerbated by the fact that in the first year of program implementation, both of the students who were consumers were known in the community as consumer advocates. At times, it was difficult to sort out the extent to which stigma or the tendency of agency personnel to react to these students in their prior consumer roles contributed to some of the problems they experienced. Interestingly, in light of this discussion, the first two consumer-students successfully graduated and are working as case managers.

What are the particular strengths that consumers and family members can bring to their professional roles? Dr. Frederick Frese, a consumer/professional, talks about the difficulties of introducing "chronically normal persons" (CNPs) into the world of persons with major mental illness where the belief structures are radically different from those of the CNP. Thus, a person who has experienced a major mental illness has a common basis for communication and is better able to teach the mentally ill person how to move toward the normal world (Frese, 1990).

The strengths that a consumer/professional bring to his or her practice are numerous. A former consumer is much more likely to appreciate, for example, what would be most helpful in a crisis situation, as in "talking down" a person who is extremely agitated or suicidal. Such finely honed sensitivity could mean the difference in preventing a hospitalization. A potential danger, however, is that the consumer/professional may fail to fully appreciate the diversity of experiences of persons with major mental illness and the individuality of a person's response. They could be trapped by their own unique experience and what "worked for them," without fully considering how another person's needs might differ.

Unfortunately for many persons with major mental illness, a considerable portion of their energies must be devoted to surviving the circumstances caused by poverty, as well as those which result from the mental illness. In some situations they are minimally assisted with their financial needs when low pay, low prestige, and limited training and experience are the requirements for the case managers who work with consumers. Case managers are frequently young and relatively inexperienced in "survival skills." To the extent that a former consumer has become "street smart" in accessing community resources, they can be extremely helpful in transmitting this knowledge to others. While case managers are likely to be knowledgeable about the formal system and formal ways of accessing it, it is the informal tricks of the trade which are likely to be most helpful to a consumer who is struggling to survive in economically depressed circumstances.

Another area where former consumers have a distinct advantage is in the area of medication compliance, which is a major issue for mental health service systems. Former consumers are much more credible and persuasive with their peers than professionals who have not shared the experience of serious mental illness. Having undergone the experience, consumer/professionals are likely to be more accurate and comprehensive in educating consumers about the side effects of medication and to help the client sort out which symptoms are related to the illness, and which to the effects of medication. It is probable that the testimony of a former consumer regarding the consequences of discontinuing medication will be more persuasive than recommendations from non-consumer/professionals whose cautions can be seen as moralizing.

In addition, consumer/professionals are likely to be more skilled at helping clients identify their personal idiosyncratic prodromal signs and the circumstances which are most likely to exacerbate their symptoms. Similarly, these professionals should be more effective at helping clients determine non-psychopharmacological methods of controlling symptoms to supplement medication, or to substitute for it, in those cases where clients are unresponsive or unreceptive to medication.

With respect to family members who become professionals there is a greater likelihood of understanding the stresses and strains placed on families, which should aid in the building of rapport. As professionals, family members should be particularly effective in psychoeducational efforts since their own experience will prepare them for the questions family members have, and will generate practical solutions to everyday problems. Family member professionals should also be especially effective in encouraging family members to share their feelings about their ill family member, drawing on personal experiences as models.

Family members can also be particularly adept at advocacy, in evaluating alternative service opportunities and accessing existing

This learning and experience was encouraged by changing the standard teacher-student roles into a more collegial relationship in which students were actively engaged in program problem solving and consultation with faculty on an ongoing basis.

resources. Designing protocols with the consumer and family around recognizing prodromal signs and developing a plan of action when these signs occur should also be an area where family member/professionals would have a particular advantage. These are all skills that can be articulated and developed with other family members.

It is important in both cases, however, that professionals who also happen to be consumers or family members do not become the "specialists" for certain tasks or jobs, such as conducting psychoeducational programs for families. It is imperative that these professionals perform the full range of professional roles.

The special needs of consumer/professionals are likely to be in such areas as additional supports, maintaining appropriate boundaries, and separating personal agendas from those of the client. Family members might encounter role confusion when working in the same mental health system where their ill family member receives care. In some circumstances these professionals might be required to act as advocates for their family members and, thus, to confront professionals with whom they prefer to maintain positive collegial relationships in their professional roles. It is not clear to what extent mental health systems are willing to respond to consumer and family member/professionals in the same way as with other professional colleagues. Nor is it certain at this point that family and consumer professionals will receive the credibility necessary to fulfill their professional responsibilities. In many instances it can be expected that other professionals will respond in a stereotyped or stigmatizing fashion, as if they were relating to these new professionals in consumer/family member roles.

One partial remedy for addressing the problems of defining future work roles, would be to develop a specific career planning process for all incoming students. While it might be of special importance to consumers and family members, it would be helpful to all students, particularly in terms of sorting out interests in direct practice, supervision, or administration. At the outset students could be helped to clarify realistic roles for themselves, given their individual interests, talents, and experience, within the framework of the training provided by the program.

Recruitment and Retention of Students

The newness of the program and the lack of awareness of its existence has contributed to the problems that consumers and family members face. Until the program is well known, special recruitment efforts will be required to interest consumers and family members. The active recruitment of consumers assumes that the program faculty have a particular obligation to assist these students to succeed without compromising program structure or requirements. These dilemmas, in fact, are similar to those associated with affirmative action programs of the past. The extent to which consumers enter the program through the normal route may influence the ease with which they can be approached like all other students in terms of expectations, while ongoing supports are built for their special needs.

In the future, the program intends to distribute announcements of the program to major national consumer organizations and the national, state, and local AMI newsletters as a recruitment strategy, which one would hope will expand the network of supports and develop a community-university partnership to increase successful training experiences.

It has already been noted that consumers and family members will probably require additional support. This additional support was, in part, provided by a strategy to maintain enthusiasm among the SMHTP students in general. Maintaining a high level of interest in the program was given a high priority in light of the special demands and expectations that were placed on students. A great deal of energy went into developing a team spirit among them. The expected outcome was the reduction of burnout and the enhancement of learning from one another. This process also provided important modeling that could be related to the functioning of effective case management teams. This learning and experience was encouraged by changing the standard teacher-student roles into a more collegial relationship in which students were actively engaged in program problem solving and consultation with faculty on an ongoing basis. One hour of the weekly lecture series was devoted to problem solving, group processing, and sharing information and concerns. These programmatic activities were augmented by regular social events between students and faculty, which strengthened the cohesiveness. This process also served to build a commitment to the philosophy of community support and a realistic view of the rewards and demands that are inherent in this work.

These efforts were highly successful in several ways. The group as a whole became a very closely knit support system. Ironically, given the prevailing perceptions regarding this work, the SMHTP students came to be considered as an elite group within the School of Social Work. There was some jealousy of the richness of their learning and mutual support. The program's existence has spread by word of mouth; consequently, recruitment has become easier each year as students and graduates recruit friends and colleagues.

The students who were consumers and family members became well integrated into the total group. Their involvement provided an unanticipated positive consequence. For example, as incidents occurred with consumers and family members (i.e., the child of a student family member was ejected from a halfway house and returned home during an acute psychiatric episode), students developed a special empathy, reacting to the situations as friends and colleagues, and not as detached "professionals." These experiences introduced students to the realities of long term mental illness beyond the learning that takes place in the field and through academic work.

However, an important point to acknowledge from the faculty perspective is that the development of the students into a cohesive team proved to be considerably more time consuming than originally anticipated. Nonetheless, in retrospect the effort has proved to be one of the most critical contributions to the program's success.

Special Supports for Consumers

It was only after the program began that it was learned that the stress of an academic program exceeds that of a job for many persons with major mental illness (Knoedler, 1988). In recruiting consumers, a key variable which was considered to be an indicator of ability to succeed in the SMHTP was successful work history. Clearly, in light of this new information, this was probably not the best indicator of the ability to handle the stresses of a graduate program. In addition, it is relevant to note that in several cases, students had to relocate. In these circumstances they were faced with the additional trauma of moving and the task of creating a new support system. It has become obvious that in the future there is a

need for an even greater exploration with consumer applicants of the stresses that are likely to be faced, and the probable supports that will be needed.

One problem in providing additional supports has been the limitations on funding for faculty time which has precluded the development of longer term extensive supports. Two strategies to overcome these gaps are the greater use of the University's Office of Handicapped Services of the University and the development of the SMHTP as a supported employment site. Currently the Office of Handicapped Services mainly concerns itself with physical disabilities and has not given any thought to assisting students with psychiatric and emotional disabilities. A great deal of education is needed by this office with respect to the needs of this population as well as the legal obligation to provide services to persons with psychiatric disabilities as a recognized disabled group. The idea of the use of supported employment in the SMHTP as a vehicle for providing supports came from one of our consumer/students who worked on a supported employment project as part of a field placement experience. It was noted that supported employment is rarely considered for jobs requiring higher levels of intellectual functioning. Many consumers have college or graduate degrees and can perform at high intellectual levels, but require the supports to manage some of the interpersonal aspects of work situations, or assistance in developing ways to mitigate their symptomatology. Otherwise, frequently they are unable to maintain such jobs.

All of our consumer/students could have made considerably better personal progress if they had had the support of a job coach during their field placement to ease the transition into new professional roles. Since students can qualify for supported employment under current Ohio regulations, the SMHTP intends to explore the possibility of treating the internship experience as a supported employment site. One would hope that this support could continue, if needed, in the initial phases of the consumer's professional career upon graduation. The student/consumer mentioned above managed to secure a job coach during the last weeks of the SMHTP and will be using this job coach in the newly acquired employment. This approach presents some exciting new opportunities for the SMHTP in providing additional supports for consumers and in expanding the professional opportunities for them.

Conclusion

Training consumers and family members to take their place as mental health professionals has not been without its difficulties. However, these problems have been clearly minimized by the success of the graduates. These students have been successful in "keeping the program honest" and in sensitizing both fellow students and faculty to the issues and needs of consumers and family members. They have also made substantive contributions to the program's content and design. While it is too soon to tell whether those who have graduated will be particularly effective in bringing about systemic improvements in the care of persons with major mental illness, certainly there has been no indication that their illness-related experiences have led to insurmountable problems. Those who have graduated have been enjoying their new roles as professionals. To this extent, at least, the SMHTP has succeeded in empowering consumers and family members, and has more than justified the effort required to recruit and retain these students in the program. It is expected that through the lessons learned from these early experiences, the SMHTP will enable consumers and family members to become even more effective in their professional roles in the future.

References

Anthony, W. (1979). *Principles of psychiatric rehabilitation.* Baltimore, MD: University Park Press.

Anthony, W., Cohen, M. R. & Cohen, B. F (1984). Psychiatric rehabilitation. In J. A. Talbott, (Ed.) *The chronic mental patient: Five years later,* pp. 137-158. New York: Grune & Stratton.

Frese, F J. (1990). *Response to incorporating the consumer's contribution to clinical training.* Proceedings of the national forum for educating mental health professionals to work with the seriously mentally ill and their families. Washington, D.C.: NIMH.

Knoedler, W. (1988). *The PACT program.* Paper presented at the meeting of the Collaboration Network, Cincinnati, Ohio.

Paulson, R. (1990). *Educating social workers to work with long-term seriously mentally ill persons and their families.* Proceedings of the national forum for educating mental health professionals to work with the seriously mentally ill and their families. Washington, D.C.: NIMH.

Stein, L. & Test, M. (Eds.) (1985). The training in community living model: A decade of experience. *New Directions for Mental Health Services Series #26.* San Francisco: Jossey-Bass.

Stroul, B. A. (1986). *Models of community support services.* Boston: Center for Psychiatric Rehabilitation.

POWER, POWERLESSNESS, AND EMPOWERMENT IN PSYCHOTHERAPY

John E . Mack

JOHN E. MACK, MD, IS PROFESSOR OF PSYCHIATRY IN THE DEPARTMENT OF PSYCHIATRY AT THE CAMBRIDGE HOSPITAL, HARVARD MEDICAL SCHOOL.

THIS ARTICLE ORIGINALLY APPEARED IN
Psychiatry, 1994, 57, 178-198
AND IS REPRINTED WITH PERMISSION.

The Captain: If the child is not mine, then I have no authority over her, and I don't want any. And that is exactly what you are aiming at! Isn't it? But perhaps you are reaching for still more—for something else, perhaps? You want the child in your power, and at the same time, have me support you. Laura. In my power, yes.... What has all this struggle of life and death been for, if not for power?

—Strindberg (1960), "The Father," Act II

Psychiatrists and other mental health professionals are working increasingly with diverse patient populations for whom the basic disorder may be less the result of internal conflict than of overwhelming or disturbing events or circumstances in the outside world. As a result, we are needing to reexamine our theories and models of psychotherapy. This paper is an attempt to contribute to this process. Many of the clinical conditions that psychiatrists and allied professionals are encountering now in both inpatient and ambulatory settings might be understood as the result of inequalities or abuse of power in relationships and an accompanying sense of powerlessness and helplessness. Appropriate therapeutic strategies to deal with these imbalances will differ from those that have been derived from psychoanalytic or psychodynamic principles developed with socioeconomically more advantaged populations in which inner conflict and conflict resolution have been stressed.

The feeling of possessing some form of personal power, the sense that one is to a degree the creator of one's own life, is essential to the sense of self. A comparison of Buddhist and psychoanalytic theories of the self suggests that power, or agency (the word *agency*, interestingly, also applies to organizations or institutions that govern our lives from outside the self) may be the most central aspect of the self (Aranow, 1989). Conversely, the experience of being overwhelmed or helpless may threaten or fragment the sense of self, leading to fears of dissolution or death.

The perspective offered here grows out of more than 35 years of experience in practicing, supervising, and teaching psychotherapy and developing mental health services with ethnically and socioeconomically diverse populations in a variety of clinical settings. These have included several inpatient and outpatient services, emergency wards, day treatment centers, a tertiary care Air Force Hospital in Japan, neighborhood clinics, services for children and families, court clinics and prisons, drug and alcohol treatment units, and facilities for the care of the chronically mentally ill. The diversity itself has helped to highlight for me the importance of power and powerlessness in human functioning and distress. In particular, I have been deeply impressed with the centrality of abuse or inequalities of power inside and outside of the treatment context as a source of human emotional disturbance and the special value of processes of enabling or empowerment in psychotherapy.

Inequalities of Power Relations

The inequalities of power relations can assume a number of forms and may take place between or among a variety of elements of personality, individuals, groups, and institutions. To some degree, clinical conditions may be defined by the nature of the inequality and the entities or agencies involved. For example, cases of childhood sexual trauma or physical abuse are expressions of unequal power relations among individuals, especially between a child and an adult, whereas the disturbing syndromes of people in oppressive organizations, or living in societies currently or formerly under colonial rule (the condition of *nervios,* for instance—Guarnaccia and Farias, 1988; Farias, 1989), reflect the abuses of power experienced by individuals in an oppressive social system. The following are categories of inequality or differences of power relations and a few of their accompanying clinical conditions that we frequently encounter in various treatment settings.

Unequal Power Between or Among Individuals

Interindividual inequality is exemplified in cases of traumatic abuse or in the troubled relationships of couples, especially where one member tyrannizes over the other, or among members of families. Many of the devices we adults deplore in ourselves and in children—such as lying, secrecy, and deception—are originally developed, individually and in groups, to redress a real or perceived inequality in the balance of power.

Disturbing Experiences of Individuals in Relation to Groups, Institutions, and Social and Political Forces

Individuals feel powerless before these forces. This would apply to women in a male-dominated society, the disorders of refugee populations, the distresses of minority groups, the victims of political tyranny, and to some degree the poor in all societies. Kleinman (1988) describes situations "where severe, economic, political and health problems create endemic feelings of

hopelessness and helplessness, where demoralization and despair are responses to actual conditions of chronic deprivation and persistent loss, where powerlessness is not a cognitive distortion but an accurate mapping of one's place in an oppressive social system, and where moral, religious, and political configurations of such problems have coherence for the local population but psychiatric categories do not" (p. 15). One of the most disturbing aspects of being hospitalized for medical or psychiatric reasons is the loss of the sense of agency, power, and autonomy.

Inequality Between the Individual and Chemical Substances

An example is alcohol, in relation to which the person feels powerless. Alcoholics Anonymous (AA) and other self-help groups that are based on the AA model recognize the centrality of the powerlessness of the individual in their therapeutic strategies (AA, *Twelve Steps, and Twelve Traditions,* 1977). A 35-year-old woman, for example, overcompensated her impulse to gorge food by self-starvation and attended OA (Overeaters Anonymous) in order to master her problem. She found the group's emphasis on discovering a higher power to be empowering, which to her meant the supportive context of the group itself and the capacity to be aware of her impulses, to observe them and gain distance and perspective, but not to act. The value of psychoactive medications in addressing the biological basis of major mental illness cannot, of course, be subsumed in the model offered here. At the same time, the psychopharmacological correction of chemical imbalance in the brain is by its very nature empowering, permitting the strengths of the personality to emerge.

Inequality Between Self and Psyche

Powerlessness or helplessness may be experienced in the relationship of the self to various forces or agencies of the psyche such as in relation to particular drives (impulse disorders of sexual deviations), an overly punitive superego (as in traditional psychoneuroses), or too exalted an ego ideal (reactive depressions). The experience of diminished functional capacity, as occurs in aging, of losing one's "powers," is likely to be particularly troubling. An 89-year-old woman who had struggled bravely and effectively with the relentless progression of her blindness remarked, "To give up power and control drives people nuts."

Reality-Related Inequality

Finally, the experience of helplessness may occur in relation to reality events or the demands of reality itself, overwhelming the ego and leading to intense pain, regression, personality fragmentation, and/or psychosis. A 22-year-old woman, for example, who had been hospitalized for the second time for an acute psychosis with delusions, became overwhelmingly distressed when her therapist went on vacation. She cried, could not sleep, shouted uncontrollably, and felt like a powerless victim. In her words, "I felt like I was in a war and they had all the weapons." Paranoid patients who become litigious, mobilizing the legal system on their behalf, do so because they feel so vulnerable and powerless to petition or negotiate for themselves in a world they experience as unjust and threatening.

The Centrality of Power

Power is one of those bridging words, like *self,* that enable us to create theoretical linkages between the person and the group, or the individual and society. At the same time, however, because of its wide scope, it is important that we be clear about how the word is being used. Power is central in nature and in human life. The sense that we have some power or effectiveness in the world, that our voices are heard, or that, at

least to a degree, we are in charge of our lives or can influence or otherwise have an impact on our surroundings or other people, is tied intimately to how we feel about ourselves. The feeling of relative personal power or powerlessness is thus closely linked with the vicissitudes of self-esteem. Institutions recognize this and use slogans for their employees like "you make a difference" in signs and company newsletters in order to maintain morale. An Advertising Council message for a teacher's association intones, "reach for the power—teach." Conversely, the feeling of powerlessness or helplessness is among the most distressing of human experiences and can, in its extreme form, become intolerable. The decision to commit suicide may occur when a person feels powerless to affect a deeply troubling life situation and sees no possibility that the circumstances can be changed.

Barbara Tuchman (1989), in an interview shortly before she died, predicted that for future historians "a sense of loss of control" will be seen to have characterized our age:

> People no longer feel that they can control their destiny, or their country's destiny, and there's bewilderment over where it's all going. For one thing, the mechanical developments in the world —the computers and so on—are beyond the average person's influence or understanding, and they're all going to have effects which the average person doesn't feel he can have any effect on. I think it bewilders people and makes them feel helpless.

To some extent our models of psychotherapy have presupposed, if not an "average expectable environment," at least a social structure and global context that offers a degree of stability or foreseeable constancy in the surrounding social and physical environment. When these fundamentals cannot be assumed, and the very fabric of social and physical existence, individual and collective, is disintegrating or threatened, all of us—patients and care-givers—are forced to address existential matters, what Erik Erikson calls "ultimate concerns" (Zock, 1990). These include basic values, choice, life, death, birth, responsibility, the nature of spirituality or God, and so forth (Kluckhohn, 1956; Lee, 1956). Power and helplessness relate closely to these ultimate matters, which may be one reason why they seem so important to consider at this time. The shared milieu of uncertainty, together with the increasing diversity of our patient populations and the frequent cultural distance between therapists and patients, makes it important to examine fully the philosophical common ground or differences of worldview between us and our patients.

Primary and Secondary Power

We use the word *power* in two quite different but related ways. I will use the terms *primary* and *secondary* power to distinguish these usages. All power derives, ultimately, from the energy sources in nature. But the expressions of primary power have retained a closer connection with these energies, reflect a harmony with them rather than an effort to control nature or others for specific purposes. Primary power is similar to what the earliest Taoist sages, Lao Tzu and Chuang Tzu, called the intelligence of nature, "that penetrating and pervading power to restore all things to their original harmony" (Heinberg 1989, p. 51). The Sioux Indian medicine man John (Fire) Lame Deer, describes primary power eloquently (Lame Deer & Erdoes, 1979):

> The Great Spirit pours a great, unimaginable amount of force into all things—pebbles, ants, leaves, whirlwinds, whatever you will. Still there is so much force left over that's not used up, that is in his gift to bestow, that has to be used wisely and in moderation if we are given some of it....all animals have power, because the Great

Spirit dwells in all of them, even a tiny ant, a butterfly, a tree, a flower, a rock. The modern white man's way keeps that power from us, dilutes it. To come to nature, feel its power, let it help you, one needs time and patience for that. Time to think, to figure it all out. You have so little time for contemplation; it's always rush, rush, rush with you. (pp. 103 & 106)

In the "force" of mind, especially in the deepest levels of the unconscious, we may discover the linkages between the human spirit or psychical energy and the primary power inherent in nature. Peoples of the earth have given different names to this basic psychical energy or power. The Dakota Indians called it *wakanda,* while the Iroquois called it *obi* and the Algonquins *inanity.* The Melanesian concept of *mana* is similar, as is Nietzsche's *will to power* (Nietzsche 1968—which is discussed later in this article), or the Hindu idea of *kundalini energy.* A classic definition of wakanda is the perception of "a universally extended, invisible, but usable and transferable life energy or universal power" (La Chapelle 1984, p. 73). Kundalini energy, which is sometimes confused with psychosis when its intensity is not understood, is experienced as a strong, vital flowing, beginning in the lower part of the body and streaming through the whole organism (Mookerjee, 1991). When the individual is prepared and does not feel terrified by its overwhelming power, this energy can be experienced as transcendent, taking the individual beyond the self, linking us to the higher forces of the universe.

What we call mystical experiences occur when there is a sense of oneness or harmony between the energy or power in our bodies, minds, and spirits and the energy of other beings and of the universe itself. This is the oceanic feeling that Freud wrote he had never experienced (Freud, 1930), perhaps because of the extreme overdevelopment in his psyche of the analytic or rational dimension.

The Freudian notion of libido relates to psychical energy but is narrower than what I mean by primary power. Jung's (1969) view of psychical energy or power is broader and closer to that of native peoples:

> The concept in question [mana, power, influence] really concerns the idea of "a diffused substance or energy upon the possession of which all exceptional power or ability or fecundity depends. The energy is, to be sure, terrible (under certain circumstances) and it is mysterious and incomprehensible; but it is so because it is vastly powerful.... (Lovejoy as quoted in Jung 1969, p.64).

Papajohn and Spiegel (1975) have shown how cultures may be characterized by the relationship which human beings experience to nature. In the United States, with our emphasis on the use of technology to solve all problems, "Man is expected to overcome the natural forces and harness them to his purpose." In Japanese and Navaho Indian societies, on the other hand, "Man's sense of wholeness is based on his continual communion with nature and with the supernatural" (Papajohn & Spiegel, 1975). In the words of the Lakota medicine man Black Elk, "Peace . . . comes within the souls of men when they realize their relationship, their oneness, with the Universe and all its powers (Heinberg, 1989, p. 37).

Secondary power is different. It is the use of force or will to dominate, coerce, or control nature or others in the service of particular purposes or desires, sometimes with highly destructive results, whether intended or not. This is the quality that Lame Deer laments in our culture, the inability to be with or let things be (Lame Deer & Erdoes 1979):

> There was great power in a wolf, even in a coyote. You have made him into a freak —a toy poodle, a Pekingese, a lap dog. You can't do much with a cat, which is like an Indian, unchangeable. So you fix it, alter it, declaw it, even cut its vocal cords so you can experiment on it in a laboratory without being disturbed by its cries. (p.109)

Psychoanalyst Hans Loewald (1978) connects what I call secondary power to conscious or secondary process thinking:

> Conscious forms of mentation are primarily—at least so it appears—responsible for our success and achievement, our domination of the forces of nature, our control over others and over ourselves. (p 69)

The extreme development of reason, intellect, and will at the expense of other human faculties such as openness, love, and intuition has helped us to master the material world and its resources, as reflected in much of our science and technology. But the effort to dominate and control nature, including one another, has contributed to the ecological and military crises that humankind now confronts.

John McPhee, in his book *The Control of Nature* (1989), describes three titanic battles waged by human beings against the forces of nature—the control of the direction of the Mississippi River, arresting a lava flow in Iceland, and blocking the erosion of the San Gabriel mountains above Los Angeles all for the purpose of protecting human settlements and interests. With each "victory" over nature came a loss, a high price in both ecological and human terms:

> Even in something as primal as a volcanic eruption, the component of human interference could apparently enter the narrative and, in complex and unpredictable geometries, alter the shape of succeeding events. After the human contribution passed a level higher than trifling, the evolution of the new landscape could in no pure sense be natural. The event had lost its status as a simple act of God. In making war with nature, there was risk of loss in winning. (p. 143)

Feminist social critic and novelist Carolyn Heilbrun (1988) captures the distinction between primary and secondary power in human relationships. For her primary power is "true" power:

> The true representation of power is not of a big man beating a smaller man or a woman. Power is the ability to take one's place in whatever discourse is essential to action and the right to have one's part matter. This is true in the Pentagon, in marriage, in friendship, and in politics. (p.17)

Tom Wolfe, in his novel *The Bonfire of the Vanities* (1987), describes beautifully the emotions associated with power of the secondary kind through the words of a public prosecutor in the Bronx:

> For it was nothing less than the Power.... It was the power of the government over the freedom of its subjects. To think of it in the abstract made it seem so theoretical and academic, but to *feel* it—to see the *looks on their faces*—as they stare back at you, courier and conduit of the Power ...to see that *little swallow of fright* in a perfect neck worth millions—well, the poet has never sung of that ecstasy or even dreamed of it...and yet we *feel* it and we know it every time they look at us with those eyes that beg for mercy or if not mercy, Lord, dumb luck or capricious generosity. (p. 591)

Organizational or institutional life, especially politics (defined in one contemporary dictionary as "use of intrigue or strategy in obtaining any position of power or control, as in a business, university, etc.") (Random House, 1967, p. 1113), is the usual arena for exercising authority and power, especially of the secondary kind. For it is in politics that there is the maximum opportunity to control, dominate, coerce, or influence external events or large numbers of people more or less legitimately. It is in the national or international political arena, of course, that secondary-power-oriented individuals find their maximum leverage. It is here that there is the greatest chance to impact the world on a large scale, including the management of life and death itself for huge numbers of people. In this age of weaponry of mass destruction, perhaps the greatest danger the planet faces is from individuals who seek to redress personal vulnerabilities or wounds through the use of coercive power in the political arena. To cause physical or emotional pain in another is a timeless way to increase one's own power while reducing another's. For the personal injuries and power needs of such leaders may find a resonance in the personal and historic wounds of a people, who may follow them to the destruction of all. In the nuclear age a wounded leader and a wounded people, especially if connected to each other through a rigid ideology that excludes contradicting information, create a deadly combination.

Investigators of the dynamics of family and social systems, especially in the 1960s and 1970s, wrote of the importance of power in human relationships, although even the 1964 *Handbook of Marriage and the Family* (Burr et al., 1979) contained no reference to "power." Discussions of power in family or social systems—defined as the ability to achieve one's intended aims or influence others in the group—relate the term to issues of control, authority, expertise, intimacy, dominance, legitimacy, and available resources (Scanzoni, 1979). Difficulties of definition seem to have led to a reduced emphasis on power in more recent studies.

Power in Psychotherapy

With but a few exceptions (Frank, 1986; Greenblatt, 1986; Horner, 1989; Heller, 1985; Person, 1988), psychoanalysis and psychodynamic psychiatry have been slow to appreciate the fundamental importance of power in human development and relationships, and in the genesis of psychopathology. We have not, therefore, evolved a body of theory and a system of therapeutic strategies that place power and powerlessness, and the methods and means of empowerment, at the forefront of our discipline. Cross-cultural studies of mental illness, and the recognition of the disempowering residua of colonialism for the peoples of developing nations, are beginning to change this perspective.

Guarnaccia and Farias's (1988) study of the syndrome of *nervios* among Central American refugees living in the United States demonstrates, as the authors themselves contend, the centrality of "issues of power, and of powerlessness" in the susceptibility to physical and emotional illness (p. 1223). The authors describe the case of "Sra. Fuentes," a 35-year-old Salvadoran woman who had come to the United States 9 years before to escape the warfare in her country. The symptoms of her illness, which were quite typical of the syndrome and which she herself called "nervios," included headaches, pain in the eyes, pain in her chest "like it is going to choke me," and "pains all over my body" (Guarnaccia & Farias, 1988, p. 1226). Questions aimed at discovering what Sra. Fuentes believed was affecting her illness revealed many social problems and personal stresses, past and present. These included the dislocation and uprooting from her homeland, family members, and support network in El Salvador; memories of the violence, killings, and losses of those she had left behind; concerns about her husband's alcoholism (she married in the United States and had an 8-year-old son) and worries about her extended family here; dissatisfaction with her factory job, where she packed boxes, felt she was underpaid, and had less control of her work than in El Salvador; verbal fighting with her boss and with other Latino workers; and the experience of exploitation and racism.

Although *nervios* was experienced by Sra. Fuentes and others in the body and expressed in somatic symptoms, the illness had several levels of meaning. Her sickness was the result of stresses at the interpersonal and familial levels and, especially, of social, economic, and political forces. An understanding of her experience of relative powerlessness before these forces is fundamental to any full appreciation of Sra. Fuentes' condition and of many others in similar situations. In a more recent study of Guatemalan refugees Farias (1989) writes of "communal powerlessness," in which the "self, as internal agent, [becomes] associated with the sociocultural milieu." Both Salvadoran and Guatemalan refugees have been reduced by violence and the destruction of their cultural and social systems "to a status of powerlessness that generates a sense of individual helplessness in the search for meaning. These circumstances define the limits of biomedical explanations and classifications and force us to relocate the analysis in the perspective of social exploitation and cultural annihilation, rather than individual systems of response to the environment" (p. 16). A few dynamically oriented clinicians have begun to consider questions of power in psychotherapeutic theory and practice. Althea Horner (1989) has considered the role of an individual's "intrinsic power" and its expres-

The feeling of possessing some form of personal power, the sense that one is to a degree the creator of one's own life, is essential to the sense of self.

sion in creativity and basic well-being. "Power," as one of her patients said, "is the ability to control your own state of emotional well-being" (p. 36).

AA and other self-help groups that have developed along the lines of the AA model recognize and apply an understanding of power and its centrality in human psychological functioning. This approach is both psychological and spiritual. In the emphasis on acceptance of powerlessness over alcohol (or whatever the compelling addicting substance or addictive behavior pattern may be), the AA model addresses the egoism of secondary power and the false sense of independent or autonomous control that are its most important manifestations. The invitation to acknowledge helplessness and make "a decision to turn our will and our lives over to the care of God as we understand Him" (AA 1977, p. 35) creates the possibility of a shift from a failed application of secondary power to participation in the experience of power of the primary kind.

The distinction between primary and secondary power helps to explain the paradox of gaining power and mastery while surrendering power to a greater source. For it is secondary power and its associated egoism that is lost, while primary power, a sharing in the power that is immanent in nature, is gained. As expressed in Taoist belief, "When there is no need to have power or gain credit, when there is no fear that we will lose our power and therefore cling to it, when we can be totally quiet...we have all the power we need" (Horner, 1989, p. 7).

The attachment to control can be seen in the alcoholic's insistence in the face of evidence to the contrary that he or she can still manage the addiction. As one 62-year-old woman described her state when she knew she must no longer use alcohol to fulfill her emotional and spiritual needs, "I wept all day, for the world as I knew it had ended and I was terrified. Was there anything on the other side?"

Another source of our potential understanding of the place of power in the clinical setting is the political process itself. Groups that are seeking to bring about social change, especially the issue-oriented citizen groups that adapt Gandhian principles of nonviolence (sometimes called "affinity groups"), have recognized the importance of creating a sense of personal empowerment among the group members. Small and large groups, not excluding AA, are particularly susceptible to the abuse of power for complex reasons that include the aggregation of power in the group, the subjection of individuals to the group will or interest, and the fulfillment of personal power needs on the part of leaders and others in the group.

Therapeutic or human growth-related groups, some of which derive from Eastern religious principles and have been influenced by the feminist movement, have also helped to introduce ideas about power and empowerment into the world of dynamic psychotherapy. The insights and analysis of Buddhist teacher Joanna Macy (1988), and of clinicians such as Jean Baker Miller (1982), Jan Surrey (1987), and Sarah Conn (1990) have been important in focusing our attention upon the centrality of empowerment through relationship in psychotherapy. The emphasis of this work is on enabling people to connect with one another, to discover their inner power or the healing power of intimacy, and the creation of new notions of community. According to Carolyn Heilbrun (1988), "The women's movement began, in fact, with discussions of power, powerlessness, and the question of sexual politics. But investigations into the qualities of womanliness have moved away from the point where male power must be analyzed and seen only in relation to female powerlessness" (p. 17).

The Neglect of Power in the History of Psychoanalysis

The failure of the psychotherapeutic community to come to terms fully with the centrality of power and powerlessness in our work may relate to the lingering influence of the early discoveries and theoretical models of psychoanalysis, from which most of our present-day psychotherapies derive. We may also be reluctant to face the social, economic, and political implications of power inequalities and abuses, including those that occur within the health care professions.

There are important differences between the clinical and societal worlds of Freud's time and the realities facing contemporary psychotherapists here and in other countries that make it easier for us to address more directly issues of power, empowerment, and abuse of power. First, Freud and his early followers were dealing—at least they thought they were—with a patient population that was, by and large, intact from the standpoint of basic ego functioning and family and community stability. This is most often not the case in our contemporary work. Second, as the explorations of the human unconscious proceeded, and exciting discoveries were emerging about the inner life, the primary interest and focus of psychoanalysts was upon intrapsychic forces, especially fantasies and dreams, and upon the analysis of internal conflict. An emphasis upon the external environment or reality has been a relatively late development in our field (Rapaport 1987). Third, early discoveries about the importance of repressed sexuality in the etiology of neuroses, and fear of the return of the repressed in the unwelcome form of an erotized transference or attachment, have made us slow to discover the potential range and therapeutic power of the nonerotized, supportive, and warm treatment relationship. Finally, the early realization of the degree to which patients invested their analysts with feelings, needs, and wishes deriving from personal historical experiences led to an emphasis on transference at the expense of a full appreciation of the transformative power of the actual therapeutic relationship. As long as inequalities of power in the client-therapist relationship are regarded primarily as transference phenomena, or as an unmodifiable dimension of the therapeutic situation, it is difficult to consider the meaning they may have in their own right. The avoidance of questions of power and powerlessness in our field may be attributed, at least in part, to the personality of Freud himself and the circumstances of his life. In *The Interpretation of Dreams* Freud recalls that his father told him when he was "ten or twelve years old" that when he was a young man he went for a walk "in the streets of your birthplace; I was well dressed, and had a new fur cap on my head. A Christian came up to me and with a single blow knocked off my cap into the mud and shouted: 'Jew! get off the pavement!'" "And what did you do?" the boy asked. "I went into the roadway and picked up my cap" was the father's "quiet reply." The scene struck the young Freud as "unheroic conduct on the part of the big, strong man who was holding the little boy by the hand." Freud contrasted this situation "with another which fitted my feelings better: the scene in which Hannibal's father, Hamilcar Barca, made his boy swear before the household altar to take vengeance on the Romans" (Freud, 1900, Vol. IV, p. 197).

The recall of this incident occurred in association to a dream of Freud's that expressed his desire to meet his friend Fliess in Rome instead of in Prague. For Rome, in turn—which Freud, like Hannibal, had yet to reach—was associated with the "Semitic" (Masson, 1985) Carthaginian general, "the favorite hero of my later school days." The identification with Hannibal captured the power and frustration associated with Freud's political ambitions. His wish, like Hannibal's to "go to Rome," had "become in my dream-life a cloak and symbol for a number of other passionate wishes" (Freud, 1900, Vol. IV, p. 196). The anti-Semitism of the Vienna of Freud's time made it seem unlikely that he would ever directly satisfy the political desires and ambitions reflected in these passages. Unable, like Hannibal, to "reach Rome," he would turn instead to "studying the unconscious" (Masson, 1985, p. 285). He would go the politicians one better and explore their and our inner drives and motivations. Quoting Virgil, he later remarked, "If I cannot bend the Higher Powers, I will move the Infernal Regions" (Freud, 1900, p. 608). Yet the example of personal and political impotence provided by Freud's father must have lingered painfully below the surface for him. There is perhaps no experience for a latency age or pubescent boy more threatening to his sense of his own power than to see his father humiliated before his eyes, whether in the outside world or by the mother within the household itself.

Carl Schorske, in his *Fin de Siecle Vienna* (1979), has shown how uneasy Freud remained about his unfulfilled political wishes, how he fled from acknowledging ambition and the desire for political power. In the interpretations of his own dreams that have clear political content Freud avoids these meanings. Complex and powerful political dramas are reduced to the conflict between fathers and sons. In Schorske's (1979) words, "Patricide

Connecting with others, or the formation of alliances, is a universal strategy that human beings use to overcome the experience of powerlessness or aloneness.

replaces regicide; psychoanalysis overcomes history. Politics is neutralized by a counter political psychology" (p. 197). And, "By reducing his own political past and present to an epiphenomenal status in relation to the primal conflict between father and son, Freud gave his fellow liberals an a-historical theory of man and society that could make bearable a political world spun out of orbit and beyond control" (p. 203).

Further evidence of Freud's avoidance of the centrality of power motivations in human psychology can be seen in his resistance to Nietzche's writings. Although he credited Nietzche with anticipating some of his own discoveries, such as the effects of repression on memory, Freud did not, or could not, stay with Nietzche's texts. He was attracted to Nietzche's writing in his student days and spent a good deal of money on his collected works in 1900, the year of Nietzche's death, but Freud, as Peter Gay (1988) notes, "treated Nietzche's writings as texts to be resisted far more than to be studied" (p. 45).

There are many reasons scattered through Freud's writings for his resistance to Nietzche, including "an excess of interest" (Nunberg & Federn, 1962, p. 359), and "the deliberate object of not being hampered" by "any sort of anticipatory ideas" (Freud, 1900, Vol. IV, pp. 15–16). But we are never quite told what it is in Nietzche's ideas that Freud is avoiding. My own suggestions on this point, therefore, are offered somewhat tentatively. In his notebooks for the years 1883–1888, gathered together as *The Will to Power,*

Nietzsche (1968) makes it clear that he regards power as central in nature and in human life. "There is nothing to life that has value," he wrote, "except the degree of power assuming that life itself is the will to power" (p. 37). Though not always precise about his meaning, for Nietzsche "will to power" meant something like the seeking of a higher, more creative, more powerful state of being, above the "herd" level. Human beings, he argued, will settle for cruder expressions of power when we cannot have or discover anything better.

In his own writings, Freud rejects Adler's emphasis on the "will to power" in the development of character and the neuroses as it "robbed sexuality of its importance and put the desire for power in its place" (Freud, 1925, p. 253). But elsewhere he seems in spite of himself to accept the centrality of power by incorporating the idea of a "will to power" in his theory of the sexual and aggressive instincts. In 1917, for example, he called "The force by which the sexual instinct is represented in the mind…something analogous to hunger, the will to power, and so on…" (Freud, 1917, p. 137); and several years later when he was working on the problem of aggression, Freud wrote that when the libido directs its energies "through the muscular apparatus towards objects in the outside world…. The instinct is then called the destructive instinct, the instinct for mastery, or the will to power" (Freud, 1924, p. 163). Freud never, however, examines power as a distinct motivational system.

One further thought concerning Freud's resistance to Nietzsche's ideas, offered more speculatively, relates to the radical nature of Nietzsche's philosophical and social enterprise. Freud, as Paul Roazen (1988) has argued, "set out, in the spirit of Nietzsche, to transform Western values" (p. 486). But the universe of Freud, as a cultured physician, was orderly, conforming to the evolving empirical science of his time, whose discov- eries offered possibilities of human better- ment. Similarly, as a bourgeois progressive Freud sought to reduce human suffering by applying his clinical discoveries to the acquisition of greater human freedom, espe- cially through sexual liberation. But Nietzsche's universe is something else, "a monster of forces without beginning, with- out end…a sea of forces flowing and rush- ing together, eternally changing" (Nietzsche, 1968, p. 550), mysterious, beyond good and evil, simultaneously destructive and cre- ative. His cosmos is Dionysian, defined as "an urge to unity, a reaching beyond per- sonality, the every day, society, reality, across the abyss of transitoriness: a passion- ate-painful overflowing into darker, fuller, more floating states; an ecstatic affirmation of the total character of life as that which remains the same… the eternal will to pro- creation, to truthfulness, to recurrence; the feeling of the necessary unity of creation and destruction" (Nietzsche, 1968, p. 539).

Power, or the will to power, is the expres- sion of cosmic energy in life, and man's pas- sions, inchoate, lawless, and difficult to confine within a materialistic scientific par- adigm, are also expressions of this primal energy. "The essential thing in the life process," Nietzsche (1968) wrote, "is pre- cisely the tremendous shaping, form-creat- ing force which *utilizes* and *exploits* 'exter- nal circumstances'" (p. 344). Nietzsche's "monster of energy" or "form-creating force" is more powerfully transforming, imprecise, threatening, and difficult to apply clinically than Freud's orderly, better- behaved sexual and destructive instincts. Yet we are coming to recognize in this post- Holocaust world of nuclear threat and cata- strophe that we are living in a universe that we experience now as perhaps more Nietzchean than Freudian, driven by the cycles of birth, death, and creation; formed more by power in its multiple incarnations than by any strictly demarcated human motivations.

A story told by Professor Henry Murray at Harvard suggests that Freud had, indeed, once considered more broadly the role of power in human psychology. During a 2-hour conversation in Vienna in 1926, Murray asked Freud how he could have put forth "such a puerile theory of human motivation," that is, one based so predominantly upon sexuality. Freud is said to have replied that Murray was "absolutely right." When he started, he said, he had defined three principle motivating forces sexuality, power, and aggression but he had come under such attack for his sexual theory that he was forced to defend it and did not get to the others (Goethals, 1988). Actually, Freud did explore the role of aggression in the later part of his life, but he never came to terms with power.

As indicated in this story, power may be considered as a desire or drive, a motivational force like sexuality or aggression. But power in the sense of agency or capability is supraordinate to our other desires, providing a necessary context for their fulfillment. Without a sense of personal power, experienced as confidence, self-assurance, optimism, a willingness to risk, determination, high intention, and so forth, in combination with a minimum of requisite skills, we experience our desires as painfully unattainable.

Sexuality, when combined with love, requires the temporary surrender of power in the service of connection and intimacy. But sexuality is often used by both men and women more in the service of power especially to hold on to, manipulate, exploit, control, or compete with others than for the fulfillment of desire or the expression of love. Scheidlinger (1989), in his work with inner-city boys in the Bronx, noted, for example, that in their search for power and self-esteem they brag of how many girls they have "knocked-up." A 61-year-old woman told me frankly that although for a number of psychological and physiological reasons she did not wish to have sexual relations with the man she cared most about, she thought strategically that she ought to go to bed with him lest he leave her in favor of a more willing partner. John Updike (1986), in his novel *Roger's Version,* captures the way sexuality may be used in order to experience a sense of personal power. Dale, noting a diminution in the ardor of his married mistress, "receives a glimmer, through his mental picture of their love play, of the possibility that women are stirred to such feats of love by the sensation of their own power, by the joy of power, and that having proved their power lessens their interest" (p. 320).

For us, the psychological professionals who have inherited the Freudian edifice, we have been given, and perhaps too willingly received, a psychology that tends to avoid politics and power, that is more bearable for us personally perhaps but does not contribute effectively to matters of power and powerlessness as they occur within and around us and our patients, and in the larger sociopolitical environment. But as theologian Glenn Tinder (1989) has written, "In its depths the life of an individual is historical and political because it is one with the lives of all human beings" (p. 85). We, in identification with Freud and his legacy, seem to have largely eschewed the political meanings that we daily confront in our patients and the larger society. Perhaps we have taken in his frustration and impotence, allowing his resistance to become our own. But whereas for Freud the realities of hierarchical, Roman Catholic, anti-Semitic Vienna made the possibilities that might follow from political commitment quite limited, we have no such excuse. The resistances to political change and the pain associated with social depredations are real for us. But the avenues available for effecting change, though involving great effort and difficulty, are far greater now than in Freud's Vienna.

Power From a Developmental Perspective

As we consider the place of power and powerlessness in our clinical work, it becomes useful to rethink infant and child development from this point of view. When we think of the situation of a newborn or small infant we readily appreciate that there is a profound discrepancy between the strength of a baby's drives and needs and its power to get what it wants. After emerging from its time in the womb when all requirements were met, a small baby enters the world in a genuinely helpless and vulnerable state, dependent on others to fulfill its basic needs. It is from this central reality, and the strategies evolved by a developing human being to deal with it, that much of our life-long preoccupation with power and powerlessness derives.

Many years ago in a paper titled "The Power of the Newborn," Erik and Joan Erikson identified the intense, mysterious feelings that a helpless newborn can inspire in its parents and others. "The baby's genuine weakness exerts a spiritual power over those around him" (Erikson & Erikson 1953, p. 2), they wrote, and "our newborns...are able to move us with mere whimpers and ever so faint smiles and even to cause crises among the strongest of us, forcing us all to be for a little while more helpfully human" (p.4). Born with an inherent but limited repertoire of strategies to enthrall its caregivers, including at first primarily cuteness, helplessness, and loud vocalization of its distress, the baby refines its capacities to charm and invite its caregivers, what the Eriksons call "his native powers of seduction." This built-in dynamic may contain the roots of our later susceptibility to enchantments and blandishments that promise to recreate the paradise, partly real and partly imagined, of intrauterine life and early parent-infant oneness.

At each stage of our lives, beginning in infancy, boys and girls, men and women, develop strategies to achieve a sense of connectedness and power in the world in relation to other people and the tasks we choose or are demanded of us. Above all, we develop skills, strengths, and defenses to avoid a repetition of the experiences of terror and pain associated with helplessness and unmet need that have occurred, beginning in infancy, with varying intensity throughout our existence. We also know that shaming and humiliating a child can cripple the development of a sense of power or agency, increasing the sense of being small, vulnerable, and weak.

According to infant researcher Daniel Stern (1985), the baby develops what he calls the "sense of a core self" in the period between 2 and 6 months of age. This includes a sense of coherence, of continuity, of affectivity, and, of special importance for our considerations here, *a sense of agency,* or of authorship and initiation of action. For the rest of the child's life this sense of agency, the antecedent of the experience of personal power, will be strengthened or weakened, reinforced or damaged, in accordance with the native gifts and acquired skills available to the individual and his or her effectiveness in applying these resources in relationships with other people and in the achievement of his or her aims. Among these skills (it is difficult to distinguish inborn from acquired capabilities as the reciprocity here is so profound) are included the continuing capacity for making positive connections with other people in a mutually satisfying way and what we varyingly call the will, self-assertiveness, or personal strength.

Each stage of development has its characteristic challenges and inherent limitations and vulnerabilities. In earliest infancy we begin to learn the limits of our powers, especially our inability to prevent those we love, and on whom we must depend, from leaving us, or from wounding us emotionally and in some cases physically. The sense of primary power that finds its expression in a reciprocity with others, or a loving harmony and wondrous connection with nature, will inevitably be found insufficient in the struggle to fulfill our wishes and secure our needs. We will be wounded and frustrated throughout our lives and thus lose confidence in the possibilities of primary power (see Schmookler, 1988, *Out of Weakness*). Secondary power tactics of manipulation, domination, aggression, control, and the possession of things and people begin to develop in infancy and may become the principal means of achieving our ends and avoiding the fear and pain associated with helplessness and loss. We know how bossy and tyrannical very young children can become when they have determined this is the only way to be heard or to get their way. One mother described her 21-month-old boy, who was frustrated with her comings and goings, sitting at her desk, calmly, "like an executive, looking at a book." He seemed to be in charge of the situation, giving orders, "asserting his power."

Power, Alliance Formation, Groups, and Politics

The people who come to us as patients are those who, at least to some degree, have accepted their limitations, or have recognized the wounds they have received in the struggle to express a sense of agency or power in the world of play, work, and human relationships. But there are certain strategies, fundamental to human life and essential for achieving a sense of power in the world, that may or may not bring people to the attention of clinicians, even when they appear to be failing in their purpose or destructive from the standpoint of others.

Connecting with others, or the formation of alliances, is a universal strategy that human beings use to overcome the experience of powerlessness or aloneness. This process is really more than a strategy, for it derives from the deepest level of our being, what or who we are as social organisms. The connection of the fetus with the mother *in utero,* and the experience of oneness in the bonding of a baby at the breast, are the *anlages* of later experiences of bonding or linking with others in pairs and larger groups. The conscious and unconscious recognition, beginning in infancy, that we are relatively powerless and vulnerable when isolated from other human beings, provides the basis for a linkage of the intrapsychic and the interpersonal, the individual, and the group. A sense of personal power can hardly exist in isolation from others. The formation of affiances to increase the experience of personal power is the basis of politics and explains why we are all, of necessity, political creatures. Among our various selves are the group or political selves (Kohut, 1978; Scheidlinger, 1990), that is, the self-in-connection for the augmentation of personal power and selfworth.

It is not yet established at what age an infant grasps that it must form alliances or linkages with the larger beings around it — its parents, other adults, and older siblings—in order to feel safe or protected. Stern (1988) implies that something like this kind of awareness begins in the first 6 months in the capacity of the baby to use affects of joy, interest, surprise, and anger "to 'play off'…many different persons in a number of contexts" (p. 18). By the beginning of the second year the baby comes to realize its relative weakness and smallness in the world, and becomes adept at forming alliances within the family, playing one member off against another, sometimes with diabolical skill. Intrafamilial alliances are continuously shifting and reforming as the power, self-esteem, and other needs of the individuals and family group change in relation to each other and the outside world.

Family alliances represent the prototype for later connectedness in group formations as varied as boys' or girls' clubs, youth organizations like the Scouts or the Nazi youth groups, self-help groups, neighborhood action committees, armies, churches, schools and academic departments, political organizations, corporations, not-for-profit foundations, and finally, nations and international organizations. Participation in one or another such group, in conjunction with the empowerment or enabling experienced through loving connections with other individuals that complete the sense of self, constitutes the principal device that human beings use to overcome their fundamental aloneness, vulnerability, and perpetual helplessness. We must belong to groups in order to live as full human beings, and this membership has intrapsychic as well as interpersonal significance. As Saul Scheidlinger (1990), one of our outstanding theorists of group psychodynamics, has shown, both gratifying and stressful group experiences are as subject to the internalization and externalization processes of the psyche as are dyadic relational encounters.

Although the types of groups in which we may participate are legion, there are characteristics they appear to share that relate to the group's function in ensuring a sense of personal power, security, and well-being. These characteristics are generally perceived to relate to the group's purpose in the world, while the psychological functions that the group fulfills for its members tend to be overlooked. Among these characteristics are the stress upon loyalty to the group itself; the group's, and especially the leader's, legitimacy; the tendency for alliances within the group or organization to shift (often obviously related to the power interests of individual members); the reluctance of individuals to use imagination or to challenge basic assumptions within the group lest this threaten membership (the fear of standing out); the tendency of individuals to fuse with or surrender identity to or within the group as in mass psychological movements; and finally, the desire of many groups to ally themselves with a higher or divine purpose or vision in order to enhance their value and power, both in the world and for its members.

The experience of personal power of individuals within a group, including, of course, its leaders, is greatly enhanced if the body or organization believes itself to be fulfilling an important, legitimate purpose on earth or in the community, especially if that purpose is believed to derive from God, a divine vision, or a higher social order. Once again the example of AA is instructive, as the psychological support of the group itself and the reference to a higher power are both instrumental in enabling alcoholics to give up their drinking through empowering the self's choosing capability (Khantzian & Mack, 1989; Mack, 1981).

George Klein (1976) was one of the foremost psychoanalytic theorists to consider the central importance of human affiliative needs, that "identity must always be defined as having aspects of both separateness and membership in a more encompassing entity" (p. 179). Certain human groups, such as nations and religious organizations, seem especially constructed to offset universal disturbing human emotions, such as loneliness, terror, and a sense of helplessness and vulnerability, which are the outgrowth of our mortality and the isolation and aloneness we experience in our daily lives. By claiming to connect themselves with a transcendent or divine purpose, such groups provide one of the principal vehicles through which frightened and vulnerable individuals may, by membership and identification, derive a sense of power and security. Nationalism in particular, the belief in the special destiny of one's own ethnonational group, has become one of the principal means through which frightened, wounded, or disenfranchised peoples gain a sense of personal identity, self-worth, and power. But at the same time, as we have come to know so well, the combination of religious exaltation of the nation state (see O'Brien, 1988) with technologically sophisticated weapons of mass destruction has brought our planet near the brink of annihilation. For our tendency to polarize reality into dichotomies of good and evil, a characteristic of human consciousness whose roots are traceable to infancy if not to the cosmic ordeal of labor and birth itself (Grof, 1985), may find expression in ideologies of enmity through which we find high value primarily in our own national group and treat other groups as at least foreign if not wicked (Mack, 1990).

Toward a Therapy of Empowerment

As mental health professionals focus on questions of power and powerlessness in clinical work, our emphasis or purpose in psychotherapy will turn increasingly to empowerment and enabling, to the means of enhancing a sense of agency in the self. We are learning, like the wizard discovered in desperation in *The Wizard of Oz,* that our patients' powers reside within themselves or in their capacities for connection with others, and that the therapeutic task is to facilitate their emergence. We may argue that this is what we already try to do, and it is true that our work is empowering whenever through empathy or other means we reduce suffering. Yet I have been struck by the degree to which we sometimes impose our views and methods upon our patients, especially on inpatient units, in order to control them or to bring about behaviors more compatible with a comfortable treatment milieu. Often we sense that this is not therapeutically effective. As one PGY III resident noted, "The more I take control, the crazier things get."

We might begin this consideration of a psychotherapy of empowerment by looking at the therapeutic situation itself. Our patients often complain to us about the inequalities of power in the treatment relationship. This is particularly obvious in inpatient settings, where the surrender of patient rights and autonomy, the imposition of rules, and the taking over of agency by the staff are all too familiar. But even in the most sophisticated dynamic psychotherapies, or in psychoanalysis itself, issues of power and control in the therapeutic situation are often voiced by our patients and clients. Often these questions are approached in terms of the patient's historic conflicts or are examined as a manifestation of a transference problem. But I would argue that something different is called for, a distinguishing of the necessary inequalities of power that relate to the greater knowledge and skills that the therapist possesses from the realities of unequal power that are expressed in the hierarchical structure of the therapeutic setting. Some of these actualities, such as the greater anchoring of the treatment around the therapist's schedule, may be difficult to avoid due to the need/satisfaction urgencies of some of our patients and the way the mental health professions have been created. But even in these instances, the troubling nature of such actualities needs to be acknowledged and explained before being subjected to transference interpretation or the exploration of the meanings of power, helplessness, inequality, and related feelings in terms of the patient's historical experience. When this is not done, the exploration itself may lead to a following of orders, rules, and expectations, a repetition of unequal power dynamics. It is precisely because our patients come to us feeling needy, vulnerable, and disempowered that we need to be sensitive to the ways in which the therapeutic encounter itself may reinforce these currents.

One man, reflecting on his analysis late in the process, generalized about what he believed patients are seeking: "Longing for the light of his own power and self-sufficiency…is the single most encouraging manifestation of the patient's intact self, which the analyst [or therapist] can never afford to lose sight of…nor dishonor by merely labeling it 'resistance'." He described his own dependent feelings, a sense of helplessness, of "lying [like a defeated warrior] at the analyst's feet."

In order to enable our patients to repair their inner wounds, griefs, and experiences of injustice, we seek to enter actively into their private worlds in a manner that is attentive to and respectful of the subtle imbalances of power that are built into the structure of the relationship. We need to examine and challenge what psychoanalyst James McLaughlin (1991) calls the "assumed position of higher objectivity and uninvolvement." When we fail to do this, we may find that we unwittingly repeat historical experiences of hurt and injustice, and begin within the therapeutic setting a new cycle of pain, frustration, humiliation, and rage that it would be wrong to analyze as merely the patient's resistance.

As we explore more deeply the processes of empowerment in psychotherapy, it might be useful to return once again to the distinction between primary and secondary power. For much of the suffering that we encounter in our work grows out of the elaborate strategies we and our patients have devised throughout our lives to substitute secondary expressions of power for primary ones. These are behaviors and mechanisms that were designed to control or ward off our desires and impulses, and to dominate and manage other people, which we created initially to avoid the pain and frustration once or repeatedly encountered when we opened ourselves to others in a natural process of spontaneously reaching out to connect with other beings and nature but were met with misunderstanding, rejection, or not at all.

Basque anthropologist Angeles Arrien

(1989) has identified three aspects of power commonly distinguished in native cultures she has studied: the power of presence, the power of communication, and the power of position. I find this classification useful in considering the tasks of the therapist in the processes of empowerment. Each of these dimensions refers to what I am calling primary forms of power.

Presence refers to the person of the therapist, how he or she appears or is experienced by the patient, the spirit or feeling that emanates from the therapist and the climate or atmosphere created in the office. Psychoanalyst Milton Viederman (1991), in his paper "The Real Person of the Analyst and His Role in the Process of Psychoanalytic Cure," stresses the "powerful effect of the real person of the analyst" and begins his conclusion by placing "the real person of the analyst in center stage," focusing on "the analyst as a *presence* [author's italics!] in the psychoanalytic situation." This emphasis, at least until recently, has been unusual on the part of a classically educated training analyst.

Communication refers to how we listen and connect through our words, entering into the patient's world without imposing our own needs or points of view, appreciating what it means really to be heard. This can be an active process of engagement and dialogue, a bringing forth of new possibilities from within the other person out of the freedom and support created in the therapeutic conversation and interaction. Exploration, recognition, and acknowledgment of experiences of powerlessness and helplessness in the therapeutic relationship and in the patient's previous life can be especially valuable for enabling patients to discover their own power. This would mean a new respect for rage, especially outrage, as an emotion that reflects a healthy response to hurt and injustice, and a step beyond powerlessness on the way to potentially meaningful or effective change.

Position refers to who we are in society or the world. This is distinguished from presence by the emphasis on what we represent in the larger environment, apart from personality or mien. It is more than title, role, or status, that one is, for example, a psychiatrist or social worker. It refers also to the stand we take on a patient's or someone else's behalf, not only in the office but in the outside world. It may be foolish to think that our patients do not know about us, who we are in our lives outside of the consulting room. The empowerment process includes our patients' identification with the stand we take, the courage we demonstrate on their behalf or on social, political, and economic issues that directly or indirectly affect their lives. A group of patients in a community meeting at a metropolitan state hospital expressed fears for their security and complained to the staff that they were not helping them. Instead of merely interpreting these communications as reflective of the patients' needs, which only annoyed them further, it could have been helpful to acknowledge the disturbing reality of recent cuts in staff that threatened patient care, and to have allied with the patients to do something useful, if not courageous, about it. But as a senior resident who worked on the unit, and saw what was occurring, observed, "We are not trained to be active."

Before concluding this discussion of a psychotherapy of empowerment, it seems essential to speak of the place of the spiritual or sacred in our work. In the course of the 19th century, in the struggle of psychotherapy to find its professional and scientific place, or to distance itself from a historical association with the mystical or the spiritistic (Ellenberger, 1970), a distinction, and then a gulf, became established between the psyche and the spirit, the material and the sacred. Yet as George Bernard Shaw (1963) says in "Major Barbara" through the ironic words of his heroine's father, a munitions manufacturer, "I think all power is spiritual." Although considerable knowledge may have been gained about the unconscious and the mechanisms through which we avoid knowing or experiencing its depths, we have also, I believe, lost something vital for understanding and empowering our patients and even one another. I have in mind a respect for the spiritual forces and needs that are a universal part of the human experience, and an attitude toward our work that might be thought of as sacred.

By sacred I mean an attitude of awe or reverence in relation to nature, especially toward human nature, which partakes of its archetypal forms, and acknowledgment of the mysterious, unknown, and even unknowable elements of the psyche. Admitting a point beyond knowing seems to be empowering for both patient and therapist, perhaps by widening and deepening the context so that new possibilities, ideas, and resources may be discovered. Although there has been great value in the discovery of phenomena such as defenses, transference, and resistance, they are the observed phenomena of a psychological system that separates subject and object and may assume an artificial distance or disconnec-

> *We are learning...that our patients' powers reside within themselves or in their capacities for connection with others, and that the therapeutic task is to facilitate their emergence.*

tion between the self and the other. Much of the world's population expresses its emotional distress in the language of the spirit and religion. Psychiatrist Farias (1989), for example, in his work with Guatemalan Indian refugees notes that "Healing depended on the powers of nature and illness resulted from weakening of the spirit due to lack of contact with the holy places, their ancestors, and the community rituals" (p. 13). An attitude of awe and reverence toward the mystery and the dignity of every person can in itself enrich the healing process (Tinder, 1989).

The attitude of humility and unknowingness for which I am calling may not, at least in the short run, improve our professional status. This cannot be helped. But it may enable us in the long run to be stronger healers and more powerful therapists. I have often observed that when we suspend knowledge, and hold quietly for a time with our uncertainty, we may enter our patients' worlds directly, bypassing as it were the mechanisms of defense, which may themselves be to a degree conceptual artefacts, products of the distances we have created in outmoded habits and models of clinical learning. This kind of direct connecting, the outcome of trust and suspended belief, may be essential for allowing us to reach, in a mutually enhancing interaction (or what Buddhist teacher Thich Nhat Hanh calls "interbeing"), like music or humor do, the mysterious unheard places in the psyche that are the sources of our patients' power.

Discussion and Conclusions

Before concluding, I would observe again that our patients, perhaps to a greater degree in these times than ever before, are engaged in unequal struggles. They feel overwhelmed and disempowered, oppressed outside and inside of themselves by forces that they cannot control or manage. The work of psychotherapy might be thought of as contributing to the redressing of the balance in the patient's favor by enhancing the sense of personal agency or empowerment. For a limited number of well-functioning individuals the imbalance may be largely intrapsychic. These are the people who have traditionally been thought of as "good candidates" for psychoanalysis or long-term individual psychotherapy. But for most of the people we see this is not the case, even allowing that the caseloads of therapists are still heavily weighted toward middle and upper echelon patients. Rather, the majority of these individuals feel themselves to be relatively powerless, or victimized, unable in varying degrees to contend with the threatening, unjust, or oppressive interpersonal, social, economic, and political forces that beset them. Living within disrupted families and fragmented communities, they feel that they lack the resources—personal, social, and economic to deal with their feelings, needs, and impulses, and the requirements of daily life.

This indicates that to be useful as therapists it would be helpful to become more familiar with the social, cultural, and institutional worlds in which our patients live and work. The training of psychiatrists in particular does not focus adequately on these realities. Perhaps we have believed they are the domain of social workers, anthropologists, and other social scientists. When supervising child psychiatry fellows, for example, I have been struck by the degree to which they must learn to be "warriors" on behalf of the children they treat, sorting out complex family and social realities, identifying sources of trauma and abuse, advocating for the child or the family in meetings with various social agencies (that word *agency* again), sometimes testifying in court, while at the same time exploring the inner experience of the child or adolescent as its development proceeds in the context of all of these forces. Although adults may function more autonomously than children, identifying the intrafamilial, social, or communal realities within which their lives are embedded is an important part of the empowerment process.

The kind of active, sometimes affectionate, entering into our patients' worlds which I believe is essential for increasing, or restoring, a sense of agency—may raise the questions about appropriate boundaries, or the worries about seduction by therapists related to directly gratifying patients' needs and wishes, that are currently so prominent in our field. In my view, the intense, sometimes justified, concern about sexual seduction and abuse of power by therapists has created an unwarranted anxiety around issues of ordinary warmth, caring, and closeness between therapists and patients that is an essential dimension of the process of therapeutic growth and empowerment. The exaggerated focus on sexualization of the relationship may inhibit the many forms of simple contact, even in some instances simple expressions of physical affection, when appropriate, that are an important part of our therapeutic work. The most vital task, in my view, is to learn to establish the emotional distance or closeness called for by the requirements of the therapeutic work in a given instance. This is a complex matter, involving the subtleties of mutuality and connection between people about which we continue to learn throughout our personal and professional lives. Above all, we struggle to know our own vulnerabilities and egoistic needs so as not to impose these on our patients or clients.

The purpose of the forms of caring and giving that I am advocating here grow naturally from our response to listening to our patients' narratives when we are not too inhibited by fears or theoretical preconceptions and admonitions. As a trusting alliance develops, we may introduce into patients' lives, sometimes for the first time, the experience of being heard and understood. It is possible, of course, for a thera-

pist to be too giving, too generous emotionally, creating unrealistic desires for gratification and becoming disempowering by undercutting patients' capacity for assuming responsibility. The greater risk in my experience has been the opposite tendency—to repeat an original deprivation in a new context of deprivation in the therapeutic setting itself.

The therapeutic alliance, although empowering in itself through the process of listening and identifying historical wounds and traumas, injustices, sources of inhibition, losses, and impoverished relationships, is also a means to an end. For at the same time, unknown or unrecognized strengths and inner resources, especially the capacity to give and receive love, develop and are put into use to redress current grievances and injustices, and to forge new relationships. Sometimes therapists need to become active in developing strategies for addressing and changing the actual problems in the world that afflict patients' lives. These involve above all, the utilization of the example of the therapeutic relationship for extending the patient's capacity for affiliation and the formation of alliances.

Many patients tell us they do not participate much in groups, that they are not "group persons." But this too is a form of relational deprivation, particularly relevant to the problems of power and powerlessness. For as I have argued, the entering into group alliances is a central dimension of human empowerment. It is an inescapable aspect of our natures that we are social creatures whose experience of power, agency, and identity grows out of our participation in groups and communities of various sorts, even though we recognize that inequalities and abuses of power occur frequently in these settings. Conversely, as lone beings, or creatures limited to dyadic relationships, we are inevitably compromised in our power.

A striking example of empowerment through group alliance formation was told to me by an outstanding grass-roots organizer in the Piedmont district of rural North Carolina. Although not a psychotherapeutic situation per se, her work illustrates the principles I am setting forth here. Linda Stout brings disenfranchised and disempowered tenant farmers and textile workers into an organization that has successfully addressed the economic and political woes that have afflicted their lives. Power for the people she works with, Linda Stout says, comes from discovering what they are capable of within themselves, scoring victories by working together within an authentic community. She, in turn, is empowered by the results that she gets. "What keeps me going," Linda says, "is when I see someone get their personal power. Wow, that keeps me going!" Similarly, researcher Alan Kay (1989), while studying the attitudes of Americans on a variety of national security issues, found that simply participating in focus groups where their views were heard gave many individuals a sense of personal power they had never had before.

I do not wish to imply that we do not seek to have our patients discover their own contribution to the problems that surround them and take appropriate responsibility for their creation—the traditional work of insight oriented psychotherapy. But in my experience, if questions along those lines are asked, or the patients' role in their afflictions is interpreted before the therapist fully grasps and acknowledges the dimensions and sources of hurt, or has identified the circumstances under which troubled feelings developed, we run the risk of repeating the original pathogenic experiences, a kind of unwitting blaming the victim. Our patients, who have often been trained to be obedient, especially in relation to powerful figures like us upon whom they must depend, are likely to comply with this process. The result, however, will not be therapeutic.

Healing and empowerment, finally, for our patients as for ourselves, develops out of the connections we make with those places that are wounded and shut away in silence, expressed only in the strategies of distancing through which wounded creatures have always protected themselves. Through acknowledgement and alliance we help to restore a sense of agency out of which can grow, like a ripple effect, the affiliations with others that secure our personal power and the sense that we can, when alone, bear our pain, knowing that it will not be forever. Perhaps this is what we do, or believe we do. But often I see us imposing our theories or points of view, using hierarchically derived power to control patients and tolerating conditions in our institutions that repeat the economic and emotional deprivations that brought our patients to us in the first place. We have enabling power as both therapists and advocates. When we fail to recognize our power or do not use it on our patients' behalf, we run the risk of being perceived as yet another group of unhelpful or even hurtful agents in an often unjust and oppressive society.

References

Alcoholics Anonymous. (1977). *Twelve steps and twelve traditions.* Alcoholics Anonymous World Services, 15th Printing.

Aranow, P. (1989). *Is there a self: Psychoanalytic and buddhist views.* Grand Rounds Presentation at The Cambridge Hospital, Cambridge, MA, November 15.

Arrien, A. (1989). Presentation to Stanislav Grof Training Workshop on the Theory and Practice of Transpersonal Psychology. Pocket Ranch, Geyserville, CA, March 22.

Burr, W.R., Hill, R., Nye, I.F., and Reiss, I.L. (1979). *Contemporary theories about the family,* Vols. I and II. Free Press.

Conn, S. (1990). Protest and thrive: The relationship between social responsibility and personal empowerment. *New England Journal of Social Policy,* Special issue: Women and Economic Empowerment.

Ellenberger, H. F. (1970). *The discovery of the unconscious.* Basic Books.

Erikson, E. H. & Erikson, J. (1953). The power of the newborn. *Mademoiselle,* June.

Farias, P. J. (1989). *Ethnopsychology of refugees: A comparison of patterns in urban Salvadoran and rural Guatemalan refugees.* Presentation at American Anthropological Association meeting, Washington, DC, November.

Frank, J. (1986). Afterword: Nuclear winter and the will to power. In L. Grinspoon, (Ed.), *The long darkness: Psychological and moral perspectives on nuclear winter.* Yale.

Freud, S. (1929). *Standard edition of the complete psychological works of Sigmund Freud.* London: Hogarth Press. Original work published: Vol. IV, 1900; Vol. V, 1900; Vol. XIV, 1914; Vol. XIX, 1917, 1924, 1925; Vol. XXI 1930.

Gay, P. (1988). *Freud: A life for our time.* Norton.

George, G. (1988). Personal communication, December 12, to whom George Murray told this story in 1970.

Grenblatt, M., (Ed.). (1986). The use and abuse of power in the administration of systems. *Psychiatric Annals,* 16(11).

Grof, S. (1985). *Beyond the brain: Birth, death and transcendence in psychotherapy.* Albany, NY: State University of New York Press.

Guarnaccia, P. J. & Farias, P. (1988). The social meanings of nervios: A case study of a Central American woman. *Social Science and Medicine,* 26(12), 1223-31.

Heilbrun, C. (1988). *Writing a woman's life.* Norton.

Heinberg, R. (1989). *Memories and visions of paradise: Exploring the universal myth of a lost golden age.* Los Angeles: Jeremy P. Tarcher.

Heller, D. (1985). *Power in psychotherapeutic practice.* Human Sciences Press.

Horner, A. (1989). *The wish for power and the fear of having it.* Aronson.

Jung, C. C. (1969). *The Structure and dynamics of the psyche: The collected works of C G. Jung,* Vol. 8. Princeton University Press.

Kay, A. (1989). *Focus groups technology: A tool for public opinion assessment.* Presentation at Center for Psychological Studies in the Nuclear Age, Academic Council Meeting, November 9.

Khantzian, E. J. & Mack, J. E. (1989). Alcoholics Anonymous and contemporary psychodynamic theory. In M. Galanter, (Ed.), *Recent developments in alcoholism,* Vol. 1. Plenum.

Klein, G. S. (1976). *Psychoanalytic theory: An exploration of essentials.* International Universities Press.

Kleinman, A. (1988). *Rethinking psychiatry: From cultural category to personal experience.* Free Press.

Kluckhohn, F. R. (1956). Dominant and variant value orientations. In C. Kluckhohn and H. A. Murray, (Eds.), *Personality in nature, society, and culture.* Knopf.

Kohut, H. (1978). Creativeness, charisma, group psychology: Reflections on the self-analysis of Freud. In P. H. Ornstein, (Ed.), *The search for the self: Selected writings of Heinz Kohut: 1950-1978,* Vol.2.

La Chappell, D. (1984). *Earth wisdom.* Silverton, CO: Finn Hill Arts.

Lame Deer, J. (1979). (FIRE), and ERDOES, R. *Lame Deer: Seeker of visions.* Pocket Books.

Lee, D. (1956). Are basic needs ultimate? In C. Kluckhorn and H. A. Murray, (Eds.). *Personality in nature, society and culture.* Knopf.

Loewald, H.W. (1978). *Psychoanalysis and the history of the individual.* Yale.

Mack, J.E. (1981). Alcoholism, A.A. and the governance of the self, In Margaret H. Bean and Norman E. Zinberg, *Dynamic approaches to the understanding and treatment of alcoholism,* pp. 128-162.

Mack, J.E. (1990). The enemy system. In: V. D. Volkan, D. A. Julius, and J. V. Montvilb, (Eds.), *The psychodynamics of international relationships, Vol. I: Concepts and theories.* Lexington Books.

McPhee, J. (1989). *The control of nature.* Farrar, Strauss, Giroux.

McLaughlin, J. (1991). Clinical and theoretical aspects of psychoanalytic enactment. *Journal of the American Psychoanalytic Association,* 39, 595-614.

Macy, J. (1988). *Despair and personal power in the nuclear age.* Philadelphia: New Society Publishers.

Masson, J.M. (Trans. and Ed.). (1985). *The complete letters of Sigmund Freud, to Wilhelm Fliess, 1887-1904.* Harvard University Press.

Miller, J. B. (1982). *Women and power.* Work in progress, Stone Center for Developmental Services and Studies, Wellesley College, No. 82-01.

Mookerjee, A. (1991). *Kundalini: The Arousal of the inner energy.* Rochester, VT: Destiny Books.

Nietzsche, F. (1968). *The will to power,* W. Kaufmann, (Ed.). Vintage.

Nunberg, H. & Federn, E. (Eds.). (1962). *Minutes of the Vienna Psychoanalytic Society,* Vol. 1, International Universities Press.

O'Brien, C. C. (1988). *Godland: Reflections on religion and nationalism.* Harvard University Press.

Papajohn, J. & Spiegel, J. (1975). *Transactions in families: A modern approach to solving cultural and generational conflicts.* Jossey-Bass.

Person, E. (1988). *Dreams of love and fateful encounters: The power of romantic passion.* Norton.

Rapaport, D. (1967). *The collected papers,* Merton M. Gill, (Ed.). Basic Books.

Random House Dictionary of the English Language, Unabridged Edition. (1967). Random House.

Roazen, P. (1988). Normality and nihilism. *Virginia Quarterly Review* (Summer).

Scanzoni, J. (1979). Social process and power in families. In W. Burr, R. Hill, I. F. Nye, and I. L. Reiss, (Eds.), *Contemporary theories about the family,* Vol. I. Free Press.

Scarry E. (1985). *The body in pain: The making and unmaking of the world.* Oxford University Press.

Scheidlinger, S. (1989). *Letter to the author,* December 28.

Scheidlinger, S. (1990). On internalization in group psychology: The group within. *Journal of the American Academy of Psychoanalysis, 18,* 494-504.

Schmookler, A. B. (1988). *Out of weakness: Healing the wounds that drive us to war.* Atheneum Books.

Schorske, C. (1979). *Fin de siecle of Vienna politics and culture.* Knopf.

Shaw, G. B. (1963). Major Barbara, Act 3. Bernard Shaw, *Complete plays with prefaces,* Vol. l. Dodd Mead.

Stern, D. N. (1987). Development of the senses of the self, Scientific Program, New England Council of Child Psychiatry, September 28. Review by A. M. Kerzner. Bulletin of the *New England Council of Child Psychiatry* (1988), 24(1), 18.

Stern D.N. (1985). *The interpersonal world of the infant.* Basic Books.

Strindberg, A. (1960). *The father, Act II.* Paulson, trans. Bantam.

Surrey, J.L. (1987). *Relationship and empowerment.* Work in progress, Stone Center for Developmental Services and Studies, Wellesley College, No. 30.

Tinder, G. (1989). Can we be good without God? *Atlantic Monthly,* December: 69-85.

Tuchman, B. (1989). Interview with by D. C. Denison. *Boston Globe Magazine,* January 1.

Updike, J. (1986). *Roger's version.* Fawcett Crest.

Viederman, M. (1991). The real person of the analyst and his role in the process of psychoanalytic cure. *Journal of the American Psychoanalytic Association, 39,* 451-489.

Wolfe, T. (1987). *The bonfire of the vanities.* Farrar, Straus, Giroux.

Zock, H. (1990). *A psychology of ultimate concern. Erik H. Erikson's contribution to the psychology of religion.* J. A. van Belzen and J. M. van der Lans, (Eds.). Atlanta: Rodopi.